MRS. GASKELL'S
OBSERVATION AND INVENTION

NEW STUDIES—2

A

The John Rylands Library, Manchester
Photograph of Mrs. Gaskell. c. 1864.

MRS. GASKELL'S
OBSERVATION AND INVENTION

A Study of Her Non-Biographic Works

by

JOHN GEOFFREY SHARPS

B.Litt. (Oxon.), M.Ed. (Psychol.), M.A. (Hons.),
F.R.A.I., F.R.Econ.S., F.R.G.S., F.R.S.A.

With a Foreword by
A. STANTON WHITFIELD
B.Litt. (Oxon.), B.Sc., Ph.D., F.R.Hist.S., F.R.S.A.

LINDEN PRESS
1970

First published 1970 by the Linden Press, Fontwell, Sussex,
and distributed by the Centaur Press Ltd.,
11-14 Stanhope Mews West, London, S.W.7.
Printed in Great Britain by T. J. Winterson Co.

40566

For

My Parents, Mr. & Mrs. J. R. Sharps
My Aunt, Mrs. L. Deighton
My Wife, Heather

PREFACE

I must begin with a general acknowledgement to all who have aided and encouraged me for more than a decade. In the particular recognitions which follow I have usually furnished an address if one does not occur elsewhere (such as in my bibliographies), if it might prove difficult to ascertain, and if important material seems involved.

My interest in Mrs. Gaskell arose at Edinburgh; appropriately, since the Scottish capital held many associations for her: there valued advice came from Mr. (now Professor) P. H. Butter, Dr. A. Melville Clark, Professor W. L. Renwick, and Dr. L. W. Sharp. It gathered strength at Oxford, a city she knew and loved, where I greatly profited from the guidance and criticism of Mr. J. B. Bamborough, Lord David Cecil, Mr. H. J. F. Jones (especially), and Dr. Joyce M. S. Tompkins.

It is pleasant to record debts to those, both past and present, whose publications bear on Mrs. Gaskell: occasionally I have noted inaccuracies in their work, though never, I trust, in a carping spirit; for no one is more conscious than myself that this study too will be subject to correction and revision. Among Gaskellians of a bygone generation I must pay homage to Esther Alice (Mrs. Ellis H.) Chadwick, Miss Elizabeth Haldane, the Rev. George A. Payne, Sir Arthur Quiller-Couch, Clement King Shorter, and Dr. (later Sir) Adolphus Ward. Contemporary scholars (with most of whom I have been privileged to correspond) include Professor Walter Allen, Dr. Miriam Allott, Professor Richard D. Altick, Alderman Thomas Beswick (of Knutsford), Miss Theresa Coolidge, Dr. Johanna Jacoba van Dullemen (Maastorenflat, 183 Schiedamse Dijk, Rotterdam 1), Mr. Martin Dodsworth, Dr. Waldo Hilary Dunn, Miss Yvonne ffrench, Dr. Margaret Ganz, Professor Gordon S. Haight, Dr. Graham Handley, Miss Annette Brown Hopkins (6303 Pinehurst Road, Baltimore, Maryland 21212), Professor Walter E. Houghton, the Countess of Huntingdon (Margaret Lane), Mr. C. A. Johnson, Miss Naomi Lewis, Mrs. J. G. Links (Mary Lutyens), Mrs. John Lock (Winifred Gérin), Mr. John Lucas,

vii

Lektor Aina Rubenius (Höganäsgat 1B, Uppsala), Mrs. Lucy Poate Stebbins, Professor Kathleen Tillotson, Mr. John R. Townsend, Professor Ross D. Waller, and Professor Edgar Wright. Special gratitude is due to Mr. J. A. V. Chapple and Professor Arthur Pollard, editors of Mrs. Gaskell's letters, who willingly placed at my disposal the fruits of their scholarship, now elegantly published by the Manchester University Press; to Miss Mildred G. Christian (721 Lowerline Street, New Orleans 18, Louisiana), whose recent information may well lead, as it has already led, to the location of unprinted Gaskell correspondence; to Professor Anne Lohrli (New Mexico Highlands University, Las Vegas, New Mexico), who examined entries in the *Household Words* Office (or Day) Book, identified 'The Growth of Good'—*Household Words*, V (3 April 1852), 54-55—as a poem by Eliza(beth) Holland (Gaskell), equated 'The Wild-Flower of the Danube'—*Household Words*, V (5 June 1852), 266-270—with Mme De Mérey's Hungarian legend [see *The Letters of Mrs Gaskell*, ed. Chapple and Pollard, 1966—hereafter *G.L.*—, No. 128 (where the form is Mme de Mery)], and confirmed 'Helena Mathewson'—*Household Words*, XVI (4 July 1857), 13-22—as a tale contributed by Meta Gaskell; to Dr. Gerald DeWitt Sanders (now at 1007 Schuyler Apts., Spartanburg, South Carolina 29301), for stimulating conversation and for passing on an interesting point about Mrs. Gaskell's schooling; to Mrs. Walter Muir Whitehill (Jane Revere Coolidge), who generously loaned all her pertinent material; and to Professor A. Stanton Whitfield, whose hospitality and kindnesses are a pleasure to recall.

With the ensuing people, formerly or currently engaged on Gaskell research, I have enjoyed communicating: Mr. F. W. Binding (32 Buttrills Road, Barry, Glamorganshire), Mrs. Dorothy W. Collin (Department of English, University of Western Australia), Miss Patricia Gingrich (681 Merrick, Apt. 109, Detroit, Michigan 48202), Mr. Edward Hall (16 Old Road West, Gravesend, Kent), Dr. Alice Harmon, Miss Anne Karminski (15 Eccleston Square, London S.W.1), Dr. John McVeagh (Department of English, University of Ibadan, Nigeria), Miss Hilda Marsden (3 Harling Bank, Kirby Lonsdale, Lancashire), Fräulein Helga Miethling (Berlin 41, Albestrasse 23), Dr. Graham Owens (16 Park Drive, Shelley, Huddersfield), Miss Joanne Rowley, and Miss Margaret Tarratt (St. Anne's College, Oxford). Here I especially want to mention Miss Catharine M. E. Halls (283 Avenue Road, Toronto 7), who accorded me ready access to her Gaskell bibliography; and Mr. J. T. Lancaster, who placed his numerous Gaskell transcripts in my hands.

The survey of primary sources at the end of this book indicates that many bodies co-operated in making material available. To the authorities of the enumerated institutions I am obligated, particularly to those whose Gaskelliana have been cited or quoted; I am grateful too for the numerous searches undertaken elsewhere on my behalf, albeit they proved fruitless. In addition to acknowledging courtesies from chief librarians and the like, I wish to thank all those with whom as a reader I came into contact : I refer to the staff of the Library of the Queen's University of Belfast, the staff of the Bodleian Library (especially Mr. Giles G. Barber, Dr. R. W. Hunt, Mr. P. Long, Mr. D. H. Merry, and Mr. D. S. Porter), the staff of the Edinburgh University Library, the staff of the Leeds University—Brotherton —Library (especially Mr. David I. Masson and Mr. H. G. Tupper), the staff of the Manchester Central Public Library (especially members in the Reference Library and in the Language & Literature Library), the staff of the Manchester University Library (especially Dr. Margaret M. Wright), the staff of The John Rylands Library (especially Dr. Frank Taylor), the staff of the National Library of Scotland, the staff of the National Library of Wales, and the staff of the Leeds City Archives Dept.

To individual holders of Gaskell material I am likewise much indebted, either directly or indirectly (through the good offices of Mr. Chapple and Professor Pollard) : a list of private collections, together with some items which are in or have passed through the hands of booksellers and auctioneers, may be found among my bibliographies. I naturally owe most to Mrs. Gaskell's great grand-daughter, Mrs. Margaret E. A. Trevor Jones (now at 56 Heol Isaf—formerly of Monkstone—Radyr, Cardiff); but I also owe much to others, such as Sir John Murray who allowed me to consult the extensive Gaskell correspondence in the archives at 50 Albemarle Street.

It may be appropriate to remark that the researches of myself and of Mrs. Whitehill (carried out in the late nineteen-twenties, before her marriage) have revealed : that there seems to be no author-publisher material in the files of Messrs. Chapman & Hall Limited, of Messrs. Harper & Row, and of Messrs. Sampson

Low, Marston & Co., Ltd.; that the family solicitors, Messrs. Tatham, Worthington & Co., are unable to assist; that Mrs. Gaskell's letters to Henry Arthur Bright—whose presentation second-edition of *The Life of Charlotte Brontë* still exists—cannot be found by his grand-daughter, Mrs. Elizabeth M. Lloyd (Barton Court, Colwall, Malvern); that the Ewarts once possessed an inscribed *Mary Barton* first edition, but few—if any—letters (a recent search by Mr. William Ewart, of Colislinn, Hawick, proving negative), though—according to Mr. W. H. Lee Ewart —the novelist probably wrote part of *Sylvia's Lovers* at their home (Broadleas, Devizes) and used a nearby village (Potterne) as a setting for one of her works; that their mother's letters to Eliza Fox were very likely purchased (and then destroyed) by the Miss Gaskells; that the Robert Hyde Greg family may well have had a few letters; that Miss Elizabeth Haldane did not own any primary material; that no letters to Mme Mary Mohl seem extant; that whatever the Rev. George A. Payne may have assembled has been dispersed; that most—if not quite everything —once owned by Miss Margaret Josephine Shaen has been printed; that the bulk of Mrs. Gaskell's letters to the William Wetmore Storys was burned by Henry James at the instigation of her daughters; and that Mr. J. A. Williams (11 Morton End Lane, Harpenden, Hertfordshire) has not come upon the letters written to his grandfather (Williams of Messrs. Williams & Norgate), formerly in the family collection.

I should now like to express gratitude for favours received from a variety of individuals and institutions, occasionally specifying their nature. Thus I am deeply obliged to : Miss Valentine Ackland; Mrs. Helen Hunt Arnold; Miss J. O. Y. Arnold; Professor T. S. Ashton; Mrs. I. K. Bennett; Mr. B. C. Bloomfield; Mrs. Mary Boardman, from whom I acquired a Book of Common Prayer containing Mrs. Gaskell's autograph and address with the date 28 June 1855; Sir Walter and Lady Bromley-Davenport; Mrs. Esmond Bryon (*née* Marion Perkins, 1 Coleman Street, Brighton 7), who informed me of a family tradition concerning Mrs. Gaskell's proposal to adopt John Wade, her great-uncle [see my article : "Charlotte Brontë and the Mysterious 'Miss H.' A Detail in Mrs. Gaskell's *Life*", *English*, XIV (Autumn 1963), 236]; Mr. Walter Carter and the Miss Carters, through whom I obtained genealogical data about the Stevenson family and also letters to a Stevenson uncle of the novelist's from his sister,

Dorothy (Mrs. George Landles), and from James Smith; Dr. W. H. Chaloner; Professor H. B. Charlton; the Cheshire County Record Office; Miss Mary Fawcett, who gave me both a photograph of Meta Gaskell and a memorial picture for Julia Gaskell; Mr. R. Sharpe France, Lancashire County Archivist, for abstracts from various Gaskell wills, including that of the Rev. William's father (which names as sons—in birth-order—William, Samuel, Robert, and John; but mentions no Henry); Miss J. Gaddum; Mrs. Elsie Graver; Mr. Richard Gilbertson (Bookseller, Bow, Crediton, Devon), for putting many Gaskelliana in my way; Miss Constance E. Green; Professor H. J. Habakkuk; Miss Lilian L. Harper, who took Mr. Chapple and myself on a fascinating tour of Mrs. Gaskell's last Manchester home, now 84 Plymouth Grove [her previous home, in Upper Rumford Street, proved inaccessible: see *Brontë Society Transactions*, XV (1967), 146-148]; Miss Dorothy Jane Harrison, her sister (Mrs. J. L. Longland, Bridgeway, Bakewell, Derbyshire), and her cousin (Dr. W. M. R. Henderson, 8 Holmewood Ridge, Langton Green, Kent), for supplying genealogies relating to their Stevenson ancestry; Dr. R. M. Hartwell; Mrs. E. Margaret Hayward (2 College Road, Exeter), Mrs. Lilian C. Tavener (20 Grosvenor Crescent, St. Leonards-on-Sea), and others, for details about their forbear— reputedly the Rev. William Gaskell's brother—Henry Gaskell (died on 5 April 1866), who took to the stage, gained fame in a Faust play (perhaps Marlowe's), and consequently assumed the surname—or, better, *nick*name—Denvil (De-n-vil); Mr. John Healy, Town Clerk of Berwick-upon-Tweed, for discovering that John Stevenson (the authoress's brother), a mariner in the service of the East India Company, was admitted to the Freedom of the Borough on 13 March 1820; Professor W. G. Hoskins; Mrs. Joanna Hutton; Admiral Sir William James; Mr. F. H. Johnson and the Town Clerk of Manchester (Mr. Philip B. Dingle), for ascertaining that the wooden mock-tombstone mentioned in an authorial footnote at the end of the sixth chapter of *Mary Barton* may have been used in any one of several Manchester churchyards of the period, the former also confirming in other respects the accuracy of the *locale* of the story; the Rev. Peter Jones, the Rev. Albert Smith (especially), the Rev. W. R. Strachan, and the Committee of the Unitarian Chapel, Brook Street, Knutsford; the Rev. G. Knight; Dr. Winifred Lamb (Borden Wood, Liphook, Hants), for permission to reproduce a Valentine sent to

Mrs. Gaskell by her publishers in 1864; Mr. John Lehmann; Mrs. LeWragg, for letting me view Hollingford House, the Knutsford home of Mrs. Gaskell's uncle, Dr. Peter Holland; Mrs. E. Lightburn (22 Woodlands Road, Hartford, Northwich, Cheshire), for her efficient typing; Mr. N. Long-Brown; the Manchester City Art Gallery (especially the Keeper of Paintings, for stating that David Dunbar's bust of—as she then was— Elizabeth Cleghorn Stevenson, though entered among their accessions, cannot be located; and for providing information about both Sir William Hamo Thornycroft, 1850-1925, who made a replica of this bust, and William John Thompson—or Thomson—1771-1845, who painted a miniature of Miss Stevenson); Miss Betty Millar and Mr. R. A. Millar; Mrs. M. E. Miller, from whom I obtained various Gaskelliana, including letters by Meta Gaskell to Thomas Seccombe regarding his edition of *Sylvia's Lovers* (1910); the National Portrait Gallery; Mrs. Marjorie Neill Newton; Miss Marjorie S. Oldham; Miss Marjorie M. Poole; the Public Record Office; Mrs. A. Roberts, for taking Dr. van Dullemen and myself through her Knutsford home, Heathwaite, where before her marriage Miss Stevenson lived with her favourite aunt, Mrs. Hannah Lumb; Mr. Alec Robertson; Mrs. Cecily M. Shipman (formerly of St. John, Jersey), for details about the Gaskells' links with Silverdale, and for agreeing that her grandfather's house there (Cove House) may have been the original of Eagle's Crag (Abermouth) in *Ruth*; the Rev. Leonard Baker Short; Miss Olive M. Simpkin; Mrs. Ethel L. Smith (22 Hillside, Southwick, Sussex), for allowing me to acquire letters by John Stevenson to his sister (Elizabeth Cleghorn Stevenson) and his aunt (Mrs. Hannah Lumb) as well as a photograph of Charles Darwin which Meta Gaskell received on 4 July 1892 from his son, William Erasmus; Mr. F. L. Summerhayes; Mr. J. Alexander Symington and his widow, Beatrice; Dr. Martha Salmon Vogeler; Mr. R. W. Walker (Little Lusteds, Stone Cross, Pevensey, Sussex), who had copied for me a long [1945] letter to his cousin, Mrs. Josephine Greenway-Vaudrey, from his great-aunt, Alice Walker, which mentions a visit paid to the Walker home, Moss Farm (Bowdon), by Florence and Julia Gaskell, their nurse, and their mother ("More like an angel than anything else —an angel in the house", according to Alice's aunt, quoted in the letter) at the time the novelist was, the Walkers thought, engaged on *Ruth* (wherein Moss Farm may feature as Milham

Grange) [a reference to lodging at Bowden (*sic*) with the Miss Walkers occurs in *G.L.*, No. 101a]; Mr. Wyndham L. Walker, who also notes the family tradition that *Ruth* was written at Moss Farm; Miss Mary Walters; Mrs. Alison M. Wareham (West Street Farm, Maynards Green, Horam, Sussex), for furnishing genealogical data about the Winkworths and for allowing me to acquire her two volumes (the first inscribed by Margaret Josephine Shaen on 15 April 1883) of the privately circulated *Letters and Memorials of Catherine Winkworth*; Mr. J. C. Way (Beech Top, Fletcher Drive, Disley, Cheshire), through whom I came to own a Wedgwood tea-pot, reputedly Mrs. Gaskell's; Colonel M. I. Williams-Ellis; Mr. J. L. Wetton (Applegarth, 39 Oriental Road, Woking, Surrey), from whom I secured a first edition of Henry Green's *Knutsford*, inscribed 'M Radcliffe with/ Mrs Gaskell's kind regards/ May 1859'; the Whitby Literary & Philosophical Society; Dr. Williams's Library, London. Nor must I omit to thank, for their helpfulness in printing requests for Gaskelliana, the editors of many newspapers and journals—such as *The Daily Telegraph and Morning Post*, *The Guardian*, the *Knutsford Guardian*, the *Manchester Evening News*, *The Spectator*, *The Sunday Times*, and *The Times Literary Supplement*.

My concluding paragraph must be reserved for my family, without whom this study would never have been commenced, continued, or concluded. To relatives dead as well as living I owe much: so I here pay tribute not only to my aunt, Mrs. Hilda Hindley, and my uncle, Mr. R. P. Deighton, but also to my late grandfather, Mr. C. H. Street, and my late aunt, Miss A. L. Jones. Above all, however, I am indebted to my parents, Mr. & Mrs. J. R. Sharps; my maternal aunt, Mrs. L. Deighton; and my wife, Heather: to them this book is dedicated.

J.G.S.

BIBLIOGRAPHICAL PRELIMINARIES AND COMMENTS ON THE CHAPPLE-POLLARD EDITION OF MRS. GASKELL'S LETTERS

(a) BIBLIOGRAPHICAL PRELIMINARIES

In the main I have applied the recommendations of William Riley Parker, compiled *The MLA Style Sheet*, rev. edn, New York: The Modern Language Association of America, 1954. To elucidate a few matters, however, the following notes may prove useful.

1. The initial footnote-reference usually accords with the corresponding bibliographical-entry: on occasions the latter may be slightly fuller; but the former should suffice for most purposes. Subsequent footnote-references are always detailed enough to facilitate identification of the relevant source.

2. If, in any form, the author's name appears on the title-page of a book or an article, then my reference gives that name in the fullest form discoverable. If the author's name does not so appear, then I have enclosed the full form within square brackets.

3. When a text quoted or cited has an editor (as well as, or instead of, an author), his name has been put before the title if the editorial aspect warranted such precedence.

4. In reproducing titles, I have retained initial capitals for all words except articles, conjunctions, and prepositions; and I have invariably retained the initial capital of the first word in a sub-title, even though this be the definite or indefinite article.

5. Places of publication and the names of publishers conform, as far as possible, to the style of the title-page. Thus, in footnotes and bibliography alike, 'Ltd' occurs as well as 'Ltd.', '&' as well as 'and'. Where only some of the volumes of a work have been published at a certain place, that place has usually been enclosed with round brackets; similarly, if a firm has shared in bringing out only some of several

volumes, then that firm has likewise been enclosed with round brackets.

6. Dates—and, if necessary, places—of publication have been surrounded by square brackets if they could not be easily ascertained from the works themselves.

7. Superior footnote-numbers, contrary to the usual English practice, precede my punctuation.

8. Single inverted commas enclose unindented quotations; but, if the quotation is itself quoted material, I have usually retained any double inverted commas found in the secondary source.

9. Although all punctuation within inverted commas belongs to the passages quoted, I have sought, as far as possible, to incorporate it in my own sentence-structure : for example, the concluding comma of a quotation has frequently been kept if, had it been absent, I should myself have needed one after the end of the extract.

10. Square brackets—[ ]—indicate non-original (often editorial) material, including surmised dates; pointed (angle) brackets — ⟨ ⟩ —intimate lacunae, usually resulting from physical damage, and surround the conjectured additions; carets —∧ ∧—flank original interlinear insertions; and single and double slashes—/ and //—mark line and page endings respectively.

11. When quoting or citing MSS, I have endeavoured to supply their press-marks if these existed and were known to me. In the footnotes I usually state whether I am dealing with an autograph letter, a fragment, or a copy; in the bibliography the term 'letter' or 'copied letter' covers an incomplete, as well as a complete, holograph or transcript. I have frequently designated line and page endings; deletions; interlinear insertions; and the like : such refinements imply an examination of autograph material (or photocopies thereof), though their absence does not necessarily mean that I have not had access to the originals.

12. As regards the dating of letters, various points deserve mention. The conventional square brackets enclose conjectures. Times of the day (*e.g.* morning) and days of the week (*e.g.* Tuesday) have seldom been recorded, if the correspondent also provides month-day and year (*e.g.* July 13, 1863). However, if the letter carries no year, any week-day present

xvi

has been noted; so has usually any day-time, if the month-day is absent. For complete dating information, recourse should be had to *The Letters of Mrs Gaskell*, ed. John Alfred Victor Chapple and Arthur Pollard, Manchester: Manchester University Press, 1966.

(b) COMMENTS ON CHAPPLE AND POLLARD, ED.

THE LETTERS OF MRS GASKELL (1966)

All Gaskellians owe an immeasurable debt to Mr. J. A. V. Chapple and Mr. (now Professor) Arthur Pollard. Their excellent work will, one trusts, soon acquire a supplement, embodying the odd correction and amplification besides new material. Meanwhile, tentatively and with due deference, I offer the ensuing notes, prefaced by some general observations; they may serve to render the edition still more useful until a more authoritative supplement appears.

1. After the editors had concluded their task, fresh letters came to light. The current situation is set forth in the second (manuscript) section of my bibliography.

2. Not every one of the late Mr. Joseph Torry Lancaster's numerous transcripts of letters by or relating to Mrs. Gaskell (source 8a in their source-list) was available to Chapple and Pollard. All of them, now in my possession, have since been *cursorily* collated. They consist of typed and of handwritten copies: almost certainly the former have the greater authority, with the latter deriving from them; and several copies only occur in typed form. However, as two or more typescripts usually exist for the same letter, distinguishing priorities poses problems. The differences, though often slight, occasionally seem important: thus one version furnishes a date for No. 264a in *The Letters of Mrs Gaskell* (abbreviatable as *G.L.*, No. 264a). Moreover, a few of these typescripts may contain, at least in some respects, better texts than their counterparts in the Gaskell Section, Brotherton Collection, Leeds University Library: such appears the case with *G.L.*, Nos. 277, 310, 636, 637.

3. Brotherton Collection miscellaneous typescripts—source 41 (d)—virtually always provide preferable texts to those incorporated in the incomplete (Brotherton Collection) typed biography of Mrs. Gaskell by Jane Revere Coolidge (now

Mrs. Walter Muir Whitehill)—source 41 (c). In general, therefore, no *G.L.* text should be based on a source 41 (c) version when a source 41 (d) one is available—as with *G.L.*, Nos. 1, 19, 36, 100, 148. A further complication arises because Chapple and Pollard list source 41 (c) for certain *G.L.* texts (Nos. 277, 558, 636, 637) which would seem to be based rather on source 41 (d).

4. Clement Shorter's privately printed *Letters on Charlotte Brontë by Mrs. Gaskell* [London : c. 1916]—source 60 (b)— contains texts which in parts may be superior to those used by Chapple and Pollard—cf. and cont. *G.L.*, Nos. 48, 55, 79, 146, 274; and No. 316 (where Shorter's text, though followed, is not quite accurately reproduced). The background to several of these letters is sketched in Clement King Shorter, 'Mrs. Gaskell and Charlotte Brontë', *Brontë Society Transactions*, Vol. V, No. 4 (Part 26 of the Society's Publications), 1916, pp. 144-149—a reprint of C.K.S., 'A Literary Letter : Mrs. Gaskell and Charlotte Brontë', *The Sphere*, Vol. LXIII, No. 819 (2 October 1915), p. 24.

5. Here and there one can suggest dating-changes, indicate misprints, notice possible misreadings, supply additional information, and so forth; yet such revisions, emendations, and annotations are neither exhaustive nor beyond dispute. Minor variants from the secondary sources unavailable to Chapple and Pollard—for instance, differences in spelling and puctuation—are rarely recorded; but I have tried to note all substantive variants : this policy accords with that of the editors. I have adopted a similar method where I have discovered the originals of letters hitherto printed from copies (*G.L.*, Nos. 166, 562): the satisfactory solution—printing afresh from the primary sources—must await a supplement to *The Letters of Mrs Gaskell*.

In the following list, the indicating numeral refers to the number of the letter in the Chapple-Pollard edition. Thus (*G.L.*, No.) 1 is the first letter, printed on pp. 1-2. Square brackets—or a single square bracket—separate my remarks from this textual material.

1	the preferable source 41 (d) has] without *my* portion . travelling companion . . . *March* 1833
2	probably [16 September 1832]
3	2nd fn. should read] W. F. Irvine
4	3rd fn.: the compositions may have been prose pieces, not poetic imitations

7	[28 March 1838]
9	3rd fn.: Marghanita Laski suggests 'white satin' repetition makes sense
11	'strike' not 'skrike' and 'which' not 'whilk' seem intended
16	perhaps [23 December 1840]
19	41 (d) source preferable
21	source is dated] Tuesday morning, before breakfast.
26	10 July [1848] fell on a Monday; so the rather illegible weekday should perhaps be read as] Monday
30	2nd fn.: *Mary Barton* appeared on 18 October 1848
34	Friday fell on 8 December
36	perhaps prior to *G.L.,* No. 34; the preferable 41 (d) source is headed] /1848./ 121, Upper Rumford St., Tuesday. [this source has] *true*; not [the source used—41 (c)—has] *true* not
48	see *G.L.,* No. 55
55	a passage similar to one herefrom occurs in source 60 (b), where it is headed, rather like *G.L.,* No. 48] 121, Upper Rumford Street, Manchester, *May* 29, 1849. [it continues] My dear Eliza, Have you read Southey's Memoirs? But of . . . wrote *Jane Eyre* and *Shirley*. Do tell me who wrote *Jane Eyre*. E. C. G. [the source used—41 (d)—has] *dama* of a lady
74	Mrs. Clark's reply of 21 August 1850 was sold at Sotheby's 29 October 1968 sale
75	Margaret Goalby identifies the Marshall residence as] Tent Lodge
76	1st fn. should read] p. xxvii
77	1st fn.: source has] Bronté [but see *G.L.,* Introduction, p. xxvii, fn. 3]
79	source 60 (b) contains a passage, similar to one herefrom, headed] Plymouth Grove, Manchester, *August* —, 1850. [which opens] My dearest Tottie, [and continues] William is at Birmingham . . . "Editorial party." Yours very affectionately, E. C. Gaskell.
92	perhaps [31 March 1851]
92 & 93	'Hale' and/or 'Hull'?
95	probably [Thursday 24 April 1851]
96	perhaps [6 or—rather—13 May 1851]
97	perhaps [22 May 1851]
97a	[pre 20—perhaps 1—June 1851]
99	perhaps [Friday 4 July 1851]
100	the preferable source 41 (d) has] Wedgwood's to keep . . . [all sources—41 (c) and 41 (d)—have] day (Friday) which
102	[post 12—perhaps 19—September 1851]
116	probably [February or (possibly c. 11-16) March 1851]
119	probably [1863]
125	should follow *G.L.,* No. 126
128	1st fn.: the legend by Mme De Mérey [*sic*] is 'The Wild-Flower of the Danube', published on 5 June 1852 in *Household Words*, V, 268-270
134	3rd fn.: Meta also alludes to a poem by her aunt, Eliza(beth) Holland, *née* Gaskell; entitled 'The Growth of Good', it appeared on 3 April 1852 in *Household Words*, V, 54-55
145	perhaps [Christmastide 1852]

146	20 December fell on a Monday; source 60 (b), headed] Manchester, *Dec.* 20, 1852. [has] My dearest Tottie, *Ruth* is . . . money) stay . . . road. However . . . one of older girls . . . angelic. Yours ever very affectionately, E. C. Gaskell.
148	the preferable TS source—41 (d)—has] you wld. be . . . cd. share it . . . we shd. not be . . . affcly., E.C.G.
149	Will is William Shaen, not William Gaskell: see Margaret Josephine Shaen's 15 January 1931 letter to Elizabeth Haldane, in the National Library of Scotland—MS. 6035, ff. 127-128
153	described in her transcript by the then owner as 8vo 4½pp.
157	written, according to the source, from Hyde Park Gardens—doubtless from No. 8 (Lady Coltman's)
166	the original letter—in the Brotherton Collection—has] ruddy kind-looking man . . . brown distant moors . . . furniture, wh^h did . . . it's consistency . . . it's place . . . *not* annoyances . . . Mr Smith & Elder . . . room on the opposite . . . his *invariable* custom . . . fancy it! only they . . . we had had a long . . . and in the dip . . . Ireland, raised . . . two pipes & a . . . that is). He was . . . masters,—or vice . . . him in his walks . . . my 4th sheet . . . him over again & again of . . . own & her sister's lives . . . she never would own . . . she *would* dress . . . on enquiry I found . . . lived for a year
180	probably [1852]
182 & 184	recipient Miss Hannah Kay
183	surely [Before 8 March ?1854]
186	recipient Emile [*sic*] Souvestre
199	probably [late (post 15) May 1854]
222	King being the family name of the Earl of Lovelace, M. C. Draper would read] this young King
225	perhaps [21 or 28 January 1855]
229	probably [16 February 1855]
230	probably [Friday 23 February 1855]
234	misprints: hence read] taken . . . Jameson
249	source has] with you that there are
267	text seems based on source 61 rather than 41 (c): cf. Appendix A
274	source 60 (b) has] *December* 15, 1855. . . . the packet of . . . she is addressing . . . [source used—41 (d)—has] her sisters' death [source 60 (b) and source 8a TSS have] her sister's death . . . [one source 8a TS has] them so long as . . . [source 60 (b) has] Williams's brother
277	source 41 (d) not 41 (c); the recipient was perhaps Leitch Ritchie; the source 8a TS has] about 3 weeks . . . upon them; namely
307	should follow *G.L.*, No. 308
310	text seems based on source 61 rather than 41 (c); the source 8a TS has] Edinburgh, for a word of advice; they may . . . but I have
315	source 8a TSS have] too indiscriminately . . . their doles
316	source has] long and scientific
330	probably [(pre 12) January 1857]
335	source 8a TSS have] it not be . . . of the second edition . . . up the little blank . . . the last page of MS (In looking . . . but she also said
*335a	no such letter

336	perhaps [(post 5) March 1865]; 1st fn.: the story may be 'Wives and Daughters'
342	Mrs. Maud Waldo Story's transcript has] Hôtel . . . Rue du Bac . . . Hôtel . . . Città
347	Tuesday fell on 31 March in 1857
368	1st fn. might have referred to p. 475, where Hill's departure on 24 August is mentioned
382	perhaps 'title' not 'little' was intended: cont. G.L., No. 87, fn.
394	source has] help her to bear much
401	source has] Given 150£
405	source 8a transcripts have recipient's address] Miss Gaskell, Plymouth Grove, Manchester, England. Affranchie. Oct. 20. 1858.
414	probably [Sunday—post 5 (possibly 6)—February 1859]
421	perhaps Mrs. Gaskell wrote] do you know the Storys
424a	source has] Noddgerie's, with [Miss von der Noddgerie is named in Max Müller's 30 March letter to Mrs. Gaskell—in The John Rylands Library, Manchester: English MS. 731/70]
444	Field [sic] is doubtless the publisher, James T. Fields
447	probably [3 November 1859]
455	doubtless [Monday 27 February 1860]
457	probably [9 or—less likely—16 March 1860]; source has] carefully looked
460	perhaps [19 March 1860]
463 & 470	recipient probably Sampson Low, whose firm published Right at Last, and Other Tales, 1860
464	1st fn.: the lady is probably Miss von der Noddgerie
466	possibly [Spring 1861]
469	possibly [29 May 1860]
471	very problematic dating: possibly [2 June 1860]
475	perhaps not all non-authorial insertions—doubtless by Florence or Julia—are noted as such
481	source 8a TSS have] Miss Bennett who . . . then on hand . . . [one source 8a TS has] Saturday's night sermon . . . [source 8a TSS have] come up and . . . six week's ago . . . in terrorem. He . . . strangers' visiting . . . heard it was to . . its name in the . . . [one source 8a TS has] awkward and he had thus saved [the other source 8a TS has] awkward and he thus saved
485	3rd fn.: Lady—Lucie (Lucy)—Duff-Gordon translated J. Wilhelm Meinhold's narrative; 4th fn.: standard authorities give 1860 as the publication-date of Norton's Notes
486	recipient probably Frederic [sic] Chapman
493	Tuesday fell on 27 August
499	source 8a TSS have] Feb. 1st . . . third volume to . . . not. (If somebody (out of my family) . . . first two volumes) . . . [one source 8a TS has] I don't want . . . [source 8a TSS have] entirely out of . . . I should be . . . you would kindly . . . unless he knew how it came [doubtless Mrs. Gaskell wrote, or meant to write, '17th' not '19th' in respect of the century where her French interests lay]
500	recipient perhaps Thomas Walker, Daily News editor (1858-1869)
502	possibly 'duly' rather than 'dee[p]ly'
505	'A Dark Night's Work' may be the relevant reference for 2nd fn.; 'Six Weeks at Heppenheim' that for 3rd fn.

516	perhaps [25 September 1862]
517	written, according to source 73, from Eastbourne in October 1862
518	2nd fn. might also have noted *A Dark Night's Work. A Novel*, New York: Harper & Brothers, 1863
519	source has] Decr 11. 1852
522	recipient Miss Isa Blagden
530	better source is [Sarah Blake Shaw] *Memorial: RGS*, Cambridge [Mass.]: University Press, 1864, pp. 149-150
532	1st fn. should read] E. M. Gordon's
535	source has] Octr 22nd
549	recipient Mme Mohl's nephew
555	Tuesday fell on 13 September in 1864
558	source 41 (d) not 41 (c)
562	The original letter—in the Harvard University Library—is headed] 46 Plymouth Grove/ February 24/ [and opens] My dear Mr Ruskin/ [there follows this paragraph, absent from the copy-text] Thank you so/ very much for what you/ have done. We sent off your/ last note,—enclosing Mr Cowper's,—/ to Mr Waterhouse, within ten/ minutes after receiving it/ I can't tell you how grateful/ I am. I want to do something/ for you, straight, slap-away./ You can't tell me what,—can/ you? / [the original has (line-endings will hereafter not be marked)] And then again about "Cranford. I am . . . say "*enjoy*" it, but that . . . pretty,—laugh . . . I knew the cat . . . the emetic &c &c. . . . it was too ridiculous . . . who had made a grand . . . Sir Ed. Cust.) . . . the young couple. But I . . . & sliding with . . . and that they had been teaching . . . places, for fear lest her . . . killed poor Capt Brown
593	indexed under Henry Arthur Bright
614	source has] hers or been touched
617	source 63 better than 41 (d); perhaps [18 August 1838]; source 63—*Good Words*, XXXVI, 612—also has] Faith, such as the rich can never imagine on earth, and love, strong as death.
620	recipient doubtless Mrs. Jane Loudon
624	somewhat misquoted in source 64, these words are actually Charlotte Brontë's—see E. C. Gaskell, *The Life of Charlotte Brontë*, 1st edn, 1857, II, 164: cf. and cont. Clement King Shorter, *The Brontës: Life and Letters*, 1908, II, 150
628	1st fn. should read] Owens College
636	source 41 (d) not 41 (c); recipient perhaps William or Robert Chambers; grouped with copies of letters to William—and to Robert—Chambers, the source 8a TS has] Yours very truly
637	source 41 (d) not 41 (c); the source 8a TS has] Jenkins' christian . . . glad indeed to learn . . . me, Yours very truly
74a	one source 8a TS has] any circumstance has . . . put it off
91a	doubtless [9 March 1851]
91b	doubtless [16 March 1851]
97+	perhaps [25 May 1851]
118a	probably] *good* . . . Rathbones
122a	one source 8a TS has] June to the 29th . . . her to-day before . . . old sad way . . . sold my stock of
144a	perhaps [21 December 1852]
144b	perhaps [Sunday 26 December 1852]
147b	perhaps [22 September 1854]

156a	one source 8a TS has] join up in our . . . Mr & Ly. Coltman
198a	probably [late (post 15) May 1854], same day as *G.L.*, No. 199; one source 8a TS has] written to Mlle Mohl [doubtless 'Mme Mohl' correct reading] . . . are clearly off a little
205+	one source 8a TS has] a rockery ['rookery' may be correct reading] and heronry . . . opened my bedroom . . . Kebles Evening Hymn
209a	one source 8a TS has] TIMES. Speaking of . . . The Major leave [changed from 'leaves'] Nelson . . . to Meta and Mrs Ewart . . . affec. Eliz. [copy-text has] Meta And Mrs Ewart . . . affec ELIZ.
242a	one source 8a TS has] wrote last on Thursday ['Sunday' may be correct reading] . . . Coate's sale . . . the way and found . . . all my goodness . . . is so good . . . Winbrock [doubtless 'Winkworth'] who
264a	one source 8a TS has] nr. Lancaster. Aug. 9th.
264b	copy-text and other source 8a TSS have] I shall most thankfully avail
267a	one source 8a TS has] about Sepr. 5th or . . . on the Monday following, October the 8th . . . Marianne is *very* much obliged
268a	one source 8a TS has] at Birstal . . . upon which time would . . . to temptations I . . . My kind regards
270a	Ellen Nussey's 22 October reply belongs to J. G. Sharps; one source 8a TS has] My Dear Miss Nussey
275+	one source 8a TS has] she has much pleasure . . . in her Memoir . . . she hopes that you will . . . sure that I can . . . thinks she will have to
275a	perhaps [c. 24 December 1855], in response to Ellen Nussey's reply of the 22nd to Meta Gaskell's 17 December 1855 letter (copies of both being among source 8a TSS); one source 8a TS has] amount of letter-writing
276a	two source 8a TSS have] no other time will . . . come. But pray [or 'come. but pray'] . . . be so very sorry . . . you here under our own roof.
276b	other source 8a TSS have] good talk-over with . . . for Mrs [or 'Mrs.'] Brontë's letters
280a	one source 8a TS has] do any letter writing . . . it is not likely . . . it will finished
294a	one source 8a TS has] My Dear Miss Nussey . . . [copy-text and another source 8a TS have] in her letter were . . . [one source 8a TS has] would be best she . . . Did *she* ever make
297a	one source 8a TS has] Dear Miss Nussey
310a	one source 8a TS has] will be so kind
322a	one source 8a TS has] the success . . . [some source 8a TSS have] told her that . . . read it to you
353a	one source 8a TS has] to you to tell . . . Tuesday eveng, . . . [two source 8a TSS have] shall all be so glad
360a	one source 8a TS has] ever very effecely.
381a	one source 8a TS has] be well hunted . . . [two source 8a TSS have] about this Miss Martineau . . . [one source 8a TS has] and with very much from me to yrself and

385a	perhaps Mrs. Gaskell wrote] you will lose the object . . . [one source 8a TS has] Brookroyd, it was . . . [two source 8a TSS have] deadly feeling of fatigue . . . [one source 8a TS has] she is gone to stay . . . New Years Day . . . brother Lt. Colonel Ewart
421a	all source 8a TSS incorrectly have the year as] /58 [one source 8a TS has] was staying with . . . the 3rd July . . . [two source 8a TSS have] that *they* had heard . . . [one source 8a TS has] determined after this to wait . . . brother (Capt. Dudley . . . mind has been . . . [perhaps Mrs. Gaskell wrote] West Kirby, Liverpool . . . [one source 8a TS has] 1830: He dies about . . . remonstrated and said . . . [two source 8a TSS have] Mr. Gaskell's kindest
447b	one source 8a TS has] sketch out a house . . . Mr *John Whitmore*
472+	one source 8a TS has] Wednesday *or* Saturday . . . Reading to *Vauxhall* . . . there for that at any rate . . . things. When [in copy-text changed in pencil to 'Where'] are . . . from Osten —curious
475a	one source 8a TS has] opened verily by . . . ½ past 2
475b	one source 8a TS has] August 25th.
484a	one source 8a TS has] 9 sharp went . . . [copy-text and other source 8a TS have] Gaskell's in particulars.
506a	one source 8a TS has] 6 *single beds* . . . while she spent . . . not then ask . . . go the Smiths
509b	1st fn. might have stated that in 1862 Derby Day fell on Wednesday 4 June
511a	a similar text occurs in source 41 (d)
p. 968	source has] She comes with her look of gentleness/ . . And I know, I know she loves me still/

Addenda

137	[(post 2—possibly 8—October) 1852]
178 & 179	46 Plymouth Grove address suggests [post 1860]
217	the Symington source TS (Leeds City Archives Dept.) provides a fuller and better text, headed] Thursday. Lea Hurst. (27 : 10 : 1854)
236	perhaps [1860]
237	perhaps [c. 1859-1860]
335	the Symington source TS (Leeds City Archives Dept.) supplies to the date] October, 1856.
365	[(pre 13—possibly 8—August) 1857]
555	1st fn.: did Meta Gaskell have in mind Mrs. Gordon's Lawrence or that (see my p. 676) of Mrs. Trevor Jones when, writing on 6 April in a letter to C. E. Norton begun on 27 March [1866] —in the Harvard University Library: bMS Am 1088 (2608)— she referred to the likeness Lawrence had taken of her mother two springs previously, which she had seen before the last sitting and which 'promised to be very like—/though the portrait only told of one side of her/ character, the nobility and heroism, and/ left all the exquisite tenderness untouched'?
564	with its envelope, the original letter, residing among Symingtoniana (Leeds City Archives Dept.), supplies the authoritative text, headed] 120 Rue du Bac/ Sunday/
630	42 Plymouth Grove address suggests [1850-1860], perhaps [1853-1860]
97+	[late May or early—possibly 1 or 8—June 1851]
267a	all source 8a TSS have (18)58 dating: the year is [1855]
362a	copy-text concludes] E.C. [other source 8a TSS conclude] E.G.
636a	the source 41 (d) counterpart does not have the recipient's name

CONTENTS

ILLUSTRATIONS

Miniature by William John Thom(p)son of Elizabeth Cleghorn Stevenson.
June 1832, Edinburgh.

FOREWORD
By
Professor A. Stanton Whitfield

FOREWORD

This admirable book is not only an act of piety to a charming lady but a tribute to the industry and perspicacity of its author.

Mrs. Gaskell was a natural social reformer. Her works, more than a century after her death, can still instruct as well as entertain. Uninfluenced by dogma and undogmatic, she tried in her way to stress the spiritual importance of trust between masters and men (or artisans, as the latter were often called). Nowadays it would be well if many of the shirking classes were provided with paperbacks of *Mary Barton* and *North and South,* whose writer coevally embraced, yet not deliberately, the ideas of Benjamin Disraeli, Karl Marx, and John Bright[1]. One of the most intelligent humanists of her age, she remained unbiassed and unbitten by the prejudices and pettinesses that assailed her masculine contemporaries; for Mrs. Gaskell was a genius who was also a gentlewoman. As such (to adapt my mentor's words of Shakespeare), she wove on the loom of Drumble a garment everlasting.

Mr. Sharps has judiciously located his subject's diverse facets. Her well-nigh infinite variety, indeed, partly explains Mrs. Gaskell's constant reputation despite the mutations of fashion. Always esteemed from *Cranford* onwards[2], she never fell into that temporary oblivion which engulfed Trollope—a time when Gladstone, possibly with Disraeli on his mind, remarked that Marie Corelli's little bit (whatever that may mean) enabled her to be sweet while others were sugarless. To persons of true culture, W. T. Stead once affirmed, the prejudices and predilections of the British public are matters as well worth study as are any of those obscure and apparently insignificant natural phenomena which scientists spend their days in investigating. Some one may therefore, I hope, paint as fine a picture of Mrs.

---

[1] Doubtless the less said the better about Victorian combinations (which in any case were concealed under crinolines).

[2] During the last five decades more than fifty books and articles have been written about Mrs. Gaskell; and in one edition alone *Cranford* has been reset and reprinted at least eight times since 1927.

3

Gaskell's literary life after death as that of Shelley's by Sylva Norman, whose study it would be an impertinence for me to praise. She has given us her *Flight of the Skylark*; Mr. Sharps will one day, perhaps, give us his *Flutterings of the Dove*—a title, I think, Lord David Cecil might appreciate.

Never out of favour, Mrs. Gaskell has seldom been underrated or unfairly assessed. Evaluation of her work, taken as a whole, has remained well-balanced; by critics from neither the left nor the right have the scales of justice been overloaded one way or the other. The reason does not lie far to seek: her output, varied in nature, proved consistent in quality. That she never wrote anything bad was the verdict of George Saintsbury, a gentleman who considered the absorption of the reader the true test of literary greatness and who covered with much gusto a wider range than any other English critic.

A.S.W.

CHAPTER 1

INTRODUCTION

CHAPTER I

INTRODUCTION

To attempt a narrow definition of our key-words, 'observation' and 'invention', appears an unprofitable task; whatever meaning these terms have when applied to the works of Mrs. Gaskell should emerge from a detailed consideration, in order of publication, of all her non-biographic writings—which is the method here employed.

Although 'observation' may be used in a dual sense, as in speaking of 'observations of' and 'observations on' (meaning thereby that the observer is more or less passive, or more or less active, respectively), it is a psychological and philosophical truism that we rarely, if ever, obtain information about the outside world without to some degree 'cooking' the data. We see what we want to see; our perceptions are coloured by our personalities. One cannot draw clear-cut distinctions between what Mrs. Gaskell observed, her way (humorous, ironical, and so forth) of observing, and her responses (moralistic or otherwise) to what she had observed. Because she was herself, she looked at and for certain things; did so in an individual way; and made her own, unique, comments on them. Something of her artistic temperament will be revealed in this study; but for the present it suffices to indicate the essence of the woman and the writer. This was done, more than half a century ago, by Dr. Adolphus Ward, one of her finest critics, when he wrote:

> . . . a distinctive quality of her own—it may be called a literary quality, because alike in her graver and in her gayer moods she was able to give literary expression to it—is her sweet serenity of soul.[1]

It is not our purpose to analyse in psychological terms Mrs. Gaskell's literary productions; rather the approach will be biographical. There is no doubt that her books were greatly

---

[1] Adolphus William Ward, ed. *The Works of Mrs. Gaskell*, 8 vols., London: Smith, Elder & Co., 1906, I, p. xlvii. This, the Knutsford Edition, will hereafter be cited as *Works*.

influenced by what she received from the world around her; for hers was an extremely sensitive and receptive mind.

> From the first she was interested in them [the people she met], so that she became observant by instinct rather than by training; she was enamored with life, much as she wished to improve ways of living.[2]

Mrs. Gaskell's susceptibility to her immediate *milieu* is well exemplified by her earliest novel. In a letter to Lady Kay-Shuttleworth, having acknowledged its gloominess to be the one great failing in *Mary Barton*[3], she continued:

> It is the fault of the choice of the subject; which yet I did not *choose*, but which was as it were impressed upon me.[4]

Something of Mrs. Gaskell's aesthetic can be inferred from her injunction 'that a thing should be always *let seen*, and not shown'[5]; and from her pleasure in finding a writer who did not make the reader see things through authorial eyes, but rather presented "the scene itself to him."[6] However, the clearest indication of Mrs. Gaskell's critical theory (in so far as she consciously held one) may be gathered from what looks to be the

[2] Lucy Poate Stebbins, 'Elizabeth Gaskell', *A Victorian Album: Some Lady Novelists of the Period*, London: Secker & Warburg, 1946, p. 97.
[3] [Elizabeth Cleghorn Gaskell] *Mary Barton: A Tale of Manchester Life*, 2 vols., London: Chapman and Hall, 1848.
[4] Our quotation was initially taken from a typescript copy of Mrs. Gaskell's letter to Lady (Janet, wife of Sir James Phillips) Kay-Shuttleworth of 16 July [1850—not 1851, as it is annotated]. This copy, belonging to the Hon. Mrs. Angela Mary James (Cutlers, Lane End, High Wycombe), corrected against the original letter, owned by the Fourth Baron Shuttleworth of Gawthorpe (Charles Ughtred John Kay-Shuttleworth, Leck Hall, Carnforth, Lancashire), appears as No. 72a in John Alfred Victor Chapple and Arthur Pollard, ed. *The Letters of Mrs Gaskell*, Manchester: Manchester University Press, 1966. (I owe an inestimable debt to Mr. Chapple and Mr. Pollard for granting me access to the proof-stages of their work when I was correcting my own proofs. I have thus been able to include references to Gaskell letters printed in this edition—hereafter abbreviated as *G.L.*, with the relevant letter-number following.)
[5] Quoted, from Mme Mohl's letter to Mrs. Gaskell of 8 July 1860, in Mary Charlotte Mair Simpson, *Letters and Recollections of Julius and Mary Mohl*, London: Kegan Paul, Trench & Co., 1887, p. 165.
[6] Quoted, from Mary Howitt's letter to her daughter of Thursday [26 December 1850], in *Mary Howitt: An Autobiography*, ed. Margaret Howitt, 2 vols., London: Wm. Isbister Limited, 1889, II, 66.

draft of her reply to a certain 'Herbert Grey' (possibly a pseudonym), a would-be philosophical novelist who seems to have asked for her views on his manuscriplt, 'The Three Paths'[7]. Most of this draft deals with novel-writing; and Mrs. Gaskell's first advice is to observe the external world rather than to examine the inner realm of 'our mental proceedings/'—introspection not being conducive to the novelist's art. After mentioning the healthy way in which Defoe sets objects, not feelings, before one, she apparently recommends 'Herbert Grey' to function like 'an Electric telegraph/', and bring the reader into touch with a hitherto unknown set of vital figures; next a complex of events should be imagined, fit for a good plot. Here she stresses the need to think about the plot, which must grow to a crisis; and warns against the introduction of unnecessary characters who do not contribute to its development ('The plot/ is like the anatomical drawing/ of an artist; he must have/ an idea of his skeleton, before/ he can clothe it with muscle/ & flesh, much more before/ he can drape it.'). She suggests that the sketch of the story be made 'a subject of labour & thought'; and that he should imagine himself 'a spectator & auditor of every/ scene & event' till for him it becomes a reality. He should then recollect, describe, and report fully and accurately so that the reader too may have this clearly before him. Mrs. Gaskell warns against any personal intrusion in his description, saying that if he thinks about the story until he can *'see it in action'* the words will follow (simplicity and conciseness here being virtues). Her main criticisms relate to his lack of plot, his overconcern with feelings, the length of his conversations ('which// *did not advance the action/*'), and his excessive reference to books—which merely served to 'impede the narration'.

How well Mrs. Gaskell observed such precepts is a matter for argument: 'everybody', as she herself reminded 'Grey', 'can preach/ better than they can practise'—in some respects, however, she appears to have followed her own advice. Certainly it

[7] This long draft, with a concluding brief and undated note to Polly [Marianne Gaskell], is in the Fales Collection at the New York University Libraries. Chapple and Pollard, who conjecture that Mrs. Gaskell was writing after 15 March 1859 (*G.L.*, No. 420), identify the novel whose MS she had received—Herbert Grey, *The Three Paths*, 2 vols., London: Hurst & Blackett, 1859.

was her general custom to make a rough outline of any tale she intended to tell: in proof whereof we have the testimony of Lady Ritchie, who recalled 'hearing one of Mrs. Gaskell's daughters say that before beginning a book her mother never failed to write down at length the sketch of the story that was to be.'[8] It also seems—certainly with respect to *Mary Barton*— that the novelist sought 'to really see the scenes'[9] she tried to describe, these being 'as real as . . . [her] own life at the time'[10]. Concerning her involvement with her characters, we may quote the author herself (who always talked 'of her personages as if they were real people'[11]).

[8] Anne Isabella Thackeray Ritchie, 'Mrs. Gaskell', *Blackstick Papers,* London: Smith, Elder, & Co., 1908, p. 215.

[9] These words, quoted by Miss Elizabeth Sanderson Haldane (*Mrs. Gaskell and Her Friends,* London: Hodder and Stoughton Limited, 1930, p. 39) appear in a letter from Mrs. Gaskell to her friend, Miss Eliza ('Tottie') Fox. We have retained the double underlining of the copy of part of this letter (*G.L.,* No. 48), dated Monday [Tuesday] 29 May 1849, found in 'Transcripts of Letters written by, to or about Mrs. E. C. Gaskell, Together with Particulars of Her Books and Other Literary Works. Magazine Articles, Press Notices, Bibliographical Records and other Miscellaneous Biographical Notes. First Collected by Clement K. Shorter to 1914, and Now Continued, Arranged and Transcribed by J. Alex. Symington, Brotherton Librarian, 1927', 2 vols., Vol. I, Section of Letters from Mrs. Gaskell to Eliza (or 'Tottie') Fox—a typescript (deposited in the Gaskell Section, Brotherton Collection, Leeds University Library) hereafter cited by its spine-title, 'Correspondence, Articles & Notes Relating to Mrs. E. C. Gaskell. Transcripts.' Our subsequent references to Brotherton copies of Mrs. Gaskell's letters to Eliza Fox are to the relevant section in the first volume of this Shorter-Symington typescript—the originals apparently having been bought by the Miss Gaskells, according to Edward Garnett's letter of 29 April 1929 to Miss Jane Revere Coolidge (now Mrs. Walter Muir Whitehill, 44 Andover Street, North Andover, Massachusetts, U.S.A.). Unfortunately Miss Haldane, one must note, was in general rather inaccurate in her quotations.

[10] Quoted by Miss Haldane (*Mrs. Gaskell and Her Friends,* p. 39)— a copy of part of Mrs. Gaskell's letter to Eliza Fox of Monday [Tuesday] 29 May 1849 (*G.L.,* No. 48) being in the Gaskell Section, Brotherton Collection, Leeds University Library.

[11] According to her friend, Miss Catherine Winkworth—*Letters and Memorials of Catherine Winkworth,* 2 vols., Clifton: E. Austin and Son (privately circulated), 1883-1886, I (ed. Her Sister [Susanna Winkworth], 1883), 383. Of her *Mary Barton* characters Mrs. Gaskell wrote, to an unnamed American correspondent in a letter of 28 April 1850 (now in the Cornell University Library), that she had realized them to herself 'so vividly/ that parting with them was/ like parting with friends.' The recipient of this letter (*G.L.,* No. 71) is identified as John Seely Hart by Chapple and Pollard.

When I had *little* children I do not think I could have written
stories, because I should have become too much absorbed in my
fictitious people to attend to my *real* ones. . . . you know how
you,—how every one, who tries to write stories *must* become
absorbed in them, (fictitious though they be,) if they are to
interest their readers in them. Besides viewing the subject from a
solely artistic point of view a good writer of fiction must have
lived an active & sympathetic life if she wishes her books to have
strength & vitality in them.[12]

To sum up, Mrs. Gaskell sought to observe what she had
invented, and what she had invented owed much to prior
observations.

It may now be well to indicate, in a general sort of way, those
topics deserving mention in approaching Mrs. Gaskell's stories
by way of 'observation'. Firstly, there is her treatment of places
intimately known, more especially Knutsford, Stratford-on-Avon,
and Manchester, as well as those, like Silverdale and Whitby,
to which she went as a visitor. Secondly, noting 'her power of
understanding and reproducing the varieties of human character
within the range of her observation'[13], we shall endeavour to
demonstrate that many of her literary personages were modelled
on real people. Thirdly, fictional episodes based on actual incidents will be noticed. Fourthly, Mrs. Gaskell's knowledge of
the structure of society, as illustrated by her writings, must
receive some attention. Fifthly, we shall consider her descriptions
of natural scenery, and her evocation of the atmosphere of a
locality. Sixthly, her eye for the telling and significant detail
will require emphasis. This list, though not exhaustive, at least
suggests some fruitful lines of approach.

We shall avoid giving any limited signification to 'invention';

[12] Quoted, from Mrs. Gaskell's letter of 25 September [1862] to a
would-be writer, in Annette Brown Hopkins, 'A Letter of Advice from
the Author of *Cranford* to an Aspiring Novelist', *The Princeton University Library Chronicle,* XV (1954), 144. The letter (*G.L.,* No. 515) from
which this extract is taken largely concerns the difficulties of following a
literary career when one has domestic duties: Mrs. Gaskell's own position
in this respect is discussed, with pertinent quotations, in Aina Rubenius,
The Woman Question in Mrs. Gaskell's Life and Works, The English
Institute in the University of Upsala: Essays and Studies on English
Language and Literature (ed. S. B. Liljegren), No. V, Upsala: A.-B.
Lundequistska Bokhandeln; Copenhagen: Ejnar Munksgaard; Cambridge,
Mass.: Harvard University Press, 1950, pp. 56-62.
[13] Ward, ed. *Works,* I, p. xlvii.

yet a contrast to 'observation' is intended. In speaking of Mrs. Gaskell's 'works of art and observation'[14] Frederick Greenwood could have used our term instead of 'art'. Susanna Winkworth very likely had the same quality in mind when, besides noting Mrs. Gaskell's 'quick keen observation,'[15] she remarked upon 'her wealth of imaginative power'[16]. Our survey will take into account her qualities as a story-teller, but, at the same time, not neglect those 'limitations . . . in her technical powers as a novelist'[17] detected by one of Mrs. Gaskell's more recent critics. Under 'invention' will be included matters of structure and technique. We shall pay heed to plots, which are often loosely constructed and ill-defined, and comment on the way she at times handled her material in the service of poetic justice. We shall, moreover, stress the frequency with which certain themes, incidents, and even proper names[18] are repeated. Although much of Mrs. Gaskell's success in character-creation came from an imaginative synthesis of illuminating *minutiae,* no case will be maintained for her as a profound or philosophical novelist: as Lord David Cecil puts it, she could not 'argue from her particular observation to discover a general conception of the laws governing human conduct'[19]. Finally, when opportunity arises, we shall try to draw attention to the poetic qualities in her fiction, her awareness of the transitoriness of things, and her occasional moments of vision.

Probably the aspect of Mrs. Gaskell's inventiveness which can with most profit here be discussed is the diversity of her output;

[14] Concluding Remarks to *Wives and Daughters* (*Works,* VIII, 759).
[15] *Memorials of Two Sisters: Susanna and Catherine Winkworth,* ed. Margaret Josephine Shaen, London, New York, Bombay, and Calcutta: Longmans, Green, and Co., 1908, p. 24—our shorter title for this work being *Memorials of Two Sisters.*
[16] *Memorials of Two Sisters,* ed. Shaen, p. 24.
[17] Arthur Pollard, 'The Novels of Mrs. Gaskell', *Bulletin of the John Rylands Library, Manchester,* XLIII (1961), 423. This article is separately published as an off-print (*The Novels of Mrs. Gaskell,* Manchester: The Librarian, The John Rylands Library; and The Manchester University Press, 1961).
[18] See Appendix VII.
[19] Edward Christian David Gascoyne Cecil, 'Mrs. Gaskell', *Early Victorian Novelists: Essays in Revaluation,* Harmondsworth, Middlesex: Penguin Books, 1948, p. 154. Lord David Cecil's valuable essay first appeared in his *Early Victorian Novelists: Essays in Revaluation,* London: Constable and Co. Ltd, 1934, pp. 195-241.

for she tried her hand at numerous literary modes. Notwithstanding the repetitions found in her books, she rarely wrote sequels to works which brought her fame : in that sense, she never repeated her successes. Perhaps the best way to demonstrate the variety of her writings is by attempting an *ad hoc* classification, with appropriate examples (several of these, of course, exemplify more than one *genre*). One may look upon Mrs. Gaskell as poet ('Sketches among the Poor. No. 1', 1837[20]), biographer (*The Life of Charlotte Brontë,* 1857), humorist (*Cranford,* 1853), sociologist ('An Italian Institution', 1863), light essayist ('Company Manners', 1854), antiquary ('Clopton Hall' piece, 1840), editor (*Mabel Vaughan* [by Maria S. Cummins], 1857), anecdotist ('Disappearances', 1851), reviewer ('Modern Greek Songs', 1854), and journalist (articles in *The Pall Mall Gazette,* 1865); one may also regard her as a writer of the regional novel (*Mary Barton,* 1848), the social-problem novel (*Ruth,* 1853), the industrial novel (*North and South,* 1855), the historical novel (*Sylvia's Lovers,* 1863), the domestic novel (*Wives and Daughters,* 1866), the pastoral idyl (*Cousin Phillis,* 1864), the moral tale ('Bessy's Troubles at Home', 1852), the gothick tale of terror ('The Grey Woman', 1861), the ghost story ('The Old Nurse's Story', 1853), the murder story (*A Dark Night's Work,* 1863), the fantasy ('Curious, if True', 1860), the travelogue ('French Life', 1864), the preface (*Garibaldi at Caprera,* by Colonel Vecchj, 1862), and even the laudatory obituary ('Robert Gould Shaw', 1863).

A concluding word on methodology may be apposite. In the present study a chronological framework has been favoured for a variety of reasons. It enables the critic to follow the sequence in which Mrs. Gaskell's literary output initially came before the public; hence, to some degree, the expectations with which one approaches every work are similar to those of its first readers. Since the order of publication, though not identical with that of composition, presumably provides a fair approximation to it, an estimate may be formed of the development of the novelist's art and dominant concerns. The details of composition and

[20] Detailed bibliographical descriptions of the works cited in this paragraph will be given when they are treated, in their proper chronological order, later in our study.

publication are sometimes themselves of interest, and such an approach permits their discussion without incongruity. It allows every work to be treated as a unity as well as a part of the canon, and ensures that the minor writings are not neglected—an important advantage, for many of Mrs. Gaskell's shorter stories have been unduly ignored. Relevant biographical information can be introduced with ease, the close connection between life and works being thereby underlined. A historical approach is helpful too in keeping both the inventive and the observational aspects of the fiction before one, thus guarding against the compartmentalization which a more analytic, non-annalistic, treatment might have engendered. There is also a practical convenience in having most of the essential points about a novel or tale set down in one place.

The Life of Charlotte Brontë[21] has been omitted from this survey. A strong case for its inclusion, on the grounds of observation, could doubtless have been made; a hostile critic, not without warrant[22], might even have urged its claims as a work of invention. However, the biography has already received much attention, from Brontë as well as from Gaskell scholars[23]. To have given it the consideration it deserves would have entailed more research, and yet further extended a study which is, perhaps, already inordinately long. Nevertheless references to this book will occur whenever pertinent links can be established between it and the rest of the canon.

[21] Elizabeth Cleghorn Gaskell, The Life of Charlotte Brontë, 2 vols., London: Smith, Elder & Co., 1857.

[22] "In the Dewsbury Reporter of December 4th, 1897, Mr Brontë is quoted as saying on one occasion to Mrs Gaskell, ' . . . You will have plenty of material and if you haven't enough, why you must invent some' "—Joanna Mary Brough Hutton, 'Items from the Museum Cuttings Book', Brontë Society Transactions, Vol. XIV, No. 3 (Part 73 of the Society's Publications), 1963, p. 30.

[23] There are, for example, a couple of excellent chapters in Annette Brown Hopkins, Elizabeth Gaskell: Her Life and Work, London: John Lehmann, 1952, pp. 158-199—our shorter title for this work being Elizabeth Gaskell.

CHAPTER II

"MY DIARY" (Composed 10 March 1835-28 October 1838)
TO *MARY BARTON* (1848)

SECTION I

"My Diary"
(Composed 10 March 1835-28 October 1838)

Although John Stevenson was pleased to hear his sister, while in her early teens, was keeping a journal[1], the only one extant was begun much later, and concerns the first years of her daughters, Marianne and Margaret Emily ('Meta'); it did not appear in print till 1923, being then privately circulated by Clement King Shorter[2]. Mrs. Gaskell intended the diary for her eldest child, Marianne, to whom she addressed the dedication[3]; but, as an important preliminary to her public writings, this personal document deserves detailed treatment. Her first and

---

[1] 'I am very glad to hear that you have begun a/ Journal & have no doubt it will be ∧a∧ very amusing/ as well as interesting one—at least I know you can/ if you like, make it so—I shall hope to have/ good long extracts from it— /': thus wrote John to Elizabeth Stevenson from Blackwall on 8 June [1827], the first two leaves of his letter, which was continued on 10 June, being in the hands of the present writer (High Bank, 12 Forest Street, Weaverham, Northwich, Cheshire). John's words apparently produced the desired effect; for, in a letter written aboard the Ship Recovery at Gravesend on 17(?) June [1827], he told Elizabeth not to be afraid of giving good long extracts from her log as anything about herself would interest him—typescript copies of this letter, one (erroneously?) dated 13 June, once owned by the late Mr. Joseph Torry Lancaster (10 Vernon Road, Harrogate), belong to the present writer. William Stevenson was equally solicitous on the same subject: in a letter from 3 Beaufort Row of 2 July [1827] he told his daughter that, should she go into Wales, he expected a diary to be kept of what she saw and remembered (typescript copies of this letter, which were formerly in the hands of Mr. J. T. Lancaster, are now possessed by the present writer). A couple of years earlier John had written to his (and Elizabeth's) aunt, Mrs. Hannah Lumb, this time from India, saying that his sister would find no difficulty in lengthening her correspondence to him if only she got 'into the habit/ of keeping a journal'—extract from a mutilated letter in the possession of the present writer, its water-mark is 1822, but the date 1825 appears above the address on the outside (verso) of the second leaf.

[2] Elizabeth Cleghorn Gaskell, *"My Diary": The early years of my daughter Marianne,* intro. Clement King Shorter, London: Privately printed by Clement Shorter, 1923. The MS of this diary is in the possession of Marianne's grand-daughter, Mrs. Margaret Evelyn Averia Trevor Jones (Monkstone, Radyr, Cardiff).

[3] *"My Diary"*, p. 5.

17

D

most devoted biographer remarked that Mrs. Gaskell's 'career affords an excellent illustration of the value of minute observation at all times and in all places'[4] : such was the case from the outset.

"My Diary" is very much a record of Mrs. Gaskell's observations of and on the psychology and physiology of her two baby girls; yet the emphasis of that record is as much subjective as objective. The parent-child relationship having prominence in her life and work alike, motherhood is, not unnaturally, highly valued by the diarist—for 'all a woman's life, at least so it . . . [seemed to her then], ought to have a reference to the period when she will be fulfilling one of her greatest and highest duties, those of a mother.'[5] Aware of her 'holy trust,'[6] she recognized 'the dear and tender tie of Mother and Daughter'[7]; and her disposition and feelings were so closely linked to her baby's that even during the writing she found Marianne's regular breathing the music of her own thoughts[8]. It is worth while to recall that Mrs. Gaskell was alone among the major early-Victorian novelists in being a mother as well as an authoress—a fact which can easily be kept in mind by reflecting that she has, almost invariably, been known to her readers by no other name than 'Mrs. Gaskell'.

With this devotion to her children is found a concern that her attachment may not become idolization. Throughout the diary Mrs. Gaskell constantly makes remarks of which the following are typical.

> . . . oh! may I not make her [Marianne] into an idol, but strive to prepare both her and myself for the change [death] that may come any day.[9]

> Lord! unto thee do I commit this darling precious treasure [Marianne]; thou knowest how I love her; I pray that I may not make her too much my idol, . . . [10]

[4] Esther Alice (Mrs. Ellis H.) Chadwick, *Mrs. Gaskell: Haunts, Homes, and Stories,* New and rev. edn, London: Sir Isaac Pitman & Sons, Ltd., 1913, p. 295—our shorter title for this work being *Mrs. Gaskell.* (The first edition appeared in 1910.)
[5] *"My Diary",* p. 10.
[6] *"My Diary",* p. 11.
[7] *"My Diary",* p. 5.
[8] *"My Diary",* p. 9.
[9] *"My Diary",* p. 11.
[10] *"My Diary",* p. 17.

> Oh! may I constantly bear in mind the words, "The Lord hath
> given, and the Lord hath taken away. Blessed be the name of
> the Lord!"[11]

Her religion required submission to divine decrees[12], and she
considered it wrong to make too much of any earthly being.

Coupled with her religious are her moral views. Miss Hopkins
has mentioned that Mrs. Gaskell's 'management of the children,
her concern for their physical and moral welfare, sounds very
modern, very much like the observations of an experienced
person, rather than the beginner'[13]. Her approach, based on
reason, is in keeping with the spirit of Unitarianism; though on
occasions she confesses to not always being able to act upon her
convictions[14], and to only partially adhering to rational rules[15].

One aspect of Mrs. Gaskell's religious morality deserves special
notice since we shall meet it later in literary form—she not only
stresses the necessity to fulfil promises[16], but also expresses a
dislike of deceit (by her distaste for distracting a child's attention
with the suggestion it look for something not there[17]). Thus she
would seem to consider any sort of convenient invention immoral, truthfulness appearing all important in her eyes. Self-
observation is as evident as observation of the babies; for Mrs.
Gaskell was careful to scrutinize her own character, being alert,
for instance, to curb faults of anger[18], jealousy[19], and im-
patience[20].

It is opportune here to take note of Mrs. Gaskell's 'theory that
when *children*, at any rate, are irritable, something is physically
the matter with them.'[21] This close connexion between bodily
and mental states may be relevantly borne in mind when we
come to consider her attitude to industrial and social conditions.
She did not, however, relinquish her sense of values by adopting
a *laissez-faire* approach to morals.

---

[11] *"My Diary"*, pp. 19-20.
[12] *"My Diary"*, pp. 27-28.
[13] Hopkins, *Elizabeth Gaskell*, p. 59.
[14] *"My Diary"*, p. 14.
[15] *"My Diary"*, p. 9.
[16] *"My Diary"*, pp. 12, 26.
[17] *"My Diary"*, pp. 12, 33.
[18] *"My Diary"*, p. 22.
[19] *"My Diary"*, p. 16.
[20] *"My Diary"*, p. 39.
[21] *"My Diary"*, p. 17.

I do not mean to say that the habit of self-control may not be given, and that at a very early age, but I think that, with certain states of the body, feelings will arise which *ought* to be controlled, and that everything physical tending to produce those peculiar states of the body should be avoided, with as much care as we would avoid anything moral tending to produce moral evil.[22]

Significantly among the traits she wished Marianne to acquire was 'a habit of fixing her attention.'[23]

If we give her habits of observation, attention and perseverance, in whatever objects her little mind may be occupied with, I shall think we are laying a good foundation, . . . [24]

From this it is an easy inference that the writer herself set great store by careful observation and scrutiny.

Before leaving *"My Diary"*, we may pertinently point out how large death bulks in the journal. Besides constant apprehensions about the fragility of human life in regard to Marianne, Mrs. Gaskell mentions the death from the croup of 'little Eddy Deane'[25] and also (at length) that of her favourite aunt[26].

My dearest Aunt Lumb, my more than mother, had had a paralytic stroke on Wednesday, March 8th. . . . on May 1st I lost my best friend. May God reward her for all her kindness to me![27]

Her own mother the diarist had lost more than thirty-five years before—a loss very deeply felt, and poignantly voiced in a letter of 13 February [1849] to George Hope, a fellow Unitarian.

"I will not let an hour pass, my dear sir, without acknowledging your kindness in sending me my dear mother's letters, the only relics of her that I have, and of more value to me than I can express, for I have so often longed for some little thing that had once been hers or been touched by her. I think no one but one so unfortunate as to be early motherless can enter into the craving one has after the lost mother."[28]

[22] *"My Diary"*, p. 14.
[23] *"My Diary"*, p. 6.
[24] *"My Diary"*, p. 24.
[25] *"My Diary"*, p. 36.
[26] *"My Diary"*, pp. 28-30.
[27] *"My Diary"*, p. 28.
[28] Quoted in His Daughter [Charlotte Hope], comp. *George Hope of Fenton Barns: A Sketch of his Life,* Edinburgh: David Douglas, 1881, p. 177. This passage is slightly misprinted in *G.L.*, No. 614.

In the late eighteen-twenties John Stevenson, Elizabeth's only surviving brother, had mysteriously disappeared while on a voyage to India[29]; and her father, of whom she had seen little before his last illness, had died in March 1829, when she was only eighteen. With the decease of Mrs. Lumb, therefore, she lost all the blood-relatives who meant most to her. The mortality theme occurs often in Mrs. Gaskell's stories; but one can appreciate the private reasons for this: she was not merely indulging a popular fashion for death-bed scenes. It is, moreover, important to remember that an early grave was much commoner then than now, among both rich and poor.

[29] For what it is worth, we may mention a letter of 10 December [1914] to Clement Shorter from Mrs. Edward Thurstan Holland (Marianne Gaskell)—now in the Gaskell Section, Brotherton Collection, Leeds University Library. Mrs. Holland states that, when she was about ten, her mother told her: that she could only just recall her brother; that he had gone to sea when (Mrs. Holland thinks she said) she was quite a young girl; and that she remembered visiting her father from Knutsford to wish her brother goodbye—she then being about twelve, in Mrs. Holland's opinion. However, various communications from John Stevenson to Elizabeth, the property of the present writer, both typescript copies (once owned by Mr. J. T. Lancaster) and original letters, indicate that John probably left England for good in 1828. Indeed his last brotherly epistle may well have been that from Beaufort Row of 16 August [1828], where he speaks of his most likely remaining in India and bids his sister farewell. In this letter (of which only typescript copies remain) John remarks that Smith & Elder, though themselves declining to publish his work, had suggested that Longman might comply—an ironical refusal in that they were to become Mrs. Gaskell's favourite publishers.

SECTION II

'On Visiting the Grave of My Stillborn Little Girl'
(Written in 1836)

Some three years after the death of her first child[1], Mrs. Gaskell composed a sonnet, 'On Visiting the Grave of My Stillborn Little Girl', first printed in the Knutsford Edition[2]—its date being given as 4 July 1836[3]. Dr. Ward forbore to comment upon this poem except to remark on its 'great tenderness and sweetness'[4]; but for our purposes we may mention that it is wholly in keeping with the devotion revealed in *"My Diary"*. The lines sprang from observation, from painfully direct personal experience, albeit recollected in tranquillity.

[1] Who was born dead in the summer of 1833 (Chadwick, *Mrs. Gaskell,* p. 135), possibly on 4 July (Arthur Pollard, *Mrs Gaskell: Novelist and Biographer,* Manchester: Manchester University Press, 1965, p. 14, fn. 1).
[2] *Works,* I, pp. xxvi-xxvii.
[3] Mrs. Gaskell apparently dated this poem 'Sunday, July 4th, 1836' (*Works,* I, p. xxvi); yet according to the perpetual calendar 4 July 1836 fell on a Monday.
[4] Ward, ed. *Works,* I, p. xxvi.

23

SECTION III

'Sketches among the Poor. No. 1' (1837)

Writing on 18 August 1838 to Mary Howitt, Mrs. Gaskell
remarked about her husband and herself :

> "We once thought of *trying* to write sketches among the poor,
> *rather* in the manner of Crabbe (now don't think this presump-
> tuous), but in a more seeing-beauty spirit; and one—the only one
> —was published in *Blackwood*, January 1837. But I suppose we
> spoke of our plan near a dog-rose, for it never went any further."[1]

The poem[2] referred to describes the prototype of Alice Wilson,
a character who appears in *Mary Barton*. It was a joint composition, so we must be careful not to regard it solely as the
work of Mrs. Gaskell. The Rev. William Gaskell was himself
poet enough to draw praise from Wordsworth[3] for his philan-

---

[1] Quoted in Margaret Howitt, 'Stray Notes from Mrs. Gaskell', *Good
Words*, XXXVI (1895), 611. Reprinted, with slight errors, by Ward (ed.
Works, I, pp. xxi-xxii), Miss Hopkins (*Elizabeth Gaskell*, p. 60), and
Mrs. Chadwick (*Mrs. Gaskell*, pp. 135-136), who explains the dog-rose
reference, this passage appears in *G.L.*, No. 12.

[2] 'Sketches among the Poor. No. 1', *Blackwood's Edinburgh Magazine*,
XLI, 48-50. About this (anonymous) contribution Mrs. Gaskell wrote
modestly over twenty years later—on 9 March [1859]—to John Blackwood,
the publisher, 'It was worth very little; but I/ was very much pleased;
and/ very proud to see it in print./ I sent some articles, in prose,/ afterwards to Blackwood,—but/ they were, as I now feel, both/ poor & exaggerated in tone; &/ they were never inserted. //'—Letter in the National
Library of Scotland (MS. 4319, ff. 9-12; the quoted passage appears on
f. 11ʳ), printed as *G.L.*, No. 417, where our extract is slightly differently
punctuated. The prose articles may have been, or arisen from, the pieces
on various poets which Mrs. Gaskell was composing in May 1836 (*G.L.*,
No. 4); however, as Chapple and Pollard imply, these latter compositions could have been preliminary to the Gaskells' proposed 'Sketches
among the Poor' series.

[3] Ross Douglas Waller, 'Letters Addressed to Mrs. Gaskell by Celebrated Contemporaries. Now in the Possession of the John Rylands
Library', *Bulletin of the John Rylands Library, Manchester*, XIX (1935),
133-134. There is a convenient reprint of this article—Ross Douglas
Waller, ed. *Letters Addressed to Mrs Gaskell by Celebrated Contemporaries Now in the Possession of the John Rylands Library*, Manchester:
The Manchester University Press; and The Librarian, The John Rylands
Library, 1935 (our shorter title being *Letters Addressed to Mrs Gaskell
by Celebrated Contemporaries*).

thropically didactic *Temperance Rhymes*[4]; he gained a reputation in Manchester for his knowledge of the Lancashire dialect, and lectured on 'The Poets and Poetry of Humble Life'[5]. Although ostensibly in the manner of Crabbe, 'Sketches among the Poor. No. 1' also recalls Goldsmith, Johnson, Cowper, Wordsworth, and Shelley[6].

The 'seeing-beauty spirit' (looking at life so as to find the poetic in it, rather than romanticizing as a reaction against mundane sordidness) is central to a great deal of Mrs. Gaskell's writings; hence her own words to Mary Howitt are especially relevant.

> "As for the Poetry of Humble Life, that, even in a town, is met with on every hand. We have such a district[7], and we constantly meet with examples of the beautiful truth in that passage of 'The Cumberland Beggar:'
>> 'Man is dear to man; the poorest poor
>> Long for some moments in a weary life
>> When they can know and feel that they have been,
>> Themselves, the fathers and the dealers out
>> Of some small blessings; have been kind to such
>> As needed kindness, for this simple cause,
>> That we have all of us a human heart.'

---

[4] [William Gaskell] *Temperance Rhymes*, London: Simpkin, Marshall and Co., 1839.

[5] *G.L.*, Nos. 191, 192, 195, 196, 197, 202, 558; 9, 10, 11, 12.

[6] Excellent indicators of Mrs. Gaskell's acquaintance with English literature are: Literary Index (b) to Chapple and Pollard, ed. *The Letters of Mrs Gaskell*; and Appendix III to Rubenius, *The Woman Question in Mrs. Gaskell's Life and Works*, pp. 284-370. For the influence of her reading on Mrs. Gaskell's writings one may contrast the case made out by Miss Rubenius (*op. cit.*, pp. 241-283) with the repudiation of literary indebtedness due to (unconscious) plagiarism found in Ward, ed. *Works*, I, pp. xlv-xlvi. Some of Mrs. Gaskell's favourite authors are listed by Mrs. Chadwick (*Mrs. Gaskell*, pp. 94, 137); the selections for a commonplace book she kept at the age of twenty-one covered, besides Shakespeare, Burns, and Wordsworth, many ballads and seventeenth-century poets—Jane Revere Coolidge (subsequently Mrs. Walter Muir Whitehill), 'Life and letters of Mrs. E. C. Gaskell', Ch. I, pp. 25-28 (an incomplete typescript in the Gaskell Section, Brotherton Collection, Leeds University Library).

[7] The Gaskells then lived at 14 Dover Street, Oxford Road, Manchester—Howitt, 'Stray Notes from Mrs. Gaskell', *Good Words*, XXXVI, 604.

"In short, the beauty and poetry of many of the common things and daily events of life in its humblest aspect does not seem to me sufficiently appreciated."[8]

This first and only sketch describes a country-woman, Mary, living in an industrial town and doing good to those around her, yet always longing to return to her country home—though never able to do so because of the constant calls made on her charity. While labouring for others, she thinks of her girlhood with a sister since dead. The poem closes with her deafness, blindness, and withdrawal from reality; she returns to the realms of childhood. The attitude of the Gaskells to such a life is quite explicit.

> To some she might prosaic seem, but me
> She always charmed with daily poesy,
> Felt in her every action, never heard,
> E'en as the mate of some sweet singing-bird,
> That mute and still broods on her treasure-nest,
> Her heart's fond hope hid deep within her breast.[9]

It is worth while noticing the part memory plays in the poem. The narrator looks back into 'childhood's days'[10] to remember Mary, who is herself recollecting her childhood. Mary's dreams and hopes refer back to past happiness, and when the phrase 'glad imaginings'[11] occurs the sense seems equivalent to 'sweet young memories'[12]. 'Fancy wild'[13] is not extravagance of invention, but rather an especially forceful memory which removes its half-conscious owner from her present surroundings to a former, country *milieu*.

There is an authentic ring about the sketch which makes it by no means rash to postulate an original, or at least several similar

---

[8] Quoted, from Mrs. Gaskell's letter to Mrs. Mary Howitt of 18 August 1838, in Howitt, 'Stray Notes from Mrs. Gaskell', *Good Words*, XXXVI, 611: the passage appears in *G.L.*, No. 12. The Wordsworth quotation is slightly inaccurate.

[9] *Works*, I, p. xxiii.

[10] *Works*, I, p. xxii.

[11] *Works*, I, p. xxv.

[12] *Works*, I, p. xxv.

[13] *Works*, I, p. xxv.

originals: perhaps, like many[14], drawn into the town by higher wages and a determination not to be a burden upon her rural parents, Mary appears a typical product of industrial urbanization. Mr. Gaskell, in the course of his ministry of fifty-six years at Cross Street Chapel, must have met scores of such women; and his wife had the additional sympathy and insight arising from her own position as a Manchester resident whose mouth watered for " 'the primrose-bordered lanes' "[15].

[14] For example, Alice Wilson in *Mary Barton* (*Works*, I, 32-33). It is worth noting that close correspondences exist between Mary of this poem and Alice Wilson of the novel: like the former (*Works*, I, pp. xxii-xxv), the latter had a clean though urban dwelling (*Works*, I, 14-16); was always willing to help others (*Works*, I, 9-10, 15, 35, 83, 225); longed to return to her rural home (*Works*, I, 179, 225), yet was constantly prevented from so doing (*Works*, I, 33-36, 86); used to recall from her childhood days not only roams with a long-dead sister but even the bees or a certain hawthorn-tree (*Works*, I, 35), such memories recurring during her last illness (*Works*, I, 250); gradually became deaf (*Works*, I, 135, 137, 139, 166, 171, 178-9), blind (*Works*, I, 166, 169, 171, 179), and clouded in her mind (*Works*, I, 249); and eventually lapsed into a second childhood (*Works*, I, 250, 312, 393-394)—a veiled blessing (*Works*, I, 250, 394)—before being quietly taken by death (*Works*, I, 393-394).

[15] Quoted, from Mrs. Gaskell's letter to Mrs. Mary Howitt of (perhaps) 18 August 1838, in Howitt, 'Stray Notes from Mrs. Gaskell', *Good Words*, XXXVI, 612. The extract occurs in *G.L.*, No. 617.

SECTION IV

' Clopton Hall ' Contribution (1840)

In 1838, after the announcement of his intended *Visits to Remarkable Places,* William Howitt received a letter from Mrs. Gaskell 'drawing his attention to a fine old seat, Clopton Hall, near Stratford-on-Avon.'[1] Mrs. Gaskell's description of a visit made in her school-days to this mansion so impressed Howitt that he incorporated what she had written into his own book[2], mentioning his correspondent was 'a fair lady'[3].

Mrs. Gaskell's sketch of Clopton House is a portrait from memory. She may have refreshed that memory by reference to something composed immediately after the visit, which must have occurred during the five years[4] Elizabeth Stevenson was at Avonbank School, very probably in 1825[5]. What immediately

---

[1] *Mary Howitt: An Autobiography,* ed. Howitt, II, 28.
[2] William Howitt, *Visits to Remarkable Places: Old Halls, Battle Fields, and Scenes Illustrative of Striking Passages in English History and Poetry,* London: Longman, Orme, Brown, Green, & Longmans, 1840, pp. 135-139.
[3] Howitt, *Visits,* p. 135.
[4] Rubenius, *The Woman Question in Mrs. Gaskell's Life and Works,* p. 19, fn. 1. The crucial evidence about the length of time she was at school in Warwickshire is Mrs. Gaskell's reference to her five years there in a letter to W. S. Landor of 22 May 1854 (now in the Forster Collection—F. MS. 215—at the Victoria & Albert Museum): *G.L.,* No. 197. Details of Elizabeth Stevenson's Stratford school, kept by Miss Maria Byerley and her sisters, appear in Phyllis D. Hicks, *A Quest of Ladies: The Story of a Warwickshire School* [Birmingham: Frank Juckes, 1949], pp. 80-88. Mrs. Gaskell's letter to Marianne of Sunday [late May or early—possibly 1 or 8—June 1851], copies of which, formerly the property of Mr. J. T. Lancaster, belong to the present writer, contains another reference to these five years at Miss Byerley's; this letter (*G.L.,* No. 97+) is dated [May 1851] by Chapple and Pollard. Elizabeth probably finished her formal schooling some time (doubtless shortly) before 14 June 1826, as is implied by a letter written to her then by one of the Miss Byerleys (almost certainly Jane Margaret), typescript copies of part of which, once possessed by Mr. J. T. Lancaster, are owned by the present writer. That she was residing at Avonbank on Thursday 15 June 1825 but at Knutsford on 12 June 1827 is attested by two of her music books, respectively so dated, in the Gaskell Collection at the Manchester Central Reference Library: MS. F. 823.894 C1.
[5] The autumn before her departure.

strikes the reader is how very 'powerful and graphic'[6] in detail
this description is: for she clearly brings before one's eyes the
building, with its colour ' "that deep, dead red almost approaching to purple" '[7]; ' "the single yellow rose and the Austrian briar
trained into something like order round the deep-set diamond-
paned windows" '[8]; the military map of Civil War times ' "hung
up, well finished with pen and ink, shewing the stations of the
respective armies, and with old-fashioned writing beneath, the
names of the principal towns, setting forth the strength of the
garrison" '[9]; ' "the wide shelving oak staircase, with its massy
balustrade all crumbling and worm-eaten." '[10] Recollections with
this degree of vividness go to support what we learn elsewhere
about the author's 'marvellous memory'[11]. When she went with
her friends to pay this visit to an old family seat, she not only
observed minutely but was able, over a decade later, to recollect
what had once been so precisely noted. Certainly she confessed
to recalling little in the chapel[12], and her memory must have
been at fault about the date of *All for Love*[13]; but whatever
interested her impressed itself upon her mind. Thus even in her
school-days she showed that historical curiosity and instinct for
research[14] which were later to distinguish *Sylvia's Lovers* and
The Life of Charlotte Brontë.

Side by side with acute observations of the house go speculations about its inmates. Here is displayed a spirit we have
already noted—that spirit which was drawn to the poetic, though
it usually took something concrete as its point of departure. Mrs.
Gaskell recalls the legend of Charlotte Clopton, who was buried
alive in the family tomb; and mentions the ' " 'eirie' feeling" '[15]

[6] *Mary Howitt: An Autobiography,* ed. Howitt, II, 28.
[7] *Works,* I, 505.
[8] *Works,* I, 505.
[9] *Works,* I, 505: the comma after 'beneath' may be a printer's error
(Howitt, *Visits,* p. 136).
[10] *Works,* I, 505-506: a small typographical error has been corrected.
[11] *Memorials of Two Sisters,* ed. Shaen, p. 24.
[12] *Works,* I, 506.
[13] *Works,* I, 506. There is no recorded 1686 edition of Dryden's play,
though one did appear in 1696—the mistake may be due to a misreading
by Howitt (*Visits,* p. 137) of what his fair correspondent had written; or,
of course, it may simply be a printer's error.
[14] *Works,* I, 507.
[15] *Works,* I, 506.

she experienced when in the haunted bedroom where Charlotte's picture hung : her *penchant* for ghost-stories remained a life-long interest[16]. Closely related are her musings over the empty nursery, which (characteristically) she calls ' "of these deserted rooms . . . the most deserted, and the saddest" '[17]—for it was ' "a nursery without children, without singing voices, without merry chiming footsteps!" '[18] It is worth quoting Mrs. Gaskell's next words, both for their intrinsic merit as a mother's expression of the *ubi sunt motif* and also for their textual interest, containing as they do a phrase which links with the title[19] of a story Mrs. Gaskell would, some years later, submit to *Howitt's Journal* —though the present context hardly suggests that story's Dickensian theme.

> "A nursery hung round with its once inhabitants, bold, gallant boys, and fair, arch-looking girls, and one or two nurses with round, fat babies in their arms. Who were they all? What was their lot in life? Sunshine, or storm? or had they been 'loved by the gods, and died young?' The very echoes knew not."[20]

[16] Margaret Howitt (ed. *Mary Howitt: An Autobiography*, II, 65) quotes from a letter her mother wrote at Christmas 1850, where she looks forward to interchanging ghost-stories with Mrs. Gaskell. See too, for a testimony to her prowess in this art, Anne Isabella Thackeray Ritchie, pref. *Cranford*, by Mrs. Gaskell, London and New York: Macmillan and Co., 1891, p. ix.

[17] *Works*, I, 507.

[18] *Works*, I, 507.

[19] 'Christmas Storms and Sunshine'.

[20] *Works*, I, 507.

SECTION V

Libbie Marsh's Three Eras (1847)

Whether or not William Howitt's recommendation that Mrs. Gaskell should 'use her pen for the public benefit'[1] led, as he supposed, to the writing of *Mary Barton,* it was almost certainly the reason why she contributed to *Howitt's Journal.* William and Mary Howitt had first met the Gaskells in 1841[2], when travelling on the Rhine; but ever since Mrs. Gaskell's letter on Clopton House a correspondence had been kept up. The Howitts were interested in the general economic and social conditions of their time; and, though any direct literary influence on Mrs. Gaskell may be discounted[3], her association with these socially-alert authors must have reinforced her own literary inclinations.

Mrs. Gaskell's first published (if not first written) story appeared in print on 5 June 1847, and was entitled 'Life in Manchester. Libbie Marsh's Three Eras.—St. Valentine's Day'[4], the author being 'Cotton Mather Mills, Esq.'[5] This culminates in a poor seamstress's present of a canary to a bed-fast little boy: it is a moving story which must have brought tears to the eyes of its original readers—whereby nothing derogatory is intended; for 'sentimental' is not the adjective one would apply. Two or three points deserve notice as indicative of what will, in later works, again be found.

Mrs. Gaskell's graphic descriptive powers, based on first-hand experience, are at once evident. Her reference, as narrator, to

---

[1] *Mary Howitt: An Autobiography,* ed. Howitt, II, 28.

[2] Chadwick, *Mrs. Gaskell,* p. 144; Hopkins, *Elizabeth Gaskell,* pp. 63-65; and *G.L.,* No. 15.

[3] For a different view, see Carl Ray Woodring, *Victorian Samplers: William and Mary Howitt,* Lawrence, Kansas: University of Kansas Press, 1952, pp. 89-90.

[4] *Howitt's Journal of Literature and Popular Progress,* I, 310-313. The three episodes, of which this is the first, were published together in [1850] —*Libbie Marsh's Three Eras. A Lancashire Tale,* London: Hamilton, Adams, and Co.; Liverpool: David Marples.

[5] Cotton Mather was a New England witch-hunter: see Chadwick, *Mrs. Gaskell,* p. 89.

33

'our neighbourhood'[6] suggests an intimate relation with her material; when pointing to the aspect of 'No. 2. —— Court, Albemarle Street'[7] and when treating the life of its inmates[8], she displays an 'insider's' point of view. She depicts Mrs. Dixon's preparation of tea in a way which shows she had herself often been present on many similar occasions, a typically realistic detail being the addition of eggs to thicken the cream[9]. The Dixons were, at that time, an affluent household, wages being high. An instance of Mrs. Gaskell's knowledge of the working life of the family is her remark that, being confined to a factory atmosphere of between seventy-five and eighty degrees[10], '[t]hey

---

[6] *Works,* I, 459.

[7] *Works,* I, 459.

[8] *Works,* I, 460-462.

[9] *Works,* I, 461.

[10] This tallies with an 1843 report by a factory superintendent, referred to by Miss Rubenius (*The Woman Question in Mrs. Gaskell's Life and Works,* p. 235). See too Peter Gaskell, *The Manufacturing Population of England, Its Moral, Social, and Physical Conditions, and the Changes Which Have Arisen from the Use of Steam Machinery; with an Examination of Infant Labour,* London: Baldwin and Cradock, 1833, p. 68, fn. Most of what is known about Peter Gaskell, whose book was an important source for Engels, may conveniently be found in William Otto Henderson and William Henry Chaloner, trans. and ed. *The Condition of the Working Class in England,* by Friedrich Engels, Oxford: Basil Blackwell, 1958, p. xiii, fn. 5 [3]. In a letter of 14 November 1958 Dr. Chaloner (Room 6, Arts Building, University of Manchester, Manchester 13) informed me that he and Dr. Henderson had considered whether Peter Gaskell and the novelist might not be related, though they could find no evidence in favour of this theory. Since then my own researches have established not only that the two writers were indeed connected, very distantly and by marriage, but also, more importantly, that the author of *Mary Barton* was aware of this connexion. The evidence is as follows. Among the papers of the late Edgar Swinton Holland was found a copy of a letter of 10 February 1838, apparently written by a Miss Margaret Holland of Mobberley to Miss Abigail Holland of Knutsford (aunt to Mrs. Gaskell); this copy subsequently appeared in William Fergusson Irvine, ed. *A History of the Family of Holland of Mobberley and Knutsford in the County of Chester with Some Account of the Family of Holland of Upholland & Denton in the County of Lancaster, from Materials Collected by the Late Edgar Swinton Holland,* Edinburgh: Privately printed at the Ballantyne Press, 1902, pp. 61-62. Trying to fulfil a request for information about the Coppock family, Margaret remarks that a medical man married Miss C., who was living near London (presumably Catherine Coppock, earlier mentioned and apparently the grand-daughter of a certain Abigail, *née* Holland—Margaret's own aunt); a little later in the letter Margaret says that Mrs. Gaskill [*sic*] and Miss Lucy Holland have just arrived, the former supplying further de-

had lost all natural, healthy appetite for simple food, and, having no higher tastes, found their greatest enjoyment in their luxurious meals.'[11]

The same kind of direct acquaintance with Manchester weavers is exemplified by Mrs. Gaskell's treatment of Libbie Marsh's purchase of the canary from a bird-fancying barber. Commenting that men like him know more than one would suppose, she remarks that, stubborn, silent, and reserved though they be 'on many things, you have only to touch on the subject of birds to light up their faces with brightness. They will tell you

---

tails about one of the Coppocks. Added support to strengthen the tenuous link is provided by a manuscript among the collection of family papers in the possession of the novelist's great grand-daughter, Mrs. Margaret Trevor Jones. The MS purports to be an extract from a letter relating to the Coppock family at Stockport, the date— February 1838—most probably referring to that of the original letter. Although the handwriting does not look like Mrs. Gaskell's, one cannot be dogmatic; possibly the MS itself is a copy. Its importance lies in the additional information given about the husband of '[t]he eldest Miss Coppock'; he is said to be 'a surgeon of the name of Gaskell,' resident in London and the author of 'a pamphlet . . . on the factory system, & the poor laws' which the writer (of the letter, or of the extract) had seen very favourably reviewed. From the 1841 Home Office Census Returns (in the Public Record Office: Bundle 1050, Vol. 2, Enumeration District 4, p. 18) for Champion Grove, Camberwell, Lambeth, it would indeed seem that Catherine was the name of the wife of a surgeon called Peter Gaskell. Perhaps, in conclusion, we ought to mention that both the printed version of Miss Margaret Holland's letter and the MS belonging to Mrs. Trevor Jones indicate a forthcoming marriage between Henry Coppock (Catherine's brother, a Stockport solicitor) and a Miss Ashton; the MS also states that she was the sister of the man murdered about two years previously. It so happens that Mrs. Gaskell was accused of having drawn on the events surrounding Mr. Ashton's death when she wrote about the murder of Henry Carson in *Mary Barton*. Her letter (*G.L.*, No. 130) of Monday 16 August [1852] to Sir John Potter, a relative by marriage of the Ashtons, denying any conscious use of the incident, may be consulted in the Manchester Central Reference Library (No. 29 in the Sir John Potter Collection of Autograph Letters); according to Mrs. Gaskell the plot of the novel was as much suggested by some similar cases at Glasgow. Further details on this subject are given in Ward, ed. *Works*, I, p. lxvii, fn.; and in Clement King Shorter, ed. *The Novels and Tales of Mrs Gaskell,* 11 vols., London (Edinburgh, Glasgow), New York, Toronto (Melbourne, and Bombay): Henry Frowde (Humphrey Milford for Vols. IX-XI), Oxford University Press, 1906-1919, I (1906), p. vii—this, 'The World's Classics' Edition, is the most inclusive collection of Mrs. Gaskell's writings, its shorter title being *Novels and Tales.*

[11] *Works*, I, 462.

who won the prizes at the last canary show, where the prize birds may be seen, and give you all the details of those funny, but pretty and interesting mimicries of great people's cattle shows.'[12]

We find in this little narrative something already noted— Mrs. Gaskell's quasi-poetic insight into humble life. She well conveys the feelings of Libbie Marsh on arrival at her new lodgings—very intense desolation and loneliness[13]. Later Libbie is shown crying by the hearth while, musing, she realizes that such a plain girl as she hardly dare cheer herself with 'bright visions of a home of her own at some future day, where, loving and beloved, she might fulfil a woman's dearest duties.'[14]

It is essential to emphasize, however, that this sympathy was not an indulgence : Mrs. Gaskell never uses Libbie as an excuse for autobiographic morbidity. Although there is the reference— as so often in her work—to dead relatives (in this instance, father, mother, and brother)[15], she does not allow her heroine to find all her consolation in star-gazing 'at the bright heavens'[16] where 'for ever and ever "the blue sky, that bends over all," sheds down a feeling of sympathy with the sorrowful'[17]—for the next paragraph opens with Libbie's noticing the suffering child in the house opposite, an observation of the everyday world and a return to reality which bring practical benefits to the boy, to his mother, and to Libbie herself. The remedy for the cripple's distress which Libbie (and Mrs. Gaskell) decided upon was to

---

[12] *Works,* I, 466. Himself an ex-prisoner, Leigh Hunt informed the author of his uneasiness at the bird-cage part of the narrative (Waller, ed. *Letters Addressed to Mrs Gaskell by Celebrated Contemporaries,* pp. 27-29). However, though confessing that the absence of any word of disapproval might seem to countenance the custom, Mrs. Gaskell half-justified its inclusion on the grounds of 'trying to draw/ from the life': as she wrote in her letter to Hunt of 13 September [1850]—now deposited at Brook Street Unitarian Chapel, Knutsford, by its owner, Professor Archie Stanton Whitfield (Plas Benar, Dyffryn, Merionethshire); and (with minor variations) printed in Archie Stanton Whitfield, *Mrs Gaskell: Her Life and Work,* London: George Routledge & Sons Ltd., 1929, p. 30, and as *G.L.,* No. 80. Our shorter title for Professor Whitfield's book will be *Mrs Gaskell.*
[13] *Works,* I, 459.
[14] *Works,* I, 461.
[15] *Works,* I, 460.
[16] *Works,* I, 462.
[17] *Works,* I, 462.

give him a canary, thereby satisfying 'his great want of an
object on which to occupy his thoughts, and which might dis-
tract his attention, when alone through the long day, from the
pain he endured.'[18] It was just the sort of solution which one
might have read in *"My Diary"*.

Libbie Marsh's second era was Whitsuntide; and the piece
appeared on 12 June 1847 in the same periodical[19]. An account
of the holiday Libbie, Mrs. Hall, and her crippled son, Franky,
spent at Dunham Park, it seems the work of a woman who
had herself made such visits, most probably in the company
of those very Sunday-School children[20] whose psalm-singing is
so charmingly described[21]. The opening paragraphs, made up
of exchanges between dwellers in the court, have a colloquial
authenticity about them; and this realistic rendering of Lancashire dialect gives the narrative added veracity[22].

Mrs. Gaskell's humorous observation of diverse reactions to
the out-of-the-ordinary is well illustrated. Libbie felt shy during
the journey to the canal, 'afraid of being seen by her employers,
"set up in a coach!" '[23], hence 'she hid herself in a corner, and
made herself as small as possible; while Mrs. Hall had exactly
the opposite feeling, and was delighted to stand up, stretching
out of the window, and nodding to pretty nearly every one they
met or passed on the footpaths'[24].

> At last she plumped down by Libbie, and exclaimed, "I never
> was in a coach but once afore, and that was when I was a-going
> to be married. It's like heaven; and all done over with such
> beautiful gimp, too!" continued she, admiring the lining of
> the vehicle.[25]

The picture Mrs. Gaskell paints of the operatives at Dunham
is delightful. She shows their good-will among themselves; their

[18] *Works,* I, 464.
[19] Cotton Mather Mills, Esq., 'Life in Manchester. Libbie Marsh's
Three Eras.—Whitsuntide', *Howitt's Journal,* I, 334-336.
[20] For Mrs. Gaskell's connexion with Manchester Sunday-School pupils,
see A. Cobden Smith, 'Mrs. Gaskell and Lower Mosley Street', *The
Sunday School Quarterly,* II (1911), 156-161.
[21] *Works,* I, 475-476.
[22] *Works,* I, 469-470.
[23] *Works,* I, 472.
[24] *Works,* I, 472.
[25] *Works,* I, 472.

ready, mutual help; and, most importantly, the spiritual effect
on their souls of this brief holiday—a holiday from 'Manchester,
old, ugly, smoky Manchester! dear, busy, earnest, working, noble
Manchester; where their children had been born, (and perhaps
where some lay buried,) where their homes were, where God
had cast their lives, and told them to work out their destiny.'[26]

An extract from the conclusion will show the seeing-beauty
spirit again at work in humble life, and provide an example of
Mrs. Gaskell's observation at a deeper-than-surface level.

> As they trod the meadow-path once more, they were joined by
> many a party they had encountered during the day, all abound-
> ing in happiness, all full of the day's adventures. Long-cherished
> quarrels had been forgotten, new friendships formed. Fresh tastes
> and higher delights had been imparted that day. We have all of
> us our look, now and then, called up by some noble or loving
> thought (our highest on earth), which will be our likeness in
> heaven. I can catch the glance on many a face, the glancing
> light of the cloud of glory from heaven, "which is our home."
> That look was present on many a hard-worked, wrinkled coun-
> tenance, as they turned backwards to catch a longing lingering
> look at Dunham woods, fast deepening into blackness of night,
> but whose memory was to haunt, in greenness and freshness,
> many a loom, and workshop, and factory, with images of peace
> and beauty.[27]

The last sketch in the 'Life in Manchester' series came out in
the following number, a week later[28]. Now the omens of death,
which Libbie had discerned on the day of the Dunham visit[29],
have had their effect. Franky's funeral procession opens the story.
What is noticeable, however, is Mrs. Gaskell's sense of the variety
of the everyday world. She foregoes any morbid concentration
on the death theme to the sacrifice of all else: not only is the
funeral set in the context of gentlemen returning to their offices
and ladies sallying forth to shop[30], but amidst the sadness of

---

[26] *Works*, I, 477: but corrected against *Howitt's Journal* (I, 336). In
general, no collating has been undertaken; however, besides differences
in the passage here quoted, one finds that, a few lines *infra*, in a piece
of dialect, the *Howitt's* ' "Sunday-school childer" ' appears as ' "Sunday-
school children" ' in Ward's Knutsford Edition (*Works*, I, 478).

[27] *Works*, I, 478-479.

[28] Cotton Mather Mills, Esq., 'Life in Manchester. Libbie Marsh's
Three Eras.—Michaelmas', *Howitt's Journal*, I, 345-347.

[29] *Works*, I, 476.

[30] *Works*, I, 479-480.

death she puts the merriment of Anne Dixon's marriage[31]. It was part of her way of observing life not to focus attention exclusively and narrowly; she was keenly aware of the multiplicity of experience.

Mrs. Gaskell—as a side issue in the tale—treats morally, though not with a heavy, moralizing pen, the problem of drink among the working classes; nor can one read much Victorian social history without realizing just how pressing a problem this was.

> In Manchester alone there are very near if not quite one thousand inns, beer-houses, and gin-vaults. Of these more than nine-tenths are kept open exclusively for the supply of the labouring population, placed in situations calculated for their convenience, decked out with every thing that can allure them, crowded into back streets and alleys, or flaunting with the most gaudy and expensive decorations in the great working thorough-fares. They are open at the earliest hour, . . . and remain open during a considerable portion of the night ministering their poisons to thousands of debilitated creatures, who flock to them, in place of seeking excitement and pleasurable stimulus in fire-side comforts and enjoyments.[32]

Moreover one is able to refer to Mr. Gaskell's own pictures of the vices of drink and the virtues of abstinence as painted in his *Temperance Rhymes*. Though Mrs. Gaskell treats the matter less luridly, her point is none the less made. Anne Dixon tells[33] Libbie that she would prefer her Bob tipsy to anyone else sober, just as he would rather have an untidy home with her than a tidy one with another—factory women being notoriously ill acquainted with domestic economy[34]. Libbie, in reply, says that Anne has no conception of what drink can do, mentioning that her own father killed his baby child during a drinking bout. Although nothing like this, of course, happened in her family, Mrs. Gaskell must have been well acquainted with the kind of

[31] *Works*, I, 483-485.
[32] Peter Gaskell, *The Manufacturing Population*, pp. 117-118. His figures are based on those of Dr. Kay—conveniently found in James Phillips Kay-Shuttleworth, *Four Periods of Public Education as Reviewed in* 1832-1839-1846-1862, London: Longman, Green, Longman, and Roberts, 1862, pp. 34-36. The figures were still high during the next two decades (*Four Periods*, pp. 133-140).
[33] *Works*, I, 483-484.
[34] Peter Gaskell (*The Manufacturing Population*, pp. 103-104) strongly supports this view.

life described by Peter Gaskell and James Kay-Shuttleworth[35].

It is worth noting that Mrs. Gaskell gives her heroine a high degree of moral sensitivity; her refusal to go to the Dixon wedding is due to a refinement in conduct which Anne failed to comprehend.

> With a heavy heart Libbie mounted the little staircase, for she felt how ungracious her refusal of Anne's kindness must appear to one who understood so little the feelings which rendered her acceptance of it a moral impossibility.[36]

There is something in the sombre tone of this last sentence which puts out of court any charge that Mrs. Gaskell was merely writing a simple goody-goody tale of an improving nature for the lower classes: the observation and analysis are not superficial enough for that.

The conclusion is so charmingly disarming that criticism of the explicit moral would be captious indeed.

> Do you ever read the moral, concluding sentence of a story? I never do, but I once (in the year 1811, I think) heard of a deaf old lady, living by herself, who did; and, as she may have left some descendants with the same amiable peculiarity, I will put in, for their benefit, what I believe to be the secret of Libbie's peace of mind, the real reason why she no longer feels oppressed at her own loneliness in the world—
>
> She has a purpose in life; and that purpose is a holy one.[37]

---

[35] Dr. Kay, who added '-Shuttleworth' on his marriage, was, of course, that Sir James Kay-Shuttleworth who helped Mrs. Gaskell to secure Brontë papers (see, for example, *G.L.*, Nos. 297, 297a, 308).

[36] *Works*, I, 485.

[37] *Works*, I, 489. One may note the Cranfordesque lady and the delightful invention of the date—Mrs. Gaskell was born on 29 September 1810.

SECTION VI

The Sexton's Hero (1847)

Still employing 'Cotton Mather Mills' as a pseudonym, Mrs. Gaskell next contributed to *Howitt's Journal* in the number for 4 September 1847[1]. Mrs. Chadwick[2] and Dr. Adolphus Ward[3] tell us all we really need to know about the background to this story. Its setting is a district where Mrs. Gaskell spent many holidays—the coast of Morecambe Bay—and it has been suggested that she actually wrote the tale during a visit to Silverdale[4]. Writing over a decade later, Mrs. Gaskell, having described her Silverdale residence, continued:

> Then at the very end of the garden is a high terrace at the top of the broad stone wall, looking down on the Bay with it's slow moving train of crossers led over the treacherous sands by the guide, a square man sitting stern on his *white* horse, (the better to be seen when day light ebbs). . . . On foggy nights the guide, (who has let people drown before now, who could not pay him his fee, . . .) may be heard blowing an old ram's horn trumpet, to guide by the sound,—[5]

[1] 'The Sexton's Hero', *Howitt's Journal*, II, 149-152. This story was sold at Capesthorne Fête, for the Benefit of Macclesfield Public Baths and Wash-houses, as a sixpenny pamphlet—*The Sexton's Hero, and Christmas Storms and Sunshine*, Manchester: Johnson, Rawson, and Co., 1850. Significantly it also appeared in *The Christian Socialist*, I (March 1851), 159-160, 167-168; so too did 'Christmas Storms and Sunshine'—*The Christian Socialist*, I (March-April 1851), 175-176, 183-184, 191-192, 199-200. Further evidence of Mrs. Gaskell's support for the Christian Social-ists is provided by her letter (*G.L.*, No. 67) to William Robson, of Warrington, asking him to help distribute their publications. This letter, post-marked 20 and 21 February 1850, is among the Gaskell material in the Morris L. Parrish Collection of Victorian Novelists at the Princeton University Library; its recipient may have been the husband of Mr. Gaskell's sister, Mrs. Nancy Robson.

[2] *Mrs. Gaskell*, pp. 232-236.

[3] Ed. *Works*, I, p. lxx-lxxii.

[4] Chadwick, *Mrs. Gaskell*, p. 232.

[5] *Letters of Mrs. Gaskell and Charles Eliot Norton*, 1855-1865, ed. Jane Revere Whitehill, London: Humphrey Milford, Oxford University Press, 1932, p. 22: *G.L.*, No. 394—but our version has been corrected against Mrs. Gaskell's original letter of Monday 10 May [and 14 May 1858] to Charles Eliot Norton, deposited in the Harvard University Library. Our short-title for Mrs. Whitehill's edition will be *Gaskell-Norton Letters*.

Although this passage was written on 10 May [1858], Mrs. Gaskell's attraction to a story with a quick-sand adventure in it goes back to her girlhood[6]; hence her thoughts not unnaturally turned to such a subject when she was considering what next to send to the Howitts. Possibly she even had the tale, or at least its outlines, already on paper, and so needed only to make a few minor alterations.

[6] In a letter of 30 July [1828], written from his father's house in Beaufort Row, John Stevenson remarked to Elizabeth: 'You have really made out a very pretty story of Captain/ Barton—it would almost make the foundation of a novel/ it was indeed a narrow escape of Kitty's and must have/ given her a tremendous fright, though I have heard ⟨and/⟩ read many stories of them, I never saw a quicksand a ⟨nd hard/⟩ -ly believed them to be so dangerous as was generally ⟨spoken/⟩ off. /'—Extract from the torn letter in the possession of the present writer. (It may be merely coincidental that, in a letter Mrs. Gaskell addressed to her sister-in-law, Eliza Gaskell, at Beaumaris, she remarked on Eliza's never having mentioned Captain Barton, and enquired whether he were still to the fore—this letter (*G.L.*, No. 9) of Tuesday morning [17 July 1838], post-marked 18 July 1838, being in the Gaskell Section, Brotherton Collection, Leeds University Library.) As is noted by Miss Rubenius (*The Woman Question in Mrs. Gaskell's Life and Works*, p. 254, fn. 4), John's letter is mentioned by Jane Revere Coolidge (subsequently Mrs. Walter Muir Whitehill) in her 'Life and letters of Mrs. E. C. Gaskell', Ch. I, pp. 31-33—an incomplete typescript of this study being deposited in the Gaskell Section, Brotherton Collection, Leeds University Library. Miss Coolidge wonders whether the story could have been a first draft of *The Sexton's Hero*, a surmise not recorded by Miss Rubenius. (Perhaps here is the place to state that Miss Coolidge, who in 1932 became Mrs. Whitehill, virtually completed her 'Life and letters of Mrs. E. C. Gaskell', which she has most kindly allowed me to read. Her address is 44 Andover Street, North Andover, Massachusetts, U.S.A.) Further evidence of Elizabeth Stevenson's youthful literary prowess is furnished by an extract from a letter the late Professor John W. Draper, of West Virginia University, wrote to Dr. Gerald DeWitt Sanders (Rt. 3, Box 7-Z, Manning, South Carolina, U.S.A.)—here requoted by the kind permission of Dr. Sanders (given in a letter of 31 January 1962 containing the extract), who in turn received consent to use the material from Professor Draper. Professor Draper recalled that the novelist's former school-fellow, his maternal grandmother, Harriet Van Ness Ludlow (*née* Maury), "used often tell us that the teachers in the school thought her [Elizabeth Stevenson's] compositions so good that instead of correcting them as themes are generally corrected, they would save her papers and read them aloud to one another." An incidental piece of information supplied by Professor Draper is that at this time Elizabeth was attending a school for young ladies kept at Chester by a certain Miss Hervey; she must then have been in her middle childhood, for she subsequently spent five years at the school of the Misses Byerley in Stratford-on-Avon (see, for example, Rubenius, *The Woman Question in Mrs. Gaskell's Life and Works*, p. 19, fn. 1).

The opening paragraphs are picturesquely evocative; and the vacation-mood of the narrator and his companion is well conveyed. Though speaking through the *persona* of the former, Mrs. Gaskell is obviously recalling her own feelings.

> It is one of the luxuries of holiday-time that thoughts are not rudely shaken from us by outward violence of hurry and busy impatience, but fall maturely from our lips in the sunny leisure of our days. The stock may be bad, but the fruit is ripe.[7]

The sexton—a kind of Wordsworthian figure, 'an accessory to the scene . . . whom . . . [they] had forgotten, as much as though he were as inanimate as one of the moss-covered headstones'[8]—breaks in upon their leisurely attempts to define a hero; and tells of the heroic Gilbert Dawson.

Mrs. Gaskell did not need to use any great inventive powers when composing the sexton's tale. Very probably she had often heard local stories along similar lines; and only had to add her own, moral, contribution by defining heroism in terms of Christianity, self-sacrifice, and non-violence.

In making literary judgements the critic, one might maintain, here faces certain difficulties, since a flawless narrative would be inappropriate from a man like the sexton. For example, concerning Letty's attitude to her erstwhile lover at the time she believed him a coward, he says:

> "When he still stuck to it he could not [fight], for that it was wrong, she was so vexed and mad-like at the way she'd spoken, and the feelings she'd let out to coax him, that she said more stinging things about his being a coward than all the rest put together (according to what she told me, sir, afterwards), and ended by saying she'd never speak to him again, as long as she lived; she did once again, though—her blessing was the last human speech that reached his ear in his wild death-struggle."[9]

It could be argued that the last words, suspense-destroying as they are, had been better left unsaid. Similarly the description[10] of Gilbert Dawson's rescue of the sexton and his wife is a little melodramatic. A little stagey too are ' "the tears down-dropping

---

[7] *Works*, I, 490.
[8] *Works*, I, 491.
[9] *Works*, I, 494.
[10] *Works*, I, 496-498.

from . . . [the] withered cheeks" [11] of the parish clerk, while he tells how Gilbert rode out to watch for the couple's return across the sands, intending to ride back unobserved had all gone well. Yet no fault can be found with that awareness of the variety in life implied by the sexton's account of the different responses to Gilbert's death.

> "His friends came over from Garstang to his funeral. I wanted to go chief mourner, but it was not my right, and I might not; though I've never done mourning him to this day. When his sister packed up his things, I begged hard for something that had been his. She would give me none of his clothes (she was a right-down saving woman), as she had boys of her own, who might grow up into them. But she threw me his Bible, as she said they'd gotten one already, and his were but a poor used-up thing. . . . "[12]

Before leaving *The Sexton's Hero*, we may note the reference to the rough rural life common during the sexton's youth[13]; the deferential (but ironical) preference of the villagers for the vicar's militant preaching over the parish clerk's Biblical pacifism[14]; and the death theme[15]. This last would, to some extent, be in keeping with the sexton's profession. Certainly his words about digging ' "a grave for a little child, who is to be buried to-morrow morning, just when his playmates are trooping off to school" '[16] seem at one with Mrs. Gaskell's realistic observation of what life is like. Nevertheless, when we learn that both the sexton's wife and daughter were carried off within a short time of each other[17] and that his sister lies in the grave-yard where he works[18], we can be forgiven for remarking that perhaps the author's inventive powers found death a congenial field for their operation a little too often.

[11] *Works*, I, 498.
[12] *Works*, I, 500.
[13] *Works*, I, 492.
[14] *Works*, I, 495.
[15] *Works*, I, 500-501.
[16] *Works*, I, 500.
[17] *Works*, I, 501.
[18] *Works*, I, 496.

SECTION VII

'Emerson's Lectures' (1847)

The next contribution to *Howitt's Journal* is conjectural only : it consists of three columns describing 'Emerson's Lectures', being attributed to 'our Manchester Correspondent' and appearing on 11 December 1847[1]. The conjecture, made by Professor Ross D. Waller, is based upon a letter from Mary Howitt to Mrs. Gaskell in which she hints that an account of Emerson's lectures would be welcome[2]. The *Howitt's* correspondent gives a vivid picture of Emerson and his manner of address. Less is said about the lectures themselves (the subject—'On men representative of Great Ideas'—embraced Swedenborg and his mysticism, Montaigne and his scepticism, and Shakespeare); but that treating Montaigne was liked best. If this account be by Mrs. Gaskell, then she gives a good report of her observations— though the subjective element is not absent, partly owing to a first-person narration.

[1] *Howitt's Journal,* II, 370-371.
[2] Fuller details may be found in Waller, ed. *Letters Addressed to Mrs Gaskell by Celebrated Contemporaries,* pp. 6-7. That Mrs. Gaskell heard Emerson lecture is attested by Catherine Winkworth—*Letters and Memorials of Catherine Winkworth,* I (ed. Her Sister [Susanna Winkworth]), 130, 132.

SECTION VIII

Letter in *Howitt's Journal* (1847)

A week after 'Emerson's Lectures' came out, a letter appeared in the same periodical, enquiring whether the *People's Journal* (with which the Howitts had been unfortunately involved financially) were indeed up for sale[1]; it was signed 'C.M.M.', initials which have been taken to stand for 'Cotton Mather Mills'[2], and was dated 'Manchester, Dec. 6th, 1847.'

---

[1] *Howitt's Journal*, II, 399.

[2] By Woodring (*Victorian Samplers: William and Mary Howitt*, p. 142). See too Waller, ed. *Letters Addressed to Mrs Gaskell by Celebrated Contemporaries*, p. 6.

SECTION IX

Christmas Storms and Sunshine (1848)

Inappropriately Cotton Mather Mills' last contribution to *Howitt's Journal* did not come out in a Christmas number[1]— inappropriately because not only does the story have a Christmas setting, but its tone and atmosphere bring to mind the Dickensian Christmas Philosophy (it recommends the spirit of friendship, with an end to quarrels and misunderstandings[2]). *Christmas Storms and Sunshine* is the story of a reconciliation between families, brought about by the severe illness of the child of one of them: for the danger of a child's death makes Mrs. Jenkins (wife of the chief compositor of the Tory *Flying Post*) soon begin to appreciate the trifling nature of the disagreements of her husband and herself with Mr. Hodgson (chief compositor of the Radical *Examiner*) and his wife[3]. The short story is not remarkable for inventiveness; nor is its humour subtle. The opening paragraph gives the key-note of the tale, indeed these first sentences suggest the lack of seriousness, the fairy-tale touch.

In the town of ——— (no matter where) there circulated two local newspapers (no matter when). Now the *Flying Post* was long-established and respectable—alias bigoted and Tory; the *Examiner* was spirited and intelligent—alias new-fangled and democratic.[4]

Two Gaskellian concerns already noticed—illness in childhood and rural memories—again find expression. Little Tommy Hodgson is seized by an attack of the croup (a complaint of which the authoress had painfully personal experience[5]), and without the aid of Mrs. Jenkins would probably have died[6].

---

[1] 'Christmas Storms and Sunshine', which appeared in the New Year's Day Number—*Howitt's Journal*, III (1848), 4-7. It was later published in pamphlet form—*The Sexton's Hero, and Christmas Storms and Sunshine*, Manchester: Johnson, Rawson, and Co., 1850.

[2] *Works*, II, 205.

[3] *Works*, II, 201-202.

[4] *Works*, II, 193.

[5] "*My Diary*", pp. 36-37; and *G.L.*, No. 7.

[6] *Works*, II, 198-202.

F

Recollections of her country childhood (the cottage home, the Portugal laurel, the orchard path, and unripe apples)[7] fill Mrs. Hodgson's mind, although (as so often in Mrs. Gaskell's fiction) she is not long allowed to indulge such memories, since reality only too forcefully brings itself to her notice. When we consider the later stories, especially *North and South* and *Cousin Phillis,* these rural remembrances will be seen as part of a strand which runs through much of Mrs. Gaskell's writing, to finish with her death in the incomplete *Wives and Daughters.*

[7] *Works,* II, 198.

SECTION X

Mary Barton (1848)

In October 1848 Chapman & Hall published *Mary Barton*:
A Tale of Manchester Life[1]. Although no author's name

[1] [Elizabeth Cleghorn Gaskell] *Mary Barton*: *A Tale of Manchester
Life*, 2 vols., London: Chapman and Hall, 1848. Initially the book was
to be called 'John Barton', according to Mrs. Gaskell's draft of a letter
to Mrs. Sam Greg (relevantly quoted in Ward, ed. *Works*, I, p. lxiii):
G.L., No. 42. However it is interesting that she should refer to her 'MS,
(a Manchester/ Love Story,)' when writing to her publisher on 2 April
[1848]. The introduction of the heroine's name was Chapman's idea, as is
shown by the novelist's letter of 17 April 1848 in which, after thanking
him for his suggestions, she remarks that he will see she has 'adopted the
additional/ title of *"Mary Barton,"* a Manchester/ Love Story': this designation was, of course, again slightly modified before publication. Both
the letters (*G.L.*, Nos. 23, 25) from which we have quoted, together with
other correspondence (c. 1848-1856) between the Gaskells and the publishing firm, are deposited in the Pierpont Morgan Library (under the
classification: Autographs-Miscellaneous-English). It is interesting to note
that the Gaskell Collection at the Manchester Central Reference Library
contains a cheap edition of the novel whose inscription by the author,
dated 3 May 1861, also testifies that its original title, 'John Barton', was
changed at the publisher's request—see Marian V. Malcolm-Hayes,
'Notes on the Gaskell Collection in the Central Library', *Memoirs and
Proceedings of the Manchester Literary and Philosophical Society* (*Manchester Memoirs*), LXXXVII (1945-1946), 157-158; and [Elizabeth Cleghorn Gaskell] *Mary Barton; A Tale of Manchester Life,* Cheap edn,
London: Chapman and Hall, 1856, p. ii (Manchester Central Reference
Library: Book No. B.R. 823.894 P2.156). From her 19 October [1848]
letter (*G.L.*, No. 28) to Chapman (in the Pierpont Morgan Library) it seems
Mrs. Gaskell proposed Stephen Berwick as a *nom de plume*; but, in his
letter of 23 October 1848, Chapman told the novelist that her 'reply
respecting the name on the title page' had arrived too late, and, not having
heard anything earlier, he had 'left the name out altogether' (a copy of
part of this letter being in Shorter and Symington, 'Correspondence, Articles
& Notes Relating to Mrs. E. C. Gaskell. Transcripts', Vol. II, Section on
Mary Barton—a typescript in the Gaskell Section, Brotherton Collection,
Leeds University Library). If she had no desire for her own name to appear,
one wonders why Mrs. Gaskell did not suggest Cotton Mather Mills
—the pseudonym by which William Howitt seems to have referred to the
writer during his early negotiations on her behalf with Chapman & Hall
(Waller, ed. *Letters Addressed to Mrs Gaskell by Celebrated Contem-
poraries*, pp. 5-6). Several points discussed in this footnote are raised in
Annette Brown Hopkins, ' "Mary Barton": A Victorian Best Seller',
The Trollopian, III (1948), 1-3, 10-11; *Elizabeth Gaskell*, pp. 69-70, 76-77.

appeared on the title-page, it was not long before Mrs. Gaskell
was recognized as the writer; she was lionized, and found herself famous. The reasons which led to her composing this two-
volume novel were diverse: her own literary talent was the
essential requirement; but biographers generally ascribe the
precipitating cause to the loss, on 10 August 1845, of her only
son, then not a year old[2]. Her husband suggested that she should
write to divert her mind from the morbid thoughts which
assailed her. In this she was doubtless encouraged by William
Howitt; and so, by the recommendation of John Forster[3] but
after being with the publishers for some time, the work was
eventually printed[4]. Most of the book was almost certainly
written between the last months of 1845 and the first months
of 1847[5].

The sub-title reminds us of the 'Libbie Marsh' contributions
to *Howitt's Journal*, since these had come out under the heading
'Life in Manchester'; very likely the short stories were written
after *Mary Barton* had been begun, even though the difference

[2] Gerald DeWitt Sanders, *Elizabeth Gaskell,* with a Bibliography by
Clark Sutherland Northup, Cornell Studies in English (ed. Joseph Quincy
Adams, Clark Sutherland Northup, and Martin Wright Sampson), Vol.
XIV, New Haven: Yale University Press for Cornell University; London:
Humphrey Milford, Oxford University Press, for Cornell University,
1929, p. 17, fn. 2.

[3] Sanders, *Elizabeth Gaskell,* p. 18.

[4] In her letter to Chapman of 2 April [1848]—see our ante-penulti-
mate footnote, *supra*—Mrs. Gaskell mildly complains that when he had
been introduced to her in January he had then promised to publish
within two or three months (*G.L.,* No. 23). Sanders (*Elizabeth Gaskell,*
p. 18) gives the date of publication as 14 October 1848; yet it was 25
October, according to Miss Hopkins—' "Mary Barton": A Victorian Best
Seller', *The Trollopian,* III (1948), 1; *Elizabeth Gaskell,* p. 70. However the book surely came out on 18 October, the Wednesday for which
it was advertised in *The Athenaeum Journal of Literature, Science, and
the Fine Arts,* No. 1094 (14 October 1848), p. 1019—a review following
in the next number (21 October 1848, pp. 1050-1051). The facts of publication are discussed in his Appendix II by Graham Owens ('Town and
Country in the Life and Work of Mrs. Gaskell and Mary Russell Mitford',
M.A. thesis, University College of North Wales, Bangor, 1953, pp. 386-
388) and in our Appendix I.

[5] The draft of Mrs. Gaskell's letter to Mrs. Sam Greg, quoted by
Ward (ed. *Works,* I, p. lxiv), would suggest that the MS of most of the
novel had been with the publisher for over fourteen months before the
book came out (*G.L.,* No. 42); and her Preface—October 1848—implies
that she began working about three years previously (*Works,* I, pp.
lxxiii-lxxiv).

in literary quality might suggest that they antedate the novel[6].
It seems worth while in this context to emphasize those advantages enjoyed by Mrs. Gaskell which were denied to Dickens
and Disraeli : she had first-hand experience of the life of the
Northern manufacturing population, whereas they resorted to
exploratory visits and Blue Books. She did not need to read the
Reports of Royal Commissions (which is not to say that she did
not do so) in order to find out how the working classes lived;
nor was her observation of strikes gained during a sociological
tourist-visit. Preliminary research and field study were unnecessary.

> " The whole tale grew up in my mind as imperceptibly as a
> seed germinates in the earth, . . . "[7]
>
> . . . I bethought me how deep might be the romance in the
> lives of some of those who elbowed me daily in the busy streets of
> the town in which I resided. I had always felt a deep sympathy
> with the care-worn men, who looked as if doomed to struggle
> through their lives in strange alternations between work and
> want; tossed to and fro by circumstances, apparently in even
> a greater degree than other men. A little manifestation of this
> sympathy, and a little attention to the expression of feelings on
> the part of some of the work-people with whom I was acquain-
> ted, had laid open to me the hearts of one or two of the more
> thoughtful among them; . . . [8]

The origins of those social-problem novels which came out
before and after *Mary Barton,* novels which dealt with the
Condition-of-England Question from a reformist stand-point,
were rarely (if ever) along the lines suggested by these quotations.
Even Mrs. Gaskell's *"hero, Mr. Kingsley"*[9] did not write *Yeast*

---

[6] In a rough sketch for *Mary Barton* (a copy of which appears in
Shorter and Symington, 'Correspondence, Articles & Notes Relating to
Mrs. E. C. Gaskell. Transcripts', Vol. II, Section on *Mary Barton*—a
typescript in the Gaskell Section, Brotherton Collection, Leeds University
Library) there is a reference to a 'day at Dunham' which, presumably,
Mrs. Gaskell preferred to develop in 'Era II' of *Libbie Marsh's Three
Eras,* for it does not enter into the novel.

[7] Quoted by Ward (ed. *Works,* I, p. lxiii) from the draft of Mrs.
Gaskell's letter to Mrs. Sam Greg (*G.L.,* No. 42).

[8] Extract from the Preface to *Mary Barton* (*Works,* I, p. lxxiii).

[9] Quoted by Miss Haldane (*Elizabeth Gaskell and Her Friends,* p. 75)
and Miss Rubenius (*The Woman Question in Mrs. Gaskell's Life and
Works,* p. 54), these words, apparently written on Tuesday [27 November
1849] to Eliza Fox, occur in a copy of part of Mrs. Gaskell's letter of
26 November 1849 (*G.L.,* No. 55) in the Gaskell Section, Brotherton
Collection, Leeds University Library.

and *Alton Locke* from sources like hers[10]. It is significant, however, that she shared with all her contemporaries who concerned
themselves with the socio-economic problems of the Industrial
and Agrarian Revolutions a propagandist purpose: they spoke
on behalf of a 'great dumb toiling class which . . . [could not]
speak'[11]; they made articulate 'the dumb deep want of the
people'[12].

> The more I reflected . . . the more anxious I became to give
> some utterance to the agony which, from time to time, con-
> vulses this dumb people; the agony of suffering without the
> sympathy of the happy, or of erroneously believing that such
> is the case.[13]

A possible method of treating *Mary Barton* as a work of
invention and observation would be to make a division between
the plot proper (Mary's love story and the Carson murder) and
that part of the novel which deals with the scenes of humble life.
Then the critical judgement could be made that, though Mrs.
Gaskell's management of the plot appears conventional, stagey,
and melodramatic, in her reporting of life among the Manchester operatives she reveals sympathetic insights found in no
other Victorian novelist. Such an approach seems to have found
some favour with Miss ffrench[14]; but the following quotation
from Lewis Melville probably best presents this line of argument.

> These sketches of humble life are fit companions of *Cranford*,
> but as the story of *Mary Barton* develops it becomes abundantly
> clear that, whereas the sketches came from the heart, the novel
> arose from a determination to write a novel, and not because the
> author had a tale to tell. In *Mary Barton*, in *Ruth*, and in *North
> and South*, there is everywhere a straining after sensational effect.
> All the stereotyped situations are introduced one after the other.
> There is the lover holding his tongue at the risk of his life to
> save his sweetheart's father from the gallows; there is the miss-
> ing witness returning at the eleventh hour, shouldering his way
> through the crowded court to the witness-box, there to testify

[10] For Kingsley's social novels see, for example, Louis François
Cazamian, *Le Roman Social en Angleterre* (1830-1850): *Dickens—Disraeli
—Mrs. Gaskell—Kingsley,* New edn, 2 vols., Paris: H. Didier [1935], esp.
II, 161-247. (The first edition, dated 1903, appeared in 1904.)
[11] Thomas Carlyle, *Chartism*, London: James Fraser, 1840, p. 5.
[12] Carlyle, *Chartism*, p. 5.
[13] Extract from the Preface to *Mary Barton* (*Works*, I, p. lxxiv).
[14] Yvonne ffrench, *Mrs. Gaskell*, London: Home & Van Thal Ltd.,
1949, pp. 23-28.

to the hero's innocence; there is the simple maid and the vile
seducer, who is foiled in one book [*Mary Barton*] and successful
in another [*Ruth*]. . . . All the devices, all the unwarrantable
coincidences of bad plays are exploited in turn; and most of
them are exploited in connexion with that sickly sentiment that
those writers who fall under the influence of Dickens never seem
able to escape.[15]

In a similar vein modern critics, as Miss Hopkins remarks, have
objected to the author's sentimental use of the reconciliation
motif—for Mr. Carson comes to terms with John Barton,
the murderer of his son, Harry. She reminds us, however, that
'in the light of instances of forgiveness accorded to enemies that
have been reported during the second world war, the reconciliation between Carson and Barton can hardly be said to falsify
human conduct.'[16] Nevertheless, knowing that readers can have
too much of a good theme, she apologises for its frequency in
Mrs. Gaskell's fiction as a whole. Miss Hopkins goes on to explain
the tendency on the ground that the writer was a practical
Christian, and so really believed that people could 'rise above
their passions and meet on a plane of rational intercourse.'[17]
Mrs. Gaskell certainly believed that principles should be 'worked
into the life,'[18] though one is tempted to ask whether, if she is
indeed so often sentimental in her reconciliations, a plea of sincerity makes a good literary excuse.

Mary Barton is, however, too complex a novel to allow
division along the foregoing lines. It is difficult to decide where
precisely to begin our study; but probably the title Mrs. Gaskell
originally intended to give the book—'John Barton'[19]—provides
a convenient starting point. In a letter of Monday [Tuesday]
29 May 1849[20], Mrs. Gaskell affirmed that the character of

[15] Lewis Melville [Lewis Saul Benjamin], 'The Centenary of Mrs.
Gaskell', *The Nineteenth Century and After: A Monthly Review Founded
by James Knowles*, LXVIII (1910), 476-477.
[16] Hopkins, *Elizabeth Gaskell*, p. 78.
[17] Hopkins, *Elizabeth Gaskell*, p. 78.
[18] *Works*, I, 301.
[19] See the draft of her letter to Mrs. Sam Greg, quoted by Ward (ed.
Works, I, p. lxiii): *G.L.*, No. 42.
[20] The relevant quotation is given by Miss Haldane (*Mrs. Gaskell and
Her Friends*, p. 39) and by Miss Rubenius (*The Woman Question in
Mrs. Gaskell's Life and Works*, pp. 242-243); that of the latter, though
not that of the former nor that printed in *G.L.*, No. 48, tallies with the
copy of part of this letter to Eliza Fox in the Gaskell Section, Brotherton Collection, Leeds University Library.

John Barton was the only one based on an actual prototype (at least, we should add, the only one of which she was then aware). When drafting a letter to Mrs. Sam Greg, she wrote as follows:

> "Round the character of John Barton all the others formed themselves; he was my hero, *the* person with whom all my sympathies went, with whom I tried to identify myself at the time, because I believed from personal observation that such men were not uncommon, and would well reward such sympathy and love as should throw light down upon their groping search after the causes of suffering, and the reason why suffering is sent, and what they can do to lighten it. . . . There are many such whose lives are magic [?tragic] poems which cannot take formal language."[21]

In the Preface[22] to the first edition, Mrs. Gaskell recalls how she became aware of the romance in the lives of those around her; how she found thoughtful operatives incensed against the rich who, they held, showed no concern for their misery. Sympathy on her part led the operatives to speak frankly, and it is one of these whom she represents in the character of John Barton.

We have the author's word for it that she had been acquainted with such a man as Barton: the subsequent quotation may serve to indicate the nature of that acquaintanceship.

> Mrs. Gaskell told Mr. Travers Madge[[23]] that the one strong impulse to write "Mary Barton" came to her one evening in a labourer's cottage. She was trying hard to speak comfort, and to allay those bitter feelings against the rich which were so common with the poor, when the head of the family took hold of her arm, and grasping it tightly said, with tears in his eyes: "Ay, ma'am, but have ye ever seen a child clemmed [starved] to death?"[24]

---

[21] Quoted by Ward (ed. *Works,* I, p. lxiii): my square brackets—the emendation being suggested to me by Dr. Joyce M. S. Tompkins; see too *G.L.,* No. 42.

[22] *Works,* I, p. lxxiii.

[23] An account of this Manchester social and religious worker may be found in Brooke Herford, *Travers Madge: A Memoir,* London: Hamilton, Adams and Compy; Manchester: Johnson & Rawson; Norwich: Fletcher & Son, 1867.

[24] Mat Hompes, 'Mrs. Gaskell', *The Gentleman's Magazine,* CCLXXIX (1895), 130-131: my square brackets. Cf. ' "Han they [the masters] ever seen a child o' their'n die for want o' food?" asked Barton, in a low deep voice.'—*Works,* I, 73. Probably Mrs. Gaskell was asked such questions more than once in the course of her work as one of the first voluntary visitors of the Manchester & Salford District Provident Society ('Advice and sympathy were the main objects of the visitors, and these objects

John Barton has, not unexpectedly, been identified with a particular cotton-spinner, R.K.[25]; whether or not correctly seems now impossible to say, especially as R.K. is not the only candidate[26]. More important for establishing Barton as an authentic type among Manchester working men are the words of the Lancashire Radical, Samuel Bamford[27], who remarked 'of John Bartons, I have known hundreds, his very self in all things except his fatal crime'[28].

Mrs. Gaskell considered John Barton's tragedy central to the novel[29], and in this she has been confirmed by recent (if not by

---

must have been well achieved when the Society numbered, as it did, amongst its visitors such characters as Mrs. Gaskell'—Hugh Colley Irvine, *The Old D.P.S. A Short History of Charitable Work in Manchester and Salford,* 1833-1933, Manchester: The Committee of the District Provident and Charity Organisation Society of Manchester and Salford [1933], p. 9). The Library of the Unitarian College (Victoria Park, Manchester 14) has part of a very astute letter Mrs. Gaskell wrote one Thursday morning [between 1850 and 1860] to the Rev. Samuel Alfred Steinthal (*G.L.,* No. 630); in it she speaks of how best to gain information about social conditions from visitors and other qualified people by sifting corn from chaff, by employing 'the art of *extracting*' in conjunction with that of rejecting.

[25] R. E. Bibby, ' "Mary Barton" and Greenheys Fields', *The Manchester City News,* 22 June 1878.

[26] It seems worth recording that Mrs. Gaskell's friend, Susanna Winkworth, in some notes on the novel (an extract from which being found in Shorter and Symington, 'Correspondence, Articles & Notes Relating to Mrs. E. C. Gaskell. Transcripts', Vol. II, Section on *Mary Barton*— a typescript in the Gaskell Section, Brotherton Collection, Leeds University Library) recalls lending the book to a Chartist couple of her acquaintance; and being struck by the similarity of John Barton to the husband, B., as she had first known him, about five years earlier, when he was a joiner in full employment: she mentions, moreover, his telling her of a passage in his own history which was very like the story of Barton's little Tom. Apparently, according to Susanna Winkworth, the couple also had a son called Jem; and they considered the fictional Jem the most interesting character in the novel and its real hero.

[27] For Bamford (1788-1872), see Henry Dunckley, ed. *Bamford's 'Passages in the Life of a Radical' and 'Early Days',* 2 vols., London: T. Fisher Unwin, 1893, I, 9-23; see too Edward Smith's article in *The Dictionary of National Biography.*

[28] *Letters Addressed to Mrs Gaskell by Celebrated Contemporaries,* ed. Waller, p. 8.

[29] She complained that no one seemed to see her 'idea of a tragic// poem' in a letter to Chapman of 1 January [1849], now in the Pierpont Morgan Library (Autographs-Miscellaneous-English). Also relevant is her reply to a certain Miss Lamont, who had apparently written to say the novel should have been called 'John Barton'. Having owned that such

her contemporary) critics[30]; he has been described, Heathcliff excepted, as 'the nearest approach to a tragic hero which the early Victorian novel permitted itself.'[31] It was the fate of Barton, initially 'resolute either for good or evil,'[32] that misery and hardship so played upon his sensibilities as to make him despair of any earthly help[33]. Eventually he ceased to hope, largely losing his mental equipoise[34]; however there remained constant an overwhelming hatred of the rich and a powerful sympathy with the poor, albeit directed by a judgement unable to distinguish between good and evil[35]. Disillusioned in his attempts to live after the Gospel precepts[36], Barton was wont to turn his thoughts unwholesomely upon the parable of Dives and Lazarus[37], which he interpreted after his own fashion, in a spirit of vengeance. Mrs. Gaskell, with convincing skill, reveals how John Barton's mind became deranged, making him violate ' "the eternal laws of God," '[38] the punishment for which was ' "an avenging conscience far more difficult to bear than any worldly privation." '[39] He had lost his son during hard times, when no nourishing food could be obtained, even though his master's luxurious style of living still seemed unchanged[40]; Mrs. Barton's death, partly brought about by her sister's thoughtless conduct, had loosened another 'of the ties which bound him down to the gentle

---

was its original title, and that to her mind Barton was the central figure, Mrs. Gaskell remarked that she had 'long/ felt that the bewildered life/ of an ignorant thoughtful/ man of strong power of sym/=pathy, dwelling in a town/ so full of striking contrasts/ as' Manchester, 'was a tragic poem'; but that the 'Mary Barton' suggestion came from London through the publisher: many people, she wrote, either overlooked or misunderstood John Barton. She mentioned that some were angry with the book, saying it would do harm; but that, though this had distressed her, she believed only good could come in the long run from an earnest expression of one's feelings, and tried not to mind greatly blame or praise. This letter of 5 January [1849] is in the Parrish Collection at the Princeton University Library. (The letters here cited are respectively G.L., Nos. 37, 39.)

[30] E.g. Kathleen Mary Tillotson, *Novels of the Eighteen-Forties*, Corrected 2nd impression, Oxford: The Clarendon Press, 1956, pp. 211-213.

[31] Arnold Charles Kettle, 'The Early Victorian Social-Problem Novel', in *From Dickens to Hardy*—Vol. VI of *A (The Pelican) Guide to English Literature*, ed. Boris Ford, 7 vols., 1954-1961—[Melbourne, London, and Baltimore:] Penguin Books, 1958, p. 181.

[32] *Works*, I, 4.	[35] *Works*, I, 196.	[38] *Works*, I, p. lxiii.
[33] *Works*, I, 111.	[36] *Works*, I, 430-431.	[39] *Works*, I, p. lxiii.
[34] *Works*, I, 194.	[37] *Works*, I, 8, 112.	[40] *Works*, I, 24-25.

humanities of earth'[41]; Parliament's rejection of the Chartist Petition, together with his own treatment in London, had further destroyed Barton's belief in humanity[42]; finally the insolence and ridicule which a deputation of strikers received at the hands of the masters was the direct cause of the murder of Harry Carson[43]. However, it is impossible to convey the acute observation and sympathetic insight with which Mrs. Gaskell treats her protagonist merely by tabulating a few key events: a quotation is required. Though the following passage may not be of the highest literary merit, no other social-problem novelist could have written it: Barton's mind is seen as a woman would see it, as something of a piece with his physical condition.

> There sat her father, still and motionless—not even turning his head to see who had entered; but perhaps he recognised the footstep,—the trick of action.
>
> He sat by the fire; the grate, I should say, for fire there was none. Some dull, grey ashes, negligently left, long days ago, coldly choked up the bars. He had taken the accustomed seat from mere force of habit, which ruled his automaton body. For all energy, both physical and mental, seemed to have retreated inwards to some of the great citadels of life, there to do battle against the Destroyer, Conscience.
>
> His hands were crossed, his fingers interlaced; usually a position implying some degree of resolution, or strength; but in him it was so faintly maintained, that it appeared more the result of chance; an attitude requiring some application of outward force to alter—and a blow with a straw seemed as though it would be sufficient.
>
> And as for his face, it was sunk and worn—like a skull, with yet a suffering expression that skulls have not![44]

Turning from 'the tragedy of a poor man's life'[45] to the industrial setting, the reader is conscious of the same sympathetic observation, the same careful recording of *minutiae,* the same graphic recreation, the same responsive sensitivity to working-class life. The opening scene, set a couple of miles from industrial Manchester, is a splendid picture of a typical May holiday as enjoyed by common people in Green Heys Fields; it is a picture which, for one reader at least, served to identify the writer by virtue of its accuracy and power[46]. Written with a

---

[41] *Works,* I, 22.   [43] *Works,* I, 208-220.   [45] *Works,* I, 432.
[42] *Works,* I, 110-115.   [44] *Works,* I, 410-411.
[46] Emily Winkworth recognized the author from her description of the fields and stile: see Shaen, ed. *Memorials of Two Sisters,* p. 31.

feeling for the countryside which reminds us of the novelist's Cheshire childhood and fondness for rural settings, its poignancy (the contrast with what has been left, and must be returned to, after all too brief an interlude) recalls the Dunham visit of *Libbie Marsh's Three Eras*. Mrs. Gaskell's introduction of the operatives and their wives—especially the Barton and Wilson families —is natural and sure: with remarkable economy she sets the story in motion, and makes her readers enter imaginatively into the lives of the characters. D. H. Lawrence and Mrs. Gaskell had, rather surprisingly, something in common[47]; for the opening chapters of *Sons and Lovers* are, in their realistic evocation of a particular working-class mentality and *milieu*, not so very dissimilar to those of *Mary Barton*.

Maria Edgeworth remarked that 'the tale shews . . . intimate knowledge of manufacturing miseries and of all those small details which can be obtained only from personal observation and which can be selected so as to produce great effect, only by the union of quiet feeling with cool discriminating judgement'[48]: similarly Samuel Bamford complimented Mrs. Gaskell on her fidelity in describing 'the dwellings of the poor, their manners, their kindliness to each other'[49]. In a letter of 8 November 1848[50], Thomas Carlyle welcomed the authoress's 'social, clear and observant charac-/-ter'; praised her use of rich new materials; found *Mary Barton* worthy of a 'place far above/ the ordinary garbage of Novels'; considered her capable of giving 'Portraits of Man-/-chester Existence still more strikingly *real*'; recommended conciseness 'not in words only, but in thought and/ conception;' and found her 'already strong' in ' "veracity", or devout earnestness of mind'.

---

[47] A link suggested in Raymond Henry Williams, *Culture and Society, 1780-1950*, London: Chatto & Windus, 1958, pp. 87-88. See too Walter Ernest Allen, 'Mrs. Gaskell in Town and Country', *The Daily Telegraph and Morning Post*, 28 October 1965, p. 20; and John Bayley, 'Why Read Mrs. Gaskell?', *Sunday Telegraph*, 14 November 1965, p. 18.

[48] *Letters Addressed to Mrs Gaskell by Celebrated Contemporaries*, ed. Waller, p. 9.

[49] *Letters Addressed to Mrs Gaskell by Celebrated Contemporaries*, ed. Waller, p. 8.

[50] Now in The John Rylands Library, Manchester (English MS. 730/14). It may be a comment on Gaskell scholarship that this letter, so often referred to by biographers, has never been accurately transcribed.

Contemporary periodical opinion likewise commended *Mary Barton* for its accuracy in depicting the living conditions of the poor[51]; even William Rathbone Greg, in many ways a hostile critic, had no complaints on this score[52]. Mrs. Gaskell favoured writings which, she thought, succeeded in presenting "the scene itself"[53] to the reader; and her own method in relating *Mary Barton* was "to really see the scenes . . . [she] tried to describe, (and they were as real as . . . [her] own life at the time) and then to tell them as nearly as . . . [she] could, as if . . . [she] were speaking to a friend over the fire on a winter's night and describing real occurrences."[54] This, then, is what Mrs. Gaskell attempted in her descriptions of life among the operatives. As she says in the Preface, her aim was 'to write truthfully'[55], without consciously supporting or attacking any partic-

---

The extracts given by Miss Hopkins (*Elizabeth Gaskell,* p. 82), Miss Haldane (*Mrs. Gaskell and Her Friends,* pp. 47-48), and Dr. Johanna Jacoba van Dullemen (*Mrs. Gaskell: Novelist and Biographer,* Amsterdam: H. J. Paris, 1924, pp. 191-192) not only differ from Carlyle's autograph, but even fail to tally among themselves. Waller, whose transscripts (like those of Aina Rubenius) are on the whole as accurate as one can expect, omits to mention Miss Haldane's inaccuracy when he refers to her book instead of quoting the Carlyle MS himself (Waller, ed. *Letters Addressed to Mrs Gaskell by Celebrated Contemporaries,* p. 12). (Our shorter title for Dr. van Dullemen's work will be *Mrs. Gaskell.*)

[51] Some account of the criticism Mrs. Gaskell's works received when they first came out may be found in van Dullemen, *Mrs. Gaskell,* pp. 191-210; esp. pp. 193-200 for contemporary reviews of *Mary Barton.* One may also refer to Josephine Gernsheimer, 'Mrs. Gaskell's Novels, Their Reception in Various Periodicals, 1848-1910', M.A. essay, Columbia University, 1934.

[52] William Rathbone Greg, Review of *Mary Barton,* in *The Edinburgh Review or Critical Journal,* LXXXIX (1849), 403, 409-410.

[53] Extract from a letter of Thursday [26 December 1850] by Mary Howitt to her daughter, in which she passes on the novelist's praise—quoted in *Mary Howitt: An Autobiography,* ed. Howitt, II, 66.

[54] Quoted by Miss Haldane (*Mrs. Gaskell and Her Friends,* p. 39), these words occur in Mrs. Gaskell's letter to Eliza Fox of Monday [Tuesday] 29 May 1849 (*G.L.,* No. 48). However we have retained the punctuation and double underlining of the typescript copy of part of this letter in the Gaskell Section, Brotherton Collection, Leeds University Library. Mrs. Gaskell also here remarks that only the character of John Barton was real; and she refers to the poem of 1837 in *Blackwood's* as being 'the germ of "Alice." '

[55] *Works,* I, p. lxxiv.

lar theory of political economy[56] : misrepresentation she seemed especially anxious to avoid[57].

It is possible to give here only two or three instances of Mrs. Gaskell's eye for relevant detail, her vivid descriptive powers, and her imaginative documentation. Typical examples occur in the second chapter, which chiefly concerns a tea-party among working-class Mancunians[58] during a prosperous period (which is in itself interesting, since very few social-problem novelists give any sense of joy in the world of the industrial lower classes). Mrs. Gaskell shows us the hospitably blazing fire; enumerates at length the articles of furniture (the room being crammed, for times are good); believes the cupboard 'full of plates and dishes, cups and saucers, and some more nondescript articles, for which one would have fancied 'their possessors could find no use'[59]; points to the gay-coloured oil-cloth; refers to 'a bright green japanned tea-tray, having a couple of scarlet lovers embracing in the middle'[60]; and so forth. When Mrs. Barton talks of buying fresh eggs, the price is noted; and the quantities of milk and rum are estimated according to their cost (a pennyworth and sixpennyworth respectively). In contrast to all this, we find a very different

---

[56] Mrs. Gaskell never claimed to present the whole truth, though she hoped her book did contain the truth and nothing but the truth. Declining to write another novel—complementary to *Mary Barton*—from the standpoint of the masters, Mrs. Gaskell put her position as follows : 'In the first place whatever power there was in Mary Barton was caused by my feeling strongly on the side which I took; now as I don't feel as strongly (and as it is impossible I ever should,) on the other side, the forced effort of writing on that side would [be *deleted*] ∧end in∧ a weak failure. I know, and have always owned, that I have represented *but one* side of the question, and no one would welcome more than I should, a true and earnest representation of the other side. I believe what I have said in Mary Barton to be perfectly true, but by no means the whole truth; and I have always felt deeply annoyed at anyone, or any set of people who chose to consider that I had manifested the whole truth; I do not think it is possible to do this in any *one* work of fiction.'—Extract from the letter, dated 16 July [1850—not 1851, as it is annotated], written by Mrs. Gaskell to Lady Kay-Shuttleworth : our quotation is based on the typescript copy belonging to the Hon. Mrs. Angela Mary James, corrected against the original letter owned by Lord Shuttleworth of Gawthorpe, which appears as *G.L.*, No. 72a. See too *G.L.*, Nos. 35, 36, 39a.

[57] See the draft of her letter to Mrs. Sam Greg, quoted by Ward (ed. *Works*, I, pp. lxii-lxiii) : *G.L.*, No. 42

[58] *Works*, I, 11-18, esp. 12-17.

[59] *Works*, I, 13.

[60] *Works*, I, 13.

picture painted in hard times; but the manner of reporting is the same.

This trial [of changing house] was spared. The collector (of himself), on the very Monday when Barton planned to give him notice of his intention to leave, lowered the rent threepence a week, just enough to make Barton compromise and agree to stay on a little longer.

But by degrees the house was stripped of all its little ornaments. Some were broken; and the odd twopences and three-pences, wanted to pay for their repairs, were required for the far sterner necessity of food. And by-and-by Mary began to part with other superfluities at the pawn-shop. The smart tea-tray, and tea-caddy, long and carefully kept, went for bread for her father. He did not ask for it, or complain, but she saw hunger in his shrunk, fierce, animal look. Then the blankets went, for it was summer time, and they could spare them; and their sale made a fund, which Mary fancied would last till better times came. But it was soon all gone; and then she looked around the room to crib it of its few remaining ornaments.[61]

A graphic passage referred to more than once by her con-temporaries[62] is that in which Mrs. Gaskell describes the journey of Barton and Wilson through unpaved streets, filled with all manner of refuse, to the cellar-home of the Davenport family[63]. Of the dwelling itself she remarks as follows.

He [Wilson] had opened a door [in the main cellar], but only for an instant; it led into a back cellar, with a grating instead of a window, down which dropped the moisture from pigsties, and worse abominations. It was not paved; the floor was one mass of bad smelling mud. It had never been used, for there was not an article of furniture in it; nor could a human being, much less a pig, have lived there many days. Yet the "back apart-ment" made a difference in the rent. The Davenports paid threepence more for having two rooms.[64]

It is not difficult to gloss Mrs. Gaskell's description of con-ditions in Manchester in the second quarter of the nineteenth century: W. H. Brown, for example, has a relevant passage.

Just think of the city when she arrived in September, 1832. Mark Phillips had been elected as the first M.P. for Man-chester, defeating William Cobbett at the poll. An inquiry revealed that there were 27,281 comfortable dwellings in the

[61] *Works*, I, 130.
[62] E.g. by Greg (*The Edinburgh Review*, LXXXIX, 407-408).
[63] *Works*, I, 65-66.
[64] *Works*, I, 70.

town; that 10,443 uncomfortable ones existed along with them, and that 18,000 people lived in cellars. Ten years later things were little better. The town authorities spent £5,000 a year on cleansing the streets—those of the first class were cleaned once a week; the second class every fortnight; and the third class once a month, while the courts and alleys were disregarded altogether. Manchester then had 132 cotton mills employing 32,413 "hands"—43 were stopped altogether and ten were on short time. Two thousand families, near where Mrs. Gaskell lived in ministerial comfort, were found to have a weekly income of 1s. 2½d. per person.[65]

Another commentator[66] remarks that Mrs. Gaskell's information came from no second-hand sources but from visiting the poor, talking to Sunday-School pupils, and engaging in general philanthropic activities with social workers like Travers Madge and Thomas Wright (the prison visitor); statistics are quoted in support of Mrs. Gaskell's faithful reporting. It would be possible, by using authors like Engels[67], Kay-Shuttleworth[68], and Redford[69], to substantiate Mrs. Gaskell's historical accuracy, although the knowledgeable mode of description and the authoritative note in the narrative really provide in themselves sufficient justification[70]. As a side-light on Mrs. Gaskell's objectivity, her seeing both aspects of the lives of the poor, it is well to recall the account of Alice Wilson's well-kept cellar[71], very different from that, already quoted, of the Davenports' abode.

Mrs. Gaskell concludes the sixth chapter with a most graphic

[65] William Henry Brown, 'Mrs. Gaskell: A Manchester Influence', *Papers of the Manchester Literary Club,* LVIII (1932), 16.
[66] A Manchester Correspondent [Mat Hompes], 'Mrs. Gaskell and Her Social Work among the Poor', *The Inquirer,* LXIX (8 October 1910), 656.
[67] Engels, *The Condition of the Working Class in England,* trans. and ed. Henderson and Chaloner.
[68] Kay-Shuttleworth, *Four Periods of Public Education.*
[69] Arthur Redford (ass. by Ina Stafford Russell), *The History of Local Government in Manchester,* 3 vols., London, New York, and Toronto: Longmans, Green and Company, 1939-1940.
[70] The unwisdom of relying solely on general historical evidence in these matters—especially if one regards J. L. and Barbara Hammond as 'two of the most reliable social historians of our time'—is manifested in D. S. Bland, '*Mary Barton* and Historical Accuracy', *The Review of English Studies,* N.S. I (1950), 58-60. Bland would have found there was no need to go into print if he had but turned to an article by John Mortimer—'Concerning the "Mary Barton" Fields', *The Manchester Quarterly,* XXXVII (1911), 1-8.
[71] *Works,* I, 15.

account of a pauper burial. What is especially remarkable, however, is that, after mentioning how a wooden tombstone was used to do duty over the common grave, she adds an authorial footnote: 'The case, to my certain knowledge, in one churchyard in Manchester. There may be more.'[72] With this kind of veracity, one would (*prima facie*) scarcely expect slip-shod observation. Nevertheless W. R. Greg attacked her for giving a very misleading picture of the relations between rich and poor. One might reply[73] that Greg is guilty of misreading in regarding John Barton's attitude as that of the average workman; yet Greg, one of the founders of the Manchester Statistical Society[74], has some claim to be heard on Manchester conditions. Having referred to medical institutions, infirmaries, dispensaries, eye and lying-in hospitals, and so forth[75], Greg goes on to mention that during the very severe periods of distress in 1842 and 1847 large-scale relief was carried out (4,000 people receiving daily supplies of rice and soup in the earlier year—a number nearly doubled in 1847, when bread and soup were distributed gratuitously for many months)[76]. Hence he feels he may state confidently:

> That a steady and religious family, like the Davenports, could have fallen into the state of helpless and squalid wretchedness which the authoress has depicted, no one acquainted with the poor of Manchester will easily believe; ... [77]

One need not rely on knowledge of Mrs. Gaskell's life to answer the innuendo that she was unaware of what Manchester did for its poor: *Mary Barton* itself does that. She was not ignorant about the existence of infirmaries—John Barton had been well treated in one[78]; she realized that soup kitchens did good work —Mrs. Aldred used two cows' heads weekly in soup-

---

[72] *Works*, I, 81, fn.—this footnote, of course, appears in the first edition (I, 111, fn.).

[73] Finding some support in William Minto, 'Mrs. Gaskell's Novels', *The Fortnightly Review*, XXX (N.S. XXIV, 1878), 358-364.

[74] Thomas Southcliffe Ashton, *Economic and Social Investigations in Manchester, 1833-1933: A Centenary History of the Manchester Statistical Society*, intro. The Earl of Crawford and Balcarres, London: P. S. King & Son, Ltd., 1934, pp. 6-8.

[75] *The Edinburgh Review*, LXXXIX, 425.

[76] *The Edinburgh Review*, LXXXIX, 425-426.

[77] *The Edinburgh Review*, LXXXIX, 426.

[78] *Works*, I, 93.

preparation[79]; she knew that the Board would give help—
Davenport had not applied from fear of being sent back to his
Buckinghamshire parish[80], but his widow had found it less for-
midable than expected[81]; she did not forget the Guardians' re-
lieving office—though John Barton preferred not to apply for
charity[82].

Although the kind of criticism voiced by Greg, *The Manchester Guardian*[83], and *The British Quarterly Review*[84] suggested
that Mrs. Gaskell's was a biased presentation of the facts, even
if the facts themselves were accurate, the novelist never sought
to engage in economic arguments, her remedy for class warfare
and disharmony being mutual understanding. On reflexion,
moreover, one is inclined to consider that she did not distort.
The manufacturers are not all painted black (Jem Wilson's
former employer, Mr. Duncombe[85], is a case in point); nor does
'approval' seem the word to apply to Mrs. Gaskell's attitude
towards Barton's murdering young Harry Carson. She saw that
both masters and men failed to regard one another as human
beings[86], and to this she assigned their lack of mutual understanding and the consequential violence and strife. What emerges
from the conversation between Mr. Carson, the economic
theorist who worked facts like fixed mathematical quantities[87],
and Job Legh, the operative who, like Mrs. Gaskell[88], disclaimed
any knowledge of political economy[89], is a change in the master's
disposition which the author clearly judged an improvement.

> [T]hose who were admitted into his confidence were aware, that
> the wish that lay nearest to his heart was that none might
> suffer from the cause from which he had suffered; that a perfect

[79] *Works*, I, 210.
[80] *Works*, I, 71.
[81] *Works*, I, 82.
[82] *Works*, I, 130-131.
[83] Review of *Mary Barton*, in *The Manchester Guardian*, 28 February
1849, p. 7; Editorial Comment on a Letter by D. Winstanley, *The Manchester Guardian*, 7 March 1849, p. 8—see Ward, ed. *Works*, I, p. lviii;
and van Dullemen, *Mrs. Gaskell*, pp. 195-196.
[84] Review of *Mary Barton*, in *The British Quarterly Review*, IX (1849),
117-136.
[85] *Works*, I, esp. 436-437.
[86] *Works*, I, 209, 425-426.
[87] *Works*, I, 448.
[88] *Works*, I, p. lxxiv.
[89] *Works*, I, 447.

understanding, and complete confidence and love, might exist
between masters and men; that the truth might be recognised
that the interests of one were the interests of all, and, as such,
required the consideration and deliberation of all; that hence
it was most desirable to have educated workers, capable of
judging, not mere machines of ignorant men; and to have them
bound to their employers by the ties of respect and affection,
not by mere money bargains alone; in short, to acknowledge the
Spirit of Christ as the regulating law between both parties.[90]

This is very different from the Carson who, when asked for an
infirmary order for one of his workmen, replied that he did not
pretend to know the names of the men he employed—he left
that to the overseer[91]. If *Mary Barton* did something to change
such attitudes, then it did much. By publishing her observations
of the life around her, Mrs. Gaskell brought a degree of enlightenment to those wealthy inhabitants of Manchester who would,
in Cobden's view, scarcely be likely to know that a man like
Thomas Wright (the prison philanthropist) was at work in the
city[92], and who, we may *a fortiori* assume, had little acquaintance with the conditions so graphically depicted in *Mary
Barton*.

We turn now, rather late in our study, to the love story. Miss
Edgeworth thought highly of this, seeing in the position of the
heroine—torn between her guilty father and her innocent lover
—'a situation fit for the highest Greek Tragedy yet not unsuited
to the humblest life of a poor tender girl'[93]. However, as has
been indicated, it was 'the tragedy of a poor man's life'[94] which

---

[90] *Works*, I, 451.
[91] *Works*, I, 77-78.
[92] For evidence of Mrs. Gaskell's high opinion of Wright, see Waller,
ed. *Letters Addressed to Mrs Gaskell by Celebrated Contemporaries,*
pp. 15-18. Further details about Wright may be found in [Thomas
Wright McDermid] *The Life of Thomas Wright, of Manchester, the
Prison Philanthropist,* pref. The Earl of Shaftesbury, Manchester: John
Heywood; London: Simpkin, Marshall, and Co., 1876. One may also
consult [Henry Morley] 'An Unpaid Servant of the State', *Household
Words*, IV (1852), 553-555—for confirming that this anonymous writer
was almost certainly Henry Morley I am indebted to Professor Anne
Lohrli (New Mexico Highlands University, Las Vegas, New Mexico,
U.S.A.), who wrote to me on 31 October 1964; the *Household Words*
Day (or Office) Book (in the Princeton University Library) merely records
the author's surname, Morley.
[93] *Letters Addressed to Mrs Gaskell by Celebrated Contemporaries,*
ed. Waller, p. 10.
[94] *Works*, I, 432.

primarily interested Mrs. Gaskell; this was what she had in mind
when she "took refuge in the invention"[95] to exclude from
remembrance the painful recollections of her son's death. The
writing of the novel had a therapeutic value for the author; but
it was also composed to help relieve the sufferings of others by
one who herself knew what suffering meant. Her treatment of
Mary's romances was of secondary importance; in the love-plot
as such there is 'nothing very striking or original.'[96]

Mrs. Gaskell never leaves the reader in any doubt about her
disapproval of Mary's flirtation with Harry Carson, the mill-
owner's handsome young son, though one understands that not
all Mary's motives sprang from vanity[97]. The scene in which
Harry, fearful of losing Mary, promises to make a great sacrifice
and marry her, with Mary's shocked reaction, is less conventional than a reference to it might suggest[98]. Nevertheless Mrs.
Gaskell's invention does not here distinguish her from the general
run of Victorian novelists. We shall come across the theme of
the elegant but essentially selfish lover and the rather roman-
tically innocent dress-maker in a later work, *Ruth*. It would
not, however, be well to leave this subject without giving an
example of the inward realism employed in describing Mary's
feelings; this rings true, and is beyond mere reporting.

> It was scarcely ten minutes since he [Jem] had entered the
> house, and found Mary at comparative peace, and now she lay
> half across the dresser, her head hidden in her hands, and every
> part of her body shaking with the violence of her sobs. She
> could not have told at first (if you had asked her, and she could
> have commanded voice enough to answer) why she was in such
> agonised grief. It was too sudden for her to analyse, or think
> upon it. She only felt, that by her own doing her life would be
> hereafter blank and dreary. By-and-by her sorrow exhausted her
> body by its power, and she seemed to have no strength left for
> crying. She sat down; and now thoughts crowded on her mind.
> One little hour ago, and all was still unsaid, and she had her
> fate in her own power. And yet, how long ago had she deter-
> mined to say pretty much what she did, if the occasion ever
> offered.[99]

[95] Quoted by Ward (ed. *Works*, I, p. lxiii) from the draft of Mrs.
Gaskell's letter to Mrs. Sam Greg (*G.L.*, No. 42).

[96] *The British Quarterly Review*, IX (1849), 125: these words are
here applied to the plot as a whole.

[97] *Works*, I, 90-91.

[98] *Works*, I, 156-158.

[99] *Works*, I, 149.

One is conscious, at the conclusion of the novel, of a certain falling off in inventive power. The marriage, emigration, and idyllic picture of Mary and Jem Wilson, together with Jem's mother, enjoying an Indian summer—with the promise that they will soon be joined by Will Wilson, with Margaret as his wife (her sight recovered), and by the botanising Job Legh—, though not entirely without justification, do give the impression of a tying-up of ends, of being the result of extra-literary requirements[100]. The ending is, in some ways, escapist[101].

We have previously referred to what Mrs. Gaskell called the 'seeing-beauty spirit'. In surveying the world around her, she looked for joy as well as sorrow; she had the sense of life as a mingled yarn. From the outset such sentiments pervade her writings. Dr. Adolphus Ward remarked that '[w]ith Mrs. Gaskell's power of observation, the quality of humour with which she was so richly endowed was in her earliest work not yet altogether able to keep pace'[102]; and this seems largely true for *Mary Barton* (the author herself realized "the fault of there being too heavy a shadow over the book"[103]): but Mrs. Gaskell was certainly aware of the variety of life, the chequered quality of human existence—an awareness poetically expressed in the following passage.

> It is a pretty sight to walk through a street with lighted shops; the gas is so brilliant, the display of goods so much more vividly shown than by day, and of all shops a druggist's looks the most like the tales of our childhood, from Aladdin's garden of enchanted fruits to the charming Rosamond with her purple

---

[100] Certainly so with respect to some of the passages following John Barton's death, according to the draft of Mrs. Gaskell's letter to Mrs. Sam Greg, quoted by Ward (ed. *Works*, I, pp. lxiii-lxiv): *G.L.*, No. 42.

[101] In the view of Maria Edgeworth (*Letters Addressed to Mrs Gaskell by Celebrated Contemporaries*, ed. Waller, pp. 10-11) and Raymond Williams (*Culture and Society*, 1780-1950, p. 91).

[102] Ward, ed. *Works*, I, p. lxvi.

[103] Quoted by Ward (ed. *Works*, I, p. lxiii) from the draft of Mrs. Gaskell's letter to Mrs. Sam Greg (*G.L.*, No. 42). Cf. 'I acknowledge,—no one feels more keenly than I do, the great fault of the gloominess of M B. It is the fault of the choice of the subject; which yet I did not *choose*, but which was as it were impressed upon me.'—Extract from a letter, dated 16 July [1850—not 1851, as it is annotated] written by Mrs. Gaskell to Lady Kay-Shuttleworth: our quotation is based on the typescript copy belonging to the Hon. Mrs. Angela Mary James, corrected against the original letter owned by Lord Shuttleworth of Gawthorpe, which appears as *G.L.*, No. 72a.

jar. No such associations had Barton; yet he felt the contrast between the well-filled, well-lighted shops and the dim gloomy cellar, and it made him moody that such contrasts should exist. They are the mysterious problem of life to more than him. He wondered if any in all the hurrying crowd had come from such a house of mourning. He thought they all looked joyous, and he was angry with them. But he could not, you cannot, read the lot of those who daily pass you by in the street. How do you know the wild romances of their lives; the trials, the temptations they are even now enduring, resisting, sinking under? You may be elbowed one instant by the girl desperate in her abandonment, laughing in mad merriment with her outward gesture, while her soul is longing for the rest of the dead, and bringing itself to think of the cold-flowing river as the only mercy of God remaining to her here. You may pass the criminal, meditating crimes at which you will to-morrow shudder with horror as you read them. You may push against one, humble and unnoticed, the last upon earth, who in heaven will for ever be in the immediate light of God's countenance. Errands of mercy —errands of sin—did you ever think where all the thousands of people you daily meet are bound?[104]

There are in *Mary Barton* three incidents which cut across the main course of the story; one might describe them as moments of vision, the infringing of another realm upon Manchester life. The first arises when John Barton, murder-bent, meets a lost child, whom he returns to its mother before going on his way[105]. The second occurs when Mary, stunned by the news of Jem's arrest, encounters a little Italian boy with a humble show-box : at first she passes by, in spite of his cries for food; but, upbraided at heart, she returns to give him all that remains in her scanty larder[106]. The third happens when Mr. Carson, intent on avenging his son's death, sees a little errand boy knock a girl down : her nurse threatens him with a policeman; but the girl herself takes his part, saying the boy did not know what he was doing[107]. It is difficult to comment on these episodes; they seem to evoke more than a reference to them implies. Perhaps one could mention the philosophy, given rather sentimental expression in Margaret's song[108], that little things have a far-reaching importance—for good or ill. Applying what Mrs. Gaskell says about another song, one might suggest that here is something 'near akin to pathos'[109].

---

[104] *Works,* I, 69-70.   [106] *Works,* I, 266.   [108] *Works,* I, 108-109.
[105] *Works,* I, 229-230. [107] *Works,* I, 427-428. [109] *Works,* I, 39.

Mrs. Gaskell's inclusive vision ensures against sentimentality. Though several instances could be given, two will suffice. Mary and Margaret are engaged on making mourning, an occasion from which emerges humour as well as sadness; for, in response to Mary's supposition that the daughters of the family could have made their own gowns, Margaret replies:

"So I dare say they do, many a one, but now they seem all so busy getting ready for the funeral; for it's to be quite a grand affair, well-nigh twenty people to breakfast, as one of the little ones told me; the little thing seemed to like the fuss, and I do believe it comforted poor Mrs. Ogden to make all the piece o' work. Such a smell of ham boiling and fowls roasting while I waited in the kitchen; it seemed more like a wedding nor a funeral. They said she'd spent a matter o' sixty pounds on th' burial."[110]

[110] *Works*, I, 49: there is a footnote to explain 'nor'. The difficulty of deciding when such explanations would be required for non-Lancashire readers, the notes being by her husband, is mentioned in Mrs. Gaskell's letter to Chapman of 17 April 1848. Unfortunately the first edition contained numerous errors—e.g. 'gotten' for 'getten'—in the dialect parts, as the author informed her publisher in a letter of 5 December 1848; however, acknowledging on Friday 7 [8] December 1848 the first half of the hundred pounds due for her novel, Mrs. Gaskell promised to send him a corrected copy that day, the day following or the subsequent Monday. All three letters (*G.L.*, Nos. 25, 33, 34) are in the Pierpont Morgan Library (Autographs-Miscellaneous-English). Nevertheless the third (1849) rather than the second (1849) of the London (Chapman and Hall) editions carried most minor emendations; and the copyright text (Leipzig: Bernhard Tauchnitz, 1849) virtually coincides with the third English edition. Below appear a sample of the variants: these include added, substituted, and deleted words; dialectal changes; new, expanded, and curtailed footnotes; varied word-order; a different chapter-motto; spelling, capitalization, punctation, and paragraph alterations.

	1st Edn	2nd Edn	3rd Edn
II, 271	know. *He*	know. He did not mean to do it. *He*	know. He did not mean to do it. *He*
II, 86	expres-/sion	word [II, 87]	word [II, 87]
II, 209	Parkside	Hollins Green	Hollins Green
II, 89	But Mary	Mary	Mary
I, 16	gotten	gotten	getten
II, 248	getten	getten	gotten
I, 314	in the street	i' th' street	i' th' street
I, 64	[*no fn. to* nobbut]	[*no fn. to* nobbut]	[*fn. to* nobbut]
I, 6	[*fn. to* nesh]	[*fn. to* nesh]	[*longer fn. to* nesh]
I, 143	[*fn. to* letting on]	[*shorter fn. to* letting on]	[*shorter fn. to* letting on]

After the murder and Jem's subsequent arrest, Mary is portrayed at home, dazed with grief yet attempting to control her sorrow; but there is nothing morbid in the treatment, especially since the appearance and coarse conduct of Sally Leadbitter[111], with her racy, slightly comic, vulgarity, provide a realistic foil for Mary's distress.

As we look at the other characters, we note how Mrs. Gaskell's observation joined with her invention to lend complexity to the tale. She took her figures from people encountered in everyday life; but their interaction, their being contrasted and brought together in different situations, this was due to her own artistic skill. She thus convinces us, by judicious selection and re-arrangent, of the living reality of her world.

Of Job Legh it is possible to see a very tentative first draft, at least as far as scientific enthusiasm is concerned, in the canary-selling barber of *Libbie Marsh's Three Eras*. Expert confirmation from Samuel Bamford on the faithfulness of her portrayal of scientific interests among the poor[112] is scarcely needed; for Mrs. Gaskell's character comes very much alive. The account of the lengths to which his botanical enthusiasm takes him (in the scorpion-killing episode[113]) and his scepticism about Will Wilson's mermaid-yarn[114] are among the memorable passages in the novel; and he is one of its author's most successful creations.

	1st Edn	2nd Edn	3rd Edn
I, 28	Mary he could not tell, in his bewildered state.	Mary he could not tell, in his bewildered state.	Mary, in his bewildered state, he could not tell.
II, 169	[*Wordsworth chapter-motto*]	[*non-Wordsworth chapter-motto*]	[*non-Wordsworth chapter-motto*]
I, 300	immovable	immovable	immoveable
II, 95	lovable	loveable	loveable
I, 106	fever wards	Fever Wards	Fever Wards
II, 308	Butterfly	Butterfly	butterfly
I, 75	aperture, there	aperture, there	aperture—there
I, 83	Let!	Let?	Let?
II, 155	One ... wind. [*two paragraphs*]	One . . . wind. [*one paragraph*]	One . . . wind. [*one paragraph*]

111 *Works*, I, 318-321.
112 *Letters Addressed to Mrs Gaskell by Celebrated Contemporaries*, ed. Waller, p. 8.
113 *Works*, I, 43-44.
114 *Works*, I, 173-175.

Mrs. Wilson, the mother of Mary's faithful lover, is another interesting individual from the working classes. Despite being quick-tempered she is not unsympathetic, since the author gives us an insight into the misery, hardship, and death which were formative influences during most of her life. The accident she received from unfenced machinery, mentioned *en passant* by John Barton[115], is an instance of how Mrs. Gaskell can make a historical point not so much for its own sake but for the purpose of the novel. Her jealous maternal love for Jem, her consequentially rather hostile attitude to Mary, her tragico-humorous belief that she was responsible for her son's acquittal—all go into composing a realistic character. The following extract indicates something of Mrs. Gaskell's approach.

> On large occasions like the present [when she learnt that Mary's father had been a murderer], Mrs. Wilson's innate generosity came out. Her weak and ailing frame imparted its irritation to her conduct in small things, and daily trifles; but she had deep and noble sympathy with great sorrows, and even at the time that Mary spoke she allowed no expression of surprise or horror to escape her lips. She gave way to no curiosity as to the untold details; she was as secret and trustworthy as her son himself; and if in years to come her anger was occasionally excited against Mary, and she, on rare occasions, yielded to ill-temper against her daughter-in-law, she would upbraid her for extravagance, or stinginess, or over-dressing, or under-dressing, or too much mirth, or too much gloom, but never, never in her most uncontrolled moments, did she allude to any one of the circumstances relating to Mary's flirtation with Harry Carson, or his murderer; and always when she spoke of John Barton, named him with the respect due to his conduct before the last, miserable, guilty month of his life.[116]

We have met Alice Wilson, sister-in-law to Jane, in 'Sketches among the Poor. No. 1'; and we have Mrs. Gaskell's own testimony[117] that she incorporated the Mary of that sketch into the

---

[115] *Works*, I, 100.

[116] *Works*, I, 440.

[117] In her letter of 9 March [1859] to John Blackwood, the publisher, now in the National Library of Scotland (MS. 4139, ff. 9-12; the relevant passage being on ff. 10ᵛ-11ʳ); and in her letter to Eliza Fox of Monday [Tuesday] 29 May 1849 (a copy of part of which being in the Gaskell Section, Brotherton Collection, Leeds University Library), where she speaks of the poem as being 'the germ of "Alice."' These letters appear respectively as *G.L.*, Nos. 417, 48.

novel[118]. Alice is more than a country-woman, longing for her rural home yet never able to return there, doing good in whatever ways she finds possible in the poor districts of Manchester. She exemplifies the patience of the poor[119], their acceptance without complaint of whatever life brings. When her death is near, the spiritual peace of the old woman pervades the sick-room[120]. However Mrs. Gaskell guards against sickly sentimentality by making use of Sally Leadbitter's comments on ' "th' canting old maid" '[121].

The figure of Esther, Mary's aunt, has by some critics[122] been considered irrelevant, whereas others have stressed her importance[123]. The 'fallen woman' *motif* was common in Victorian literature; indeed it is a theme which Mrs. Gaskell herself used more than once in her work. With her, however, personal experience[124] rather than literary convention directed the choice; it was not a matter of being fashionable in an artistic sense. Opinions may differ as to the staginess or otherwise of Esther; but she is the significant reminder of what Mary herself might so easily have become, had she been seduced by Harry Carson. Professor Stanton Whitfield[125] has remarked that no prostitute ever talked like Esther, yet against this one must put the graphic description of her life on the streets[126]. Such cases as hers were very common[127]. Even here Mrs. Gaskell's treatment is neither sentimental nor merely scientifically documentary— one wonders which other contemporary industrial novelist would

[118] There are verbal parallels: for instance the account in the poem of the old woman's childhood (*Works* I, pp. xxiii-xxiv) may be compared with a similar account in the novel (*Works,* I, 35).

[119] *Works,* I, 86, 164.

[120] *Works,* I, 254.

[121] *Works,* I, 104.

[122] Such as Maria Edgeworth (*Letters Addressed to Mrs Gaskell by Celebrated Contemporaries,* ed. Waller, p. 11).

[123] For example, Tillotson, *Novels of the Eighteen-Forties,* 1956, pp. 64-65.

[124] For Mrs. Gaskell's first-hand knowledge, see our remarks on *Ruth.*

[125] Whitfield, *Mrs Gaskell,* pp. 119-120.

[126] *Works,* I, 140-143, 181-190.

[127] There is a useful section on this subject in Rubenius, *The Woman Question in Mrs. Gaskell's Life and Works,* pp. 176-216.

have had imagination enough to invent a trade-name for the prostitute.

> Jem wandered far and wide that night, but never met Esther. The next day he applied to the police; and at last they recognised under his description of her, a woman known to them under the name of the "Butterfly," from the gaiety of her dress a year or two ago.[128]

This passage acquires pathos if one recalls Esther's encounter with John Barton, when 'most of all, he loathed the dress; and yet the poor thing, out of her little choice of attire, had put on the plainest she had, to come on that night's errand'[129]—a pathos which receives additional force if Esther's pawn-shop clothes-changing[130] (in an attempt to appear respectable before her niece) is also borne in mind.

Margaret Jennings stands in marked contrast to Mary Barton, especially since the love between herself and Will Wilson is of so modest a nature as to render her incapable of appreciating Mary's position in regard to Harry Carson[131]. Her moralistic point of view is not that of the author who, though she can understand Margaret's touch of Puritanism, does not fully endorse it. Margaret's lover, the sailor nephew of Alice Wilson, is given a couple or so good yarns to tell[132], and his testimony in court possesses importance for the plot[133]; nevertheless what strikes the Gaskell scholar in his case is the first occurrence of the 'returning sailor' *motif*, a theme which runs through several later stories. Mrs. Gaskell's own brother disappeared at sea in mysterious circumstances; so it is tempting to posit that, doubtless at sub-conscious levels, a lifelong wish that he might one day come home found expression in her writings. Her picture of Ben Sturgis, which shows an insight into nautical types and manners, is also of interest—but then the Stevensons had several links with the sea[134]. One could describe the following scene as viewed through eyes at once nautical, maternal and, therefore, feminine—the reference to the sail-cloth sheets comes from a

---

[128] *Works,* I, 454.   [130] *Works,* I, 274.   [132] *Works,* I, 172-178.
[129] *Works,* I, 141.   [131] *Works,* I, 289-290.   [133] *Works,* I, 382-385.
[134] See Ward, ed. *Works,* I, p. xvi; VI, p. xvi. Mrs. Gaskell's pride in her supposedly Viking blood and Scandinavian ancestry is mentioned in Ritchie, pref. *Cranford,* by Mrs. Gaskell, p. x.

sailor's observation of things, whereas the comment on the well-aired bed certainly betokens the wife and mother.

> . . . Mrs. Sturgis led her [Mary] into a little room redolent
> of the sea and foreign lands. There was a small bed for one son,
> bound for China; and a hammock slung above for another, who
> was now tossing in the Baltic. The sheets looked made out of
> sail-cloth, but were fresh and clean in spite of their brownness.
> Against the wall were wafered two rough drawings of vessels
> with their names written underneath, on which the mother's
> eyes caught, and gazed until they filled with tears. But she
> brushed the drops away with the back of her hand, and in a
> cheerful tone went on to assure Mary the bed was well aired.[135]

Mrs. Gaskell's *penchant* for deaths has already been noted (the previous quotation contains an ominous allusion). In *Mary Barton* the list of people who die is remarkably long—Mrs. Barton (whose son had died before the tale begins), Davenport, the Wilson twins, George Wilson, young Carson, Alice, John Barton, and Esther—so long indeed as to prompt almost every scholar to criticize the author on this score. The cause was biographic rather than literary: it was not that Mrs. Gaskell was satisfying a popular Victorian taste, rather thoughts of mortality seem to have been constantly in her mind after the death of her only son. Though she spoke little of the loss, it was "the never ending sorrow"[136] of her life. Relevant here are her words in the draft of her letter to Mrs. Greg.

> "The tale was formed, and the greater part of the first volume
> was written when I was obliged to lie down constantly on the
> sofa, and when I took refuge in the invention to exclude the
> memory of painful scenes which would force themselves upon
> my remembrance."[137]

Under such circumstances it should cause no surprise that the invention often encompassed morbid themes. Nevertheless one

---

[135] *Works,* I, 365.

[136] Quoted by Miss Rubenius (*The Woman Question in Mrs. Gaskell's Life and Works,* p. 198, fn. 3) from a copy of part of Mrs. Gaskell's letter to Eliza Fox of 26 April 1850 (in the Gaskell Section, Brotherton Collection, Leeds University Library)—not from the letter itself, as Miss Rubenius states—: *G.L.,* No. 70. See too, in this connexion, Haldane, *Mrs. Gaskell and Her Friends,* pp. 239-240; Hopkins, *Elizabeth Gaskell,* p. 66; and *G.L.,* Nos. 25a, 16a.

[137] Quoted by Ward (ed. *Works,* I, p. lxiii): *G.L.,* No. 42.

ought constantly to remember the very high Manchester mortality-rate, double that found in rural areas[138]. Mrs. Gaskell's treatment is not stereotyped. In the following description John Barton's reaction to his wife's death is far from being a stock response; especially noteworthy are the imaginative use of everyday detail and the intuitive apprehension of his psychological condition.

> He tried to realise it—to think it possible. And then his mind wandered off to other days, to far distant times. He thought of their courtship; of his first seeing her, an awkward beautiful rustic, far too shiftless for the delicate factory work to which she was apprenticed; of his first gift to her, a bead necklace, which had long ago been put by, in one of the deep drawers of the dresser, to be kept for Mary. He wondered if it was there yet, and with a strange curiosity he got up to feel for it; for the fire by this time was well nigh out, and candle he had none. His groping hand fell on the piled-up tea-things, which at his desire she had left unwashed till morning—they were all so tired. He was reminded of one of the daily little actions, which acquire such power when they have been performed for the last time by one we love. He began to think over his wife's daily round of duties: and something in the remembrance that these would never more be done by her, touched the source of tears, and he cried aloud.[139]

Even Esther's death[140], which a superficial reading might condemn as melodramatic[141], has a certain pathos when, recalling our previous comments, we see 'fallen into what appeared simply a heap of white or light coloured clothes, fainting or dead, . . . the poor crushed Butterfly'[142].

Most studies make no mention of the murder-mystery in *Mary Barton*, yet it is necessary to remark how well Mrs. Gaskell's inventive powers handle this part of the plot. The reader at first feels inclined to attribute the murder to John Barton, since this follows naturally from the Trade Union oath and lot-drawing[143]. Subsequently Esther's discovery at the scene of the crime of the scrap of paper in Jem's handwriting[144], taken with his des-

---

[138] Kay-Shuttleworth, *Four Periods of Public Education*, pp. 155-159.
[139] *Works*, I, 20-21.
[140] *Works*, I, 455-457.
[141] ffrench, *Mrs. Gaskell*, p. 24.
[142] *Works*, I, 456.
[143] *Works*, I, 220.
[144] *Works*, I, 270-272.

peration on being rejected by Mary[145] and his violent encounter
with Henry Carson[146], raises doubts; moreover Mary's reaction
to Esther's giving her the paper is ambiguous[147]. It is only later
that we are really convinced of John Barton's guilt by Mary's
search in her father's room for other evidence[148]. Mrs. Gaskell
neatly connects Esther's scrap of paper with a Valentine from
Jem to Mary, on the back of which she had copied some verses
by Samuel Bamford for her father[149]—an incident the reader
had all but forgotten as it seemed a triviality at the time (but
then Mrs. Gaskell makes use of the trivial in the best detective-
story manner).

Worthy of mention is (to use Mrs. Gaskell's own phrase) 'the
racy Lancashire dialect'[150] of the novel. Some of our quotations
have illustrated this already; for one does not have to read
far in *Mary Barton* before coming upon examples. Mrs. Gaskell,
or rather her linguistically knowledgeable husband[151], glossed
those words they considered her non-Lancashire reading-public
might find difficult[152]. More important than the use of individual
words, however, is the syntactical flow of the dialogue, lending
a strong degree of verisimilitude to the story[153].

Although the narrator is no puppet-master, she does from
time to time remind the reader of her presence. There is, firstly,
the frankly autobiographic comment. A good example is her
parenthesis on dreams, at the conclusion of which she refers to
'that land where alone I may see, while yet I tarry here, the
sweet looks of my dear child'[154]. A second interpolation of the

---

[145] *Works,* I, 148-149.
[146] *Works,* I, 203-208.
[147] *Works,* I, 278-281.
[148] *Works,* I, 282-283.
[149] *Works,* I, 127.
[150] *Works,* I, 430.
[151] Whose 'Two Lectures on the Lancashire Dialect' were appended
to the fifth edition (1854) of *Mary Barton; A Tale of Manchester Life,*
London: Chapman and Hall.
[152] E.g. *Works,* I, 5, 12, 33, 34, 36, 37, etc. See *G.L.,* Nos. 25, 36.
[153] There is 'A Note on Mrs. Gaskell's Use of Dialect' in Sanders,
Elizabeth Gaskell, pp. 145-155.
[154] *Works,* I, 311. For a reference to personal agony, see *Works,*
I, 284: a sentiment—that grief comes because of, not despite, the fact
that its cause cannot be remedied—, here parenthetically expressed, is,
perhaps significantly, completely dramatized in *Ruth,* Mrs. Gaskell's next
novel, being there put into the heroine's mouth (*Works,* III, 48).

same kind is her contrast between the urban setting where Mary found herself and the rural beauty of the place (most probably Silverdale[155]) where the novel was being written[156]. There is, however, another type of authorial comment, this time of the usual sort. Thus, when describing the trial scene and Mary's countenance on that occasion, she states that, not being present herself, she learnt of it from another[157]. Yet Mrs. Gaskell does not confine herself to what an onlooker could have observed. For instance—and this instance is also an artistic flaw—after mentioning Mary's initial reactions to Esther's showing her the incriminating Valentine, she remarks:

> I must tell you; I must put into words the dreadful secret which she believed that bit of paper had revealed to her. Her father was the murderer.[158]

So far, therefore, Mrs. Gaskell's inventive competence does not appear altogether assured: on occasions the author seems, somewhat incongruously, to mix the subjective with the objective; and at times the woman takes over from the story-teller, replacing the narrator's impersonality by characteristics of her own.

---

[155] See Chadwick, *Mrs. Gaskell*, pp. 231-232.
[156] *Works*, I, 286.
[157] *Works*, I, 375-376.
[158] *Works*, I, 282.

CHAPTER III

HAND AND HEART (1849) TO *CRANFORD* (1851-1853)

SECTION I

Hand and Heart (1849)

In July 1849 'Hand and Heart' came out in *The Sunday School
Penny Magazine*[1]. It is, not unnaturally, a work of an improving
nature, an attempt to recommend charity and patience by
enrolling invention in the service of morality. Relevant here is
Mrs. Gaskell's connexion with the scholars of Lower Mosley
Street[2], since this seems just the sort of thing she probably composed on many occasions, in an *ad hoc* manner, at that Sunday
School. The author herself appears to have been rather fond
of the story; for she wrote[3] to an unnamed correspondent (possibly a friend of F. D. Maurice) that she hoped he would like it.
Together with *Libbie Marsh's Three Eras*, *The Sexton's Hero*,
Christmas Storms and Sunshine, and *Bessy's Troubles at Home*,
it made up a group of tales she described to the same correspondent as 'all moral/ & sensible'.

The title was no doubt suggested by the words of good Mrs.
Fletcher, who, when her son begins to recount his many excellent deeds, cuts him short.

> "Let not thy left hand know what thy right hand doeth."
> He was silent in a moment.
> Then his mother spoke in her soft low voice: "Dearest Tom,
> though I don't want us to talk about it, as if you had been
> doing more than just what you ought, I am glad you have seen
> the truth of what I said: how far more may be done by the
> loving heart than by mere money-giving; and every one may
> have the loving heart."[4]

Tom's mother dies; and he is taken to his uncle's, where his
patient humility and acts of kindness transform that riotous,

[1] *The Sunday School Penny Magazine,* II, 121-123, 141-144, 181-184,
201-205, 221-226. It ran from July to August, and from October to
December, 1849; and was signed.
[2] Details are given in Smith, 'Mrs. Gaskell and Lower Mosley Street',
The Sunday School Quarterly, II (1911), 156-161.
[3] In a letter of 27 July [1854 or 1855], now in the Berg Collection at
the New York Public Library. Chapple and Pollard put this letter (*G.L.*,
No. 260) in [1855].
[4] *Works,* III, 546.

unruly household. Mr. Fletcher begins to say grace and no longer
frequents the public-house[5]; Mrs. Fletcher picks up domestic
tips from Tom[6]; the children are reformed[7].

As might be expected, the incidents are trivial and commonplace. Help for the scold of the court[8]; flowers and Bible-reading
for lame Harry, confined to his cellar[9]; a resolution not to tell a lie
about a broken window[10]—these are typical, strung together
without much consideration for anything, except the illustration
of practical Christianity. Yet there is nothing unpleasantly
didactic in Mrs. Gaskell's manner; nor does her sense of humour
desert her. She can, for instance, show how Tom's dreams of
being the Prince of Wales were rudely shattered by his mother's
suggestion that he should pick flowers in the fields[11]. *Hand and
Heart*[12] is in the *Libbie Marsh* tradition, and parallels are not
lacking. One finds similarities between lame Harry and the
crippled Franky (both received flowers[13]), between Mrs. Jones
and Mrs. Hall (both scolds), between the Dixon household
and the Fletcher family (both rough and dirty). More generally,
the same benevolent philosophy of life is the keynote in each
tale.

---

[5] *Works*, III, 556.
[6] *Works*, III, 556.
[7] *Works*, III, 556.
[8] *Works*, III, 540-542.
[9] *Works*, III, 544-546.
[10] *Works*, III, 551-553.
[11] *Works*, III, 543-544.
[12] Published as a fourpenny pamphlet—*Hand and Heart; and Bessy's
Troubles at Home*, London: Chapman and Hall, 1855. It seems worth
noting that the phrase 'heart and hand' appears in *Ruth* (*Works*, III,
174), and that the phrase 'heart or hand' occurs in *Mary Barton* (*Works*,
I, 9).
[13] *Works*, III, 544-545; I, 476.

SECTION II

' The Last Generation in England ' (1849)

In July 1849 there also came out (in *Sartain's Union Magazine*[1]) 'The Last Generation in England' : it was 'by the author of "Mary Barton" '[2], having been 'communicated for Sartain's Magazine by Mary Howitt.'[3] This contribution, the result, as Mrs. Gaskell says, of 'a wish in . . . [her] to put upon record some of the details of country town life, either observed by . . . [herself], or handed down to . . . [her] by older relations'[4], will at once be recognized by devotees of *Cranford* as a preliminary to that more famous work.

In 'The Last Generation in England' the town's name is merely indicated by a dash; but there appears little difficulty in making the attribution, since the omitted word must surely be 'Knutsford'. The account is avowedly autobiographic, being jottings from memory by one who had lived with the people described. Little attempt is made at literary presentation; Mrs. Gaskell seems rather to have put down her recollections as they came to mind. She gives the social background to the country town, emphasizing its feminine character and the careful distinctions maintained among the various classes of society; she refers to the card-parties, with their peculiar etiquette, and mentions old customs and bye-gone social manners. Every circumstance and occurrence related will, the writer promises, be 'strictly and truthfully told without exaggeration.'[5] Thus the authorial seal of authenticity is conferred on the fitting out of an unfortunate cow in a flannel waistcoat[6]; the concealing of

[1] V, 45-48. The article was brought to light by Professor Waller. See Ross Douglas Waller, 'Articles by Mrs. Gaskell', *The Times Literary Supplement*, 25 July 1935, p. 477; Professor Waller, in this letter, mentions his discovery of two articles ('The Last Generation in England' and 'Martha Preston') contributed by Mrs. Gaskell to *Sartain's Union Magazine*: see also his remarks in 'Notes and News', *Bulletin of the John Rylands Library, Manchester*, XX (1936), 25-27.
[2] *Sartain's Union Magazine*, V, 45.   [4] *Sartain's Union Magazine*, V, 45
[3] *Sartain's Union Magazine*, V, 45.   [5] *Sartain's Union Magazine*, V, 45.
[6] *Sartain's Union Magazine*, V, 45-46.

tea-trays underneath a couch[7]; and the adventures of a piece of lace, swallowed by, but retrieved from, a cat[8]. We shall meet these again in *Cranford* itself, where other evidence of Mrs. Gaskell's drawing on life will be noted; however we may here remark that the famous lace became a Gaskell heirloom—to be 'inspected with awe' by Miss Hopkins[9].

In *Cranford* Mrs. Gaskell fails to mention the lady who left money in her will for the construction of a flag pavement—though not one broad enough to allow 'linking'; yet it is something upon which most writers about Knutsford quaintness comment. This typically Cranfordian bequest of Lady Jane's is included in 'The Last Generation in England'[10], thereby providing further evidence of the author's veracity, and making the historical identification with Knutsford beyond dispute.

In selecting from what she had herself observed or been told, Mrs. Gaskell had an eye for the quaint, the curious, and the eccentric. She had a keen appreciation of individuality, and realized that in her day life was rapidly changing. The effects on nineteenth-century England of the Industrial Revolution—seen in terms of change in the village and drift to the town; the growth of suburbia; the end of independent, largely self-sufficient, rural economies; the break-up of organic communities; the desiccation of distinctively regional and provincial ways of life; the decay of country arts and crafts—are now commonplaces to social historian and literary critic alike. Mrs. Gaskell however, writing without benefit of hindsight, was by 1849 already noticing what was taking place: she fully recognized that her age was very much one of transition. Hence she could remark :

> . . . even in small towns, scarcely removed from villages, the phases of society are rapidly changing; and much will appear strange, which yet occurred only in the generation immediately preceding ours.[11]

[7] *Sartain's Union Magazine*, V, 47.
[8] *Sartain's Union Magazine*, V, 46.
[9] *Elizabeth Gaskell*, p. 105.
[10] *Sartain's Union Magazine*, V, 47. The lady was Lady Jane Stanley (see Henry Green, *Knutsford, Its Traditions and History: with Reminiscences, Anecdotes, and Notices of the Neighbourhood,* London: Smith, Elder, & Co.; Macclesfield: Swinnerton & Brown; Knutsford: John Siddeley, 1859, pp. 144-145).
[11] *Sartain's Union Magazine*, V, 45.

SECTION III

' Martha Preston ' (1850)

'Martha Preston' was published anonymously in *Sartain's Union Magazine*[1] in February 1850. Most probably Mrs. Gaskell wrote it late the preceding year, in response to a letter from Mrs. Mary Howitt of 20 October[2]. This was the contribution which, with certain changes, appeared in *Household Words*[3] from 6 October to 20 October 1855 under the title 'Half a Life-Time Ago'; but the relation between these two versions will not be considered until the latter story comes under review.

The tone and manner of 'Martha Preston' is easy, colloquial, conversational. Mrs. Gaskell begins with the personal statement that she had recently twice visited the Lakes; and then, after some introductory scenic description, goes on to relate a tale current among the inhabitants of that district. She purports to be passing on to her American readers what she had herself heard, and frequently reminds them of her function as an intermediary by phrases like 'I have learnt'[4]; 'from the account I heard'[5]; 'old people have told me'[6]; 'I was told'[7]; 'when first I saw the cottage, and heard the history.'[8] Although this emphasis on the factual basis for her story could be merely a literary device, used to gain the reader's attention and make plausible a heroic exploit, it appears more likely that Mrs. Gaskell was indeed recounting a local Loughrigg tale, the bare bones of which were most probably true. What she may well have done was to supply fictitious names. Thus one finds

---

[1] VI, 133-138.

[2] Waller, ed. *Letters Addressed to Mrs Gaskell by Celebrated Contemporaries*, p. 7: see also Waller, 'Articles by Mrs. Gaskell', *The Times Literary Supplement*, 25 July 1935, p. 477; and Waller's note in the *Bulletin of the John Rylands Library, Manchester*, XX (1936), 25-27.

[3] XII, 229-237, 253-257, 276-282.

[4] *Sartain's Union Magazine*, VI, 133.

[5] *Sartain's Union Magazine*, VI, 135.

[6] *Sartain's Union Magazine*, VI, 136.

[7] *Sartain's Union Magazine*, VI, 136.

[8] *Sartain's Union Magazine*, VI, 138.

inverted commas when the heroine (' "Martha Preston" '[9]) is first mentioned, the implication being that hers is a pseudonym (though one wonders why Mrs. Gaskell chose the surname of her Skelwith landlady[10]). As further support for the hypothesis, there is the use of first Thomas[11] and then John[12] for the Christian name of Martha's father : a mistake probably due to *ad hoc* invention of names during the actual writing. Moreover Mrs. Gaskell may have also invented to fill out the narrative— for example, the dialogue, relatively sparse and scarcely dialectal, must surely have been of her own composing—but the plot itself was, we suggest, ready-made.

Mrs. Gaskell's visit in the summer of 1849 to Skelwith Bridge can easily be substantiated; for on 9 July of that year we find Edward Quillinan writing from Loughrigg Holme to Henry Crabb Robinson :

> . . . I had been dining that day [Monday 2 July] at your namesake's Captain Robinson's R.N. from whose table I went to an evening party at D[r] Davy's, where [Lisketh How, Ambleside[13]]

---

[9] *Sartain's Union Magazine,* VI, 133.

[10] Preston. In a letter *(G.L.,* No. 182) of Tuesday 7 March [1854] to Miss Hannah Kay (owned by Mrs. Douglas Walker, 100 Avenue de New York, Paris XVI[e]) Mrs. Gaskell remarked that the Prestons had been friends of her family ever since they first stayed with them five years earlier. Her letter *(G.L.,* No. 439a) of Monday [29 August 1859] to Charles B. P. Bosanquet (in the Manchester University Library) indicates that it was through the Arnolds and the Wordsworths that the Gaskells came to lodge with Mrs. Preston of Mill Brow, a Stateswoman whose family, according to report, had lived on the same land and in the same house for over two centuries.

[11] *Sartain's Union Magazine,* VI, 133.

[12] *Sartain's Union Magazine,* VI, 134.

[13] Probably, see Edith Julia Morley, ed. *The Correspondence of Henry Crabb Robinson with the Wordsworth Circle* (1808-1866), *the Greater Part Now for the First Time Printed from the Originals in Dr. Williams's Library, London,* 2 vols., Oxford: The Clarendon Press, 1927, II, 773. Lasketh how [*sic*], Ambleside, is given as the address of John Davy by Kelly *(Post Office Directory of Westmoreland, Cumberland, Northumberland, and Durham: with Maps Engraved Expressly for the Work, and Corrected to the Time of Publication,* London: Kelly and Co., 1858, p. 3); but Mrs. Gaskell herself speaks of Lesketh How—in a letter of 25 October [1852] to Miss Carpenter (in the Berg Collection at the New York Public Library), and in a Friday [(post 2—possibly 8—October) 1852] letter to Eliza Fox, the relevant passage from which is quoted by Miss Haldane *(Mrs. Gaskell and Her Friends,* p. 241), whose transcript tallies fairly well with the copy of part of this letter in the Gaskell Section, Brotherton Collection, Leeds University Library. Mrs. Gaskell's letters

I met Mrs Gaskell (Mary Barton), Mrs Fletcher, & some other pleasant persons.[14]

Quillinan, like so many others, thought Mrs. Gaskell 'a *charming* person'[15]; and he invited her, two of her daughters, and a friend (probably Selina Winkworth[16]) to tea on the following Wednesday[17]. In a letter of 14 October 1849, likewise to Crabb Robinson, Quillinan wrote:

> He [Froude] was lodged, as I was informed for I did not see him, at a farm-house at or near Skilwith Bridge [*sic*].—Mrs Gaskill [*sic*], the author of Mary Barton, was also for some weeks in that neighbourhood, & I got Mr W. to meet her & her husband (a Unitarian minister at Manchester) She is a very pleasing interesting person.[18]

As Mrs. Chadwick[19] and Professor Waller[20] indicate, Mill Brow, Skelwith, was Mrs. Gaskell's place of residence in 1849. The reference to her meeting with Wordsworth is relevant, since it

---

appear respectively as *G.L.*, Nos. 138, 137: Chapple and Pollard identify the recipient of the first, Mary Carpenter; and conjecture [?October 1852] as the date of the second.

[14] Quoted in Morley, ed. *The Correspondence of Henry Crabb Robinson with the Wordsworth Circle*, II, 698: my square brackets. Cf. *Autobiography of Mrs. Fletcher with Letters and Other Family Memorials*, ed. The Survivor of Her Family [Mary Richardson], Edinburgh: Edmonston and Douglas, 1875, p. 274—here is quoted a letter from Mrs. Fletcher, written [from Lesketh How (*sic*)] to her daughter, in which she refers to a proposed meeting with Mrs. Gaskell and her party at Lancrigg.

[15] Quoted in Morley, ed. *The Correspondence of Henry Crabb Robinson with the Wordsworth Circle*, II, 700. Charlotte Brontë mentioned that this epithet was generally used of Mrs. Gaskell—see Thomas James Wise and John Alexander Symington, *The Brontës: Their Lives, Friendships and Correspondence*, 4 vols., Oxford: Basil Blackwell for The Shakespeare Head Press, 1932, III, 254: letter to Mrs. Smith of 1 July 1851.

[16] *Memorials of Two Sisters*, ed. Shaen, 1908, p. 47.

[17] See Morley, ed. *The Correpondence of Henry Crabb Robinson with the Wordsworth Circle*, II, 700.

[18] Quoted in Morley, ed. *The Correspondence of Henry Crabb Robinson with the Wordsworth Circle*, II, 705: my square brackets. At Lesketh How on 20 July 1849 Wordsworth contributed to Mrs. Gaskell's autograph album (Waller, ed. *Letters Addressed to Mrs Gaskell by Celebrated Contemporaries*, p. 34).

[19] *Mrs. Gaskell*, p. 217.

[20] Ed. *Letters Addressed to Mrs Gaskell by Celebrated Contemporaries*, p. 59; see too p. 60.

has a bearing on the opening sentences of 'Martha Preston'.

> Within the last few years I have been twice at the Lakes. There
> is a road leading to Grasmere, on the least known side of
> Loughrigg, which presents a singular number of striking and
> dissimilar views. First of all, on departing from the highway
> to Langdale, you climb a little hill; and there below you, in a
> sort of grassy basin on the side of Loughrigg, lies Wordsworth's
> favourite Loughrigg tarn; the "Speculum Dianae" as he loves to
> call it; oval, deep, and clear as her mirror should be.[21]

Having established the autobiographic background, we can
now consider the work itself. The first part continues along the
lines suggested by our last quotation: the reader enjoys a
miniature conducted tour of the Loughrigg district, culminating
in a view of Grasmere. Obviously drawing on personal observation, Mrs. Gaskell manages this descriptive narration well; she
then turns her attention to a picturesque old hillside cottage,
graphically presented amidst its fauna and flora. It is with the
inhabitants of this cottage, past and present, that the story is
concerned.

Since 'Martha Preston' cannot easily be consulted, a summary
of the tale, based largely on Professor Waller's convenient
résumé[22], will not be out of place.

Martha Preston's mother, who busied herself more with domestic matters than with her children, died suddenly when her daughter was fifteen. Johnnie, Martha's brother, felt his mother's death
least, because his sister had been accustomed to act *in loco paren-
tis*. Some years later (in 1818), Martha became engaged to Will
Hawkshaw, who had been a casual worker for her father. After
two or three more years, Mr. Preston quietly died, from his
death-bed charging Martha to be both mother and father to
his son, who was eight years younger than she. Johnnie, following an attack of typhoid fever, became an idiot; whereupon
Will suggested that he should be confined in an asylum—which

---

[21] *Sartain's Union Magazine*, VI, 133. On Wednesday [1 August
1849] the Gaskells were among a party who walked across Loughrigg
Fell, as Stephen Winkworth, one of the number, told his sister,
Catherine, in a letter of 4 August 1849, relevantly quoted in Her Sister
[Susanna Winkworth], ed. *Letters and Memorials of Catherine Wink-
worth*, I (1883), 194.
[22] To be found in 'Notes and News', *Bulletin of the John Rylands
Library, Manchester*, XX, 27.

would have brought the property into the hands of his prospective wife, and so, he hoped, to himself. Martha, however, refused to sanction the scheme, and Will married elsewhere (his bride being a rich man's daughter). Johnnie, after causing his sister years of anxiety, eventually died; hence Martha, who in terms of wealth had prospered, was left alone. One winter night, attracted by her dog's actions, she came upon a child lying lost and exhausted in the snow; he proved to be no other than the son of her former lover. Thereafter young John Hawkshaw often visited Martha, whose money later made it possible for him to marry the girl of his choice, without the need of a long engagement. The young couple then went to live with her, and she became a granny to their children.

Professor Waller comments: "It is a simple human story, told without sentimentality, and seeming to be in substance a record of fact"[23]—with the latter opinion we find ourselves in agreement; but we cannot entirely endorse the first part of the quotation. Although, as previously mentioned, Mrs. Gaskell appears to invent very little, at times she allows her own (maternal) feelings to colour the narrative. There is, too, a tendency towards melodrama and spurious emotionalism, a tendency to strain after a desired effect. Some extracts will illustrate these defects.

> She was growing old alone; with a most loving nature, she had none to love as she could have done, had God permitted her to have husband and children; and sometimes in the deep midnight she cried aloud to heaven in her exceeding grief that she had never heard a child's murmuring voice call her "Mother."[24]

> And he [Johnnie] recovered! But oh, wo! as he recovered, his wandering lost senses were not restored. The neighbours sighed and shook their heads, and looked mysteriously, . . . [25]

> There will not be a grave in Grasmere churchyard, more decked with flowers—more visited with respect, regret, and tears, and faithful trust, than that of Martha Preston when she dies.[26]

One would, however, scarcely want to stress such occasional

---

[23] Quoted in 'Notes and News', *Bulletin of the John Rylands Library, Manchester*, XX, 27.
[24] *Sartain's Union Magazine*, VI, 137.
[25] *Sartain's Union Magazine*, VI, 135.
[26] *Sartain's Union Magazine*, VI, 138.

lapses, if lapses they be. Rather one would wish to notice the keen appreciation shown for the moral fibre of the self-sacrificing heroine, whose devotion to duty must have appealed strongly to Mrs. Gaskell. The author's moral sensibility, as well as her sense of humour, also finds expression in the characterization of Mr. and Mrs. Preston—especially in those little touches which were doubtless gratuitous additions to the historical prototypes. Certainly in the following extract the point of view is all her own.

> . . . Jane [Preston] had to go to market, to see after the cows and the dairy, to look after the sheep on the fell, and was a busy, bustling, managing woman; the "gray mare" some people said. If she had had time, she would have been fond of her children, but as it was, on week days they were rather in her way. John Preston was reserved and quiet; a man of few words, but sensible, conscientious, and thoroughly upright. He never talked about his duty; people did not in those days; but it might be seen that it was the rule of his life; . . . [27]

[27] *Sartain's Union Magazine,* VI, 134.

SECTION IV

Lizzie Leigh (1850)

On 31 January 1850 Charles Dickens wrote to request from Mrs. Gaskell 'the least result of . . . [her] reflection or observation in respect of the life around'[1] her; he was seeking contributions for his new journal—whose aim, he told the novelist, would be 'the raising up of those that are down, and the general improvement of our social condition.'[2] In consequence 'the authoress of Mary Barton (a book that most profoundly affected and impressed . . . [Dickens])'[3] sent him 'Lizzie Leigh', the first story to be serialized in *Household Words*[4]. For this she received £20, which was duly handed over to Mr. Gaskell who promised some of it for, significantly, her Refuge[5]. Dickens considered the tale 'very good, but long'[6], and brought it out between 30 March and 13 April. Unfortunately we cannot altogether endorse his favourable opinion.

The central theme of *Lizzie Leigh*[7] brings the Esther *motif* in *Mary Barton* to mind; for, albeit Lizzie's profession subse-

---

[1] *The Letters of Charles Dickens*, ed. Walter Dexter, 3 vols., Bloomsbury: The Nonesuch Press, 1938, II, 202.

[2] *The Letters of Charles Dickens*, ed. Dexter, II, 202.

[3] *The Letters of Charles Dickens*, ed. Dexter, II, 202.

[4] *Household Words. A Weekly Journal. Conducted by Charles Dickens*, I, 2-6, 32-35, 60-65. 'Lizzie Leigh', like all Mrs. Gaskell's subsequent contributions to *Household Words*, was anonymous.

[5] Rubenius, *The Woman Question in Mrs. Gaskell's Life and Works*, pp. 31, 33. For Mrs. Gaskell's concern with unfortunate girls, see Annette Brown Hopkins, 'Dickens and Mrs. Gaskell', *The Huntington Library Quarterly*, IX (1946), 357-358; *Elizabeth Gaskell*, p. 131. See too our discussion of this matter when *Ruth* is examined. In a letter of Sunday [19 June 1853] to Mrs. Julius Salis Schwabe (*G.L.*, No. 162)—now in the Gaskell Collection at the Manchester Central Reference Library (MS. F. 928.23 G47/4)—Mrs. Gaskell mentions talking '(apropos of Ruth) a good/ deal about the difficulty of reclaiming/ this class, *after they had once taken to/ the street life*'.

[6] *The Letters of Charles Dickens*, ed. Dexter, II, 207: letter to William Henry Wills of 28 February 1850. At this date Dickens had seen 'a great part' of the MS.

[7] [Elizabeth Cleghorn Gaskell] *Lizzie Leigh; and Other Tales*, Cheap edn, London: Chapman and Hall, 1855. (Apparently the first dated edition.)

quent to her seduction[8] is never explicitly named, the hints provided[9] leave the reader in little doubt. Invention follows the conventional lines (though, by ending her life in good works and repentance, Lizzie is spared the conventional death). Nor does the language in which the crisis is described redeem it from melodrama : Mrs. Gaskell is so evidently describing what she never observed, and what she was incapable of concretely imagining, that the lapse into a third-rate novelist's technique is most painfully apparent.

> She stood with wild, glaring eyes by the bedside, never looking at Susan, but hungrily gazing at the little, white, still child. She stooped down, and put her hand tight on her own heart, as if to still its beating, and bent her ear to the pale lips. Whatever the result was, she did not speak; but threw off the bedclothes wherewith Susan had tenderly covered up the little creature, and felt its left side.
> Then she threw up her arms, with a cry of wild despair.
> "She is dead! she is dead!"
> She looked so fierce, so mad, so haggard, that, for an instant, Susan was terrified; the next, the holy God had put courage into her heart, and her pure arms were round that guilty, wretched creature, and her tears were falling fast and warm upon her breast.[10]

Mrs. Gaskell's attitude to Lizzie's plight is, as expected, sympathetic; those male characters who initially adopt a strictly moralistic standpoint (Lizzie's father[11] and brother[12]) are contrasted with Mrs. Leigh and Susan Palmer, whose reactions are anti-Pharisaic[13].

The mother-daughter devotion is thematically important in that Mrs. Gaskell's own strong family feelings doubtless influenced the lines the invention took. We have seen how close were her maternal bonds with the young Gaskell children, and the same concern for a united family was present throughout her life : this concern reveals itself in her private correspondence, especially that carried on with Marianne Gaskell, the

---

[8] *Works,* II, 222-223.
[9] *Works,* II, 235-236.
[10] *Works,* II, 232.
[11] *Works,* II, 211-212.
[12] *Works,* II, 237.
[13] *Works,* II, 220, 225.

eldest daughter[14]. Mrs. Gaskell had at first decided Lizzie
should completely abandon her offspring; but on Dickens' advice
this was changed—Lizzie being made to put the baby into Susan
Palmer's hands, and from time to time send small gifts for its
support. Dickens rightly considered that, as originally planned,
the story unpleasantly contrasted Mrs. Leigh's devotion to her
daughter with that daughter's treatment of her own child[15].

The most convincing part deals with the rural life led by the
Leigh family before Mrs. Leigh's decision to seek in Manchester
her lost daughter. The funeral procession and Samuel Orme's

---

[14] See, for example, the substantial collections of letters to Marianne
in the Gaskell Section, Brotherton Collection, Leeds University Library
(a relevant quotation may be found in Rubenius, *The Woman Question
in Mrs. Gaskell's Life and Works*, p. 69, fn. 3); in the Yale University
Library; and in the possession of Mrs. Margaret Trevor Jones. The
present writer possesses an extensive collection of transcripts of Mrs.
Gaskell's letters, mostly to Marianne, once the property of the late Mr.
J. T. Lancaster. All these and several others are printed by Chapple and
Pollard (ed. *The Letters of Mrs Gaskell*), whose Indexes must be consulted.

[15] This point, perhaps owing to a slightly inaccurate transcript of the
relevant part of Dickens' letter to Mrs. Gaskell of 14 March 1850 (*The
Letters of Charles Dickens,* ed. Dexter, II, 210), seems to have been misunderstood by Miss Hopkins—'Dickens and Mrs. Gaskell', *The Huntington Library Quarterly,* IX (1946), 360; *Elizabeth Gaskell,* pp. 137-138.
It may be well, therefore, to quote from the original letter, now in The
John Rylands Library, Manchester (English MS. 729/2).

> I am strongly of opinion that as Lizzie/
> is not to die, she ought to put that child/
> in Susan's own arms, and not lay it down/
> at the door. observe!—The more forcibly and/
> strongly and affectingly, you exhibit her mother's/
> love for her, the more cruel you will make/
> this crime of desertion ∧ in her. ∧ The [same *deleted*] sentiment/
> which animates the mother, will have been/
> done violence to by the daughter; and you/
> cannot set up the [first *deleted*] ∧one∧, without pulling down/
> the other.   /
>   The slightest alteration will suffice to//
> set this right. If you will make it, in your answer,/
> I should prefer it to *our* doing it; but rely/
> upon it, it will do Lizzie an immense/
> service,—and I am sure you would do anything/
> to serve her! I am quite confident of its/
> removing an objection otherwise certain to/
> suggest itself—and the better you write, the/
> stronger it is. I can't tell you how earnestly/
> I feel it.   /

unwillingness to settle his lease-terms with the bereaved mother (there being no fun in driving a hard bargain under the circumstances)—these[16] point to an intimate acquaintance with country life. Nor is the Manchester section without some good things, such as the Dickensian introduction[17] of the rather tipsy Mr. Palmer[18], whose failure as a greengrocer was the great event in his life[19]. Another merit to note is Mrs. Gaskell's use of dialect, as in Mrs. Leigh's moving expression of undying devotion towards her erring daughter[20]—the realistic dialogue, free from stock phraseology, there acting as a safe-guard against sentimentality.

Before leaving *Lizzie Leigh*, we may with profit recall those specifically feminine details which an authoress might be expected to have observed—the clean hearth and the boiling kettle[21]; the Sunday clothes worn by Mrs. Leigh for her visit to Susan Palmer[22]; the baby-clothes made out of a woman's gown[23]; the matches left on the dresser[24].

[16] *Works*, II, 208-210.
[17] 'Lizzie Leigh' was, in fact, attributed to Dickens: see Hopkins, *Elizabeth Gaskell*, pp. 97-98; Northup's Bibliography to Sanders, *Elizabeth Gaskell*, p. 171; and the Bibliography to Whitfield, *Mrs Gaskell*, p. 226.
[18] *Works*, II, 215.
[19] *Works*, II, 216.
[20] *Works*, II, 239.
[21] *Works*, II, 207-208.
[22] *Works*, II, 220.
[23] *Works*, II, 224-225.
[24] *Works*, II, 231.

SECTION V

' The Well of Pen-Morfa ' (1850)

Dickens was so pleased with Mrs. Gaskell's first *Household Words* contribution that, in letters dated 3 July[1] and 7 August[2], 1850, he pressed her for others; the first of these appeared in the numbers for 16 November and 23 November[3]. Since it seems quite possible that *Lizzie Leigh* was, in part at least, written before *Mary Barton*[4], 'The Well of Pen-Morfa' may have been the first story for whose production Dickens' requests were entirely responsible.

'The Well of Pen-Morfa' is not well-planned, perhaps because it was an early effort refurbished[5] for periodical publication—though more probably hasty composition accounts for the lack of attention to points of construction. Mrs. Gaskell possessed a fairly intimate knowledge of Wales. Not only had she toured there on her honeymoon; she had also, as a young girl, visited Plas Penrhyn, the home of her uncle Holland[6]. In addition, after her marriage, she spent holidays in Wales, during one of which her son died at Portmadoc. It is, indeed, a visitor to

[1] *The Letters of Charles Dickens*, ed. Dexter, II, 220.
[2] *The Letters of Charles Dickens*, ed. Dexter, II, 225.
[3] *Household Words*, II, 182-186, 205-210.
[4] So think Ward (ed. *Works*, II, pp. xxiv-xxv), Mrs. Chadwick (*Mrs. Gaskell*, p. 138), and Miss Rubenius (*The Woman Question in Mrs. Gaskell's Life and Works*, p. 66, fn. 1). The story is mentioned by Mrs. Gaskell in her letter of 12 November [1850] to Lady Kay-Shuttleworth; she there appears to like the tale, but no light is thrown upon its mode of composition (*G.L.*, No. 83).
[5] As conjectured by Miss Rubenius (*The Woman Question in Mrs. Gaskell's Life and Works*, p. 180). A passage in Mrs. Mary Howitt's 20 October [1849] letter to the author suggests that Mrs. Gaskell may have had many manuscripts lying by her for years; the letter (in The John Rylands Library, Manchester: English MS. 730/43) is cited by Waller (ed. *Letters Addressed to Mrs Gaskell by Celebrated Contemporaries*, p. 7), though he does not refer to this particular passage.
[6] See Jane Revere Coolidge (subsequently Mrs. Whitehill), 'Life and letters of Mrs. E. C. Gaskell', Ch. I, p. 10—an incomplete typescript of which is deposited in the Gaskell Section, Brotherton Collection, Leeds University Library (the finished draft being in the hands of Mrs. Whitehill)—; and *G.L.*, No. 9.

Portmadoc who tells the tale; so one may assume with some safety that Mrs. Gaskell is drawing on personal recollections[7].

The first part comprises a sketch of the scenery, the inhabitants, their dwellings, and their manners, as these appeared to an English traveller with an eye for homely detail and a feeling for '*Welsh* Wales'[8]. The description, an individual's impressions rather than a guide-book exposition, establishes an intimacy between the writer and her public—the next quotation being typical of Mrs. Gaskell's almost conversational tone.

> . . . Here were an old couple, who welcomed me in Welsh, and brought forth milk and oat-cake with patriarchal hospitality. Sons and daughters had married away from them; they lived alone; he was blind, or nearly so; and they sat one on each side of the fire, so old and so still (till we went in and broke the silence) that they seemed to be listening for death.[9]

Following her topographic and anthropological introduction, Mrs. Gaskell goes on to mention the Wordsworthian-like figure of a local beauty who, seduced in London while in domestic service, had returned home to bear a deformed child (at the time of writing, dead for fifteen years). Restrained in manner, this brief narrative, for whose truth Mrs. Gaskell vouches[10], possesses pathos without sentimentality.

Most of the *Household Words* contribution, however, concerns the title-story itself. 'The Well of Pen-Morfa' proper is another local tale, set 'a lifetime ago'[11]—the tale of beautiful Nest Gwynn, jilted by her lover when, having fallen while carrying water from the well, she was crippled for life, unable ever to fulfil those duties required of a farmer's wife. Very likely Mrs. Gaskell obtained an outline of Nest's misfortunes from the older inhabitants—a supposition supported when she mentions that

> "as beautiful as a summer's morning at sunrise, as a white sea-gull on the green sea wave, and as Nest Gwynn," is yet a saying in that district.[12]

Although the central features, therefore, were probably

---

[7] Chadwick, *Mrs. Gaskell*, p. 182.
[8] *Works*, II, 242.
[9] *Works*, II, 242.
[10] *Works*, II, 244.
[11] *Works*, II, 245.
[12] *Works*, II, 245.

historical (certainly the well[13] and the farmhouse named 'The
End of Time'[14] are still identifiable[15]), the details, more especially
the states of mind of Nest and her mother, as well as the moral
message must have been of Mrs. Gaskell's inventing. However
it seems regrettable that she did not maintain the condensed
manner of the first sketch, and so confine her contribution to
one number of *Household Words*.

Nevertheless the title-story should not be disparaged unduly.
Worthy of commendation are the ironic description of Nest's
high-spirited merriment, whose smiles some people, having by
their own vanity initially misinterpreted them, held to be signs
of flirtation[16]; the picture of Nest in her blue cloak going for
water[17]; the evocation of the rural background when Mrs.
Gwynn talks to her daughter's lover, the owner of that farm
so poetically called 'The End of Time'[18]; and the reference to
the old Welsh custom of putting salt on the breast, and candles
at the head and feet, of the dead[19]. Even so, the over-all effect
is rather weak. What, briefly told, could have been a memorable local tragedy seems, in effect, a rather tedious, long-winded,
diffuse piece of writing.

Since, in outline at least, this story may well be true, criticism
of the invention loses much of its force; yet there is little attempt
to weave convincingly together the several strands of the narrative. Mrs. Gaskell did not see the need to emphasize some
elements and pass by others. As a case in point, one has only
to mention the space devoted to David Hughes whose *rôle,*
though functional, could have been considerably curtailed. Nor
does the dialogue greatly redeem the tale. Mrs. Gaskell makes
no effort to convey the flavour of the Welsh (which would,
perhaps, have meant translating the original Welsh into a
Welshified English), the most realistic speeches being given to

[13] *Works,* II, 245.
[14] *Works,* II, 246.
[15] The well, in use to-day, is that of St. Bueno; on the Portmadoc-
Criccieth Road one may find the 'End of Time' farm—in Welsh, *Penam-
ser.* I am indebted for this information to Colonel M. I. Williams-Ellis
(Wern, Portmadoc, N. Wales), who wrote to me on 8 September 1960.
[16] *Works,* II, 246.
[17] *Works,* II, 247-248.
[18] *Works,* II, 249-250.
[19] *Works,* II, 259.

an idiot[20]. Neither do explicit authorial comments generally enhance the literary quality of the work, as may be demonstrated by the following quotation.

> Edward Williams was for a long time most assiduous in his inquiries and attentions; but by-and-by (ah! you see the dark fate of poor Nest now), he slackened, so little at first that Eleanor blamed herself for her jealousy on her daughter's behalf, and chid her suspicious heart.[21]

20 *Works,* II, 264-266.
21 *Works,* II, 249.

SECTION VI

The Moorland Cottage (1850)

In December 1850 Chapman and Hall published *The Moor-land Cottage*[1]—a Christmas book, probably written in haste for an exacting Mr. Chapman[2]. As Miss Haldane remarks, this was very likely the Christmas tale which moved Matthew Arnold

[1] [Elizabeth Cleghorn Gaskell] *The Moorland Cottage,* London: Chapman & Hall, 1850. An undated letter Mrs. Gaskell sent from (Miss Fox's) 3 Sussex Place, Regents Park to (presumably) Chapman—now in Pierpont Morgan Library (Autographs-Miscellaneous-English)—indicates that her publisher had chosen 'The Fagot' as the title of a tale she wished called 'December Days', the latter name being more sugges-tive, in her view, of its quiet tone. This may refer to the story published as *The Moorland Cottage,* perhaps after another alternative designation, 'Rosemary' (see our next footnote), had also been considered but finally rejected. However 'December Days' (*aliter* 'The Fagot') and/or 'Rose-mary' could have been the title(s) of the Christmas story which, in a letter written one Saturday [(pre Summer) 1850], Mrs. Gaskell agreed with her correspondent (probably a publisher, possibly Chapman) she was incapable of writing (well)—this letter being in the hands of the present writer. The afore-mentioned letters (*G.L.,* Nos. 87, 66) from Mrs. Gaskell are respectively dated [?December 1850] and [?Early 1850] by Chapple and Pollard.

[2] Hopkins, *Elizabeth Gaskell,* pp. 99-100: cf. Sanders, *Elizabeth Gaskell,* p. 34. Such was indeed the case if, in the following extract, 'Rosemary' became *The Moorland Cottage.* 'I am almost sorry you know I am going to publish another [story] because I don't think you will like it. Mr. Chapman asked me to write a Xmas Story, "recommending benevolence, charity, etc", to which I agreed, why I cannot think now, for it was very foolish indeed. However I could not write about virtues to order, so it is simply a little country love-story called Rosemary, which will I suppose be published somewhere in November, and not be worth reading then; it is bad to make a bargain beforehand as to time or subject, though the latter I have rejected.'—Extract from Mrs. Gaskell's letter of 25 September [1850] to Lady Kay-Shuttleworth, based on the typescript copy belonging to the Hon. Mrs. Angela Mary James, corrected against the original letter owned by Lord Shuttleworth of Gawthorpe: *G.L.,* No. 81. Another likely reference to the same tale occurs in Mrs. Gaskell's letter to Eliza Fox of Tuesday [27] August 1850: there she speaks of having 'been writing a story for Xmas; a *very foolish* en-gagement' which she was angry with herself for doing but which, having promised, she had done—the relevant quotation given by Miss Haldane (*Mrs. Gaskell and Her Friends,* p. 235) has been slightly modified to agree with the virtually complete copy of this letter (*G.L.,* No. 79) in the Gaskell Section, Brotherton Collection, Leeds University Library.

"to tears, and the tears to complacent admiration of his own sensibility."[3]

The reader will readily agree with Charlotte Brontë about the fresh beauty of the book's opening[4]. Mrs. Gaskell conjures up the moorland setting with a detailed description of the scenery and the cottage[5]; and one feels one is participating in eye-witness observations. Then the introduction of the Brownes, especially the *en passant* reference to Mrs. Browne's customary crying over her husband's grave as a thing expected of her[6], brings the life of the family intimately before one. The dialogue between the two children which ensues reveals Mrs. Gaskell's insight into the minds of the young as well as her sense of the humorous in the mundane. It is just the sort of thing she would have noticed with her own children.

> "I wish it would always rain on Sundays," said Edward one day to Maggie, in a garden-conference.
> "Why?" asked she.
> "Because then we bustle out of church, and get home as fast as we can, to save mamma's crape; and we have not to go and cry over papa."[7]

The first chapter conveys the differing temperaments of the children (Edward's selfishness, Maggie's generous self-abnegation); the favouritism Mrs. Browne showed her son; the gruff kindness of the servant, Nancy; the importance of Mr. Buxton's visit for the family—all this being in Mrs. Gaskell's best manner.

---

[3] Quoted by Ward (ed. *Works*, I, p. xlvi) and, as written from Mrs. W. E. Forster to Dr. Arnold [*sic*], by Miss Haldane (*Mrs. Gaskell and Her Friends*, p. 79); however the fuller extracts given by both authors differ not only between themselves, but also from the copy of part of Mrs. W. E. Forster's letter to Mr. Thomas Arnold of 30 December 1850, found in Shorter and Symington, 'Correspondence, Articles & Notes Relating to Mrs. E. C. Gaskell. Transcripts', Vol. II, Section of Extracts from Letters Relating to Mrs. Gaskell and Her Work—a typescript in the Gaskell Section, Brotherton Collection, Leeds University Library. For Arnold's letters to Mrs. Gaskell, see Waller, ed. *Letters Addressed to Mrs Gaskell by Celebrated Contemporaries*, pp. 35-37.

[4] See Haldane, *Mrs. Gaskell and Her Friends*, p. 78; and Wise and Symington, *The Brontës: Their Lives, Friendships and Correspondence*, III, 194, 204: letters to Mrs. Gaskell of 4 January 1851 and 22 January 1851.

[5] *Works*, II, 267-268.

[6] *Works*, II, 268.

[7] *Works*, II, 269.

The author was writing about what she had experience of, a rural community and its social relations.

In the next chapters one notes the acute sociological analysis of Mr. Buxton's immediate forbears with regard to their conduct as wealthy yeomen. His grandfather had built the place at Combehurst, but felt rather ashamed at what seemed like stepping out of his social position[8]; his father and mother had gradually filled the house with ornaments, and opened out the rooms[9]; he himself had not, as had the county people, gone to college[10], though he was able to marry 'the grand-daughter of Sir Henry Biddulph'[11]; his own son was expected to go to Oxford[12], and did indeed go to Cambridge[13]. A single sentence will display Mrs. Gaskell's awareness of the social *milieu* she so admirably depicts.

> He [Mr. Buxton] sat like a king (for, excepting the rector, there was not another gentleman of his standing at Combehurst), among six or seven ladies, who laughed merrily at all his sayings, and evidently thought Mrs. Browne had been highly honoured in having been asked to dinner as well as to tea.[14]

Mrs. Gaskell's Knutsford upbringing among the Holland family, whose origins were not very different from those of Mr. Buxton[15], must have served her well in much of her writings on country life. Not only was her eye for rural beauties acute, she also possessed a keen appreciation for the *minutiae* of social intercourse both within and between classes. Typical here is the rejoinder she assigned to Mrs. Browne respecting the parental attitude of Mr. Buxton, whose sole objection to Maggie as a wife for his son was on the score of social standing[16].

> "Mr. Buxton is quite put out about it," said Mrs. Browne querulously; "and I'm sure he need not be, for he's enough of money, if that's what he wants; and Maggie's father was a clergyman, and I've seen 'yeoman,' with my own eyes, on old Mr. Buxton's (Mr. Lawrence's father's) carts; and a clergyman is above a yeoman any day. . . . "[17]

[8] *Works*, II, 281. [11] *Works*, II, 287. [13] *Works*, II, 308.
[9] *Works*, II, 281. [12] *Works*, II, 297. [14] *Works*, II, 286.
[10] *Works*, II, 282.
[15] Irvine, ed. *A History of the Family of Holland of Mobberley and Knutsford in the County of Chester with Some Account of the Family of Holland of Upholland & Denton in the County of Lancaster, from Materials Collected by the Late Edgar Swinton Holland*, esp. pp. 69-82.
[16] *Works*, II, 324. [17] *Works*, II, 325-326.

It can hardly be said that the plot-invention is satisfactory. Although the opening, childhood scenes do, in a sense, prepare for Edward's forgery by their early revelation of his moral nature, the romance between Frank and Maggie has insufficient preliminary preparation. Similarly the concluding paragraph of the book[18], which speaks of the power exerted for gentleness, holiness, and patience by the memory of Mrs. Buxton, lacks that force which ought to have been bestowed upon it by all that had gone before. The time-gap between the first chapter, where the future lovers are but children, and the later part, where they are twenty-three[19] and almost nineteen[20], is inadequately filled. Nor does the concluding chapter have, from a structural point of view, much to recommend it: the ship-fire compares unfavourably with the mill-fire in *Mary Barton*; and the melodramatic death of the rascal brother, Edward, seems most contrived—one feels that, having arranged for Maggie to be absent from her lover for nearly a year[21], Mrs. Gaskell resorted to the improbable to escape from an untenable position. Charlotte Brontë's view that the book gathered power in its progress and closed in pathos[22] will scarcely bear critical scrutiny.

Swinburne had occasion to comment on George Eliot's reticence concerning 'that sufficiently palpable and weighty and direct obligation'[23] which the writer of *The Mill on the Floss* owed to the author of *The Moorland Cottage*. Certainly both heroines have the same Christian name; there is a similar sort of brother-sister relationship, with a tendency in the sister towards self-sacrifice[24]; and a charge of plagiarism has a *prima facie* plausibility. Nevertheless it is safe to say that the case for direct literary borrowing is about as strong as that made out by

[18] *Works*, II, 383.
[19] *Works*, II, 345.
[20] *Works*, II, 352.
[21] *Works*, II, 361-362, 366.
[22] See Haldane, *Mrs. Gaskell and Her Friends*, p. 78; and Wise and Symington, *The Brontës: Their Lives, Friendships and Correspondence*, III, 204: letter to Mrs. Gaskell of 22 January 1851.
[23] Algernon Charles Swinburne, *A Note on Charlotte Brontë*, London: Chatto & Windus, 1877, p. 31.
[24] *Works*, II, 295-296.

Miss Rubenius for indebtedness in the reverse direction[25]. Yet Swinburne's note is valuable to the extent that it implies how well Mrs. Gaskell managed the brother-sister aspects of the story. Although one hesitates to place undue emphasis on what Mrs. Gaskell said about her own relations with her step-mother, step-brother, and step-sister, the following quotation is not wholly without relevance to *The Moorland Cottage.*

> "Long ago I lived in Chelsea occasionally with my father and stepmother, and *very, very* unhappy I used to be; and if it had not been for the beautiful, grand river, which was an inexplicable comfort to me, and a family of the name of Kennett, I think my child's heart would have broken. . . . "[26]

Slight though this evidence be, it is not altogether fanciful to detect autobiographic echoes when Maggie is portrayed as neglected and criticized by Mrs. Browne who, at the same time, makes much of Edward. Moreover Maggie, like Miss Stevenson, found solace in nature. There seems, for example, a personal reminiscence in the following observation.

> . . . She forgot her little home griefs to wonder why a brown-purple shadow always streaked one particular part in the fullest sunlight; why the cloud-shadows always seemed to be wafted with a sidelong motion; or she would imagine what lay beyond those old grey holy hills, which seemed to bear up the white clouds of heaven on which the angels flew abroad. . . . [27]

Perhaps such a passage should also be taken in conjunction with those tales about Mrs. Gaskell's childhood—'of departures from the house and of hours of solitary misery in the sand-pits and among the whin-bushes of the Heath.'[28] It appears, then,

[25] Miss Rubenius (*The Woman Question in Mrs. Gaskell's Life and Works,* pp. 257-259) suggests that *Sylvia's Lovers* shows the influence of *Adam Bede* and *Scenes from Clerical Life.* However George Eliot, with the composition of *Scenes from Clerical Life* and *Adam Bede* in mind, did remark that her 'feeling towards Life & Art had some/ affinity with the feeling which had/ inspired "Cranford" & the earlier/ chapters of "Mary Barton".'—Letter to Mrs. Gaskell of 11 November 1859, now in The John Rylands Library, Manchester (English MS. 731/62), mentioned by Waller (ed. *Letters Addressed to Mrs Gaskell by Celebrated Contemporaries,* p. 39).

[26] Quoted in Howitt, 'Stray Notes from Mrs. Gaskell', *Good Words,* XXXVI (1895), 606: *G.L.,* No. 616.

[27] *Works,* II, 293.

[28] Conrad S. Sargisson, 'Mrs. Gaskell's Early Surroundings, and Their Influence on Her Writings', *The Bookman* (London), XXXVIII (1910), 246.

not unlikely that Mrs. Gaskell was drawing on her own past experiences, was giving literary form to poignant recollections.

In some ways *The Moorland Cottage* has links with Mrs. Gaskell's last work, *Wives and Daughters*. The character of Mrs. Browne, the curate's widow, looks forward to that incomparable curate's widow of the later book, the never-to-be-forgotten Mrs. Gibson (as by her second marriage she became). Both ladies have a vividness and vitality which, in Mrs. Gaskell's case, so often suggests a portrait from life. Doubtless these were composite characters, in the sense that memories and observations of more than one person went into their making, though, from what has been said, it seems not unlikely that the author had the second Mrs. Stevenson very much in mind. One must, however, point out that Mrs. Browne's characterization is far less successful than that of Mrs. Gibson, of whom she is but an early sketch. Although the humorous-ironical treatment of Mrs. Browne's behaviour and bearing ('all her sugary manner'[29]) is admirable, her inclusion in the semi-tragic events of Edward's forgery and subsequent death, which occupy so important a place in the latter half of the book, appears out of keeping. This inconsistency can best be indicated by setting two passages side by side, each in its way typical of the incompatible *rôles* provided for Mrs. Browne.

> Mrs. Browne was much obliged to Mr. Buxton for giving her so decent an excuse for following her inclination, which, it must be owned, tended to the acceptance of the invitation. So, "for the children's sake," she consented. But she sighed, as if making a sacrifice.[30]

> Mrs. Browne looked round and saw Maggie. She did not get up from her place by his head; nor did she long avert her gaze from his poor face. But she held Maggie's hand, as the girl knelt by her and spoke to her in a hushed voice, undisturbed by tears, Her miserable heart could not find that relief.
> "He is dead!—he is gone!—he will never come back again! If he had gone to America—it might have been years first—but he would have come back to me. But now he will never come back again; never—never!"[31]

The parallelism between the two books extends to the love

[29] *Works,* II, 291.
[30] *Works,* II, 276.
[31] *Works,* II, 382.

affairs. Frank Buxton's alliance to Maggie Browne evokes disapproval from Mr. Buxton, much as a possible union between
Roger Hamley and Molly Gibson at first gains little favour
from the squire: in both instances the young man's father
looked upon marriage as a means towards social advancement.
Just as Mr. Buxton has affinities with Squire Hamley, so too
does Mrs. Buxton, set in her *milieu* of sick-bed holiness and
gentleness[32], find a literary kinswoman in that squire's wife.

There are, in Erminia, hints of the character of Cynthia
Kirkpatrick. The following passage could well have come out
of *Wives and Daughters,* with the appropriate name-changes.

> As they sat on the floor, Mrs. Buxton thought what a pretty
> contrast they made; Erminia [Cynthia], dazzlingly fair, with her
> golden ringlets and her pale-blue frock: Maggie's [Molly's] little
> round white shoulders peeping out of her petticoat; her brown
> hair as glossy and smooth as the nuts that it resembled in colour;
> her long black eye-lashes drooping over her clear, smooth cheek,
> which would have given the idea of delicacy, but for the coral
> lips that spoke of perfect health; and when she glanced up, she
> showed long, liquid, dark-grey eyes. The deep red of the cur-
> tain behind threw out these two little figures well.[33]

Erminia's *penchant* for ' "a man with some deep, impenetrable
darkness round him; something one could always keep wonder-
ing about" '[34] is an attitude Cynthia would certainly have
understood.

It seems worth noticing two characters of a sort we shall
encounter again. Nancy, the Brownes' devoted servant, is the
first: gruff, shrewd, kindly, out-spoken, with a trick of swearing
to sweeten the blood[35]. The second is Edward Browne: a selfish
brother; a spend-thrift, exacting son[36]; and a clever, flashy,
wholly worldly, would-be lawyer[37]. In passing, we may mention
that Mrs. Gaskell's opinion of legal men generally contrasts
most unfavourably with her evident esteem for doctors, even
though she had relatives in both professions. Already, during the
Mary Barton court-scene, she had displayed the former in an
unflattering light, whereas in the same book the latter appeared
entirely worthy of respect—as they do in all her fiction. We shall
subsequently deal with this point at greater length.

---

[32] *Works,* II, 284-289. [34] *Works,* II, 321. [36] *Works,* II, 328.
[33] *Works,* II, 285. [35] *Works,* II, 317. [37] *Works,* II, 309-311.

We can conclude by noting that, here and there, the author's personal values manifest themselves in this work. She realized the dangers of reverie, in the case of Maggie, with its attendant passivity[38]; her own morality seems to have been a sort of ethical pragmatism, stressing action rather than reflection, conduct rather than belief. She also appreciated that, for charity's sake, every judgement must take fully into account the element of temptation, ' "the 'What's resisted' of Burns" '[39].

[38] *Works*, II, 293.
[39] *Works*, II, 337.

SECTION VII

' The Heart of John Middleton ' (1850)

'The Heart of John Middleton', appearing in the number for 28 December 1850, was Mrs. Gaskell's next contribution to *Household Words*[1]. Dickens, who supplied the title[2], thought it 'the best thing of hers'[3] he had seen, 'not excepting Mary Barton'[4]; however he objected to the unhappy ending[5]. Mrs. Gaskell, for her part, was quite willing to change the conclusion —though her offer came too late[6]. Here, one cannot help thinking, Dickens had his eye more on what suited the Christmas season than on what the artistic demands of the tale required.

With 'The Heart of John Middleton' Mrs. Gaskell returned to the Lancashire (albeit not the Manchester) she knew so well. The setting is the vicinity of Pendle Hill—Sawley (identified by the reference to the Peel Mills[7]) being Whalley; the Bribble, the river Ribble. In spite of mentioning factory work, with its long hours[8], unsuitability for women[9], petty tyranny[10] and victimization[11], the story is, in its central interest, religious rather than industrial.

John Middleton, erstwhile poacher and riotous liver (not unlike the sexton, of *The Sexton's Hero,* in his earlier days), undergoes a double conversion—being turned from his wild ways by his love for the virtuous, gentle Nelly[12], and being drawn to an evangelical brand of Christianity by the words of a hillside

---

[1] II, 325-334.
[2] *The Letters of Charles Dickens*, ed. Dexter, II, 250: letter of 12 December 1850 to W. H. Wills.
[3] *The Letters of Charles Dickens*, ed. Dexter, II, 250.
[4] *The Letters of Charles Dickens*, ed. Dexter, II, 250.
[5] *The Letters of Charles Dickens*, ed. Dexter, II, 250.
[6] *The Letters of Charles Dickens*, ed. Dexter, II, 255: letter of 20 December 1850 to Mrs. Gaskell.
[7] By Ward (ed. *Works*, II, p. xxvii).
[8] *Works*, II, 384.
[9] *Works*, II, 392.
[10] *Works*, II, 389-390.
[11] *Works*, II, 396.
[12] *Works*, II, esp. 385-395.

preacher[13]. Here Mrs. Gaskell's treatment of religious psychology
is eminently successful. She evinces a remarkably sympathetic
awareness of the mind of Middleton when, under the sway of
Old Testament tales of violent vengeance, he waits for a chance
to repay Dick Jackson : it is an insight scarcely expected from
the respectable wife of a refined Unitarian minister. Yet, con-
trariwise, her presentation of New Testament Christianity (the
religion of charity, where forgiveness replaced the *lex talionis*),
as embodied in the figure of Nelly, is far less convincing.

Mrs. Gaskell wisely employs Middleton to relate the story,
making him use that 'rough kind of Bible language'[14] common
among Lancashire people and especially apposite in his case.
Consequently the highly dramatizing mode of narration appears
justifiable; for this seems the very way in which such a person
would be likely to tell his own tale. The description of a storm
in terms of spiritual violence[15] is, for example, warranted by
Middleton's anthropomorphically religious beliefs.

In her scenic descriptions Mrs. Gaskell is obviously depicting
from personal observation; for the character of her hero, however, she would, equally obviously, have had to turn to invention. Even if the outlines of the tale had some basis in fact,
the psychological colouring was all her own. Perhaps here Mrs.
Chadwick may be allowed to comment.

> Mrs. Bridell-Fox, a daughter of W. J. Fox, once a noted Unitar-
> ian minister, and afterwards a member of Parliament for
> Oldham, and a friend of the Gaskells, mentions in some graphic
> memories, having walked with Mrs. Gaskell until long past
> midnight over the Fells, which divide Lancashire and Yorkshire,
> "where the wild winds came down and whistled round the
> cottage of John Middleton, till his hard heart was melted within
> him by the death of his sweet invalid wife." This reference
> goes to prove that most of Mrs. Gaskell's stories were founded
> on fact.[16]

It was not uncommon for Mrs. Gaskell to use the same
material, in slightly varied forms, more than once in her work.

---

[13] *Works,* II, 400-403
[14] *Works,* II, 388.
[15] *Works,* II, 403.
[16] Chadwick, *Mrs. Gaskell,* p. 183. The 'graphic memories' Mrs.
Chadwick cites and quotes from are contained in Eliza F. Bridell-Fox,
'Memories', *The Girl's Own Paper,* XI (19 July 1890), 660.

This habit of developing and refurbishing is not necessarily a sign of poverty of invention (Shakespeare did the same thing); but the inclination must be kept in mind when Mrs. Gaskell's literary position is under assessment. The present work contains an illustration of the tendency. Dr. Adolphus Ward[17] was the first to call attention to the parallel between the scene where Nelly shields John from a stone thrown by Dick Jackson, herself receiving the blow, and that similar episode[18] in *North and South* where Margaret Hale protects John Thornton in like manner.

There is, in 'The Heart of John Middleton', a second literary parallel, remarked upon by Mrs. Chadwick[19]. Mrs. Gaskell had a great love of country traditions and sayings, legends and beliefs —well exemplified in her letter of 18 August 1838 to Mary Howitt[20]. It was therefore quite natural that, in her *Life of Charlotte Brontë*, she should have the following.

> I remember Miss Brontë once telling me that it was a saying round about Haworth, "Keep a stone in thy pocket seven year; turn it, and keep it seven year longer, that it may be ever ready to thine hand when thine enemy draws near."[21]

Turning back to 'The Heart of John Middleton', we find:

> But I forgot not our country proverb—"Keep a stone in thy pocket for seven years; turn it, and keep it for seven years more; but have it ever ready to cast to thine enemy when the time comes."[22]

Nevertheless there seem good artistic grounds for Gaskell's use of this Yorkshire proverb in her Lancashire tale. It reminds readers of the stone-throwing incident, already mentioned, with an inverse appropriateness; it also adds local flavour to the

[17] Ed. *Works,* II, pp. xxvii-xxviii.
[18] The parallel passages are given more or less accurately in Whitfield, *Mrs Gaskell,* p. 195—the relevant references being *Works,* II, 394: cf. IV, 211-212.
[19] *Mrs. Gaskell,* pp. 182-183.
[20] Quoted in extracts in Howitt, 'Stray Notes from Mrs. Gaskell', *Good Words,* XXXVI (1895), 606-611; much of this (*G.L.,* No. 12) is reproduced, on the whole accurately, in Sanders, *Elizabeth Gaskell,* pp. 38-41.
[21] *The Life of Charlotte Brontë,* 1st edn, 1857, I, 12.
[22] *Works,* II, 400.

story. One wonders whether she made a note of the saying at the time she heard it from Miss Brontë[23], or whether this is just another example of that 'marvellous memory'[24] which so impressed her acquaintances.

[23] Miss Rubenius (*The Woman Question in Mrs. Gaskell's Life and Works*, p. 259, fn. 2) reminds us that Charlotte Brontë told Mrs. Gaskell the proverb, probably when they first met in August 1850.

[24] *Memorials of Two Sisters*, ed. Shaen, p. 24.

SECTION VIII

'Mr. Harrison's Confessions' (1851)

'The Last Generation in England' was a collection of Knutsford recollections rather than a work of fiction with a Knutsford setting; however between February and April 1851 Mrs. Gaskell did publish, in *The Ladies' Companion*[1], just such a story. Probably the periodical form of publication explains, even if it does not excuse, the episodical nature of the plot; for the author's inventive powers failed to weave together its several threads into a wholly satisfactory narrative. This lack of unity is most easily demonstrated by pointing to the concluding chapters, where marriages are arranged, usually with little, or at best insufficient, preparation, and in a manner which has regard neither to probability nor to consistency. If the work raised no serious issues, such a fairy-tale ending might be defensible; but, since Mrs. Gaskell mixes the tragic (or pseudo-tragic) with the comic, no apologetics are possible along these lines. Whatever virtues the tale possesses, they are not of the structural sort.

Mrs. Gaskell's acquaintance with medical men was wide: not only were both her uncle and her cousin such (Mr. Peter Holland and his son, Sir Henry[2]); her great-uncle (Peter Colthurst[3]) and her brother-in-law (Samuel Gaskell[4]) were likewise members

[1] 'Mr. Harrison's Confessions', *The Ladies' Companion and Monthly Magazine*, III, 1-11, 49-56, 97-106. The contribution was anonymous. At its inception Mrs. Gaskell had felt unable to write for this periodical, as appears from a letter to her of 20 October 1849 by the editor, Mrs. Jane Loudon, the first part of which is in The John Rylands Library, Manchester—English MS. 731/112.

[2] See Sir Henry Holland, *Recollections of Past Life*, London: Longmans, Green, & Co., 1872.

[3] Chadwick, *Mrs. Gaskell*, p. 41.

[4] A specialist in mental diseases who became head of an asylum in Lancaster, according to Jane Revere Coolidge (subsequently Mrs. Whitehill), 'Life and letters of Mrs. E. C. Gaskell', Ch. II, p. 5—an incomplete typescript of which is deposited in the Gaskell Section, Brotherton Collection, Leeds University Library; the finished draft being in the hands of Mrs. Whitehill. In 1849 he seems to have been a London Commissioner in Lunacy—Her Sister [Susanna Winkworth], ed. *Letters and Memorials of Catherine Winkworth*, I (1883), 183, fn.

113

of the fraternity. Especially important is her connexion with her uncle, whom she used to accompany on his rounds[5], in the course of which she must, albeit unconsciously, have gained that wealth of experience which as a writer she later turned to good use. 'Mr. Harrison's Confessions' is a convincing picture of the life of a country doctor. We find, for example, a realistic description of the case of John Brouncker[6]—with knowledgeable passing references to the *Lancet*[7], Sir Astley Cooper[8], and Sir Everard Home[9]. More importantly, there is a shrewd appreciation of the part played by social manners and professional decorum in the daily affairs of a general practitioner[10]. The narrator around whom the story revolves is himself a surgeon, and Mrs. Gaskell uses her *persona* with considerable skill.

The opening scene—a fireside conversation between two old medical students[11]—effectively introduces the reader to the atmosphere of the tale. Throughout Mrs. Gaskell shows herself to advantage in treating varied social types: a neat instance is the scene in which Jack Marshland makes his unceremonious entry into a Duncombe drawing-room where a game with conversation-cards is in progress[12].

Despite the general excellence of her treatment of Mr. Harrison and his *milieu,* there are moments when Mrs. Gaskell loosens her hold. An illustration of this is the motherly tone he adopts in talking of little Walter Hutton's attack of croup— a complaint with which Mrs. Gaskell was herself[13] only too familiar. One feels that the authoress is putting inappropriate words into her narrator's mouth, is writing personally rather than fictionally, is indulging herself to the detriment of the story.

> " . . . She [Sophy Hutton] was on her knees by the warm bath, in which the little fellow was struggling to get his breath, with a look of terror on his face that I have often noticed in young children when smitten by a sudden and violent illness. It seems as if they recognised something infinite and invisible, at whose

5 Chadwick, *Mrs. Gaskell*, p. 14.
6 *Works,* V, 452 ff.
7 *Works,* V, 422, 452.
8 *Works,* V, 413.
9 *Works,* V, 416.
10 E.g. *Works,* V, 416.
11 *Works,* V, 405.
12 *Works,* V, 438-442.
13 See, for example, *"My Diary"*, pp. 27, 36-37; and *G.L.*, No. 7.

bidding the pain and the anguish come, from which no love can shield them. It is a very heart-rending look to observe, because it comes on the faces of those who are too young to receive comfort from the words of faith, or the promises of religion. Walter had his arms tight round Sophy's neck, as if she, hitherto his paradise-angel, could save him from the grave shadow of Death. Yes! of Death! . . . "[14]

As another indication that, at times, Mrs. Gaskell forgot to tell the tale consistently from Mr. Harrison's point of view, we may mention his being given two Christian names (Will[15] and Frank[16]). This slip of the pen, or slip of the mind, slight though it may at first appear, does suggest an incomplete absorption with the central character and therefore, by implication, with the work as a whole.

Mrs. Gaskell's observations of Knutsford life are responsible for her success with Duncombe: all is brought before the reader with a reality which is never questioned—the social structure (five-sixths of the ' " 'householders of a certain rank' " '[17] being women); the typical atmosphere of a rural auction[18]; the gossip and prejudice[19] as well as the charm of a little country town where ' "everybody is so sympathetically full of the same events" '[20]; the picturesque old-world streets and Mayence-style houses[21]; the Dutch-like interior picture presented by a vicarage parlour[22].

Turning to the characters, one can point to a similar realism, though without the suggestion that Mrs. Gaskell was merely incorporating Knutsford people directly into the story. Mrs. Holland, the eldest of her daughters, was of the opinion that she never consciously based her characters upon specific individuals—although many of their attributes were so like those of their 'originals' as to cause the family to make identifications[23].

[14] *Works*, V, 434-435.
[15] *Works*, V, 405.
[16] *Works*, V, 440.
[17] *Works*, V, 414.
[18] *Works*, V, 461-462.
[19] *Works*, V, 481.
[20] *Works*, V, 454.
[21] *Works*, V, 407-408.
[22] *Works*, V, 417-418.
[23] See Edna Lyall [Ada Ellen Bayly], 'Mrs. Gaskell', in *Women Novelists of Queen Victoria's Reign: A Book of Appreciations,* London: Hurst & Blackett, Limited, 1897, p. 144.

Possibly Mrs. Gaskell was a sort of artistic alchemist : sometimes
she produced the pure gold, by fusing into a composite fictional
personage traits taken from several different people whom she
actually knew, or had known; on other occasions, no doubt,
nothing was transmuted. The characters here, however, are not
fully developed, and so warrant but a passing glance. Mr.
Hutton, the vicar, is rather a shadowy figure; nor are most of
his family portrayed at length. His son, Walter, does indeed
come alive, yet the unfortunate sentimental death-bed scene
mars the force of his presentation; Sophy, the vicar's eldest
daughter, seen through the infatuated eyes of Mr. Harrison, is
sufficient for her part. The Bullock family have considerable
vitality, especially their head, a solicitor with leanings like Mrs.
Gaskell's father[24] towards scientific, though not very successful,
agriculture. All the medical men are, in their different ways,
convincing, as are the ladies of Duncombe.

Since, in 'Mr. Harrison's Confessions', Mrs. Gaskell's comic
gifts bulk large for the first time, although to be sure they were
not absent in earlier work, we may consider them in a little
detail. 'The tale is', in the opinion of Miss Hopkins[25], 'pure
farce'; but this opinion needs qualification. Certainly one finds
many farcical situations : there is the episode where Jack Marshland drinks black-currant wine believing it port, his consequential face-pulling being excused on the grounds of a professed
teetotalism[26]; there is the scene in which Mr. Harrison kneels
before Caroline Tomkinson to test a weakness of the heart[27]
which proved emotional rather than physical[28]. Nevertheless the
story contains more than farce; Miss Hopkins herself goes on,
in apparent contradiction, to mention Mrs. Gaskell's 'light,
satirically humorous tone'[29]. However some of Mrs. Gaskell's
humour is undeniably a little heavy-handed—the position of
Mr. Harrison, allegedly engaged to three ladies[30], none of whom

[24] See Chadwick, *Mrs. Gaskell*, pp. 1-2, 5-6; and Sanders, *Elizabeth
Gaskell*, p. 2.
[25] *Elizabeth Gaskell*, p. 112.
[26] *Works,* V, 442.
[27] *Works,* V, 450.
[28] *Works,* V, 468-470.
[29] *Elizabeth Gaskell*, p. 112.
[30] *Works,* V, 473.

he loved, may have its funny side; but when Mr. Morgan is by rumour reputed to be on the point of marriage[31] the reader feels this is too much of a good thing. Yet there is another side. Mrs. Gaskell's treatment of Mrs. Rose is, for instance, in her best humorous manner. With a smile one recalls that lady looking over her shoulder as she shows her late husband's miniature to Mr. Harrison[32]; mixing her medical terms when discussing Brouncker's injuries[33]; holding up a hand-screen in preparation for Mr. Harrison's expected proposal[34].

In her opening chapter Mrs. Gaskell skilfully evokes the kindness of Duncombe in a way which also brings out its amusing aspect. As soon as he arrived, enquiries were made concerning Mr. Harrison's health, the first to ask being a certain Mrs. Munton. Thereupon he beguiled himself by guessing the lady's characteristics from so suggestive a surname; soon after came the Miss Tomkinsons.

> "I don't know why, but the Miss Tomkinsons' name had not such a halo about it as Mrs. Munton's. Still it was very pretty in the Miss Tomkinsons to send and inquire. I only wished I did not feel so perfectly robust. I was almost ashamed that I could not send word I was quite exhausted by fatigue, and had fainted twice since my arrival. If I had but had a headache, at least! I heaved a deep breath: my chest was in perfect order; I had caught no cold; so I answered again—
> "'Much obliged to the Miss Tomkinsons; I am not much fatigued; tolerably well: my compliments.' "[35]

The tone and manner of the above passage are not omnipresent. In the character of Miss Horsman, for example, Mrs. Gaskell shows a less genial aspect of Duncombe. Miss Horsman delighted to cast aspersions upon the moral and professional qualities of Mr. Harrison. On the other hand ' "she was really kind among the poor," '[36] although even here ' "she could not help leaving a sting behind her" '[37]. To illustrate further, Mrs. Gaskell's treatment of the superficially sweet and sugary Miss Caroline Tomkinson indicates clearly her real disposition: this

[31] *Works,* V, 475.
[32] *Works,* V, 423.
[33] *Works,* V, 460.
[34] *Works,* V, 466-467, 470-471.
[35] *Works,* V, 409.
[36] *Works,* V, 459.
[37] *Works,* V, 459.

is done by a typically feminine method, by observing Miss
Caroline's behaviour with children (those of the invalid Brouncker).

> "Just then the children came in, dirty and unwashed, I have
> no doubt. And now Miss Caroline's real nature peeped out. She
> spoke sharply to them, and asked them if they had no manners,
> little pigs as they were, to come brushing against her silk gown
> in that way? She sweetened herself again, and was as sugary as
> love when Miss Tomkinson returned for her, . . . "[38]

One of the memorable events in 'Mr. Harrison's Confessions'
is the picnic to the nearby old hall. Mrs. Chadwick aptly
remarks upon the 'choice descriptions of country scenery, showing that Mrs. Gaskell must have been a keen observer of
nature'[39]; she identifies the hall with Tabley[40]—an identification
confirmed by Mrs. Gaskell's own account[41] of visits made
there. Observation of a different sort is found in Mrs. Gaskell's
sketch of the townspeople as they waited for the pleasure-seekers
to depart; the sense of a 'social occasion' is excellently rendered.

> " . . . The sympathetic shopkeepers, standing at their respective
> doors with their hands in their pockets, had, one and all, their
> heads turned in the direction from which the carriages (as Mrs.
> Bullock called them) were to come. There was a rumble along
> the paved street; and the shopkeepers turned and smiled, and
> bowed their heads congratulatingly to us; all the mothers and
> all the little children of the place stood clustering round the
> door to see us set off."[42]

[38] *Works*, V, 458-459.
[39] *Mrs. Gaskell*, p. 186.
[40] *Mrs. Gaskell*, p. 187.
[41] Quoted by Margaret Howitt—'Stray Notes from Mrs. Gaskell', *Good
Words*, XXXVI (1895), 605-606—from Mrs. Gaskell's letter of May
1838 to William and Mary Howitt: *G.L.*, No. 8.
[42] *Works*, V, 425.

SECTION IX

' Disappearances ' (1851)

On 7 June 1851 an article entitled 'Disappearances' came out in *Household Words*[1]. Mrs. Gaskell, having read about recent police detective work, was moved to reflect that the mysterious disappearances of former days were no longer possible. She mentions how easily, through the good offices of a plain-clothes detective, a cousin of hers, who frequently changed his address, was located by a friend[2]. Such a state of affairs had, quite clearly, put an end to romances after the fashion of *Caleb Williams*[3].

Mrs. Gaskell then proceeds to relate several mysteries of which she had heard. For this interest there was, no doubt, a personal explanation : her own brother, John Stevenson, had himself disappeared without any trace—captured, according to one family tradition[4], by pirates. The disappearance *motif* is of thematic importance in Mrs. Gaskell's work; stories of disappearances haunted her 'imagination longer than any tale of wonder'[5]. Their importance for our author's invention of plots must constantly be borne in mind; and it is well to examine at some length the present *Household Words* contribution.

The first incident—told to Mrs. Gaskell by an aristocratic old lady (perhaps that same Knutsford resident who was mentioned in 'The Last Generation in England'[6])—concerns the disappearance of a paralytic old man from a chair outside his cottage[7]. With the credentials of her informant as a warrant for the tale's veracity, Mrs. Gaskell gives such confirming details as the month of the year, the lay-out of the village street, and the whereabouts of the old man's relatives at the time of his

[1] III, 246-250.
[2] *Works*, II, 410-411.
[3] *Works*, II, 412.
[4] Sanders, *Elizabeth Gaskell*, p. 7, fn. 1.
[5] *Works*, II, 413.
[6] *Sartain's Union Magazine*, V (1849), 47-48.
[7] *Works*, II, 412-414.

disappearance. Were it not that she claims to have heard the story as a child, one would conclude Mrs. Gaskell had immediately written down what had been related—though she may, indeed, have done just this; for her brother had wished her to keep a journal[8]. At any rate a retentive memory rather than inventive skill seems to have been responsible for the narrative. Nonetheless the Rev. William Maskell suggested that in Mrs. Gaskell's 'account, guarded as it claims to be by so much of corroborative proof, almost every particular rests on imagination'[9]. Maskell[10] held that she had given a garbled version of the mysterious disappearance, in 1768, of Owen Parfitt, a tailor living at Shepton Mallet, in Somerset. Although there is no date-discrepancy, the lively *raconteuse* being about seventy when she told the tale to little Elizabeth Stevenson, the charge that Mrs. Gaskell's account is merely a distortion of the Parfitt mystery cannot be sustained. To cite but one significant difference, Parfitt disappeared in Somerset while living with his sister, whereas the *Household Words* paralytic, who lived with his son and daughter, disappeared in Shropshire (where Mrs. Gaskell's informant's father had an estate). Yet even granting what need not be granted—namely that the two stories are related in some way—, one sees no reason at all to impugn Mrs. Gaskell's veracity, or to tax her with too free an invention; if any distorting had been done, the old lady seems most likely to have done it.

The next anecdote[11], as the others, Mrs. Gaskell claims to be 'correctly repeated'[12] and believed by her 'informants to be strictly true'[13]. It tells how an attorney strangely vanished after

[8] John Stevenson's keenness for his sister to keep a diary is, as we have noted, expressed in his letter to Elizabeth of 8 and 10 June [1827] as well as in his letter to Aunt Lumb of 1825. Both MSS are in the hands of the present writer: the former is incomplete; the latter, mutilated.

[9] William Maskell, 'The Mystery of Owen Parfitt', *Odds and Ends*, London: James Toovey, 1872, p. 78.

[10] 'The Mystery of Owen Parfitt', *Odds and Ends*, pp. 74-94. A similar account, where the month of the disappearance is given as May, can be found in Samuel Butler, *The Life and Letters of Dr. Samuel Butler, Head-Master of Shrewsbury School 1798-1836, and Afterwards Bishop of Lichfield, in So Far as They Illustrate the Scholastic, Religious, and Social Life of England*, 1790-1840, 2 vols., London: John Murray, 1896, I, 90-99; see also Ward, ed. *Works*, II, pp. xxviii-xxix.

[11] *Works*, II, 414-415.   [12] *Works*, II, 414.   [13] *Works*, II, 414.

having collected rents for a local squire; and it includes a death-bed confession from a butcher-cum-grazier, this leading to the discovery of the attorney's skeleton in a sandy heath, close to his house in a small country town. Dashes instead of names, the mention of a heath, the reference to a small country town—all bring Knutsford inevitably to mind : recourse to the Rev. Henry Green's book[14] provides the expected confirmation. His account[15] differs in some details from that of Mrs. Gaskell. For example, he says that the murderer was an inn-keeper (though the man may well have subsequently become a butcher and grazier, or indeed followed all three callings at the same time); and he reports—what Mrs. Gaskell omits—that the murderer was, when drunk, conscience-stricken at the scene of the crime, and claimed to have a vision of his victim. Of the two stories, Mrs. Gaskell's is much more sober than that of the Unitarian minister; and this very sobriety gives her narrative the appearance of truth.

Mrs. Gaskell then compares[16] a Lincolnshire tale of a vanishing bridegroom with a similar Festiniog tradition, adding that, in the latter, the bride sat daily at a certain window awaiting her lover's return. With humour Mrs. Gaskell comments that, in her day, the electric telegram and the detective policeman would soon bring home a disappearing bridegroom.

The penultimate anecdote[17] has for its subject the strange disappearance, some time between 1820 and 1830, of a North Shields medical student. After including graphic local details—she mentions, for instance, 'the alleys (or "chares") which lead down from the main street . . . to the river'[18]—Mrs. Gaskell repeats the general belief that Dr. G.'s apprentice could have been taken by boat to Edinburgh, there to fall victim to Burke and Hare.

A fortnight later, in the 'Chips' column of Household Words[19], further information was published under the heading

[14] Knutsford, Its Traditions and History: with Reminiscences, Anecdotes, and Notices of the Neighbourhood.
[15] Green, Knutsford, pp. 93-94.
[16] Works, II, 415-416.
[17] Works, II, 416-417.
[18] Works, II, 416.
[19] III, 305-306. The Household Words Day Book (in the Princeton University Library) suggests that W. H. Wills was responsible for the appearance of this piece, which information I owe to Professor Anne Lohrli.

'A Disappearance'[20]. A correspondent (whose sister was the daughter-in-law of Dr. G.) wrote that about a year and a half after he had vanished (murdered, as the G.'s thought), the youth had sent word he was doing well in America. Such, however, was not the end of the affair; for on 21 February 1852, again in the 'Chips' section, there was printed 'A Disappearance Cleared Up'[21]. This article contained a letter from John Gaunt, with an additional note by his brother, William—both being sons of the patient whose medicine the apprentice had delivered just before disappearing. John enclosed an account of a public meeting, held on 9 May 1834 (seven years after the disappearance), at which documents were read proving the young man had died from cholera on 12 November 1832, while in the service of the East India Company; and he related how his family had been persecuted by those who, like the boy's parents, believed they had made away with the lad. The account thus slightly conflicts with Mrs. Gaskell's, which included neither the apprentice's enlistment with the East India Company nor the North Shields meeting; moreover she suggested that only the boy's mother was alive when he vanished, whereas Gaunt claimed that both parents died afterwards, still comparatively young. There is also a conflict with the statement of Dr. G.'s distant relative, who professed to have heard about the apprentice some eighteen months after his disappearance, though Gaunt's letter implied a seven years' silence; nor did she refer to the boy's enlistment or the meeting in the town.

Entitled 'Character-Murder'[22], yet a third relevant 'Chip' came out on 8 January 1859, its ostensive aim being to counteract spiteful rumours against the Gaunts, recently revived when some old bones were found in the grounds of a Mechanics' Institute. Details of the case and of the ensuing ill-founded gossip were reiterated (based on the amalgamated accounts of

[20] Reprinted less fully in *Works*, II, 420-421.
[21] *Household Words*, IV, 513-514. Professor Anne Lohrli informs me that the *Household Words* Day (or Office) Book (in the Princeton University Library) records the item as having been communicated, no payment being entered.
[22] *Household Words*, XIX, 139-140. The *Household Words* Day Book (in the Princeton University Library) names its anonymous author as Morley—almost certainly Henry Morley, according to Professor Anne Lohrli.

Mrs. Gaskell and the Gaunt brothers); and for the first time the names of the physician and his apprentice were given as Dr. Greenhow and John Margetts. It was hinted that a scandalous version of the story (Mrs. Gaskell's) had found its way into the third volume of *Household Words*, thus affording an opportunity in the fourth for a public refutation (by the Gaunts). Although seemingly designed to give a *coup de grâce* to persistent accusations against the Gaunt family, 'Character-Murder' unfortunately failed to distinguish between what had and had not been said in the initial 'Disappearances' account—at least so Mrs. Gaskell thought. She took umbrage in consequence, and wrote to W. H. Wills (assistant editor of *Household Words*): no explanation nor any satisfactory apology was forthcoming[23].

Mrs. Gaskell's article concludes with a story[24] she had obtained from the elder spinster daughter of a Manchester attorney, Mr. S. A Manchester squire, owner of Garrat Hall[25], vanished while visiting London; subsequently he secretly communicated with his son and heir, revealing that he had married a shopkeeper's daughter and relinquished all his previous family ties. This is the longest of Mrs. Gaskell's anecdotes, and there seems no reason to doubt its truth. The considerable detail given suggests that she may well have written it down soon after its narration by old Miss S.

[23] This information is contained in a passage—unprinted, but briefly summarized, by Mrs. Whitehill (ed. *Gaskell-Norton Letters*, pp. 30-31)— in Mrs. Gaskell's letter to Charles Eliot Norton of 9 March [1859], now in the Harvard University Library. Mrs. Gaskell's annoyance at the affair made her unwilling for Dickens to have a story she was then in the middle of—probably *A Dark Night's Work*. This last was subsequently published anonymously from 24 January to 21 March 1863 in *All the Year Round. A Weekly Journal. Conducted by Charles Dickens. With Which Is Incorporated 'Household Words'* (VIII, 457-465, 481-485, 505-510, 529-533, 553-562; IX, 1-7, 25-32, 49-57, 73-84), although we here (*G.L.*, No. 418) find Mrs. Gaskell signifying to Norton that she did not want to be among the contributors to the new periodical, about which she had already received a circular. Dickens, on the other hand, was keen to have both her and her story—see his letter to Wills of 28 April 1859, in which there is a probable reference to what he later published as 'A Dark Night's Work' (*The Letters of Charles Dickens*, ed. Dexter, III, 100).

[24] *Works*, II, 417-420.

[25] Details of Garrett Hall [*sic*] may conveniently be found in William Farrer and John Brownbill, ed. *The Victoria History of the County of Lancaster*, 8 vols., 1906-1914, IV (London: Constable and Company Limited, 1911), 240.

SECTION X

Cranford (1851-1853)

On 13 December 1851 'Our Society at Cranford' appeared in *Household Words*. Mrs. Gaskell 'never meant/ to write more'[1] : yet this was to be the first of a series of nine sketches which came out irregularly until 21 May 1853[2]. In that year, with a few minor changes, these pieces were brought together in one volume[3]. Since the original (periodical) form of publication did not detrimentally affect the artistic quality of the composition, it seems wiser to consider *Cranford* as a whole rather than to treat every section chronologically. Chronology has here little place[4]. Whatever unity exists is a unity of sentiment : one can speak meaningfully of the *Cranford ethos*.

In *Cranford* Mrs. Gaskell brought before her Victorian readers a world of recollections. To them it must have seemed as if she were writing of a time ' "long years ago" '[5] : this phrase, and another of Mr. Peter's—' "more than half a lifetime, and yet it seems like yesterday" '[6]—could aptly apply to the chronology of the whole work, for the very vagueness is appropriate. In the first chapter the narrator's Cranfordesque questions (asking such things as whether a cow dressed in flannel is ever seen in London[7]) immediately suggest the slight unreality of the town.

---

[1] Mrs. Gaskell's letter of 24 February [1865] to John Ruskin (in the Harvard University Library: Autograph File). Chapple and Pollard base their text (*G.L.*, No. 562) on an incomplete and slightly inaccurate manuscript copy, probably made by Meta Gaskell for Ward, who (ed. *Works*, II, pp. xi-xii) printed a lengthy extract.
[2] *Household Words*, IV (1851-1852), 265-274, 349-357, 588-597; V (1852), 55-64; VI (1853), 390-396, 413-420; VII (1853), 108-115, 220-227, 277-285.
[3] [Elizabeth Cleghorn Gaskell] *Cranford,* London: Chapman & Hall, 1853.
[4] For chronological inaccuracies, see Whitfield, *Mrs Gaskell,* pp. 139-140.
[5] *Works,* II, 187.
[6] *Works,* II, 187: a minor typographical error has been corrected.
[7] *Works,* II, 6.

For Gaskell scholars the perennial problem is the relation of
Cranford to Knutsford. The most notable work has been done
by the Rev. George Andrew Payne, whose ' "Cranford" Notes'[8]
provide many useful data for an examination of Mrs.
Gaskell's literary debt to Knutsford people and places; the Honourable
Beatrix Tollemache is another important writer on Knutsford-
Cranford connexions. The list of magazine articles runs into
pages[9]. Summarizing this research, one may say that undoubtedly Mrs. Gaskell drew heavily upon her Knutsford childhood.
Although there is some disagreement about the identifications,
the originals of Miss Debõrah Jenkyns and Miss Matty are
generally held to be Miss Mary and Miss Lucy Holland,
daughters of Dr. Peter Holland and cousins to the authoress[10].
Thus the 'heroine' at least, namely Miss Matty, had a factual
starting-point. Similarly somebody somewhere has, it is safe to
say, identified most of the other major characters : the narrator
with Mrs. Gaskell; poor Peter with John Stevenson; Captain
Brown with Captain Hill; the Honourable Mrs. Jamieson with
Lady Jane Stanley (the lady, mentioned in 'The Last Generation in England', who disliked 'linking'); Mrs. Fitz-Adam with
Mrs. Lumb; Mr. Thomas Holbrook with Mr. Peter Leigh.
In some cases the resemblance seems close, in others less so.
We must, however, admit that most of the evidence is lacking,
and that the prudent course is to suspend judgement—with a
warning against ridiculing eager seekers after originals, whose
identifications ought, perhaps, to receive the benefit of any
doubt.

One of the most forceful testimonies to Mrs. Gaskell's direct
use of fact in fiction is found in Green's *Knutsford*. We need
make no apology for quoting the passage at length; for it has
become a *locus classicus* in Gaskell criticism.

> . . . Mrs. Gaskell, the author of *Mary Barton*, of *the Sexton's
> Hero*, of *Ruth*, of *North and South*, and of several other tales

---

[8] George Andrew Payne, *Mrs. Gaskell and Knutsford*, 2nd edn, Manchester: Clarkson & Griffiths, Ltd.; London: Mackie & Co. Ld. [1905],
pp. 39-43. Our subsequent citations give the publication-date as 1905.

[9] See the Bibliographies of Northup (to Sanders, *Elizabeth Gaskell*) and
Whitfield.

[10] See Ward, ed. *Works*, II, pp. xix-xxii; Chadwick, *Mrs. Gaskell*, p.
27; and Payne, *Mrs. Gaskell and Knutsford*, 1905, pp. 39-40.

of deep interest, may be claimed as belonging to this town, during her infancy and early life up to the time of her marriage. There is one work of hers, *Cranford*, which in my judgment, while depicting life in almost any country town, is especially descriptive of some of the past and present social characteristics of Knutsford. I know that the work was not intended to delineate this place chiefly or specially, but a little incident within my own experience will show the accuracy of the pictures as applied to our town. A woman of advanced age, who was confined to her house through illness, about three years ago, asked me to lend her an amusing or cheerful book. I lent her *Cranford*, without telling her to what it was supposed to relate; she read the tale of Life in a Country Town; and when I called again, she was full of eagerness to say:—"Why, Sir! that Cranford is all about Knutsford; my old mistress, Miss Harker, is mentioned in it; and our poor cow, she did go to the field in a large flannel waistcoat, because she had burned herself in a lime pit."[11]

In this instance the extent of Mrs. Gaskell's invention was to change a letter—Miss Harker became Miss Barker[12]. Recalling that Mrs. Gaskell 'knew the cat that/ swallowed the lace, that be=/=longed to the lady, that sent/ for the doctor,'[13] we may safely assume that another *prima facie* improbable Cranfordism did in truth take place. Of a further far-fetched story Mrs. Gaskell wrote to Ruskin, 'I will tell her [Ruskin's mother] a bit/ more of "Cranford" that I did/ not dare to put in, because I/ thought people would say it/ was too ridiculous, and yet/ which really happened in/ Knutsford.'[14] It seems, indeed, that it was not uncommon for Mrs. Gaskell to mention Cranfordisms in her correspondence, as when, writing to John Forster, she remarked:

. . . Shall I tell you a Cranfordism. An/ old lady[,] a M[rs] Frances Wright[,] said to/ one of my cousins "I have never been able/ to spell since I lost my teeth". . . . /[15]

[11] Green, *Knutsford, Its Traditions and History: with Reminiscences, Anecdotes, and Notices of the Neighbourhood*, p. 114.
[12] *Works*, II, 6.
[13] Mrs. Gaskell's 24 February [1865] letter to Ruskin, in the Harvard University Library—cf. and cont. Ward, ed. *Works,* II, p. xi: *G.L.,* No. 562.
[14] *Ibidem.*
[15] This letter (*G.L.,* No. 195) to Forster of Wednesday night [17 May 1854] is in the National Library of Scotland (MS. 2262, ff. 34-40; the quotation being on f. 39v). Sometimes the Cranfordisms applied to herself, as when she wrote that her 'ancles ached with talking'—in a letter to Eliza Fox of Monday [Tuesday] 29 May 1849 (*G.L.,* No. 48), a copy of part of which is in the Gaskell Section, Brotherton Collection, Leeds University Library.

Mrs. Gaskell's keen observation of life in the little Cheshire town was, therefore, an important element in *Cranford*: Knutsford fact appears, at times, stranger than fiction. This real quaintness was responsible for that early contribution to *Sartain's*, in which Mrs. Gaskell did little more than write up her reminiscences. Following 'The Last Generation in England' came 'Mr. Harrison's Confessions', where some attempt was made to go beyond mere recollected incidents by inventing a very loose plot. Thereafter came *Cranford*.

In *Cranford* there is no complex plot. The chapters tend to fall together (often in pairs), partly owing to the initial division for instalment-publication; however the reader is scarcely conscious of this, and the book lends itself extremely well to piecemeal reading. Mrs. Gaskell admitted[16] that it was the only work of hers she could read again; and implied that the comic episodes, especially, afforded excellent sick-bed entertainment. Indeed what remains in the mind is not a consecutive narrative, but rather a series of sayings and situations, related by virtue of being Cranfordesque.

Mrs. Gaskell's success in *Cranford* arose as much from her skill in choosing as from her power of inventing: she used incidents selected from memory; and the principle of selection was whether they would be in keeping with the over-all atmosphere. Usually the result of Knutsford experiences and recollections, events at Cranford did, nonetheless, sometimes have a different origin. It may be well to give an illustration of Mrs. Gaskell's debt to another source as a warning against ascribing everything to the influence of Knutsford. The illustration can be made by comparing the following passages: the parallel needs no comment.

> If she [Miss Matty] was made aware that she had been drinking green tea at any time, she always thought it her duty to lie awake half through the night afterward (I have known her take it in ignorance many a time without such effects), and consequently green tea was prohibited the house; yet to-day she herself asked for the obnoxious article, under the impression that she was talking about the silk.[17]

16 In her 24 February [1865] letter to Ruskin (in the Harvard University Library)—quoted, from a copy, by Ward (ed. *Works*, II, p. xi): *G.L.*, No. 562. Cf. [Leonard Huxley] *The House of Smith Elder*, 1923, p. 81.
17 *Works*, II, 145-146.

As may be imagined Miss Brontë was none too easy a visitor.
This [the visit paid to Plymouth Grove in June 1851] was the
occasion on which she was asked if she preferred tea or coffee.
"Tea" was the reply, "but please see that there is no green tea
mixed with it, as I am never able to sleep after partaking of a
cup of tea that has the least particle of green leaf." Mrs. Gaskell
in vain recommended a mixture of green and black blended,
which in fact was the tea she was making use of. Besides, it was
too late to make a change, and the ordinary tea was used. Next
morning the guest was asked how she had slept. There was a
general smile when she said "Splendidly," and a similar tea was
used to the end of the visit![18]

One recalls then, from one's reading of *Cranford,* an assort-
ment of incidents which have a unity of tone : the cow dressed
in flannel[19]; the lace-swallowing cat[20]; poor Peter's shooting a
cherubim[21]; Miss Matty's exchanging her sovereigns for the
worthless bank-note[22]; Mr. Mulliner's appropriating the *St.
James's Chronicle*[23]; the reading of old letters by firelight[24].
All these have the *Cranford* flavour. Comic or pathetic, they
are all recollected in tranquillity, all more or less viewed nostalgically. Likewise one remembers the *Cranford* sayings—Martha's
definition of reason (' "Reason always means what some one
else has got to say." '[25]); Mary's *naive* belief in the family in-
fallibility ('But I was right. I think that must be an hereditary
quality, for my father says he is scarcely ever wrong.'[26]); Miss
Matty's comment on hearing that Mr. Hoggins was about to
marry Lady Glenmire (' "Two people that we know going to

[18] Haldane, *Mrs. Gaskell and Her Friends,* pp. 133-134. Apparently
the ultimate source for this anecdote was Miss Meta Gaskell; but she
seems to have put the incident now in 1853, now in 1851: see the
reports found, respectively, in Marion Leslie, 'Mrs. Gaskell's House and
Its Memories', *The Woman at Home*: *Annie S. Swan's Magazine,* Vol.
V, No. 45 (June 1897), pp. 765-766, and in Sarah A. Tooley, 'The
Centenary of Mrs. Gaskell', *The Cornhill Magazine,* N.S. XXIX (1910),
325. The episode occurred during Charlotte Brontë's second (1853) visit,
according to the account in Esther Alice (Mrs. Ellis H.) Chadwick, *In
the Footsteps of the Brontës,* London: Sir Isaac Pitman & Son, Ltd.,
1914, p. 450.
    [19] *Works,* II, 6.
    [20] *Works,* II, 94-95.
    [21] *Works,* II, 191-192.
    [22] *Works,* II, 147-149.
    [23] *Works,* II, 89-90.
    [24] *Works,* II, 49-59.
    [25] *Works,* II, 155.
    [26] *Works,* II, 177.

L

be married. It's coming very near!" '[27]); Miss Matty's request
for a sort of cap like the widowed Mrs. Jamieson's (' "I only
meant something in that style; not widows', of course, but
rather like Mrs. Jamieson's." '[28]).

The Cranfordian attitude to life is difficult to define. The
tragic colouring is not absent, since one has but to mention
Captain Brown's fatal accident[29], followed by his elder daughter's
death-bed scene[30]. There is too the pathos of Miss Matty's love
affair[31] of long ago with Mr. Holbrook, who likewise dies[32].
Pervasive is Mrs. Gaskell's own tolerant humour. Perhaps, however, the essential *Cranford* philosophy is embodied in the two
following passages, both of which refer to Miss Matty.

> No! there was nothing she could teach to the rising generation
> of Cranford, unless they had been quick learners and ready
> imitators of her patience, her humility, her sweetness, her quiet
> contentment with all that she could not do.[33]

> Ever since that day there has been the old friendly sociability
> in Cranford society; which I am thankful for, because of my
> dear Miss Matty's love of peace and kindliness. We all love Miss
> Matty, and I somehow think we are all of us better when she
> is near us.[34]

The unselfishness exemplified by Miss Matty is also illustrated
by the generosity of the ladies of Cranford; in her hour of need
they collect for her what they can spare—although in secret,
so as not to injure her feelings of independence[35]. The same
spirit is displayed by the maid, Martha, who pressed for an
immediate marriage with Jem Hearn in the hope of having
Miss Matty lodge with them[36]. As a specific against sentimentality, Mrs. Gaskell does not neglect the touch of humour; yet,
it is obvious, the way of life taken by Miss Matty is the one
she herself favoured. How a Manchester business-man appeared

[27] *Works*, II, 137.
[28] *Works*, II, 47.
[29] *Works*, II, 19-20.
[30] *Works*, II, 23-24.
[31] *Works*, II, esp. 27-36.
[32] *Works*, II, 47.
[33] *Works*, II, 158.
[34] *Works*, II, 192.
[35] *Works*, II, 164-169.
[36] *Works*, II, 160-163.

in the light of this philosophy the next quotation will show; it
is a fundamental criticism of worldly wisdom, couched in language of the utmost naivety.

> But to return to Miss Matty. It was really very pleasant to see
> how her unselfishness and simple sense of justice called out the
> same good qualities in others. She never seemed to think any
> one would impose upon her, because she should be so grieved to
> do it to them. I have heard her put a stop to the asseverations
> of the man who brought her coals by quietly saying, "I am sure
> you would be sorry to bring me wrong weight;" and if the coals
> were short measure that time, I don't believe they ever were
> again. People would have felt as much ashamed of presuming
> on her good faith as they would have done on that of a child.
> But my father says "such simplicity might be very well in Cran-
> ford, but would never do in the world." And I fancy the world
> must be very bad, for with all my father's suspicion of every
> one with whom he has dealings, and in spite of all his many
> precautions, he lost upwards of a thousand pounds by roguery
> only last year.[37]

Mrs. Gaskell admirably recreates the social atmosphere
of Cranford, so well epitomized in the phrase ' "elegant
economy" '[38]. The opening chapter is a piece of masterly scene-
setting; having just a touch of irony to give aesthetic distance,
it is pervaded with the sympathetic humour of a writer who
must have on many occasions observed at first hand the social
behaviour there described. The social manners of Mr. Holbrook
are presented with that same 'tact, . . . observation, . . . delicacy
and . . . loving appreciation of absurdities'[39] shown in her pictures of Cranford card- and tea-parties. The gentility of *Cranford*
has nothing of the shabby genteel : the view that 'money-spend-
ing [was] always "vulgar and ostentatious" '[40] may indeed have
'a sort of sour-grapeism'[41] about it; but it points to a system
of values worthy of respect. The social 'placing' of Mrs.
Jamieson, most discreetly managed, is an excellent illustration
of how Mrs. Gaskell's humorous irony coloured her mode of
observing, of how description can work at more than one level.

---

[37] *Works*, II, 174.
[38] *Works*, II, 4. The phrase had already been foreshadowed by H. F.
Chorley (see Rubenius, *The Woman Question in Mrs. Gaskell's Life and
Works*, p. 247, fn. 5).
[39] ffrench, *Mrs. Gaskell*, p. 45.
[40] *Works*, II, 4.
[41] *Works*, II, 4.

I saw Mrs. Jamieson eating seed-cake, slowly and considerately, as she did everything; and I was rather surprised, for I knew she had told us, on the occasion of her last party, that she never had it in her house, it reminded her so much of scented soap. She always gave us Savoy biscuits. However, Mrs. Jamieson was kindly indulgent to Miss Barker's want of knowledge of the customs of high life; and, to spare her feelings, ate three large pieces of seed-cake, with a placid, ruminating expression of countenance, not unlike a cow's.[42]

The life of Cranford is the life of its ladies, those 'holders of houses above a certain rent'[43], those Amazons in whose possession the town lay. Nevertheless Mrs. Gaskell manages to give the sense of a real community. We find references to the surgeon (Mr. Hoggins[44]), the rector (Mr. Hayter[45]), and the railway official (Captain Brown[46]), as well as to such minor male characters as Lord Mauleverer[47] and Major Jenkyns[48]. More importantly, perhaps, she makes her readers aware of several diverse groups in Cranford. Servants are, of course, essential to the ladies; and they, in their train, have the inevitable followers—'handsome young men'[49] who 'abounded in the lower classes.'[50] Shopkeepers too are mentioned: one, Mr. Johnson[51], owned the shop where Miss Matty had to decline purchasing silk for a new dress, having exchanged her sovereigns for the Town-and-County-Bank note. A carter appears to announce the death of Captain Brown[52]. Nor does the outer world as a whole fail to impinge on the feminine society of Cranford: the Town and County Bank failed[53], with dire consequences for Miss Matty; Signor Brunoni visited the town 'to exhibit his wonderful magic in the Cranford Assembly Rooms'[54]; the Aga Jenkyns returned[55], full of stories of his Eastern travels. In this way Mrs. Gaskell prevents the Cranford ladies from being confined within a closed circle—indeed the narrator (like the authoress at the time of writing) was herself a non-resident.

With Mary Smith Mrs. Gaskell achieved a considerable advance in her *persona* method of story-telling. Explicit and obtrusive authorial comments find no place in *Cranford*: whatever autobiographic remarks Mrs. Gaskell makes appear wholly

[42] *Works,* II, 79-80. [47] *Works,* II, 15. [52] *Works,* II, 19.
[43] *Works,* II, 1. [48] *Works,* II, 32. [53] *Works,* II, 153.
[44] *Works,* II, 20. [49] *Works,* II, 29. [54] *Works,* II, 98.
[45] *Works,* II, 106. [50] *Works,* II, 29. [55] *Works,* II, 180.
[46] *Works,* II, 4. [51] *Works,* II, 142.

in keeping with this character who could say, as could Mrs. Gaskell herself, 'For my own part, I had vibrated all my life between Drumble and Cranford'[56]—'Manchester and Knutsford' in other words. Although everything is seen through Mary's eyes, Mrs. Gaskell succeeds in giving her readers a point of view other than that of the rather *naïve* narrator. This has already been illustrated, incidentally, by some of our previous quotations; but it is worth while to demonstrate further. For example, Mary Smith, discussing Captain Brown's eccentricity in carrying an old lady's dinner in the street, seems to identify herself with the typical Cranford reaction—yet her words evoke quite a different response in the reader.

> . . . it was rather expected that he would pay a round of calls, on the Monday morning, to explain and apologise to the Cranford sense of propriety: but he did no such thing: and then it was decided that he was ashamed, and was keeping out of sight.[57]

A closely related point is made by Miss ffrench, who reminds us that 'Mary Smith, . . . in her character of impartial observer, is best able to display'[58] subdued irony with great effect. Though Mary's observations of and on Cranford society often acquire, for the reader, a humorous and ironic tone, Mrs. Gaskell's treatment is never satirical: perhaps 'Chaucerian' is the word to describe it.

Dr. Clara Schnurer, discussing possible literary influences on *Cranford,* remarked that it was 'her accurate transcript of minutiae'[59] which saved Mrs. Gaskell's villages from the artificiality of Goldsmith's; and went on to add that '[s]he described in full the feelings of women, the dress, the details of their domestic arrangements.'[60] While hesitating to endorse the view that feelings are fully described (the inner thoughts of no-one but Mary Smith are related), we can wholly subscribe to the commendation of Mrs. Gaskell's factual details, always seen through a woman's eyes. For instance, there is the observation

---

[56] *Works,* II, 185.
[57] *Works,* II, 12-13.
[58] ffrench, *Mrs. Gaskell,* pp. 45-46.
[59] Clara Schnurer, 'Mrs. Gaskell's Fiction', Ph.D. dissertation, University of Pittsburgh. Pennsylvania, 1932, p. 96.
[60] *Ibidem.*

of women's dresses: the attire of Miss Jessie (Brown) was 'about two pounds per annum more expensive than Miss Brown's'[61]; ' "ten pounds would have purchased every stitch she [Lady Glenmire] had on—lace and all" '[62]; Mary gave Miss Matty 'a pretty, neat, middle-aged cap'[63] instead of 'the sea-green turban'[64] she desired. Of realistic household details there are many examples, perhaps Miss Matty's alternating use of two candles[65] being among the most amusing. The following, at once humorous and accurate in its observation, is characteristic of this aspect of Mrs. Gaskell's method.

> In a few minutes tea was brought. Very delicate was the china, very old the plate, very thin the bread and butter, and very small the lumps of sugar. Sugar was evidently Mrs. Jamieson's favourite economy. I question if the little filigree sugar-tongs, made something like scissors, could have opened themselves wide enough to take up an honest, vulgar good-sized piece; and when I tried to seize two little minnikin pieces at once, so as not to be detected in too many returns to the sugar-basin, they absolutely dropped one, with a little sharp clatter, quite in a malicious and unnatural manner.[66]

For a domestic commonplace conveying a sense of both pathos and reality, we can turn to the cowslip-wine incident: Mrs. Jenkyns and Matty were preparing cowslip wine when Peter, having been thrashed by his father, came to bid good-bye before leaving home. From that time, Miss Matty remarked, she could never abide either the wine or the flowers.

> " . . . I remember, a few days after, I saw the poor, withered cowslip flowers thrown out to the leaf heap, to decay and die there. . . . "[67]

In the same connexion perhaps the saddest among the old letters was that 'little simple begging letter from Mrs. Jenkyns to Peter, addressed to him at the house of an old schoolfellow,

[61] *Works*, II, 7.
[62] *Works*, II, 91.
[63] *Works*, II, 98.
[64] *Works*, II, 98.
[65] *Works*, II, 50. This habit was apparently suggested by the candle-economy of the writer's own aunt, Mrs. Lumb—Flora Masson, 'The Gaskell Centenary. The Novelist's Career', *The Manchester Guardian*, 29 September 1910.
[66] *Works*, II, 93.
[67] *Works*, II, 64.

whither she fancied he might have gone.'[68] It had been returned unopened.

As a general summary of Mrs. Gaskell's method, the words of Dr. Adolphus Ward cannot be bettered : 'Rarely have fact and fiction—*Wahrheit und Dichtung*—been more deftly interwoven than in "Cranford,"—the joint product of quick observation, tender remembrance, and fresh imaginative power.'[69] Ward goes on to quote Thomas Arnold to the effect that Mrs. Gaskell was no mere photographer. A similar verdict appeared in Lady Thackeray Ritchie's excellent introduction to the 1891 edition of *Cranford*—an edition also memorable by reason of Hugh Thomson's illustrations, themselves an appreciative comment on the text.

> *This power of living in the lives of others* [she has been talking of *Mary Barton*] *and calling others to share the emotion, does not mean, as people sometimes imagine, that a writer copies textually from the world before her, I have heard my father say that no author worth anything, deliberately, and as a rule, copies the subject before him. And so with Mrs. Gaskell. Her early impressions were vivid and dear to her, but her world, though coloured by remembrance and sympathy, was peopled by the fresh creations of her vivid imagination, not by stale copies of the people she had known.*[70]

---

[68] *Works,* II, 67.

[69] Ward, ed. *Works,* II, p. xvi.

[70] Ritchie, pref. *Cranford,* by Mrs. Gaskell, pp. xvii-xviii. The Preface is printed in italic type.

CHAPTER IV

BESSY'S TROUBLES AT HOME (1852) TO
' THE SCHOLAR'S STORY ' (1853)

SECTION I

Bessy's Troubles at Home (1852)

In January 1852 Mrs. Gaskell's second contribution to *The Sunday School Penny Magazine*[1] began to appear. *Bessy's Troubles at Home*[2] opens as the heroine bursts in upon her mother, 'a pale, sick woman'[3], with news of having obtained a charity-order for her—thereby making the invalid's heart flutter, and causing her to choke. This stock sick-bed situation, unrelieved by any sort of imaginative rendering, is scarcely a propitious beginning to the tale; indeed the tale is really a fable, whose moral is that ' "when you want to be of service to others, don't think how to please yourself." '[4]

Mrs. Gaskell invented a plot which did what was required: it illustrated the concluding moral, without appearing too didactically contrived. Mrs. Gaskell's familiarity with the domestic conditions of her Sunday-School pupils is well exemplified by the glimpses she gives of a typical working-class household: Jem whittling his wood[5]; Bill and Mary learning their lessons[6]; Mary preparing the porridge[7]. The characters in themselves are convincing; and the dialogue is adequate. Of its kind, *Bessy's Troubles at Home* seems a good specimen. Mrs. Gaskell once[8] described the tale as 'complete rubbish', and called the children who liked it 'great geese'; on another occasion[9] she termed it

---

[1] 'Bessy's Troubles at Home', *The Sunday School Penny Magazine*, N.S. II (January-April 1852), 7-12, 21-24, 41-45, 61-64.
[2] Published for fourpence—*Hand and Heart; and Bessy's Troubles at Home*, London: Chapman and Hall, 1855.
[3] *Works,* III, 514. [5] *Works,* III, 519. [7] *Works,* III, 523.
[4] *Works,* III, 535. [6] *Works,* III, 524-525.
[8] In a letter, written to Marianne one Wednesday morning [(post 11 February) 1852], copies of which, once owned by Mr. J. T. Lancaster, are in the hands of the present writer. Chapple and Pollard date this letter (*G.L.*, No 114a), doubtless correctly, [18 February 1852].
[9] In a letter of 27 July [1854 or 1855] to an unnamed correspondent (possibly a friend of F. D. Maurice), now in the Berg collection at the New York Public Library. Chapple and Pollard put this letter (*G.L.*, No. 260) in [1855].

'rather/ good for nothing'. Nevertheless appreciation from children, for whom it was primarily designed, testifies to the measure of the story's success.

SECTION II

' The Old Nurse's Story ' (1852)

Mrs. Gaskell's first ghost story came out in the 1852 Extra Christmas Number of *Household Words*[1]; she delighted to tell such stories[2], and 'The Old Nurse's Story' is a fine example of her skill.

The primary critical point to make is that Mrs. Gaskell authenticates the supernatural by means of a realistic technique. The narration is quite straightforward. We see everything through the eyes of an old nurse, whose personality (established in the opening paragraph[3]) is not that of a highly imaginative character. As a result Mrs. Gaskell's invented supernaturalism is set forth in terms of down-to-earth observation. How the author made good use of mundane details, of factual touches entirely in keeping with the temperament of the old nurse, can best be demonstrated by a few random quotations.

> They [the orphan's guardians] were my poor young mistress's own cousin, Lord Furnivall, and Mr. Esthwaite, my master's brother, a shopkeeper in Manchester; not so well-to-do then as he was afterwards, and with a large family rising about him.[4]

> Miss Furnivall was an old lady not far from eighty, I should think, but I do not know. She was thin and tall, and had a face as full of fine wrinkles as if they had been drawn all over it with a needle's point. Her eyes were very watchful, to make up, I suppose, for her being so deaf as to be obliged to use a trumpet.[5]

---

[1] 'The Old Nurse's Story', *A Round of Stories by the Christmas Fire,* pp. 11-20.

[2] Mrs. Gaskell claimed to have herself seen a ghost, in a letter to Eliza Fox of Monday [Tuesday] 29 May 1849 (*G.L.,* No. 48), the relevant passage being quoted by Miss Haldane (*Mrs. Gaskell and Her Friends,* p. 55), whose transcript, except for omissions, follows more or less closely the copy of part of this letter in the Gaskell Section, Brotherton Collection, Leeds University Library: a full account of the incident may be found in Augustus John Cuthbert Hare, *The Story of My Life,* 6 vols., London: George Allen, 1896-1900, II (1896), 224-227.

[3] *Works,* II, 422-423.

[4] *Works,* II, 423.

[5] *Works,* II, 426.

> I thought at first, that it might be Miss Furnivall who played, unknown to Bessy; but one day, when I was in the hall by myself, I opened the organ and peeped all about it and around it, as I had done to the organ in Crosthwaite Church once before, and I saw it was all broken and destroyed inside, though it looked so brave and fine; and then, though it was noon-day, my flesh began to creep a little, and I shut it up, and run away pretty quickly to my own bright nursery; . . . [6]

In such passages, the ordinary incidentals (the prosperous Manchester shopkeeper; the ear trumpet; the organ in Crosthwaite Church) give substance and body to the narrative, provide a concrete and commonplace framework for the ghost story proper.

Not in itself complex, the plot is well managed so as to prepare for the important last scene. Mrs. Gaskell introduces the wild setting of the lonely house and its strange inhabitants (Miss Furnivall and Mrs. Stark, 'with their grey, hard faces, and their dreamy eyes, looking back into the ghastly years that were gone'[7]); goes on to add to her preliminary hints of strangeness the mysterious organ-playing of the old lord (the dead father of Miss Furnivall)[8]; proceeds to relate the extraordinary disappearance of Rosamond, and her curious tale of the other little girl in the snow and the weeping lady; and concludes with the graphically rendered climax, where the phantoms re-enact a terrible bygone scene of anger, hatred, and cruelty. Taken in its context, the final moral (' "What is done in youth can never be undone in age!" '[9]) makes a fitting ending to the tale : the spectres had haunted Miss Furnivall's mind for half a century; their ultimate materialization caused her death.

It seems appropriate, as illustrative of Mrs. Gaskell's artistic method, her mode of invention, to examine Dickens' proposals regarding the conclusion.

> A very fine ghost-story indeed. Nobly told, and wonderfully managed.
> But it strikes me (fresh from the reading) that it would be very new and very awful, if, when the narrator goes down into the parlor on that last occasion, she took up her sleeping charge in her arms, and carried it down—if the child awoke when the

[6] *Works,* II, 430.
[7] *Works,* II, 442.
[8] *Works,* II, 429-431.
[9] *Works,* II, 445.

noises began—if they all heard the noises—but *only the child*
saw the spectral figures, except that they all see the phantom
child.* I think the real child crying out what it is she sees, and
describing the phantom child as shewing it all to her as it were,
and Miss Furnivall then falling palsy-stricken, would be a very
terrific end.

What do you say to this? If you don't quite and entirely
approve, it shall stand as it does. If you do quite and entirely
approve, shall I make the necessary alteration in the last two
MS pages, or will you?

....

(*The real child in a kind of wildness to get at it all the time,
and held by the nurse.)[10]

My interpretation of this, and of Dickens' subsequent letters[11]
to Mrs. Gaskell, is that they caused Mrs. Gaskell to agree to
changes in her original conclusion so that: (1) the narrator
carried the child into the parlour; (2) the child awoke on hearing
the noises; (3) they all heard the noises; (4) the child, still held
by the nurse, wildly struggled to get at the phantom little girl
—all these incidents, of course, appear in the printed version[12].
Mrs. Gaskell, however, refused to sanction any alteration to the
effect that only the child (herself through the mediation of the
phantom girl) should see the spectres[13]. In suggesting that the
description of the spectre-figures of the old lord and the elder
Miss Furnivall be put into the mouth of the child, Dickens
weakened rather than strengthened the ending. The reason
is as follows. If the incident where Lord Furnivall drives out
his daughter and her child, with the younger Miss Furnivall
standing by in triumphant scorn, had been shown only to Rosa-

---

[10] *The Letters of Charles Dickens,* ed. Dexter, II, 428: letter to Mrs.
Gaskell of 6 November 1852.

[11] Dated 9 November 1852 (*Letters,* II, 428-429), 1 December 1852
(*Letters,* II, 433), 6 December 1852 (among the Autographs in the
General Collection at the Manchester Central Reference Library), and
17 December 1852 (*Letters,* II, 434-435).

[12] *Works,* II, 443-445.

[13] That none of Dickens' suggestions was incorporated seems the view
of Miss Hopkins—'Dickens and Mrs. Gaskell', *The Huntington Library
Quarterly,* IX (1946), 364-365; *Elizabeth Gaskell,* p. 138. In passing one
may note, perhaps with some relevance, that Miss Hopkins had not herself read the tale very closely; for she mentions that the old lady, Miss
Furnivall, had in her youth been implicated in a crime committed
'against her younger sister' (*The Huntington Library Quarterly,* IX, 364),
whereas the Miss Furnivall of the story was herself the younger sister
(*Works,* II, 439).

mond (the real child), who would then have related it to the other living people, the immediacy of this dramatic re-enactment would have been entirely lost. Instead of herself being an actor, the phantom child would have simply called up a vision of the past for the benefit of Rosamond, who would in her turn have told the others what she saw[14]. Mrs. Gaskell's graphic and forceful presentation of this powerful conclusion therefore amply justifies her refusal to follow the last of Dickens' proposals[15]. Her clear and vivid rendering of the scene is but a further instance of that eye for detail we have already so often encountered in Mrs. Gaskell's work.

[14] For a psychologico-moral explanation of Mrs. Gaskell's refusal to use the Dickens ending (namely that Mrs. Gaskell thought the guilty Miss Furnivall should see the spectres), see Hopkins, 'Dickens and Mrs. Gaskell', *The Huntington Library Quarterly*, IX, 365; *Elizabeth Gaskell*, p. 138.

[15] In a letter of 11 December 1852, declining to write for another periodical, Mrs. Gaskell remarked that she contributed to *Household Words* 'as a personal mark of respect/ & regard to Mr Dickens'. She continued: 'I choose my own subjects/ when I write, and treat/ them in the style that/ I myself prefer. But half a// dozen papers in H.W. are all/ I ever wrote for any periodical/ as I dislike & disapprove of/ such writing ∧for myself∧ as a general/ thing. /'—Extract from a letter to an unknown correspondent (in the Parrish Collection at the Princeton University Library). Chapple and Pollard read the year of this letter (*G.L.*, No. 519) as 1862; however, paleography apart, its contents seem more appropriate to 1852.

SECTION III

' The Shah's English Gardener ' (1852)

The number of *Household Words*[1] for 19 June 1852 contained 'The Schah's English Gardener'[2], in effect an expansion of notes taken during a conversation with the head gardener at Teddesley Park[3], near Penketh in Staffordshire. Mr. Burton supplied his observations of Persian life; and Mrs. Gaskell worked them up into a magazine article.

All that needs to be noted is the mass of informative detail in the account, a further indication of Mrs. Gaskell's concern for factual accuracy. Having regard to its intrinsic interest, she no doubt thought that a straightforward description seemed required; so she wisely let the facts speak for themselves. Nevertheless her engaging sense of humour is not entirely absent, as the following juxta-positioning proves.

> . . . The great-grandfather of the present Shah, Aga Mohammed, the founder of the Kujur dynasty, had large baskets-full of the eyes of his enemies presented to him after his accession to the throne.
>
> Let us change the subject to attar of roses; though all the perfumes of Arabia will not sweeten the memory of that last sentence. . . . [4]

---

[1] V, 317-321.

[2] It has the title 'The Shah's English Gardener' in Ward's Knutsford Edition (*Works*, VII).

[3] The Lord Hatherton's seat, where Mrs. Gaskell had probably stayed that year from Tuesday [30 March] to [Tuesday] 6 [April], as proposed in her Sunday afternoon [28 March 1852] letter to Meta (*G.L.*, No. 118a), copies of which, once owned by Mr. J. T. Lancaster, belong to the present writer. Mr. Burton was head gardener at Teddesley from September 1851 to May 1853, according to Lord Hatherton's estate account book; an estate cash book gives his Christian name as John: both books are in the Staffordshire County Record Office (D260/M/E/73, 54).

[4] *Works*, VII, 598-599.

145

SECTION IV

Ruth (1853)

By April 1852 Mrs. Gaskell was able to provide an outline of her next novel for Charlotte Brontë who, though she protested against the death of the heroine, seemed most favourably impressed.

> The sketch you give of your work (respecting which I am, of course, dumb) seems to me very noble; and its purpose may be as useful in practical result as it is high and just in theoretical tendency. Such a book may restore hope and energy to many who thought they had forfeited their right to both, and open a clear course for honourable effort to some who deemed that they and all honour had parted company in this world.[1]

Ruth[2] was published in January 1853[3], Miss Brontë holding back *Villette* to comply with Mrs. Gaskell's pitiful request that

---

[1] Quoted in Wise and Symington, *The Brontës: Their Lives, Friendships and Correspondence*, III, 332: letter to Mrs. Gaskell of 26 April 1852.

[2] [Elizabeth Cleghorn Gaskell] *Ruth. A Novel*, 3 vols., London: Chapman & Hall, 1853.

[3] Sanders, *Elizabeth Gaskell*, pp. 48, (Northup) 174; and Hopkins, *Elizabeth Gaskell*, p. 119. In a letter of Friday [(post 2—possibly 8—October) 1852], Mrs. Gaskell mentions Chapman's having written 'that Mr. Forster had given him the MS. of Ruth and that the first 2 vols. *were printed;*' the entire novel, according to her letter of Tuesday 20 [21] December 1852, had by then gone to the printers—the relevant quotations by Miss Haldane (*Mrs. Gaskell and Her Friends*, pp. 242, 243) tallying fairly well with the copies of parts of these letters, both to Eliza Fox, in the Gaskell Section, Brotherton Collection, Leeds University Library. Publication was to follow within a month of Edward Chapman's receiving the completed MS, by the terms of the agreement of 23 August 1852 between author and publisher—the memoranda of which being in the Parrish Collection at the Princeton University Library and in the Pierpont Morgan Library (Autographs-Miscellaneous-English). (The foregoing letters appear respectively as *G.L.*, Nos. 137, 146, Chapple and Pollard dating the first [?October 1852]; in their Appendix F they refer to the memorandum in the Pierpont Morgan Library.) John Forster's letter to Mrs. Gaskell of 21 December 1852 indicates that by that time the last of the proofs had reached him—a copy of part of this letter being in the Gaskell Section, Brotherton Collection, Leeds University Library.

it should not clash with her story[4]. Having the printed work before her, Miss Brontë saw no reason to modify her previous opinion on its social usefulness and philanthropic intention[5]. This book is, even more than *Mary Barton,* a novel with a purpose; but, as also with *Mary Barton,* the public was divided[6] —chiefly on moral grounds, for Mrs. Gaskell treats at length a *motif* we have already noted, that of the fallen woman.

The purpose of *Ruth* was both to protest against the double standard of Victorian sexual morality and at the same time to plead for a more charitable, a more truly Christian, attitude towards the 'betrayed' mother, whose child the novelist saw as a possible means of redemption rather than as a badge of shame. During her life in Manchester, Mrs. Gaskell had become acquainted with the problem of seduced girls, and done what she could on their behalf. Possibly the first letter she received from Dickens was a response to her appeal, which went by way of Mr. Burnett, 'for a pros=/=pectus of Miss Coutt's refuge for/ Female prisoners'[7]—an appeal made on behalf of 'people desirous of/ establishing a similar refuge in/ Manchester.'[8] Furthermore the earliest extant letter to Mrs. Gaskell

---

[4] See Wise and Symington, *The Brontës: Their Lives, Friendships and Correspondence,* IV, 36: letter of 19 January 1853 from Charlotte Brontë to Ellen Nussey.
[5] See Wise and Symington, *The Brontës: Their Lives, Friendships and Correspondence,* IV, 34-35, 48-49: letters to Mrs. Gaskell of 12 January 1853 and [February 1853].
[6] See Ward, ed. *Works,* III, pp. xii-xviii; van Dullemen, *Mrs. Gaskell,* pp. 200-207; Haldane, *Mrs. Gaskell and Her Friends,* pp. 62-68; *Memorials of Two Sisters,* ed. Shaen, pp. 103-104; Rubenius, *The Woman Question in Mrs. Gaskell's Life and Works,* pp. 211-216; Waller, ed. *Letters Addressed to Mrs Gaskell by Celebrated Contemporaries,* pp. 19-20; and *G.L.,* Nos. 148-154.
[7] Quoted, from a letter which Mrs. Gaskell wrote to Dickens some years later—on 8 January [1850]—, by Edgar Johnson (ed. *Letters from Charles Dickens to Angela Burdett-Coutts, 1841-1865, Selected and edited from the collection in the Pierpont-Morgan Library, with a critical and biographical introduction,* London: Jonathan Cape, 1953, p. 160), whose transcript has been checked (and slightly corrected) against the original letter—No. 640 in the Burdett-Coutts Collection (MA 1352) at the Pierpont Morgan Library: *G.L.,* No. 61.
[8] Quoted by Johnson (ed. *Letters from Charles Dickens to Angela Burdett-Coutts,* 1841-1865, p. 160), whose transcript has been checked against Mrs. Gaskell's original letter to Dickens of 8 January [1850]: *G.L.,* No. 61.

from Dickens (a letter of 9 January 1850) was 'in reply to her request for his assistance in getting an unfortunate girl off to Australia.'[9] Helped by Miss Coutts, Mrs. Gaskell seemed confident of success in this emigration scheme[10]. Here there seems a striking, perhaps a significant, parallel between fact and fiction; for the unfortunate girl, Pasley by name, resembles[11] in several ways the heroine of *Ruth*. Coming from respectable families, Ruth was an orphan and Pasley virtually so; both were apprenticed to dress-making, having mistresses who paid scant attention to the real moral well-being of their charges; pretty and not seventeen, each was seduced by a man socially her superior.

[9] Hopkins, 'Dickens and Mrs. Gaskell', *The Huntington Library Quarterly*, IX (1946), 358. This letter is in the Berg Collection at the New York Public Library (*The Huntington Library Quarterly*, IX, 358, fn. 3).

[10] In her letter to Dickens of Saturday 12 January [1850]—No. 641 in the Burdett-Coutts Collection (MA 1352) at the Pierpont Morgan Library —quoted by Johnson (ed. *Letters from Charles Dickens to Angela Burdett-Coutts*, 1841-1865, pp. 162-163): *G.L.*, No. 62. The relevant letters to Miss Coutts from Dickens of 10 January and 14 January, 1850, appear in *Letters from Charles Dickens to Angela Burdett-Coutts*, 1841-1865, ed. Johnson, pp. 159-160.

[11] According to Mrs. Gaskell's account in her letter to Dickens of 8 January [1850], quoted by Johnson (ed. *Letters from Charles Dickens to Angela Burdett-Coutts*, 1841-1865, pp. 160-162). Almost certainly Pasley is the unfortunate girl mentioned by Mrs. Gaskell when writing to Eliza Fox on Tuesday [27 November 1849]—in a letter of 26 November 1849—and on Tuesday 24 [22] January 1850; copies of parts of these two letters are in the Gaskell Section, Brotherton Collection, Leeds University Library, relevant and fairly accurate quotations being given by Miss Rubenius (*The Woman Question in Mrs. Gaskell's Life and Works*, p. 56, fn. 1), though she misdates the second letter and does not seem to realize that only one girl is involved. Neither reference adds anything pertinent for a comparison with Ruth. (These three letters appear respectively as *G.L.*, Nos. 61, 55, 63.) In this connexion it is interesting that Mrs. Esther Hare should have written to Mrs. Gaskell: 'Your letter pleasantly confirms the conviction I felt on reading Ruth, that your own experience of life had taught you the truths which you have so frankly expressed.'— a copy of this letter of 12 March 1853 being found in Shorter and Symington, 'Correspondence, Articles & Notes Relating to Mrs. E. C. Gaskell. Transcripts', Vol. II, Section of Extracts from Letters Relating to Mrs. Gaskell and Her Work (a typescript in the Gaskell Section, Brotherton Collection, Leeds University Library). On the other hand, doubtless after consulting the author who was with her at the time, Mlle Ida Mohl wrote to her aunt, Mme Mary Mohl: 'J'ai lu Ruth ces jours ci, Dieu que c'est triste, cela a l'air de si vrai, pourtant c'est tout de son invention.'—this extract from her Heidelberg letter of 4 November 1858 having been made by Miss Jane Revere Coolidge (subsequently Mrs. Whitehill) before the destruction of the Mohl letters during World War II.

Ruth attempted suicide, Pasley confessed to having hoped for death; later each encountered her seducer in unexpected circumstances. Clearly Mrs. Gaskell had little need to fabricate events such as resulted in Ruth's unhappy plight; she had but to observe and listen to the ones she tried to aid.

Yet, as far as its central theme is concerned, *Ruth* is not artistically a success : invention fails in its attempt to come to the aid of morality. Mrs. Gaskell commenced her work rather ill-equipped for what lay before her : in the nature of things she lacked first-hand experience of seduction, and her imagination could not supply the deficiency. It was not so much a Victorian concern for the exigences of family reading which made her gloss over the essential details—she recognized that, reticent as it was, *Ruth* must be a forbidden book in her own household[12]—it was rather her personal inability to deal with the London period, during which Ruth lost her virtue. Mrs. Gaskell completely shirked the difficulty. Chapter IV closes with Ruth's departure with Mr. Bellingham for a destination unknown to her; the next chapter opens, several months later, with the arrival of Ruth and Mr. Bellingham in a little North Wales village. By omitting any treatment (psychological or otherwise) of the important intervening events, Mrs. Gaskell makes much of her subsequent study of Ruth's spiritual and moral regeneration somewhat meaningless. Before her seduction the heroine is presented as an innocent child, scarcely conscious of there being anything ethically wrong in her association with Mr. Bellingham; after her seduction she seems unaware that she is living in sin, the realization of which is gradually forced upon her by the reactions of others. Thereafter her life with the Bensons appears as a process of purification; but it is a period of repentance for a sin she can herself only describe as such

---

[12] As she told her sister-in-law, Mrs. Nancy Robson, in a [(pre 27) January 1853] letter (*G.L.*, No. 148), most of which is in the possession of Mrs. Margaret Trevor Jones (quotations—from the somewhat inaccurate, though complete, copy in the Gaskell Section, Brotherton Collection, Leeds University Library—appearing in Hopkins, *Elizabeth Gaskell,* pp. 123-124; and Rubenius, *The Woman Question in Mrs. Gaskell's Life and Works,* p. 213, fn. 1): however Mrs. Gaskell seems to have had in mind careful guidance rather than absolute proscription, at least as far as her eldest child was concerned; for she added that she meant to read the novel 'with MA/ some quiet time or other'.

long after its commission. Admittedly Mrs. Gaskell does, in large measure, make plausible and convincing the period of moral goodness and redemption; yet this success is achieved because she knew from her own religious experience what Christian penance and good works were like, not because she could appreciate, could fully enter into, the state of mind which would result from that particular kind of fall from virtue with which *Ruth* is primarily concerned. Mrs. Gaskell's artistic unsureness, her failure of nerve in regard to the central issue, in regard to the very *raison d'être* of the novel, may have been in Clough's mind when he described the book to Miss Blanche Smith as "rather cowardly—and 'pokey' in its views"[13] : his modification of this opinion is really little more than a rephrasing which takes into account good intentions while underlining the questionable nature of the religious psychology.

> I don't say it is what I called it yesterday [19 April 1853]—it is really very good—but it *is* a little too timid—I think—. Ruth did well—but there is also another way and a more hopeful way —Such at least is my feeling—I do not think she has got the whole truth—I do not think that such overpowering humiliation should be the result in the soul of the not *really guilty*, though misguided, girl any more than it should be, justly, in the judgement of the world— . . . [14]

Characteristically Mrs. Gaskell made the illegitimate child of the union the instrument for Ruth's redemption—an instance of maternal feelings finding literary expression. The child, Leonard, has been called 'a neurotic little prig'[15]; and the scene where Ruth reveals to him the facts of his birth has been condemned as '[m]ost unnatural'[16]—even though Charlotte Brontë thought it heart-piercing[17]. Seldom is the boy considered apart from his mother. The novelist sought mainly to present Leonard through Ruth's eyes; and, influenced by memories of her own children, Mrs. Gaskell's—as distinct from Ruth's—sentiments often

[13] *The Correspondence of Arthur Hugh Clough,* ed. Frederick Ludwig Mulhauser, 2 vols., Oxford: The Clarendon Press, 1957, II, 417.

[14] *The Correspondence of Arthur Hugh Clough,* ed. Mulhauser, II, 418: my square brackets.

[15] ffrench, *Mrs. Gaskell,* p. 53.

[16] Van Dullemen, *Mrs. Gaskell,* p. 126.

[17] See Wise and Symington, *The Brontës: Their Lives, Friendships and Correspondence,* IV, 48: letter of [February 1853] to Mrs. Gaskell.

coloured the presentation. The tone of the following passage,
for example, recalls that of *"My Diary"*.

> "Ah, my darling!" said Ruth, falling back weak and weary. "If
> God will but spare you to me, never mother did more than I
> will. I have done you a grievous wrong—but, if I may but live,
> I will spend my life in serving you!"
> "And in serving God!" said Miss Benson, with tears in her
> eyes. "You must not make him into an idol, or God will,
> perhaps, punish you through him."
> A pang of affright shot through Ruth's heart at these words; had
> she already sinned and made her child into an idol, and was there
> punishment already in store for her through him? But then the
> internal voice whispered that God was "Our Father," and that
> He knew our frame, and knew how natural was the first outburst
> of a mother's love; so, although she treasured up the warning,
> she ceased to affright herself for what had already gushed forth.[18]

However the book contains more objective observations, indicating Mrs. Gaskell's knowledge of child psychology. When
Leonard tells a falsehood, the authoress—but not her characters
—is aware of fantasy as natural at a certain stage of development[19]; and the picture of the little Bradshaw girls, with their
curiosity about the relationship between Mr. Farquhar and
their sister[20], seems equally true.

'The inner side of Dissenting life is very cleverly pourtrayed.'[21]
This judgement by Baron Bunsen points to an especial excellence in *Ruth*. Although the social purpose may not be altogether successful, the picture of Nonconformity is a fine achievement. Here Mrs. Gaskell, without any inhibiting factors, could
describe what she had observed, as a minister's wife, from the
inside.

In this world Mr. Bradshaw is the most prominent figure, a
figure whose various prototypes (we may assume him to be a
composite character) Mrs. Gaskell must have met almost daily
in the course of her 'ministerial' life. Without being bitingly
satirical, she neatly conveys her own attitude—ironical yet in

---

[18] *Works*, III, 161.
[19] *Works*, III, 200.
[20] *Works*, III, 215-217.
[21] Quoted in Shaen, ed. *Memorials of Two Sisters*, p. 99. A Muscovite
priest of the Greek Orthodox Church surprised Arthur Stanley by his
knowledge of the relations between Dissenting ministers and their congre-
gations—a knowledge gained from *Ruth* (*Gaskell-Norton Letters*, ed.
Whitehill, p. 15: *G.L.*, No. 384).

some ways appreciative—to the patronizing pew-renter, the moralizing utilitarian, the self-righteous Nonconformist, the politician with a tender conscience who looked the other way when shady methods were mentioned. Herself emotionally uninvolved, the novelist's observation was objective and detached. A few quotations will illustrate the manner, at once descriptive and evaluative, by which she creates Bradshaw both as a Dissenting type and as an individual in his own right.

> . . . then all the congregation stood up, and sang aloud, Mr. Bradshaw's great bass voice being half a note in advance of the others, in accordance with his place of precedence as principal member of the congregation. His powerful voice was like an organ very badly played, and very much out of tune; but as he had no ear, and no diffidence, it pleased him very much to hear the fine loud sound.[22]

> The first evening spent at Mr. Bradshaw's passed like many succeeding visits there. There was tea, the equipage for which was as handsome and as ugly as money could purchase. Then the ladies produced their sewing, while Mr. Bradshaw stood before the fire, and gave the assembled party the benefit of his opinions on many subjects. The opinions were as good and excellent as the opinions of any man can be who sees one side of a case very strongly, and almost ignores the other.[23]

> Stained by no vice himself, either in his own eyes or in that of any human being who cared to judge him, having nicely and wisely proportioned and adapted his means to his ends, he could afford to speak and act with a severity which was almost sanctimonious in its ostentation of thankfulness as to himself.[24]

We may conclude by quoting the paragraph where Mrs. Gaskell records his characteristic reactions on hearing that a clerk from the Star Insurance Company is waiting to see him—a clerk who may bring information proving Bradshaw's son fraudulent. It admirably suggests in its commonplace yet significant detail the fundamental fibre of the man.

> When the errand-boy had closed the door, Mr. Bradshaw went to a cupboard where he usually kept a glass and a bottle of wine (of which he very seldom partook, for he was an abstemious man). He intended now to take a glass, but the bottle was empty;

[22] *Works,* III, 152.
[23] *Works,* III, 187.
[24] *Works,* III, 209.

and, though there was plenty more to be had for ringing, or even
simply going into another room, he would not allow himself to
do this. He stood and lectured himself in thought.[25]

A very different aspect of Dissent is represented by the Rev.
Thurston Benson and his sister, Faith. In characterizing Mr.
Benson, Mrs. Gaskell probably drew less on her knowledge of
Mr. Gaskell than on memories of Mr. Stevenson, who was himself for a time a Unitarian preacher[26]. Between Mr. Benson
and Mr. Hale (the clergyman in *North and South*) there is no
very close over-all parallelism; yet the former is at least akin
to the latter in his tendency to introspection, his scrupulous
conscience, and his preference for lengthy theoretical consideration rather than immediate practical action. Mrs. Gaskell's
attitude to Thurstan Benson's moral qualities is ambivalent. On
the one hand, she portrays him as a minister of God, a Christian in the fullest sense of the word : he brings, in the best
Nonconformist tradition, the poor to his chapel, 'drawn there
by love for Mr. Benson's character, and by a feeling that the
faith which made him what he was could not be far wrong'[27].
On the other hand, she clearly condemns[28] that lack of faith
which caused him to condone a falsehood when Ruth was
passed off as a widow to all the members of his congregation.
In this respect Mrs. Gaskell's treatment of the minister is indicative of her inability to arrive at a satisfactory solution to
the problem of the fallen woman. If society at large had held
different views, then the pure Christianity of Mr. Benson would
never have been soiled by falsehood. As things were, he considered it too cruel that she should bear the social consequences
of her sin. Ruth's re-instatement by means of her typhus-
nursing is, in effect, a shrinking from, and a shirking of, the
difficulty. Since Mrs. Gaskell (and Mr. Benson) rescued Ruth
from suicide only to attend at her death-bed, the novelist
virtually confesses her failure to improve upon Goldsmith's
advice to the lovely woman who stoops to folly and finds too
late that men betray.

[25] *Works,* III, 395.
[26] Ward, ed. *Works,* I, p. xvi; Chadwick, *Mrs. Gaskell,* pp. 3-4; and
Sanders, *Elizabeth Gaskell,* pp. 1-2.
[27] *Works,* III, 151-152.
[28] *Works,* III, 121, 344-345.

When dealing with the minister's household affairs, Mrs. Gaskell had no socio-moral problems to encounter, and was fully able to exploit that inside knowledge afforded by her position, as both the wife of the Rev. William Gaskell and, in her own right, an experienced household-manager. She can well appreciate the position of Miss Benson, whose brother (like her own husband[29]) spent much of his time in 'the solitary comfort of his study'[30]. Faith's essentially practical nature is akin to Mrs. Gaskell's. Although the economies necessary in consequence of Mr. Benson's reduced income, after Ruth lost her post as governess, were not elegant in the *Cranford* sense, Mrs. Gaskell used a method similar to that employed in the earlier work : there is the same eye for detail, the same observation of *minutiae*. She points to the replacing of the parlour carpet by a large hearth rug[31]; mentions the change from a meat to a vegetable diet[32]; and recalls Cranford ways by referring to the candle on either side of which sat Faith and Ruth[33]. This feeling for domestic detail is excellently illustrated in the picture she gives of the Benson establishment, describing the architectural lay-out of the place as well as its furnishings and atmosphere. Bearing in mind that this house compares exactly with the one where, as Miss Stevenson, she had enjoyed Newcastle hospitality from the Rev. William Turner[34], we may legitimately take the following scene autobiographically.

> The curtains were drawn in the parlour; there was a bright fire and a clean hearth; indeed, exquisite cleanliness seemed the very spirit of the household, for the door which was open to the kitchen showed a delicately-white and spotless floor, and bright glittering tins, on which the ruddy fire-light danced.
> From the place in which Ruth sat she could see all Sally's movements; and though she was not conscious of close or minute observation at the time (her body being weary, and her mind full of other thoughts), yet it was curious how faithfully that scene remained depicted on her memory in after years.[35]

[29] *Gaskell-Norton Letters,* ed. Whitehill, p. 7: *G.L.,* No. 374—see too No. 570.
[30] *Works,* III, 378.
[31] *Works,* III, 374.
[32] *Works,* III, 377.
[33] *Works,* III, 378.
[34] Chadwick, *Mrs. Gaskell,* pp. 106-107.
[35] *Works,* III, 135.

Sally, one of Mrs. Gaskell's very successfully created servant-characters, fully deserves Charlotte Brontë's praise—"an 'apple of gold,' deserving to be 'set in a picture of silver.' "[36] Mrs. Gaskell's knowledge of servants resulted from practical experience in domestic management—we remember that 'her actual household cares were a positive delight to her'[37]; that she 'trained a succession of young women into first-rate cooks'[38]; and that the Gaskells' 'own old dear English Hearn'[39] was with the family for half a century[40]. Embarrassed by riches, one can mention only a few respects in which Mrs. Gaskell shows her readers Sally's vitality. There is, to begin, the graphic initial description of the Bensons' maid[41]; there is the comic account of how she received her first proposal which, though sorely tempted by the chance to use her ham-curing recipe, she declined[42]; there is her amusing yet moving recollection of how she had had her will drawn up so as to contain as many law-words as possible, but in a phrasing which left all to Mr. Benson and his sister[43]; there is the heroic sacrifice of her savings-withdrawal when the Bensons were in straitened circumstances[44] (one remembers that Miss Matty's servant was equally steadfast in her mistress's hour of need[45]); there is her conscious superiority over Dissenters and their ways from the knowledge that her father was a parish clerk[46]. As a further help to establishing Sally as one of the most memorable and lovable characters in *Ruth,* her dialectal speech is both racy and vigorous. For example, on learning that her mistress has disgraced her by appearing before the rector in old attire, in clothes unworthy of the mistress of the late parish-clerk's daughter, she breaks forth, casting aside Faith's excuse that she had been working and that the call was unexpected.

[36] Quoted in Wise and Symington, *The Brontës: Their Lives, Friendships and Correspondence,* IV, 35: letter to Mrs. Gaskell of 12 January 1853.

[37] *Memorials of Two Sisters,* ed. Shaen, p. 24.

[38] *Memorials of Two Sisters,* ed. Shaen, p. 24.

[39] *Gaskell-Norton Letters,* ed. Whitehill, p. 25: *G.L.,* No. 401.

[40] Chadwick, *Mrs. Gaskell,* p. 150.

[41] *Works,* III, 133-136.

[42] *Works,* III, 164-169.

[43] *Works,* III, 192-194.

[44] *Works,* III, 375-377.

[45] *Works,* II, 154-156, 160-163.

[46] *Works,* III, 165.

"You might ha' letten me do the jelly; I'se warrant I could ha'
pleased Ruth as well as you. If I had but known he was coming,
I'd ha' slipped round the corner and bought ye a neckribbon, or
summut to lighten ye up. I'se loth he should think I'm living
with Dissenters, that don't know how to keep themselves trig and
smart."[47]

Besides Newcastle-on-Tyne, which provided material for the
Eccleston section of *Ruth* (even the typhus-fever was probably
based on the 1831 Asiatic cholera epidemic which may have
caused Miss Stevenson to leave the town[48]), Knutsford, Silverdale, and Wales are all of some importance. Knutsford's chief
contribution was the picturesque description of Brook Street
Chapel[49]—a description which brought vividly before Mrs.
Stanley (the Bishop's wife, the Dean's mother) "the old chapel
on Adam's Hill at Knutsford . . . —the diamond-paned windows, overshadowing tree, and outside steps."[50] To the accuracy
of Mrs. Gaskell's observation yet further testimony is borne by
a former minister of Brook Street Chapel, the Rev. George A.
Payne[51].

The importance of Silverdale as the prototype of Abermouth
finds visible confirmation in the frontispiece to the third volume
of the Knutsford Edition (*Ruth and Other Tales*, &c.), since
there Dr. Adolphus Ward used a water-colour by Meta Gaskell
to illustrate 'The "Abermouth" Sands'. Meta, like the other
daughters, spent happy summers with her mother at Lindeth
Tower, Silverdale, and in all possibility it was during one of
these holiday visits that she painted her picture. Mrs. Gaskell's
descriptive excellence, her poetic regard for seascape and landscape, her ability to suggest the atmosphere of a locality, all this
rightly deserves the reader's appreciation. What one remembers
about the meeting on the sands between Ruth and Bellingham
(the scene where he proposes marriage) is not so much the words
spoken, the emotions felt, the moral considerations involved—
not, in other words, those very things which were of importance

---

[47] *Works*, III, 432.
[48] Chadwick, *Mrs. Gaskell,* pp. 116-117.
[49] *Works*, III, 150-151. There is a passage in *Mary Barton* where
possibly Mrs. Gaskell had the same chapel in mind (*Works*, I, 312).
[50] Quoted, from her letter to Mrs. Gaskell of 12 March 1853, by
Ward (ed. *Works*, III, p. xvi).
[51] *Mrs. Gaskell and Knutsford,* 1905, pp. 34-36.

for *Ruth* as a social-problem novel, for *Ruth* as a book with a
purpose—but rather 'the grey, silvery rocks, which sloped away
into brown moorland, interspersed with a field here and there
of golden, waving corn'[52]; the 'purple hills, with sharp, clear
outlines, touching the sky'[53]; 'the ceaseless murmur of the salt
sea waves'[54]. Mrs. Gaskell's keen eye for natural objects, her
close and sympathetic observation, and her sensitivity to the
moods of the sea can be illustrated by a few sentences, poetic
in their power of evocation.

> The tide had turned; the waves were slowly receding, as if loth
> to lose the hold they had, so lately, and with such swift bounds,
> gained on the yellow sands. The eternal moan they have made
> since the world began filled the ear, broken only by the skirl of
> the grey sea-birds as they alighted in groups on the edge of the
> waters, or as they rose up with their measured, balancing motion,
> and the sunlight caught their white breasts. There was no sign
> of human life to be seen; no boat, or distant sail, or near shrimper.
> The black posts there were all that spoke of men's work or labour.
> Beyond a stretch of the waters, a few pale grey hills showed like
> films; their summits clear, though faint, their bases lost in a
> vapoury mist.[55]

Dr. Adolphus Ward's other illustration is appropriately of the
Vale of Ffestiniog—visited by Mrs. Gaskell on her honeymoon[56];
it was here that Marianne contracted the scarlet fever which
was to kill her little brother[57]. The dual nature of Mrs. Gaskell's
association with Ffestiniog has a parallel in the novel, where it
is a scene of both joy and sadness. Mrs. Gaskell's delight in
mountainous scenery finds ample expression in the Welsh sections[58]; for she could appreciate the grandeur and majesty, as
well as the softer aspects, of nature. With this appreciation went
delicacy of perception and observation: Ruth, for example,
even in the midst of the agony which followed Bellingham's
desertion, then noticed and long afterwards 'remembered the
exact motion of a bright green beetle busily meandering among
the wild thyme near her, and she recalled the musical, balanced,
wavering drop of a skylark into her nest, near the heather-bed
where she lay.'[59] It is this sort of truth—to nature as well as

---

[52] *Works,* III, 292.   [54] *Works,* III, 293.   [55] *Works,* III, 292-293.
[53] *Works,* III, 292.
[56] See, for instance, Hopkins, *Elizabeth Gaskell,* pp. 51, 54.
[57] See, for instance, Hopkins, *Elizabeth Gaskell,* p. 66.
[58] E.g. *Works,* III, 64.   [59] *Works,* III, 93.

to psychology—which authenticates the reality of Ruth's feelings of despair after Bellingham's desertion.

The other consequence of Mrs. Gaskell's Welsh experience was to bring her forward as authoress-commentator, usually with unfortunate results. For instance, in the passage given below, the concluding sentence is worse than redundant: first-hand observation makes its presence felt in the very wording of the description; the dismal autobiographic ending serves only to mar what has gone before.

> He led the way into a large bow-windowed room, which looked gloomy enough that afternoon, but which I have seen bright and bouyant with youth and hope within, and sunny lights creeping down the purple mountain slope, and stealing over the green, soft meadows, till they reached the little garden, full of roses and lavender-bushes, lying close under the window. I have seen— but I shall see no more.[60]

If autobiographic comments, directly imported into a descriptive passage, are artistically out of place, even more out of keeping are Mrs. Gaskell's explicit authorial remarks upon the moral situation. This didacticism leads at best to redundancy, at worst to bathos. Often she anticipates the outcome of actions by her comments on them; and the seriousness of her approach prevents that irony of tone or consideration *sub specie aeternitatis* which might, in a different writer, have provided the justification for such obtrusiveness. Her invention, her imaginative powers, her grasp of her materials were, it seems, insufficient to allow the story to present its own message—that, though transgressors inevitably suffer by breaking the laws of God, the human response should always be one of charity. Mrs. Gaskell felt she must herself point the moral, and personally underline the need for a fully Christian attitude towards women like Ruth. There are very many instances of this; an examination of two will suffice to indicate its artistic dangers.

When Ruth and Mr. Bellingham revisit Ruth's former home, they meet old Thomas, once her father's servant. Mrs. Gaskell makes good use of this character, whom she presents realistically before the reader. Bellingham's disdainful manner to him hints at flaws in his own nature, whereas Ruth's child-like misinterpretation of Thomas's Biblical quotation (concerning the devil's

[60] *Works*, III, 63.

going about as a roaring lion seeking whom he may devour)
shows an innocent non-comprehension of the potential dangers
of her *liaison* with Bellingham. Nevertheless, despite this success,
Mrs. Gaskell must needs add a moralizing tail-piece.

> The poor old labourer prayed long and earnestly that night for
> Ruth. He called it "wrestling for her soul;" and I think that his
> prayers were heard, for "God judgeth not as man judgeth."[61]

A further illustration of the same fault occurs as a comment
on the decision of Thurstan and Faith to pass Ruth off as a
widow. The dialogue has been convincing, the argument for
the deception forcefully clinched by Faith's reference to the
illegitimate Thomas Wilkins, who threw down the register containing the facts of his birth and baptism. Then Mrs. Gaskell
indulges in a piece of rhetorical moralizing, whose phraseology
brings to mind the endeavours of the author who, said Catherine
Winkworth, carefully went over the last hundred pages 'to
take out superfluous epithets and sentences, of which there were
certainly enough . . . to give . . . a slightly sentimental twang.'[62]

---

[61] *Works,* III, 50-51.
[62] *Letters and Memorials of Catherine Winkworth,* I (ed. Her Sister
[Susanna Winkworth], 1883), 369. Cf. 'I am so glad you liked "Ruth." I
was so anxious about her, and took so much pains over writing it, that
I lost my own power of judging, and could not tell whether I had done
it well or ill. I only knew how very close to my heart it had come from.
I tried to make both the story and the writing as quiet as I could, in
order that "people" (my great bugbear) might not say that they could not
see what the writer felt to be a very plain and earnest truth, for romantic
incidents or exaggerated writing.'—Extract from Mrs. Gaskell's letter of
10 February [1853] to Monckton Milnes, quoted in Thomas Wemyss Reid,
*The Life, Letters, and Friendships of Richard Monckton Milnes, First
Lord Houghton,* 2nd edn, 2 vols., London, Paris & Melbourne: Cassell
& Company, Limited, 1890, I, 481. (The first edition appeared in 1890.)
Mrs. Gaskell's distrust in her own critical powers led her, perhaps mistakenly, to ask assistance from friends: on 25 March 1851 Catherine
Winkworth wrote to her sister, Mrs. Emma Shaen, 'I can't help fearing
that Mr. Forster and we shall spoil "Ruth" in itself, as well as for ourselves, by talking it all over with Lily as it goes on, and being summoned
to give judgment and advice upon it.'—*Letters and Memorials of Catherine Winkworth,* I, 285. Forster himself wrote to reassure the novelist that
every part he had read measured up to the work's conception and purpose,
that she was quite right in taking the pains she did, and that he detected
nothing false or exaggerated, all such temptations having been foreborne
—a copy of part of his letter (though without any indication of its date)
being in the Gaskell Section, Brotherton Collection, Leeds University
Library. (Mrs. Gaskell's letter to Milnes appears as *G.L.,* No. 152.)

Ah, tempter! unconscious tempter! Here was a way of evading the trials for the poor little unborn child, of which Mr. Benson had never thought. It was the decision—the pivot, on which the fate of years moved; and he turned it the wrong way. But it was not for his own sake. For himself, he was brave enough to tell the truth; for the little helpless baby, about to enter a cruel, biting world, he was tempted to evade the difficulty. He forgot what he had just said, of the discipline and the penance to the mother consisting in strengthening her child to meet, trustfully and bravely, the consequences of her own weakness. He remembered more clearly the wild fierceness, the Cain-like look, of Thomas Wilkins, as the obnoxious word in the baptismal registry told him that he must go forth branded into the world, with his hand against every man's, and every man's against him.[63]

The closely related stylistic mannerism of using 'loaded' epithets to convey religious and ethical attitudes is an unfortunate by-product of Mrs. Gaskell's doctrinal explicitness. One especially notices such terminology when she is treating the mother-child relationship in the manner of a maternal moralist who sees therein the means for Ruth's redemption. It is, however, remarkable that Mrs. Gaskell should, in a moment of insight, allow the worldly lawyer, Hickson, to make the very criticism that could with justice be raised against parts of her own writing.

"... I say once more, if Mr. Donne is the man for your purpose, and your purpose is a good one, a lofty one, a holy one" (for Mr. Hickson remembered the Dissenting character of his little audience, and privately considered the introduction of the word "holy" a most happy hit), ... [64]

The introduction of such words as 'holy' was, in the author's case, usually the reverse of a happy hit[65].

Taken as a whole, the structure of *Ruth* is very weak; the work fails as an artistic unity. Mrs. Gaskell's over-all inventing and plotting, intended to serve a specific religious and moral purpose, did not succeed in embodying that purpose in the substance of the book. She shirked the seduction, and thereby made the account of Ruth's redemption lack its very *raison d'être*. Nevertheless there are passages which stand out by virtue

[63] *Works,* III, 121.
[64] *Works,* III, 252-253.
[65] For example, in *Works,* III, 99 ('holy words'), 127 (' "no holy or self-denying effort" '), 140 ('holy ground').

N

of the imaginative perception which went to their making,
passages which bear the mark of Mrs. Gaskell's genius, which
illustrate her eye for the significant. Of these the most memorable is that describing a gargoyle in the Abermouth church,
noticed by Ruth in the midst of the mental turmoil which
resulted from her re-encountering Bellingham (*alias* Donne)
many years after he had left her abandoned in Wales. This is
the finest single piece we can quote from *Ruth*, being the product
of a poetic sensibility more than once displayed in that novel.
We see Mrs. Gaskell entering into her heroine's mind, observing
the face with Ruth's eyes, conveying the indefinable yet powerful meaning which this sculptured countenance possessed for
the tormented girl.

> When they sat down for the reading of the first lesson, Ruth
> turned the corner of the seat so as no longer to be opposite to
> him [Bellingham]. She could not listen. The words seemed to be
> uttered in some world far away, from which she was exiled and
> cast out: their sound, and yet more their meaning, was dim and
> distant. But in this extreme tension of mind to hold in her be-
> wildered agony, it so happened that one of her senses was pre-
> ternaturally acute. While all the church and the people swam
> in misty haze, one point in a dark corner grew clearer and clearer
> till she saw (what at another time she could not have discerned at
> all) a face—a gargoyle I think they call it—at the end of the arch
> next to the narrowing of the nave into the chancel, and in the
> shadow of that contraction. The face was beautiful in feature
> (the next to it was a grinning monkey), but it was not the features
> that were the most striking part. There was a half-open mouth,
> not in any way distorted out of its exquisite beauty by the intense
> expression of suffering it conveyed. Any distortion of the face by
> mental agony implies that a struggle with circumstance is going
> on. But in this face, if such struggle had been, it was over now.
> Circumstance had conquered; and there was no hope from mortal
> endeavour, or help from mortal creature, to be had. But the eyes
> looked onward and upward to the "hills from whence cometh our
> help." And though the parted lips seemed ready to quiver with
> agony, yet the expression of the whole face, owing to these
> strange, stony, and yet spiritual eyes, was high and consoling. If
> mortal gaze had never sought its meaning before, in the deep
> shadow where it had been placed long centuries ago, yet Ruth's
> did now. Who could have imagined such a look? Who could
> have witnessed—perhaps felt—such infinite sorrow and yet dared
> to lift it up by Faith into a peace so pure? Or was it a mere
> conception? If so, what a soul the unknown carver must have had;
> for creator and handicraftsman must have been one; no two minds
> could have been in such perfect harmony. Whatever it was—how-
> ever it came there—imaginer, carver, sufferer, all were long

passed away. Human art was ended—human life done—human
suffering over; but this remained; it stilled Ruth's beating heart
to look on it.[66]

It would be misleading if one were not to emphasize the
exceptional quality of this extract as against the general level
of the book. It seems wise, therefore, to give a more typical
instance of Mrs. Gaskell's sensitive observation. In the following
quotation we may note how the details the author chooses are
at once factually and artistically right for their context—that of
Ruth expectantly waiting outside Bellingham's sick-room.

A soft grey oblong of barred light fell on the flat wall opposite
to the windows, and deeper grey shadows marked out the tracery
of the plants, more graceful thus than in reality. Ruth crouched
where no light fell. She sat on the ground close by the door; her
whole existence was absorbed in listening: all was still; it was
only her heart beating with the strong, heavy, regular sound of
a hammer. She wished she could stop its rushing, incessant clang.
She heard a rustle of a silken gown, and knew it ought not to
have been worn in a sick-room; for her senses seemed to have
passed into the keeping of the invalid, and to feel only as he
felt.[67]

Another instance of Mrs. Gaskell's ability to seize on essential
details is her admirable power of making change meaningful,
of giving reality to the passage of time: the wild hop Mr.
Benson had planted when Leonard was but a child in arms
grew to become 'a garland over the casement'[68]; the iron-grey
hair of Mr. Bradshaw turned white during the period his pew
was unoccupied[69]; when Ruth first arrived in Eccleston, the

---

[66] *Works*, III, 279-280. The passage may connect, albeit somewhat
tenuously, with Mrs. Gaskell's description of 'an exquisitely painted picture
of a dead child . . . with the most woeful expression of pain on its little
wan face, . . . too deeply stamped to be lost even in Heaven . . . not the
quiet lovely expression of angelic rest, but the look of despairing agony'
—her description of this picture, owned by Bishop Lee of Manchester,
appearing in a letter to Eliza Fox of 26 April 1850 (a copy of part of
which is in the Gaskell Section, Brotherton Collection, Leeds University
Library): *G.L.*, No. 70. Mrs. Gaskell's portrayal of the gargoyle—'which
symbolizes for Ruth a hope and a peace'—is considered 'an almost Hardy-
like leap of the imagination' by Edgar Wright (*Mrs. Gaskell: The Basis
for Reassessment*, London, New York, and Toronto: Oxford University
Press, 1965, p. 78—hereafter cited as *Mrs. Gaskell*).

[67] *Works*, III, 82.

[68] *Works*, III, 206.

[69] *Works*, III, 418.

Bensons' neighbour could take walks with his daughter, yet with 'the lapse of life and time'[70] he became permanently confined to a 'large, cushioned easy-chair'[71].

There has been, in several of our quotations, a poetic quality. Certain descriptions carry significance beneath the surface observation; some suggest that gentle melancholy which is at times present in Mrs. Gaskell's writings, a nostalgic longing and regret; others point to a delicacy of perception, and illustrate the author's *penchant* for the picturesque. It may be appropriate, therefore, to consider a closely related tendency— Mrs. Gaskell's attraction to popular superstitions and customs. The landlady at Llan-dhu remarks to Ruth that the turning point for sick people never falls on an even number of days, but rather ' "on the third, or the fifth, or the seventh, or so on" '[72]; Sally scolds Leonard's mother for bringing ill-luck by shedding salt tears on him before he has been weaned[73]. The most interesting example, however, occurs when Thurston Benson, having told Ruth of his love of Welsh traditions and legends (some of which being ' "very fine and awe-inspiring, others very poetic and fanciful" '[74]), relates the beliefs surrounding the foxglove. Illuminating, in a study of how Mrs. Gaskell's own interests and experiences found expression in her work, is the parallelism between the incident just mentioned and an anecdote in one of the author's letters. Recalling the use made of Charlotte Brontë's proverb in 'The Heart of John Middleton', we may note this further instance of Mrs. Gaskell's invention providing a context which could, with little difficulty, incorporate something that had years before caught her fancy. A lengthy quotation will facilitate close comparison.

> "For instance," said he, touching a long bud-laden stem of foxglove in the hedge-side, at the bottom of which one or two crimson-speckled flowers were bursting from their green sheaths, "I dare say, you don't know what makes this fox-glove bend and sway so gracefully. You think it is blown by the wind, don't you?" He looked at her with a grave smile, which did not enliven his thoughtful eyes, but gave an inexpressible sweetness to his face.

[70] *Works,* III, 389.
[71] *Works,* III, 389.
[72] *Works,* III, 81.
[73] *Works,* III, 172.
[74] *Works,* III, 68.

"I always thought it was the wind. What is it?" asked Ruth innocently.

"Oh, the Welsh tell you that this flower is sacred to the fairies, and that it has the power of recognising them, and all spiritual beings who pass by, and that it bows in deference to them as they waft along. Its Welsh name is Maneg Ellyllyn—the good people's glove; and hence, I imagine, our folk's-glove or fox-glove."[75]

"I was once saying to an old, blind country-woman how much I admired the foxglove. She looked mysteriously solemn as she told me they were not like other flowers; they had 'knowledge' in them! Of course I inquired more particularly, and then she told me that the foxglove knows when a spirit passes by and always bows the head. Is not this poetical! and of the regal foxglove with its tapering crimson bells. I have respected the flower ever since."[76]

To conclude our examination of *Ruth,* it is necessary for the sake of the thematic and typological aspect of Mrs. Gaskell's invention at least to note, albeit in a cursory and miscellaneous manner, some of those *motifs* and character-figures, found in this book, which appear elsewhere in Mrs. Gaskell's writings.

Most important as regards the plot is the lie told by the Bensons in their pretence that Ruth was a young widow. From the outset Mrs. Gaskell makes known her own disapproval of this deceit[77]. Later the conversation between Mr. Bradshaw and Mr. Benson[78] when the secret is out demonstrates the usual Gaskell moral : that lying, even with the intent that good may come, is scarcely defensible—nor indeed is good likely to come. In some form or other the lie *motif* occurs in several of Mrs. Gaskell's works; for example, in her next major novels, *North and South* and *Sylvia's Lovers*, there is a failure to tell the truth on the part of respectively the heroine and the 'hero'.

The situation of the worldly yet morally weak brother with a more virtuous sister, already seen in *The Moorland Cottage,* appears in the sub-plot of *Ruth*. Richard Bradshaw's career of hypocritical moralizing and secret indulgence culminates in the

---

[75] *Works,* III, 68.
[76] Quoted, from a letter by Mrs. Gaskell to Mrs. Mary Howitt of 18 August 1838, in Howitt, 'Stray Notes from Mrs. Gaskell', *Good Words*, XXXVI (1895), 610: *G.L.,* No. 12.
[77] *Works,* III, 121.
[78] *Works,* III, 344-348.

crime of forgery[79]. Mrs. Gaskell seems to have had an inclination for introducing into her stories selfish sons and unselfish daughters.

Since the selfish son was likely, as in *Ruth,* to be connected with the legal profession, we may again note Mrs. Gaskell's apparently habitual dislike of lawyers—certainly they rarely appear to advantage in her work. In the present novel, besides Richard Bradshaw, there is the clever and worldly Mr. Hickson, a briefless barrister professing great contempt for the corrupt practices of the law, practices he hoped to cure by returning reformist Members to Parliament with the aid of bribery[80].

If those of the legal fraternity almost invariably show themselves to ill effect, then the reverse is true of doctors. Most of the medical men in *Ruth* appear eminently practical, doing whatever good lies in their power—as when Mr. Jones concerns himself with needful prescriptions while Mrs. Morgan discourses on immorality[81]; as when Mr. Wynne's feasible suggestion that she should nurse the sick[82] leads to Ruth's re-instatement in society. Mr. Davis, the principal Eccleston surgeon, is drawn at greatest length, and plays a quite important part. Being himself illegitimate[83], he could sympathize with Leonard's position, and offer to take him on as an apprentice, thereby providing a neat solution to the problem of what should become of the boy. A different aspect of Mr. Davis, but one typical of doctors, is his humorous-ironical trait. Mrs. Gaskell must have observed this closely in practitioners she knew; and she brings it out extremely well when she makes him chuckle over the rival surgeon's literal interpretation of the following words.

> "I could not answer it to Mr. Cranworth [the Tory candidate whom Mr. Davis himself supported] if I had brought his [Liberal] opponent round, you know, when I had had such a fine opportunity in my power. Now, with your patients, and general Radical interest, it will be rather a feather in your cap; for he may want

[79] John Forster's letter to Mrs. Gaskell of 12 November 1852 suggests that the author considered the forgery incident merely an episode, whereas Forster regarded it as quite essential for the story by reason of the position in which it placed Benson and the Bradshaws. The relevant passage (from a copy of part of this letter in the Gaskell Section, Brotherton Collection, Leeds University Library) is quoted by Miss Rubenius (*The Woman Question in Mrs. Gaskell's Life and Works,* p. 35).

[80] *Works,* III, esp. 251-253.   [82] *Works,* III, 384.
[81] *Works,* III, 77.   [83] *Works,* III, 437.

a good deal of care yet, though he is getting on famously—so
rapidly, in fact, that it's a strong temptation to me to throw him
back—a relapse, you know."[84]

As previously noticed, Mrs. Gaskell must have gained an
insight into the ways of medical life from her relatives in the
profession. With lawyers she had, no doubt, slightly less intimate
acquaintance. Though two of her daughters married barristers,
they did not do so till the eighteen-sixties.

In conclusion we must make a passing reference to Mrs.
Gaskell's love of the historical. This may be accomplished by
quoting the passage that follows Mrs. Gaskell's description of
Fordham—a description, at once architectural and social, which
opens the book.

> The traditions of those bygone times, even to the smallest social
> particular, enable one to understand more clearly the circum-
> stances which contributed to the formation of character. The daily
> life into which people are born, and into which they are ab-
> sorbed before they are well aware, forms chains which only one
> in a hundred has moral strength enough to despise, and to break
> when the right time comes—when an inward necessity for inde-
> pendent individual action arises, which is superior to all outward
> conventionalities. Therefore, it is well to know what were the
> chains of daily domestic habit, which were the natural leading-
> strings of our forefathers before they learnt to go alone.[85]

An early statement of the close connexion between conduct
and *milieu* has doubtless its own significance in such a social-
problem novel as *Ruth*. However the point we wish to stress
is the general importance Mrs. Gaskell attached to the influence
of environment on character. The first chapter of her *Life of
Charlotte Brontë*, for example, shows the emphasis she placed
upon the Yorkshire social and topographic setting as a necessary preliminary to any understanding of that strange literary
family at Haworth. Similarly *Sylvia's Lovers* opens with a fine
evocation of Monkshaven, an appropriate context for such a
sombre tale. As the passage quoted also implies, Mrs. Gaskell
had a feeling for the antique; but her interest was not merely
antiquarian. In *Ruth*, as in so many of her books, she was a
historian of the recent past, of that period known to the passing generation, of that time which the author felt vaguely to
be a lifetime, or half a lifetime, ago.

[84] *Works,* III, 443.   [85] *Works,* III, 2.

SECTION V

'Cumberland Sheep-Shearers' (1853)

Mrs. Gaskell's 'Cumberland Sheep-Shearers' came out in *Household Words*[1] on 22 January 1853; it is an account, cast in autobiographic form, along the lines suggested by its title. When the Gaskells lodged near Keswick—whose neighbourhood[2] provides a setting for the sheep-shearing—is difficult to define precisely, though Ward[3] testifies to the historicity of the stay. Their acquaintance with the Lakes in general can, however, easily be established.

In discussing 'Martha Preston', we referred to Mr. and Mrs. Gaskell's 1849 Lake District holiday, during which they met Wordsworth[4]. The following year the novelist was at Briery Close, Windermere—the residence of Sir James and Lady Kay-Shuttleworth—arriving there late one Tuesday afternoon [20 August][5], and remaining three days, in which time she 'went to see all . . . [her] old friends at/ Skelwith and elsewhere.'[6] From late July to mid-August, 1851, Mr. and Mrs. Gaskell, Marianne, and Meta were at their 'old lodgings in . . . [a] nice/ farm house at Skelwith at the entrance/ to the Langdales'[7]. Whether

---

[1] VI, 445-451.   [2] *Works*, III, 455-457.   [3] Ed. *Works*, III, p. xxv.

[4] Through the good offices of Edward Quillinan: see his letter of 14 October 1849, quoted in Morley, ed. *The Correspondence of Henry Crabb Robinson with the Wordsworth Circle* (1808-1866), II, 705.

[5] According to Mrs. Gaskell's letter to Catherine Winkworth of Sunday evening [25 August 1850—this date being given in different ink at the end of the letter], now in the Gaskell Section, Brotherton Collection, Leeds University Library; the relevant quotation appears, more or less accurately, in Haldane, *Mrs. Gaskell and Her Friends*, p. 123. The letter occurs as *G.L.*, No. 75.

[6] As she told Mrs. J. A. Froude in a [(late August) 1850] letter, the requisite part of which (*G.L.*, No. 78, dated [c. 25 August 1850] by Chapple and Pollard) is in the Berg Collection at the New York Public Library.

[7] So she wrote to Mrs. Nancy Robson on Monday [1 September 1851], this letter (*G.L.*, No. 101) being in the Gaskell Section, Brotherton Collection, Leeds University Library. According to the same letter the Gaskells had first spent ten days at Holborn Hill, near Broughton in Furness.

or not she, her husband, and their four children spent the
summer of 1852 near Keswick (as Mrs. Chadwick[8] and Dr.
Sanders[9] suggest), she may have crossed the Cumberland border
in the autumn, either while she was visiting Mrs. Fletcher at
'Lancrigg/ Grasmere/'[10], or when she was at 'Dr. Davy's, Lesketh
How, Near Ambleside.'[11]

All things considered, 1849 appears the most likely date for
the Keswick sojourn on which Mrs. Gaskell's article was based.
She remarks that the 'party consisted of two grown-up persons
and four children, the youngest almost a baby'[12]—which would
have been true in July, when the youngest daughter (Julia
Bradford) would have been less than three years old; this would
tally too with the time given in the opening sentence : 'Three
or four years ago'[13]. Nevertheless it is conceivable that the
Cumberland holiday occurred the summer before : Mrs. Gaskell

---

[8] *Mrs. Gaskell,* p. 189.

[9] *Elizabeth Gaskell,* p. xiv.

[10] The heading of her letter of 25 October [1852] to Miss Carpenter,
now in the Berg Collection at the New York Public Library. Writing to
Marianne one Saturday morning [2 October 1852], Mrs. Gaskell, having
mentioned Mrs. Fletcher's invitation to visit her 'any day after the/ 15th',
remarked that she had named the eighteenth in her reply—this letter to
Marianne being in the collection of Mrs. Margaret Trevor Jones. Mrs.
Fletcher had earlier proposed a visit before May that year—as Mrs.
Gaskell informed Marianne in a Sunday afternoon letter (in the Gaskell
Section, Brotherton Collection, Leeds University Library)—though there
seems no evidence that it was ever paid; this letter also indicates that
Mrs. Gaskell had recently engaged a new maid, Isabella Postlethwaite of
Legberthwaite, near Keswick—whose name suggests that of Isabel Cros-
thwaite, a girl appearing in the present article (*Works,* III, 466). These
letters respectively occur as *G.L.,* Nos. 138, 135, 107; Chapple and Pollard
identify the recipient of the first as Mary Carpenter, and give [Early
November 1851] as the date of the third.

[11] The address given on a Friday [(post 2—possibly 8—October)
1852] letter to Eliza Fox; the relevant quotation is given by Miss Haldane
(*Mrs. Gaskell and Her Friends,* p. 241), whose transcript tallies fairly
well with the copy of part of this letter in the Gaskell Section, Brotherton
Collection, Leeds University Library. This letter (*G.L.,* No. 137) is dated
[?October 1852] by Chapple and Pollard. Besides lodging with Mrs.
Fletcher and at Lesketh How, Mrs. Gaskell also stayed at Fox How,
Ambleside, with Mrs. Arnold—*G.L.,* Nos. 139-140; and Her Sister
[Susanna Winkworth], ed. *Letters and Memorials of Catherine Winkworth,*
I (1883), 369, fn.

[12] *Works,* III, 456.

[13] *Works,* III, 455.

at least was away from home early 'that July[14]; and the opening words of 'Martha Preston'[15] suggest a pre-1849 visit to the Lakes. Despite such dating problems, however, there seems no reason to doubt her material was gathered at first hand.

'Cumberland Sheep-Shearers' exemplifies Mrs. Gaskell's characteristic virtues, 'keen observation'[16] and 'graphic description'[17]; it is, Dr. Adolphus Ward notes, 'a singularly true and characteristic reproduction of out-of-the-way English country life, animated by the poetic touch which makes the difference between the picture and the photograph.'[18] In it she recaptures the atmosphere of the hot July day; makes the reader appreciate the scenic beauty; conjures up the holiday mood of country people at shearing time; introduces named individuals (which enhances the everyday realism of the sketch); and provides an informed account of farming methods and problems, as seems appropriate from a grand-daughter of Samuel Holland of Sandlebridge. Everywhere an interested and interesting observer reveals herself—one who is shrewd, perceptive, appreciative, and not without a sense of humour. What ought chiefly to be stressed in analysing her way of viewing the scene is the blend of the poetic with the realistic; for the Cumberland sheepmen are seen in the context of a bucolic tradition. Mrs. Gaskell refers to 'a sort of rural Olympics'[19], to 'Greek' meeting 'Greek'[20], to 'the Eleusinian circle'[21], and (with a smile) to the farmer's 'pipe

---

[14] 'Gale Cottage/'—a possible Lakeland abode—seems the heading of Mrs. Gaskell's letter to Edward Chapman on Monday 10 July [1848], now in the Pierpont Morgan Library (Autographs-Miscellaneous-English); however the faded ink of the letter (*G.L.*, No. 26) causes difficulty in deciphering its address and its date—read as Tuesday, July 10th [1848], by Chapple and Pollard. We may note that in a letter (*G.L.*, No. 73) penned a couple of years later—[?July 1850] according to Chapple and Pollard—Mrs. Gaskell told Eliza Fox about two middle-aged women 'from a retired Cumberland farmhouse' who proposed to visit London for the first time (perhaps acquaintances from her sheep-shearing days) —a copy of part of this letter being in the Gaskell Section, Brotherton Collection, Leeds University Library.

[15] *Sartain's Union Magazine*, VI (1850), 133.
[16] Chadwick, *Mrs. Gaskell*, p. 189.
[17] Chadwick, *Mrs. Gaskell*, p. 189.
[18] Ward, ed. *Works*, III, p. xxv.
[19] *Works*, III, 460.
[20] *Works*, III, 461.
[21] *Works*, III, 466.

(not Pandean)'[22]. It is not that she idealizes the work of the shearers and shepherds—she knows about such things as the 'obscene eggs'[23] of 'the common flesh-fly'[24]—but rather 'that she brings out the poetry in their lives by her seeing-beauty spirit, is aware of the richness, energy, worth, and customary values embodied in 'this vital pastoralism[25].

[22] *Works*, III, 470.
[23] *Works*, III, 468.
[24] *Works*, III, 468.
[25] It seems interesting that Wordsworth, mentioned in this article (*Works*, III, 458, 470), should have used the phrase 'a "Homeric/ family" ' to describe the Prestons—Skelwith Statespeople, with whom the Gaskells began to lodge in 1849 (*G.L.*, No. 182)—according to Mrs. Gaskell's letter (*G.L.*, No. 439a) of Monday [29 August 1859] to Charles B. P. Bosanquet, now in the Manchester University Library. The same letter contains a detailed account, from a tourist's stand-point, of the Keswick district.

SECTION VI

'Bran' (1853)

A poem in octosyllabic couplets, 'Bran' appeared in *Household Words*[1] on 22 October 1853. Possibly, like 'Sketches among the Poor. No. 1', this was jointly produced by husband and wife (who may have met the original Breton tale while holidaying in France that summer[2])[3]. The ballad relates how the hero's mother crossed the sea to ransom her son, only to discover a lifeless Bran; for, misled by a deceitful jailor, he had died in despair of her ever arriving. The conclusion illustrates those traditional beliefs of Brittany which represent the dead as re-appearing in the guise of birds. Doubtless Mrs. Gaskell was drawn to the tale by its inherent poetry and pathos, by the devotion of Bran's mother, and by the legendary returning of the dead. The versification is competent, and the narrative easy-flowing.

[1] VIII, 179-181. It is reprinted in *Novels and Tales*, X (1915), 447-452.
[2] Sanders, *Elizabeth Gaskell*, p. 59.
[3] In her letter of 31 October 1964 Professor Anne Lohrli informed me that there is an ambiguity about the entry for this contribution in the *Household Words* Day (or Office) Book (in the Princeton University Library). Because of the paleographical difficulty in deciding whether 'Mr' or 'Mrs' should be read, the authorship may be ascribed to husband or wife; but the poem clearly came through (*per*) Mrs. Gaskell, which (as Professor Lohrli remarked to me in a 6 January 1968 letter) suggests she did not submit this item as her own work.

SECTION VII

'Morton Hall' (1853)

'Morton Hall' came out in the numbers of *Household Words*[1] for 19 and 26 November 1853. It has not been possible to identify the mansion which gives the story its title[2], although the locality is obviously near Manchester—the Drumble of the tale (this name recalling *Cranford,* which had been earlier serialized in the same periodical). The piece possesses little structural unity and cohesion : old stories and Knutsford memories seem to have been used to fill up column-space rather than as material for a literary artist's shaping spirit.

A typically Cranfordian lady, the narrator is Miss Bridget Sidebotham, who lives with her spinster sister, Ethelinda; the characteristic Knutsford note is early sounded by Bridget's remark that the pulling down of the old hall would be a worse piece of work 'than the Repeal of 'the Corn Laws[3]. The following passage exemplifies the serious-humorous aspect of the storyteller, whose words carry amusing overtones of which she is herself unaware.

> ... were the Sidebothams [like the Morton family, whose followers they were] marked with a black mark in that terrible mysterious book which was kept under lock and key by the Pope and the Cardinals in Rome? It was terrible, yet, somehow, rather pleasant to think of. So many of the misfortunes which had happened to us through life, and which we had called "mysterious dispensations," but which some of our neighbours had attributed to our want of prudence and foresight, were accounted for at once, if we were objects of the deadly hatred of such a powerful order as the Jesuits, of whom we had lived in dread ever since we had read the "Female Jesuit."[4]

Here the use of the surname, the feminine mentality which seized upon a 'romantic' explanation for misfortune, the reference to a Gothick novel—all might have come from the rather

---

[1] VIII, 265-272, 293-302.
[2] Ward, ed. *Works,* II, p. xxxi.
[3] *Works,* II, 446.
[4] *Works,* II, 446-447.

naïve narrator in *Cranford,* as might the subsequent reference to an Alderney cow[5].

However most of what is related in the first chapter seems hardly in keeping with such a Cranfordesque atmosphere, though Mrs. Gaskell does something to remove it from too direct an association with the Miss Sidebothams by presenting it as Bridget's remembrance of what the Morton housekeeper, Mrs. Dawson, had told her mother. This concerns the marriage between a cavalier, Sir John Morton, and the daughter of the Puritan who had supplanted him in his hall during the Interregnum; their subsequent quarrels; and her curse on the house. The working out of the curse is then illustrated by Bridget's account of the sorrowful plight to which in her own day the Mortons were reduced. By means of another marriage, the final outcome is a happy reconciliation. The curse *motif,* though traditional, seems worth noting since it appears elsewhere in Mrs. Gaskell's work. As a tale of family ruin, the story is well told : but its narrator should not have been a woman like Bridget Sidebotham; for her dual nature produces incongruous effects. Such a quaintly humorous, Cranfordesque character is scarcely the person, in her capacity as a faithful tenant, to assist at the laying-out of Miss Phillis Morton, following the latter's death from starvation[6]. If Mrs. Gaskell had separated the gruesome from the humorous, if she had made two distinct contributions to *Household Words,* her success would have been more complete[7]. Nevertheless there are good things in 'Morton Hall', and it would be ungenerous to pass on without noticing some of them.

Firstly there are fine strokes of personal and natural observation : people, talking merrily in the sunlight, grow silent in the

[5] *Works,* II, 448. According to her letter (*G.L.,* No. 132) of Friday [10 September 1852] to Marianne (in the possession of Mrs. Margaret Trevor Jones), Mrs. Gaskell, like Cranford's Miss Betsy Barker (*Works,* II, 6), kept an Alderney cow.

[6] *Works,* II, 469.

[7] But not in the opinion of John Forster. His letter to Mrs. Gaskell of 21 November 1853 (a copy of part of which is in the Gaskell Section, Brotherton Collection, Leeds University Library) suggests not only that he disagreed with the author in considering the second chapter inferior to the first—it being, in his view, if anything, better—but also that he found the whole tale a pleasing unity, with 'the sad and the smiling ... charmingly intermixed'.

shade[8]; a little girl cries, upon dreaming that the dead person for whom she had gone into mourning was alive again, in case her new frock should be taken away[9]; the impoverished squire, out of a sense of dignity and pride, repressed his hacking cough if anyone was near[10].

Another merit is the use made of the narrator for conveying anti-Drumble attitudes, such as resentment against industrial innovations to the rural scene. Unobtrusively managed factual documentation suggestive of a concrete locality ('Our farm stood where Liverpool Street runs now . . . '[11]) makes the reader keenly aware of both the old country setting and the latter-day urban development. Remarks like 'she was a Drumble person'[12] (an explanation for bad manners) and the labelling of cotton-spinners as 'fools'[13] for buying eggs at high prices, by coming as natural *en passant* comments in the narrative, serve to keep the character of the narrator before one's eyes. With traditional ways of thought Mrs. Gaskell was well acquainted; and a wide understanding of conservative attitudes and points of view is frequently found in her writings. She had, one supposes, so completely digested such aspects of the Knutsford *milieu* as to be able to introduce them without effort, without having to think about what she was doing. Therefore, in spite of the narrator's standpoint being far more quaintly *naïve* than that of the author, the latter might easily, one feels, have echoed a sentiment like the following.

> We thought it would have been prettier if he [General Morton] had hired John Cobb, the Morton builder and joiner, he that had made the squire's coffin, and the squire's father's before that. Instead, came a troop of Drumble men, knocking and tumbling about in the Hall, and making their jests up and down all those stately rooms.[14]

Although the comic element is not successfully integrated with the sombre grimness of much of the tale, certain humorous

[8] *Works*, II, 450.
[9] *Works*, II, 465.
[10] *Works*, II, 465.
[11] *Works*, II, 447.
[12] *Works*, II, 464.
[13] *Works*, II, 465.
[14] *Works*, II, 473.

passages seem fit to stand alone, independent of the story proper.
There is the entertaining account of the feast prepared for the
Puritan ministers, followed by their retreat before Sir John's
bad language—an account whose humour is enhanced by a
string of Old-Testament-style Christian names which reaches
its climax in Master Help-me-or-I-perish Perkins[15]. Then there
is Cordelia Mannisty's education at the hands of three eccentric maiden aunts, all differing in their ideas on the subject:
here one finds a reference to Miss Sophronia's reading to
Cordelia passages from a book on which she was engaged, 'to
be called "The Female Chesterfield; or, Letters from a Lady of
Quality to her Niece" ' [16]—an incident which, besides being in-
trinsically amusing, reminds one that the married sister of Mrs.
Gaskell's Stratford teachers, Mrs. William Parkes (née Frances
Byerley), had originally intended her Domestic Duties to be cast
in epistolary form[17]. There is, again, the delightful theory that
the higher (anatomically) a bodily pain, the more aristocratic
its nature[18]; unfortunately Lord Toffey proved an exception,
being lame and suffering from gout[19].

'Morton Hall' contains, like Cranford, its verbal witticisms,
its brilliant turns of phrase. To parallel Martha's ' "Reason
always means what some one else has got to say" '[20], we can
quote Bridget as follows.

> If there is one thing I do dislike more than another, it is a person
> saying something on the other side when I am trying to make up
> my mind—how can I reason if I am to be disturbed by another
> person's arguments?[21]

We ought, before leaving this story, to mention some minor
characters, deserving notice not so much for their own importance as for their exemplification of certain recurring Gaskellian

---

[15] Works, II, 456.
[16] Works, II, 476.
[17] Mrs. William Parkes, Domestic Duties; or, Instructions to Young
Married Ladies, on the Management of Their Households, and the Regulation of Their Conduct in the Various Relations and Duties of Married
Life, London: Longman, Hurst, Rees, Orme, Brown, and Green, 1825,
p. iv.
[18] Works, II, 483-484.
[19] Works, II, 484.
[20] Works, II, 155.
[21] Works, II, 484.

types. Besides the Sidebotham sisters (who might have lived in Cranford) and their 'dear little brother'[22] who died young (a familiar *motif*), we should note that 'frail, delicate lady'[23] who married Squire Morton, 'a great invalid'[24] not living long (the ailing-wife theme being not uncommon in the Gaskell canon—for our authoress was a Victorian novelist). The profligate son appears in the shape of the young squire, John Marmaduke Morton, who 'played high at college'[25] and so helped to aggravate the family financial difficulties. Furthermore the marriage which concludes the tale, that between the aristocratic Cordelia Mannisty and a Drumble manufacturer (albeit one with a respectable ancestry)[26], hints at what would be developed at greater length in *North and South*.

[22] *Works*, II, 459.
[23] *Works*, II, 459.
[24] *Works*, II, 461.
[25] *Works*, II, 462.
[26] *Works*, II, 487-489.

SECTION VIII

'Traits and Stories of the Huguenots' (1853)

'Traits and Stories of the Huguenots', published in *Household Words*[1] on 10 December 1853, need not long detain us. It consists of historical anecdotes from the time of the Proclamation of the Edict of Nantes to within the author's own memory. A considerable part is taken up by Mrs. Gaskell's recounting what she had heard from a friend, of Huguenot descent, about that lady's family history[2]. Although one cannot substantiate this authorial affirmation by reference to any particular informant, there seems no reason to doubt that Mrs. Gaskell was, as she claimed, retelling rather than inventing. Though she probably made slight changes to render the account more graphic (as with the detailed and vivid description of Farmer Lefebvre's ride home to prevent his daughter's being confined to a nunnery[3]), Mrs. Gaskell is scarcely likely to have made important original alterations to the narrative. Indeed, since her general comments imply she was merely passing on 'traditions . . . heard and collected'[4], a strong presumption exists that little was added in the passing on. Of another anecdote, dealing with a meeting between a husband and his wife after years of absence, Mrs. Gaskell states that it too was told her by her friend[5]; and, to authenticate the story of an ingenious escape made by a Huguenot couple and their child, she adds 'their descendants may be reading this very paper.'[6]

For Gaskell scholars the chief value of the article lies in exemplifying its author's attraction to curious tales (one may relevantly recall 'Disappearances') and her keen interest in various aspects of French life and history.

[1] VIII, 348-354.
[2] *Works,* II, 492-496.
[3] *Works,* II, 494-495.
[4] *Works,* II, 492.
[5] *Works,* II, 497.
[6] *Works,* II, 499.

SECTION IX

'My French Master' (1853)

Mrs. Gaskell's next contribution to *Household Words*[1], occupying the numbers for 17 and 24 December 1853, also has a French flavour about it. Couched in the form of an old lady's reminiscences about the fortunes of her former language teacher, 'My French Master' has no intricate, elaborate plot; one feels rather that Mrs. Gaskell was inventing as she went along—a supposition receiving some support from the narrator's sister's being inconsistently called both Mary[2] and Fanny[3]. It appears quite probable that the second chapter (and article) was written after the first had already gone to press.

If one is seeking an autobiographic basis, there may be some relation between the 'amateur' farmer's losses[4] and Mr. Stevenson's not very profitable attempts at scientific agriculture[5]; furthermore this same man, the narrator's father, died from paralysis[6], as did the author's own father[7]. Mrs. Chadwick[8] has expressed her belief that the prototype of M. de Chalabre was M. Rogier, the Knutsford dancing-master at the time of Mrs. Gaskell's girlhood. Green's account[9] of the Frenchman is too brief to afford sufficient data for a detailed comparison; but it is not unlikely that Rogier provided a point of departure for the character of M. de Chalabre, especially as the former's association with the Count D'Artois (later Charles X) brings to mind that of M. de Chalabre with the Count de Provence (Louis XVIII)[10]. Moreover the idyllic description of country life found in the first chapter recalls Knutsford during Mrs. Gaskell's

[1] VIII, 361-365, 388-393.
[2] *Works*, II, 510.
[3] *Works*, II, 517.
[4] *Works*, II, 506.
[5] Chadwick, *Mrs. Gaskell*, pp. 4-5.
[6] *Works*, II, 520, 524.
[7] Chadwick, *Mrs. Gaskell*, pp. 95-96.
[8] *Mrs. Gaskell*, pp. 20-22.
[9] Green, *Knutsford, Its Traditions and History: with Reminiscences, Anecdotes, and Notices of the Neighbourhood*, pp. 134-136.
[10] *Works*, II, 518.

childhood : the treatment is light, humorous, retrospective with
a touch of pathos; the narrator looks back over the years, her
past observations are recollected in tranquillity.

The story itself was possibly suggested to Mrs. Gaskell when
she was visiting Mme Mohl[11] in the Rue du Bac, Paris. Certainly Mme Mohl seems an obvious candidate for the lady
mentioned at the outset.

> Three years ago I was in Paris. An English friend of mine who
> lives there—English by birth, but married to a German professor,
> and very French in manners and ways—asked me to come to her
> house one evening.[12]

Although there appears to be no other evidence for a Parisian
visit some time in 1850-1851, Mrs. Gaskell had known Mme
Mohl for several years[13]; and one need have few qualms about
making the identification, especially as Mme Mohl (*née* Mary
Clarke) had also taken a German husband, Julius Mohl, Professor of Persian at the *Collège de France*. The description of
the behaviour of the lady in 'My French Master' is quite in
keeping with what we should expect from Mme Mohl; for the
former's desire to see poetic justice done, through a union
between the daughter of an *émigré* and the grandson of the
man who had taken over his estate (a theme not unlike that of
'Morton Hall'), is entirely characteristic of Mme Mohl—a
woman who, enjoying the company of young people, 'was
always ready to be interested in their love affairs, or to help
on a marriage.'[14]

It seems, then, that the basic ingredients which went to the
making of 'My French Master' were Knutsford memories and

[11] For Mme Mohl, see Kathleen O'Meara, *Madame Mohl, Her Salon
and Her Friends: A Study of Social Life in Paris*, London: Richard
Bentley & Son, 1885; and Simpson, *Letters and Recollections of Julius
and Mary Mohl.*
[12] *Works*, II, 527.
[13] Writing a Christmas later to Eliza Fox, Mrs. Gaskell remarked that
she had known Mme Mohl 'a little for many years'. The relevant passage
—from a copy of part of this letter (*G.L.*, No. 222) of Monday 24 [25]
December 1854 in the Gaskell Section, Brotherton Collection, Leeds
University Library—is quoted, with comments though slightly inaccurately,
by Miss Rubenius (*The Woman Question in Mrs. Gaskell's Life and
Works*, p. 41, fn. 3).
[14] O'Meara, *Mme Mohl*, p. 136.

a love-story which could easily have come from the *salon* of
Mme Mohl. As previously surmised, Mrs. Gaskell probably
began without having a well-developed plan before her, much
of the invention being *ad hoc* in consequence. However the
reader can scarcely feel disappointment : for there are many
Gaskellian touches of humour and pathos—the cipher-talk of
the narrator's parents before their children, who, nevertheless,
realized what the circumlocutions imported and the reason for
this hieroglyphic language[15]; the graphic outward illustration
of M. de Chalabre's inner state, on hearing about the execution
of Louis XVI, through the limp and unstarched appearance of
his white muslin frills and ruffles[16]; the same Frenchman's
omission of 'de' from his name as a token of his changed
social position[17]; the primary concern of the narrator's father
(when in his second childhood) being the choice of a daily pud-
ding[18]. Such instances, which lend solidity to the narrative,
could be multiplied; they are just the things which the narrator (who is very like the author) would have observed and
taken note of.

If one were to try to pick out the best in 'My French Master',
what might without incongruity be found in *Cranford* or *Cousin
Phillis*, then one would fix upon that evocation of rural felicity,
viewed retrospectively as being the happiness experienced half a
lifetime ago, which is felt immediately the first few paragraphs
are read. Soon one comes to the incident where M. de Chalabre
helps a countrywoman over a style and carries her basket[19],
which strongly recalls Captain Brown's helping a poor old inhabitant of Cranford to carry her dinner[20] : the same spirit of
charity, going far beyond mere good manners, is exemplified
by both. Here too, as later in *Cousin Phillis,* one enjoys an
idyllic background (fields of clover, fragrant evening walks,
posies of carnations, lessons on the lawn)[21] owing much to
Mrs. Gaskell's golden memories of the Cheshire and Warwick-

---

[15] *Works,* II, 512-513.
[16] *Works,* II, 513.
[17] *Works,* II, 522.
[18] *Works,* II, 521.
[19] *Works,* II, 509-510.
[20] *Works,* II, 12-13.
[21] *Works,* II, 508-510.

shire countryside. This is in the pastoral tradition of Goldsmith, Cowper, and Wordsworth : nor must Tennyson be forgotten; for the author of *Cranford* had made Mr. Holbrook draw particular attention to that poet's graphic natural description, his acute observation of form and shade[22].

---

[22] *Works,* II, 41-42.

SECTION X

'The Squire's Story' (1853)

Visitors to Knutsford are still shown the house once occupied by Higgins, the eighteenth-century highwayman[1]; appropriately enough it is next to the one where, before her marriage, Elizabeth Stevenson lived with her aunt. 'The Squire's Story', which came out in *Another Round of Stories by the Christmas Fire*, the 1853 Extra Christmas Number of *Household Words*[2], is based upon local legends about this colourful character.

Scarcely disguised under the name of Barford (on the Derby Road), Knutsford provides the setting for the story—complete with *George Inn*[3] and a Cranfordesque maiden lady[4]. The name 'Barford', we may note in passing, was doubtless suggested (perhaps unconsciously) by the place in Warwickshire where Mrs. Gaskell's schoolmistresses had kept a teaching-establishment before their move to Stratford—the village appears in *Lois the Witch*. Although the social context is satisfactory (made actual by such things as the deferential attitude of the townspeople towards the gentry[5]; the convincing hunting scenes[6]; and the realistic representation of the Barford attorney, particularly in relation to his employers, the county gentry[7]), the story, considered as a whole, does not succeed. Mrs. Gaskell used the Higgins tradition—there being little necessity for her to invent

---

[1] A good summary of the Higgins traditions is given by Green (*Knutsford, Its Traditions and History: with Reminiscences, Anecdotes, and Notices of the Neighbourhood*, pp. 119-130); a more easily accessible account is provided by Ward (ed. *Works*, II, pp. xxxii-xxxiii).

[2] Pp. 19-25. From his letter to Mrs. Gaskell of 19 September 1853 it seems the only injunction Dickens laid on the author was that her tale, like its predecessor—'The Old Nurse's Story'—in the past (1852) Extra Christmas Number, should be suited to fireside-telling at Christmas, though without necessarily having either a seasonal reference or a moral (*The Letters of Charles Dickens*, ed. Dexter, II, 490).

[3] *Works*, II, 532.

[4] *Works*, II, 539.

[5] *Works*, II, 532-533.

[6] *Works*, II, 535-536.

[7] *Works*, II, 541-542.

anything—but failed to make her central character come alive.
The narrator is, according to the tale's title, a squire, though the
inference is doubtless invalid since presumably Dickens gave
the story a name which would fit in with the group as a whole
(i.e. with 'The Schoolboy's Story', 'The Old Lady's Story', and
so forth); at all events the narrator neither shows skill *qua*
narrator, nor exhibits distinctive personal qualities—'squiresque'
characteristics—to compensate for his incompetent story-telling.
In support of such an unfavourable judgement we may quote
the following passage.

> The gentleman was tall, well-dressed, handsome; but there was a
> sinister cold look in his quick-glancing, light blue eye, which a
> keen observer might not have liked. There were no keen observers
> among the boys and ill-conditioned gaping girls.[8]

Here Mrs. Gaskell evidently wanted to hint at Higgins' real
nature, to suggest that he was not all he seemed; yet she does
so in a rather obvious and *naïve* manner, as if she were describing a stage villain. Another instance of the same defect is
provided by the next quotation, where melodramatic dialogue
increases one's sense of the writer's ineptness.

> "Oh! it was a shocking, terrible murder!" said Mr. Higgins, not
> raising his look from the fire, but gazing on with his eyes dilated
> till the whites were seen all round them. "A terrible, terrible
> murder! I wonder what will become of the murderer? I can
> fancy the red glowing centre of that fire—look and see how
> infinitely distant it seems, and how the distance magnifies it into
> something awful and unquenchable."[9]

It is a major criticism of this tale that its central figure is
theatrical and unreal; he is a historical person in whom we
cannot believe. Mrs. Gaskell seems to have thrown together the
legendary material without attempting to organize and order it[10].

---

[8] *Works,* II, 533.
[9] *Works,* II, 544.
[10] A glaring instance of hasty composition is the fact that within the
same paragraph we read both that Catherine is Squire Hearn's only child
and that he has a son and heir (*Works,* II, 537)—a point remarked upon
by Miss Rubenius (*The Woman Question in Mrs. Gaskell's Life and
Works,* p. 137, fn. 3) and by Professor Archie Stanton Whitfield (ed. *The
Sexton's Hero and Other Tales,* by Elizabeth Cleghorn Gaskell, 3rd edn,
[Tokyo:] The Hokuseido Press [1932], 'Additions and Corrections' slip).

Even where she does appear to have added something of her own—the way in which Higgins was eventually found out—, there is little subtlety in the invention : is it likely that the hard-drinking Higgins would, before murdering an old lady, tap a barrel of her ginger wine, take a drink, and then wrap the spigot round with a piece of paper which might identify him as the killer[11]? One must of necessity make an invidious comparison between this use of an incriminating scrap of paper and the way Mrs. Gaskell employed a tell-tale Valentine in *Mary Barton*[12], where, as wadding for the murderer's gun, it functions as an ambiguous clue. In the novel she has some pretensions to be considered a promising detective-writer; no such claims can be made for the author of 'The Squire's Story'.

---

[11] *Works*, II, 548.
[12] *Works*, I, 270-283.

SECTION XI

'The Scholar's Story' (1853)

The same 1853 Extra Christmas Number of *Household Words*[1] contained 'The Scholar's Story'[2], a translation into octosyllabic couplets of one of the Breton ballads collected by the Vicomte de la Villemarqué. Possibly William Gaskell, as a linguist, produced the initial rendering, this being subsequently versified with the help of his wife, who probably supplied the brief prose introduction[3]. The narrative tells of a priest's treachery towards his cousin—a knight who, as a result of the clerk's deceit, kills his lady, believing she has played him false and, by her neglect, caused the death of their child. Perhaps this contribution was submitted together with 'The Squire's Story', and Dickens thought it would do well enough for the same number.

[1] *Another Round of Stories by the Christmas Fire*, pp. 32-34.
[2] Reprinted in *Novels and Tales*, X, 453-462.
[3] The translation is attributed to William Gaskell and the introduction to Elizabeth by Professor Archie Stanton Whitfield—*Mrs Gaskell*, p. 236; major entry for Elizabeth Cleghorn Gaskell, *née* Stevenson (1810-1865), in *The Cambridge Bibliography of English Literature*, ed. Frederick Noel Wilse Bateson, 4 vols., Cambridge: The University Press, 1940, III, 428. Professor Whitfield (Plas Benar, Dyffryn, Merionethshire) tells me he cannot recall his authority for these ascriptions; however he thinks the information may have come from someone in Manchester, possibly John Albert Green or Professor C. H. Herford. His own opinion is that doubtless Mr. Gaskell did the original translating, with his wife assisting in the later versifying. That Green was Professor Whitfield's source is strongly suggested by the following: 'Mr. Green has unearthed . . . "The Scholar's Story" in the Christmas Number of *Household Words*, 1853, which he tells us is based upon a Breton ballad translated by Mr. Gaskell, and containing some introductory remarks by Mrs. Gaskell'—Esther Alice (Mrs. Ellis H.) Chadwick, 'The Gaskell Collection at Manchester', *The Bookman* (London), XLI (1911), 45. The Miss Gaskells may have assisted Green's researches; they are named in his Preface to the Gaskell catalogue whose relevant ('The Scholar's Story') entry credits William with the translation and Elizabeth with its introduction—John Albert Green, *A Bibliographical Guide to the Gaskell Collection in the Moss Side Library*, Manchester: Reference Library, King St.; Moss Side Library, Bradshaw Street, 1911, p. 50. The *Household Words* Office Book (in the Princeton University Library) designates the author as Mrs. Gaskell.

CHAPTER V

'MODERN GREEK SONGS' (1854) TO
'A CHRISTMAS CAROL' (1856)

P

SECTION I

'Modern Greek Songs' (1854)

'Modern Greek Songs', which came out in *Household Words*[1] on 25 February 1854, was in effect a review of Claude Fauriel's *Chants Populaires de la Grèce Moderne*[2]. Quite probably Mrs. Gaskell's association with Mme Mohl led to her reading Fauriel's book; for Fauriel had, when alive, been a close friend of Miss Clarke, before her marriage to Julius Mohl[3]. Apparently unaware of the English version by Charles Brinsley Sheridan[4], Mrs. Gaskell begins by opining that some account of a book she had found interesting would perhaps not displease her readers, especially since it was currently out of print.

What Mrs. Gaskell gives is a general survey of the work, together with summaries of parts which particularly took her fancy. The emphasis is appreciative rather than critical, no attempt being made at an impersonal, 'objective' estimate— indeed the typically Gaskellian touches are among the most charming things in 'Modern Greek Songs'. Very soon she draws upon her own experience; for a discussion of Fauriel's description of household feast-day ceremonies brings to mind the time she was invited by a Greek family living in England to attend their Easter Day celebrations. A sentence from this brief digression shows how appropriately Mrs. Gaskell could incorporate into the article something she had herself observed, and in such a way as to grace it with a touch of poetry and romance.

---

[1] IX, 25-32.

[2] Claude-Charles Fauriel, *Chants Populaires de la Grèce Moderne, Recueillis et Publiés, avec une Traduction Française, des Eclaircissements et des Notes*, 2 vols., Paris: Firmin Didot, Père et Fils (and Dondey-Dupré, Père et Fils), 1824-1825.

[3] Simpson, *Letters and Recollections of Julius and Mary Mohl*, pp. 10-12; and O'Meara, *Madame Mohl, Her Salon and Her Friends*, pp. 52-64.

[4] Charles Brinsley Sheridan, *'The Songs of Greece', from the Romaic Text, Edited by M. C. Fauriel, with Additions. Translated into English Verse*, London: Longman, Hurst, Rees, Orme, Brown, and Green, 1825.

> In one corner of the small English drawing-room there was spread
> a table covered with mellow-looking sweetmeats, all as if the
> glow of sunset rested on their amber and crimson colours; and
> there were decanters containing mysterious liquids to match.[5]

Although Mrs. Gaskell's response to Fauriel was primarily
that of a fellow literary-artist—feeling, as she did, the poetry
inherent in the ceremonials, as well as that of the accompanying songs[6]—, it is characteristic that she should miss no opportunity of seeing the humorous aspect of things. Thus she can
smile at the custom whereby an ardent suitor might declare his
passion by throwing an apple at the lady of his choice[7]. There
is one instance of Mrs. Gaskell's digressive humour which,
being especially interesting for the source-seeker, requires attention.

Discussing the Greek practice of singing funeral songs, Mrs.
Gaskell remarks that at times some of the mourners, 'in a form
. . . used from time immemorial,'[8] implore the newly dead to
take messages to those who have gone before. The custom makes
her recall a similar Highland superstition, and hence 'Mrs.
Hemans's pathetic little poem on this subject'[9] ('The Message
to the Dead', Dr. Adolphus Ward[10] reminds us). Instead of
going on to give a touching little anecdote—as, when one recalls
her own bereavements, she might have done—, Mrs. Gaskell
proceeds to entertain her readers with a funny story. We have
here yet another example of her versatility, her surprising
many-sidedness. Since she makes plain that this anecdote was
none of her own inventing, we might content ourselves by
simply taking her word for it; however her veracity is confirmed by a trustworthy witness—Mr. Gaskell. The relevant evidence occurs in the ensuing extracts (the first from Mrs. Gaskell's article, the second from a lecture by her husband).

> It is rather too abrupt a turn from the deep pathos of the faith-
> ful love implied by this superstition, to a story of something of a

---

[5] *Works*, III, 472.
[6] *Works*, III, 476-477.
[7] *Works*, III, 474-475.
[8] *Works*, III, 478.
[9] *Works*, III, 478.
[10] Ed. *Works*, III, p. xxx.

similar kind, which fell under the observation of a country minister in Lancashire, well known to some friends of mine. A poor man lay a-dying, but still perfectly sensible and acute. A woman of his acquaintance came to see him, who had lately lost her husband, and who was imbued with the idea mentioned above. "Bill," said she, "where thou art bound to thou'lt maybe see our Tummas; be sure thou tell him we have getted th' wheel o' the shandry mended, and it's mostly as good as new; and mind thou say'st we're getten on vary weel without him; he may as weel think so, poor chap!" To which Bill made answer, "Why woman! dost 'oo think I'se have nought better to do than go clumping up and down the sky a-searching for thy Tummas?" To those who have lived in Lancashire the word "clumping" exactly suggests the kind of heavy walk of the country people who wear the thick wooden clogs common in that county.[11]

In Icelandic, 'klumbr," like "klump" in Swedish, and "klomp" in Dutch, signifies a mass or clod; and the Lancashire man speaks of a "clump of wood," and of "clumpin' clogs." I suppose it is to something like this that Stowe refers when he says, "he brought his wooden shoes or *clampers* with him." And to this source, as I know of none in Anglo-Saxon, I refer the Lancashire verb "to clump." The meaning of the word will be gathered from a short conversation which a minister in this county once overheard between a poor man on his death-bed, and a farmer's wife who had come to visit him. "Well," she said, "when yo getten theer, yo'll may-happen see eawr Tummus; and yo'll tell 'im we'n had th' shandry mended, un a new pig-stoye built, un at we dun pratty weel beawt him." "Beli' me, Meary!" he answered, "dost 'think at aw's ha nowt for t'do, bo go *clumpin'* up un deawn t'skoies a seechin' yore Tummus!" The Flemings, I believe, have the same word "klompen," and this might therefore, perhaps, with equal justice, be ascribed to the Frisian.[12]

[11] *Works*, III, 479.
[12] William Gaskell, *Two Lectures on the Lancashire Dialect,* London: Chapman and Hall, 1854, pp. 28-29. (These lectures also appeared appended to the cheap—fifth—edition of [Elizabeth Cleghorn Gaskell] *Mary Barton; A Tale of Manchester Life,* London: Chapman and Hall, 1854: see *G.L.*, Nos. 191, 195. In 1854 threepenny-pamphlet form, they bore as a cover-style *The Lancashire Dialect, Illustrated in Two Lectures,* London: Chapman and Hall; Manchester: Abel Heywood.) Some copies have the variant 'may happen' for 'may-happen' in this passage.

SECTION II

'Company Manners' (1854)

Saturday 20 May 1854 saw Mrs. Gaskell's next contribution to *Household Words*[1], a contribution which again owes not a little to her friendship with Mme Mohl. Some articles on Mme de Sablé by Victor Cousin, which initially appeared in the *Revue des Deux Mondes*[2] and were later published in book-form[3], caused Mrs. Gaskell to reflect upon 'the art of keeping a *salon*; and doubtless her acquaintance with Cousin (an *habitué* of Mme Mohl's own *salon*[4]) induced her to read the articles. Having referred to Cousin and his work, Mrs. Gaskell mentions 'the views of other French people about *salon*-entertainment, it being likely that much of this material was collected in the drawing-room of Mme Mohl. She concludes with her own thoughts on the subject.

'Company Manners' provides autobiographic *data* of two sorts: the first, chiefly historical; the second, rather more psychological. As an example of 'the former, we may point to Mrs. Gaskell's Welsh reminiscences. When she recalls the hospitality in her youth prevalent 'in the very heart and depth of Wales,'[5] she seems to have drawn on memories of what she had observed during visits to her cousin, Samuel Holland (1803-1892), at his home, Plas Penrhyn (close to Minffordd,

---

[1] IX, 323-331.
[2] Claude Henri Victor Cousin, 'La Marquise de Sablé et les Salons Littéraires au XVIIᵉ Siècle'; 'Histoire Littéraire.—La Marquise de Sablé et La Rochefoucauld'; 'La Marquise de Sablé.—III.—Mme de Sablé et Mme de Longueville'; 'La Marquise de Sablé.—IV.—Port-Royal et Mme de Longueville, dernière partie', *Revue des Deux Mondes*, 2nd Series, V (1854), 5-36, 433-472, 865-896; VI (1854), 5-36.
[3] Claude Henri Victor Cousin, *Madame de Sablé: Etudes sur les Femmes Illustres de la Société du XVIIᵉ Siècle*, Paris: Didier, 1854. Here there is an appendix (pp. 305-459), following the *Revue* articles, which contains miscellaneous letters by and to Mme de Sablé, and also letters from Mme de Longueville to Mme de Sablé.
[4] Simpson, *Letters and Recollections of Julius and Mary Mohl*, p. 30; and O'Meara, *Mme Mohl, Her Salon and Her Friends*, p. 65.
[5] *Works*, III, 501.

199

near Penrhyndeudraeth, Merionethshire)[6]. In the same category
are the recollections she gives of delightful tea parties, held in
the children's old schoolroom, with her host telling marvellous
tales of voyages of discovery[7]; here too Mrs. Gaskell is evidently speaking from personal experience, even though it is
difficult to specify the particular household. Over against such
personal, autobiographic anecdotes one can set passages which
reveal something of Mrs. Gaskell's mentality and temperament.
In this sense 'Company Manners' is very characteristic of its
writer; for it is just the sort of article which, knowing her
nature, one might have supposed she would write. To convey
some idea of the author's personality one cannot do better than
quote an assessment by Susanna Winkworth, an assessment from
which only Jane Welsh Carlyle[8] and Prosper Mérimée[9] could
be expected to dissent.

> She was a noble-looking woman, with a queenly presence, and her
> high, broad, serene brow, and finely-cut mobile features, were
> lighted up by a constantly-varying play of expression as she
> poured forth her wonderful talk. It was like the gleaming ripple
> and rush of a clear deep stream in sunshine. Though one of the

[6] *The Memoirs of Samuel Holland, One of the Pioneers of the North
Wales Slate Industry* [ed. William Llewelyn Davies], The Merioneth
Historical and Record Society (Cymdeithas Hanes a Chofnodion Sir
Feirionnydd), Extra Publications (Cyhoeddiadau Ychwanegol), Series
(Cyfres) I, Number (Rhif) 1 [Dolgelley (Dolgellau), 1952], p. 23; see too
pp. 20, fn. 6, 30-31. Samuel Holland here (p. 23) mentions that his cousin
was working on a novel during one of her visits: this may have been
Mary Barton or (more probably) *Ruth*, but 'The Well of Pen-Morfa' and
(especially) 'The Doom of the Griffiths', though short stories, are also
possible candidates.

[7] *Works*, III, 503-504.

[8] Mrs. Carlyle detected 'an atmosphere of moral dulness about' Mrs.
Gaskell: see the relevant passage, from a letter to Thomas Carlyle, quoted,
with a few minor differences, by Whitfield (*Mrs Gaskell*, 1929, p. 35),
and by Lawrence and Elisabeth Mary Hanson (*Necessary Evil: The Life
of Jane Welsh Carlyle*, London: Constable, 1952, pp. 407, 589) who claim
in their Preface to have examined all the available important MSS—
their dating being 7 September 1851; Professor Whitfield's, 13 September
1851. A letter containing these extracts, however, is dated 12 September
1851 in Alexander Carlyle, ed. *New Letters and Memorials of Jane Welsh
Carlyle, Annotated by Thomas Carlyle*, intro. James Crichton-Browne, 2
vols., London and New York: John Lane, The Bodley Head, 1903, II, 28.

[9] Mérimée found her morose and lachrymose: see the reviewer's relevant quotation in 'The Letters of Prosper Mérimée', "French Writing To-
day" Special Section, *The Times Literary Supplement,* 26 March 1954,
p. xiii; and Whitfield, *Mrs Gaskell*, p. 40.

most brilliant persons I ever saw, she had none of the restless-
ness and eagerness that spoils so much of our conversation nowadays. There was no hurry or high-pressure about her, but she
seemed always surrounded by an atmosphere of ease, leisure, and
playful geniality, that drew out the best side of every one who
was in her company. When you were with her, you felt as if you
had twice the life in you that you had at ordinary times. All her
great intellectual gifts,—her quick keen observation, her marvellous memory, her wealth of imaginative power, her rare felicity
of instinct, her graceful and racy humour,—were so warmed and
brightened by sympathy and feeling, that while actually with her,
you were less conscious of her power than of her charm.[10]

This eulogy serves as an admirable comment on, as an excellent
summing-up of, the woman who composed 'Company Manners'.
Mrs. Gaskell presents herself (albeit unobtrusively) as a truly
considerate hostess, taking every care of the 'material' aspects—
the dinner itself and the physical *décor*—yet at the same time
realizing that an enjoyable evening depends for its success even
more on 'pleasant conversation and happy social intercourse'[11].
One may aptly apply to Mrs. Gaskell (the hostess who unconsciously reveals herself in the article) the very words she uses to
characterize Mme de Sablé.

> ... Mme de Sablé cooked sweetbreads for her friends in a silver
> saucepan; but never to fatigue herself with those previous labours.
> She knew the true taste of her friends too well; they cared for her,
> firstly, as an element in their agreeable evening—the silver sauce-
> pan in which they were all to meet; the oil in which their several
> ingredients were to be softened of what was harsh or discordant
> —very secondary would be their interest in her sweetbreads.[12]

In 'Company Manners' Mrs. Gaskell scatters *en passant*
several practical hints for the lady of the house. She recommends foot-men for waiting-on, since they can carry heavy
loads more easily and so move more silently and with greater
decorum than women[13]; she states her preference for real as
against artificial flowers[14]; she gives her advice about the best

---

[10] *Memorials of Two Sisters,* ed. Shaen, pp. 23-24.
[11] *Works,* III, 496.   [12] *Works,* III, 498.   [13] *Works,* III, 499-500.
[14] *Works,* III, 497. Ironically it was *artificial* flowers she found at
(probably) the first dinner given by Dickens to which she was invited,
according to Jane Welsh Carlyle, quoted in David Alec Wilson, *Carlyle
at His Zenith* (1848-53)—*Life of Carlyle,* Vol. IV—, London: Kegan Paul,
Trench, Trubner & Co., Ltd.; New York: E. P. Dutton & Co., 1927, p.
89. She dined on Saturday 12 May 1849 (*op. cit.,* p. 88; and *G.L.,* No. 47).

use of books as aids to conversation[15]. Yet it is the vivacious
sparkle rather than any utilitarian content which makes this
Household Words contribution so eminently readable. There is
the author's belief that she once ate a white kid glove[16]; and
there is her longing to burst out with a nonsense word during
'sensible' (platitudinous) talk[17]—certainly as the wife of a
Unitarian minister, and therefore having to visit 'a good deal
among a set of people who piqued themselves on being rational'[18], she must have had her fill of cant, earnestness, and trite-
ness. There is, too, the amusing description of a feather-blowing
game, suggested by some daring *belle* at a mutual-improvement
party when details were being given of some new scientific
discovery (details which, Mrs. Gaskell comments, 'were all and
each of them wrong, as I learnt afterwards'[19]).

Despite the (in general) humorous tone, Mrs. Gaskell does
on one occasion depart slightly from her accustomed tolerance
to disapprove of attempts 'to say brilliant rather than true
things'[20] by those seeking to be clever rather than good. Here she
may, perhaps, seem to display that 'moral dulness'[21] of which
Mrs. Carlyle complained; but in reality the position is far
otherwise. Usually a complete stranger to any sentiment of
hatred or animosity, she nevertheless had an intense dislike for
people who revealed no depth of feeling, who displayed no
real enthusiasm for any subject, who were witty at the most
superficial levels, who satirized others only to draw attention
to their own verbal brilliance, their own smart turns of phrase.
Undoubtedly Mrs. Gaskell must have encountered many such
in the social circles to which she belonged. We have met this
type of person in *Ruth,* where Mr. Hickson is shown speaking
eloquently on the side of expediency[22]; and we shall come
upon a similar sort of conversationalist in *North and South.*

---

[15] *Works,* III, 511-512.
[16] *Works,* III, 499.
[17] *Works,* III, 507.
[18] *Works,* III, 507.
[19] *Works,* III, 509.
[20] *Works,* III, 508.
[21] *New Letters and Memorials of Jane Welsh Carlyle,* ed. Carlyle, II,
29. See too Whitfield, *Mrs Gaskell,* p. 35; and Hanson and Hanson,
Necessary Evil: The Life of Jane Welsh Carlyle, p. 407.
[22] *Works,* III, 251-255.

Readers of Mrs. Gaskell should note her disapproval of such worldly, flippant attitudes. Here, as elsewhere, what she wrote appears to have been greatly influenced by what her observation and experience provided.

SECTION III

North and South (1854-1855)

What is probably the first extant reference to 'North and South', serialized in *Household Words*[1] between 2 September 1854 and 27 January 1855, occurred as early as 3 May 1853, in a letter from Charles Dickens[2], where there is a hint that he too was attracted by the same subject. His interest apparently resulted in 'Hard Times', which directly preceded Mrs. Gaskell's story in the weekly numbers of the magazine. According to Mrs. Gaskell's own testimony she had had the plot and its characters in her head some time before she began writing[3]. Indeed it seems to have been her custom to plan her novels, in outline at least: preliminary sketches were prepared for both *Ruth*[4] and *Mary Barton*[5].

Having an overall scheme in view did not preclude Mrs. Gaskell from making changes of detail. At a certain stage she considered introducing a new character, as is shown by one of

[1] X, 61-68, 85-92, 109-113, 133-138, 157-162, 181-187, 205-209, 229-237, 253-259, 277-284, 301-307, 325-333, 349-357, 373-382, 397-404, 421-429, 445-453, 469-477, 493-501, 517-527, 540-551, 561-570.

[2] *The Letters of Charles Dickens,* ed. Dexter, II, 459: letter to Mrs. Gaskell.

[3] See her statement in a letter to Mrs. Jameson, quoted in Beatrice Caroline (Mrs. Steuart) Erskine, ed. *Anna Jameson: Letters and Friendships* (1812-1860), London: T. Fisher Unwin, Ltd., 1915, p. 296. The original of this letter (*G.L.*, No. 225), written one Sunday evening [January 1855], is now in the Yale University Library (MS Vault Sect. 16); its complete quotation by Mrs. Erskine (ed. *op. cit.,* pp. 296-297) is fairly accurate.

[4] Charlotte Brontë mentions receiving the sketch of *Ruth* (see Wise and Symington, *The Brontës: Their Lives, Friendships and Correspondence,* III, 332).

[5] There is a copy of a rough sketch for *Mary Barton* in Shorter and Symington, 'Correspondence, Articles & Notes Relating to Mrs. E. C. Gaskell. Transcripts', Vol. II, Section on *Mary Barton*—a typescript in the Gaskell Section, Brotherton Collection, Leeds University Library. See our Appendix I.

her letters to Forster[6]; but in the event this female figure was
reserved for *Sylvia's Lovers*. Similarly she asked Catherine
Winkworth whether she should facilitate the failure of the
manufacturer, Thornton, by making a fire burn down his mills
and house[7]; however she must have subsequently decided against
doing so. Knowing that Dickens in his story intended to cover
a similar field (the social conditions in Northern England), she
enquired whether or not he planned to introduce a strike[8];
finding he had 'no intention of striking'[9], she did. Thus it
appears that minor matters and details of secondary importance
were invented as the occasion arose, albeit within a framework
long conceived of. To reveal Mrs. Gaskell at work, inventing
as she went along, we shall quote from one of her letters to
Mrs. William Shaen (Emily Winkworth).

[6] This letter of Sunday [23 April 1854] is in the British Museum (Add.
MS. 38794, ff. 263-266). Relevant, if slightly inaccurate, quotations are
given by both Miss Haldane (*Mrs. Gaskell and Her Friends,* p. 152) and
Miss Rubenius (*The Woman Question in Mrs. Gaskell's Life and Works,*
p. 258). This letter appears as *G.L.,* No. 191.
[7] When writing on Saturday evening [14 October 1854], in a letter,
apparently begun on Wednesday evening [11 October 1854], post-marked
15 and 16 October 1854, now in the Gaskell Section, Brotherton Collection, Leeds University Library. It is relevantly quoted by Miss Rubenius
(*The Woman Question in Mrs. Gaskell's Life and Works,* p. 36) and,
more fully but even less accurately, by Miss Haldane (*Mrs. Gaskell and
Her Friends,* pp. 103-104). The letter occurs as *G.L.,* No 211.
[8] In her letter to John Forster of Sunday [23 April 1854]—now in the
British Museum (Add. MS. 38794, ff. 263-266)—Mrs. Gaskell expressed
her relief on finding Dickens was 'not going to have a strike' (f. 265ᵛ)—
the relevant passage being quoted by Miss Haldane (*Mrs. Gaskell and Her
Friends,* p. 152) and, briefly as well as less accurately, by Miss Rubenius
(*The Woman Question in Mrs. Gaskell's Life and Works,* p. 153, fn. 2).
Writing on 18 April 1854 (a copy of part of this letter being in the Gaskell
Section, Brotherton Collection, Leeds University Library), Forster had told
her, regarding the possibility of both authors' treating industrial discontent,
that he regretted the likelihood of a clash, and would suggest she might
write to Dickens, mentioning her own intention and asking for his views
on the advisability of her work following his (in *Household Words*);
Forster had remarked, however, that he did not anticipate the objection
she did, since her strike would have its own *raison d'être*. Mrs. Gaskell's
Sunday letter to Forster appears as *G.L.,* No. 191.
[9] *The Letters of Charles Dickens,* ed. Dexter, II, 554: letter to Mrs.
Gaskell of 21 April 1854—Dexter encloses the year within square brackets;
yet 1854 clearly occurs in the original letter, now in The John Rylands
Library, Manchester (English MS. 729/20). See too our last footnote.

I've got to (with Margaret—I'm off at her now following your
letter) when they've quarrelled, silently, after the lie and she
knows she loves him, and he is trying not to love her; and Frederick is gone back to Spain and Mrs. Hale is dead and Mr. Bell
has come to stay with the Hales, and Mr. Thornton ought to be
developing himself—and Mr. Hale ought to die—and if I could
get over this next piece I could swim through the London life
beautifully into the sunset glory of the last scene. But hitherto
Thornton is good; and I'm afraid of a touch marring him; and
I want to keep his character consistent with itself, and large and
strong and tender, and *yet a master*. That's my next puzzle. I am
enough on not to hurry; and yet I don't know if waiting and
thinking will bring any new ideas about him.[10]

One may say that, in *North and South*[11], Mrs. Gaskell
became artistically aware of herself. Although for some purposes it is sensible to group this novel with *Mary Barton,* since
they both treat the Condition-of-England Question, a crafts-
man's concern is revealed in *North and South* which is not
found to the same degree in *Mary Barton,* or, indeed, in *Ruth.*
The celebrated quarrel with Dickens[12] regarding the need to
conform to *Household Words* space-demands illustrates the
author's consciousness of her literary responsibility. Previously
she had been more or less content to submit to his editorial
advice; now we find her adamant, stipulating to Wills that the
proofs should not be touched "even by Mr. Dickens."[13]
It would falsify to call *Mary Barton* a working-class love
story, yet there is truth in describing *North and South* as a
middle-class romance. This at least serves as a warning not to
place it too readily alongside Mrs. Gaskell's first two novels, each
recognized by her contemporaries as having been written with a
purpose; for it is upon the personal relationship between the
heroine, Margaret Hale, a country-parson's daughter, and John
Thornton, a self-made captain of industry, that the plot hinges.
The greater part of one's interest is engaged by the development

---

[10] Quoted, from Mrs. Gaskell's letter (*G.L.,* No. 217) of 27 October
1854, by Miss Haldane (*Mrs. Gaskell and Her Friends,* p. 97), who puts
in italics what is here in roman, and *vice versa.*
[11] [Elizabeth Cleghorn Gaskell] *North and South,* 2 vols., London:
Chapman and Hall, 1855.
[12] Full details are given by Miss Hopkins—'Dickens and Mrs. Gaskell',
The Huntington Library Quarterly, IX (1946), 357-385; *Elizabeth Gaskell,*
esp. pp. 135-157.
[13] Quoted by Dickens, in a letter to Wilkie Collins of 24 March 1855
(*The Letters of Charles Dickens,* ed. Dexter, II, 646).

of the love-theme, a gradual growth from mutual hostility to the most powerful affection. Mrs. Gaskell displays a remarkable grasp of the psychology of sentiment—remarkable especially because her previous work gave little hint of this capacity. One is at a loss to offer any explanation for such insights into the human heart, except by mentioning that Marianne and Meta (her two eldest daughters, born respectively on 12 September 1834 and 5 February 1837) would be of an age for their mother to concern herself in their relations with men. Margaret Hale, when the story begins, is eighteen years old[14]; so in that respect maternal feelings may have stimulated, provided *data* for, artistic invention. However what remain of Mrs. Gaskell's letters to her daughters[15] will not sanction our over-straining this hypothesis, though they do reveal her regard for their general behaviour, with conduct towards the opposite sex more or less taken for granted in the advice at large.

Mrs. Gaskell begins the love-plot by describing Mr. Henry Lennox and the events leading to his proposal of marriage; the relationship between him and Margaret acts as a contrast for what is to follow, that between herself and Thornton. The reader is left in no uncertainty about the genuineness of Lennox's love (we have such a minor yet indicative detail as his attraction to an Italian word-list because it had been copied out in her hand[16]); there are, nonetheless, important qualifications. Firstly, a want of real passion is suggested. His very declaration[17], while proclaiming that his better and deeper sentiments had found an outlet through contact with Margaret, has, even so, a touch of irony about it, implying a certain reservation, a lack of whole-hearted self-giving. Her immediate response to his offer is doubtless intended to be that of the reader also.

---

[14] *Works,* IV, 5.
[15] A number of such letters (chiefly to Marianne) may be found in the Gaskell Section, Brotherton Collection, Leeds University Library; in the Yale University Library; and in the possession of Mrs. Margaret Trevor Jones: there is an extensive collection of transcripts of Mrs. Gaskell's letters, mostly to Marianne, once owned by Mr. J. T. Lancaster and now belonging to the present writer. All these and several others are printed by Chapple and Pollard (ed. *The Letters of Mrs Gaskell*), whose Indexes must be consulted.
[16] *Works,* IV, 23.
[17] *Works,* IV, 29-31.

Margaret could not answer this. The whole tone of it annoyed her. It seemed to touch on and call out all the points of differ-ence which had often repelled her in him; while yet he was the pleasantest man, the most sympathising friend, the person of all others who understood her best in Harley Street. She felt a tinge of contempt mingle itself with her pain at having refused him.[18]

However Margaret's primary reaction, as she herself recog-nized, had been one of sorrow at the proposal's ever having been made—a sorrow shared by Lennox, who 'seemed for a moment to have slid over the boundary between friendship and love; and, the instant afterwards, to regret it nearly as much as she did, although for different reasons.'[19]

Lennox contemplated another bid for Margaret's hand when, after all those trials in Milton-Northern which followed upon the Hales' quitting their beloved Helstone vicarage, she once more returned, though with mother and father both dead, to the old, familiar, Harley-Street *milieu*. Mrs. Gaskell admirably brings out his essential egotism.

From this time the clever and ambitious man bent all his powers to gaining Margaret. He loved her sweet beauty. He saw the latent sweep of her mind, which could easily (he thought) be led to embrace all the objects on which he had set his heart.[20]

Perhaps she overplayed her hand with the emphatically pejora-tive 'clever and ambitious'; but the last sentence does its work well enough.

It is appropriate to notice that Lennox was a lawyer. Mrs. Gaskell almost invariably looked on his profession with distrust, apparently thinking that the legal mind was peculiarly worldly, calculating, clever, and ambitious. We have already pointed to the flashy Mr. Hickson, in *Ruth*[21]; and those brilliant verbal displays, aiming at wit rather than truth, which were censured in 'Company Manners'[22], also find echoes in the conversation of Lennox and his smart friends.

These dinners were delightful; but even here Margaret's dissatis-faction found her out. Every talent, every feeling, every acquire-ment; nay, even every tendency towards virtue, was used up as materials for fireworks; the hidden, sacred fire exhausted itself in

[18] *Works,* IV, 31.
[19] *Works,* IV, 234.
[20] *Works,* IV, 495.

[21] *Works,* III, 251-255.
[22] *Works,* III, 508.

sparkle and crackle. They talked about art in a merely sensuous way, dwelling on outside effects, instead of allowing themselves to learn what it has to teach. They lashed themselves up into an enthusiasm about high subjects in company, and never thought about them when they were alone; they squandered their capabilities of appreciation into a mere flow of appropriate words.[23]

Margaret's response to such superficial, though glittering, talk is made explicit in a subsequent conversation with Lennox. He, having noticed her disapproval of his friends' witty advocacy of what was obviously wrong, nevertheless remarked :

> "But it was very clever. How every word told! Do you remember the happy epithets?"
> "Yes."
> "And despise them, you would like to add. Pray don't scruple, though he is my friend."
> "There! that is the exact tone in you that"—she stopped short.[24]

Two of Mrs. Gaskell's daughters married lawyers, though not till many years after the publication of *North and South*. However Mrs. Gaskell would, without doubt, have obtained long before then a considerable knowledge of members of the profession—gained by dining in their presence, paying calls on their wives, and so forth. After the success of *Mary Barton*, when she was lionized in London circles, she must have been especially well placed to observe ambitious, rising young barristers and their ways.

Thornton, both in himself and in his relations with Margaret, is of a very different order; since his love cannot be dissociated from his general character, to this we must now turn. One of his most important qualities is a fundamental honesty, revealed in every facet of his life. At one level it is seen in his refusal to endanger other people's money in a speculative venture which, if brought off, would have prevented his own ruin[25]; here, Mrs. Gaskell hints, someone like Lennox might have acted differently[26]. At another level it is shown when he declined to take advantage of an opportunity to escape acknowledging his failure in business[27]. His rectitude is further manifested when, instead of dismissing out of hand a most unlikely story, told by

---

[23] *Works*, IV, 486-487.
[24] *Works*, IV, 487.
[25] *Works*, IV, 505-509.
[26] *Works*, IV, 514.
[27] *Works*, IV, 514.

a workman well known as a trouble-maker, he investigated the matter and found he had been told the truth[28]. Thornton's tenderness towards Mr. Hale during their conversation after Mrs. Hale's death illustrates his religious integrity.

> Mr. Thornton said very little; but every sentence he uttered added to Mr. Hale's reliance on and regard for him. Was it that he paused in the expression of some remembered agony, Mr. Thornton's two or three words would complete the sentence, and show how deeply its meaning was entered into. Was it a doubt—a fear—a wandering uncertainty seeking rest, but finding none—so tear-blinded were its eyes—Mr. Thornton, instead of being shocked, seemed to have passed through that very stage of thought himself, and could suggest where the exact ray of light was to be found, which should make the dark places plain.[29]

How very different is this from the casual references to ' "imaginary doubts" '[30] and ' "uncertain fancies" '[31] made by Lennox, who seemed to assess Mr. Hale's resignation for conscience' sake largely in terms of the annoyance it must surely have caused Margaret[32].

Contrasting Thornton's offer with the one she had received from Lennox, Margaret realized his passionate proposal sprang from a love which had grown out of antagonism and opposition. The mill-owner's declaration seems far from fortuitous, not simply the result of an attempt to provide the conventional solution to a compromising situation. For some time the perceptive reader had been aware of certain pointers and clues, designed to indicate to the onlooker, if not to the participants themselves, the way things would go. It is not so much the debates and disputes upon which Margaret and Thornton engaged which are here of importance, it is rather the hints and innuendoes which tell the tale. There was, for example, something which compelled Thornton, on first meeting Margaret, to change his mind about going in search of Mr. Hale, and instead remain to talk with her[33]—something which also made him irritated when she did not second her father's invitation that he should join them for lunch, even though it would have been most inconvenient to him to stay[34]. Similarly,

---

28 *Works*, IV, 379-389.
29 *Works*, IV, 327-328.
30 *Works*, IV, 454.
31 *Works*, IV, 454.
32 *Works*, IV, 454.
33 *Works*, IV, 70-71.
34 *Works*, IV, 72.

during his first tea-taking with the Hales, Thornton, having watched Mr. Hale use his daughter's finger and thumb as sugar-tongs, half-longed for Margaret to serve him in the same way[35] : it is just the sort of action which a potential lover would be likely to have noticed. One could easily multiply such examples of Mrs. Gaskell's observant eye for the psychologically meaningful.

In treating Thornton when fully aware of his affections, Mrs. Gaskell is equally satisfactory as a novelist of sentiment; there is, for instance, an excellent account of his vain attempts to forget Margaret after she had refused him[36]. However the following quotations will sufficiently support our praise. Firstly there is the description of Thornton's behaviour in Margaret's presence after she had declined his offer.

> He never looked at her; and yet, the careful avoidance of his eyes betokened that in some way he knew exactly where, if they fell by chance, they would rest on her. If she spoke, he gave no sign of attention, and yet his next speech to any one else was modified by what she had said; sometimes there was an express answer to what she had remarked, but given to another person, as though unsuggested by her.[37]

Thornton's feelings, when he imagines Margaret in love with another, are just as convincingly rendered.

> Just before Mr. Thornton came up to Mrs. Boucher's door, Margaret came out of it. She did not see him; and he followed her for several yards, admiring her light and easy walk, and her tall and graceful figure. But, suddenly, this simple emotion of pleasure was tainted, poisoned by jealousy. He wished to overtake her, and speak to her, to see how she would receive him, now she must know he was aware of some other attachment. He wished too, but of this wish he was rather ashamed, that she should know that he had justified her wisdom in sending Higgins to him to ask for work, and had repented him of his morning's decision.[38]

On Margaret's side the course of love follows a rather similar pattern, though with her it is more delayed. The first suggestion of a changed attitude towards Thornton, subsequent to her rejecting his proposal, is her surprise at Frederick Hale's mistaking him for a shopman; she hastily corrects this error, yet reflects that she too, at their first meeting, had thought of him

---

[35] *Works,* IV, 91.   [37] *Works,* IV, 283.
[36] *Works,* IV, 245-246.   [38] *Works,* IV, 389-390.

in much the same way (' "not quite a gentleman; but that was hardly to be expected" '39)40. Later she finds herself putting Mr. Thornton's disapproval on a par with Divine displeasure, though scarcely caring to admit why 'he haunted her imagination so persistently'41. Mrs. Gaskell supplies a subtle analysis of Margaret's state of mind, indicating what really lay behind her desire for Thornton's good opinion42. A further stage is marked by the following sentence.

> Margaret had to pull herself up from indulging a bad trick, which she had lately fallen into, of trying to imagine how every event that she heard of in relation to Mr. Thornton would affect him: whether he would like it or dislike it.43

To add pathos to Margaret's position, there is her fondness for her cousin's little boy—a fondness which, even so, 'gave her a taste of the feeling that she believed would be denied to her for ever.'44 By means like these the author keeps Margaret's half-conscious but unacknowledged love for Thornton in view, thereby preparing for the final scene45 where, as she herself remarked, all went 'smash in a moment'46 between them both.

Although realistically presenting the relations between hero and heroine, Mrs. Gaskell gives a rather conventional kind of complication to the love-plot by means of a misunderstanding (Thornton's belief that Margaret had directed her affections elsewhere)—yet in such a way as not to stretch probability too far. Functionally more important is the part assigned to Mr. Bell. He first suspected that Thornton and Margaret might have a *tendresse* for each other47; he furthered the aforementioned misunderstanding by a confident affirmation that Frederick was not in Milton-Northern at the time of Mrs. Hale's death48; his

---

39 *Works,* IV, 73.
40 *Works,* IV, 304-305.
41 *Works,* IV, 339.
42 *Works,* IV, 383-384.
43 *Works,* IV, 413.
44 *Works,* IV, 485.
45 *Works,* IV, 518-521.
46 Quoted in Erskine, ed. *Anna Jameson*: *Letters and Friendships* (1812-1860), p. 296. Mrs. Gaskell's original letter (*G.L.,* No. 225), written to Mrs. Jameson one Sunday evening [January 1855], is now in the Yale University Library—MS Vault Sect. 16.
47 *Works,* IV, 401.
48 *Works,* IV, 429.

words, attempting to persuade an apparently indifferent Thornton of Margaret's worth, ironically expressed Thornton's own
sentiments[49]. Bell is, in many ways, the centre of the action,
about whom all the other characters turn : through his good
offices the Hales went to Milton-Northern[50]; by means of his
legacy[51] Margaret came to marry Thornton.

Mrs. Gaskell recognized two possible criticisms of the love-
plot. Firstly she knew that the exigencies of serial-publication
had cramped her style, bringing about a perhaps too hasty
conclusion[52]. Certainly there does seem something hurriedly contrived about the final coming-together of Margaret and Thornton, though, on reflexion, one might well agree with the author
that, given two such people, this sort of ending is not at all
improbable[53]. The second objection, to be inferred from a
remark by Parthenope Nightingale[54], namely that Margaret,
while making Thornton happy, will not be so herself, hardly
requires serious consideration. Unfavourable opinions about the
after-life of its characters make little difference to the achievement of the novel. Mrs. Gaskell's first attempt at a large-scale
love-story is signally successful.

Even when Mrs. Gaskell had written quite a large part of
her work, she "had", according to Dickens, "left the title of
the story blank."[55] Possibly Forster suggested 'North and South'
as being suitable[56]; but it was Dickens[57] who saw to it that the

[49] *Works*, IV, 430.
[50] *Works*, IV, 41-42.
[51] *Works*, IV, 492.
[52] See Appendix II.
[53] See her Sunday evening [January 1855] letter to Mrs. Jameson,
quoted in Erskine, ed. *Anna Jameson: Letters and Friendships* (1812-
1860), pp. 296-297. The original letter (*G.L.*, No. 225) is, as we have
noted, now in the Yale University Library.
[54] In a letter, written to Mrs. Gaskell from Embley one Saturday night
[1855], now in the Gaskell Section, Brotherton Collection, Leeds University Library. It is relevantly and fairly accurately quoted in Haldane, *Mrs.
Gaskell and Her Friends*, p. 105.
[55] Quoted—in Hopkins, 'Dickens and Mrs. Gaskell', *The Huntington
Library Quarterly*, IX (1946), 370; *Elizabeth Gaskell*, p. 146—from his
letter to Mrs. Gaskell of 2 July 1854 in the Berg Collection at the New
York Public Library.
[56] The opinion of Miss Haldane (*Mrs. Gaskell and Her Friends*, p.
108). However Dickens, on 3 May 1853, had promised Mrs. Gaskell to
'think of a name' (*The Letters of Charles Dickens*, ed. Dexter, II, 459).
[57] See the instructions to Wills in his letter of 30 July 1854 (*The Letters
of Charles Dickens*, ed. Dexter, II, 572).

serial came out beneath this heading rather than under 'Margaret Hale' (probably the one offered by the author[58] on analogy with her first two novels, each of which was called after its heroine). Perhaps critics[59] have been inclined to make a little too much play with this title, so it will be well to recall how the phrase is introduced.

Margaret Hale, the daughter of a country clergyman who resigned his living for conscientious reasons, goes with her family to the industrial town of Milton-Northern (Manchester). She there chances to encounter a middle-aged workman, and, in the course of their first real conversation together, the subsequent dialogue occurs.

> "Thank yo, miss. Bessy'll think a deal o' them flowers; that hoo will; and I shall think a deal o' yor kindness. Yo're not of this country, I reckon?"
> "No!" said Margaret, half sighing. "I come from the South —from Hampshire," she continued, a little afraid of wounding his consciousness of ignorance, if she used a name which he did not understand.
> "That's beyond London, I reckon? And I come fro' Burnley-ways, and forty miles to th' North. And yet, yo see, North and

---

[58] Mrs. Gaskell speaks of 'Margaret' in her Sunday [23 April 1854] letter to John Forster (in the British Museum—Add. MS. 38794, ff. 263-266) and in her letter to Mrs. William Shaen (Emily Winkworth) of 27 October 1854 (quoted in Haldane, *Mrs. Gaskell and Her Friends,* p. 97); she refers to 'M. Hale' in a [(pre 15) May 1854] letter to Forster (the relevant part being in the British Museum—Add. MS. 38794, ff. 267-268) and in the Saturday evening [14 October 1854] passage of her letter to Catherine Winkworth, apparently begun on Wednesday evening [11 October 1854], post-marked 15 and 16 October 1854 (in the Gaskell Section, Brotherton Collection, Leeds University Library): in this connexion, pertinent if slightly inaccurate quotations are given by Miss Haldane (*Mrs. Gaskell and Her Friends,* pp. 152; 154, 103) and Miss Rubenius (*The Women Question in Mrs. Gaskell's Life and Works,* pp. 258; 35). The aforesaid letters occur respectively as *G.L.,* Nos. 191, 217; 192 (dated [? 8-14 May 1854]), 211: also relevant for the novel's title are *G.L.,* Nos. 200, 218 ('Margaret'); 195 ('Margaret Hale'); 220 ('Death & Variations'). See too Dickens' remarks in his letter to Mrs. Gaskell of 2 July 1854 (quoted in Hopkins, 'Dickens and Mrs. Gaskell', *The Huntington Library Quarterly,* IX, 370; *Elizabeth Gaskell,* p. 146) and in that to her of 26 July 1854 (*The Letters of Charles Dickens,* ed. Dexter, II, 571).
[59] Notably Miss Elizabeth Dorothea Cole Bowen (intro. *North and South,* by Mrs. Gaskell, London: John Lehmann, 1951, pp. v-viii).

South has both met and made kind o' friends in this big smoky place."[60]

One must, however, resist the temptation to make a crude contrast; for there are in the novel at least five distinct *milieux* —London (Harley Street), Hampshire (Helstone), and the three worlds of Milton-Northern.

North and South opens and closes with the Harley-Street set. Mrs. Chadwick[61] has pointed out that visits to her uncle, Swinton Holland of Park Lane, and her cousin, Sir Henry Holland of Lower Brook Street, very likely supplied Mrs. Gaskell with material for these 'delightful sketches of London drawing-room life'[62]. Moreover the author's own lionizing, after the publication of *Mary Barton*, should also be taken into account. In treating this world, Mrs. Gaskell shows herself as a social satirist, albeit a mild one. She admirably conveys the superficiality of the existence led by Mrs. Shaw and her daughter. To Edith one of the most important problems for her future married life at Corfu would be how to keep the piano in good tune[63]; her mother, apparently enjoying the romance of the engagement more than Edith herself, was wont to sigh emphatically in the midst of the comfortable surroundings she enjoyed as a widow, as if to suggest that 'love had not been her motive for marrying the General.'[64] Mrs. Gaskell's analysis of Mrs. Shaw (who takes on a representative quality) is exquisitely humorous and psychologically acute.

> . . . Mrs. Shaw welcomed him in her gentle kindly way, which had always something plaintive in it, arising from the long habit of considering herself a victim to an uncongenial marriage. Now that, the General being gone, she had every good of life, with as few drawbacks as possible, she had been rather perplexed to find an anxiety, if not a sorrow. She had, however, of late settled upon

---

[60] *Works,* IV, 82-83: also relevant is a subsequent exchange between Margaret and Higgins (*Works,* IV, 363-365). Part of the novel may have been written in Hampshire; for, according to Miss Haldane (*Mrs. Gaskell and Her Friends,* p. 108), some of the work was done at Embley (the Nightingales' estate on the edge of the New Forest)—though this could be a slip of the pen for Lea Hurst, the Nightingales' residence to which Mrs. Gaskell was invited in Autumn 1854 'so that she might have a quiet time for writing "North and South" ' (*op. cit.,* p. 89).

[61] *Mrs. Gaskell,* pp. 20, 97, 99.

[62] Chadwick, *Mrs. Gaskell,* p. 99.

[63] *Works,* IV, 1.   [64] *Works,* IV, 3.

her own health as a source of apprehension; she had a nervous little cough whenever she thought about it; and some complaisant doctor ordered her just what she desired—a winter in Italy. Mrs. Shaw had as strong wishes as most people, but she never liked to do anything from the open and acknowledged motive of her own good will and pleasure; she preferred being compelled to gratify herself by some other person's command or desire. She really did persuade herself that she was submitting to some hard external necessity; and thus she was able to moan and complain in her soft manner, all the time she was in reality doing just what she liked.[65]

We have already glanced at another aspect of the London social world, that evoked by a reference to Mr. Henry Lennox and his clever friends. Mr. Lennox was rightly disdainful[66] of the idle but amiable behaviour of his brother, the Captain; yet his own worldly ambition offers no positive alternative in Mrs. Gaskell's eyes: both modes of conduct are described in such a way as to call forth slight contempt.

It would be possible to expatiate at length on Mrs. Gaskell's Harley-Street descriptions, especially on those telling turns of phrase whereby the author discreetly reveals her own moral stand-point. Into that luxurious household, one learns, 'the bare knowledge of the existence of every trouble or care seemed scarcely to have penetrated. The wheels of the machinery of daily life were well oiled, and went along with delicious smoothness.'[67] Indeed to Margaret it seemed that 'the very servants lived in an underground world of their own, of which she knew neither the hopes nor the fears; they only seemed to start into existence when some want or whim of their master and mistress needed them.'[68]

The Hampshire village of Helstone provides the second type of environment. These Helstone scenes flank the central, industrial, part of *North and South*. The settings for the novel are presented much in this order: London, Helstone, Milton-Northern, Helstone, London—presented, that is to say, in the two-volume edition; for the second Helstone section ('Helstone Revisited', we may call it) was the one major innovation when the novel came out in book-form[69]. Thus, by the symmetry of Mrs. Gaskell's plot-devising, the story comes full circle.

[65] *Works,* IV, 11.   [68] *Works,* IV, 445.
[66] *Works,* IV, 485.   [69] See Appendix II.
[67] *Works,* IV, 444.

As regards the Helstone *milieu,* the point to emphasize is
that Mrs. Gaskell presents this rural setting realistically rather
than idyllically. Certainly Margaret is, at times, given to ideal-
izing Helstone, as when she confesses to Lennox that it ' "is
like a village in a poem" '[70]; but Mrs. Gaskell, although mentioning that on her return home many of Margaret's rosy
expectations were fulfilled, does not neglect the less pleasant
aspects of the rustic scene. During summer days Margaret could
roam in the forest with enjoyment, visiting old people, nursing
babies, engaging generally in out-of-door activities[71]. Yet life
indoors had its drawbacks—Mrs. Hale was somewhat discon-
tented with her position as the wife of a poor clergyman[72],
feeling especially the absence of intercourse with cultivated
people[73]; Margaret herself found it difficult to fill up the
autumnal evenings[74]. Worst of all, perhaps, was Mr. Hale's
introspective self-absorption, the signs of his being bewildered
and overpowered, his significant sighing aloud[75].

Nevertheless the most memorable parts of the first Helstone
section are delightful and pleasing. There is the picture of the
countryside in late July[76]; the sketching expedition of Margaret
and Henry Lennox into the forest[77]; and the parsonage dinner,
with desert taken in the garden with bucolic simplicity[78]. When
the Hales have to leave Helstone, Mrs. Gaskell is at her best,
describing the inevitable melancholy occasioned by such a departure. Excellently done is the poetic evocation of Margaret's
nostalgia on walking in the beloved vicarage-garden : a blend
of serenity, pastoral beauty, tranquillity, quiet recollection, and
accurate observation, this passage is too long for complete quotation; but something of the atmosphere is rendered in the
following extract.

> There was a filmy veil of soft dull mist obscuring, but not hiding,
> all objects, giving them a lilac hue, for the sun had not yet
> fully set; a robin was singing—perhaps, Margaret thought, the
> very robin that her father had so often talked of as his winter
> pet, and for which he had made, with his own hands, a kind of
> robin-house by his study-window. The leaves were more gorgeous

[70] *Works,* IV, 9.   [75] *Works,* IV, 16.
[71] *Works,* IV, 16.   [76] *Works,* IV, 15-16.
[72] *Works,* IV, 16-19.   [77] *Works,* IV, 24-26.
[73] *Works,* IV, 17.   [78] *Works,* IV, 27-28.
[74] *Works,* IV, 18-19.

than ever; the first touch of frost would lay them all low on the
ground. Already one or two kept constantly floating down,
amber and golden in the low slanting sun-rays.[79]

Besides such long poetic passages, Mrs. Gaskell makes use, as
in her earlier work, of little details which have the poetry of
the everyday about them. One instance is the touching irony
that the weeping servants, seeing Margaret apparently calm and
collected in giving orders, should think her indifferent to the
removal from Helstone[80]; another is the beauty of Margaret's
action in relinquishing her last chance of looking at the old
church spire, for she acknowledged her father's greater right
to the window of their departing carriage[81]. A little later Mrs.
Gaskell brings out the pathos of Mrs. Hale's reaction (' "Dear!
how altered!" '[82]) on seeing the familiar London shop where,
many years before, she had bought her wedding things; further
pathos arises because, by a strange quirk of fortune, she spied
in the street Henry Lennox, and told her daughter.

> Margaret started forwards, and as quickly fell back, half-smiling
> at herself for the sudden motion. They were a hundred yards
> away by this time; but he seemed like a relic of Helstone—he
> was associated with a bright morning, an eventful day, and she
> should have liked to have seen him, without his seeing her—with-
> out the chance of their speaking.[83]

Since Mr. Hale's resignation has such important consequences, beginning with the family removal from Helstone, it is
appropriate to say something about that event. In the printed
versions of *North and South*[84], little explanation is afforded
beyond his quoting a passage from Joshua Oldfield[85] and his
admission of an inability ' "to make a fresh declaration of con-

---

[79] *Works*, IV, 59.
[80] *Works*, IV, 59.
[81] *Works*, IV, 63.
[82] *Works*, IV, 64.
[83] *Works*, IV, 64.
[84] Dickens *may* have caused some cutting (see his letters to Mrs. Gaskell
of Thursday Evening 16 [15] June 1854, 26 July 1854, 20 August 1854—*The
Letters of Charles Dickens,* ed. Dexter, II, 562, 571, 582—; see too our
Appendix II); but this is a moot point. That no changes were made is the
view of Miss Hopkins—'Dickens and Mrs. Gaskell', *The Huntington Library Quarterly,* IX (1946), 372; *Elizabeth Gaskell,* p. 147.
[85] *Works*, IV, 37.

formity to the Liturgy" [86] : Mrs. Gaskell was not a novelist to
engage in polemic disputation, least of all on religious questions;
as she remarked to Charles Eliot Norton, 'about doctrines . . .
we can never be certain in this world.'[87] Thus, with the early
chapters before her, Charlotte Brontë found no 'narrowness of
views or bitterness of feeling towards the Church or her Clergy,'[88]
but rather a 'defence of those who conscientiously differ from
her, and feel it a duty to leave her fold.'[89] There was little
need for much originality of invention in this episode. Doubts
were, at the time, in the air generally; yet specific instances are
not lacking: it is unnecessary to claim that Mr. Hale's case is
based on any *one* of these, only to show that Mrs. Gaskell had
plenty of material at hand. Her own father, William Stevenson, following the example of his friend, the Rev. George
Wicke[90], had scruples about being paid to preach, and so resigned from the ministry. Her friend, Travers Madge, had the
same conscientious reasons for turning from the profession[91].
Then, too, one must take into account the influence of J. A.
Froude, whom 'Mr Hale . . . resembles . . . in not a few
features'[92], and who, like the former Helstone vicar, was employed as a tutor by a manufacturer[93]. We are most fortunate

---

[86] *Works,* IV, 38. In a [(post 15) May 1854] letter to Marianne, a copy
of which, once owned by Mr. J. T. Lancaster, belongs to the present
writer, Mrs. Gaskell acknowledged that, despite feeling more devotional
at Church than at Chapel, she considered certain parts of the Litany
contrary to her faith; for, not believing Christ co-equal with the Father,
she deemed it wrong for her to worship Him as God. This letter (*G.L.*,
No. 198a) is dated [May-June 1854] by Chapple and Pollard. (A copy of
The Book of Common Prayer, bearing Mrs. Gaskell's autograph and dated
28 June 1855, is in the hands of the present writer.)
[87] *Gaskell-Norton letters,* ed. Whitehill, p. 33: *G.L.,* No. 418.
[88] Quoted in Wise and Symington, *The Brontës: Their Lives, Friendships and Correspondence,* IV, 153: letter to Mrs. Gaskell of 30 September 1854.
[89] Quoted in Wise and Symington, *The Brontës: Their Lives, Friendships and Correspondence,* IV, 153: letter to Mrs. Gaskell of 30 September 1854.
[90] Sanders, *Elizabeth Gaskell,* pp. 1-2.
[91] Chadwick, *Mrs. Gaskell,* pp. 154, 165; and Herford, *Travers Madge:
A Memoir,* pp. 30-31.
[92] Whitfield, *Mrs Gaskell,* p. 25; see too p. 125.
[93] Whitfield, *Mrs Gaskell,* p. 25. Other relevant information on Froude
(1818-1894) in this connexion may be found in Waldo Hilary Dunn,
James Anthony Froude: A Biography, 2 vols., Oxford: The Clarendon
Press, 1961-1963, I, 151-167, 186; Shaen, ed. *Memorials of Two Sisters,*

in having Mrs. Gaskell's views on Mr. Hale, especially since her words imply that his behaviour may well have been based on the author's own experience.

> Mr. Hale is not a 'sceptic'; he has *doubts*, and can resolve greatly about great things, and is capable of self-sacrifice in theory; but in the details of practice he is weak and vacillating. I know a character just like his, a clergyman who has left the Church from principle, and in that did finely; but his daily life is a constant unspoken regret that he did so, although he would do it again if need be.[94]

The second Helstone section, that dealing with Margaret's return in the company of Mr. Bell, most appropriately opens with a description of what Margaret could see from the carriage window: the 'hamlets sleeping in the warm light of the pure sun'[95]; at the passing stations but few people, suggesting 'they were too lazily content to wish to travel;'[96] spectators whose only occupation seemed to be watching the trains go by[97]; the hot air dancing 'over the golden stillness of the land,'[98] while

---

pp. 45-47, 63-66, 74; Albert F. Pollard's *Dictionary of National Biography* article; and Rubenius, *The Woman Question in Mrs. Gaskell's Life and Works*, pp. 246-247—Miss Rubenius (*op. cit.*, p. 247) has an extract from Froude's 5 January [1862] letter to Mrs. Gaskell which refers to his and his first wife's strange feelings on finding photographed in *North and South* the—presumably their—little Green Heys drawing-room (not "dining room", as appears in the quotation, which does not quite follow the original letter in The John Rylands Library, Manchester: English MS. 730/30); however, she (*op. cit.*, p. 17) sees in Mr. Hale's reluctance to face anxiety one of Mr. Gaskell's traits. Perhaps this is the place to record that, according to verbal information received from Professor Whitfield, Margaret Hale was to some degree based on Froude's first wife, Charlotte Grenfell (Mrs. Kingsley's sister), whom he met just before becoming a tutor to the children of the Manchester manufacturer, Samuel Dunkinfield Darbishire (Dunn, *Froude*, I, 155-157). 'Manchester and its ways were distasteful to her', wrote Froude (quoted in Dunn, *Froude*, I, 168); but he himself found the place no more congenial (see the relevant quotations in Dunn, *Froude*, I, 165, 167). Professor Whitfield tells me that in a letter he received from Charlotte's daughter, Miss Georgina Margaret Froude, she acknowledged the identification.

[94] Quoted in William Pole, ed. and completed *The Life of Sir William Fairbairn, Bart., F.R.S., LL.D., D.C.L. . . . Partly Written by Himself*, London: Longmans, Green, and Co., 1877 [1876], p. 461. Pole's extract from Mrs. Gaskell's letter to Fairbairn (*G.L.*, No. 249) is dated [? Summer 1855] by Chapple and Pollard.

[95] *Works*, IV, 459.   [97] *Works*, IV, 460.
[96] *Works*, IV, 459.   [98] *Works*, IV, 460.

'farm after farm was left behind'[99]. Here Mrs. Gaskell's achievement is to call forth in the reader responses similar to those elicited in Margaret.

> Every mile was redolent of associations, which she would not have missed for the world, but each of which made her cry upon "the days that are no more," with ineffable longing. The last time she had passed along this road was when she had left it with her father and mother—the day, the season, had been gloomy, and she herself hopeless, but they were there with her. Now she was alone, an orphan, and they, strangely, had gone away from her, and vanished from the face of the earth. ... [100]

The 'Helstone Revisited' part proper shows both Mrs. Gaskell's deep affection for the English countryside and the objectivity of that appreciation. There is the delightfully charming description of the *Lennard Arms,* offering traditional rural hospitality and rich rural fare[101]; there is, too, Margaret's farewell visit to the vicarage garden, from which she gathered 'a little straggling piece of honeysuckle'[102]—an incident strangely moving. This aspect of Helstone owes much to Margaret's colouring, to the eye of the beholder.

> The common sounds of life were more musical there than anywhere else in the whole world, the light more golden, the life more tranquil and full of dreamy delight.[103]

On the other hand Mrs. Gaskell makes the necessary qualifications, and does so with a degree of complexity.

In the first place Margaret herself experiences sadness and melancholy: aged trees have been felled[104]; a new tidy cottage has replaced the rude one of former days[105]; she feels the instability of all human things[106]. A different point of view is afforded by Mr. Bell, with his old-fashioned *penchant* for natural simplicity and unsophisticated education[107]. Mrs. Gaskell does not, however, condone his indulgence in this rather academic, Rousseauesque romanticizing; and indicates the perils of rustic ignorance through Betty Barnes' superstitious belief in the magical powers of a cat-roasting ritual[108]. Yet the incursion of nineteenth-

99   *Works,* IV, 460.
100 *Works,* IV, 460.
101 *Works,* IV, 460-463.
102 *Works,* IV, 479.
103 *Works,* IV, 479-480.

104 *Works,* IV, 463.
105 *Works,* IV, 463.
106 *Works,* IV, 464, 478-479.
107 *Works,* IV, 465.
108 *Works,* IV, 466.

century practical Christianity, represented by the new incumbent
and his spouse, spreading temperance and systematic instruction, is not, Mrs. Gaskell hints, wholly commendable nor
deserving an unqualified welcome, worthy though it be. The
landlady's description[109] of the teetotal vicar and his recipe-
dispensing wife is an excellent preparation for the visitors' encounter with Mrs. Hepworth at the remodelled village-school,
where Margaret is invited to take the class. Surely the author
of *Hard Times* must have smiled on reading the following.

> Margaret bent over her book, and seeing nothing but that—
> hearing the buzz of children's voices, old times rose up, and
> she thought of them, and her eyes filled with tears, till all at
> once there was a pause—one of the girls was stumbling over
> the apparently simple word "a," uncertain what to call it.
> "A, an indefinite article," said Margaret mildly.
> "I beg your pardon," said the Vicar's wife, all eyes and ears;
> "but we are taught by Mr. Milsome to call 'a' an—who can
> remember?"
> "An adjective absolute," said half-a-dozen voices at once. And
> Margaret sate abashed. The children knew more than she did.
> Mr. Bell turned away, and smiled.[110]

When Mrs. Hepworth proposed that Margaret and Mr. Bell
should see the changes made at the parsonage, 'the word "improvements" had half slipped out of her mouth, but she substituted the more cautious term "alterations" '[111]. Mrs. Gaskell's
mode of viewing other innovations suggests a similar implicit
value-judgement : these observations comment as well as describe.

The sources of Mrs. Gaskell's Helstone episodes are the same
as gave rise to nearly all her scenes of country life. One has
but to recall the Knutsford-Sandlebridge girlhood, the Stratford
days at Avonbank, and her habitual love of rural England. The
Hampshire setting may be due to her acquaintance with the
Nightingales, who once resided in the New Forest district[112];
but, even without such a possibility, the personal element is
obvious enough in her writing. There was no need to invent

[109] *Works*, IV, 462-463.
[110] *Works*, IV, 468.
[111] *Works*, IV, 469.
[112] Haldane, *Mrs. Gaskell and Her Friends*, p. 108.

Margaret's Helstone experiences; for, as a fugitive from Manchester, Mrs. Gaskell must have undergone them, long after she ceased to live in the country. From first-hand knowledge she fully realized how hard was the lot of an agricultural labourer[113]; yet she could, at the same time, appreciate the peace, colour, and beauty of the rural landscape.

The central portion of *North and South* is occupied by Milton-Northern—the Manchester of *Mary Barton,* under a different name and at a slightly later stage in its industrial development. In the town's graphic introduction, Mrs. Gaskell picks out the significant details—those very characteristics she must herself have often observed with respect to Manchester.

> . . . a deep lead-coloured cloud hanging over the horizon . . . the air had a faint taste and smell of smoke . . . long, straight, hopeless streets of regularly-built houses, all small and of brick. Here and there a great oblong many-windowed factory stood up, like a hen among her chickens, puffing out black "unparliamentary" smoke . . . here every van, every wagon and truck, bore cotton, either in the raw shape in bags, or the woven shape in bales of calico. People thronged the footpaths, most of them well-dressed as regarded the material, but with a slovenly looseness which struck Margaret as different from the shabby, threadbare smartness of a similar class in London.[114]

Other distinctly Northern qualities had, a little previously, been mentioned in regard to Heston, the nearby watering-place, with the same telling realism.

> . . . everything looked more "purpose-like." The country carts had more iron, and less wood and leather about the horse-gear . . . The colours looked greyer—more enduring, not so gay and pretty. There were no smock-frocks, even among the country-folk . . . In such towns in the south of England, Margaret had seen the shopmen, when not employed in their business, lounging a little at their doors, enjoying the fresh air, and the look up and down the street. Here, if they had any leisure from customers, they made themselves business in the shop—even, Margaret fancied, to the unnecessary unrolling and re-rolling of ribbons.[115]

---

113 *Works,* IV, 364.
114 *Works,* IV, 66-67.
115 *Works,* IV, 65.

In Milton-Northern Margaret encounters life of two different sorts—broadly, that represented by the Higgins family and that typified by the Thorntons (one recalls, as a kind of comparison from *Mary Barton*, the Bartons and the Carson family).

We have already cited Margaret's first conversation with Higgins; for this contains the phrase which gave the novel its title[116]. In what sense, therefore, does Higgins stand for the North? Sir William Fairbairn both suggests an answer and at the same time pays tribute to Mrs. Gaskell's veracious observation.

> "Poor old Higgins, with his weak consumptive daughter, is a true picture of a Manchester man. There are many like him in this town, and a better sample of independent industry you could not have hit upon. Higgins is an excellent representative of a Lancashire operative—strictly independent—and is one of the best characters in the piece."[117]

Higgins, however, is far from being merely a stock character, introduced as a counter on the side of labour in the struggle against capital. Mrs. Gaskell, so realistic in her treatment of working-class life in *Mary Barton*, had lost none of her touch in *North and South*. Nevertheless this, her latest novel, contains proportionately less concerning the squalor and misery of operatives and their families: firstly, because the story is narrated from a middle-class point of view (chiefly that of Margaret, partly that of Thornton); secondly, because there had been some amelioration of social conditions and a general rise in living-standards. In 1842 Joseph Adshead could bring out his *Distress in Manchester*[118], and devote a chapter ('Narratives of Suffering'[119]) to examples of starvation, prolonged sickness, destitution, celler-dwelling, nakedness, extensive clothes-pawning, and moral deterioration—this was the period treated in *Mary Barton*. By the early fifties an improvement had undoubtedly

---

[116] Higgins used the phrase a second time (*Works,* IV, 365).
[117] Quoted in Ward, ed. *Works,* IV, p. xx.
[118] Joseph Adshead, *Distress in Manchester. Evidence (Tabular and Otherwise) of the State of the Labouring Classes in* 1840-42, London: Henry Hooper, 1842.
[119] Adshead, *Distress in Manchester,* pp. 25-41.

R

come about for many Manchester working-people; it was related
to England's increased commercial prosperity[120].

Mrs. Gaskell's intimate acquaintance with the physical and
spiritual conditions of working-class households seems well
exemplified in her descriptions of the abode and beliefs of the
Higgins family. The material side is represented by the slatternly
younger daughter, 'busy at the wash-tub, knocking about the
furniture in a rough capable way'[121]; and by the large fire,
burning as a mark of hospitality despite the heat of the day[122].
Of religious import is the other daughter, Bessy, with her
apocalyptic visions, haunted by that same parable of Dives and
Lazarus which bulked so large in the mind of John Barton. The
following extracts illustrate how admirably, in dialectal dialogue, Mrs. Gaskell can convey the fatalistic, morbid yet grimly
humorous, aspects of the debased Methodism in which the girl
believed[123].

[120] For fuller details, see Ward, ed. *Works,* IV, pp. xiv-xv; John Harold
Clapham, *An Economic History of Modern Britain,* 3 vols., Cambridge:
The University Press, 1926-1938, esp. I (*The Early Railway Age,* 1820-
1850, 1926), 536-602, II (*Free Trade and Steel,* 1850-1886, 1932), 440-488;
Ronald Max Hartwell, 'Interpretations of the Industrial Revolution in
England: A Methodological Enquiry', *The Journal of Economic History,*
XIX (1959), 229-249; Ronald Max Hartwell, 'The Rising Standard of
Living in England, 1800-1850', *The Economic History Review,* 2nd Series,
XIII (1961), 397-416; Eric John Ernest Hobsbawm and Ronald Max Hartwell, 'The Standard of Living during the Industrial Revolution: A Discussion', *The Economic History Review,* 2nd Series, XVI (1963), 119-146;
and A. J. Taylor, 'Progress and Poverty in Britain, 1780-1850: A Reappraisal', *History,* XLV (1960), 16-31. 'That in Great Britain, during the
six years 1851-56, there has been established a Rise of Wages for all kinds
of Handicraft and Factory Labour of between 15 and 20 per cent. on the
rates current for some time prior to 1851' was the authoritative conclusion of Thomas Tooke and William Newmarch (*A History of Prices,
and of the State of the Circulation, during the Nine Years* 1848-1856—
Vols. V-VI of *The History of Prices from* 1792 *to the Present Time,* 6
vols., 1838-1857—2 vols., London: Longman, Brown, Green, Longmans,
& Roberts, 1857, II, 176): they further remark 'that the largest per-centage
of increase has occurred in the Wages of Unskilled Labour;—and that to
some considerable extent, more especially in the better cultivated districts,
there has been, during the same six years, a decided tendency to a rise in
the Wages of Agricultural Labour' (*op. cit.,* II, 176-177).
[121] *Works,* IV, 104.
[122] *Works,* IV, 115.
[123] Margaret (*Works* IV, 162) probably expresses Mrs. Gaskell's own
view: that God allots joy and sorrow more or less equally (see her
explicit opinion, in contra-distinction to that of Charlotte Brontë, in *The
Life of Charlotte Brontë,* 1st edn, 1857, II, 302-303).

. . . "Some's pre-elected to sumptuous feasts, and purple and fine linen—may be yo're one on 'em. Others toil and moil all their lives long—and the very dogs are not pitiful in our days, as they were in the days of Lazarus. But if yo' ask me to cool yo'r tongue wi' th' tip of my finger, I'll come across the great gulf to yo' just for th' thought o' what yo've been to me here."[124]

" . . . Sometimes I'm so tired out I think I cannot enjoy heaven without a piece of rest first. I'm rather afeared o' going straight there without getting a good sleep in the grave to set me up."[125]

Over against these ' "Methodee fancies" '[126] is set the pragmatic philanthropy of Higgins, a rationalist who tested Christianity by its fruits, in the manner of John Barton.

" . . . when I see the world going all wrong at this time o' day, bothering itself wi' things it knows nought about, and leaving undone all the things that lie in disorder close at its hand—why, I say, leave a' this talk about religion alone, and set to work on what yo' see and know. That's my creed. It's simple, and not far to fetch, nor hard to work."[127]

The problem of drink, raised in *Libbie Marsh's Three Eras,* is, through Bessy, again presented. Yet the reader should notice how sympathetically Mrs. Gaskell makes the presentation —not as a middle-class condemnation, not as a tract-like set-piece, but rather as a sensitive analysis of drinking, showing insight into that particular escape from the drabness of reality. In the ensuing passage we have more than a telling indictment of modern industrial life from a writer whose observation went below the surface of working-class existence, from an authoress who could appreciate the feelings of women as well as those of men (something virtually impossible for Disraeli and Kingsley). We have creation, not description; the novelist's experience seems truly at one with that of her character.

" . . . There are days wi' you as wi' other folk, I suppose, when yo' get up and go through th' hours, just longing for a bit of a change—a bit of a fillip, as it were. I know I ha' gone and bought a four-pouder out o' another baker's shop to common on such days, just because I sickened at the thought of going on for ever wi' the same sight in my eyes, and the same sound in my ears, and the same taste i' my mouth, and the same thought (or no thought, for that matter) in my head, day after day, for ever.

---

[124] *Works,* IV, 177.
[125] *Works,* IV, 117.
[126] *Works,* IV, 104.
[127] *Works,* IV, 105; cf. 268. Yet he believed in God, if not in life beyond the grave (*Works,* IV, 268-270).

I've longed for to be a man to go spreeing, even if it were only
a tramp to some new place in search o' work. And father—all
men—have it stronger in 'em than me to get tired o' sameness
and work for ever. And what is 'em to do? It's little blame to
them if they do go into th' gin-shop for to make their blood flow
quicker, and more lively, and see things they never see at no
other time—pictures, and looking-glass, and such like. ..."[128]

Before turning from Bessy and her troubles, we ought to
note a detail which, trivial in itself, is indicative of that historical accuracy noticed so often in Mrs. Gaskell's writings. We
have seen that, in *Mary Barton,* she attempted to give a faithful account of how Manchester operatives lived by letting the
facts speak for themselves. This aspect of her work should,
therefore, no longer need labouring; nevertheless one more
instance may be allowed. Bessy, talking of her consumption,
sought its cause in the cotton-fluff, a by-product of the carding
process, which had affected her lungs. Having remarked that
the expense of installing a ventilating wheel was too great for
most masters, she went on to say that even some hands were
averse to its use.

" ... I've heard tell o' men who didn't like working in places
where there was a wheel, because they said as how it made 'em
hungry, at after they'd been long used to swallowing fluff, to
go without it, and that their wage ought to be raised if they were
to work in such places. ..."[129]

Beside this we may put the following, taken from a modern
study of the factory system.

Efforts to improve the factories had to be carried out in face
of the opposition of the very workers whom it was intended to
benefit. One millowner was threatened with a strike because he
installed a ventilating machine, and the spinners said that it
increased their appetites; ... [130]

The only other working-class family in *North and South* is
that composed of John Boucher, the improvident operative and
unwilling Unionist, his sickly, helpless wife, and their eight
children. Perhaps Mrs. Gaskell introduced the Bouchers to

[128] *Works,* IV, 160-161.
[129] *Works,* IV, 119.
[130] William Harold Hutt, 'The Factory System of the Early Nineteenth
Century', in *Capitalism and the Historians,* ed. Friedrich August von
Hayek, London: Routledge & Kegan Paul Limited, 1954, p. 186.

maintain the truthfulness of her picture of the Manchester poor; certainly they are just the sort of people against whom William Rathbone Greg delighted to inveigh. Boucher was his own worst enemy, despised alike by Higgins[131], the Unionist, and Hamper[132], the master. He is at once a tragic and a comic figure. The comedy comes out well in the following unflattering but racy comparison by Higgins.

> " ... Th' Union's the plough, making ready the land for harvest-time. Such as Boucher—'twould be settin' him up too much to liken him to a daisy; he's liker a weed lounging over the ground—mun just make up their mind to be put out o' the way. ... "[133]

Boucher's tragic aspect receives most emphasis when he takes steps to put himself out of the way—by lying face downwards in a ditch which scarcely contained sufficient water to drown him. Mrs. Gaskell's account is grimly graphic in detail.

> They put the door down carefully upon the stones, and all might see the poor drowned wretch—his glassy eyes, one half-open, staring right upwards to the sky. Owing to the position in which he had been found lying, his face was swollen and discoloured; besides, his skin was stained by the water in the brook, which had been used for dyeing purposes. The fore part of his head was bald; but the hair grew thin and long behind, and every separate lock was a conduit for water.[134]

However, whereas in *Mary Barton* the leading characters had come from the lower orders, in *North and South* people from that section of society occupy only part of the stage, and even then not the most important. One may make the following distinction. The Bartons and the Legh family are interesting for their own sakes, and for the sake of their environment; a slice of economic history is made meaningful, text-book figures become real people, are imaginatively re-created. In *North and South* Mrs. Gaskell had forgotten none of this skill: she continued to observe the conditions around her with a keen and sympathetic eye. Nonetheless the later work appears more truly the product of a *novelist*. The author's presence is scarcely felt, dramatization seems more complete, and a greater objectivity is obtained; the reader tends to associate himself with the middle-class characters, and the atmosphere is more decidedly

---

[131] *Works,* IV, 158.
[132] *Works,* IV, 349.
[133] *Works,* IV, 348.
[134] *Works,* IV, 350.

bourgeois. We are looking through the eyes of Margaret Hale and, to a less degree, those of John Thornton : their responses become our responses; their interests, our interests; their thoughts, our thoughts. The middle-class manufacturer and critic, William Rathbone Greg, remarked that he liked *North and South* more than *Mary Barton,* adding that Mrs. Gaskell had "taken the right tone"[135] though conceding that it was not "as thorough a work of genius as 'Mary Barton' "[136]. Certainly that earliest novel, especially its first part, was original in a way *North and South* was not; for *North and South* was in a tradition—a tradition which could accommodate Jane Austen, Charlotte Brontë, and Henry Fothergill Chorley[137], but not, paradoxically, 'the author of *Mary Barton*'.

Most of the central portion of *North and South* is set in a *milieu* far different from that of the Higgins family or the Bouchers. It is the world conjured up by a reference to ' "John Thornton of Milton" '[138] and ' "Thornton o' Marlborough Mill" '[139]; a world of utilitarianism, self-help, and *laissez-faire*; a world of industrial progress, political economy, and rugged individualism. In this context we must consider Thornton as manufacturer, not lover; hence it is useful to conjecture whether Mrs. Gaskell had, when creating the mill-owner, any particular person in mind. For Thornton *qua* lover, there could, in the nature of things, scarcely have been a model, since such aspects of his character would spring directly from the novelist's imagination. Yet, even if Mrs. Gaskell invented the amatory experiences, she could very well have had a concrete starting-point for Thornton *qua* industrialist and economic theorist.

Mrs. Chadwick, whose views are always worthy of respect, implies[140] that James Nasmyth influenced the drawing of

---

[135] Quoted in Ward, ed. *Works,* IV, p. xix.

[136] Quoted in Ward, ed. *Works,* IV, p. xix.

[137] For this seemingly arbitrary grouping Miss Rubenius is responsible, since the influence on *North and South* of these three authors is discerned by her (*The Woman Question in Mrs. Gaskell's Life and Works,* pp. 247-255).

[138] *Works,* IV, 133.

[139] *Works,* IV, 159.

[140] Chadwick, *Mrs. Gaskell,* p. 148. For Nasmyth, see *James Nasmyth, Engineer: An Autobiography,* ed. Samuel Smiles, London: John Murray, 1883. Like Thornton (*Works,* IV, 97), Nasmyth began his career as a

John Thornton. She rightly points out[141] that in *North and South*[142] there is an unmistakable reference to Nasmyth, as the inventor of the steam hammer, even though his name is not mentioned. Like Thomas Wright, to whose prison rescue-work and philanthropy Mrs. Gaskell had previously—in *Mary Barton*[143]—referred (similarly without mentioning him by name), Nasmyth was a friend of the Gaskells; it is, therefore, an easy inference that much relevant information could have been collected from this source.

More recently a second candidate has been proposed as a prototype for Thornton. David Shusterman[144], while recognizing that Thornton could well be a composite character, has urged the claims of the author's friend and critic, William Rathbone Greg. Perhaps one of his strongest arguments is that, like Thornton, W. R. Greg suffered from business reverses—yet this would also apply to his brother, Samuel[145], with whom Mrs. Gaskell was likewise acquainted[146]. Shusterman further maintains,

---

capitalist by laying something aside from an income of only fifteen shillings a week (*Memorials of Two Sisters*, ed. Shaen, p. 134).

[141] Chadwick, *Mrs. Gaskell*, p. 147.

[142] *Works*, IV, 92-93.

[143] *Works*, I, 181.

[144] David Shusterman, 'William Rathbone Greg and Mrs. Gaskell', *Philological Quarterly*, XXXVI (1957), 268-272.

[145] See the article on him by George Clement Boase in *The Dictionary of National Biography*; his dates were 1804-1876.

[146] On 16 July [1850] Mrs. Gaskell wrote to Lady Kay-Shuttleworth saying why she was not able to write a book—complementary to her first novel—from the point of view of the manufacturers. She explained that she lacked the necessary strength of feeling to present the employers' case convincingly; and that she would merely do harm by undertaking such a work, when she had not the experience needed to decide which benevolent theory would in practice produce the best results (for both masters and men). Having referred to Sam Greg and his Utopian (if not very success-ful) schemes, she remarked: 'I think he, or such as he, might almost be made the hero of a fiction on the other side of the question[—]the trials of the conscientious rich man, in his dealings with the poor. And I should like some *man*, who had a man's correct knowledge, to write on this subject, and make the poor intelligent work-people understand the infinite anxiety as to right and wrong-doing which I believe that riches bring to many.' (Perhaps, when Mrs. Gaskell came to write *North and South*, she had the trials of Sam Greg still at the back of her mind.) Our quotation from Mrs. Gaskell's letter to Lady Kay-Shuttleworth of 16 July [1850—not 1851, as it is annotated] is based on the typescript copy belonging to the Hon. Mrs. Angela Mary James, corrected against the original letter owned by Lord Shuttleworth of Gawthorpe, which appears as *G.L.*, No. 72a.

not without some *prima facie* plausibility, that Thornton's
opinions, as propounded in the novel, resemble those found in
Greg's writings on industrial and social questions. Nevertheless,
for a corrective, it is doubtless advisable to quote from an article
which came out twenty-six years before Shusterman's.

> One of the ablest polemics directed against *Mary Barton* was the
> article by William R. Greg in the *Edinburgh Review*, for April,
> 1849. . . . The novelist took these strictures in very good part
> however, and without directly admitting her culpability in mis-
> representing the relationship between employer and employee,
> she put into practice in her next novel on the subject certain prin-
> ciples enjoined by Greg. However, the similarity between precept
> and practice observable in the article and in the novel respect-
> ively may be due merely to coincidence. As already stated, bet-
> ween the publication of *Mary Barton* and *North and South,*
> social consciousness had begun to apprehend the need for amelior-
> ation of conditions among the working classes, so that the more
> equable picture described in *North and South* may actually owe
> little or nothing to Greg's objections to the novelist's earlier treat-
> ment.[147]

Thornton is an entirely convincing figure, and clearly first-
hand observation went into his making. In such circumstances
one need scarcely seek for further models among Manchester
manufacturers of Mrs. Gaskell's acquaintance[148]. That she had
at least one of these at the back of her mind is confirmed by
Meta's testimony.

> Miss Gaskell does not think that her mother consciously put real
> people into her books, although many people fancied themselves to
> have been prototypes of her characters. Once at an evening party
> a gentleman came up to Mrs. Gaskell and, bowing low, said, 'I
> understand, madam, that you have done me the honour to put
> me into your new book!' He referred to the character of Thornton
> in 'North and South.' Mrs. Gaskell was in an awkward position,
> but tactfully turned the conversation. The fine character of
> Thornton had been suggested by a philanthropist in Manchester,
> but it was not the gentleman who bowed before her.[149]

[147] Annette Brown Hopkins, 'Liberalism in the Social Teachings of Mrs.
Gaskell', *The Social Service Review*, V (1931), 64.
[148] Professor Whitfield (*Mrs Gaskell*, pp. 81-83) has printed a letter
from Mrs. Gaskell (owned by him, but deposited at Brook Street Unitarian Chapel, Knutsford) in which she gives advice about how to gain an
insight into local industry—the firms mentioned indicate the width of
her experience and the breadth of her knowledge. This letter of 9 March
[1864] occurs as *G.L.*, No. 549.
[149] Tooley, 'The Centenary of Mrs. Gaskell', *The Cornhill Magazine*,
N.S. XXIX (1910), 324. The episode is also recounted in 'The Gaskell
Centenary', *The Manchester City News*, 3 September 1910.

Mrs. Gaskell was, as far as the labour disputes went, quite able to appreciate the manufacturer's point of view : numerous passages could here be cited, endless quotations made—but one reference will suffice to substantiate the claim. During his first long conversation with Margaret Hale and her father[150], Thornton paints in glowing colours the romance of manufacture, the adventure of commerce; he sketches the immediate past-history of the cotton industry, drawing with bold lines the power and extravagance of the early cotton-lords; he describes in laudatory terms the rewards brought by prudence and self-denial, taking his own case as an appropriate illustration. All this Mrs. Gaskell presents in a sympathetic light, not necessarily approving everything Thornton says, yet nonetheless providing him with emotionally convincing language. While in some ways it would have been easy to turn such highly-charged dialogue into bombast, Mrs. Gaskell skilfully retains the realism; she makes Thornton *mean* what he professes.

Upon the socio-economic arguments, largely those of *laissez-faire* and the Manchester school, which throughout the novel are voiced by Thornton, there seems at the present time little cause to comment. Mrs. Gaskell, perhaps better than some of her critics[151], realized the complexity of the situation. Wisely she saw that there was no ready-made blue-print solution for class antagonism; her own emphasis was always on personal contact and mutual recognition of difficulties. Since *North and South* is almost always classified (along with *Mary Barton, Sybil, Yeast,* and the like) as a social-problem novel, it is necessary, however, to touch on a few related issues. Our treatment makes no claims to be exhaustive, it can only try to show that Mrs. Gaskell was not unaware of contemporary conditions.

To the initial instalment of *North and South*[152] were prefixed

---

[150] *Works,* IV, 91-98.

[151] On this matter one may contrast the slightly patronizing tone adopted in, for example, Miriam Allott, *Elizabeth Gaskell,* Writers and Their Work (ed. Bonamy Dobrée), No. 124, London, Cape Town, Melbourne, New York, and Toronto: Longmans, Green & Co. for The British Council and the National Book League, 1960, pp. 8-9, with the commendation in Hopkins, 'Liberalism in the Social Teachings of Mrs. Gaskell', *The Social Service Review,* V (1931), 57-73, and in Josephine Johnston, 'The Social Significance of the Novels of Mrs. Gaskell', *The Journal of Social Forces,* VII (1928), 224-227.

[152] *Household Words,* X, 61.

some lines from Tennyson, possibly of the author's own choosing but sanctioned 'by an editorial *imprimatur*[153], which do not appear in the first (book-form) edition. The tenor of these lines is condemnation for partial, one-sided views, with the recommendation that 'All parties work together' : such was Mrs. Gaskell's own social philosophy—a philosophy based on personal experience, a practical application of Christian teachings.

Mrs. Gaskell's criticisms of Thornton's rugged individualism, usually put into Margaret's mouth, are obvious enough. Perhaps they were her own first instinctive responses to Manchester industrialism[154], as when, for instance, she remarks upon the bitterness of the class struggle[155], or urges personal co-operation in opposition to the isolation and proud, independent self-sufficiency of the ' "Darkshire Egos" '[156]—in other words she reminds her readers that no man is an island.

Mrs. Gaskell's was an inclusive vision, her social criticism was far-ranging, and she tried not to take a biased view of things. The workers were, in some ways, just as wrong-headed as their masters. In *Mary Barton* the dangers of Unionism had been fully recognized, and they are not forgotten in *North and South*. Considered in their corporate capacity, the operatives were no less tyrannous than the employers : Boucher is one of their victims. The Christian-Socialist charge against an inherent defect of Unionism—class consciousness—is cogently made by Mr. Hale[157]. Nor are the non-industrial *bourgeoisie* exonerated. By neatly employing the *tu quoque* argument, Thornton can turn the tables on Margaret.

> "But why," asked she, "could you not explain what good reason you had for expecting a bad trade? I don't know whether I use the right words, but you will understand what I mean."
> "Do you give your servants reasons for your expenditure, or your economy in the use of your own money? We, the owners of capital, have a right to choose what we will do with it."[158]

This was, no doubt, a very valid point, especially at a time

---

[153] *The Letters of Charles Dickens,* ed. Dexter, II, 580: letter to Wills of 19 August 1854.
[154] Doubtless the opinion of Mrs. Chadwick (*Mrs. Gaskell,* pp. 139-142).
[155] *Works,* IV, 94.
[156] *Works,* IV, 143.
[157] *Works,* IV, 276.
[158] *Works,* IV, 137.

when there were employed in domestic service 'more than twice as many women and girls as [in] all the textile industries put together'[159]. Nor, moreover, are agricultural labourers in the South idealized at the expense of Northern operatives (and agriculture was, we must recall, the greatest 'industry' of the mid-nineteenth century[160]) : Margaret at once disillusions Higgins when the latter, being unemployed, contemplates going South[161].

Mrs. Gaskell's presentation of the intellectual and industrial atmosphere of Milton-Northern appears eminently successful. In treating labour-capital disputes she avoids a narrow approach, and sees the conflict in human terms. The solution she suggests finds its concrete embodiment in Thornton's personal relations with Higgins[162], an intercourse described by Thornton as ' "beyond the mere 'cash nexus.' " '[163] This individual contact led to Higgins' working extra (unpaid) hours during his employer's financial crisis[164]; and later, when eventually the gates had to be closed, both he and his fellows expressed their readiness to work again for Thornton, should that ever be possible[165]. The specific example of co-operation given in the novel[166] is the establishment of a factory dining-room. Here the mill-owner acted as a sort of steward, while the actual control was in the hands of the men themselves (at whose initiative the scheme was put into effect—although, ironically, the original, basic idea had been mooted by Thornton, only to be laid aside because of objections from Higgins). Mrs. Gaskell was realist enough to imply that schemes like this were no more than ' "experiments" '[167]; and her view would almost certainly coincide with that expressed by Thornton at the end of the tale. In both cases it was a view resulting from personal experience.

[159] Clapham, *An Economic History of Modern Britain*, II, 464. The 1851 figure for female domestics was 905,000 (*op. cit.*, II, 24; see too p. 23).

[160] Clapham, *An Economic History of Modern Britain*, II, 22-24. The second largest 'industry' was, of course, domestic service—see our last footnote.

[161] *Works*, IV, 363-364.

[162] *Works*, IV, 500-502.

[163] *Works*, IV, 515.

[164] *Works*, IV, 502-503.

[165] *Works*, IV, 516.

[166] *Works*, IV, 431-433.

[167] *Works*, IV, 515 : the term is Thornton's.

> "And you think they [plans formed and worked out with both
> sides acting together] may prevent the recurrence of strikes?"
> "Not at all. My utmost expectation only goes so far as this—
> that they may render strikes not the bitter, venomous sources of
> hatred they have hitherto been. A more hopeful man might
> imagine that a closer and more genial intercourse between classes
> might do away with strikes. But I am not a hopeful man."[168]

We have now dealt with the differing but related spheres of
Higgins and Thornton, which has involved some consideration of Mrs. Gaskell's general attitude towards industrial questions. One aspect of the Manchester scene still remains for
attention, that associated with Mrs. Thornton. In a sense this
is part of the Thornton *milieu*, as opposed to that of Higgins;
yet it has affinities with the very different world of Mrs. Shaw.
Both are social rather than industrial, private rather than
public, parochial rather than national. We have pictures of
drawing-room life in Milton-Northern just as we had of drawing-
room life in London.

Between the idle vanity of Fanny Thornton's existence and
the futile life led by the Carson women in *Mary Barton* there
is much resemblence. Mrs. Gaskell must have known many
female relatives of Manchester manufacturers who, finding
themselves free from domestic tasks, lacked the cultural where-
withal to profit from their leisure. The introduction of Thornton's sister is revealing in this connexion.

> Some one was practising up a morceau de salon, playing it very
> rapidly, every third note, on an average, being either indistinct,
> or wholly missed out, and the loud chords at the end being half
> of them false, but not the less satisfactory to the performer.[169]

When treating Fanny's mother, Mrs. Gaskell deals with a
very different kind of personage; yet in essence her method
seems the same. The novelist's eye for distinctive domestic details
and meaningful *minutiae* is focussed upon Mrs. Thornton as
upon the insignificant Fanny. Thus a description of her dress
not only increases the general air of verisimilitude but, more
importantly, suggests the nature of the woman; for that lady's
nature appears well indicated by her choice of clothes ('stout
black silk, of which not a thread was worn or discoloured'[170]).

---

[168] *Works*, IV, 516.
[169] *Works*, IV, 88.
[170] *Works*, IV, 87; see too p. 131.

Substance as well as utility is also the keynote of the Thornton home. The picture of their drawing-room—which might easily have appeared in 'Company Manners' as an example of what to avoid—points to the values of its occupants. The complete passage[171] is too long for quotation; but a couple of sentences will demonstrate what Mrs. Gaskell is doing. In describing this material embodiment of a whole mode of life, she both observes and assesses; hand in hand with the detailed account goes the social evaluation.

> The walls were pink and gold; the pattern on the carpet repre-
> sented bunches of flowers on a light ground, but it was carefully
> covered up in the centre by a linen drugget, glazed and colour-
> less. . . . The whole room had a painfully spotted, spangled,
> speckled look about it, which impressed Margaret so unpleasantly
> that she was hardly conscious of the peculiar cleanliness re-
> quired to keep everything so white and pure in such an atmos-
> phere, or of the trouble that must be willingly expended to secure
> that effect of icy, snowy discomfort.[172]

Everything speaks of purposeful ostentation, of conspicuous consumption—in striking contrast with the Hale drawing-room[173] where all was warmth, ease, and comfort. Effectively to drive home the difference, two extracts may be juxta-posed; both illustrate how significant little touches can be.

> In the middle of the room, right under the bagged-up chandelier,
> was a large circular table, with smartly-bound books arranged at
> regular intervals round the circumference of its polished surface,
> like gaily coloured spokes of a wheel.[174]

> Pretty baskets of work stood about in various places: and books,
> not cared for on account of their binding solely, lay on one table,
> as if recently put down.[175]

The concluding comparison in each quotation has a peculiarly clinching effect; in a sense it typifies an entire way of life.

On the other hand, Mrs. Gaskell reveals aspects of Mrs. Thornton which call forth a sympathetic response in the reader.

---

[171] *Works,* IV, 130-131.

[172] *Works,* IV, 130-131.

[173] *Works,* IV, 90.

[174] *Works,* IV, 131. One may relevantly mention the reference to the use of books in 'Company Manners' (*Works,* III, 511-512), where the author expresses her own views—in keeping, of course, with those of the Hales.

[175] *Works,* IV, 90.

John Thornton's mother is far from being a caricature. Her past struggles, after her husband's bankruptcy, win respect: from her son's narration of these trials we learn of his obvious devotion to ' "such a mother as few are blest with; a woman of strong power, and firm resolve." '[176] When trouble arises at the mill, she remains calm and steadfast[177]; when John finds himself in dire financial straits, she gives him every possible comfort[178]. All this is admirably executed by the authoress, whose sympathetic powers allowed her to appreciate Mrs. Thornton's mentality. Perhaps we may best exemplify such success by a striking little incident, yet another instance of Mrs. Gaskell's imaginative use of small domestic events. Mrs. Thornton, anticipating John's marriage to Margaret, carefully divided her linen, bearing the initials of George and Hannah Thornton, from what, being her son's, bore his.

> Some of those marked G. H. T. were Dutch damask of the old kind, exquisitely fine; none were like them now. Mrs. Thornton stood looking at them long—they had been her pride when she was first married. Then she knit her brows, and pinched and compressed her lips tight, and carefully unpicked the G. H. She went so far as to seach for the Turkey-red marking-thread to put in the new initials; but it was all used—and she had no heart to send for any more just yet.[179]

The foregoing account ought to have given some indication of how well Mrs. Gaskell conveys the total Milton-Northern *milieu*, knowing it as she did during many years of residence in Manchester. Her descriptions go beyond mere reportage, have a value other than that of historical sociology—though this latter is abundantly present. We do not read her novels primarily as sociological treatises, and it would be unwise in the extreme for a critic to stress unduly this aspect of Mrs. Gaskell's work. Nevertheless a final plea must be entered. When the writer of a recent study on Mrs. Gaskell can remark, as a matter of course, that 'we do not read her social novels to-day for any far-reaching analysis of the situations that drove her to write them'[180], one must make a distinction. That we do not read her novels solely

[176] *Works,* IV, 97.
[177] *Works,* IV, 205-218.
[178] *Works,* IV, 505-508.
[179] *Works,* IV, 248.
[180] Allott, *Elizabeth Gaskell,* pp. 8-9.

or chiefly for their social analysis is true; but the implication that there is *no* social analysis of any depth is patently at odds with the facts. If the context were forgotten, who could confidently deny that the following did not come from a novelist familiar with Veblen?

> "Why, they [the wives of the manufacturers] took nouns that were signs of things which gave evidence of wealth—housekeepers, under-gardeners, extent of glass, valuable lace, diamonds, and all such things; and each one formed her speech so as to bring them all in, in the prettiest accidental manner possible."[181]

Much might be said about aspects of *North and South* which can now receive only a passing mention. The plot to some degree depends, like that of *Ruth,* on deception (the lie *motif*)[182]. ' "Poor Frederick" '[183] Hale, a former naval officer virtually exiled from England, recalls ' "poor Peter" '[184] Jenkyns in *Cranford,* and hence the author's own sea-faring (though never returning) brother. The introduction of Leonards[185], his accidental death, and the subsequent police investigations show Mrs. Gaskell's interest, albeit here little developed, in mystery and detection. The benevolent medical man appears in the shape of Dr. Donaldson[186]; and Mrs. Hale[187] fills the *rôle* of the ailing mother. The at times humorous, at all times faithful, Dixon[188] is the *North and South* contribution to Mrs. Gaskell's gallery of devoted domestics. Nor are the expected deaths lacking—Mr. Hale[189], Mrs. Hale[190], Boucher[191], Mrs. Boucher[192], Bessy Higgins[193], and Mr. Bell[194] come readily to mind. Then again, there is, as in *Mary Barton,* a scene of violent action—in this case the riot and attack on Thornton's mill[195]. Recognizably Gaskellian

[181] *Works,* IV, 198.
[182] *Works,* IV, 323 ff.
[183] *Works,* IV, 14.
[184] *Works,* II, 59.
[185] *Works,* IV, 300 ff.
[186] *Works,* IV, 136 ff.
[187] *Works,* IV, 13 ff.
[188] *Works,* IV, 20 ff.
[189] *Works,* IV, 417-418.
[190] *Works,* IV, 296.
[191] *Works,* IV, 349-350.
[192] *Works,* IV, 385.
[193] *Works,* IV, 257.
[194] *Works,* IV, 491.
[195] *Works,* IV, 203-213.

features are thus present. The author's invention had worked on familiar material, producing her distinctive types of character and tricks of plotting. Such elements, requiring notice, do not demand emphasis; the achievement of the novel lies elsewhere. Nonetheless one must, as a final comment, remark that these instances of recurring characters and favourite themes are put to excellent service, as a closer examination would prove.

SECTION IV

'An Accursed Race' (1855)

On 25 August 1855 'An Accursed Race' came out in *Household Words*[1]; this article was afterwards incorporated into the *Round the Sofa*[2] group, appearing as a paper drawn up for the Edinburgh Philosophical Society by a certain Mr. Dawson[3], who gave a preliminary reading before a drawing-room assembly. Since the *Round the Sofa* framework was, in effect, a device for gathering together miscellaneous literary pieces, we shall consider its constituent writings in their appropriate chronological positions.

The title of the present *Household Words* contribution applies to the Cagots, inhabitants of France (including Brittany), the Pyrenees district, and parts of Spain and Austria. Mrs. Gaskell mentions the superstitions and suppositions centring on this outcast people, and relates several curious anecdotes. The interest of the article is twofold: it is another manifestation of the antiquarian streak in the writer's nature, and a further indication of her Unitarian devotion to tolerance.

Adolphus Ward has dealt at length with Mrs. Gaskell's and other sources[4], so nothing needs adding on this score. According to Dr. Sanders, the account was probably written 'from information obtained on one of her trips to France'[5]. It seems possible to be a little more specific: for the essayist refers to the work of M. Emile Souvestre with respect to Breton prejudice against the Cagot people[6]; and in a letter to M. Emil [*sic*] Souvestre,

---

[1] XII, 73-80.
[2] [Elizabeth Cleghorn Gaskell] *Round the Sofa*, 2 vols., London: Sampson Low, Son & Co., 1859.
[3] *Works*, V, 217.
[4] Ward, ed. *Works*, V, pp. xvi-xix.
[5] Sanders, *Elizabeth Gaskell*, p. 62.
[6] *Works*, V, 229.

S

dated 'Samedi, Mars 18th' [1854][7], she recalls their agreeable conversation at the house of Mme Mohl.

'An Accursed Race' deserves comment only in one other regard. Its concluding moral consists of the following four lines, taken from a Stratford epitaph.

> "What faults you saw in me,
>   Pray strive to shun;
> And look at home; there's
>   Something to be done."[8]

Here Mrs. Gaskell was apparently recalling a verse which had, many years previously, made a deep impression on the young schoolgirl, Elizabeth Stevenson[9]—so deep, in fact, that a quarter of a century or so afterwards it came to mind as an appropriate plea for self-examination, an apposite warning against acquiring the prejudices of others, and a fitting reminder not to rest content with insular complacency. In fine, her quotation aptly sums up the message which her article held for readers of *Household Words*.

[7] This letter, serving to introduce to him W. R. Greg (for whom Mrs. Gaskell had written a letter of introduction to Souvestre), was discovered in the first volume of a *Mary Barton* first edition; it is fully quoted in Morris Longstreth Parrish, *Victorian Lady Novelists: George Eliot, Mrs. Gaskell, the Brontë Sisters. First Editions in the Library at Dormy House, Pine Valley, New Jersey, described with Notes,* London: Constable and Company Limited, 1933, pp. 57-58. The letter is in the Morris L. Parrish Collection of Victorian Novelists at the Princeton University Library; it appears as *G.L.*, No. 186.

[8] *Works*, V, 235.

[9] Chadwick, *Mrs. Gaskell*, pp. 216-217.

SECTION V

'Half a Lifetime Ago' (1855)

'Half a Life-Time Ago' came out in *Household Words*[1] from 6 October to 20 October 1855. Apparently it was divided into three parts by Wills, though Dickens suggested that the first section might with advantage be split into two chapters—provided Mrs. Gaskell were willing[2].

Professor Ross D. Waller did not, in either his *Times Literary Supplement* letter[3] or his *Bulletin of the John Rylands Library* note[4], link the story with 'Martha Preston' (the contribution to *Sartain's Union Magazine*[5] which he had discovered while editing Gaskell material in The John Rylands Library). This connexion was made by Miss Hopkins[6] who, however, did not engage upon a detailed comparison. We have examined 'Martha Preston' at its proper chronological place in the Gaskell canon; but for the present purpose some recapitulation is doubtless desirable. Professor Waller's view was, it will be recalled, that 'Martha Preston' "is a simple human story, told without sentimentality, and seeming to be in substance a record of fact."[7] Mrs. Gaskell's explicit statement at the beginning of that piece mentions two recent visits to the Lake District[8], thereby encouraging her readers to take the factual basis on trust; and, when discussing 'Martha Preston' and 'Cumberland Sheep-

---

[1] XII, 229-237, 253-257, 276-282.

[2] *The Letters of Charles Dickens,* ed. Dexter, II, 693: letter to Wills of 25 September 1855—see too p. 691: letter to Henry Morley of 21 September 1855. This point is noted by Miss Hopkins—'Dickens and Mrs. Gaskell', *The Huntington Library Quarterly,* IX (1946), 376; *Elizabeth Gaskell,* p. 152.

[3] 'Articles by Mrs. Gaskell', *The Times Literary Supplement,* 25 July 1935, p. 477.

[4] *Bulletin of the John Rylands Library, Manchester,* XX (1936), 25-27, esp. 27.

[5] VI (1850), 133-138.

[6] *Elizabeth Gaskell,* pp. 101, 255.

[7] Quoted in 'Notes and News', *Bulletin of the John Rylands Library, Manchester,* XX, 27.

[8] *Sartain's Union Magazine,* VI, 133.

Shearers', we substantiated at least one of these visits[9]. More-over in 'Martha Preston' the writer was at pains to make clear she was retelling a local story.

About the final form assumed by this tale no problems arise : it was incorporated into the *Round the Sofa* network where, unchanged from the *Household Words* version ('Half a Life-Time Ago'), it was narrated by Mrs. Preston[10], the wife of a Westmoreland squire[11]. The genesis and early stages do, how-ever, present certain difficulties.

Mrs. Gaskell, we conjectured, probably heard a true story along the lines of 'Martha Preston' while near Skelwith, this later suggesting itself as suitable for her second *Sartain's* con-tribution. She may have included a few minor alterations—very possibly of names, perhaps of places too—and then narrated from memory, providing a personal introduction yet telling the tale much as she herself had received it. Her method was, no doubt, a more or less direct reiteration, with little attempt to elaborate : indeed 'bald' seems an appropriate epithet for the narrative. Her audience being primarily American, there was no obligation to fictionalize the facts for the sake of any living people concerned.

When planning the *Household Words* version, Mrs. Gaskell doubtless realized that the characters ought not to be identifiable, especially since the periodical's wide circulation might make recognition quite likely. We can surmise, therefore, that she would certainly effect changes in the names of characters and places—and these are, in fact, different from those in 'Martha Preston', even granted that the latter may have been left undisguised—as well as modifications in the plot itself. Never-theless the impression of verisimilitude is retained, an impression achieved in 'Martha Preston' partly by means of numerous realistic details, conceivably designed for that very purpose.

[9] Relevant references include: Morley, ed. *The Correspondence of Henry Crabb Robinson with the Wordsworth Circle* (1808-1866), II, 698, 700, 705; *Autobiography of Mrs. Fletcher with Letters and Other Family Memorials,* ed. The Survivor of Her Family [Mary Richardson], p. 274; *Memorials of Two Sisters,* ed. Shaen, p. 47; Her Sister [Susanna Wink-worth], ed. *Letters and Memorials of Catherine Winkworth,* I (1883), 192-194, 197-199; Waller, ed. *Letters Addressed to Mrs Gaskell by Celebrated Contemporaries,* pp. 34, 59-60; and *G.L.*, Nos. 26, 49, 182.
[10] *Works,* V, 277.   [11] *Works,* V, 6.

We may, then, hazard that 'Half a Lifetime Ago'[12] developed in the following stages :—(1) an actual instance of heroism and self-sacrifice on the part of a Westmoreland daleswoman; (2) the version recounted to Mrs. Gaskell by local inhabitants; (3) Mrs. Gaskell's relating of the tale, from memory (perhaps helped by notes taken at the time) and with various slight amendments, for her American reading public; (4) her working over the *Sartain's* material in an attempt to put any possible literary detectives off the scent, without sacrificing the appearance of historical veracity.

Probably Mrs. Gaskell's first move was to transpose her scenes from the Loughrigg district (lying northward of Skelwith Bridge) to the region around Oxenfell and Blea Tarn (which are respectively to the south and to the west of Skelwith Bridge). One can neatly indicate this topographic change by saying that, whereas in 'Martha Preston' the heroine's cottage was certainly in Westmoreland, in 'Half a Lifetime Ago' the heroine, living between Skelwith and Coniston, strictly resided within the Lonsdale hundred of Lancashire[13]. It may be convenient to summarize other divergencies.

The most noticeable difference of technique is that in 'Martha Preston' the narrator's presence is felt, whereas for 'Half a Lifetime Ago' everything is in the third person. We have already noted the name-changes as between the two versions; but there is also some alteration of the characters themselves. Although Susan Dixon does in her attributes correspond to Martha Preston, her mother displays a maternal devotion towards young William which is altogether absent from Mrs. Preston's attitude to her son; moreover in the earlier story it is Mr. Preston who enjoins his daughter to care for her brother, whereas in 'Half

---

[12] Ward dispenses with the hyphen in his Knutsford Edition (*Works,* V).
[13] Joseph Aston, *The Lancashire Gazetteer: an Alphabetically Arranged Account of the Hundreds, Market Towns, Boroughs, Parishes, Townships, Hamlets, Gentlemens' Seats, Rivers, Lakes, Mountains, Moors, Commons, Mosses, Antiquities, &c. in the County Palatine of Lancaster; Together with Historical Descriptions of the Chief Places, with their Fairs, Markets, Local and Metropolitan Distances, Charters, Church Livings, Patrons, &c.,* London: Longman, Hurst, Rees, and Orme; County of Lancaster: All booksellers, 1808, map frontispiece. Though geographically her farmhouse must have been in Lancashire, Susan Dixon is throughout the tale regarded as a Stateswoman inhabiting 'one of the Westmoreland dales' (*Works,* V, 278).

a Lifetime Ago' it is Mrs. Dixon who exacts the death-bed promise. In 'Martha Preston' Mr. Preston is presented as wholly worthy and upright; Mr. Dixon, on the other hand, is prone to occasional bouts of drinking[14], and is less kind to his son. Even though William Hawkshaw is shown to be unworthy of Martha, the reader does initially form a more favourable impression of him than is possible in the case of Susan's suitor, Michael Hurst, whose selfishness early betrays itself. In 'Martha Preston' only little Willie suffers from typhoid fever; in the later version typhus attacks father, daughter, and son—the first fatally. Nor is the rescue episode the same in both. Martha, helped by her dog, successfully rescues the son of her former lover; he recovers, and eventually brings his wife to live with Martha, she acting as a sort of grandmother to their children. Susan, on the other hand, unaided drags to shelter the lifeless body of William Hurst, whose widow and children she takes into her own home.

One would not wish to emphasize what Mrs. Gaskell seemingly invented for purposes of disguise and deception, since, from the literary point of view, these are not of the highest importance. The concluding rescue episode has, for example, equal merit in each tale : when everything is taken into account, neither is inherently improbable. The realistic touches expected from Mrs. Gaskell are present to confer an air of plausibility and an aspect of truth. Thus when Susan Dixon hears the cry for help, she neglects none of those practical details which to a daleswoman would be second nature—putting a new candle in the lantern, changing her shawl for a maud, leaving the door on the latch, and so forth[15]. As regards the preliminary (ante-rescue) part, the greater length of the *Household Words* contribution allowed Mrs. Gaskell to develop her characters more than had been possible in the *Sartain's* article. We find Michael

---

[14] Works, V, 280-281. It may be merely coincidental that, according to a letter Mrs. Gaskell wrote one Monday [29 August 1859] to Charles B. P. Bosanquet, Mr. Preston, the husband of her Skelwith landlady, sometimes turned to drink, being nonetheless a fine fellow when sober. In this letter she also mentions that it was the Arnolds and the Wordsworths who long ago had arranged for the Gaskells to lodge with Mrs. Preston of Mill Brow, a Stateswoman whose family, so she had heard, had lived on the same land and in the same house for over two centuries: Mrs. Gaskell's letter (*G.L.*, No. 439a) is in the Manchester University Library.

[15] *Works*, V, 321.

Hurst's final break with Susan made more convincing, by virtue of preparatory hints about his innate selfishness and the superficiality of his love[16], than its equivalent in the briefer treatment of William Hawkshaw. Similarly additional space permitted Mrs. Gaskell to devote more attention to the *milieu*; for the peculiar features of a district always attracted her. In this respect one finds a good analysis of Westmoreland and Cumberland statesmen, whose characteristics she had evidently observed with interest, especially since, like the habits of those very different people with whom her first *Sartain's* article had been concerned, they were 'the characteristics of a class now passing away from the face of the land'[17].

Mrs. Gaskell was both a perceptive observer of local groups and a sensitive antiquary; she felt the romance of regionalism, and was moved by the poignancy of change. Indeed her very title is poetic. Many of her stories seem to be set in a time which, though passed, can still be remembered, some vague period not yet part of history; these tales, like the present one, might well appropriately open with the words 'Half a lifetime ago'[18]. With additional elbow-room, Mrs. Gaskell had the opportunity to evoke distance in space as well as in time. Here the dialectal dialogue is important, even though it scarcely differs from that of the Lancashire stories proper (a similarity partly explicable from the border context). Thus to have Mrs. Dixon, on her death-bed, using words like ' "dree" '[19] and ' "lile" '[20] (both of which occur in a contemporary dialect glossary[21]) lends to the scene a Northern flavour. Perhaps the most memorable part of 'Half a Lifetime Ago' is not the rescue incident; nor the description of Susan's struggles with her idiot brother; nor the chequered course of Susan's love for, and estrangement from, Michael Hust; nor yet the tragico-humorous

---

[16] *Works*, V, 286, 291, 292, 294, 298.
[17] *Works*, V, 281.
[18] *Works*, V, 278.
[19] *Works*, V, 283.
[20] *Works*, V, 283.
[21] The glossary of Westmoreland and Cumberland words in Mrs. Ann Wheeler, *The Westmoreland Dialect in Four Familiar Dialogues, in Which an Attempt Is Made to Illustrate the Provincial Idiom*, New edn, London: John Russell Smith, 1840, pp. 93-175, esp. pp. 118, 140.

scene[22] where Mrs. Gale tries to make Susan see reason, and put
Willie away in the asylum as her brother proposes. What rather
comes to mind as the essence of the tale is Susan's quiet heroism
in following her conscience, finely illustrated by the clap-bread
episode. After she knew all was finished between herself and the
man she loved, Susan turned to an accustomed task for Westmoreland daleswomen, the making of clap-bread. As expected,
Mrs. Gaskell has all the details right; but, though these incidentals have their place in creating circumstantial truthfulness,
the real force of the scene is in terms of human and moral
values: it springs from the few words spoken. Recalling old
Germanic ideals, perhaps we are not altogether fanciful if we
discern in the ensuing conversation between two Westmoreland
women something of their remote ancestors' Stoicism and appreciation of the transience of things.

> "Lass!" said Peggy [her servant] solemnly, "thou hast done
> well. It is not long to bide, and then the end will come."
> "But you are very old, Peggy," said Susan, quivering.
> "It is but a day sin' I were young," replied Peggy; . . . [23]

Taken in the context, no better example could be found in the
depths reached by that language, Biblical in its pregnant
economy, characteristic of such folk in their moments of crisis.
All is simply stated; nothing is melodramatic, high flown, or
sentimentalized. It is not without significance that Mrs. Gaskell
should have earlier mentioned that 'grave, solid books'[24], like
Paradise Lost and *The Pilgrim's Progress,* were the wonted reading of the class to which Susan belonged.

[22] *Works,* V, 308-311.
[23] *Works,* V, 311-312.
[24] *Works,* V, 280.

SECTION VI

'The Poor Clare' (1856)

'The Poor Clare', later incorporated into the *Round the Sofa* group as the narrative of Signor Sperano[1], first appeared between 13 December and 27 December 1856 in *Household Words*[2]. Almost certainly this tale of the supernatural had been intended for the numbers of the previous Christmas; but, being at that time incomplete, it was appropriately reserved until the next December[3].

The telling of ghost stories seems to have been a favourite Christmas recreation among Mrs. Gaskell and her friends[4]; certainly it was a practice in which she was proficient—so proficient as to disconcert Charlotte Brontë[5]. We have already examined 'The Old Nurse's Story', one of whose virtues lay in the author's maintaining plausibility by means of matter-of-fact incidentals; in 'The Poor Clare' this success is repeated. Mrs. Gaskell supplies the tale with a substantiating background, and has as its narrator an unimaginative lawyer; moreover she includes several historical references, which reinforces the impression of veracious reporting. The extraordinary elements, therefore, appear less so when taken in their commonsensical context.

Clearly Mrs. Gaskell was familiar with that part of Lancashire where the opening scenes are laid : she had earlier, in 'The Heart of John Middleton', used a neighbouring district as a setting. In such circumstances, one naturally looks for correspondences between fact and fiction; some can be found,

[1] *Works*, V, 327-328.
[2] XIV, 510-515, 532-544, 559-565.
[3] This supposition is suggested by a letter of 2 January 1856 from Dickens to Mrs. Gaskell (*The Letters of Charles Dickens*, ed. Dexter, II, 719-720). Dickens there (*op. cit.*, II, 719) hopes that he will see the end of the story she could not finish for Christmas—'that of 1855' (Hopkins, *Elizabeth Gaskell*, p. 153), not 'that of 1856' as is stated in Hopkins, 'Dickens and Mrs. Gaskell', *The Huntington Library Quarterly*, IX (1946), 376.
[4] *Mary Howitt: An Autobiography*, ed. Howitt, II, 65-67.
[5] Haldane, *Mrs. Gaskell and Her Friends*, pp. 136-137.

249

others cannot—which is not to say they do not exist. On the other hand, certain apparent parallels may be purely fortuitous and unintended by the author. Perhaps, however, all that is really needed is to show that Mrs. Gaskell was not working *in vacuo*, that her invention had several factual starting-points.

We have often remarked upon Mrs. Gaskell's powers of scenic description. Her ability to evoke a locality is again illustrated in the opening chapter. There she gives a graphic sketch of that wild region known as the Trough of Bowland, and provides a picturesque account of Starkey Manor-house. Whether or not she had any particular residence in mind is difficult to determine—partly because not all the old halls of the district have survived. The principal seat of the Starkie family at the time of the tale was Huntroyde, built near Pendle Forest in the late sixteenth century[6]; and, since the manor-house of the story seems to date initially from pre-Stuart times[7], this tempting identification may be put forward. Of a slightly later period, although within the confines of the Forest of Bowland, is Browsholme[8]— but this was never in the possession of the Starkie family. It seems that Mrs. Gaskell used the Forest as a location for the manor-house of a well-known Lancashire family; both the Forest and the name of Starkey (the spelling varies) would be recognized by her readers as authentic, yet their conjunction was of her own inventing. Mrs. Gaskell mentions that the Starkey residence was originally a tower—of a sort common in that part of Lancashire which had most to fear from the Scots[9].

[6] Thomas Dunham Whitaker, *An History of the Original Parish of Whalley, and Honor of Clitheroe. To Which Is Subjoined an Account of the Parish of Cartmell*, ed. John Gough Nichols and Ponsonby A. Lyons, 4th edn, rev. and enlarged, 2 vols., 1872-1876, II (London: George Routledge and Sons; and Lynch Conway Gent, 1876), 44.

[7] *Works*, V, 329.

[8] Whitaker, *Whalley*, ed. Nichols and Lyons, I (London: George Routledge and Sons; Manchester: L. C. Gent, 1872), 336-340. It is worth noting that when Catherine Winkworth and the Gaskells were touring Yorkshire in 1852 they read about the great families of the district—also open to Scottish invasion—in Whitaker's *History of Craven*: see *Letters and Memorials of Catherine Winkworth*, I (ed. Her Sister [Susanna Winkworth], 1883), 358.

[9] When at Silverdale Mrs. Gaskell had for her larder the lower storey of (she affirmed) "an old Square Tower, or 'Peel'—a remnant [?] of the Border towers."—*Gaskell-Norton Letters*, ed. Whitehill, p. 22: *G.L.*, No. 394 (our square brackets). In fact Lindeth Tower, whose ground-floor served as Mrs. Gaskell's larder, was a much more recent edifice than she

In respect of historical architecture Mrs. Gaskell shows herself a careful observer; for, besides the description of the hall, she refers to the peculiar construction of nearby cottages[10], perhaps built for family retainers—which suggests such cottages were still to be seen in the mid-nineteenth century. As regards the historicity of the Patrick Byrne Starkey[11] of the tale, no Starkie seems to have borne that name in the early eighteenth (or any other) century; moreover the family, far from being Catholics, during the latter half of the seventeenth century 'appear to have been Puritans.'[12] The Sherburnes of Stonyhurst[13], on the other hand, were well-known adherents to the old religion.

The later part of the narrative takes place in Antwerp between the end of the War of Spanish Succession and the beginning of that of the Austrian Succession. Adolphus Ward opines that the exact time 'is left conveniently vague'[14]; and Clement Shorter implies it is 'soon after the Rebellion of 1745'[15]. We have here unexpected carelessness from both scholars, who can almost always be relied upon for their accuracy. Shorter seems to consider the period to be just before the writing down of the account (12 December 1747[16]), whereas the writer explicitly states he is looking back over the years; Dr. Ward, though not falling into this error, apparently does not notice that Mrs. Gaskell put two dates (1711 and 1718)[17] in the body of the tale, which thus permits some sort of chronological estimation. We may surmise that the Antwerp revolt of the story[18] occurred in the early seventeen-twenties. Pirenne confirms that there was discontent in the Austrian Netherlands following the Third Barrier Treaty

---

implied (Chadwick, *Mrs. Gaskell*, p. 227); but doubtless her words were influenced by thoughts of Scottish raids and of the nearby ruined Arnside Tower (Chadwick, *Mrs. Gaskell*, pp. 228, 235).

[10] *Works*, V, 330. For an account of the domestic architecture of Lancashire, see Whitaker, *Whalley*, ed. Nichols and Lyons, II, 566-575.

[11] *Works*, V, 331.

[12] William Farrer and John Brownbill, ed. *The Victoria History of the County of Lancaster*, 8 vols., 1906-1914, VI (London: Constable and Company Limited, 1911), 500.

[13] *Works*, V, 378.

[14] Ward, ed. *Works*, V, p. xxi.

[15] Shorter, ed. *Novels and Tales*, IX (1913), p. xiii.

[16] *Works*, V, 329.

[17] *Works*, V, 339, 343.

[18] *Works*, V, 386.

of 15 November 1715[19]; and, although at the time indicated by Mrs. Gaskell there was no Antwerp rioting of sufficient importance for him to record, we do find at a slightly earlier date (c. 1717) 'une émeute provoquée à Anvers par les fabricants de soie'[20]. As for Mrs. Gaskell's historical accuracy in her references to the Jesuit father and the Order of Poor Clares, we know that the Jesuits first came to the city in 1562[21], and the Clares in 1455[22]. Concerning the Clares one can quote Dr. Adolphus Ward to the effect that their community 'at Levenshulme, within a quarter of an hour's walk from Plymouth Grove, ... may have suggested to Mrs. Gaskell the form given by her to the final episode of her story.'[23]

The foregoing historical prolegomena are not intended to demonstrate that Mrs. Gaskell did some research before writing, but rather to show that the background was authentic, that she had got her facts as near correctness as mattered for the task in hand. The Lancashire and Netherlands scenes were written by an author who was attracted to the past; and this concern with bygone times had advantages for some one treating the supernatural. Indeed it is quite likely that Mrs. Gaskell's love of old legends suggested the theme of the tale. Perhaps, while in the district, she heard traditions about East Lancashire witchcraft—perhaps even about the demoniacal possession in 1594 of the household of Nicholas Starkie[24]. From such origins, we may hazard, the story took its beginning.

The theme of 'The Poor Clare' is a variation of the *Doppelgänger motif*[25]. Bridget Fitzgerald's curse on Squire Gisborne, who had killed her spaniel, caused her grand-daughter (the

[19] Jean Henri O. L. M. Pirenne, *Histoire de Belgique*, 7 vols., 1900-1932, V (2nd and rev. edn, Brussels: Maurice Lamertin, 1926), 172-174.

[20] Pirenne, *Histoire*, V, 192.

[21] [Jean-Baptiste Christyn] *Histoire Générale des Païs-Bas, Contenant la Description des XVII Provinces*, New edn, 4 vols., Brussels: François Foppens, 1720, I, 184 ('les Jesuites qui y vinrent l'an 1562').

[22] [Christyn] *Histoire*, I, 185 ('les Clarisses [y vinrent] l'an 1455').

[23] Ward, ed. *Works*, V, p. xxi.

[24] John Harland and Thomas Turner Wilkinson, compiled and ed. *Lancashire Folk-Lore: Illustrative of the Superstitious Beliefs and Practices, Local Customs and Usages of the People of the County Palatine*, London: Frederick Warne and Co.; New York: Scribner and Co., 1867, pp. 92-98.

[25] See Frank Laurence Lucas, *Literature and Psychology*, London, Toronto, Melbourne, Sydney, and Wellington: Cassell & Company Ltd, 1951, pp. 89, 122, 133.

child of Gisborne's union with Mary Fitzgerald) to be afflicted with an evil apparition, the double of herself. In this way Mrs. Gaskell invented a plot whose construction brings to mind the principles of Greek tragedy, if we may compare small things with great; certainly there is tragic irony and poetic justice— human blindness and blasphemy producing an effect exactly opposite to that intended.

From a formal view-point, this can claim to be one of the author's best-planned works. Improbabilities do not here, as they may elsewhere, seem merely *ad hoc* contrivances; rather they are central to the whole scheme. Apparent coincidences, in reality the work of the powers of darkness, thus acquire an especial appropriateness; they both reinforce, and are in turn reinforced by, the more obviously supernatural elements.

Since the narrator of 'The Poor Clare', like that of 'The Old Nurse's Story', is not a highly imaginative person, extraordinary events *ipso facto* assume an air of plausibility. Mrs. Gaskell skilfully handles this common device for dealing with the other-worldly. In the course of a matter-of-fact unfolding of the story—the manner is most apposite for the lawyer-narrator —there are significant hints, just sufficient to arouse the reader's attention, suggesting something mysterious will ensue. There is, for instance, the narrator's avowed intention of telling a 'strange story'[26], followed by his seeming reluctance to come on to the important characters[27]; there is the darkness surrounding Bridget (the fear in which the villagers held her, her reputation for witchcraft, the prosperity which was the lot of those who showed her kindness, the bad fortune which befell those who did her ill)[28]; there are the drops of blood from her dead dog which ominously stained its killer's shooting-dress[29]; there is Squire Gisborne's shock on learning that the woman who had cursed him was called Fitzgerald[30]. Such examples could be multiplied; but, as we have pointed out, they occur in a quasi-historical narrative, and are recounted autobiographically as matters of fact. In making her narrator appear to give a straight-

26 *Works*, V, 329.
27 *Works*, V, 333.
28 *Works*, V, 337-342, 369.
29 *Works*, V, 341.
30 *Works*, V, 341-342.

forward account of what he had discovered or observed, Mrs. Gaskell succeeds to the full. He plausibly explains that some earlier occurrences had to be gathered from the villagers, one of whose interests was, characteristically, to discover how much Squire Starkey had tipped the lad who directed him and his party to the manor-house[31]. Being himself an important figure in the tale, the story-teller can vouch for its truth, so the reader feels inclined to take all he says on trust. Moreover his legal background accustomed him to adopt an objective view of things, as when, in questioning Bridget, he tried to keep 'up her attention to details'[32]; as when, while going in search of her, he noted that his 'feet left prints in the sprinkling of hoar-frost that covered the ground'[33].

In general the characters are adequate for their *rôles*, except, perhaps, Lucy Gisborne, whose misfortune it was to suffer from the demoniacal double. One can best indicate the nature of her deficiency by saying she looks rather too much like a Victorian heroine[34] incongruously placed in an eighteenth-century context. Bridget Fitzgerald (like John Barton[35], ' "one powerful for good as for evil" '[36]) is forcefully presented and of central importance. We have spoken of the narrator who, we may notice in passing, happens to be one of the few lawyers displayed by Mrs. Gaskell in a favourable light. In her portrayal of clergymen she was never partizan: here one finds an urbane Jesuit[37] and a Field-ingesque, beer-drinking, witch-detesting, anti-Catholic parson[38]. Each, though slightly sketched, seems wholly in keeping with the period, as does the narrator's uncle, an attorney interested in antiquities and heraldry[39]. In keeping too with the eighteenth-century setting are the gentry—the Starkeys[40], Squire Gisborne[41], and Sir Philip Tempest[42].

Before leaving 'The Poor Clare', we must commend Mrs. Gaskell's graphic picture of the Antwerp mob[43], both in riot against the Austrians and in haste to carry food to the starving Poor Clares: crowd scenes are usually, though not invariably,

[31] *Works*, V, 332.
[32] *Works*, V, 349.
[33] *Works*, V, 346.
[34] *Works*, V, 368, 371.
[35] *Works*, I, 4.
[36] *Works*, V, 378.
[37] *Works*, V, 377.
[38] *Works*, V, 372.
[39] *Works*, V, 343.
[40] *Works*, V, 329-334.
[41] *Works*, V, 339.
[42] *Works*, V, 339.
[43] *Works*, V, 386-390.

well done in her work. A final point to mention, albeit scarcely deserving attention were it not for parallels elsewhere, is the use of Mignon, her daughter's spaniel, to arouse from stupor the grief-stricken Bridget Fitzgerald[44]. There are several instances in Mrs. Gaskell's writings where a mother gains comfort or is brought back to her senses by receiving a child (usually a baby) into her arms. In the present case we have a slight variation on this technique for facilitating a return to reality[45]; it can, no doubt, be related to the maternal feelings of the authoress.

[44] *Works*, V, 335.
[45] E.g. *North and South* (*Works*, IV, 355), *Wives and Daughters* (*Works*, VIII, 672-673); a baby is pinched to bring about the same result in *Sylvia's Lovers* (*Works*, VI, 417). See too *Ruth* (*Works*, III, 350, 407).

SECTION VII

'A Christmas Carol' (1856)

On 27 December 1856, the same day as saw the conclusion of 'The Poor Clare', there was published in *Household Words*[1] 'A Christmas Carol'. These quatrains Clement Shorter attributed to Mrs. Gaskell[2] and reprinted as hers[3]. However, according to Professor Lohrli[4], he misinterpreted the relevant entry (of 27 December by W. H. Wills) in the *Household Words* Office (or Day) Book. This entry, whose author-column remains blank, follows that for 'The Poor Clare', where the authorship is clearly indicated; hence Shorter—in ignorance of the entry-system employed—naturally assumed Mrs. Gaskell had supplied both contributions. Since, because of its anonymity, the poem may just conceivably be by Mrs. Gaskell, it need not be omitted from our study.

A widow relates her story to some children, telling how her husband had died a hero's death, soon to be followed, on Christmas Eve, by his son. The woman sees her child as born again in heaven, just as Christ was born on earth. Hence she can say:

> "Thus I celebrate, alone and silent,
> On the Christmas Eve, a double birth;
> Thanking God, who took my child to Heaven;
> Praising God, who sent His child on Earth."[5]

Dr. Sanders finds the literary qualities of the work negligible[6], despite 'a certain beauty . . . for which . . . [the poet's] religious beliefs are responsible'[7]; nevertheless one might claim

---

[1] XIV, 565.
[2] Initially in his MS list of her *Household Words* contributions, to be found among Shorter's biographical and bibliographical notes on the novelist (in the Gaskell Section, Brotherton Collection, Leeds University Library).
[3] *Novels and Tales*, X, 463-466.
[4] Anne Lohrli, '*Household Words* and Its "Office Book"', *The Princeton University Library Chronicle*, XXVI (1964), 38.
[5] *Household Words*, XIV, 565.
[6] Sanders, *Elizabeth Gaskell*, pp. 62-63.
[7] Sanders, *Elizabeth Gaskell*, p. 63.

T

that this concept of a double birth is a little out of the ordinary,
and rather poetic in a non-Victorian sense. The season and
subject could easily have combined to produce sickly, sentimental
verses; these were avoided. Although one would not wish to
make absurd claims for the use of a metaphysical conceit, there
may be invention of a slightly witty sort, a hint of unlooked-
for mental flexibility, in the last line of the next extract. Whilst
what has gone before suggests one should take the reference
as being to the dead husband and his (perhaps posthumous)
child, the capitalization points to a different—divine—interpretation, possibly that uppermost in the mind of the author.

> "Then I mourn'd for him as one distracted—
> Sinfully, despairingly, I mourn'd—
> Till my love fix'd on another object,
> From the Maker to His creature turn'd."[8]

An interesting aspect is the widow's almost idolatrous love
for her baby, with God's chastening her through the child's
death. Mrs. Gaskell, we have previously seen, had feared she
might make too much of her own baby (Marianne), and the
same apprehension was expressed by Ruth[9]; moreover, like the
widow, she had lost her son (William) at a tender age[10]. Thus,
even if Mrs. Gaskell did not compose the verses, she may have
read them with pleasure.

---

[8] *Household Words,* XIV, 565.

[9] See too, on this point, Rubenius, *The Woman Question in Mrs.
Gaskell's Life and Works,* p. 198, fn. 3.

[10]   Concerning his death she believed not 'even Heaven itself' could
'obliterate the memory of that agony'—quoted, from Mrs. Gaskell's letter
to 'dearest Fanny' (doubtless her cousin, Mrs. Frances Holland) of Tuesday
[(perhaps 23 February or 2 March) 1847; rather than 1846, as conjectured],
in Sotheby's Sale Catalogue for 29 October 1968: this letter (Lot 451)
was bought by Francis Edwards Ltd., 83 Marylebone High Street, London
W.1.

CHAPTER VI

'THE SIEGE OF THE BLACK COTTAGE' (1857)
TO 'THE MANCHESTER MARRIAGE' (1858)

SECTION I

'The Siege of the Black Cottage' (1857)

Charles A. Durfee, when compiling his *Index to 'Harper's New Monthly Magazine'*, ascribed[1] to Mrs. Gaskell 'The Siege of the Black Cottage', which had been published anonymously in February 1857[2]. According to Miss Hopkins, any such ascription must remain 'extremely doubtful'[3]; but a different view can, nonetheless, be maintained. Some of Mrs. Gaskell's short stories in *Household Words* and *All the Year Round* only came to light when the account books were examined[4]; and presumably Durfee's attribution was based on similar evidence. Moreover neither of Mrs. Gaskell's first two contributions to *Harper's*—'Lizzie Leigh'[5] and 'A Love Affair at Cranford'[6]— appeared as her work : hence the absence of the writer's name gives little weight to the case against Gaskellian authorship.

A careful reading of 'The Siege of the Black Cottage' tends to confirm Durfee's indexing. Certainly (to put things no higher) there is no internal evidence for supposing him mistaken. On the other hand there is nothing so distinctly Gaskellian as to preclude further argument. The style does not seem out of keeping with that of writings indisputably by Mrs. Gaskell, though her easy-flowing prose was, in the main, free from idiosyncrasies—this being one of her virtues.

As regards content, one can again point to nothing so unmistakably from Mrs. Gaskell's pen as to convince a doubter.

---

[1] *Index to 'Harper's New Monthly Magazine'*, *Alphabetical, Analytical, and Classified, Volumes I. to LXX. Inclusive from June, 1850, to June,* 1885, compiled by Charles Augustus Durfee, New York : Harper & Brothers, 1886, pp. 235, 255.

[2] *Harper's New Monthly Magazine*, XIV, 334-341.

[3] Hopkins, *Elizabeth Gaskell*, p. 337.

[4] Ward, ed. *Works*, VII, pp. xi-xii.

[5] '[From Household Words.]/ Lizzie Leigh', *Harper's New Monthly Magazine,* I (June 1850), 38-50. As the heading states, the story first appeared (from 30 March to 13 April 1850) in *Household Words* (I, 2-6, 32-35, 60-65).

[6] *Harper's New Monthly Magazine*, IV (March 1852), 457-464. This was the same sketch as had first come out on 3 January 1852 in *Household Words*, IV, 349-357

There are, to be sure, a brother at sea[7] and a mother who exacts a death-bed promise[8]; yet to consider these peculiar to our author would be ridiculous. The story itself, telling how a girl of eighteen or so defended herself in a lonely cottage against two disreputable characters bent on robbery, has a remote affinity with the burglary episode in 'The Crooked Branch'; since this last was based on fact, then a real attack may here also have resulted in a short story. However such a supposition must remain merely speculative.

There are vivid touches of the sort one might expect from Mrs. Gaskell. One recalls the graphic description of the Black Cottage, protected from the elements by the pitch and tar whose colour gave it its name[9]; the blackguardly gentility of Jerry, a ruffian possessing 'a bald head with some very ugly-looking knobs on it'[10]; Shifty Dick's terse comment on what would happen to Bessie when they had broken in (' "[W]e'll mash you!" '[11]); the narrator's quasi-comic action of putting her cat to bed in time of danger[12]; the 'sensation' caused by the appearance through the roof of a 'heavy, hairy hand . . . armed with . . . [a] knife'[13]; and, finally, the half-crazed Bessie's remnant of sense in keeping the wind to her back as she escaped from the Black Cottage to Moor Farm[14].

Like some of Mrs. Gaskell's tales, this story has a concluding moral. It is such as she could have written—but then so could many others. Since the ostensive purpose of the epistolary narrative is to enlighten a young lady who was puzzled that a stone-mason's daughter should have married a gentleman-farmer[15], the concluding moral appears less out of place than it might otherwise have been.

7 *Harper's New Monthly Magazine*, XIV, 334.
8 *Harper's New Monthly Magazine*, XIV, 334.
9 *Harper's New Monthly Magazine*, XIV, 334-335.
10 *Harper's New Monthly Magazine*, XIV, 336.
11 *Harper's New Monthly Magazine*, XIV, 337.
12 *Harper's New Monthly Magazine*, XIV, 338.
13 *Harper's New Monthly Magazine*, XIV, 339.
14 *Harper's New Monthly Magazine*, XIV, 340.
15 *Harper's New Monthly Magazine*, XIV, 334.

You will now, perhaps, be ready to admit that a woman may possess neither beauty, birth, wealth, nor accomplishments, and yet, in spite of those disadvantages, may still have attractions of her own in the eyes of a sensible man.[16]

It remains to note one passage which does have a Gaskellian ring about it; for certainly the views expressed would readily have come from such a sympathetic student of the ways and habits of humble folk as was the author of *Mary Barton*.

I had seen enough of poverty and poor men to know what a terrible temptation a large sum of money is to those whose whole lives are passed in scraping up sixpences by weary hard work. It is one thing to write fine sentiments in books about incorruptible honesty, and another thing to put those sentiments in practice, when one day's work is all that a man has to set up in the way of an obstacle between starvation and his own fireside.[17]

[16] *Harper's New Monthly Magazine*, XIV, 340-341.
[17] *Harper's New Monthly Magazine*, XIV, 337.

SECTION II

Mrs. Gaskell, ed. *Mabel Vaughan*
[by Maria Susanna Cummins] (1857)

The Life of Charlotte Brontë excepted, the only new work
indubitably by Mrs. Gaskell published in 1857 was an annotated
(and Englished) edition of *Mabel Vaughan*[1], for which she also
wrote a preface[2]. Before considering the Preface, we ought to
notice that this was the first time she dealt with Sampson Low,
Son & Co.— probably Low took the initiative. Subsequently
Round the Sofa was brought out by the 'rascally publisher'[3],
Mrs. Gaskell's relations with his firm being rather unhappy[4].

One purpose of the editor's prefatory remarks was to indicate
the value of novels in promoting Anglo-American friendship.
By strengthening mutual understanding, they can bring about
increased sympathy. The truth such fiction embodies she held
to be:

[1] Elizabeth Cleghorn Gaskell, ed. *Mabel Vaughan,* by The Author of
The "Lamplighter" [Maria Susanna Cummins], London: Sampson Low,
Son, and Co., 1857. September was the month of publication, according
to Michael Thomas Harvey Sadleir (*Excursions in Victorian Bibliography,*
London: Chaundy & Cox, 1922, p. 213).

[2] Gaskell, ed. *Mabel Vaughan* [by Cummins], pp. v-viii. The Preface
is reprinted in *Novels and Tales,* X, 467-470.

[3] So described, for trying to pass off as new this republication of her
Household Words stories, by Mrs. Gaskell in a [Sunday (post 5—possibly
6—February) 1859] letter to Mrs. Nancy Robson, now in the Yale Univer-
sity Library—MS Vault Sect. 16. The letter (*G.L.,* No. 414) is dated
[February 1859] by Chapple and Pollard. Even by late 1857 Mrs. Gaskell
had reasons for believing Low 'rather a/ "tricky man" '—as is indicated by
her letter of Monday [7] December [1857] to Charles Eliot Norton (in the
Harvard University Library), the relevant passage being quoted by Mrs.
Whitehill (ed. *Gaskell-Norton Letters,* pp. 10-11), who tactfully substitutes
X for the publisher's name which, as in this letter (*G.L.,* No. 384), Mrs.
Gaskell usually spelled 'Lowe'.

[4] Mrs. Gaskell's lack of confidence in their straightforwardness is voiced
in her letter to Norton of 3 September [1858]—this passage is not printed,
though its omission is indicated, by Mrs. Whitehill (ed. *Gaskell-Norton
Letters,* p. 29). The full text (*G.L.,* No. 403) is given by Chapple and
Pollard who, unlike Mrs. Whitehill but in accordance with the reading of
the original letter (in the Harvard University Library), enclose the year of
the date within square brackets.

the truth that, however different may be national manifestations
of the fact, still, below accents, manners, dress, and language, we
have
   "All of us one human heart."[5]

This Wordsworthian thought, which had been in Mrs. Gaskell's
mind when, much earlier, she was reflecting on the poetry of
humble life[6], now suggested itself as an appropriate response
to national differences. Better acquaintanceship led, she believed, to a fuller appreciation of our common humanity.

It seems worth while to give a further extract from this preface, which has relevance for Mrs. Gaskell's own writings.
There we have often noticed a use of graphic domestic details;
an attraction towards old customs and traditions; a concern
with ethical issues and cases of conscience; and sympathetic
attempts to observe from the inside the life of diverse characters,
be they masters or men, from town or country, of high station
or low.

> Through the means of works of fiction we obtain glimpses into
> American home-life; of their modes of thought, their traditional
> observances, and their social temptations, quite beyond and apart
> from the observations of travellers, who, after all, only see the
> family in the street, or on the festival days, not in the quiet
> domestic circle, into which the stranger is rarely admitted.[7]

With but little adaptation, these words could aptly be applied
to, for instance, *Ruth*, or *North and South*, or *Mary Barton*;
the function of the industrial or social-problem novel was, in
her view, interpretative not didactic, informative rather than
polemic. Yet what we have quoted will apply, in some degree,
to almost all her work; Mrs. Gaskell was, in the widest sense,
a social novelist, a novelist who wrote about society.

---

[5] Gaskell, ed. *Mabel Vaughan* [by Cummins], p. viii.
[6] These words (albeit slightly misquoted—"a" for "one") end the
extract from Wordsworth's 'The Old Cumberland Beggar' (1800) which
Mrs. Gaskell included in her letter to Mrs. Mary Howitt of 18 August
1838—quoted in Howitt, 'Stray Notes from Mrs. Gaskell', *Good Words*,
XXXVI (1895), 611: *G.L.*, No. 12. Again slightly misquoted, they appear
in *G.L.*, No. 255; and, correctly, in *North and South* (*Works*, IV, 500).
[7] Gaskell, ed. *Mabel Vaughan* [by Cummins], p. vii.

SECTION III

'The Doom of the Griffiths' (1858)

January 1858 saw Mrs. Gaskell's 'The Doom of the Griffiths' come out in *Harper's New Monthly Magazine*[1]; it was later incorporated into the *Round the Sofa* group, its narrator there being Miss Duncan[2]. The nature of this work, promised to *Harper's* more than a year previously, is indicated by the author's letter of Monday [7] December [1857] to Charles Eliot Norton: 'The story, per se, is an old rubbishy one,—begun when Marianne was a baby,—the only merit whereof is that it is founded on fact.'[3] Since Marianne was born on 12 September 1834, her mother probably put pen to paper in the middle or later eighteen-thirties. She may have jotted down a local tradition heard during one of her Welsh holidays; indeed, according to her daughter, the tale was written 'at Plas Penrhyn near Tremadoc, where the author often stayed with her cousin Mr. Samuel Holland'[4]. Of such visits we said something when considering 'The Well of Pen-Morfa': 'The Doom of the Griffiths' is set in the same district. Before examining its literary merits, we must look at the authenticity of its point of departure.

[1] XVI, 220-234. On 26 October 1857 Mrs. Gaskell completed her manuscript (53 folios), which the next day she despatched to Sampson Low, Son & Co.; without the author's permission, Low forwarded it to Messrs. Harpers, then in financial difficulties, he having done other ' "*dodgy*" things' in Mrs. Gaskell's view, as Marianne informed Charles Eliot Norton when, enclosing Low's acknowledgement of the story, she wrote on her mother's behalf requesting him, if necessary, to look into the matter: Marianne Gaskell's letter of Friday 30 October 1857 and that from Low of 29 October 1857 are in the Harvard University Library—located bMS Am 1088 (3491) and Autograph File respectively. That Norton took action is evidenced by the thanks Mrs. Gaskell expressed in her letter (*G.L.*, No. 384) to him of Monday [7] December [1857]: the relevant passage from this letter (in the Harvard University Library) is quoted by Mrs. Whitehill (ed. *Gaskell-Norton Letters*, pp. 10-11) who substitutes X for Low's name—his firm being agents for Harpers (*op. cit.*, p. 29: *G.L.*, No. 403).

[2] *Works*, V, 235-236.

[3] *Gaskell-Norton Letters*, ed. Whitehill, p. 10. Mrs. Gaskell's letter to Norton of Monday [7] December [1857] occurs as *G.L.*, No. 384.

[4] Shorter, ed. *Novels and Tales*, IX, p. xii.

In relating the traditional basis of the curse whose tragic consequences for a later generation form her subject, Mrs. Gaskell apparently takes it for granted that a distant ancestor of the Owen Griffiths of her tale could have been implicated with David Gam in the Machynlleth plot to murder Owen Glendower. As there is no reason to suppose David Gam ever did attempt to kill Glendower at the 1404 Parliament[5], the historical origin of the story can be called in question. However probably all Mrs. Gaskell intended to convey was, not that she was sure of the facts as such, but that she was not inventing. In effect, she was recounting what had been told her, what her informants held to be true.

A further preliminary note is needed to save Mrs. Gaskell from the charge of simulating an interest in, and knowledge of, Welsh affairs—needed because the *Harper's* article contains (compositorial) errors which might lead an attentive reader to suspect the writer possessed no first-hand acquaintance with Wales and things Welsh. For example, the proper name 'Angharad' appears as 'Augharad'[6] owing, no doubt, to a misreading of Mrs. Gaskell's hand, in which 'u' and 'n' are virtually indistinguishable. Perhaps a mistake of a similar sort explains why what a nearly contemporary reference-book gives as 'Ynyscynhaiarn'[7] is printed as 'Ynysynhanarn'[8].

Since we have often mentioned Mrs Gaskell's love of old legends and customs—as in our treatment of *Ruth* (which also has, for several of its chapters, a Welsh background)—, there is no necessity to reiterate how much she was attracted by the things of long ago, especially if we bear in mind that her first published prose work was a sketch of Clopton Hall.

The basic material, we have noted, was none of Mrs. Gaskell's inventing. She realized its similarity to the legendary content of 'the old Greek dramas which treat of a family fore-doomed by an avenging Fate'[9]; so her task, like that of the

---

[5] See the article on 'Dafydd Gam' (d. 1415) by Sir John Edward Lloyd, in *The Dictionary of Welsh Biography, Down to* 1940, 1959, p. 101.

[6] *Works*, V, 242.

[7] *Worrall's Directory of North Wales, Comprising the Counties of Anglesey, Carnarvon, Denbigh, Flint, Merioneth, and Montgomery, with Chester, Shrewsbury, Oswestry, and Aberystwith,* Oldham: John Worrall, 1874, p. 239.

[8] *Works*, V, 239.   [9] *Works*, V, 249.

Ancients, was to expand in an interesting way. On her own estimate, she was not very successful; nor have later critics seen fit to quarrel with such an assessment.

What spoils 'The Doom of the Griffiths' is a melodramatic handling of the crucial scene, where Squire Griffiths discovers his son is married to a woman he can only describe as a harlot. This whole episode appears theatrical in tone, and stereotyped in execution. The author has recourse to exclamation marks to indicate the emotions she fails to evoke, as the ensuing extract demonstrates.

> All this was said with such rapidity that Owen had no time for the words that thronged to his lips. "Father!" (he burst forth at length) "Father, whosoever told you that Nest Pritchard was a harlot told you a lie as false as hell! Ay! a lie as false as hell!" he added, in a voice of thunder, while he advanced a step or two nearer to the Squire.[10]

Besides this central defect, there are other faults in the narrative : the sentimentalized death of a little child, whose eyes are, inevitably, 'filmy'[11]; and authorial over-insistence, evidenced by explicit comments out of place in their contexts[12]. Nevertheless the story has its virtues.

The characters are not, as we might expect, merely stock figures; their actions have a high degree of plausibility. Mrs. Gaskell shows how Owen's indulged childhood, followed by his father's second marriage, with its unhappy consequences for the issue of the first (a favourite Gaskellian theme, whose personal implications have already been studied[13]), led to his becoming engaged to a girl below him socially, yet with whom he found those domestic joys so markedly absent in his father's house[14]. Similarly successful is the portrayal of Nest's father, the shrewd, worldly-wise fisherman, with dreams of his daughter as mistress of Bodowen[15]. Even the selfish son of Mrs. Griffiths by her first

---

[10] *Works*, V, 260.
[11] *Works*, V, 261. Perhaps Mrs. Gaskell is too fond of associating filmy eyes with death or death-like states—*Mary Barton* alone contains at least three examples of this (*Works*, I, 78, 361, 456).
[12] *Works*, V, 258, 268.
[13] This particular instance of the 'remarriage *motif*' is also noted by Miss ffrench (*Mrs. Gaskell*, p. 101).
[14] *Works*, V, 257-259.
[15] *Works*, V, 255-256.

marriage, slightly sketched though he be[16], has a reality which
suggests that such a one may have been observed in the flesh.
Mrs. Gaskell was able to vitalize the shadowy figures of an
old legend; and with her central character, Owen, she displayed
a considerable degree of sympathetic participation.

Miss Hopkins tells us that '[t]he beauty of the tale lies in
the vivid descriptions of the Welsh country and Welsh manners
that spring from the author's recollections of her early married
life'[17]. Rural landscapes are here, as in *The Moorland Cottage*,
associated with a mood of sadness and melancholy, comfort
being received from nature. There is probably a strong autobiographic element in such meditative-descriptive passages; so it
may be well to remind ourselves that Mrs. Gaskell's connexion
with Wales was formed long before her marriage. On the other
hand, we must not forget how deeply she felt the loss of her
only son which, though it took place nearly eleven years after
Marianne's birth, would undoubtedly colour all memories of
Portmadoc, and hence influence her final polishing-up of the
tale prior to publication. The next extract, for instance, sounds
a subjective note heard more than once in 'The Doom of the
Griffiths'.

> [Owen often lay] indulging in gloomy and morbid reveries. He
> would fancy that this mortified state of existence was a dream,
> a horrible dream, from which he should awake and find himself
> again the sole object and darling of his father. And then he
> would start up and strive to shake off the incubus. There was the
> molten sunset of his childish memory; the gorgeous crimson piles
> of glory in the west, fading away into the cold calm light of the
> rising moon, while here and there a cloud floated across the west-
> ern heaven, like a seraph's wing, in its flaming beauty; the earth
> was the same as in his childhood's days, full of gentle evening
> sounds, and the harmonies of twilight—the breeze came sweeping
> low over the heather and blue-bells by his side, and the turf was
> sending up its evening incense of perfume. But life, and heart,
> and hope were changed for ever since those bygone days![18]

Before leaving Mrs. Gaskell's poetic pieces of natural description, we ought to mention her graphic and evocative picture of
a certain 'deep crystal pool'[19], with its circumference bordered
by water-lilies. Perhaps it is not fortuitous that this should

16 *Works*, V, 245-246.
17 Hopkins, *Elizabeth Gaskell*, p. 250.
18 *Works*, V, 248.   19 *Works*, V, 262.

bring to mind that other pool, likewise fringed with water-lilies, so picturesquely depicted in *Ruth*[20]. On both occasions Mrs. Gaskell may have been recalling what she had once observed very closely indeed.

In 'The Doom of the Griffiths' one discovers the author's characteristic touches of realism : some appear due to direct observation; others seem the product of pseudo-observation, feigned for literary purposes. The distinction is difficult to draw. What Mrs. Gaskell did was firstly to authenticate the story from personal experience, then to provide it with an internal (Defoesque) plausibility. Examples of the first method are her introduction of Welsh phrases in the dialogue (as when the hostess of the inn quotes an old proverb[21]) and her knowledge of the topography of the region; there is, too, her remark that the sweetbriar, planted by Owen and his wife, may still be seen[22]. Having a more specifically fictional *raison d'être* are details like Nest's blue stockings (' "bought at Llanrwst fair" '[23]) and Owen's closing the eyes and binding up the jaw of his dead father[24].

[20] *Works*, III, 72-73. Mrs. Chadwick (*Mrs. Gaskell*, pp. 228-229) sees here memories of Deepdale Pool, Silverdale.
[21] *Works*, V, 253.
[22] *Works*, V, 258.
[23] *Works*, V, 272.
[24] *Works*, V, 270.

SECTION IV

'An Incident at Niagara Falls' (1858)

In June 1858 there appeared in *Harper's New Monthly Magazine*[1] 'An Incident at Niagara Falls'. 'By Mrs. Gaskell'[2] according to the attribution preceding the text, to the List of Contents[3], and to the *Index to Harper's*[4], this story is, like 'The Siege of the Black Cottage', in Miss Hopkins' view an 'extremely doubtful'[5] candidate for admission to the Gaskell canon.

Where literary taste is arbiter, ascriptions must remain beyond the realm of certainty. Having carefully read the tale, however, one finds nothing out of keeping with Mrs. Gaskell's style and manner, there being no obvious incongruities with the rest of her work. Moreover in the previous January 'The Doom of the Griffiths' had come out in the same periodical, for which it was said to have been '[w]ritten exclusively'[6]. 'The Doom of the Griffiths' was later included in *Round the Sofa*; but the present story would have proved far too short for that collection. The possibility remains, therefore, that in response to a request for further material Mrs. Gaskell despatched 'An Incident at Niagara Falls' to *Harper's*. If it be objected that, as distinct from 'The Siege of the Black Cottage', this work implied special knowledge of a foreign background, one could reply that such 'special knowledge' only amounted to gazetteer-type information and an awareness that dollars and cents were common currency across the Atlantic[7]. One could also remind the objector that, if Mrs. Gaskell felt herself competent to edit for an English public Maria S. Cummins' American novel, *Mabel Vaughan*, she would scarcely have shrunk from writing a tale with a Niagara setting.

[1] XVII, 80-82.
[2] *Harper's New Monthly Magazine,* XVII, 80.
[3] *Harper's New Monthly Magazine,* XVII (1858), p. iv.
[4] *Index to 'Harper's New Monthly Magazine',* compiled by Durfee, pp. 227, 255.
[5] Hopkins, *Elizabeth Gaskell,* p. 337.
[6] *Harper's New Monthly Magazine,* XVI (1858), 220.
[7] *Harper's New Monthly Magazine,* XVII, 82.

U

Strictly a dialogue between Madame Percival and the narrator, the story is virtually a monologue by the former, since the narrator's *rôle* is confined to asking a single question[8]. Madame Percival relates how, nine or ten years before, she had been among those who saw the rescue of two men, stranded on one of the small islands formed from rock and drift wood just above the Falls. It is an account of unpretentious heroism, such as could easily have come from the same pen as *The Sexton's Hero*.

Madame Percival convincingly establishes herself as an eyewitness, and her report is graphic. Beyond this, little need be said, except to call attention to the conduct of their rescuer after the ship-wrecked pair had been safely brought ashore. Rejecting a valuable collection made on his behalf, he contented himself with offering for sale, at half-a-dollar a-piece, some six or seven walking sticks, to be made out of branches he had cut from trees on the island[9]—a touch which would have surely delighted Mrs. Gaskell, even if she were not the author.

Speculation about the genesis of 'An Incident at Niagara Falls' must be yet more hazardous than that concerning its authorship. If Mrs. Gaskell wrote it, she may have heard an anecdote along these lines from one of her American friends, possibly from William Wetmore Story or Charles Eliot Norton[10] during her Rome visit of 1857. At any rate the tale perhaps possesses at least some factual basis rather than being wholly the product of invention.

---

[8] *Harper's New Monthly Magazine*, XVII, 82. It seems worth noting that Madam Percival is the name of a character in [Cummins] *Mabel Vaughan*, ed. Mrs. Gaskell, p. 83.

[9] *Harper's New Monthly Magazine*, XVII, 82.

[10] That Niagara held attractions for Mrs. Gaskell is evidenced by her letter to Norton of 10 June 1861 (*Gaskell-Norton Letters*, ed. Whitehill, p. 82: *G.L.*, No. 488).

SECTION V

My Lady Ludlow (1858)

'My Lady Ludlow', which came out in *Household Words*[1] between 19 June and 25 September 1858, was, that same year, published as a book in America[2]; the following year it became the major story in the *Round the Sofa* volumes, where its narrator[3], Margaret Dawson, is one of the leading figures in the Edinburgh 'frame' setting. As with the other constituent tales, we shall consider *My Lady Ludlow* here, in its proper chronological place.

Most critics[4] seem agreed that this is one of the author's worst-planned works; only by courtesy can it be called a novel. Mrs. Gaskell was aware of its structural defects, which (through the narrator) she sought to defend against Aristotelian strictures by explicitly professing to provide 'neither beginning, middle, nor end.'[5] Elsewhere the mode of narration is both explained and partly excused:

> I have wandered away from time and place. I tell you all the
> remembrances I have of those years just as they come up, and I
> hope that, in my old age, I am not getting too like a certain
> Mrs. Nickleby, whose speeches were once read out aloud to me.[6]

[1] XVIII, 1-7, 29-34, 51-56, 85-89, 99-104, 123-128, 148-153, 175-181, 205-211, 247-252, 277-282, 299-305, 327-332, 341-346.

[2] Elizabeth Cleghorn Gaskell, *My Lady Ludlow. A Novel,* New York: Harper & Brothers, 1858. The unauthorized publication of this edition, a piracy for which she held Sampson Low responsible, brought to an end Mrs. Gaskell's dealings with the firm of Harpers, according to Meta Gaskell's letter of 27 January [1859] to Charles Eliot Norton—now in the Harvard University Library: bMS Am 1088 (2644). Nevertheless Mrs. Gaskell, who herself mentions this American piracy in a letter of 19 January [1859] to Thurston Holland (now in the possession of his granddaughter, Mrs. Margaret Trevor Jones), subsequently had books published by both parties. Chapple and Pollard date the last letter (*G.L.,* No. 409) Janry [?]19 [1859].

[3] *Works,* V, 8.

[4] E.g. Ward (ed. *Works,* V, pp. xiv-xvi), Mrs. Chadwick (*Mrs. Gaskell,* pp. 77-82), and Miss ffrench (*Mrs. Gaskell,* p. 74).

[5] *Works,* V, 9: cf. *Works,* V, 8 (' "no story at all, neither beginning, nor middle, nor end, only a bundle of recollections" ').

[6] *Works,* V, 48

Apparently Mrs. Gaskell was inventing as she went along, despatching parts as soon as they had been composed. Such a supposition receives support from a letter written by Dickens to Wills on 9 August 1858, in which the editor hopes 'Mrs. Gaskell will not stop, for more than a week at all events.'[7] Internal evidence also bears out this hypothesis; for there are several inconsistencies[8] of a sort that would scarcely have been over-looked if the author had had access to the earlier portions of her manuscript. Thus Lady Ludlow's sole surviving child is at first called ' "Rudolph, the present Lord Ludlow" '[9], and later appears as 'Ughtred Mortimer, Earl Ludlow'[10]; the Birmingham Baptist baker is introduced as ' "Mr. Lambe," '[11] only to be afterwards referred to as ' "Brooke, that dissenting baker from Birmingham" '[12]; even the spelling of a proper name varies as between ' "Connington" '[13] and ' "Conington" '[14].

The chief and most obvious structural fault is the long digres-sion, told by Lady Ludlow for the flimsiest of reasons, which occupies nearly a third of the work. This tale within a tale is a story of Revolutionary France, and has every appearance of having been included solely to draw out the weekly numbers. Since the digression is virtually a separate composition, we shall defer our examination thereof until the title-story proper has been considered. Nevertheless it seems relevant to notice that the digression likewise contains internal inconsistencies. For ex-ample, there is confusion about Christian names (Morin *fils*

---

[7] *The Letters of Charles Dickens,* ed. Dexter, III, 36.

[8] A few are noted, sometimes between the 'frame' of *Round the Sofa* and *My Lady Ludlow* itself, by Mrs. Chadwick (*Mrs. Gaskell,* pp. 77-78) and Ward (ed. *Works,* V, p. xiv, fn.: where, however, the first example owes some of its cogency to Ward's misquoting; what Margaret Dawson in fact said was that she 'never was at sea'—*Works,* V, 51). As was noted by the late Mr. J. T. Lancaster (in papers now belonging to the present writer), although the audience initially appear largely ignorant of Lady Ludlow's life and locality (*Works,* V, 7-9), when concluding the narrative Margaret Dawson assumes her hearers probably know that the Rev. Henry Gregson is Vicar of Hanbury and married to the daughter of Mr. Gray and Miss Bessy (*Works,* V, 216).

[9] *Works,* V, 11.
[10] *Works,* V, 169.
[11] *Works,* V, 141.
[12] *Works,* V, 177.
[13] *Works,* V, 11.
[14] *Works,* V, 176.

being called both Jean[15] and Victor[16]). Moreover, on occasions, phrases like ' "as I said" ' are misused; for either nothing has in fact been said, or, if it has, it is contradicted by the later statement : the hero, Clément, was never said to have returned to the gardener, after having been turned away from the Hôtel Duguesclin, as is later assumed[17]; nor, at the time, was there any doubt that Virginie was asleep[18] during the conversation she is afterwards reported as having overheard[19]. It is, therefore, not unreasonable to conclude that Mrs. Gaskell was writing in a more or less *ex tempore* fashion, with consequential short-comings in over-all planning and construction.

As well as lacking Aristotelian unity, *My Lady Ludlow* fails to attain that unity of tone and mood which was such a distinctive feature of *Cranford*. Nonetheless a reference to *Cranford* is not wholly out of place. Like *Cranford*, *My Lady Ludlow* owes much to Knutsford memories, though recollections of Stratford, where Mrs. Gaskell spent her schooldays, are equally relevant. Yet this later story does not succeed in conjuring up a unique world, does not evoke that peculiar atmosphere so admirably achieved in *Cranford*. The causes for the failure are diverse : most obviously, the long irrelevant digression, which bisects the story proper; secondly, the element of historical realism; thirdly, the society being less conspicuously feminine; fourthly, the lack of the curious blend of pathos and humour so pervasive in *Cranford*. Perhaps Mrs. Gaskell's heart was not fully engaged; certainly her mind seems not to have been. Although *My Lady Ludlow* possesses something of the aroma of *Cranford*, that distinctive essence is at once diluted and dispersed. The reader comes upon passages which have a Cranfordian flavour about them; but these occur piecemeal throughout the work. It is to such passages, however, that we must now give our attention.

Appropriately there is an early reference to old lace, which recalls the famous lace swallowed by the Cranford cat[20]. Furthermore, the tone in which manufacturers are mentioned and the doubt as to whether such people can be supposed to have had ancestors are both reminiscent of Cranford gentility.

15 *Works*, V, 88.
16 *Works*, V, 105.
17 *Works*, V, 113.

18 *Works*, V, 111.
19 *Works*, V, 121.
20 *Works*, II, 94-95.

My mother was always said to have good blood in her veins; and when she wanted to maintain her position with the people she was thrown among—principally rich democratic manufacturers, all for liberty and the French Revolution—she would put on a pair of ruffles, trimmed with real old English point, very much darned to be sure—but which could not be bought new for love or money, as the art of making it was lost years before. These ruffles showed, as she said, that her ancestors had been Somebodies, when the grandfathers of the rich folk, who now looked down upon her, had been Nobodies—if, indeed, they had any grandfathers at all.[21]

Quite a number of Cranfordesque incidents centre on Miss Galindo, an old maid whose kinship we may easily discern with the ladies of Cranford, and with those of Duncombe also. Significantly she is introduced[22] after more than half the story has been told, so it seems legitimate to infer that Mrs. Gaskell resorted to her as a device for spinning out the narrative; nevertheless she proves to be one of its most memorable characters, being what the eighteenth century called an original—an eccentric spinster, with a peppery temper and a fundamentally kind nature. As a typical Cranfordism, we may quote the following : whether or not it was of Mrs. Gaskell's inventing we cannot say, though, bearing in mind Knutsford ways, one would be rash to deny that she could not have observed something similar.

She wore a white muslin apron, delicately embroidered, and put on a little crookedly, in order, as she told us, even Lady Ludlow, before the evening was over, to conceal a spot whence the colour had been discharged by a lemon-stain. This crookedness had an odd effect, especially when I saw that it was intentional; indeed, she was so anxious about her apron's right adjustment in the wrong place, that she told us straight out why she wore it so, and asked her ladyship if the spot was properly hidden, at the same time lifting up her apron and showing her how large it was.[23]

As further instances of Miss Galindo's Cranfordesque characteristics, one could cite her failure to keep to the point[24]; her trick of talking to herself[25]; her device of attaching an ink-mixture to the house-door in order to have it well shaken, especially from slamming caused by lost tempers[26]; her habit

---

[21] *Works*, V, 9-10.
[22] *Works*, V, 129.
[23] *Works*, V, 134.

[24] *Works*, V, 136.
[25] *Works*, V, 137.
[26] *Works*, V, 140.

of whistling, swearing, and sticking a pen behind the ear so
that Mr. Horner might forget she was a female clerk[27]. More
interesting, because they have parallels in Mrs. Gaskell's previous work, are the poor-scolding and husband-fearful passages.
In that early anticipation of *Cranford*, 'Mr. Harrison's Confessions', Miss Tomkinson was wont to tax the villagers with
improvident extravagance, an especial cause for concern being
the use of fresh butter[28]; Miss Galindo too was accustomed to
rebuke where she thought she saw a disregard for domestic
economy, and she would 'question closely respecting the weekly
amount of butter'[29]. Both ladies revealed a fundamental goodness of heart: the former, by taking no exception to a forthright retort from a woman she had scolded[30]; the latter, by
seeing the joke that a duck, which always poked herself where
she was not wanted, should be called after her[31]. The general
distrust of men by Cranford ladies finds an echo in Miss
Galindo's reaction to the coming of Captain James, the new
estate-manager.

> "He's not above thirty; and I must just pack up my pens and my
> paper, and be off; for it would be the height of impropriety for me
> to be staying here as his clerk. It was all very well in the old
> master's days. But here am I, not fifty till next May, and this
> young, unmarried man, who is not even a widower! Oh, there
> would be no end of gossip. Besides, he looks as askance at me
> as I do at him. My black silk gown had no effect. He's afraid I
> shall marry him. But I won't; he may feel himself quite safe
> from that. And Mr. Smithson has been recommending a clerk
> to my lady. She would far rather keep me on; but I can't stop.
> I really could not think it proper."[32]

In fine, Miss Galindo is the most delightful of characters, wholly
within the *Cranford* tradition and complete with typically
charming *obiter dicta* (as when, *en passant*, she remarks: ' "My

[27] *Works*, V, 143-144.
[28] *Works*, V, 457-458.
[29] *Works*, V, 131.
[30] *Works*, V, 457-458.
[31] *Works*, V, 131-132.
[32] *Works*, V, 183-184.

dear, I have often thought of the postman's bringing me a letter as one of the pleasures I shall miss in heaven." [33]).

In Lady Ludlow Mrs. Gaskell successfully brings to life one of the grand aristocratic ladies of Regency England. It has been suggested[34] that she was based on Lady Jane Stanley, sister to the twelfth Earl of Derby; so perhaps a relevant extract may be taken from Green's *Knutsford* to give some idea of her ladyship's character.

> Lady Jane was beloved by her household, and admired by the whole neighbourhood, but she had very strict notions of propriety, and of the courtesies of life,—and would not have them infringed. It was her custom to walk out in state with a gold-headed cane, or rather staff in her hand; and she was very tenacious of the right which her noble birth gave her of keeping the wall from whomsoever she met.[35]

Mrs. Gaskell's introductory picture of Lady Ludlow is worth quoting at length, not merely for the reference to the gold-headed stick but also for the detailed attention paid to the countess's attire. This description brings her graphically before the reader; it also provides clues as to her personality : at the same time the historical period and social *milieu* are unobtrusively suggested. We have in the past remarked upon Mrs. Gaskell's concern with articles of clothing, careful observation of which being most natural in an authoress.

> She was very small of stature, and very upright. She wore a great lace cap, nearly half her own height, I should think, that went round her head (caps which tied under the chin, and which we called "mobs," came in later, and my lady held them in great contempt, saying people might as well come down in their nightcaps). In front of my lady's cap was a great bow of white satin ribbon; and a broad band of the same ribbon was tied tight round her head, and served to keep the cap straight. She had a fine Indian muslin shawl folded over her shoulders and across

[33] *Works*, V, 179. Cf. "As he opened a note which his servant brought to him, he said, 'An odd thought strikes me:—we shall receive no letters in the grave.' "—*Boswell's 'Life of Johnson', Together with Boswell's 'Journal of a Tour to the Hebrides' and Johnson's 'Diary of a Journey into North Wales'*, ed. George Birkbeck Hill, rev. and enlarged by Lawrence Fitzroy Powell, 6 vols., Oxford: The Clarendon Press, 1934-1950, IV (1934), 413.

[34] By Mrs. Chadwick (*Mrs. Gaskell*, p. 70).

[35] Green, *Knutsford, Its Traditions and History: with Reminiscences, Anecdotes, and Notices of the Neighbourhood*, p. 145.

her chest, and an apron of the same; a black silk mode gown, made with short sleeves and ruffles, and with the tail thereof pulled through the placket-hole, so as to shorten it to a useful length: beneath it she wore, as I could plainly see, a quilted lavender satin petticoat. Her hair was snowy white, but I hardly saw it, it was so covered with her cap: her skin, even at her age, was waxen in texture and tint; her eyes were large and dark blue, and must have been her great beauty when she was young, for there was nothing particular, as far as I can remember, either in mouth or nose. She had a great gold-headed stick by her chair; but I think it was more as a mark of state and dignity than for use; for she had as light and brisk a step when she chose as any girl of fifteen, and, in her private early walk of meditation in the mornings, would go as swiftly from garden alley to garden alley as any one of us.[36]

It would not be difficult, though it would be lengthy, to demonstrate how sympathetically Mrs. Gaskell portrays Lady Ludlow. There is her feudal attitude towards the tenantry[37], symbolized by her sitting in a chair of state, surmounted with a countess's coronet[38]; there is her Anglican orthodoxy, so strict as to forbid the use of any prayers but those in the Prayer Book —and even those could be read in a private house only by one in Holy Orders[39]; there is a Coverleian eccentricity which prompted her, when so disposed, to stand up at her pew-door and inform the parson that no discourse would that morning be required[40]; there is the aristocratic *hauteur* provoked by all that savoured of democracy. Yet Lady Ludlow is never presented as a caricature of a noble dowager, which would not have been difficult; instead she stands forth as a complex character, in whose existence the reader can readily believe. To illustrate this complexity, one can instance her attitude to the imprisonment of Job Gregson, a local ne'er-do-well. On first hearing from her vicar, Mr. Gray, that a newly appointed J.P., Harry Lathom, had committed Gregson on seemingly insufficient evidence, her natural response was to support the magistrate[41]; but, notwithstanding loyalty to her order, with the discovery that an injustice had been done the countess did not hesitate to remedy matters, albeit in a somewhat high-handed fashion[42]. Indeed throughout, by means of little personal

[36] *Works*, V, 15-16.
[37] *Works*, V, 50-51.
[38] *Works*, V, 43.
[39] *Works*, V, 18.

[40] *Works*, V, 20.
[41] *Works*, V, 30-34.
[42] *Works*, V, 35-40.

touches, Mrs. Gaskell succeeds in making Lady Ludlow's humanity come alive—as when, after an outspoken outburst by Mr. Gray (in support of a school of which her ladyship disapproved) had brought on a coughing-fit, she at once offered some bottles of Malmsey to fortify his health[43].

The concreteness of Lady Ludlow, dependent in part upon the complexity of the character, must certainly owe much to the author's first-hand experience of such august, aristocratic ladies. We have spoken of the possible identification with Lady Jane Stanley, though there may well have been several prototypes for Lady Ludlow. One recalls that aristocratic old lady[44] who told Mrs. Gaskell of a mysterious disappearance: she had known Major André, and frequented the Old Whig Society which gathered round the beautiful Duchess of Devonshire; moreover her father's estate lay in Shropshire. Clement Shorter[45] posited as Lady Ludlow's original the Bold Dame of Cheshire; but Lady Bromley-Davenport[46] opts for Lady Hatherton. Cumulative rather than conflicting, this sort of external testimony does what is required: it reinforces internal indications that personal observation went into the portrayal of her ladyship. Relevant too is the influence the countess exercised over the village school[47], itself initially opposed by her. Very much the same kind of benign patronage seems to have been

---

[43] *Works*, V, 151.

[44] *Works*, II, 412-413.

[45] Ed. *Novels and Tales*, IX, pp. viii-ix.

[46] In a letter of 17 July [1962] from Capesthorne Hall, Macclesfield, Cheshire, Lenette F. Bromley-Davenport informed Mr. Arthur Pollard (Department of English, Manchester University) of the 'family belief that Mrs Davenport was the model for Lady Ludlow'—cf. Pollard, *Mrs Gaskell: Novelist and Biographer*, p. 173, fn. 1. Certainly Mrs. Gaskell knew well the beautiful Mrs. Davenport, mentioned frequently in her correspondence, and was much impressed with a Capesthorne graced by this '*dama* of a lady' (so described in a passage written on Tuesday [27 November 1849] in Mrs. Gaskell's letter to Eliza Fox of 26 November 1849, a copy of part of which is in the Gaskell Section, Brotherton Collection, Leeds University Library—'*dama*' appears as '*dame*' in *G.L.*, No. 55). On 11 February 1852 Mrs. Edward Davies Davenport (*née* Caroline Anne Hurt, d. 1897) married Edward John Littleton, Baron Hatherton (d. 1863); thereafter she took charge of Teddesley (*Gaskell-Norton Letters*, ed. Whitehill, p. 13: *G.L.*, No. 384). For information about his kinswoman I am deeply indebted to Sir Walter Henry Bromley-Davenport, M.P. for Knutsford.

[47] *Works*, V, 199.

customary among the ladies of the Egerton family in regard to the Knutsford school situated near the entrance to Tatton Park[48]. It is evident that, in her treatment of aristocratic life, Mrs. Gaskell laboured under no Dickensian disadvantages.

Despite structural defects and minor inconsistencies, no account being taken of individual successes like Miss Galindo and Lady Ludlow, and with all its mirthful incidents absent, *My Lady Ludlow* would still make interesting reading. The nature of this interest is, in the widest sense, social; for here one finds illustrated English life at the turn of the eighteenth century. Such illustrations came naturally from the pen, and are far from being exemplary anecdotes, consciously didactic after the manner of lady political economists; hence for the modern reading-public, possibly even more than for that of the mid-nineteenth century, *My Lady Ludlow* has additional value by virtue of its quasi-historical component.

It is generally held that Mrs. Gaskell drew heavily upon memories of her Avonbank school days. The point was most forcefully made by Mrs. Chadwick[49], whose findings have been endorsed, rather than added to, by later scholars. Thus Lady Ludlow herself may owe traits to Miss Maria Byerley, one of the sisters who were Miss Stevenson's teachers at Stratford[50]; furthermore her ladyship's residence has features in common with the House of St. Mary[51] (Avonbank School)—for instance, both were so constructed that rooms led out of one another[52]—, and the reference to Lady Ludlow's copious chinaware[53] is in accord with the close connexion between the Byerleys and the Wedgwood family[54]; Lady Ludlow's companion-cum-housekeeper at Hanbury Court (Mrs. Medlicott[55]) is said[56] to have

---

[48] Chadwick, *Mrs. Gaskell*, pp. 42, 48; Green, *Knutsford, Its Traditions and History: with Reminiscences, Anecdotes, and Notices of the Neighbourhood*, p. 16; Payne, *Mrs. Gaskell and Knutsford*, 1905, p. 38; and Beatrix Lucia Catherine Tollemache, *Cranford Souvenirs and Other Sketches*, London: Rivingtons, 1900, pp. 5-6.

[49] *Mrs. Gaskell*, pp. 65-82.

[50] The opinion of Phyllis D. Hicks (*A Quest of Ladies: The Story of a Warwickshire School* [Birmingham: Frank Juckes, 1949], p. 81).

[51] Chadwick, *Mrs. Gaskell*, pp. 67-69.

[52] *Works*, V, 42: cf. Hicks, *A Quest of Ladies*, p. 81.

[53] *Works*, V, 45-46.

[54] Chadwick, *Mrs. Gaskell*, p. 78.

[55] *Works*, V, 15.

[56] By Mrs. Chadwick (*Mrs. Gaskell*, p. 66).

had her original in Mrs. Mortimer, the Avonbank housekeeper; finally the small community of gentlewomen which gathered round Lady Ludlow has recognizable affinities with a boarding-establishment for young ladies. In addition to this convincing array of correspondences, certain passages seem to possess a distinctly autobiographic flavour—although these are not out of keeping with the character of the tale's narrator. Of such passages the most striking is that where Margaret Dawson recalls her reactions, as a girl of sixteen, on first entering her little whitewashed bedroom; both Mrs. Chadwick[57] and Professor Whitfield[58] quote this account[59] at length, as a piece of autobiographic reminiscence. To conclude with the obvious, by introducing such place-names as Barford[60], Birmingham[61], and Warwick[62], Mrs. Gaskell leaves the reader in no doubt as regards the general locality; indeed for this her ladyship's title is of itself sufficient.

Having to some extent established the authenticity of its *milieu*, we can now investigate the historical interest in *My Lady Ludlow*. What may be termed the 'lady of the manor' aspect has already been touched on in regard to the countess; but her two estate managers, Mr. Horner and Captain James, deserve attention. Mr. Horner, devoted to the well-being of the Hanbury family, whose constant grudge was the mortgage incurred on her ladyship's hereditary estate for the benefit of her husband's Scottish lands[63], is a typically English figure; and Mrs. Gaskell must have known not a few of his fellows. Set over against him is his successor, Captain James, whose first attempts at scientific farming[64] proved as unsuccessful as did those of the writer's father. Perhaps we may quote a passage which, as well as memorably summing up one's impression of these two characters, illustrates Mrs. Gaskell's occasional moods of sombre reflexion—moods which reveal a philosophic depth

[57] *Mrs. Gaskell,* p. 72.
[58] *Mrs Gaskell,* pp. 7-8.
[59] *Works,* V, 17. Both Mrs. Chadwick and Professor Whitfield slightly misquote the relevant passage.
[60] *Works,* V, 36.
[61] *Works,* V, 52.
[62] *Works,* V, 58.
[63] *Works,* V, 49-51.
[64] *Works,* V, 197.

not usually looked for in our author, yet nonetheless characteristically English.

> And Mr. Horner was dead, and Captain James reigned in his
> stead. Good, steady, severe, silent Mr. Horner, with his clock-
> like regularity, and his snuff-coloured clothes, and silver buckles!
> I have often wondered which one misses most when they are dead
> and gone—the bright creatures full of life, who are hither and
> thither and everywhere, so that no one can reckon upon their
> coming and going, with whom stillness and the long quiet of the
> grave, seems utterly irreconcilable, so full are they of vivid motion
> and passion—or the slow, serious people, whose movements, nay,
> whose very words, seem to go by clockwork; who never appear
> much to affect the course of our life while they are with us, but
> whose methodical ways show themselves, when they are gone,
> to have been intertwined with our very roots of daily existence.
> I think I miss these last the most, although I may have loved the
> former best. Captain James never was to me what Mr. Horner
> was, though the latter had hardly exchanged a dozen words with
> me at the day of his death.[65]

Of the village scene generally Mrs. Gaskell succeeds in presenting a realistic picture; although this is achieved by means
of a few significant details, these have a wealth of experience
behind them. References are made with an ease and assurance which in themselves provide sufficient authentication. An
example is the treatment of a minor character like Job Gregson,
a poacher and squatter who, after the manner of the Ishmael-
like John Middleton[66], had led a Hobbesian existence[67] before
he was won over by Mr. Gray's kindness. What is especially
noteworthy is the objectivity of Mrs. Gaskell's manner, there
being neither middle-class denigration nor sentimental indulgence—in reading her descriptions of the poor, it is always worth
while to recall that, at the outset of her career, she took Crabbe
for a model. Her truthfulness of vision is further evidenced by
a recognition of unpleasant facts: she tells how widespread
were brutality and ignorance, swearing and cursing, even
among the village children[68], though, as she later notes, some
moral improvements were effected by the Evangelical Mr.
Gray[69].

Perhaps, from the socio-historic stand-point, the most important feature is religion in its several aspects. As a necessary pre-

[65] *Works,* V, 210-211.   [68] *Works,* V, 147.
[66] *Works,* II, 385.   [69] *Works,* V, 211-212.
[67] *Works,* V, 164.

liminary, one must here stress how ably Mrs. Gaskell conceals
her Unitarian beliefs; it is a measure of her literary skill
that the author's religious persuasion cannot be arrived at from
reading her work. Indeed one of Mrs. Gaskell's most engaging
characteristics is her humorous treatment of Nonconformity.
Just as, in *Cranford,* the Aga Jenkyns had implied that Dissenters were worse than heathens[70], so here, in *My Lady Ludlow,*
Miss Galindo confesses that she had always looked upon them
' "almost as if they were rhinoceroses." '[71] Besides the Anglican
orthodoxy of Lady Ludlow, with her consequential dislike of
Dissent, the Church of England finds its representatives in the
four clergymen. First in point of time is the eighteenth-century
Parson Hemming, a figure who might easily have come out of
Fielding or Smollett. Mrs. Gaskell neatly suggests the nature
of the man and his age by a few words from Lady Ludlow.

> " . . . Why, in my grandfather's days, the parson was family
> chaplain too, and dined at the Hall every Sunday. He was helped
> last, and expected to have done first. I remember seeing him take
> up his plate and knife and fork, and say, with his mouth full all
> the time he was speaking: 'If you please, Sir Urian, and my lady,
> I'll follow the beef into the housekeeper's room'; for, you see,
> unless he did so, he stood no chance of a second helping. A
> greedy man, that parson was, to be sure! . . . "[72]

Lady Ludlow goes on to relate how, by a grim jest typical of
the period, he was forced to eat a rook soaked in vinegar.

The Hanbury incumbent at the time of Margaret Dawson's
arrival was Mr. Mountford, who can be compared with Parson
Woodforde in fact[73], and with the more worldly Barsetshire
ecclesiastics in fiction. The few paragraphs[74] devoted to defining
his character are among the best in the work. A clergyman who
loved good living and enjoyed good hunting, he preferred to
send a dinner to a sick parishioner rather than make all con-

---

[70] *Works,* II, 192.
[71] *Works,* V, 141.
[72] *Works,* V, 60.
[73] In one respect only—a fondness for over-warm rooms—Mr. Mountford (*Works,* V, 25) had another factual counterpart in the Rev. William
Gaskell (who kept his study very hot, as his wife told his sister, Mrs. Nancy
Robson, in a letter of Wednesday [10 May 1865]—now in the Gaskell
Section, Brotherton Collection, Leeds University Library—: *G.L.,* No.
570, dated [?10 May 1865] by Chapple and Pollard).
[74] *Works,* V, 22-24.

cerned uncomfortable by an unwelcome visit—a policy admirable from every point of view, except the pastoral. There is little need to underline the historical truth of such a sketch—a truth Bishop Blomfield felt all too keenly when, in 1824, he found clerical fox-hunting 'almost a religion in Cheshire'[75], and was informed by a clergyman whom he had rebuked for drunkenness: "But, my Lord, I never was drunk on duty."[76] Besides the historical there is also a psychological truthfulness, as the next quotation indicates.

> There was a great deal of good in Mr. Mountford, too. He could not bear to see pain, or sorrow, or misery of any kind; and, if it came under his notice, he was never easy till he had relieved it, for the time, at any rate. But he was afraid of being made uncomfortable; so, if he possibly could, he would avoid seeing any one who was ill or unhappy; and he did not thank any one for telling him about them.[77]

Mr. Mountford's successor, Mr. Gray, was of a very different mould. Mrs. Chadwick[78] thinks that he may have been based on the Rev. William Turner, who established the first Sunday School at Newcastle-on-Tyne; certainly Mr. Gray's Evangelical enthusiasm for education supplies a possible connexion. The highly strung nature of this Hanbury incumbent, with his extreme moral and religious sensitivity, is, however, rather more suggestive of Travers Madge[79] who, like Mr. Gray, wore himself out in the service of others. Yet, notwithstanding the accuracy of any particular identification, Mr. Gray ought rather to be taken as typical of the Evangelical wing of the Established Church, which reacted strongly against the earlier 'high and dry' tendencies. Mrs. Gaskell enjoyed an extensive intercourse with members of the Church of England, and once confessed her only religious antipathy was 'to the Calvinistic

[75] Alfred Blomfield, ed. *A Memoir of Charles James Blomfield, D.D.,* *Bishop of London, with Selections from His Correspondence*, 2 vols., London: John Murray, 1863, I, 103.
[76] Quoted in Blomfield, ed. *A Memoir of Bishop Blomfield*, I, 105.
[77] *Works*, V, 23.
[78] *Mrs. Gaskell*, p. 71.
[79] For Madge, see Herford, *Travers Madge: A Memoir.*

or Low Church creed'[80]; this dislike may explain why on occasions Lady Ludlow exercised her wit at Mr. Gray's expense, as
when, in protest at his calling Sunday the Sabbath, she remarked that 'he was all for Judaism against Christianity.'[81] Mrs.
Gaskell does, nonetheless, endorse the vicar's general educational
and religious aims, and acknowledges his sincerity and self-
sacrifice; by the end of the story all recognize his spiritual
worth.

In striking contrast to Mr. Gray is the fawning Mr. Crosse,
a time-serving curate who officiated during the vicar's illness.
Mrs. Gaskell devotes a most telling paragraph to this unpleasant
clergyman, a character having affinities with Trollope's Mr.
Slope. Here again Mrs. Gaskell succeeds in depicting a cleric

[80] Letter of 16 April 1861 to Charles Eliot Norton (*Gaskell-Norton
Letters*, ed. Whitehill, p. 78: *G.L.*, No. 485). This lack of religious fellow-
feeling with Calvinists, voiced to Charles Bosanquet, was earlier mentioned in Mrs. Gaskell's letter to Marianne of Tuesday 19 October [1858];
and she referred to meeting 'all the cursing Evangelicals' during a call
on Bishop Lee of Manchester in a letter to Eliza Fox of 26 April 1850:
the first letter (*G.L.*, No. 405) and a copy of part of the second (*G.L.*,
No. 70) are in the Gaskell Section, Brotherton Collection, Leeds University
Library. Perhaps one should add that despite her general religious liberalism—for she was, on her own admission (in an undated letter [*G.L.*, No.
593] to Mr. Bright [in the Yale University Library: MS Vault File]), 'not
(*Unitarianly*)/ orthodox'—Mrs. Gaskell became gravely concerned when
Marianne, during her 1861-2 winter in Rome, fell under the 'evil influence'
of Monsignor Manning, as is revealed by her letter (*G.L.*, No. 504) of
22 April [1862] to Charles Eliot Norton (in the Harvard University
Library—the relevant passage being omitted, though the omission is indicated, in Whitehill, ed. *Gaskell-Norton Letters*, p. 98). Marianne's
attraction to Roman Catholicism and the family anxiety occasioned
thereby (both having abated by Autumn 1862) are mentioned, directly
or obliquely, in other correspondence, such as: Mrs. Gaskell's [early 1862]
letter (*G.L.*, No. 500a) to Marianne (copies of which, once belonging to
Mr. J. T. Lancaster, are owned by the present writer); Norton's letter to
Meta of 20 March 1862 (in the Harvard University Library: bMS Am
1088.2); Norton's letter to Mrs. Gaskell of 30 March 1862 (*Gaskell-Norton
Letters*, ed. Whitehill, p. 97); Meta's letter to Norton of Sunday 20 April
[1862]—in the Harvard University Library: bMS Am 1088 (2603)—;
Marianne's letter to Norton of 21 April 1862—in the Harvard University
Library: bMS Am 1088 (3492)—; Mrs. Gaskell's letter (*G.L.*, No. 507) of 9
May [1862] to William Wetmore Story (in the Texas University Library);
Meta's letter to Norton of Monday 21 [20] October to 30 or 31 October
[1862]—in the Harvard University Library: bMS Am 1088 (2604)—; and
Mrs. Gaskell's letter (*G.L.*, No. 560) to Norton of 5 February 1865 (in the
Harvard University Library—the relevant passage being omitted, though
the omission is indicated, in Whitehill, ed. *Gaskell-Norton Letters*, p. 120).
[81] *Works*, V, 21.

who has significance as a representative figure of the period—'a man who dropped his *h*'s, and hurried through the service, and yet had time enough to stand in my lady's way, bowing to her as she came out of church, and so subservient in manner . . . that, sooner than remain unnoticed by a countess, he would have preferred being scolded, or even cuffed.'[82]

In sum, social history confirms, and is made graphic by, Mrs. Gaskell's picture of these religious and educational aspects of village life. Perhaps it is not inappropriate to suggest a comparison with John Galt's *Annals of the Parish* (1821).

Especially refreshing is Mrs. Gaskell's freedom from those Victorian sexual inhibitions which acted as restrictions, not to say distortions, in her earlier works, particularly the ones written with a purpose. Possibly the distancing effect of the historical setting relieved her from the necessity of being narrowly moralistic; but more probably her lack of self-conscious embarrassment was perfectly natural where no special pleading was required. For example, when the account of Miss Galindo's illegitimate ward comes to be told, there is no disconcerting change of tone on the author's part: more specifically, one can point to the scene where Dr. Trevor tells his wife that her brother has left a natural daughter[83]—the doctor speaks in a professional, matter-of-fact way, and Mrs. Trevor's reaction is astonishment rather than indignation or shame. Elsewhere Mrs. Gaskell even appears to be making fun of Victorian decorum and primness, as the following passage suggests.

> After we had worked away about an hour at the bureau, her ladyship said we had done enough for one day; and, as the time was come for her afternoon ride, she left me, with a volume of engravings from Mr. Hogarth's pictures on one side of me (I don't like to write down the names of them, though my lady thought nothing of it, I am sure), and upon a stand her great Prayer-book open at the evening psalms for the day, on the other.[84]

Such a quotation serves to remind us that, as in *Cranford* and many of her tales, Mrs. Gaskell tells the story through a narrator who recalls events from the past—in this instance,

---

[82] *Works*, V, 160.
[83] *Works*, V, 193-194.
[84] *Works*, V, 45.

Margaret Dawson. Though Margaret takes little direct part in the action, she is useful for bringing off some of the author's humorous effects; she is able, by virtue of her position, to confer plausibility on the incidents which she narrates, and upon which she can comment.

Much else could be said about *My Lady Ludlow,* especially by way of citing examples of delicate humour and gentle irony; one must, however, content oneself with merely mentioning these excellences, in which the story is rich. At the same time, one ought to remark that they occur in a somewhat piecemeal fashion, almost as if Mrs. Gaskell were putting down, rather at random, such choice anecdotes and comic incidents as came to mind on the spur of the moment—products of memory or invention, as the case might be. Nevertheless there is one passage which, amusing in itself, also deserves notice by reason of its echoing something very similar in *Ruth.* In that earlier work the maid, Sally, recalls[85] how, holding the flesh wicked and the spirit all important, she neglected domestic duties for the sake of prayers and her immortal soul; yet her mistress made her see that *laborare* was compatible with *orare. My Lady Ludlow* parallels, even as regards the proper name, this Gaskellian variation on the parable of Mary and Martha. Here[86] Miss Galindo, after having unsuccessfully argued with Sally (seduced by Mr. Gray into Evangelical ways) that true godliness need not entail allowing the beef to roast to a cinder, tried a more effective means of persuading her maid that things spiritual should not interfere with carnal matters like ordering a pound of butter.

Presumably the interlude of Clément and Virginie, the tale within a tale, was included largely from space-filling motives. Almost certainly Mrs. Gaskell would have published it separately had it not been for external pressure, since only by the flimsiest of reasons has it any excuse for appearing where it does. Even though Mrs. Gaskell, using Lady Ludlow as narrator, scatters here and there comments, typical of her ladyship, on the folly of educating the lower orders above their station, such admonitory interruptions are as out of place in the digression as is the digression itself in the story proper. We have

85 *Works,* III, 173-175.   86 *Works,* V, 144-145.

previously remarked upon those small errors of detail which support the view that the Clément-Virginie episode was hastily written; it doubtless proved a last-minute addition to the design of *My Lady Ludlow*.

From a formal aspect, this long anecdote of love and betrayal in Revolutionary France is chiefly noteworthy for Mrs. Gaskell's use of the 'point of view' technique. The primary narrator is, strictly, Margaret Dawson, who retells the events related by Lady Ludlow. Lady Ludlow herself drew heavily upon the reports of Le Fèbvre[87], Pierre Babette[88], and Fléchier[89]. Of these last, only Pierre played an important part in the action; Le Fèbvre apparently gathered the outlines of the story during his stay in France; Fléchier relied principally upon what the old gardener had told him. Although Lady Ludlow to some extent dovetails the three accounts into one another, the several points of view are, nonetheless, quite well preserved. Hence there is— for example in the rather melodramatic treatment of young Morin's wild love for Virginie[90]—considerable textual support for the following statement by Lady Ludlow.

> "And now I must take up the story as it was told to the Intend-ant Fléchier by the old gardener Jacques, with whom Clément had been lodging on his first arrival in Paris. The old man could not, I dare say, remember half as much of what had happened as Pierre did; the former had the dulled memory of age, while Pierre had evidently thought over the whole series of events as a story—as a play, if one may call it so—during the solitary hours in his after-life, wherever they were passed, whether in lonely camp watches, or in the foreign prison, where he had to drag out many years."[91]

Rather unusually for Mrs. Gaskell, the Clément-Virginie episode owes far more to plot than to character. Despite minor inconsistencies, the narrative holds the reader's attention by its intrinsic interest: stories of aristocrats in danger of the guillo-tine, from their very nature, seem to have an initial advantage in this respect. Briefly, Mrs. Gaskell's method was firstly to arouse curiosity regarding Clément's indifference and languor

---

[87] *Works*, V, 84-93.
[88] *Works*, V, 94-113.
[89] *Works*, V, 113-124.
[90] E.g. *Works*, V, 101-102, 111-112.
[91] *Works*, V, 113.

after his escape from France[92]; then hint of a strange relationship between him and his cousin, Virginie, to whom, however,
he was not betrothed[93]; next suggest, by means of his mother's
fears and forebodings, that his voyage to rescue Virginie would
never succeed[94]; subsequently tell of Mme de Créquy's constant
watchfulness, her senses all acute, aware of any unusual sound
in expectation of his return[95]; and finally confirm all suspicions
and anxieties by a few simple words[96]. From then onwards,
since the eventual outcome is known, Mrs. Gaskell's task was to
describe what happened to Clément in such a way as to keep
the reader tense and alert, always in dread for her hero's safety.
Here too Mrs. Gaskell makes good use of significant hints : she
implies that Mme Babette is not entirely loyal[97], thereby suggesting danger from that quarter; yet, when fate does strike, it
is not quite as anticipated. Like the author of an exciting
detective story, Mrs. Gaskell maintains a constant state of
apprehension; in her case, however, since the conclusion is
foreknown, all interest and suspense are centred on the means
whereby that conclusion is brought about.

Nothing need be said concerning the characters beyond noting their adequacy for the plot. The plot itself was most likely
of the author's own devising—although possibly she heard
something on similar lines during one of her French visits, or
perhaps from the eccentric Knutsford dancing master, M. Rogier
(Rogier may even figure in the tale as Le Fèbvre, who also
gave dancing lessons[98])[99].

It seems well to conclude with a few remarks about some of
the incidents. According to Mrs. Chadwick the scene where,
as a boy, Clément, in response to a challenge from Urian,
climbed a chimney to bring down a starling's nest[100] is based on
an anecdote concerning Clive of India who, while at Market
Drayton, 'alarmed the inhabitants by climbing a high steeple,

---

[92] *Works,* V, 70.
[93] *Works,* V, 72-73.
[94] *Works,* V, 77-79.
[95] *Works,* V, 82-83.
[96] *Works,* V, 83-84.
[97] *Works,* V, 85.
[98] *Works,* V, 84.
[99] For Rogier, see Green, *Knutsford, Its Traditions and History: with
Reminiscences, Anecdotes, and Notices of the Neighbourhood,* pp. 134-136.
[100] *Works,* V, 63-64.

in order to extract a stone from the mouth of a gargoyle.'[101] The implausibility of this supposition diminishes when Mrs. Gaskell is found, in a letter of 2 April [1849] to Geraldine Jewsbury[102], recounting a similarly daring escapade by Robert Clive (a great friend of the Holland family), whose traditional exploits had to be spoken of under one's breath. In passing we may note the reference to Master Urian, drowned at sea[103] : this can be related to the disappearing-sailor *motif*, as well as to Mrs. Gaskell's personal grief over the death of her only son —indeed Lady Ludlow mourns not only for Urian[104], but for all her nine children[105]. Not unexpectedly, the cause of the five infant deaths ('the cruel system which forbade the mother to suckle her babies'[106]) is mentioned by the authoress.

Effective both historically and artistically are those realistic touches which give substance and body to the Clément-Virginie episode : they serve, instead of a fuller characterization, to make the narrative convincing. To suggest the climate of Revolutionary France one has Mme Babette's analysis of the attitude of the old nobility towards the ordinary people[107]; the graphic description of prison conditions[108], with the interesting parenthesis (which may be due to what Mrs. Gaskell had heard in France, or to what she had learnt about English prisons from Thomas Wright) that ' "the look of despair and agony . . . passed away from the women's faces sooner than it did from those of the men" '[109]; the semi-comic but most truth-like incident where Clément's arms were ' "pinioned behind him with a woman's garter, which one of the viragos in the crowd had made no scruple of pulling off in public" '[110]—Mrs. Gaskell having previously hinted at the moral licence of the times[111].

---

[101] Chadwick, *Mrs. Gaskell*, p. 59.
[102] Quoted, fairly accurately, in T[heresa] C[oolidge], 'Mrs. Gaskell to Ruskin', 'Library Notes' Section, *More Books*, XXIII (1948), 229. This letter (*G.L.*, No. 43) is in the Boston Public Library.
[103] *Works*, V, 62.
[104] *Works*, V, 65.
[105] *Works*, V, 167.
[106] *Works*, V, 169.
[107] *Works*, V, 112.
[108] *Works*, V, 114-123.
[109] *Works*, V, 116.
[110] *Works*, V, 114.
[111] *Works*, V, 109.

SECTION VI

Right at Last ('The Sin of a Father', 1858)

'The Sin of a Father', a short story which came out in *Household Words*[1] on 27 November 1858, was called *Right at Last*[2] when published in book-form. Since presumably it was Dickens who supplied the first title and the author who made the change[3], this alteration is not without significance.

To readers of the periodical the original designation probably suggested mystery and immorality. With certain expectations thus aroused, they would have been on the watch for dark hints and veiled meanings—nor are these wanting. Firstly there is Professor Frazer's uneasiness about his ward's proposed wedding with Dr. James Brown, concerning whom little was known[4]; after the marriage, Dr. Brown had strange fits of morbidity[5]; Christie displayed a dislike for Crawford, her fellow servant[6]; on being robbed by Crawford, the doctor was curiously reluctant to prosecute[7]; when on trial Crawford tried to catch his master's notice, at the same time behaving in an oddly insolent way[8]. By such means Mrs. Gaskell engages one's interest and makes one alert for any clues as to the nature of the mystery.

The change of title perhaps implies that the author wished the focus of attention to lie less on the detective aspect of the

[1] XVIII, 553-561.

[2] [Elizabeth Cleghorn Gaskell] *Right at Last, and Other Tales*, London: Sampson Low, Son & Co., 1860. It appeared on 10 May, according to Sadleir (*Excursions in Victorian Bibliography*, p. 208).

[3] When sending the few lines she hoped would serve instead of a preface or introductory chapter for the book, Mrs. Gaskell apparently did not refer to its title, this not being named in her covering letter to the publisher of 16 April 1860 (now in the Manchester Central Reference Library—MS. F. 928.823 G.47/9); but, in an earlier business note of Saturday [14 April 1860], mentioned in the same letter (*G.L.*, No. 463), she may have done so.

[4] *Works*, VII, 279-280.

[5] *Works*, VII, 285.

[6] *Works*, VII, 285.

[7] *Works*, VII, 292.

[8] *Works*, VII, 294.

tale than on its moral teaching (that honesty is the best policy). There is, too, the suggestion that together with a satisfactory ethical conclusion goes domestic contentedness: the hero and heroine can live in harmony and happiness, everything is all right in the end. This last implication is, no doubt, illustrated by our final view of Mrs. Brown, standing at 'the dining-room window with a baby in her arms, and her whole face melted into a smile of infinite sweetness.'[9]

Domesticity mingled with mystery is, then, the impression given by *Right at Last*. It is not a story one would wish to re-read, and in all likelihood Miss Hopkins is correct in supposing it 'to be an example of what Mrs. Gaskell considered "good enough for *Household Words*." '[10] However the plot is competently enough contrived for the purpose in hand, even if no great originality of invention is displayed—Dr. Brown's father had been transported for forgery, hence his fits of depression, and his fear of Crawford, who discovered the secret. Perhaps, with *Great Expectations* in mind, we should mention that Mr. Brown, the forger, made a fortune after his transportation[11]; but any literary debt would not be on Mrs. Gaskell's side.

Since the hero and the heroine's uncle are both medical men, and since the opening scene is set in the Scottish capital, Mrs. Gaskell's connexions with their profession and that city seem equally important. The plight of the wife of a ruined Edinburgh lawyer (reduced to cleaning her own doorstep)[12] apparently provided the germ for the story, where[13] it received the transformation expected from a cousin of Sir Henry Holland, M.D. (Edinburgh[14]). Certainly Mrs. Gaskell could speak of a doctor's life from the inside, as is illustrated by the ensuing extract, where her eye for the significant surveys the furnishings of Dr. Brown's consulting-room from both a professional and a

---

[9] *Works*, VII, 299.

[10] Hopkins, *Elizabeth Gaskell*, p. 251. Mrs. Gaskell speaks of a story she had begun (probably *A Dark Night's Work*) as being 'good enough/ for *H[ousehold] W[ords]*' in a letter to George Smith of 23 December [1859] —now in the archives of Sir John Murray at 50 Albemarle Street, London W.1.—: *G.L.*, No. 451a.

[11] *Works*, VII, 296.

[12] See Ward, ed. *Works*, VII, p. xxvii; and Shorter, ed. *Novels and Tales*, X, p. viii.

[13] *Works*, VII, 299.

[14] Holland, *Recollections of Past Life*, pp. 20, 22, 28, 32.

feminine point of view. The parentheses, which might well have come as retrospective remarks from the doctor's wife, are in keeping with the author's sympathetic involvement, with her humorous participation and fellow-feeling for the young practitioner at the outset of his career.

> His consulting-room (how grand it sounded!) was completely arranged, ready for stray patients; and it was well calculated to make a good impression on them. There was a Turkey-carpet on the floor, that had been his mother's, and was just sufficiently worn to give it the air of respectability which handsome pieces of furniture have when they look as if they had not just been purchased for the occasion, but are in some degree hereditary. The same appearance pervaded the room: the library-table (bought second-hand, it must be confessed), the bureau—that had been his mother's—the leather chairs (as hereditary as the library-table), the shelves Crawford had put up for Doctor Brown's medical books, a good engraving on the walls, gave altogether so pleasant an aspect to the apartment that both Doctor and Mrs. Brown thought, for that evening at any rate, that poverty was just as comfortable a thing as riches.[15]

The only feature deserving notice is the contrast between the morally strong wife and her apparently irresolute and weak-willed husband. Miss Rubenius[16] sees this as illustrative of Mrs. Gaskell's gradual change from the early ideal of a passive, submissive wife (as in *Lizzie Leigh*) to one who acts with a sense of ethical responsibility, following her own concepts of duty. It is difficult to accept such a thesis. Even granted the validity of the procedure (inferring from her fiction the author's private views about the most desirable *rôle* for a wife), one must stress that in general all Gaskellian heroines display greater force of personality than do the men; whether or not they are *married* heroines— usually, of course, they are not—seems irrelevant. Those female characters with whom Mrs. Gaskell was most concerned almost invariably show presence of mind, have eminently practical natures, and possess considerable moral fibre: figures of more marginal importance may or may not conform to Victorian standards of conjugal obedience; but here generalizations are out of place.

---

[15] *Works*, VII, 283.
[16] *The Woman Question in Mrs. Gaskell's Life and Works*, pp. 73-76.

SECTION VII

'The Manchester Marriage' (1858)

'The Manchester Marriage' was incorporated into the framework of *A House to Let*[1], the Extra Christmas Number of *Household Words* which came out on 7 December 1858; like *Right at Last*, it was probably written during Mrs. Gaskell's visit to Heidelberg in the autumn of that year[2]. Having, in connexion with the previous tale, referred to Miss Rubenius' discussion of the author's treatment of married women, we ought to note that here the wife, in contradistinction to Mrs. Brown in *Right at Last*, is an excellent example of conjugal passivity, being 'implicitly obedient to those whom she loved both by nature and habit'[3]; but *The Woman Question in Mrs. Gaskell's Life and Works* contains no mention of 'The Manchester Marriage'.

There is a resemblance between the subject of this story and that of Tennyson's *Enoch Arden* (1864)—a resemblance which, according to Dr. Adolphus Ward[4], struck Mrs. Gaskell when she read the poem. The theme of the returning husband ought, however, rather to be seen in the light of Mrs. Gaskell's disappearance *motif*, of which it is an instance; moreover the parallelism with the case of John Stevenson seems quite close. The writer's brother vanished while on a voyage to India, whereas Frank Wilson was presumed lost, after he had sailed

---

[1] Pp. 6-17.
[2] Whitehill, ed. *Gaskell-Norton Letters*, p. 30, fn. 2: however Mrs. Whitehill seems (misleadingly) to suggest that Mrs. Gaskell wrote the whole of *A House to Let*. 'Mme Gaskell écrit quelque chose pour le Christmas number des Household words—je ne sais ce que c'est—Elle est très occupée—il faut que ce soit fini demain.' So wrote Mlle Ida Mohl (daughter of Robert, the brother of Julius) from Heidelberg on 4 November 1858 to her aunt, Mme Mary Mohl (this relevant extract having been made by Miss Jane Revere Coolidge—subsequently Mrs. Whitehill—before the destruction of the Mohl letters during World War II). See too *G.L.*, No. 418.
[3] *Works*, V, 522.
[4] Ed. *Works*, V, p. xxiv.

'for the East Indies and China'[5]. In *Cranford,* we recall, the sailor also returned.

From a critical as distinct from a thematic stand-point, it cannot be said that the central situation (that brought about by the husband's returning to find his wife happily remarried) deserves much serious attention; certainly, should such attention be given, it must inevitably result in an unfavourable judgement. Although the events immediately surrounding the return of Frank Wilson provide the core of the story, are indeed its very *raison d'être,* not only does the author fail to exploit them to the full, but she handles them in so theatrical a fashion as to produce something bordering on melodrama. Wilson returns, sees his crippled daughter (who contrasts strikingly with his wife's healthy son by her second marriage), leaves the house, and later drowns himself[6]. There is little about his mental turmoil: nor does Mrs. Gaskell present an ethical dilemma; for a faithful maid-servant is the only other person aware of his existence until after his convenient suicide. There follows a hasty conclusion, whose final paragraph has a disconcertingly sentimental tone[7].

In its structure, 'The Manchester Marriage' is far from satisfactory. Besides mismanagement of the most important section, a sense of proportion is absent from the work as a whole. This defect in scale is partly, no doubt, due to Mrs. Gaskell's composing more or less as she wrote (significantly the same maid is first called Bessy[8], afterwards Mary[9]). The lack of adequate planning also reveals itself by inordinately long preliminaries. Here, though in a sense Mrs. Gaskell's invention is praiseworthy, since she provides a convincing narrative of the fortunes of Alice as well as a realistic contrast between her two husbands, the technical demands of a short story are nonetheless neglected. Structurally, the tale is lopsided; as regards the length of the parts, it lacks proper proportion; in terms of artistic achievement, the emphasis falls at the wrong place.

On the other hand it would be misleading to neglect such good things as Alice's faithful servant, whom Dr. Adolphus Ward[10] takes to be the true heroine. There is too the very

[5] *Works,* V, 495.
[6] *Works,* V, 505-521.
[7] *Works,* V, 523.
[8] *Works,* V, 505.
[9] *Works,* V, 513.
[10] Ed. *Works,* V, p. xxiv.

realistic characterization of Mr. Openshaw, a Manchester business man whose professed contempt for lazy Londoners[11], eminently practical disposition[12], and reliance on strength of voice rather than on force of logic[13] combine in the veritable type of the self-made, self-educated, forthright Northerner: in his portrayal Mrs. Gaskell clearly put her Manchester observations to good effect. Most memorable is the passage where Mr. Openshaw proposes.

> "Mrs. Frank, is there any reason why we two should not put up our horses together?"
> Alice stood still in perplexed wonder. What did he mean? He had resumed the reading of his newspaper, as if he did not expect any answer; so she found silence her safest course, and went on quietly arranging his breakfast, without another word passing between them. Just as he was leaving the house, to go to the warehouse as usual, he turned back and put his head into the bright, neat, tidy kitchen, where all the women breakfasted in the morning—
> "You'll think of what I said, Mrs. Frank" (this was her name with the lodgers), "and let me have your opinion upon it to-night."[14]

What follows is equally entertaining, especially as Mr. Openshaw takes out his watch and times the few minutes allowed for the consideration of his proposal[15] when, in the evening, the offer is repeated (' "Well, Mrs. Frank," he said, "what answer? Don't make it too long; for I have lots of office-work to get through to-night." '[16]).

For a shrewd comparison of two types of married love, it is worth while to quote the following passage, which illustrates how, even in a minor work, Mrs. Gaskell had sane and sensible things to say about human sentiment.

> Mr. Openshaw required no demonstration, no expressions of affection from her. Indeed, these would rather have disgusted him. Alice could love deeply, but could not talk about it. The perpetual requirement of loving words, looks, and caresses, and misconstruing their absence into absence of love, had been the great trial of her former married life.[17]

Familiarity with the author's past suggests that two fictional

[11] *Works,* V, 492.
[12] *Works,* V, 498.
[13] *Works,* V, 498.
[14] *Works,* V, 500-501.

[15] *Works,* V, 502.
[16] *Works,* V, 501.
[17] *Works,* V, 503.

features may have autobiographic parallels. In the early part of the story[18] Alice Wilson is said to have been on difficult terms with the second wife of her husband's father, who, nevertheless, became more friendly when Alice helped to nurse the dying Captain Wilson[19]: with this we can compare Elizabeth Stevenson's unhappy London visits to her father, who had married again, especially since, like the second Mrs. Wilson, the second Mrs. Stevenson realized the value of a female relative during her husband's illness[20]. Another link between literature and life may be established if we relate Ailsie, Alice's bedfast daughter who suffered from an affliction of the spine[21], with Marianne Lumb, the cripple who was so eager that her baby cousin, Elizabeth, should join her at Knutsford[22]. In this last

[18] *Works*, V, 493-494.

[19] *Works*, V, 495.

[20] Her praise of her step-daughter's conduct was expressed in a letter to Mrs. Hannah Lumb of 15 June 1829, from which Meta Gaskell sent Clement Shorter the relevant extract (handwritten, but not apparently by Meta), quite accurately quoted by Miss Hopkins (*Elizabeth Gaskell,* pp. 28-29)—this extract being in the Gaskell Section, Brotherton Collection, Leeds University Library.

[21] *Works*, V, 496.

[22] Her letter of 1 or 2 November 1811, suggesting this, seems not to be extant; but Miss Hopkins (*Elizabeth Gaskell,* pp. 22-24) quite accurately reproduces Meta Gaskell's transcript—now in the Harvard University Library: bMS Am 1088 (4490). Besides Meta's copy, there are two others (both in the Gaskell Section, Brotherton Collection, Leeds University Library)—a complete typescript one, and part of a handwritten one (almost certainly done by the copyist of the letter from the second Mrs. Stevenson, and sent—probably in a complete state—by Meta to Shorter). All three copies differ slightly from one another, though the Brotherton typescript is based on the Harvard transcript. According to an undated fragment by Meta to Shorter (in the Gaskell Section, Brotherton Collection, Leeds University Library), part of her covering note for the copies of the letters from the second Mrs. Stevenson and Marianne Lumb, the latter maimed herself for life when, as a little child, overjoyed at seeing her mother approach, she leapt from her nurse's arms through an open window and fell on hard ground. Hannah Lumb's daughter died unmarried at the age of twenty-one, according to the Pedigree of the Hollands of Mobberley and Knutsford found in Irvine, ed. *A History of the Family of Holland,* between p. 36 and p. 37. Her death almost certainly occurred in Spring 1812. In a letter from Townhill Farm [Bradford] of 8 April [1812] to her son, John William, Sarah Whittaker (*née* Buck) wrote that her sister-in-law Mrs. Francis Sharpe (*née* Martha Whittaker) had sent 'melancholly tidings from Knutsford of/ the sudden Death of Poor Mary Anne Lumb/ who went to Halifax with her Mother—& died/ there of a Days illness (Spasms)', apparently 'before the object of her Journey (making her will)// was accomplishd'. Mrs. Whittaker

connexion we may note that Alice Wilson's maternal feelings are somewhat over-stressed by the authoress. It seems not altogether uncharitable to remark that here, as elsewhere, Mrs. Gaskell would have done well to be more reticent; as she herself remarks, 'How that mother loved that child, it is not for words to tell!'[23]—unfortunately the attempt was made.

---

added that her death would not only deprive Mrs. Lumb 'of her sole companion &/ chief object of affection' but also perhaps greatly abridge 'the means of rendering her future/ life comfortable'. This letter is in the Edward Hall Collection at the Wigan Central Library—M 1006(d) E.H.C. 205—; a transcript of the relevant part (differing little from the original) may conveniently be found in Edward Hall, ed. " 'Cranford' again: The Knutsford Letters, 1809-1824", p. 35a—a typescript in the Manchester Central Reference Library (MS. F. 823.89 G69). During his editing and annotating of these Knutsford Letters (addressed by members of his family to the Rev. John William Whittaker, 1790-1854), Mr. Hall kept Mrs. Gaskell and her writings constantly in view. Of the young Elizabeth Stevenson there is no mention, beyond a passing reference to Mrs. Lumb's 'little niece'—quoted by Hall (ed. " 'Cranford' again", p. 83) from a Knutsford letter of 17 March 1815 which was sent to John William by his aunt, Catharine Whittaker (an unmarried sister of Dr. Peter Holland's second wife, Mary), and which is now in the Edward Hall Collection at the Wigan Central Library (M 1005 E.H.C. 204). On the other hand Hall points to many links between this Knutsford correspondence and *Cranford*. Although one may not accept all his conjectures—such as the claim that Miss Catharine (Kate) Whittaker was, in part at least, "the prototype of 'Aunt Matty' " (" 'Cranford' again", Introduction, p. iv)—there do seem interesting parallels between epistolary fact and Gaskellian fiction. Thus franks, in demand at Knutsford, were also in request at Cranford (" 'Cranford' again", p. 4, Footnotes, p. i; *Works*, II, 57); both Miss Mary Anne (Marianne) Lumb and Miss Deborah appear to have acted in *Old Poz* (" 'Cranford' again", p. 9, Footnotes, p. ii; *Works*, II, 27); Knutsfordians, like Cranfordians, were acquainted with Quadrille (" 'Cranford' again", pp. 39-40, Footnotes, p. iv; *Works*, II, 94); the Knutsford incumbency of the Rev. Oswald Leycester recalls the time when Mr. Jenkyns was 'the rector of Cranford' (" 'Cranford' again", p. 75, Footnotes, p. v; *Works*, II, 52); ginger lozenges were useful in Knutsford and Cranford alike (" 'Cranford' again", p. 170, Footnotes, p. vii; *Works*, II, 178); news of a bank-failure caused concern to Mrs. Sharpe, of Heathside, Knutsford, just as it did to Miss Matty (" 'Cranford' again", p. 180, Footnotes, pp. vii-viii; *Works*, II, 153); a committee of Knutsford ladies brings to mind the ladies' committee presided over by Mary's father and (we may add) 'the meeting of the Cranford ladies' whose charitable purpose was to help Miss Matty (" 'Cranford' again", p. 199, Footnotes, p. viii; *Works*, II, 134, 169); finally—a parallel not drawn by Mr. Hall—the biting tongue of Dr. Peter Holland suggests the 'slightly sarcastic' Mr. Gibson (" 'Cranford' again", Introduction, p. v, Footnotes, p. vi; *Works*, VIII, 40).

[23] *Works*, V, 497.

CHAPTER VII

ROUND THE SOFA (1859) TO 'SIX WEEKS AT HEPPENHEIM' (1862)

SECTION I

Round the Sofa (1859)

In 1859 the two volumes of *Round the Sofa*[1] appeared: the first was taken up by 'My Lady Ludlow'; the second, by 'An Accursed Race', 'The Doom of the Griffiths', 'Half a Life-Time Ago', 'The Poor Clare', and 'The Half-Brothers'. Of these, all except the last have been considered in the order in which they originally came before the general public. Apparently the concluding tale had not previously been printed; but it may have been read in manuscript by the author's friends[2]—at least so the Preface suggests.

> Most of these Stories have already appeared in *Household Words:* one [presumably 'The Doom of the Griffiths'], however, has never been published in England, and another [presumably 'The Half-Brothers'] has obtained only a limited circulation.[3]

[1] [Elizabeth Cleghorn Gaskell] *Round the Sofa,* 2 vols., London: Sampson Low, Son & Co., 1859. March was the month of publication (Sadleir, *Excursions in Victorian Bibliography,* p. 208).

[2] That Mrs. Gaskell's work did sometimes circulate in manuscript seems evidenced by John Ruskin's remark about having 'read a little pretty book of' hers 'in the M.S.', a remark made in his letter to the author of 6 July 1865 (a copy of part of which being in Shorter and Symington, 'Correspondence, Articles & Notes Relating to Mrs. E. C. Gaskell. Transcripts', Vol. II, Section of Extracts from Letters Relating to Mrs. Gaskell and Her Work—a typescript in the Gaskell Section, Brotherton Collection, Leeds University Library).

[3] Preface to *Round the Sofa,* I, p. iii. Mrs. Gaskell's [Sunday (post 5 —possibly 6—February) 1859] letter (*G.L.,* No. 414) to Mrs. Nancy Robson (now in the Yale University Library—MS Vault Sect. 16) suggests that Sampson Low, her 'rascally publisher', was trying to pass off as new this 'REpubli=/=cation of H W Stories', she having 'sold the/ right of republication to him/ in a hurry to get 100£ to take/ Meta abroad out of the clatter/ of tongues consequent on her/ breaking off her engagement./' From her letter of 25 July [1858] to Charles Eliot Norton, one may suppose that initially Mrs. Gaskell hoped to obtain £150 for republishing her 'Household Words Stories, under the title of Round the Sofa'—*Gaskell-Norton Letters,* ed. Whitehill, p. 26: *G.L.,* No. 401 (Chapple and Pollard misprint the sum as £105, this letter being in the Harvard University Library). These stories—excluding 'The Doom of the Griffiths', though possibly including 'The Half-Brothers'—may have earlier appeared in *My Lady Ludlow and Other Tales,* 2 vols., London: Smith, Elder & Co. [1859] (listed in Northup's Bibliography to Sanders, *Elizabeth Gaskell,* p.

Before treating the only story which seems to have been published for the first time, we must say something about the framework for these narratives.

---

180); I have never seen this book, but its scarcity could provide an alter-
native explanation for the 'limited circulation' obtained by (presumably)
'The Half-Brothers'. In this connexion it is interesting that the wily Low
later brought out his *Round the Sofa* group as Elizabeth Cleghorn
Gaskell, *My Lady Ludlow, and Other Tales; Included in "Round the
Sofa."*, New edn, London: Sampson Low, Son & Co., 1861 (Northup's
Bibliography in Sanders, *Elizabeth Gaskell*, p. 182); however 'New Edition'
does not appear on the title-page of all copies published that year. *G.L.*,
No. 414 is dated [February 1859] by Chapple and Pollard.

Sub-Section a

The Frame

As early as 1 May 1855 Dickens had written that Mrs. Gaskell might collect her 'stories etc. in Household Words, and republish them separately'[1]; the following September a cheap edition came out—*Lizzie Leigh; and Other Tales,* the publishers being Chapman & Hall, the same as for the periodical. In a letter of 25 July [1858] to Charles Eliot Norton, we find her writing that, trying to raise £150, she would reprint her 'Household Words Stories, under the title of Round the Sofa'[2].

The introductory pages provide the Edinburgh context. Most probably the author, in order to give some sort of setting to stories which, having been written on different occasions, possessed no unifying principle in themselves, recalled those evenings she had spent in Edinburgh drawing-rooms when, as 'a girl of eighteen or nineteen'[3], she first stayed in that city. From such memories she could sketch a plausible background for the telling of her tales. Besides her own happy associations, Edinburgh must have endeared itself to the author by reason of its connexion with the early married life of Mr. and Mrs. Stevenson; about this their daughter would have learnt not only from her own relatives, but also from those people, such as Mrs. Eliza Fletcher[4], who had known the Stevensons at that time. If the picture of Mrs. Dawson's drawing-room owes much to Elizabeth Stevenson's observations of Scottish society in the late twenties and early thirties[5], then doubtless her father's recollections of that period at the opening of the century when, as well as private tutoring, 'he and his wife established a board-

---

[1] *The Letters of Charles Dickens,* ed. Dexter, II, 656: cf. *G.L.,* No. 235.
[2] *Gaskell-Norton Letters,* ed. Whitehill, p. 26: *G.L.,* No. 401 (Chapple and Pollard misprint the sum as £105, this letter being in the Harvard University Library).
[3] Ward, ed. *Works,* V, p. xiii.
[4] *Autobiography of Mrs. Fletcher with Letters and Other Family Memorials,* ed. The Survivor of Her Family [Mary Richardson], p. 271.
[5] Miss Stevenson visited friends of her parents at Edinburgh on two successive winters, according to the letter Meta Gaskell dictated to Elizabeth Gaskell Norton for Clement Shorter on 25 November 1909 (in the Gaskell Section, Brotherton Collection, Leeds University Library).

ing house for University students in Drummond Street'[6] lie
behind Mrs. Gaskell's graphic account of Miss Greatorex's
lodgings; for, despite differences in character, the Cromer-Street
landlord, Mr. Mackenzie, had also been wont to coach 'young
men preparing for the University'[7]. It is hardly necessary to
remind ourselves of yet another family connexion with Edinburgh University—namely that the author's cousin, Sir Henry
Holland, studied medicine there.

The narrator in *Round the Sofa* responds to the city in a
way very similar to that likely in the case of the young Elizabeth Stevenson. She had, for instance, 'to exchange . . . romps
in the garden and rambles through the fields for stiff walks in
the streets'[8] where decorum required neat bonnet-strings and a
straight shawl. There is too the country girl's failure to understand that, in a town, it was economically wise to choose
only such fabrics as the dirty atmosphere would make little
impression on[9].

Mrs. Gaskell's observation, at once close and humorous, of
the lodgings and its inmates (the cadging landlord[10], his stingy
sister[11], and their sorely tried maid[12]) is in her best domestic
manner. Typically feminine are her references to 'a hard, slip-
pery, black horsehair sofa, which was no place of rest; an old
piano, serving as a sideboard; a grate, narrowed by an inner
supplement, till it hardly held a handful of the small coal
which could scarcely ever be stirred up into a genial blaze.'[13]

As regards the little circle of friends who collected in the
Dawson drawing-room, Mrs. Gaskell had, so to speak, to work
back from the stories. Ideally their characterization should have
been determined by the tales they were to tell, the narratives,
except possibly the last, being chronologically prior to their narrators.

Mrs. Dawson (so styled by courtesy[14]) is the only character
who seems truly in keeping with her story; certainly she is the
only one to be portrayed at any length. Yet even so Mrs.
Gaskell does little more than make her a sofa-confined invalid,

[6] Chadwick, *Mrs. Gaskell*, p. 5.   [11] *Works*, V, 3.
[7] *Works*, V, 2.   [12] *Works*, V, 3.
[8] *Works*, V, 1.   [13] *Works*, V, 2.
[9] *Works*, V, 2.   [14] *Works*, V, 4.
[10] *Works*, V, 2-3.

thereby providing a link with the narrator in *My Lady Ludlow* who, it will be recalled, was crippled as a result of having jumped from a stile[15]. There is, we may note in passing, a further, but unintended, link: Mrs. Dawson's Indian wall-paper[16] bears the same design as Lady Ludlow's[17]—an interesting illustration of unconscious repetition (whether the author had originally invented or observed such a pattern one cannot say). For the rest, the connexion between the tales and their tellers is usually contingent rather than necessary. 'An Accursed Race' becomes a paper Mrs. Dawson's medical brother intends for the Philosophical Society[18]; 'The Doom of the Griffiths' is recounted by the governess, Miss Duncan, as a Welsh story heard in her youth[19]; 'Half a Lifetime Ago'[20] is related by Mrs. Preston, the wife of a Westmoreland squire[21]; 'The Poor Clare', told by the Italian exile, Signor Sperano[22], is said to have been found among papers bequeathed to him by the old priest who had welcomed him to England, and whom he had nursed during a fatal attack of cholera[23]. As the concluding tale, 'The Half-Brothers', appears to be the only one that had not previously been printed[24], here, one may suppose, was an opportunity for congruence between story and narrator: nevertheless the probability is rather that Mrs. Gaskell had the tale lying by her, perhaps ready for periodical publication, should the occasion arise. The narrator, Mr. Preston[25], is a *Westmoreland* squire[26], whereas the story itself has a *Cumberland* setting[27]; it seems, therefore, that the squire's county was chosen so that

[15] *Works*, V, 40-41.

[16] *Works*, V, 5.

[17] *Works*, V, 45.

[18] *Works*, V, 217.

[19] *Works*, V, 236.

[20] Ward, as we have noted, dispenses with the hyphen in his Knutsford Edition (*Works*, V).

[21] *Works*, V, 277.

[22] Identified as Agostino Ruffini, the friend and fellow-exile of Mazzini, in Masson, 'The Gaskell Centenary. The Novelist's Career', *The Manchester Guardian*, 29 September 1910.

[23] *Works*, V, 327-328.

[24] As already noted, it may have been contained in *My Lady Ludlow and Other Tales*.

[25] *Works*, V, 390.

[26] *Works*, V, 6.

[27] *Works*, V, 391.

his wife could with propriety tell 'Half a Lifetime Ago', with its Westmoreland background[28]. If 'The Half-Brothers' had been written when the *Round the Sofa* compilation was being put together, surely Mrs. Gaskell would have given it a different location? To this tale we must now turn.

[28] *Works,* V, 278.

Sub-Section b

'The Half-Brothers' (1859)

There is not, in 'The Half-Brothers', a great deal which calls for attention. It is a simply told tale of self-sacrifice: Gregory, who, after his mother's death, though not cruelly treated by his step-father, received little loving care, gives his life to save his half-brother, the narrator, who had lost himself in a snow storm on the Cumberland Fells. The feelings of terror and fear of imminent death are well enough suggested[1], and the heroism of Gregory described with reticence[2]. In sum, it is the negative virtues that one finds oneself mentioning; theatrical attitudes are not struck, and sentimental pitfalls are avoided.

Here and there in the narrative are things to praise: the slight but graphic pictures of a funeral procession in the snow[3]; the unquestioning recognition by William Preston of his obligation to look after his step-son ('That was, as it were, in the bond when he had wedded my mother.'[4]); the author's understanding of animals, implied by the treatment of Gregory's collie, Lassie[5]; the concluding paragraph, which tells how, as a recompense to Gregory and as a penance to himself, William Preston acknowledged his step-son's right to be buried alongside Mrs. Preston, while he himself should lie at their feet[6].

Regarding those incidents and situations which call for notice because of their relation to Mrs. Gaskell's life and work in general, one can refer to the death of Gregory's little sister from scarlet fever[7] and to the unhappy position of the child whose parent married for a second time[8]. These are mentioned only because of the importance for the author of her son's death (also from scarlet fever) and her father's re-marriage: their occurrence in the short story may be quite fortuitous and without autobiographic significance. It is perhaps making a similarly tenuous comparison to suppose that Mr. Preston's kicking of Lassie, followed by the sense of shame which caused

---

[1] *Works*, V, 399-400.
[2] *Works*, V, 401-403.
[3] *Works*, V, 392.
[4] *Works*, V, 397.

[5] *Works*, V, 400-403.
[6] *Works*, V, 404.
[7] *Works*, V, 391.
[8] *Works*, V, 394-398

him to tax the dog's master with careless training[9], has more than an accidental resemblance to Colonel Gisborne's shooting of Mignon, even though this also was followed by a fit of remorse which sought alleviation in the same manner—by finding fault with the animal's owner[10]. Finally, as an instance of those verbal repetitions which are at times found in Mrs. Gaskell's writings, we can compare the following: the first quotation is from the present tale; the second, from *My Lady Ludlow*.

> My father sent to Carlisle for doctors, and would have coined his heart's blood into gold to save her, . . . [11]

> . . . if he [Morin *fils*] had married Virginie, he would have coined his life-blood for luxuries to make her happy; . . . [12]

[9] *Works*, V, 400.
[10] In 'The Poor Clare' (*Works*, V, 340).
[11] *Works*, V, 395.
[12] *Works*, V, 98.

SECTION II

Lois the Witch (1859)

From 8 October till 22 October 1859, 'Lois the Witch' appeared in *All the Year Round*[1]; in 1861 it was published separately[2]. *Lois the Witch* is founded upon fact: the late seventeenth-century witch trials did unfortunately take place; and so Mrs. Gaskell's task was, to quote Dr. Adolphus Ward, that 'of making truth seem probable'[3], a task in which she admirably succeeded. Since the New England background is of some importance, it may be well to consider what attracted our author to this subject and its setting.

Mrs. Gaskell, it will be recollected, adopted in several of her early writings the pseudonym of Cotton Mather Mills; hence, at least by the late eighteen-forties, she must have been acquainted with the work of that celebrated divine, Dr. Cotton Mather, among whose numerous publications are tracts on the Salem witch-wonders. Further evidence of the author's interest in such matters is provided by a letter to her from John Gorham Palfrey, dated (probably, though indistinctly) 21 June 1856[4]; in this letter Palfrey, having mentioned that only one copy of Calef's *More Wonders of the Invisible World*[5] was then available in London, promised to send, on his return to America, whatever he could bearing on the witch trials. It is also relevant to notice that

---

[1] *All the Year Round. A Weekly Journal. Conducted by Charles Dickens. With Which Is Incorporated 'Household Words'*, I, 564-571, 587-597, 609-624. This, like all Mrs. Gaskell's subsequent contributions to *All the Year Round*, was anonymous.

[2] Elizabeth Cleghorn Gaskell, *Lois the Witch and Other Tales*, Copyright edn, Leipzig: Bernhard Tauchnitz, 1861.

[3] Ward, ed. *Works*, VII, p. xix.

[4] Quoted in part, more or less accurately, though wrongly dated, by Miss Hopkins (*Elizabeth Gaskell*, p. 365), who locates the letter in The John Rylands Library, Manchester—English MS. 731/81. The watermark appears to be 1855.

[5] Robert Calef, *More Wonders of the Invisible World: or, The Wonders of the Invisible World, Display'd in Five Parts*, London: Nath. Hillar; and Joseph Collyer, 1700.

315

Professor Whitfield[6] has conjectured that the subject of *Lois the Witch* was suggested by the author's American friend, William Wetmore Story, who, like Nathaniel Hawthorne, was himself born at Salem.

In the main Mrs. Gaskell gives a very accurate account of what happened during the delusion, displaying that careful concern for historical research which we shall meet again in *Sylvia's Lovers,* and which is best exemplified in her *Life of Charlotte Brontë.* Palfrey's communication points to a desire to obtain full information, so the numerous correspondences between details in the story and what actually took place should cause the reader no surprise. Although source-finding can often yield very inconclusive results, there does seem a *prima facie* case for supposing that one of Mrs. Gaskell's reference books was *Lectures on Witchcraft*[7], written by a fellow Unitarian, the Rev. Charles W. Upham, Junior Pastor of the First Church in Salem. The first part of Upham's work contains an account of what happened at Salem Village and its environs; the second, which provides some explanation of these events from a scientifically rational and liberal stand-point, treats of witchcraft at large. We may note that, during his general disquisition on the delusion, Upham refers to Sir Matthew Hale[8] and Matthew Hopkins[9]: the former is mentioned by Mrs. Gaskell in 'The Poor Clare'[10]; the latter occurs in the present tale, though, by some error, his surname is spelt 'Hopkinson'[11]. Instead of listing what Mrs. Gaskell appears to have culled from Upham—the details are unobtrusively incorporated into her narrative, without any show of pedantry—, it will doubtless prove more instructive to quote first the historian and then the novelist on the same subject—the interesting way in which one of the supposed witches managed to survive during the persecution.

---

[6] *Mrs Gaskell,* p. 198.
[7] Charles Wentworth Upham, *Lectures on Witchcraft, Comprising a History of the Delusion in Salem, in* 1692, Boston: Carter, Hendee and Babcock, 1831.
[8] Upham, *Lectures on Witchcraft,* p. 174.
[9] Upham, *Lectures on Witchcraft,* p. 169.
[10] *Works,* V, 362.
[11] *Works,* VII, 164.

One adventurous and noble spirited young man found means to effect his mother's escape from confinement, fled with her on horseback from the vicinity of the jail, and secreted her in the Blueberry Swamp, not far from Tapley's brook in the Great Pasture; he protected her concealment there until after the delusion had passed away, provided food and clothing for her, erected a wigwam for her shelter, and surrounded her with every comfort her situation would admit of. The poor creature must, however, have endured a great amount of suffering, for one of her larger limbs was fractured in the all but desperate enterprise of rescuing her from the prison.[12]

One young man found means to effect his mother's escape from confinement, fled with her on horseback, and secreted her in the Blueberry Swamp, not far from Taplay's Brook [sic], in the Great Pasture; he concealed her here in a wigwam which he built for her shelter, provided her with food and clothing, and comforted and sustained her, until after the delusion had passed away. The poor creature must, however, have suffered dreadfully; for one of her arms was fractured in the all but desperate effort of getting her out of prison.[13]

Concerning the minor characters in the story, there seems no reason to dispute those identifications with real people made

---

[12] Upham, *Lectures on Witchcraft*, pp. 35-36.

[13] *Works*, VII, 200. 'Tapley's brook' (f. 107) is the reading according to the author's manuscript (in the Harvard University Library: fMS Eng 1010—including an ornamental title-page, 118 folios, the last folio not being in Mrs. Gaskell's hand). A very cursory collation of this manuscript—itself bearing marks of revision, mainly (e.g. 'about [six *deleted*] ∧four∧ years old' MS, f. 17) though not wholly (e.g. 'by Pastor [Nolan. *deleted*] Tappau./' MS, f. 103), from Mrs. Gaskell's pen—, the *All the Year Round* text, and the version published in *Right at Last, and Other Tales* (1860) suggests that occasionally the *All the Year Round* compositors seem to have misread their copy (e.g. 'malig=/=nant' MS, f. 33; 'indignant' *A.Y.R.*, I, 589; 'inhuman' *Right at Last*, p. 128) and omitted the odd word (e.g. 'But to' MS, f. 117; 'To' *A.Y.R.*, I, 624; 'To' *Right at Last*, p. 239); that there may have been authorial and/or editorial modifications at the *All the Year Round* proofs-stage (e.g. 'danger to those/ who went out to reclaim them' MS, f. 20; 'danger of reclaiming them' *A.Y.R.*, I, 569; 'danger of reclaiming them' *Right at Last*, p. 108); that the *All the Year Round* text apparently underwent revision prior to reprinting (e.g. 'God's hands' MS, f. 71; 'God's hands' *A.Y.R.*, I, 612; 'God's disposal' *Right at Last*, p. 182). A careful comparison between the texts of those tales by Mrs. Gaskell initially printed in periodicals and their later book-versions might perhaps indicate a policy of revision in minor matters (especially stylistic ones) but not in matters of substance; however no such detailed comparison has been undertaken by the present writer, whose interest in the *Lois the Witch* text arose from an enquiry by Miss Patricia Gingrich (681 Merrick, Apt. 109, Detroit, Michigan 48202, U.S.A.).

by Dr. Adolphus Ward[14] and Mrs. Chadwick[15]; nevertheless the
author effected such small changes as were necessary for her
plot—as when Mr. Nolan is said to be 'a tall, pale young man'[16]
although his prototype, George Burroughs, by then 'had passed
the prime of life'[17]. Judge Sewall and other participants appear
under their own names; and Cotton Mather himself plays a
brief, but not altogether historically accurate, part in the affair
(although, in his case, this licence is legitimate, both because
of Mather's involvement in other instances of witchcraft and
also because of the effective use to which the author puts that
godly divine, so highly regarded by the Puritans of the time).

Since the general background is important, something must
be said concerning the story's excellence in this respect. On the
level of natural description Mrs. Gaskell displays her accustomed
skill: there are, for example, evocative accounts[18] of the gloomy
forests, with their threats of Indians and worse dangers. Of
more consequence, however, is her success in conveying the
claustrophobic atmosphere of Salem; in proof whereof we may
quote part of her astute analysis of those factors which aided the
birth and growth of the delusion.

> . . . It was prevalently believed that there were manifestations
> of spiritual influence—of the direct influence both of good and
> bad spirits—constantly to be perceived in the course of men's
> lives. Lots were drawn, as guidance from the Lord; the Bible
> was opened, and the leaves allowed to fall apart; and the first
> text the eye fell upon was supposed to be appointed from above
> as a direction. Sounds were heard that could not be accounted
> for; they were made by the evil spirits not yet banished from the
> desert-places of which they had so long held possession. Sights,
> inexplicable and mysterious, were dimly seen—Satan, in some
> shape, seeking whom he might devour. And, at the beginning of
> the long winter season, such whispered tales, such old temptations
> and hauntings, and devilish terrors, were supposed to be pec-
> uliarly rife. Salem was, as it were, snowed up, and left to prey
> upon itself. . . . [19]

In her diagnosis of the mania, Mrs. Gaskell is at pains to

[14] Ed. *Works,* VII, pp. xxi-xxii. Ward (incorrectly) gives the
Christian name of Burroughs as Stephen.

[15] *Mrs. Gaskell,* pp. 89-90.

[16] *Works,* VII, 151.

[17] Upham, *Lectures on Witchcraft,* p. 101.

[18] *Works,* VII, 124, 133-134.

[19] *Works,* VII, 147.

understand the mentality of the Puritans: she appreciates, but does not approve, their characteristically morbid and introspective habits of mind; she follows, without endorsing, those trains of thought which led to accusations of witchcraft. Her own attitude seems akin to Upham's. She can comprehend how the delusion could take hold of people, how even the 'witches' believed in the reality of the supernatural[20]—indeed the heroine herself, though wrongfully accused, is at one point shown as doubting her own innocence[21].

Lois the Witch affords one of the most structurally satisfying of Mrs. Gaskell's plots, perhaps partly owing to the author's having to work within a historical framework. She was equipped with the general outlines of the Salem witch-wonders, so her task was, in effect, to invent a particular story which would serve as a concrete instance. She chose to tell how a young English girl from Barford (where, interestingly, the Byerley sisters had kept a school before their move to Stratford[22]), having lost both parents, went to live among Puritan relatives in New England, and was there subsequently accused of witchcraft and hanged. That Mrs. Gaskell invented Lois Barclay's personal history appears certain; to substantiate her fictitiousness one may mention that, contrary to what the author says[23], there never was a seventeenth-century Barford incumbent called Mr. Barclay (the heroine's father)[24].

Among the technicalities of plotting, designed to engage the reader's attention in the story as such, Mrs. Gaskell's most important device is the use of ominous hints and dark suggestions, especially appropriate for the *milieu* of superstition and supernatural belief. Very early in the tale Captain Holdernesse, who introduces Lois to the New World, refers to the tendency for people, frightened by real dangers, to imagine unreal ones also[25]; thereupon Lois tells how she once saw a witch in Barford put to the water test[26]. On entering Salem, Lois apparently

[20] *Works*, VII, 162-164.
[21] *Works*, VII, 192.
[22] Hicks, *A Quest of Ladies*, pp. 54-71, esp. p. 56.
[23] *Works*, VII, 111.
[24] According to information received in a letter of 12 April 1961 from the present incumbent, the Rev. Gerald Knight (Barford Rectory, Warwick). See too Hicks, *A Quest of Ladies*, p. 56.
[25] *Works*, VII, 121.   [26] *Works*, VII, 122.

causes a little child to stumble, by means of the evil eye[27]; later she innocently instructs her cousin in those traditional arts of divination whereby a maiden may discern her future husband[28]. When her cousin, Manasseh, has a strange dream, betokening a violent death for Lois if she will not marry him[29], her fate seems assured. These and similar forebodings create a sense of doom, wholly in keeping with the Calvinistic views on foreknowledge and predestination expressed by Manasseh[30], which further serve to enhance the tragic force of the tale. Moreover Mrs. Gaskell never fully explains how the delusion arose: rather she allows her readers to draw their own conclusions from the strange pact between the Indian servant, Nattee, and Faith Hickson[31]; from the veiled threat of the former somehow to get rid of Pastor Tappau[32]; and from such 'minor' points in the confession of Hota, Tappau's Indian servant, as her admitting to malpractices like breaking crockery by means of carefully adjusted strings[33].

In general, the characters are subordinate to the plot: and one finds that it is usually their specifically Puritan qualities which the author stresses; for these minister to the central theme. A word or two must, nevertheless, be said regarding some of the more important figures. The child, Prudence Hickson, seems, rather like 'the elfish Robert'[34] (in 'The Doom of the Griffiths'), to have the 'impish antics'[35] of a mischievous changeling; she is the chief cause of Lois's destruction[36]. The unrequited love of her sister for Pastor Nolan, turned upon itself by his apparent attraction towards Lois, prevents Faith's clearing Hota from imputations of witchcraft[37]. Their mother, Mrs. Hickson[38], is an excellent picture of the God-fearing

[27] *Works*, VII, 125.
[28] *Works*, VII, 139: another instance of the author's interest in old superstitions and beliefs.
[29] *Works*, VII, 154-155.
[30] *Works*, VII, 188-189.
[31] *Works*, VII, 150-151.
[32] *Works*, VII, 157-158.
[33] *Works*, VII, 170.
[34] *Works*, V, 264.
[35] *Works*, VII, 127.
[36] *Works*, VII, 184-185.
[37] *Works*, VII, 178.
[38] *Works*, VII, 126 ff.

Puritan, stern yet upright. More interesting, however, is her son, Manasseh, who illustrates the potential dangers of a religion built on Calvinistic doctrine, with its belief in predestination and reliance upon the inner voice. Mrs. Gaskell makes a subtle study of the mingling of religious and sexual sentiments in his mind; the process begins when, through ostensibly reading from a large (doubtless theological) folio, he casts furtive glances at his newly arrived cousin[39]. In this connexion we may quote from the passage where Manasseh first 'proposes' to Lois, at the same time noting how appropriate to the speaker is the style.

> "It is borne in upon me—verily, I see it as in a vision—that thou must be my spouse, and no other man's. Thou canst not escape what is fore-doomed. Months ago, when I set myself to read the old godly books in which my soul used to delight until thy coming; I saw no letter of printer's ink marked on the page, but I saw a gold and ruddy type of some unknown language, the meaning whereof was whispered into my soul; it was, 'Marry Lois! marry Lois!' And, when my father died, I knew it was the beginning of the end. It is the Lord's will, Lois, and thou canst not escape from it."[40]

The quotation also illustrates the near-comedy upon which Mrs. Gaskell's treatment of the Puritans at times almost inevitably verges. It is not so much that the author seeks to poke fun at their religious habits; for this would hardly have been in keeping with the central tragic theme : nor would such levity be characteristic of a writer who constantly shows respect towards beliefs sincerely held, albeit different from her own. Nonetheless we must take full account of what Dr. Adolphus Ward had in mind when he spoke of 'an exquisite blending of delicate humour with deep pathos'[41]. Early in the story Captain Holdernesse indicates to Lois (and the reader) what may be expected.

> "They are a queer set, these New Englanders," said Captain Holdernesse. "They are rare chaps for praying; down on their knees at every turn of their life. Folk are none so busy in a new country, else they would have to pray like me, with a 'Yo-hoy!' on each side of my prayer, and a rope cutting like fire through my hand. . . . "[42]

[39] *Works*, VII, 126.   [41] Ward, ed. *Works*, VII, p. xviii.
[40] *Works*, VII, 145.   [42] *Works*, VII, 114.

Besides providing an element of mirth and gusto, the captain acts as a healthy norm against which Puritan aberrations can be judged. The following passage demonstrates the dual function of Holdernesse; in passing we may also note that it is typical of Mrs. Gaskell's method—the humour being 'that of an observer rather than a comedian.'[43]

> First, dough was set to rise for cakes; then came out of a corner-cupboard—a present from England—an enormous square bottle of a cordial called Gold-Wasser; next, a mill for grinding chocolate —a rare, unusual treat anywhere at that time; then a great Cheshire cheese. Three venison-steaks were cut ready for broiling, fat cold pork sliced up and treacle poured over it; . . . Lois wondered where would be the end of the provisions for hospitably receiving the strangers from the old country. At length everything was placed on the table, the hot food smoking; but all was cool, not to say cold, before Elder Hawkins (an old neighbour of much repute and standing, who had been invited in by Widow Smith to hear the news) had finished his grace, into which was embodied thanksgiving for the past, and prayers for the future, lives of every individual present, adapted to their several cases, as far as the elder could guess at them from appearances. This grace might not have ended so soon as it did, had it not been for the somewhat impatient drumming of his knife-handle on the table, with which Captain Holdernesse accompanied the latter half of the elder's words.[44]

Lois the Witch does, indeed, contain a surprising number of humorous incidents, mostly dependent for their effects on Puritan solemnity, which is allowed to speak for itself. One cannot imagine Mrs. Gaskell writing such passages with a mocking smile, however much her tongue may have been in her cheek.

In the present discussion it seems worth while to point out how well Mrs. Gaskell manages the man-woman relationship, how civilized is her approach, how understanding her manner. The touch of humour—found, for example, in her description of Pastor Nolan's visit to the Hickson household after his long absence from Salem—seems a necessary ingredient for this sort of amatory success: it acts as a specific against any possible Victorian embarrassment touching things sexual. The complete passage loses from piecemeal quotation; but the ensuing extract

[43] K. L. [Kathleen and Letitia] Montgomery, 'Elizabeth Cleghorn Gaskell', *The Fortnightly Review*, XCIV (N.S. LXXXVIII—1910), 459.
[44] *Works*, VII, 116-117.

will exemplify the author's urbanity of tone and her appreciation of the humour inherent in such a situation.

> [Pastor Nolan, having been greeted by Lois, is left alone with Faith Hickson.] His wonder was that of a carnal man—who that pretty stranger might be, who had seemed, on his first coming, so glad to see him, but had vanished instantly, apparently not to reappear. And, indeed, I am not sure if his perplexity was not that of a carnal man rather than that of a godly minister, for this was his dilemma. It was the custom of Salem (as we have already seen) for the minister, on entering a household for the visit which, among other people and in other times, would have been termed a "morning call," to put up a prayer for the eternal welfare of the family under whose roof-tree he was. Now this prayer was expected to be adapted to the individual character, joys, sorrows, wants, and failings of every member present; and here was he, a young pastor, alone with a young woman; and he thought— vain thoughts, perhaps, but still very natural—that the implied guesses at her character, involved in the minute supplications above described, would be very awkward in a *tête-à-tête* prayer;
> . . . [45]

Something has already been said about Mrs. Gaskell's achievement both in evoking the Puritan ethos and in giving a convincing picture of the mental climate which favoured the Salem trials. The psychology of the delusion, itself an enthralling subject[46], was well understood by the author of *Lois the Witch*. She realised the dangers of the imagination, for which she prescribed a remedy often mentioned in her fiction; perhaps it may even have some bearing upon Mrs. Gaskell's own work as a creative writer. Her solution was to attend to present realities, to observe with care the concrete and close at hand. Because Lois felt desolate and lonely in a strange land, Captain Holdernesse determined to cheer her up by talking 'about hard facts, connected with the life that lay before her'[47]; when in tears owing to an inhospitable welcome from the Hicksons, she herself tried to 'divert her thoughts by fixing them on present objects'[48]; after a visionary outburst by Manasseh, Lois 'by simple questions on practical affairs . . . led him back, in her unconscious wisdom, to the subjects on which he had always

---

[45] *Works*, VII, 152.
[46] Discussed in Marion Lena Starkey, *The Devil in Massachusetts: A Modern Enquiry into the Salem Witch Trials,* London: Robert Hale Limited [1952].
[47] *Works*, VII, 114.
[48] *Works*, VII, 128.

shown strong practical sense'[49]; what, during her imprisonment, brought Lois back from 'the wild, illimitable desert in which her imagination was wandering'[50] was the 'weight of iron on her legs'[51]—which weight, Mrs. Gaskell characteristically notes, the jailer stated 'to have been "not more than eight pounds." '[52]

[49] *Works*, VII, 173.
[50] *Works*, VII, 192.
[51] *Works*, VII, 192: cf. Upham, *Lectures on Witchcraft*, p. 76.
[52] *Works*, VII, 192: cf. Upham, *Lectures on Witchcraft*, p. 76.

SECTION III

'The Crooked Branch'
('The Ghost in the Garden Room', 1859)

In the 1859 Extra Christmas Number of *All the Year Round,* called *The Haunted House*[1], that tale which Mrs. Gaskell was later to reprint as 'The Crooked Branch'[2] appeared with the inappropriate title of 'The Ghost in the Garden Room'—inappropriate because there is nothing of the supernatural about it.

The narrative is apparently Mrs. Gaskell's refashioning of a true story told her in 1849 by Mr. Justice Erle and Mr. Tom Taylor[3]; since Taylor was on the northern circuit in the later eighteen-forties[4], the date of the events related may thus be approximately established. Her plot having been supplied, Mrs. Gaskell's task was to invent incidentals, to develop the characters, and to establish a convincing background.

As its second title implies, this tale concerns the ignoble member of a family tree: the black-sheep who returns, not as a penitent prodigal, but as a plunderer, intent on robbing his aged parents. The remaining figure in the domestic tragedy is the old people's niece, who stands in virtuous contrast to her disreputable cousin. The general theme is rather similar to that of *The Moorland Cottage*; and Mrs. Gaskell may have been aware of this resemblance when she came to relate 'The Crooked Branch'.

Perhaps significantly, if one recalls its source, the intended

---

[1] Pp. 31-48. The (slightly corrected) manuscript (65 folios) of this story is in the Manchester University Library Special Collections—Exhibition Hall MSS. Post-marked 22 November 1859 (f. 65ᵛ), it was addressed to W. H. Wills.

[2] In [Elizabeth Cleghorn Gaskell] *Right at Last, and Other Tales,* London: Sampson Low, Son & Co., 1860, pp. 241-318.

[3] According to her own statement in a letter (*G.L.,* No. 452) to George Smith of Tuesday 27 December [1859], now in the archives of Sir John Murray.

[4] See Charles Kent's article on Taylor (1817-1880) in *The Dictionary of National Biography.*

high-light of the story is the court scene, where Mr. and Mrs. Huntroyd are forced to testify against their son[5]. It is, therefore, a major criticism that this legal drama should border on the melodramatic: in which connexion we may note that Henry Irving once gave a dramatic reading from the story—'its effect was quite extraordinary.'[6] The dialogue (counsel's questions to the old people and their replies) seems adequate enough; what is disastrous is the author's commentary. For example, Mrs. Gaskell tries to suggest the emotional reactions of the judge; but her stage-directions are worse than redundant: she produces theatrical effects by means of stereotyped *clichés*, and calls forth stock responses with the aid of hackneyed phraseology. Two short quotations will serve as illustrations.

> "Go on!" said the judge. "What is right and legal must be done." But, an old man himself, he covered his quivering mouth with his hand as Nathan, with grey, unmoved face, and solemn, hollow eyes, placing his two hands on each side of the witness-box, prepared to give his answers . . . [7]

> . . . Again the counsel apologised, but the judge could not reply in words; his face was quivering all over, and the jury looked uneasily at the prisoner's counsel.[8]

Although its intended climax is not satisfactory, the earlier part of 'The Crooked Branch' has considerable merit. The discovery and capture of the burglars—a necessary preliminary for the trial scene—is made exciting and thrilling; and Mrs. Gaskell's preparation for the attempted robbery—her tracing of the degeneration of Benjamin Huntroyd—is likewise convincingly rendered.

In the same line as Edward Browne[9] and Richard Bradshaw[10], Benjamin is one of Mrs. Gaskell's weak-willed, ne'er-do-well young men, whose profligacy ends in crime. As so often in her work, a morally reprehensible character is associated with

[5] *Works,* VII, 254-258. Miss Hopkins (*Elizabeth Gaskell,* p. 259) appears to think—erroneously—that Benjamin is in the dock; earlier she (*op. cit.,* p. 258) mistakenly located the setting of the tale as the West, not the North (*Works,* VII, 209), Riding of Yorkshire.

[6] Ward, ed. *Works,* VII, p. xxiv.

[7] *Works,* VII, 254-255.

[8] *Works,* VII, 256.

[9] In *The Moorland Cottage* (*Works,* II, 268 ff.).

[10] In *Ruth* (*Works,* III, 183 ff.).

the law; for it is noteworthy that Benjamin should choose a legal career rather than follow his father's calling. The most potent means used to suggest his essential nature is his treatment of those who had done most for him. Thus he made love to his cousin chiefly to wheedle gold from his parents, though Bessy's prettiness did not make the task unpleasant[11]; yet his underbred gallantry lasted only while she was within kissing-distance[12]. To extract his father's hard-earned savings, he exploited parental affection by threatening to emigrate unless the money were forthcoming[13]. On the last evening before his departure to London, he brushed off Mrs. Huntroyd's touch of endearment.

> "Thou'rt tired, my lad!" said she, putting her hand fondly on his shoulder; but it fell off, as he stood up suddenly, and said—
> "Yes, deuced tired! I'm off to bed." And with a rough, careless kiss all round, even to Bessy, as if he was "deuced tired" of playing the lover, he was gone; leaving the three to gather up their thoughts slowly, and follow him upstairs.[14]

What remains most memorable in 'The Crooked Branch', however, is not so much the story itself as those episodes, incidents, and details which betoken the writer's loving knowledge of country folk and their ways. Dr. Adolphus Ward has reminded us of Mrs. Gaskell's debt to the authoress of the privately printed *Country Conversations*[15] (those 'admirable transcripts of actual talks with poor people which had been

---

[11] *Works,* VII, 213.
[12] *Works,* VII, 213.
[13] *Works,* VII, 225.
[14] *Works,* VII, 230.
[15] [Georgine Tollet] *Country Conversations,* pref. William Clive Bridgeman, London: T. Richards, 1881. This was 'not the work of an inventive genius. The writer had a singularly accurate memory, a sense of quiet humour, and keen powers of observation; but of the faculty which creates she had no share. Her sole object was to preserve the exact expressions of those whose histories of themselves and of their affairs she had found so interesting.'—Original Preface, 1881, in William Clive Bridgeman, intro. *Country Conversations: The Humour of Old Village Life in the Midlands* [by Georgine Tollet], London: John Murray, 1923, pp. 9-10.

read to her in manuscript'[16]) for the humour resulting from that incomparable honesty which makes the middle-aged Nathan Huntroyd, when proposing to the sweet-heart of his youth, conclude with these remarks:

" . . . I'll not mislead thee. It's dairy, and it might have been arable. But arable takes more horses nor it suited me to buy, and I'd the offer of a tidy lot of kine. That's all. If thou'll have me, I'll come for thee as soon as the hay is gotten in."[17]

Yet the humour is really of Mrs. Gaskell's own creating. The whole episode is in her best manner, and so, finding that something she had once heard fitted the context, she put the borrowing to good effect.

In the next quotation Mrs. Gaskell's description is at once simple, factual, and concrete: homely details of attire and appearance are observed in such a way as not merely to present, like a slice of life, the scene itself, but also to convey character, to suggest dispositions and feelings in terms of dress and outward show.

Hester stood there, in answer to the good sound knock his good sound oak-stick made: she, with the light full upon her, he in shadow. For a moment there was silence. He was scanning the face and figure of his old love, for twenty years unseen. The

[16] Ward, ed. *Works,* VII, p. xxv. It is interesting to notice that Mrs. Gaskell received an invitation-note of Sunday [26 February 1860] from a certain G. H. Tollet, on the back of which she wrote part of a [Monday 27 February 1860] letter to Marianne (now in the possession of Mrs. Margaret Trevor Jones): *G.L.,* No. 455 (dated [Late February 1860] by Chapple and Pollard). Writing to Marianne one Monday morning, she mentions a forthcoming visit to the Tollets, Betley Hall, near Crewe; and, in an undated letter to Marianne, refers to her intention of going with Meta to the Tollets at Betley Hall, Newcastle, Staffordshire (Betley Hall lies about midway between Crewe and Newcastle): both these letters (*G.L.,* Nos. 202, 247), respectively dated [5 June 1854] and [?c. 19 June 1855] by Chapple and Pollard, are in the Gaskell Section, Brotherton Collection, Leeds University Library—see too *G.L.,* Nos. 205+; 246, 248. Although unable to help greatly in identifying the Georgine Tollet of *Country Conversations,* the Staffordshire County Record Office report that a Georgina Tollet was the sixth child of George Tollet of Betley Hall (her parents having married in 1795), and suggest she may have been the Miss Tollet whom directories list as living at Betley Hall till the early eighteen-eighties.

[17] *Works,* VII, 210: cf. the conversation held in 1857 between Georgine Tollet and Mrs. Harland, where the latter tells how her son's offer of marriage came to be refused (" "Why, mother," says he, "she'd understood mine was a harable; and she *will not* marry to a dairy." '—*Country Conversations,* 1923, pp. 20-21).

comely beauty of youth had faded away entirely; she was, as I
have said, homely-looking, plain-featured, but with a clean
skin, and pleasant frank eyes. Her figure was no longer round,
but tidily draped in a blue and white bed-gown, tied round her
waist by her white apron-strings, and her short red linsey petticoat showed her tidy feet and ankles. Her former lover fell into no ecstasies. He simply said to himself, "She'll do"; and
forthwith began upon his business.[18]

By frequent references to domestic details, little touches which
only a country-woman would be likely to include, Mrs. Gaskell
localizes her story, giving it substance and reality. This concretion—her own specific contribution—is especially evident in
such things as the old creepie stool, Bessy's accustomed fire-side
seat[19]; Nathan's wedding-coat, worn thereafter as his habitual
Sunday garb[20]; the old stocking used to store ready cash[21], over
against which was set what Hester Huntroyd 'thought of with
secret pride as " money i' th' bank" '[22] : furthermore Mrs. Gaskell's own appreciation of, and feeling for, traditional forms of
life come out well in incidentals like Nathan's wonted going
out of an evening 'to see "what mak' o' weather it wur" '[23]
and the family custom of sitting around the fire-side to listen
while the old farmer read a chapter from the Scriptures, wearing
'his horn spectacles, the tallow candle between him and the
Bible'[24].

As a concluding laudatory comment we may mention what
the quotations have already in part exemplified—the author's
ear for country dialect. In the following passage the dialogue
is fully functional as regards characterization and plot, a dead
metaphor becomes vital when extended into a full-blooded
rural comparison, and the essential honesty of the English yeoman is admirably conveyed; here we can relevantly recall a
certain *Mr.* Holbrook who returned to the Cranford postmis-
tress any letters addressed to him as Thomas Holbrook, *Esq.*[25]

---

[18] *Works,* VII, 210.
[19] *Works,* VII, 214, 219.
[20] *Works,* VII, 236.
[21] *Works,* VII, 219.
[22] *Works,* VII, 228.
[23] *Works,* VII, 239.
[24] *Works,* VII, 240.
[25] *Works,* II, 34.

He was out of breath by this time. His son took his father's first words in dogged silence; it was but the burst of surprise he had led himself to expect, and did not daunt him for long.

"I should think, sir"—

" 'Sir'—whatten for dost thou 'sir' me? Is them your manners? I'm plain Nathan Huntroyd, who never took on to be a gentleman; but I have paid my way up to this time, which I shannot do much longer, if I'm to have a son coming an' asking me for three hundred pound, just meet same as if I were a cow, and had nothing to do but let down my milk to the first person as strokes me."[26]

---

[26] *Works*, VII, 224-225.

SECTION IV

'Curious if True' (1860)

Mrs. Gaskell's first contribution to *The Cornhill Magazine*[1], 'Curious, if True', came out in the second (February 1860) number. Her *début* could scarcely have been more fortunate. The title was suggested by Smith[2], the author herself commenting "it just makes people have a notion that it *might* be true, which is what is wanted from the beginning."[3]

'Curious if True'[4] is a fairy tale for adults, a blend of the fantastic and the supernatural in every way delightful. Criticism seems almost superfluous; yet it is instructive to examine Mrs. Gaskell's methods, if only to illustrate the diversity of her talent. For this her own comment provides a convenient starting point.

The contribution purports to be an 'Extract from a Letter from Richard Whittingham, Esq.'[5] Whittingham himself is therefore the narrator, and he claims to be recounting what befell him during a visit to Tours, made as part of his quest in tracing the descendants of Calvin, to whom he believed himself connected. Characteristically Mrs. Gaskell supplies plenty of local colour to authenticate what she wants to seem possible; and throughout the narrative are scattered French phrases[6] such as would come naturally from the pen of an Englishman acquainted with France. The narrator is convincingly portrayed, so his own concreteness lends added reality to what

---

[1] I, 208-219. This, like all Mrs. Gaskell's subsequent contributions to *The Cornhill Magazine,* was anonymous.

[2] For Mrs. Gaskell's relations with George Smith and *The Cornhill,* see the admirable chapter (where good use is made of letters from Mrs. Gaskell, at present in the archives of Sir John Murray) in Hopkins, *Elizabeth Gaskell,* pp. 200-224, esp. pp. 205-206.

[3] Quoted by Ward (ed. *Works,* VII, p. xxv).

[4] Ward dispenses with the comma in his Knutsford Edition (*Works,* VII).

[5] The sub-title. We may note that a certain Mrs. Whittington took the baby Elizabeth to Knutsford, there to live with Mrs. Lumb (Chadwick, *Mrs. Gaskell,* p. 12).

[6] E.g. *table-d'hôte, salle à manger, tourelles, battants, salon, patois* (*Works,* VII, 259, 260, 261, 262, 263, 264).

he relates. The following quotation illustrates Mrs. Gaskell's technique, the last words being particularly successful in this respect.

> . . . the aspect of my fellow-guests was unprepossessing enough to make me unwilling to enter into any *tête-à-tête* gamblings with them. So I usually rose from table early, and tried to make the most of the remaining light of the August evenings in walking briskly off to explore the surrounding country; the middle of the day was too hot for this purpose, and better employed in lounging on a bench in the Boulevards, lazily listening to the distant band, and noticing with equal laziness the faces and figures of the women who passed by.[7]

Whittingham tells how, having lost his way during an evening stroll, he entered into a *château*, where a ball was in progress. Gradually the reader realizes that all the guests appear to have the guise of fairy-tale characters, though the narrator does not. Hence the narrative acts at two different levels. Whittingham reports simply and directly what he sees, making no comments and drawing no inferences therefrom; the reader, however, is aware of overtones which escape the *naïve* narrator. Yet Mrs. Gaskell never intrudes with authorial explanations. Her achievement lies in making Whittingham's account itself susceptible of two sorts of interpretation. Instances are the presentation of the Sleeping Beauty (the beautiful princess whose propensity to sleepiness is ascribed to the bad habits of her youth[8]), Cinderella (the lame old lady who attributed her swollen feet to having once forced them into very little slippers[9]), and Puss in Boots (the retainer to the Marquis de Carabas who most oddly reminded the narrator of a great Tom-cat[10]). To illustrate how even the dialogue can be taken in two ways, often with humorous effect, we shall quote from the conversation between Whittingham and Mme de Retz where the latter explained that the exact shade of her husband's beard had not been caught on canvas.

> " . . . You observe, the colouring is not quite what it should be."
> "In this light the beard is of rather a peculiar tint," said I.

[7] *Works*, VII, 260.
[8] *Works*, VII, 269.
[9] *Works*, VII, 270.
[10] *Works*, VII, 265-266.

"Yes; the painter did not do it justice. It was most lovely, and gave him such a distinguished air, quite different from the common herd. . . . "[11]

Although there is much comic deflation and debunking in the realistic treatment of these fairy-tale figures—especially by means of Tom Thumb's disrespectful remarks[12]—, there is too that poetic quality, that awareness of romance, which had early appeared in Mrs. Gaskell's sketch of Clopton Hall, and which remained a constant factor throughout her work. When, for example, the narrator is led into the *château,* he is conscious of 'a mighty rushing murmur (like the ceaseless sound of a distant sea, ebbing and flowing for ever and for ever), coming forth from the great vacant galleries that opened out on each side of the broad staircase, . . . as if the voices of generations of men yet echoed and eddied in the silent air.'[13] We have already noticed how Mrs. Gaskell's love of old traditions and legends, as evidenced by her non-fictional writings, frequently found literary expression; so it is not surprising that what first occurred in a letter to Mary Howitt should, over two decades later, be more or less repeated in this short story (itself cast in epistolary form). The relevant extracts provide further proof of how closely incorporation of this kind was made.

"Moreover, I know a man who has seen the Fairies and tells the story in the prettiest possible way. And if you were on Alderley Edge, the hill between Cheshire and Derbyshire, could not I point out to you the very entrance to the cave where King Arthur and his knights lie sleeping in their golden armour till the day when England's peril shall summon them to her rescue."[14]

. . . and for aught I knew he [Jack the Giant-killer] lay enchanted with King Arthur's knights, who lie entranced, until the blast of the trumpets of four mighty kings shall call them to help at England's need.[15]

It is a virtue in 'Curious if True' that the mystery is never resolved. Did Whittingham dream merely? Or was he perhaps

[11] *Works,* VII, 276.
[12] *Works,* VII, 266-269.
[13] *Works,* VII, 262.
[14] Quoted, from a letter of 18 August 1838 by Mrs. Gaskell to Mrs. Mary Howitt, in Howitt, 'Stray Notes from Mrs. Gaskell', *Good Words,* XXXVI (1895), 610: *G.L.,* No. 12.
[15] *Works,* VII, 273.

transported into the past, there to attend at a fancy-dress ball where all the aristocrats played their parts with consummate skill? Or was it that, by some strange psychic phenomenon, the childhood fairy-tale figures in the mind of a provincial French girl somehow peopled an old *château* on the anniversary of her death? Or were the servants just indulging in a costume party? Indeed, to increase the mystery, Mrs. Gaskell appears to have scattered her clues so as to suggest several solutions: the story ends with the narrator lying in the grass, listening to the birds and insects[16]; the porter[17], as well as his master[18] and mistress[19], was seemingly attired in old-fashioned dress, and he[20], again like Mme de Retz[21] and her second husband[22], spoke in what the narrator took to be *Marché au Vendredi* provincial *patois*; 'Cinderella', despite her aristocratic-looking face, had coarse-grained hands, less clean than they might have been[23]; Whittingham saw the phantom of a little peasant girl, whose hand was, apparently, being licked by the wolf that killed her[24].

[16] *Works*, VII, 277.
[17] *Works*, VII, 261.
[18] *Works*, VII, 264.
[19] *Works*, VII, 263.
[20] *Works*, VII, 262.
[21] *Works*, VII, 263.
[22] *Works*, VII, 264.
[23] *Works*, VII, 264.
[24] *Works*, VII, 274. This figure is taken to be Little Red Riding Hood by Mrs. Chadwick (*Mrs. Gaskell*, p. 278), but may be interpreted otherwise.

SECTION V

The Grey Woman (1861)

Between 5 January and 19 January 1861, 'The Grey Woman' came out in *All the Year Round*[1]; it was published in book-form four years later[2]. Perhaps this story was already in Dickens' hands as early as 28 November 1860, when he wrote to Miss Georgina Hogarth that a certain contribution by Mrs. Gaskell was 'much too long'[3] for his Christmas number.

Miss Rubenius' discovery—that, in the original manuscript[4], Mrs. Gaskell claims: "(The story I am going to relate is true as to it's main/ facts, and as to the consequence ∧of those facts∧ from which this tale/ takes it's title.)/"[5]—once again reminds us how much of her work had a historical origin. Most biographers[6] seem to hold that *The Grey Woman* resulted from Mrs. Gaskell's Heidelberg sojourns in Autumn 1858 and Summer 1860[7]; it is, however, just as likely that she was drawing on material gathered during her first Rhineland tour, made with Mr. Gaskell in 1841[8]. Of this 1841 Heidelberg visit she wrote to her sister-in-law, Eliza, that it was the custom for her party to exchange with the Howitts (whom she had then met personally for the first time) 'the most frightening & wild stories/ . . .

---

[1] IV, 300-306, 321-328, 347-355.

[2] Elizabeth Cleghorn Gaskell, *The Grey Woman. And Other Tales,* Illus. edn, London: Smith, Elder and Co., 1865. It appeared in October, according to Sadleir (*Excursions in Victorian Bibliography,* p. 210).

[3] *The Letters of Charles Dickens,* ed. Dexter, III, 193.

[4] Now in The John Rylands Library, Manchester—English MS. 876. The manuscript shows occasional signs of revision, especially as regards proper names.

[5] Quoted by Rubenius (*The Woman Question in Mrs. Gaskell's Life and Works,* p. 279), but corrected against the first folio of the original MS.

[6] Chadwick, *Mrs. Gaskell,* p. 279—but cont. p. 144—; Rubenius, *The Woman Question in Mrs. Gaskell's Life and Works,* p. 80, fn. 2; Sanders, *Elizabeth Gaskell,* p. 110; Ward, ed. *Works,* VII, p. xxvii; and Whitfield, *Mrs Gaskell,* p. 64.

[7] See *G.L.,* Nos. 401, 403-405a, 418, 421, 444, 485; 465, 472a-475a, 476, 480.

[8] A view once supported by Mrs. Chadwick (*Mrs. Gaskell,* p. 144).

—some *such* fearful ones—all true'[9]. Perhaps, therefore, it was one of these which, nineteen years later, she thought would be suitable for the Christmas readers of *All the Year Round*, but which, nevertheless, proved too long for that purpose. She may have obtained the outlines of the tale exactly as she describes herself as doing in *The Grey Woman* itself. In the district there were indeed 'quaint old mills'[10] like the one to which Mrs. Gaskell resorted[11], and she gives enough circumstantial details to imply that she is speaking from experience—mentioning, for example, the date as '184—'[12], referring to the 'summer-storm'[13] which drove everyone out of the mill-garden (the first of which, incidently, would have been inappropriate for the Heidelberg holidays of both 1858 and 1860; the second, for that in Autumn 1858), and even noting the miller's 'great crimson umbrella.'[14] Altogether these first few pages, telling how Mrs. Gaskell came upon the story of the Grey Woman, have every appearance of being in the main an account of what did happen. If there is anything of the author's own adding, it is her statement that a manuscript (the story itself) was given her by the miller, whereas more probably she heard the tale from the man's lips. We may then suggest, not entirely without warrant, that *The Grey Woman* is based upon a strange story a German miller related concerning an unfortunate member of his family; Mrs. Gaskell later cast this narrative into autobiographic form, presenting it as an abbreviated and translated version of what many years previously the Grey Woman had written down for her daughter's benefit. The first-person device was a happy stroke: it endows the events recounted with an additional truthfulness, and permits the author to evoke her Gothick thrills to the best effect. Furthermore the time-spans and necessary summaries are,

[9] As Mrs. Gaskell told her sister-in-law, Mrs. Charles Holland (Eliza Gaskell), in a letter written one Monday morning [1841]—the incomplete MS being in the Gaskell Section, Brotherton Collection, Leeds University Library. The relevant extract is given, fairly accurately, by Miss Hopkins (*Elizabeth Gaskell*, p. 65). Chapple and Pollard give [Late 1841] as their date for this letter (*G.L.*, No. 15)—complete copies of which, once owned by Mr. J. T. Lancaster, belong to the present writer.

[10] *Mary Howitt: An Autobiography*, ed. Howitt, I, 297.

[11] *Works*, VII, 300.

[12] *Works*, VII, 300.

[13] *Works*, VII, 301.

[14] *Works*, VII, 302.

by this means, not felt as intrusions or stop-gaps on the author's part; and the simplicity of the story-telling seems entirely in keeping with the unsophisticated character of the narrator.

The Grey Woman is in the 'Gothick' tradition, thus affording yet another instance of Mrs. Gaskell's surprising variety. Even though the bare bones of the plot were fact not fancy, she had to develop and adapt, to clothe the framework and put flesh on the skeleton. That she was moved to do so indicates the diversity of her talent. The expected machinery is present— M. de la Tourelle, the robber-leader[15] with aristocratic airs[16] and Byronic moods[17]; his wife, virtually a prisoner in the mountain *château*; the rooms she was not permitted to enter[18]; violent death among the servants[19]; a corpse stripped for plunder[20]; mistaken identity resulting in murder[21]; killing for vengeance[22]; decapitation of the villains[23]. All of this rather hackneyed stock-in-trade Mrs. Gaskell handles with a professional skill. The most 'sensational' episode (that in which the heroine, hiding beneath a table, hears her husband and his fellow *Chauffeurs* jokingly talk of their cruel deeds, and herself touches the hand of a corpse)[24] is thrilling in the best manner. Mrs. Gaskell, by her first-person presentation, makes the reader identify himself with Mme de la Tourelle in her terrifying situation : there is the obscurity ('they were doing something—I could not see what —to the corpse'[25]) which allows the imagination full play with its fears, as well as those telling psychological details which authenticate the experience ('my brain was numb to the sense of what they said, unless I myself were named; and then, I suppose, some instinct of self-preservation stirred within me, and quickened my sense'[26]).

Although this scene surpasses everything else, the rest of the narrative serves well enough to keep the reader in suspense, which is its primary purpose. For this Mrs. Gaskell must take all credit. Dr. Adolphus Ward, who believed *The Grey Woman* probably had its source in some French version of the story of

[15] *Works,* VII, 330.
[16] *Works,* VII, 309-310.
[17] *Works,* VII, 316, 318, 320.
[18] *Works,* VII, 315-316.
[19] *Works,* VII, 322.
[20] *Works,* VII, 327-332.
[21] *Works,* VII, 348-351.
[22] *Works,* VII, 358.
[23] *Works,* VII, 360.
[24] *Works,* VII, 326-333.
[25] *Works,* VII, 329.
[26] *Works,* VII, 332.

Schinderhannes (whom Mrs. Gaskell does mention[27]) or some such robber-chief, nevertheless went on to add that 'there is no reason whatever for supposing that by far the most interesting portion of it—the escape of Anna and her faithful, self-sacrificing maid Amante from the robbers' castle, and their long and almost desperate flight—was not the original invention of the writer.'[28] Our own views on the genesis of the tale scarcely conflict with this last hypothesis.

In a sense *The Woman in White* could be described as the Gothick domesticated; and it is, perhaps, significant that this novel should have been serialized in *All the Year Round* from 26 November 1859[29] to 25 August 1860[30]—in other words, not long before the time when, one presumes, Mrs. Gaskell wrote her own contribution. The marriage of Miss Laura Fairlie to Sir Percival Glyde is paralleled, at a less mundane level, by that between Anna Scherer and M. de la Tourelle: both ladies, owing to family and other pressures, marry men for whom no real warmth is felt; each later finds her true partner in some one who has helped in her time of danger. There can, of course, be no suggestion of literary indebtedness; but it may be that Collins' story, 'probably the most popular novel written in England during the nineteenth century'[31], brought to Mrs. Gaskell's mind a tale she had heard, nearly twenty years before, during her stay at Heidelberg. It created, so to speak, the necessary conditions for crystallization.

Despite the prevailing mood of fear, Mrs. Gaskell manages to introduce into the narrative touches of humour, though appropriately they occur early in the story. There is, for example, the following piece of irony, which in retrospect assumes tragic tones once the actual consequences of the wedding have been related.

[27] *Works*, VII, 347.
[28] Ward, ed. *Works*, VII, p. xxxi.
[29] *All the Year Round*, II, 95-104.
[30] *All the Year Round*, III, 457-468.
[31] Nuel Pharr Davis, *The Life of Wilkie Collins*, Urbana: University of Illinois Press, 1956, p. 216: a statement based on [Leonard Huxley] *The House of Smith Elder*, pref. I[sabel] M[arion] S[mith], London: Privately printed, 1923, p. 152.

> So we were married, in the Court chapel, a privilege which
> Madame Rupprecht had used no end of efforts to obtain for us,
> and which she must have thought was to secure us all possible
> happiness, both at the time and in recollection afterwards.[32]

There is also the amusing predicament of the miller's housekeeper, to whom, in their flight from the *Chauffeurs,* Amante
and Anna apply for shelter. She finds herself at a loss whether
or not to admit these strangers.

> She was not an unkindly woman; but her thoughts all travelled
> in one circle, and that was, that her master, the miller, had told
> her on no account to let any man into the place during his
> absence, and that she did not know if he would not think two
> women as bad; . . . [33]

When considering 'The Poor Clare', we noted how Mrs.
Gaskell used suggestive hints to engage her readers' attention;
in the present tale the same method is employed. There is,
most obviously, the initial puzzle about why the lady whose
portrait hung in the mill[34] should have turned grey: this is
followed by the Grey Woman's strange opposition to her daughter's marrying Henri[35]. Thereafter comes the personal narrative
of Anna Scherer—beginning with the statement that Babette
Müller was responsible for all her suffering[36], and going on to
relate how she happened to marry M. de la Tourelle, with
whom, for some reason, she never entirely felt at ease[37]. Analysis along these lines could be continued; but the essential point
is that Mrs. Gaskell successfully used such means to thicken
the plot, and thereby make her readers keep on turning over
the pages. However, we may specially commend the final paragraph[38], where one discovers that the suitor for Anna's daughter's hand is none other than the son of a man M. de la Tourelle had murdered. Taken in the context of the tale as a whole,
this revelation comes with a gratifying appropriateness.

As minor matters, albeit doubtless not without importance
for a general study of Mrs. Gaskell's work, we may first refer
to two internal inconsistencies, indications of hasty composition—Dr. Adolphus Ward notices[39] that Anna, although a

---

[32] *Works,* VII, 313.
[33] *Works,* VII, 337.
[34] *Works,* VII, 302-303.
[35] *Works,* VII, 303-304.
[36] *Works,* VII, 306.
[37] *Works,* VII, 311.
[38] *Works,* VII, 361.
[39] Ward, ed. *Works,* VII, p. xxviii, fn.

Lutheran like her second husband[40], bade her daughter seek
advice from 'the good priest Schriesheim'[41]; and the eyes of M.
de la Tourelle are at one point said to be grey[42], at another
blue[43] (but then eyes do seem to vary in this way[44], the significant point here being their paleness with overtones of icy
cruelty). Next we should notice that, as often in her writings, the
authoress appears influenced by her maternal experience, although
in the present instance[45] such sentiments are not out of place in
a narrative avowedly written by a mother for the sake of her
daughter. Concerning the characters it will suffice to mention
that Amante is the typically Gaskellian loyal servant, transposed
from her more usual domestic setting; and that such marginal
figures as the robber, Lefebvre[46], were presumably of Mrs. Gaskell's own inventing—certainly this is in his case implied by
the surname which occurs in other of her works[47].

[40] *Works,* VII, 359.
[41] *Works,* VII, 304.
[42] *Works,* VII, 316.
[43] *Works,* VII, 320.
[44] The heroine of *Cousin Phillis* has also, we may note, eyes which at
one time appear grey; at another, blue (*Works,* VII, 9, 70; 31).
[45] *Works,* VII, 319-320, 331, 355.
[46] *Works,* VII, 316.
[47] In 'Traits and Stories of the Huguenots' (*Works,* II, 492 ff.), and,
in the form Le Fèbvre, in *My Lady Ludlow* (*Works,* V, 84).

SECTION VI

Mrs. Gaskell, pref. *Garibaldi at Caprera,*
by Colonel Vecchj (1862)

The first piece of Mrs. Gaskell's published in 1862 was
her Preface to *Garibaldi at Caprera*[1] (an idyllic account of the
Liberator's domestic life by Colonel Vecchj, who had lived with
him on the island from 24 January to 18 August 1861). All the
proceeds from the sale of this volume were, at the General's
wishes, to be devoted to establishing elementary schools for
Neapolitan girls, since he believed good female education was 'the
best method of raising the character of the people'[2].

For our purposes little need be said regarding the Preface.
It illustrates that widespread English sympathy for the Italian
patriot in which such a liberal-minded lady as Mrs. Gaskell
might be expected to have joined; indeed her name could be
found on a committee of ladies formed to provide help for
Garibaldi's sick and wounded[3]. She must, moreover, almost cer-

[1] Elizabeth Cleghorn Gaskell, pref. *Garibaldi at Caprera,* by Colonel
C. Augusto Vecchj, trans. [L. and M. Ellis], Cambridge and London:
Macmillan and Co., 1862, pp. v-xi. The Preface is reprinted in *Novels and
Tales,* X, 471-475. The volume came out in February or March, according
to Sadleir (*Excursions in Victorian Bibliography,* p. 213): announced as
appearing immediately, it was on a list of forthcoming books in *The
Athenaeum Journal of Literature, Science, and the Fine Arts,* No. 1790
(15 February 1862), p. 235; a fortnight later it was among new publications
advertized in the same journal (No. 1792, p. 295). In a letter (*G.L.,*
No. 502a) of 1 April [1862] to Henry Morley (in the Manchester University
Library), Mrs. Gaskell remarked that she was glad he liked the book, but
that she had no right to his thanks since the editing had been forced on
her rather than undertaken voluntarily.
[2] Mrs. Gaskell, pref. *Garibaldi at Caprera,* by Vecchj, p. vii.
[3] In a letter to his absent wife of 25 July 1860, Mr. Gaskell says he
has agreed to Mrs. Gaskell's *name* being used, although he has made it
clear that she will not be able to do anything—a copy of this letter being
in Shorter and Symington, 'Correspondence, Articles & Notes Relating to
Mrs. E. C. Gaskell. Transcripts', Vol. I, Section of Letters from the Rev.
William Gaskell (a typescript in the Gaskell Section, Brotherton Collection, Leeds University Library): the original is in the Rutgers University
Library—MS A Symington Collection .G2535.

tainly have met Joseph Mazzini, a close acquaintance[4] of the
Gaskell's friend and solicitor, William Shaen. It is, incidentally,
interesting to note that she was among those who heard Kossuth
when that fugitive Hungarian leader spoke at the Manchester
Free Trade Hall[5].

Besides recommending the book to the public, Mrs. Gaskell
provides thumb-nail sketches of people mentioned by Vecchj. She
also remarks that she can vouch for the veracity of all he says[6]—
a sufficient testimonial, coming from one whose standards of
accuracy were so high.

[4] Shaen, ed. *Memorials of Two Sisters,* p. 32, fn. 1. See too Haldane,
Mrs. Gaskell and Her Friends, pp. 251-252: cf. and cont. *G.L.,* No. 157.
[5] *Autobiography of Mrs. Fletcher with Letters and Other Family Memorials,* ed. The Survivor of her Family [Mary Richardson], pp. 292-293;
and *Letters and Memorials of Catherine Winkworth,* I (ed. Her Sister
[Susanna Winkworth],1883), 303-305. There are references to Kossuth in
Mrs. Gaskell's letters to Eliza Fox of [Autumn 1849] and Monday [(post
11 November) 1851]: the relevant quotations given by Miss Haldane (*Mrs.
Gaskell and Her Friends,* pp. 232, 252-253) tally fairly well with the
copies of parts of these letters in the Gaskell Section, Brotherton Collection, Leeds University Library; but she (*op. cit.,* p. 252) misdates the
second letter, whose recipient is unnamed—these letters (*G.L.,* Nos. 51,
108a) are respectively dated [?Early November] 1849 and Monday [?17
November 1851] by Chapple and Pollard, who designate the recipient of
the second ?Eliza Fox.
[6] Mrs. Gaskell, pref. *Garibaldi at Caprera,* by Vecchj, p. vi.

SECTION VII

'Six Weeks at Heppenheim' (1862)

Mrs. Gaskell's second[1] contribution to *The Cornhill Magazine*[2] appeared in May 1862. 'Six Weeks at Heppenheim' was, according to Miss Meta Gaskell[3], planned and probably written more than three years before, during her mother's autumnal stay at Heidelberg; yet Mrs. Gaskell's letter to Smith of 18 March [1862][4], in which she promises to do her best to write a good story if he should need copy, shows that nothing was composed, at least on paper, before the spring. Since Mrs.

---

[1] Not the first, as is mistakenly said by Miss Hopkins (*Elizabeth Gaskell*, p. 259).

[2] V, 560-587.

[3] In a letter to Clement Shorter, of which the relevant fragment is in the Gaskell Section, Brotherton Collection, Leeds University Library. However Meta's memory seems not entirely trustworthy: she puts this visit in the winter (late autumn) of 1858-9, saying she thinks it lasted for thirteen weeks; whereas Mrs. Gaskell affirmed she left Heidelberg on 6 December 1858, having been there over nine weeks (*Gaskell-Norton Letters*, ed. Whitehill, pp. 34, 77, 79); furthermore she not only misdates her mother's Rhineland tour of 1841 as 1839 or 1840, but also states, erroneously, that Mrs. Gaskell stayed in Germany on only two occasions, yet she was, for example, again at Heidelberg in the summer of 1860 (*Gaskell-Norton Letters*, ed. Whitehill, p. 63). The relevant passage from Meta's letter (slightly longer than the fragment in the Brotherton Collection) is quite accurately quoted in Shorter, ed. *Novels and Tales*, VIII (1913), pp. x-xi; a briefer but fairly exact quotation is given by Miss Rubenius (*The Woman Question in Mrs. Gaskell's Life and Works*, pp. 78-79), though she (*op. cit.*, p. 78, fn. 3) implies there is no MS in the Brotherton Collection. We may note that Mlle (Ida or Anna) Mohl, writing from Heidelberg on [Friday] 1 October [1858] to (probably) Julius Mohl, her uncle, mentioned that Mrs. Gaskell had been there since Sunday [26 September] and been established in lodgings for two days (the relevant extract having been made by Miss Jane Revere Coolidge—subsequently Mrs. Whitehill—before the destruction of the Mohl letters during World War II); of the delights of her second (1860) Heidelberg holiday Mrs. Gaskell wrote in a letter of 14 December 1860 to the Rev. Edward Everett Hale (owned by his grand-daughter, Miss Nancy Hale, and deposited in the Sophia Smith Collection at the Smith College Library): other pertinent references to these respective Heidelberg sojourns include *G.L.*, Nos. 401, 403-405a, 418, 421, 444, 485; 465, 472a-475a, 476, 480.

[4] Now in the archives of Sir John Murray, this letter (*G.L.*, No. 501) is given [?1862] for the year of its date by Chapple and Pollard.

Gaskell liked to publish her best work in *The Cornhill*[5], one
might expect this tale to possess some merit—nor are such
expectations disappointed.

With the narrator she achieved a notable success. Although
he explicitly states that his part is 'little more than that of a
sympathising spectator'[6] and that, having himself little to do with
the story, his function is only to 'name . . . things, and repeat
. . . conversations,'[7] he is something more than a camera. As
well as observing, he also comments on, and mentally participates
in, the action.

In order that he may become intimate with the Heppenheim
inn-servant, Thekla, and so learn her love-secrets, Mrs. Gaskell
has to obtain for him a privileged position. This she does by the
happy expedient of making him fall ill during his travels, and
have as his chief nurse the kind, hard-working maid. Miss Hopkins[8] has implied that it is a flaw for the narrator to have to
intrude upon the girl's privacy so that the reader can discover the
reason for her distress; but in truth the narrator's behaviour
appears the most normal thing in the world. Having noticed the
servant's sobbing and looks of sadness[9], and having seen her
with a letter that apparently caused tears[10], he had his curiosity
quite naturally aroused; added to which was his own morbid condition[11], the result of long illness. In such a context one can
readily accept what Mrs. Gaskell makes him say concerning the
circumstances leading up to his enquiry about the letter.

> I became like a spoilt child in my recovery: every one whom I
> saw for the time being was thinking only of me, so it was perhaps
> no wonder that I became my sole object of thought; and at last
> the gratification of my curiosity about this letter seemed to me
> a duty that I owed to myself.[12]

The background (in which we may include the narrator) to
Thekla's personal history is rendered entirely convincing. Dr.
Adolphus Ward has remarked upon 'this singularly truthful little

5 Hopkins, *Elizabeth Gaskell*, p. 155.
6 *Works*, VII, 363.
7 *Works*, VII, 369.
8 *Elizabeth Gaskell*, p. 277.
9 *Works*, VII, 367.
10 *Works*, VII, 371.
11 *Works*, VII, 365, 367.
12 *Works*, VII, 372.

picture of real life'[13] which 'bears a striking testimony to Mrs. Gaskell's extraordinary quickness and accuracy of observation.'[14] The identity of the narrator—an Oxonian touring Germany, prior to commencing his study of the law—is persuasively established at the outset. Mrs. Gaskell had herself, during her travels, most probably met models for this character—such as, for example, Charles B. P. Bosanquet, a Balliol man and a pupil of Jowett's[15], whom she encountered at Heidelberg in 1858 before the commencement of his legal studies in the following year[16]. Perhaps what most forcefully invests the narrator with credibility is the graphic account of his mental state on recovering from fever[17]; there is, for instance, the acute sensitivity described in the following extract.

> She [the landlord's sister] meant to do everything kindly, I am sure; but a sick-room was not her place; by a thousand little maladroitnesses she fidgeted me past bearing: her shoes creaked, her dress rustled; she asked me questions about myself which it irritated me to answer; she congratulated me on being so much better, while I was faint for want of food which she delayed giving me, in order to talk.[18]

Much of this attention to *minutiae* must have come from the author's own experience, if not as a patient then as a sympathetic nurse. Besides attending her children in their sickness (especially her son, whose death was caused by scarlet fever, contracted from his sister), she watched over Mrs. Lumb during her aunt's last illness[19]. The reader of *Ruth* will recall that there too the rustling of a woman's dress was mentioned as something which should not have been heard in a sick-room[20].

With the more general setting Mrs. Gaskell succeeds at two levels: the realistic and the idyllic. Localizing detail is abundantly present; even where Dr. Adolphus Ward claims to have detected a historical error, Mrs. Gaskell's accuracy can be vin-

---

[13] Ward, ed. *Works,* VII, p. xxxii.
[14] Ward, ed. *Works,* VII, p. xxxii.
[15] *Gaskell-Norton Letters,* ed. Whitehill, p. 77: *G.L.,* No. 485.
[16] *Gaskell-Norton Letters,* ed. Whitehill, pp. 77, 79: *G.L.,* No. 485—see too *G.L.,* No. 405.
[17] *Works,* VII, 365-368.
[18] *Works,* VII, 368.
[19] *"My Diary"*, pp. 29-30; and *G.L.,* No. 5.
[20] *Works,* III, 82.

dicated[21]. Thus one finds information about a German girl's bridal contribution (household linen and hardware)[22], as well as references[23] to the legalities, customs, and usages of grape-growing and harvesting; a police requirement is mentioned[24]; and we are told 'there are no enclosures along the Bergstrasse'[25]—an observation typical of the grand-daughter of Samuel Holland, the Cheshire farmer. On the other hand Mrs. Gaskell does not neglect the poetic aspect of the countryside, expressed in her bucolic treatment of the vintage[26], an annual festival at once Christian and pagan in its associations. Both by reason of its quasi-archetypal significance and also because it is echoed in *Cousin Phillis*[27]—the English idyll with which 'Six Weeks at Heppenheim' has some affinities—, we shall quote from this description of a traditional harvest scene.

> . . . I could see the men and women on the hill-side drawing to
> a centre, and all stand round the pastor, bare-headed, for a
> minute or so. I guessed that some words of holy thanksgiving
> were being said, and I wished that I had stayed to hear them,
> and mark my especial gratitude for having been spared to see
> that day. Then I heard the distant voices, the deep tones of the
> men, the shriller pipes of women and children, join in the Ger-
> man harvest-hymn, which is generally sung on such occas-
> ions;* . . . [28]

This *milieu,* both concretely and poetically realized, provides the context for Thekla's tale. One may venture the generalization that, in many of Mrs. Gaskell's stories, the setting confers plausibility on the action; we can believe in the incidents because the incidentals are so true to life. The theme of a good woman devoted to, and ready to make sacrifices for, a ne'er-do-well is not uncommon in her work, although usually (as in *The*

---

[21] Ward (ed. *Works,* VII, p. xxxii) remarks that Herr Müller gave his sovereign an inferior title—Duke instead of Grand Duke (*The Cornhill Magazine,* V, 580)—which he corrects in his edition (*Works,* VII, 393); however Mrs. Gaskell was well aware of the correct title, which she had already mentioned (*The Cornhill Magazine,* V, 572; *Works,* VII, 380).

[22] *Works,* VII, 376-377.

[23] *Works,* VII, 380-381, 392-393, 395-398.

[24] *Works,* VII, 389.

[25] *Works,* VII, 393.

[26] *Works,* VII, 395-400.

[27] *Works,* VII, 15.

[28] *Works,* VII, 398: the text of the hymn is given in an authorial foot-note.

Moorland Cottage) they are related by blood. In 'Six Weeks at Heppenheim', however, Thekla is portrayed as having deep affection for a childhood friend, who to impartial eyes is clearly unworthy of her. When she eventually discovers his true character, she wonders whether, even so, she is not morally bound to marry him; but the narrator successfully persuades her against such a course. All this Mrs. Gaskell manages extremely well, bringing out the touch of humour implicit both in the young narrator's acting as a sort of father confessor[29] and in his romantic scheme[30] to effect a happy union between the pair. At the same time she makes convincing the successive mental states of the heroine—unable to distinguish true sentiment from superficial, egotistical sentimentality[31]; drawn by pity to a man bereft of general regard and esteem[32]; half-wishing to be convinced despite herself that she should not leave the inn[33]; unconsciously feeling that her rejection of the landlord's ill-timed marriage-offer was not altogether wise[34].

It is the ending which one would criticize, if one wished to find fault with Mrs. Gaskell's invention. Plainly her problem was to find a way of bringing together Thekla and Fritz Müller (the landlord). This would in itself form a fitting conclusion; but the means whereby it is effected—the illness of little Max Müller, whom Thekla nurses back to health[35]—appears contrived. This improvised use of a favourite *motif* is disconcerting; for it is on a lower artistic level than what has gone before. Unlike little Walter (of 'Mr. Harrison's Confessions'[36]), Max does recover; but his sickness seems so obviously a device that our feelings are in no way engaged. However it would be ungenerous to linger over the only major defect in this charming pastoral.

As regards a possible factual starting-point, one can say two things. Firstly Mrs. Gaskell may well have heard a tale along these lines during her German holidays; she always enjoyed talking with people and, as Professor Whitfield remarks, 'it is

[29] *Works*, VII, 374.
[30] *Works*, VII, 383-384.
[31] *Works*, VII, 377.
[32] *Works*, VII, 391.
[33] *Works*, VII, 389-390.
[34] *Works*, VII, 393-394.
[35] *Works*, VII, 399-402.
[36] *Works*, V, 434-436.

interesting to note that she knew a girl named Thekla.'[37] Even more relevant is the fact that Mrs. Gaskell apparently set out for Heidelberg "to take/ Meta abroad out of the clatter/ of tongues consequent on her/ breaking off her engagement./"[38] Hence

[37] Whitfield, *Mrs Gaskell*, p. 64. This Thekla was, however, the very lovely and elegant nineteen-year-old daughter of Frau von Pickford; she is mentioned by Mrs. Gaskell in a letter, describing the 1841 Rhineland tour, written to her sister-in-law, Mrs. Charles Holland (Eliza Gaskell), one Monday morning [1841]. Miss Hopkins (*Elizabeth Gaskell*, pp. 64-65) quotes—fairly accurately—from this letter (the incomplete MS being in the Gaskell Section, Brotherton Collection, Leeds University Library); but, though including an extract about Frau von Pickford, she has no quotation concerning the lady's daughter. Chapple and Pollard note August 1841 as the date for this letter (*G.L.*, No. 15) given in complete copies which, once owned by Mr. J. T. Lancaster, belong to the present writer.

[38] Quoted by Miss Rubenius (*The Woman Question in Mrs. Gaskell's Life and Works*, p. 79) from a copy of an undated letter by Mrs. Gaskell to Mrs. Nancy Robson, now in the Gaskell Section, Brotherton Collection, Leeds University Library); and checked against the original [Sunday (post 5—possibly 6—February) 1859] letter in the Yale University Library—MS Vault Sect. 16. In 1857 Meta became engaged to Captain Hill, an officer in the Indian Army; the next year she broke with him. The family maintained a natural reticence about this affair, so details are difficult to come by; but we shall subsequently, whenever appropriate, refer to the subject. Here we may fill in some *lacunae*, the result of Mrs. Jane Revere Whitehill's tactful editing of Mrs. Gaskell's letters to Charles Eliot Norton (deposited in the Harvard University Library). According to a passage in Mrs. Gaskell's letter of 28 September 1857—unprinted, though the omission is indicated, by Mrs. Whitehill (ed. *Gaskell-Norton Letters*, p. 7)—Captain Hill had left the Gaskells on 24 August, and Meta was to go out in October, November or December 1858 to marry him at Alexandria; the couple were to live in India till the captain became eligible for a pension of £200 p.a. in May 1862, when it was hoped that (not unlike Captain Brown in *Cranford*) he would get an appointment as a manager of railways or an inspector of railroads. From Mrs. Gaskell's letter of Monday [7] December [1857]—the passage is omitted in Whitehill, ed. *Gaskell-Norton Letters*, p. 17—we learn that Captain Hill was in command of a regiment of sappers and miners. However on Monday 10 May [1858] Mrs. Gaskell wrote to Norton (the passage being omitted in Whitehill, ed. *Gaskell-Norton Letters*, p. 23) that Meta had heard things about Hill from his sisters which had made her change her opinion about his character so much that she would sever their engagement unless—which seemed impossible—he could furnish a satisfactory explanation; Meta herself, Mrs. Gaskell said, was far from well, though more from disappointment in the captain's character than from wounded affection. After Meta ended their relationship, Captain Hill became engaged to a certain Miss Matilda Wilson. He was to marry her in England in April 1861, according to Mrs. Gaskell's letter of 10 December 1860 (again the passage is omitted in Whitehill, ed. *Gaskell-Norton Letters*, p. 73), and Meta, wishing to avoid an encounter, would pay no London visits then. The last relevant passage omitted by Mrs. Whitehill (ed. *Gaskell-Norton*

Thekla's predicament as to whether or not to marry her first love could, as Miss Rubenius implies[39], find a parallel in the family history of the Gaskells themselves.

Letters, p. 78) appears in Mrs. Gaskell's letter of 16 April 1861; there we read that the earnest and religious Mr. Bosanquet had brought back some of Meta's faith in *man*kind, lost in consequence of discovering Hill's nature. These letters respectively occur as *G.L.*, Nos. 414 (dated [February 1859] by Chapple and Pollard), 374, 384, 394 (concluded on Friday 14 May [1858]), 480, 485.

[39] Rubenius, *The Woman Question in Mrs. Gaskell's Life and Works*, pp. 79-80.

CHAPTER VIII

A DARK NIGHT'S WORK (1863) TO 'CROWLEY CASTLE' (1863 : 1906)

SECTION I

A Dark Night's Work (1863)

Between 24 January and 21 March 1863 'A Dark Night's Work' came out in *All the Year Round*[1] : Dickens supplied the 'Dark' of the title[2] which, though displeasing to the author[3], Smith retained when his firm published the story separately in the same year[4]. Probably Dickens had already seen most of the manuscript as early as 30 April 1862[5], the author then being paid

---

[1] VIII, 457-465, 481-485, 505-510, 529-533, 553-562; IX, 1-7, 25-32, 49-57, 73-84.

[2] *The Letters of Charles Dickens,* ed. Dexter, III, 320: letter from Dickens to Wills, written in Paris on 21 November 1862. 'The title of it is " A Night's/ Work," ' wrote Mrs. Gaskell on 30 September [1862] to an American firm (possibly Harper & Brothers, who published the New York edition in 1863)—the relevant letter (*G.L.,* No. 518) being in the Parrish Collection at the Princeton University Library.

[3] I said when I saw that/ he had gone right against my// distinct/ desire, & called/ a night's work/ a *dark* night[']s/ work, that I w^d/ never publish/ with him [Smith] again;/ . . . '—extract from a letter by Mrs. Gaskell to her daughter, Marianne, written one Monday evening [1 June 1863]. This letter is in the possession of Marianne's grand-daughter, Mrs. Margaret Trevor Jones, and appears as *G.L.,* No. 524; in their Appendix F Chapple and Pollard record a £200 receipt of 6 March 1863 for the entire copyright of *A Night's Work* [*sic*], so presumably Smith was free to use any title he chose.

[4] Elizabeth Cleghorn Gaskell, *A Dark Night's Work,* London: Smith, Elder and Co., 1863. On 25 April 1863 this book was advertized as ready in *The Athenaeum Journal of Literature, Science, and the Fine Arts,* No. 1852, p. 564.

[5] By this date Dickens had ' the entire manuscript under his eye ', according to Miss Hopkins—' Dickens and Mrs. Gaskell ', *The Huntington Library Quarterly,* IX (1946), 381; *Elizabeth Gaskell,* p. 153. However she misinterpreted her (limited) evidence. In an [October 1862] letter to George Smith, Mrs. Gaskell speaks of having to write an ending for a (probably) one-volume work (half-finished four years before); she mentions she had that spring sent her incomplete MS to *All the Year Round,* been paid for it, though informed the story would not be immediately required. Of this letter the relevant fragment (whose ending overlaps with the beginning of an extract from the same letter given in Ward, ed. *Works,* I, pp. xxxvii-xxxviii) is in the archives of Sir John Murray, as are two letters to Smith, of 23 December [1859] and of Tuesday 27 December [1859], which may also refer to *A Dark Night's Work*; the former mentions a story, good enough for *Household Words* [*sic*] but not for *The Cornhill Magazine,* of which 120 pages had been

(perhaps) £150[6]; but, since this tale was to open all the nine numbers in which it appeared, the long interval between payment and publication was dictated by editorial policy (Mrs. Gaskell's predecessor in the privileged opening position being Wilkie Collins, whose 'No Name' ended on 17 January)[7].

Mrs. Gaskell's compositions often have a personal or historical point of departure: here the factual basis is, according to Mrs. Chadwick[8], a Knutsford murder recorded by the Rev. Henry Green[9]. As she indicates, there are certain similarities between this local killing and what is presented in the story. In both accounts some one in the legal profession is done to death and his body buried, the deed remaining undiscovered for many years;

---

written for a year and a half. The probability that *A Dark Night's Work* was begun (late) in 1858 is increased by a passage—incompletely summarized by Mrs. Whitehill (ed. *Gaskell-Norton Letters*, pp. 30-31) —from Mrs. Gaskell's letter to Norton of 9 March [1859]. The author there states that a story she intended to fill forty manuscript pages seemed likely to occupy two hundred, of which over half were written: Mrs. Whitehill (ed. *Gaskell-Norton Letters*, p. 31, fn. 1) suggests that this story may have been *Lois the Witch*; yet it seems safe to reject her tentative identification since the manuscript of *Lois the Witch* is much shorter, occupying 117 pages (on 118 folios, including the ornamental water-colour title-page, in the Harvard University Library— fMS Eng 1010). References to *A Dark Night's Work* may be found in *The Letters of Charles Dickens*, ed. Dexter, III, 100 (possible), 320, 335, 337, 339: letters to Wills of 28 April 1859, 21 November 1862, 18 January 1863, 19 January 1863, 1 February 1863. The afore-mentioned letters by Mrs. Gaskell appear respectively as *G.L.*, Nos. 517 (dated [?Late September 1862] by Chapple and Pollard), 451a, 452, 418; see too No. 430.

[6] Her [incomplete *A Dark Night's Work*] manuscript, for which £150 had been offered, reached London on Monday [28 April 1862]—according to what Mrs. Gaskell wrote to Marianne on Thursday [1 May 1862] in a letter, begun on (apparently) Wednesday [30 April 1862] and postmarked 4 and 5 May 1862, in the Gaskell Section, Brotherton Collection, Leeds University Library. The letter occurs as *G.L.*, No. 505, though Chapple and Pollard do not take Mrs. Gaskell's words as referring to this story.

[7] From the fragment of Mrs. Gaskell's [October 1862] letter to George Smith (in the archives of Sir John Murray) it seems that originally Mrs. Gaskell was led to believe her story would follow one then being treated for to succeed 'No Name', but that—these negotiations apparently coming to nothing—she was later told it would be desirable for her conclusion to be ready by the end of the month. As has been noted, this letter (*G.L.*, No. 517) is dated [?Late September 1862] by Chapple and Pollard.

[8] *Mrs. Gaskell*, pp. 284-285.

[9] *Knutsford, Its Traditions and History: with Reminiscences, Anecdotes, and Notices of the Neighbourhood*, pp. 93-94.

nevertheless there are numerous differences of detail. Perhaps what most strongly attracted the novelist was that the historical murderer, conscience-stricken near his victim's hidden grave, once came close to revealing his guilt by declaring he could see the dead man : in the end he made a death-bed confession. The theme of remorse may have been for Mrs. Gaskell the main interest of the crime[10]. Certainly her own fictional treatment is psychological rather than detective-criminal in its emphasis—we know all the facts about Dunster's death, our attention is rather directed upon its causes and consequences.

Mrs. Gaskell's presentation of Mr. Wilkins, the Hamley attorney, is a study in moral degeneration; its chief merit lies in putting the 'murderer' (the killing was accidental) squarely within a concrete *milieu*. We are shown how the man's character was largely the product of his past and the social forces to which he was subjected. Hamley, the county town where Mr. Wilkins was brought up, is generally held[11] to be Knutsford under yet another guise; but the treatment is different from that found in *Cranford* : closer affinities are rather with Barford of 'The Squire's Story' and Hollingford of *Wives and Daughters*. Mrs. Gaskell presents a convincing picture of this rural society, paying special attention to the relations between a professional man and a condescending squirearchy. It was his refusal to accept the traditional network of due deference which brought about the solicitor's ruin. The way in which Mrs. Gaskell handles such a theme suggests that, in some respects, she was the feminine counterpart to Trollope in Victorian fiction.

The customary behaviour of a respectable country attorney is well illustrated by the following sentence, which tells how Mr. Wilkins senior was wont to conduct himself towards the local gentry.

> He visited among them in a way which no mere lawyer had ever done before; dined at their tables—he alone, not accompanied by his wife, be it observed; rode to the meet occasion-

---

[10] Writing (probably) about this story on 9 March [1859], when it was approximately half-finished, Mrs. Gaskell told Norton that, though the plot was too melodramatic, she had grown interested in the tale and could not ' put it aside.' The relevant passage is not printed, though it is briefly summarized, in Whitehill, ed. *Gaskell-Norton Letters*, pp. 30-31. The letter appears as *G.L.*, No. 418.

[11] By, for example, Mrs. Chadwick (*Mrs. Gaskell*, p. 35), Miss ffrench (*Mrs. Gaskell*, pp. 80-81), and Miss Hopkins (*Elizabeth Gaskell*, p. 13).

ally, as if by accident, although he was as well mounted as any
squire among them, and was often persuaded (after a little
coquetting about "professional engagements," and "being wanted at the office") to have a run with his clients; nay, once
or twice he forgot his usual caution, was first in at the death,
and rode home with the brush.[12]

In other words, the elder Mr. Wilkins, recognizing that, for a
professional man, he was accorded unusual favours, enjoyed
without abusing this rather privileged position. Careful not to
overstep the mark, he never introduced his wife into a circle to
which she could not personally aspire[13], and his own acceptance
he duly acknowledged by a respectful, slightly apologetic, manner.

The first part of *A Dark Night's Work* traces his son's refusal
to comply with such conventions. By deft strokes, Mrs. Gaskell
indicates how Edward Wilkins found himself out of harmony
with the society about him. All hopes to practise at the bar had,
for financial reasons, to be abandoned[14]; his ambition to go to
Christ Church had likewise to be relinquished[15]. On his return
from a Continental tour, he found that the squires looked as-
kance at him, while their 'heirs (whom he had licked at Eton)
called him an upstart behind his back.'[16] When he married the
penniless, but aristocratic, Miss Lamotte, her uncle, even in the
act of consenting, had some bitter and insolent things to say[17].
His wife's cousins, in spite of borrowing his horses and drinking
his wine, 'caught their father's habit of sneering at his profession.'[18] Mr. Wilkins, who felt fitted to shine in society, was led
by such treatment to indulgence in the current sensuality ('Socia-
bility in that county at that time meant conviviality.'[19]). Thereafter it was a matter of progressive deterioration. He aped the

[12] *Works*, VII, 404.
[13] The specifically *social* implications are missed if one conjectures
that Mrs. Gaskell had a 'habit of her husband in mind when she remarked on the slight to Mrs. Wilkins in *A Dark Night's Work*' (Rubenius, *The Woman Question in Mrs. Gaskell's Life and Works*, p. 26,
fn. 1). Neither the authoress nor Mrs. Wilkins would have considered
such conduct in any way a slight.
[14] *Works*, VII, 405.
[15] *Works*, VII, 405.
[16] *Works*, VII, 408.
[17] *Works*, VII, 409-410.
[18] *Works*, VII, 410.
[19] *Works*, VII, 410.

habits of the squires, wasting time in hunting and field-sports which should have been devoted to legal concerns[20]; he claimed the right to bear arms (a costly privilege)[21], and set up a brougham where his father had been content with a mere gig[22]; his nature was coarsened[23], and heavy drinking became habitual[24]. Hence extravagance and conviviality, which began as attempts to secure a status above that conferred by birth and profession, eventually became for Mr. Wilkins ends in themselves : his dissatisfaction with the local social system resulted in evils worse than those of the people he affected to despise. Mrs. Gaskell supplies an astute analysis of the situation. She appreciated the difficulties of a talented man in a squirearchical and ossified community; but at the same time she realized that, once ethical values were jettisoned in the attempt to obtain a higher position, the latter state was worse than the former. The Hamley way of life may be exemplified with two quotations, which of themselves testify to the novelist's acute observations of (Cheshire) society, observations unconsciously made by one bred in the traditions described. The first concerns the Hamley assembly-rooms, and it was most likely suggested by personal memories of the *George* at Knutsford; we may note too with what sympathetic understanding the sentiments of Mr. Wilkins are rendered.

> Into those choice and mysterious precincts no town's person was ever allowed to enter; no professional man might set his foot therein; no infantry officer saw the interior of that ball or that card room. The old original subscribers would fain have had a man prove his sixteen quarterings before he might make his bow to the queen of the night; but the old original founders of the Hamley assemblies were dropping off; minuets had vanished with them, country dances had died away, quadrilles were in high vogue—nay, one or two of the high magnates of ——shire were trying to introduce waltzing (as they had seen it in London, where it had come in with the visit of the Allied sovereigns), when Edward Wilkins made his *début* on these boards. He had been at many splendid assemblies abroad; but still the little old ball-room attached to the George Inn in his native town was to him a place grander and more awful than the most magnificent saloons he had seen in Paris or Rome.[25]

The second passage reveals its author's appreciation of those

---

20 *Works*, VII, 420-421.
21 *Works*, VII, 421-422.
22 *Works*, VII, 422.
23 *Works*, VII, 435.
24 *Works*, VII, 435, 452, 456.
25 *Works*, VII, 406-407.

obligations, acknowledged as matters of course by the gentry, which, though often trivial in nature, were nonetheless preferable to the disdainful insolence of onlookers who professed to be above such things.

> . . . most of his associates had their duties to do, and did them with a heart and a will, in the hours when he was not in their company. Yes! I call them duties, though some of them might be self-imposed and purely social; they were engagements they had entered into, either tacitly or with words, and that they fulfilled. From Mr. Hetherington, the Master of the Hounds, who was up at—no one knows what hour, to go down to the kennel and see that the men did their work well and thoroughly, to stern old Sir Lionel Playfair, the upright magistrate, the thoughtful, conscientious landlord—they did their work according to their lights; there were few laggards among those with whom Mr. Wilkins associated in the field or at the dinner table. . . . Only Mr. Wilkins, dissatisfied with his position, neglected to fulfil the duties thereof. He imitated the pleasures, and longed for the fancied leisure of those about him; leisure that he imagined would be so much more valuable in the hands of a man like himself, full of intellectual tastes and accomplishments, than frittered away by dull boors of untravelled, uncultivated squires—whose company, however, be it said by the way, he never refused.[26]

To extricate himself from the business difficulties to which his professional neglect had given rise, Mr. Wilkins was compelled to engage a clerk[27], whom he had later to admit into full partnership[28]. It is this clerk, Dunster by name, who is killed. His death is largely accidental, being the unforeseen result of an angry blow[29]; yet some preparation was necessary, for the quarrel had to seem probable. Mr. Wilkins' moral decline does, to be sure, offer a general cause; but Mrs. Gaskell stresses more particularly his antipathy towards Dunster. Characteristically she shows him irritated by apparent trifles, just those very things which, in daily intercourse, would prove most disturbing.

> He rather cherished than repressed his nervous repugnance to the harsh measured tones of Mr. Dunster's voice; the latter spoke with a provincial twang which grated on his employer's sensitive ear. He was annoyed at a certain green coat which his new clerk brought with him, and he watched its increasing shabbiness with a sort of childish pleasure. But by-and-by Mr.

[26] *Works,* VII, 435.
[27] *Works,* VII, 421.
[28] *Works,* VII, 436-437.
[29] *Works,* VII, 462.

Wilkins found out that, from some perversity of taste, Mr.
Dunster always had his coats, Sunday and working-day, made
of this obnoxious colour; and this knowledge did not diminish
his secret irritation.[30]

Furthermore Dunster's efficiency and punctuality were a kind
of standing rebuke to Mr. Wilkins[31], and served to add fuel to
his animosity. His dislike of Dunster was shared by his daughter,
Ellinor[32], and his coachman, Dixon[33]. When, therefore, the
clerk mysteriously vanished, there was no one to speak a good
word for him[34]; indeed the gossip which his strange disappearance occasioned recalls the subject matter of Mrs. Gaskell's own
article on this topic.

> . . . she [Miss Munro, Ellinor's governess] gave Ralph the
> account of the event universally received and believed in by
> the people of Hamley. How Mr. Dunster had never been liked
> by any one; how everybody remembered that he could never
> look them straight in the face; how he always seemed to be
> hiding something that he did not want to have known; how
> he had drawn a large sum (exact quantity unknown) out of
> the county-bank only the day before he left Hamley, doubtless
> in preparation for his escape; how . . . [35]

Whereas the first third of the novel prepares for Dunster's
death, the remainder works out its consequences. These may be
roughly classified as the immediate effects of the crime upon
those most concerned and the later events resulting from the
discovery of the body—a discovery which, we may note, came
about through the construction of a railway (the Knutsford line
was opened on 12 May 1862[36]).

After Mr. Wilkins had accidentally killed Dunster, he, his
daughter, and Dixon disposed of the corpse, and thenceforth
found themselves bound together in a conspiracy of silence. Both

[30] *Works*, VII, 423. Mrs. Gaskell, we may notice, mentioned the 'detest-
able bottle green coats' formerly worn by Francis William Newman, such
coats in her view never showing off a man, in a letter to Eliza Fox written
one Sunday evening (a copy of part of which being in the Gaskell Section,
Brotherton Collection, Leeds University Library): this letter (*G.L.*, No. 53)
is dated [25 November 1849] by Chapple and Pollard, who designate its
recipient as ?Eliza Fox.
[31] *Works*, VII, 422-423.
[32] *Works*, VII, 427, 442, 458.
[33] *Works*, VII, 427, 463, 556-557.
[34] *Works*, VII, 474-475.
[35] *Works*, VII, 486.
[36] Payne, *Mrs. Gaskell and Knutsford*, 1905, p. 12, fn. 1.

Ellinor[37] and her father[38] embarked on courses of deceit, entailing conscious efforts to act in a natural manner (a variation on Mrs. Gaskell's favourite lie *motif*); and a common guilty secret 'made their mutual presence a burdensome anxiety to each.'[39] Dixon also suffered, as his own forceful idiom makes plain.

> " . . . It has aged me above a bit. All my fifty years afore were but as a forenoon of child's play to that night. Measter, too—I could a-bear a good deal; but measter cuts through the stable-yard, and past me, wi'out a word, as if I was poison, or a stinking foumart. . . . "[40]

Nor are the consequences of the crime merely psychological. The shadow of this terrible concealment brings on Ellinor's illness[41], further increases her father's tendency to drink[42], and is ultimately responsible for the breaking-off of her engagement to an up-and-coming young lawyer, Ralph Corbet[43].

When, some eighteen years later[44], the body is discovered, Dixon is sentenced to death for murder, but saved through Ellinor's intervention. Thus, after an interval of comparative peace—though the memory haunted both their minds—a second period of intense anguish begins. The story does, however, end on a note of serenity.

Between the murder in *A Dark Night's Work* and that in *Mary Barton* there are certain resemblances, over which it is well

---

[37] *Works*, VII, 467.
[38] *Works*, VII, 473.
[39] *Works*, VII, 473.
[40] *Works*, VII, 480.
[41] *Works*, VII, 474-479.
[42] *Works*, VII, 484.
[43] *Works*, VII, 511-512.
[44] Apparently (*Works*, VII, 455, 589)—the murder took place in 1829 (*Works*, VII, 533) and the body was found *more than* fifteen years afterwards (*Works*, VII, 532). However Mrs. Gaskell's chronology was not especially accurate since, as Miss Rubenius remarks, 'Miss Munro . . . remains forty years old for a considerable period' (*The Woman Question in Mrs. Gaskell's Life and Works*, p. 137, fn. 3—e.g. *Works*, VII, 415: cont. 518). Likewise the chronology of Ellinor's return to England is confusing in that a day (Wednesday) seems to have been completely passed over (*Works*, VII, 555: cont. 559-561). One can also discover dating-errors in the account of her Italian holiday—for instance, although March has arrived (*Works*, VII, 548), the date is 27 February (*Works*, VII, 555). Another incongruity arises from the fact that Dunster had 'a provincial twang' (*Works*, VII, 423), although he had been bred in London and worked there before going to Hamley (*Works*, VII, 478, 421).

to pause; for in both books Mrs. Gaskell's invention seems to
have expressed itself along similar lines. Like John Barton, Edward Wilkins declines physically as well as mentally after the
crime; like Mary Barton, his daughter shows courage and presence of mind[45] on his behalf; wrongly accused of murder, both
Jem Wilson and Dixon[46] refuse to clear themselves—the one
because of his love, the other because of his loyalty—(as against
the former, so against the latter[47] is there strong circumstantial
evidence); in each case the heroine secures the prisoner's freedom,
since Mary's recalling Will for the trial leads to Jem's acquittal
and Ellinor's interview with the judge[48] ensures Dixon's pardon.
Although one finds many obvious differences, perhaps the point
chiefly to stress is that in both works the psychological effects of
moral evil are explored. On a smaller scale something of the
same sort occurs in *North and South,* where Margaret Hale,
after her brother had accidentally caused a railway-man's death,
is caught up in a web of deceit by protecting him. Indeed Ellin-
or's reflections on the baseness of deception and the virtues of
veracity[49] might very well have come from the heroine of *North
and South.*

Since we have mentioned *Mary Barton,* a book in which Mrs.
Gaskell several times offers authorial comment, it seems appropriate to remark that *A Dark Night's Work* contains more of such
explicit comment than had appeared in the stories immediately
preceding it. This aspect is illustrated by the following passage,
which has the additional interest of 'inverting' one of the main
themes in *Mary Barton*[50]. In her first novel Mrs. Gaskell's aim
was to make the wealthy realize what trials the poor had to
bear; in *North and South* she attempted to show how both
classes had their difficulties; here she stresses rather the worries
of the well-to-do.

---

[45] E.g. *Works,* VII, 471.
[46] *Works,* VII, 557, 567.
[47] *Works,* VII, 552, 557.
[48] *Works,* VII, 579-586.
[49] *Works,* VII, 477-478.
[50] Writing to Miss Ewart one Tuesday in 1848, Mrs. Gaskell made it
clear that in *Mary Barton* she had sought to represent the subject in the
light some workmen, as she knew from personal experience, considered
true, but that she dared not claim this to be the abstract, absolute
truth; she remarked that there was surely no harm in directing attention
to evils connected with the manufacturing system, adding, however, that

Some country people at work at the roadside, as the father and daughter passed along, stopped to admire their bright, happy looks; and one spoke of the hereditary handsomeness of the Wilkins family (for the old man, the present Mr. Wilkins's father, had been fine-looking in his drab breeches and gaiters, and with his usual assumption of a yeoman's dress). Another said it was easy for the rich to be handsome; they had always plenty to eat, and could ride when they were tired of walking, and had no care for the morrow to keep them from sleeping at nights. And, in sad acquiescence with their contrasted lot, the men went on with their hedging and ditching in silence.

And yet, if they had known—if the poor did know—the troubles and temptations of the rich; . . . Well, there was truth in the old heathen saying, "Let no man be envied till his death."[51]

If *A Dark Night's Work* has affinities with *Mary Barton*, it also possesses a literary kinship with *North and South*. The lie *motif* has been noticed; but more important is the parallel between Mr. Lennox (Margaret Hale's rejected suitor) and Mr. Corbet, who jilted Ellinor Wilkins. We have previously remarked upon Mrs. Gaskell's habit of portraying legal men in an unfavourable light. She generally stresses their calculating ambition, and indicates their lack of deep affections. Hence, even when in love, Ralph Corbet retains some capacity for a dispassionate assessment of the situation; he can, as it were, find time to look at things objectively, to make the rational decision in a cool hour. Mrs. Gaskell's reading of Corbet's character is one of the

---

she deeply felt the wickedness of exciting class against class which, if done by her, had been an unconscious sin. A copy of part of this letter is in Shorter and Symington, 'Correspondence, Articles & Notes Relating to Mrs. E. C. Gaskell. Transcripts', Vol. II, Section on *Mary Barton*—a typescript in the Gaskell Section, Brotherton Collection, Leeds University Library. Those best acquainted with how the poor thought and felt acknowledged the truth of the novel, which was what the author desired since evils once recognized were half-way to being cured: so Mrs. Gaskell informed her cousin, Edward Holland, in a letter (*G.L.*, No. 39a) of 13 January 1849—copies of which, once owned by Mr. J. T. Lancaster, belong to the present writer. The letter (*G.L.*, No. 36) to Miss Ewart, whom they identify as Mary Ewart, is dated [?Late 1848] by Chapple and Pollard; but their source is slightly less authoritative than the Shorter-Symington typescript, where weekday and year are given: a [pre December] dating may be conjectured; for internal evidence suggests this letter was written somewhat before that of Friday 7 [8] December 1848 to which (*G.L.*, No. 34) Chapple and Pollard make reference from it.

[51] *Works*, VII, 451.

best things in the story. While rarely explicitly condemning his behaviour, she insinuates the attitude she wishes the reader to assume by means of what she chooses to describe. On first introducing him, she mentions how Ralph induced his father to engage a special tutor; the logical approach he adopted suggests well enough the young man's temperament.

> The good-natured old squire was rather pressed for ready money; but, sooner than listen to an argument instead of taking his nap after dinner, he would have yielded anything. But this did not satisfy Ralph; his father's reason must be convinced of the desirability of the step, as well as his weak will give way.[52]

Numerous quotations could be supplied to demonstrate how Mrs. Gaskell implies that, fundamentally, Ralph is unworthy of Ellinor, even though, in the eyes of the world, his conduct is never immoral, only an instance of enlightened self-interest. The egotism implicit in such a mode of life comes out when he declines to take a cigar from Mr. Wilkins.

> "No! I never smoke." Mr. Corbet despised all these kinds of indulgences, and put a little severity into his refusal, but quite unintentionally; for, though he was thankful he was not as other men, he was not at all the person to trouble himself unnecessarily with their reformation.[53]

Perhaps some estimate of Corbet's prudential nature can be gathered by listing a few typical traits and incidents. He rebuked Ellinor for familiarity with the coachman[54]; he feared lest, if his engagement were widely known, this would militate against his reputation for wisdom[55]; he schemed to discover what dowry Ellinor might expect[56]; he endeavoured, but failed, to inculcate his *fiancée* with his own craving for success in life[57]; he inevitably sought for the baser motives in human behaviour[58]; a good conversationalist, he usually avoided topics which aroused deep

---

[52] *Works,* VII, 417.
[53] *Works,* VII, 438.
[54] *Works,* VII, 424: cf. Mr. Bellingham's displeasure with Ruth for a similar offence (*Works,* III, 48-49).
[55] *Works,* VII, 445.
[56] *Works,* VII, 446-447.
[57] *Works,* VII, 453-454.
[58] *Works,* VII, 491.

feelings[59]; treating people like 'human stepping-stones'[60], he only dined out where he might expect to gain materially thereby. Perhaps, however, Corbet's character is best indicated by a single phrase in the next extract. At bottom wishing, from reasons of expediency, to be quit of his engagement, he was provided with an excellent excuse to jilt Ellinor when Mr. Wilkins, much the worse for drink, behaved towards him in an ungentlemanly manner, and told him to leave the house.

> Ralph half turned to take him at his word, and go at once; but then he " gave Ellinor another chance," as he worded it in his thoughts; but it was in no spirit of conciliation that he said— " You've taken too much of that stuff, sir. You don't know what you're saying. If you did, I should leave your house at once, never to return."[61]

Taken in the whole context, that phrase about giving ' "Ellinor another chance" ' is the most telling condemnation of Corbet. It illustrates how truly Mrs. Gaskell, like many authoresses, could observe weaknesses in masculine morality.

Thereafter Corbet rises in his profession, and later makes a prudent marriage—though years of calculated endeavour have left their mark[62]. The first time Ellinor sees him after his wedding, at which she had been a secret witness[63], is for a moment from a carriage window[64], much in the manner that Margaret Hale, when passing through London, caught a glimpse of Henry Lennox[65]. The last occasion on which they meet is on professional terms (here too one finds some slight similarity to *North and South*); for Ellinor seeks his help in securing a pardon for Dixon. Mrs. Gaskell manages this final interview with considerable delicacy : there is the humour of an awkward situation, the embarrassed judge feeling obliged to insist that Ellinor should meet his wife, yet relieved when she declines[66]—he being not at all anxious for Lady Corbet to know his caller's identity[67]. There is, too, the touch of pathos.

[59] *Works*, VII, 493.
[60] *Works*, VII, 499.
[61] *Works*, VII, 506.
[62] *Works*, VII, 530.
[63] *Works*, VII, 530-532.
[64] *Works*, VII, 546.
[65] *Works*, IV, 64.
[66] *Works*, VII, 581.
[67] *Works*, VII, 586.

> Married judge though he was, he was not sure if she had not more charms for him still in her sorrow and her shabbiness than the handsome stately wife in the next room, whose looks had not been of the pleasantest when he left her a few minutes before. He sighed a little regretfully, as Ellinor went away. He had obtained the position he had struggled for, and sacrificed for; but now he could not help wishing that the slaughtered creature laid on the shrine of his ambition were alive again.[68]

In a sense the contrast to Ralph Corbet is supplied by Canon Livingstone, the clergyman who assists Ellinor on her return to England at the time of Dixon's trial, and whom she eventually marries. Miss ffrench is doubtless right in speaking of 'a flat note of anti-climax in the introduction of the clerical hero'[69]— if, instead of ' introduction ', one reads ' re-introduction '; for the first appearance of Mr. (as he then was) Livingstone produces a delightfully comic effect. What could be better than Mrs. Gaskell's mildly ironic description of his post-prandial romanticizing on the Victorian ideal of domestic felicity?

> He had thought her very pretty and agreeable during dinner; but after dinner he considered her bewitching, irresistible. He dreamed of her all night, and wakened up the next morning to a calculation of how far his income would allow him to furnish his pretty new parsonage with that crowning blessing, a wife. For a day or two he did up little sums, and sighed, and thought of Ellinor, her face listening with admiring interest to his sermons, her arm passed into his as they went together round the parish; her sweet voice instructing classes in his schools—turn where he would, in his imagination Ellinor's presence rose up before him.[70]

After this skit on masculine vanity, one feels slightly disappointed that, in the end, Ellinor should become the angel in the canon's house[71].

Dickens, presumably in a fit of editorial petulence, once remarked that he wished "the fair Ellinor were not so horribly like Mrs. Gaskell!"[72] What exactly he meant by such a remark

---

[68] *Works*, VII, 585.
[69] ffrench, *Mrs. Gaskell*, p. 93.
[70] *Works*, VII, 456.
[71] *Works*, VII, 589-590.
[72] Quoted, from a letter of 1 February 1863 to Wills (now in the Huntington Library), by Miss Hopkins—' Dickens and Mrs. Gaskell ', *The Huntington Library Quarterly*, IX (1946), 380; *Elizabeth Gaskell*, p. 152.

is not easy to say. Miss Hopkins[73] has suggested he had in mind the heroine's firmness of purpose (in other words, obstinacy); if so, he was not strictly accurate. Certainly Ellinor has affinities with the resolute heroines of Mrs. Gaskell's other novels: but probably her most outstanding quality is loyalty, first to her father, then to Dixon. It is, however, not of her that one would first think when considering the merits of *A Dark Night's Work*. Although she provides the continuous thread of the narrative, there is little to say about the drawing of her character; her part is, on the whole, that of a sufferer rather than an initiator of events. Yet, even so, Mrs. Gaskell establishes her authenticity by such humanizing strokes as the inventory of her secret, personal treasures, contained in an old, shabby writing-case, a present from her father, without which she never travelled[74]. On the psychological plane, one comes across such touches as the description of her feelings on sending a parcel to her erstwhile lover, now married to another.

> She chose out the book, and wrapped and tied it up with trembling hands. *He* might be the person to untie the knot. It was strangely familiar to her love, after so many years, to be brought into thus much contact with him.[75]

Miss Munro and Dixon are the only other important characters, neither of whom need long detain us. Miss Munro, Ellinor's faithful governess, is a sort of blend between a Gaskellian loyal servant and a Cranfordesque maiden lady; her *rôle* may have been invented so that Ellinor could, after her father's death, recuperate at East Chester, a cathedral town with which the governess (a precentor's daughter[76]) had childhood connexions. In this way Mrs. Gaskell can, with probability, introduce a period of comparative calm between the immediate consequences of Dunster's death and the later turmoil caused by the discovery of his body. The atmosphere of a Cathedral Close was not something the novelist had previously tried to

---

[73] 'Dickens and Mrs. Gaskell', *The Huntington Library Quarterly*, IX, 380; *Elizabeth Gaskell*, p. 152.
[74] *Works*, VII, 541-542, 578.
[75] *Works*, VII, 541. Mrs. Gaskell expressed a comparable sentiment in her letter to Charles Eliot Norton of 5 February 1865 (*Gaskell-Norton Letters*, ed. Whitehill, p. 119: *G.L.*, No. 560).
[76] *Works*, VII, 522.

evoke; yet she does so with considerable skill, perhaps drawing on observations made during her own visits to a Cathedral Close, such as when she heard an Assize Sermon and dined at the Deanery with the Judges[77]. She realized how, to one troubled like Ellinor, regular attendance at the daily services would act as a stabilizing factor, beneficial both psychologically and physiologically[78].

Dixon is in some ways the counterpart to Miss Munro; for he too is faithful to the family he serves. In him Mrs. Gaskell once more displays her knowledge of devoted servants. She must have seen many such faithful rural ' retainers ' during her youth in Knutsford: at any rate she seems to regard him as typical of an earlier generation[79], when the bond which held a man to his master was as much customary as financial, both having grown up together[80]. As a single instance of how keenly Mrs. Gaskell must have noticed the habits of men like Dixon, we may quote his remarks on pointing out to Ellinor the grave

[77] Information contained in, or easily inferred from, a letter, begun by Meta Gaskell and completed by her mother, written to Marianne from Mrs. Lyall's, The Close [Winchester], on [Thursday] 28 February [and Friday 1 March 1861]. This letter is in the collection of Mrs. Margaret Trevor Jones. In (apparently) 1861 Mrs. Gaskell, together with Marianne, spent a day in another cathedral town, Salisbury; there they ' lunched at the Deanery ', according to Marianne's letter of 13 March [1864] to the Rev. R. S. Oldham——now in the possession of the present writer. The former letter appears as *G.L.*, No. 484 (its year given as [?1861] by Chapple and Pollard); see too *G.L.*, Nos. 455, 457, 484a.

[78] *Works*, VII, 525. Cf. 'Meta & I [went in March 1860] to Winchester,/ where I fell ill of bronchitis, and had to/ burrow into bed within two hours of my/ arriving at the house we were going to stay/ at. I was there for several weeks, lying/ in bed, and looking out into the beauti/ = ful Cathedral Close, with the branches of its/ great trees sweeping slowly across my win = / = dows as the wind swayed them, and the/ sound of the chanted services in the Ca = / = thedral came to me faintly, morning &/ evening. My hostess [Mrs. Lyall] was the widow of the/ Dean of Canterbury, who preceded Alford—/and I felt it very curious, how I became/ not mere[ly] clerical, but canonical in my/ way of thinking, before I left the Close. I/ found myself inclined to resent any/ disturbance of the vested interest of the/ dignified clergy by whom I was surround/ = ed, & to consider enquiry as to the distri/ = bution of the Church funds, as sacrilegious// impertinence.'—written by Mrs. Gaskell in a letter to the Rev. Edward Everett Hale of 14 December 1860 (owned by Miss Nancy Hale, and deposited in the Sophia Smith Collection at the Smith College Library).

[79] *Works*, VII, 537.
[80] *Works*, VII, 574-575.

of his only love, a pretty scullery-maid, beside whom he wished to be buried. In addition to the realistic idiom, the author makes this incident come alive by a master stroke, insignificant though it might at first seem—Dixon's cleaning the lettering (an unconscious action on his part, one supposes, and yet, for that very reason, especially worth recording).

> " I put this stone up over her with my first savings," said he, looking at it; and then, pulling out his knife, he began to clean out the letters. "I said then as I would lie by her. And it'll be a comfort to think you'll see me laid here. I trust no one'll be so crabbed as to take a fancy to this 'ere spot of ground."[81]

In conclusion something must be said about the literary and autobiographic elements. We have already touched upon the former, indicating connexions with Mrs. Gaskell's earlier work; nevertheless it is worth mentioning, in a somewhat piecemeal fashion, a few more examples of the same thing. At this stage in our general study, a child's death[82] may be taken as a common Gaskellian feature, as may the slightly sentimental treatment of a husband's losing his wife[83]. A meal *al fresco*[84] echoes similar idyllic repasts in *North and South*[85] and ' My French Master'[86]. Dunster[87], like Mr. Holbrook[88], was guilty of eating with his knife. Both Mr. Ness (the Hamley clergyman)[89] and the Rev. Thurston Benson[90] appear to have enjoyed holidaying in Wales. A grandiose will, made when the testator was in better financial circumstances[91], brings back memories of Mr. Hilton's empty bequests[92]. On leaving her country home Ellinor could, through the carriage window, catch a last glimpse of the church spire[93]—a bitter pleasure Margaret Hale denied herself in de-

---

[81] *Works*, VII, 543.
[82] *Works*, VII, 413, 415, 578.
[83] *Works*, VII, 412.
[84] *Works*, VII, 454.
[85] *Works*, IV, 28. See too 'Mr. Harrison's Confessions' (*Works*, V, 419).
[86] *Works*, II, 510. See too 'French Life' (*Works*, VII, 651).
[87] *Works*, VII, 487.
[88] *Works*, II, 40.
[89] *Works*, VII, 514.
[90] *Works*, III, 67-68.
[91] *Works*, VII, 515.
[92] *Works*, III, 37. We may also note that there is another will in *Ruth* (*Works*, III, 192-194, 377) and that a will-making scene appears in *Sylvia's Lovers* (*Works*, VI, 84-86).
[93] *Works*, VII, 524.

ference to her father's greater claim[94]. For each of these heroines a shattering experience makes a hitherto important event
seem to belong ' to the old life of yesterday '[95], ' like a dream,
a thing beside her actual life.'[96]

Mrs. Gaskell's 1857 Italian tour provides most of the new
personal material in *A Dark Night's Work*. When she, her two
eldest daughters, and Catherine Winkworth were sailing from
Marseilles to Civita Vecchia, on the second night of their
voyage the boiler burst, and they had to return to Marseilles,
their journey being considerably lengthened in consequence[97].
This incident finds its fictional counterpart, though in reverse:
engine-trouble forces the steamer, taking Ellinor from Civita
Vecchia to Marseilles, back to the former port on the first
night, thereby delaying the heroine's return to England[98]. The
account of Ellinor's holiday also owes much to Mrs. Gaskell's
own visit to Rome; but there is one incident in particular
which deserves attention. One cannot do better than quote first
the description of this incident given by Miss Meta Gaskell, and
then the version which appears in the story.

> " We reached Rome late at night on February 23, 1857, and
> drove through the dark strange streets to the Casa Cabrale,
> where the Storys were living, who had so kindly invited us [to
> visit them]. Next morning it was all brilliant sunshine and colour
> and wild gaiety. We were taken down by the Storys to a
> balcony in the Corso, from which we were to see the great
> day of the Carnival—Shrove Tuesday. The narrow street was
> filled with a boisterous crowd of Romans, half mad with
> excitement at the confetti-throwing and horse-racing. Suddenly
> against this turbulent background there stood out the figure
> of a young man just below the balcony, smiling up at my
> mother, whom he knew he was to see there, and whom he
> easily distinguished from the others. It is fifty-three years since
> that day, and yet even now I can vividly recall the sweet,
> welcoming expression on the radiant face. He was brought on

---

[94] *Works*, IV, 63. In this case it was the sight of the church tower.
[95] *Works*, VII, 467.
[96] *Works*, IV, 46. The obverse of this phrase occurs in *Ruth*, where
the heroine, rapt in recollection, ' believed her actual life to be the
dream ' (*Works*, III, 47).
[97] *Memorials of Two Sisters*, ed. Shaen, p. 170——not p. 140, as
is given in Rubenius, *The Woman Question in Mrs. Gaskell's Life and
Works*, p. 28, fn. 3.
[98] *Works*, VII, 562.

AA

to the balcony, but how little he and my mother thought, as they greeted one another, that until her death they were to be most true and intimate friends."[99]

So March came round; Lent was late that year. The great nosegays of violets and camellias were for sale at the corner of the Condotti, and the revellers had no difficulty in procuring much rarer flowers for the belles of the Corso. The embassies had their balconies; the attachés of the Russian Embassy threw their light and lovely presents at every pretty girl, or suspicion of a pretty girl, who passed slowly in her carriage, covered over with her white domino, and holding her wire mask as a protection to her face from the showers of lime *confetti*, which otherwise would have been enough to blind her; . . . The crowd below was at its wildest pitch; the rows of stately *contadini* alone sitting immovable . . . Masks and white dominoes, foreign gentlemen, and the riff-raff of the city, slow-driving carriages, showers of flowers, most of them faded by this time, every one shouting and struggling at that wild pitch of excitement which may so soon turn into fury. The Forbes girls had given place at the window to their mother and Ellinor, who were gazing, half-amused, half-terrified, at the mad parti-coloured movement below; when a familiar face looked up, smiling a recognition; and "How shall I get to you?" was asked, in English, by the well-known voice of Canon Livingstone.[100]

Miss Rubenius has conjectured that the character of Canon Livingstone may have been 'inspired by the open admiration and warm friendship of C. E. Norton, who accompanied Mrs. Gaskell and her daughters during most of their Italian tour, and with whom Mrs. Gaskell kept up a correspondence during the

---

[99] Quoted in Sara Norton and Mark Antony DeWolfe Howe, ed. *Letters of Charles Eliot Norton, with Biographical Comment*, 2 vols., London: Constable & Co. Limited; Boston and New York: Houghton Mifflin Company, 1913, I, 155: editors' square brackets. This passage is less fully but fairly accurately reprinted by Whitfield (*Mrs Gaskell*, p. 58). A manuscript version of the account, apparently written by Meta Gaskell to or for Miss Sara Norton and differing slightly from the printed text, is in the Harvard University Library: bMS Am 1088.1 (809). The sight of Norton's upturned, smiling face clearly impressed Mrs. Gaskell (*Gaskell-Norton Letters,* ed. Whitehill, p. 85: *G.L.,* No. 488) as well as Meta, who herself recalled the incident on at least three other occasions—in letters to Charles Eliot Norton of [c. 1867 (relevantly quoted in White-hill, ed. *Gaskell-Norton Letters,* p. xix)], 28 October 1886, and 22 April [1900], all deposited in the Harvard University Library: bMS Am 1088 (2610 [seemingly the end of a letter], 2630, 2633).

[100] *Works,* VII, 548-549.

rest of her life.'[101] This seems, however, to be pushing correspondences too far; as is, perhaps, her relating Mr. Wilkins' habit of visiting without his wife to Mr. Gaskell's custom of dining out alone[102]. A more likely link between the Gaskells and *A Dark Night's Work* may be discovered in the Miss Beauchamps—the elder (pretty, seventeen, one shoulder higher than the other, fond of dancing, liking *tête-à-tête* talking if her mother were not nearby, silent in her father's presence)[103] suggesting Marianne in her younger days[104]; the next sister (wonderfully clever, reputably knowing all the governess could teach, having private lessons in Greek and mathematics from her father)[105] bringing Meta Gaskell to mind[106].

[101] Rubenius, *The Woman Question in Mrs. Gaskell's Life and Works*, p. 28, fn. 3.

[102] Rubenius, *The Woman Question in Mrs. Gaskell's Life and Works*, p. 26, fn. 1.

[103] *Works*, VII, 529.

[104] An impression based on reading her mother's letters, such as the undated [February or March 1851] fragment (in the Gaskell Section, Brotherton Collection, Leeds University Library) in which she tells Marianne to learn dancing if her schoolmistress thinks it will help to bring her '*naughty* shoulders down'; the letter (copies of part of which, once owned by Mr. J. T. Lancaster, belong to the present writer), written one Sunday afternoon [9 March 1851] to Marianne, in which she enquires after her shoulders, drawing diagrams of how they ought, and ought not, to look; and the letter (in the Gaskell Section, Brotherton Collection, Leeds University Library), written one Monday [7 April 1851] to Marianne, in which she emphatically asks 'ARE your shoulders lower?', going on to allow a further quarter of dancing or exercises, should such be of help in bringing them down. These letters appear respectively as *G.L.*, Nos. 116 (in a footnote Chapple and Pollard draw attention to their misdating of this letter), 91a (wrongly dated [10 March 1851]), 93.

[105] *Works*, VII, 529.

[106] An impression based on reading her mother's letters, such as that to Norton of 9 March [1859] in which she speaks of Meta, 'a noble beautiful character', her working away at German and Greek, and her reading 'carefully many books' (*Gaskell-Norton Letters*, ed. Whitehill, p. 32); that of 21 March [1859] to Eliza Fox (relevantly quoted—from the copy of part of this letter in the Gaskell Section, Brotherton Collection, Leeds University Library—in Rubenius, *The Woman Question in Mrs. Gaskell's Life and Works*, p. 104) in which she refers to Meta's studying Greek and German; and that (in the Gaskell Section, Brotherton Collection, Leeds University Library), written on Wednesday 19 [May 1852] to Marianne, where she mentions Meta's 'beginning mathe=/=matics with Papa'. These letters appear respectively as *G.L.*, Nos. 418, 421 (to Eliza Bridell-Fox, Chapple and Pollard using her married name), 126.

SECTION II

Sylvia's Lovers (1863)

Published in 1863[1], *Sylvia's Lovers*[2] was the product of several years' writing. Its origin lay in the visit Mrs. Gaskell paid to Whitby during late October and early November 1859 —a visit whose purpose was not, as has been sometimes postulated[3], to gather material for a work of historical fiction, but rather to improve Julia's health, she having outgrown her strength[4]. Nevertheless Mrs. Gaskell knew her publishers wanted a three-volume novel[5], so her mind would be more than usually receptive to whatever chance might provide. Having recently spent a summer holiday at Auchencairn ' in an old house, (larger than a farm-house,) that had belonged to a smuggler, in the palmy days of smuggling,'[6] she was well equipped to

---

[1] In February, according to Ward (ed. *Works,* VI, p. xiii), Thomas Seccombe (pref. *Sylvia's Lovers,* by Mrs. Gaskell, London: G. Bell & Sons, Ltd., 1910, p. xl), and Mrs. Chadwick (*Mrs. Gaskell,* p. 288); in March, according to Sadleir (*Excursions in Victorian Bibliography,* p. 209) and Northup (in his Bibliography to Sanders, *Elizabeth Gaskell,* p. 184): 20 February 1863 was the publication-day advertized in *The Athenaeum Journal of Literature, Science, and the Fine Arts,* No. 1842 (14 February 1863), p. 212; the next number of this magazine (21 February 1863, p. 273) carried a notice stating the book was ready, it being reviewed a week later (No. 1844, p. 291). In Autumn 1862, February seems to have been the publication-date uppermost in the author's mind, as is suggested both by her [October 1862] letter to George Smith (the relevant fragment being in the archives of Sir John Murray) and by what Meta Gaskell wrote to Charles Eliot Norton on 30 or 31 October in a letter begun on Monday 21 [20] October [1862]—now in the Harvard University Library: bMS Am 1088 (2604). Mrs. Gaskell's letter (*G.L.,* No. 517) is dated [?Late September 1862] by Chapple and Pollard.

[2] Elizabeth Cleghorn Gaskell, *Sylvia's Lovers,* 3 vols., London: Smith, Elder and Co., 1863.

[3] By, for instance, Sanders (*Elizabeth Gaskell,* p. 116) and Mrs. Chadwick (*Mrs. Gaskell,* p. 251).

[4] The reason given in Mrs. Gaskell's letter of 2 November [1859] to George Smith, written from Mrs. Rose's, 1 Abbey Terrace, Whitby (now in the archives of Sir John Murray—referred to in Hopkins, *Elizabeth Gaskell,* p. 364): *G.L.,* No. 446.

[5] *Gaskell-Norton Letters,* ed. Whitehill, p. 39: *G.L.,* No. 444. See too *G.L.,* Nos. 430, 432, 433.

[6] *Gaskell-Norton Letters,* ed. Whitehill, pp. 38-39: *G.L.,* No. 444.

appreciate the atmosphere of Whitby, and hence profit as a writer from its influences. These influences were both scenic and historical.

The historical consisting of the traditional and the factual, it would have been with the former, one supposes, that the author first came into contact, through her acquaintance with Whitby inhabitants. It was her custom to question people in the places she visited, her engaging manner easily winning confidence : such conversations often formed the basis for a short story; and the debt her *Life of Charlotte Brontë* owes to interviews with Yorkshire folk needs no stressing. *Sylvia's Lovers* probably grew out of similar talks. The coda to the book mentions that a garbled version of the truth ('the form into which popular feeling, and ignorance of the real facts, . . . moulded the story'[7]) was current half-a-century or more after the events had taken place; and that a certain lady, from conversing with the bathing-woman in charge of the Public Baths[8], learned what subsequently became of the chief figures. There is both pathos and irony in this passage; for it insinuates how easily a tragedy can be distorted into something different. Besides supplying the novel with an appropriate conclusion, it may hint at its origin, since the lady interlocutor was very likely the author herself[9].

Whether or not Mrs. Gaskell did hear an unhappy legend (somewhat along the lines of her own short story, 'The Manchester Marriage') which she expanded into *Sylvia's Lovers,* what she certainly must have heard about in Whitby was the 1793 riot, caused by hostility to the practices of the press-gang[10]; this had led to an attack on the local 'rendez-vous', in consequence of which an old man of seventy, William Atkinson, was hanged at York Castle[11]. During her stay in Whitby Mrs. Gaskell seems to have ascertained all she could about the affair.

[7] *Works,* VI, 530.

[8] Built in 1825-1826 (George Young, *A Picture of Whitby and Its Environs,* 2nd edn, Whitby: Horne and Richardson, 1840, p. 219).

[9] Doubtless the opinion of Miss Hopkins (*Elizabeth Gaskell,* p. 270).

[10] For a general account of impressment, see J. R. Hutchinson, *The Press-Gang Afloat and Ashore,* London: Eveleigh Nash, 1913; the Whitby incident is mentioned by Hutchinson (*op. cit.,* pp. 220-222, 272).

[11] *Criminal Chronology of York Castle; . . . ,* compiled with assistance from William Knipe, York: C L. Burdekin; London: Simpkin, Marshall, & Co., 1867, pp. 128-129.

Her first and obvious source was the family, called Rose, in whose house she was lodging. In the early years of this century the daughters of the family remembered ' with distinctness their grandmother, Mrs. Huntrods, who was a walking repository of the history and traditional lore of the " haven under the hill," being closeted day after day with Mrs. Gaskell at 1 Abbey Terrace.'[12] Other residents she is said[13] to have interviewed included the Unitarian minister, Mr. Watson; Mrs. Bradley, the bookseller; and the well-known Whitby character, fat old ' Fish Jane '. The novelist also consulted one of the oldest inhabitants, Mr. John Corney, who wrote saying he had spoken with an old tradesman who well remembered the execution of Atkinson[14]; in return for such service, as well as for his kindness in lending her Young's *History of Whitby*[15], the author presented him with an autographed copy of *Sylvia's Lovers,* 'acknowledging "much valuable assistance given during the writing of this book." '[16] Not content with information from local people, Mrs. Gaskell applied to the Admiralty, and obtained a transcript of a letter from Lieutenant Atkinson describing the attack on the gang's head-quarters[17]. Furthermore she made enquiries respecting the verdict passed on the accused, carried out research in the British Museum, and communicated with General Perronet Thompson and Sir Charles Napier on the practice of impressment[18].

---

[12] Seccombe, pref. *Sylvia's Lovers,* by Mrs. Gaskell, p. xxviii.

[13] By Seccombe (pref. *Sylvia's Lovers,* by Mrs. Gaskell, pp. xxviii, xxxiv) and Mrs. Chadwick (*Mrs. Gaskell,* p. 254).

[14] Ward, ed. *Works,* VI, p. xxiii.

[15] George Young, *A History of Whitby, and Streoneshalh Abbey; with a Statistical Survey of the Vicinity to the Distance of Twenty-five Miles,* 2 vols., Whitby: Clark and Medd; London: Longman and Co., and R. Fenner; Edinburgh: Oliphant, Waugh and Co., 1817.

[16] Chadwick, *Mrs. Gaskell,* p. 254. Mrs. Chadwick apparently saw the inscription she quotes; but she erroneously gives Mr. Corney's Christian name as George (the appropriate North Riding Electoral Lists and Directories of the period include John Corney as a Whitby householder and shopkeeper, George being nowhere mentioned). A slightly different version of this inscription appears in Joseph Rodgers, "Mrs. Gaskell's 'Sylvia's Lovers' ", *Notes and Queries,* CIX (10th Series, I—March 1904), 188.

[17] The text is quoted in Ward, ed. *Works,* VI, pp. xxiii-xxiv. More or less accurately, it is reprinted in Sanders, *Elizabeth Gaskell,* pp. 116-117; and (not so fully) in Shorter, ed. *Novels and Tales,* V (1909), pp. vi-vii.

[18] Ward, ed. *Works,* VI, pp. xxiv-xxvi.

It seems, therefore, that in constructing the plot of *Sylvia's Lovers* the author wove together two strands—a local tale (in fact a variant of what we should now think of as the *Enoch Arden* theme) and the historically verifiable Whitby riot of 1793. Neither was of her own inventing; but what she made out of them was a masterpiece in fiction.

Mrs. Gaskell's other Whitby debt was to the locality itself; the influence upon her of the sea and moors, as well as that of the situation of the town, is beautifully exemplified by numerous descriptive passages. For example, the first chapter, inviting comparison with that famous opening to *The Life of Charlotte Brontë,* is a wonderful evocation of the Yorkshire port and its environs. Topographically, historically, and socially, the background is sketched with the novelist's wonted skill, a reminder of what she had already achieved in works like *Ruth* and *The Moorland Cottage*. A quotation from Dr. Adolphus Ward seems relevant: 'It is curious', he remarks, ' that *Sylvia's Lovers*, which brings to mind the profession of Mrs. Gaskell's grandfather (Captain Stevenson),' as well, he might have added, as that of her uncles[19] and brother, ' also recalls the descriptive powers of the author of *The Seasons,* who (as a genealogical

---

[19] From details given elsewhere by Ward (ed. *Works,* I, p. xvi; VI, p. xvi) as well as from information generously supplied by the late Mr. Walter Carter, the late Miss Dorothy Jane Harrison, Dr. William Malcolm Robertson Henderson (8 Holmewood Ridge, Langton Green, Kent), and other descendants of Mrs. Gaskell's paternal grandfather, it appears that three sons of Post-Captain Joseph Stevenson (1719-1799, married in 1769 to Isabella Thomson, 1743-1806) entered the Royal Navy. These uncles of the novelist were: Lieutenant Joseph Stevenson (born 1772, died a prisoner of war at Dunkirk); Lieutenant John Thomson Turner Stevenson (born 1780, drowned escaping from Dunkirk); and Robert Stevenson (1776-1818, married in 1803 to Elizabeth Wilson, 1779-1875), a surgeon who subsequently practised at Berwick. The Yale University Library (MS Vault Sect. 16) contains part of a [(pre 8 March) 1854] letter from Mrs. Gaskell—*G.L.*, No. 183 (dated [Before 15 March ?1854] by Chapple and Pollard)—asking Marianne to call, while in London, at 55 Gordon Square, there to visit her (Mrs. Gaskell's) first cousin, Marianne, the daughter of her uncle, Dr. Stevenson of Berwick, and married to a Mr. Mannisty, Q.C. [*sic*]; according to Mrs. Gaskell, Marianne's sister was Mrs. Church, who had died at Torquay during the previous two months, and her brother was Joseph Stevenson, the Leighton-Buzzard clergyman: this family, Mrs. Gaskell told her daughter, were her only relatives on her father's side. (Thus the letter seems to suggest, somewhat erroneously, that Dr. Stevenson was alive after 1818.) The Stevenson family tree records that: Mary Anne Stevenson (born 1817, died in London 1892) married Sir Henry Manisty

statement in her own handwriting attests) was a near kinsman of her grandmother.'[20]

As regards particular correspondences between fact and fiction, one can affirm that Mrs. Gaskell's portrayal of Monkshaven is unmistakably based on what she had observed at Whitby. Seccombe[21] and Mrs. Chadwick[22] have listed parallel after parallel, so little need be said on this score; indeed, to anyone familiar with Whitby, it is abundantly clear that ' Mrs. Gaskell neither laboured, nor invented, her *mise-en-scène*.'[23] She

---

(1808-1890), a Judge of the High Court; Elizabeth Stevenson (1812-1853) married the Rev. W. M. H. Church; Joseph Stevenson (1806-1895), S.J., married Mary Ann Craig (1811-1869). We may note that Elizabeth Wilson Church, wife of William Montague Higginson Church, died at Torquay on 13 December 1853 (according to Somerset House records): that details about Sir Henry Manisty, who became a Q.C. on 7 July 1857, are given in John Andrew Hamilton's article in *The Dictionary of National Biography*: and that information on Joseph Stevenson, Leighton-Buzzard incumbent from 1849 to 1862, can be found in Ward, ed. *Works*, I, p. xvii; Chadwick, *Mrs. Gaskell*, p. 2; and Thompson Cooper's article in *The Dictionary of National Biography*. The late Mr. Carter's sister generously gave to the present writer a few letters, written in the seventeen-nineties by her great-grandmother, Dorothy Stevenson (Mrs. George Landles, 1774-1805), that mention, *inter alia*, a son born (late 1798) to her brother, William, and his wife (the novelist's parents); Miss J. Carter cannot, however, trace the family-tree (compiled by a deceased cousin) from which her brother gathered his genealogical data. Miss Harrison had, in addition to her family-tree (made by a maternal uncle, W. A. C. Henderson, Dr. Henderson's father), a notebook of remembrances, composed in 1895 by her great-grandmother, Robina Dorothy Stevenson (Mrs. Andrew Henderson, secondly Mrs. Alexander Roberts, 1818-1898), the posthumous daughter of Dr. Robert Stevenson of Berwick, and a portrait of Mrs. Church which was presented to Robina Dorothy by Mrs. Gaskell, her first cousin; the first two items now belong to her sister, Mrs. J. L. Longland (Bridgeway, Bakewell, Derbyshire). Dr. Henderson's family-tree, initially assembled by his father, states that in 1827 John Stevenson, Mrs. Gaskell's brother, was lost at sea in (according to a pencil annotation) a ship [the *Northumberland?*] that took Napoleon to St. Helena. John's birthdate, not given in the tree, was entered as 27 November 1798 in an Appendix to the Corstorphine Parish Register of Births and Baptisms (information gathered by Miss Jane Revere Coolidge—now Mrs. Whitehill—from, she believes, a note of Shorter's, and incorporated in her typescript, 'Life and letters of Mrs. E. C. Gaskell', Ch. I, p. 20: this Register is not now with the Corstorphine Kirk Session Records).

[20] Adolphus William Ward, ' In Memoriam Elizabeth Cleghorn Gaskell ', *The Cornhill Magazine*, N.S. XXIX (1910), 463, fn. 1.

[21] Pref. *Sylvia's Lovers*, by Mrs. Gaskell, pp. xxviii-xxxiv.

[22] *Mrs. Gaskell*, pp. 260-277.

[23] Seccombe, pref. *Sylvia's Lovers*, by Mrs. Gaskell, p. xxxiv.

did, of course, make some minor changes, either for literary
purposes (as in stating that one half of the prototype of Foster's
shop was at the time used for selling drapery[24]) or perhaps
simply through ignorance (as when she estimates the current—
1860's—'Monkshaven' population at about fifteen thousand,
and says that towards the end of the eighteenth century it
would have been only half that number[25]). The most striking
testimony to Mrs. Gaskell's use of her Whitby observations is
found in Canon Alfred Ainger's account of what happened
when Du Maurier was commissioned to illustrate *Sylvia's
Lovers*[26].

> As all readers of Mrs. Gaskell are now aware, 'Monkshaven,'
> the scene of the story, is identical with the favourite watering-
> place, Whitby, on the Yorkshire coast. Whitby was to become in
> later years a special haunt of du Maurier, and its ways and
> doings to appear in delightful fashion in 'Punch.' But in 1863
> he had no personal knowledge of the place, or of its identity
> with Monkshaven. Happening one day to talk over the task
> before him with Mr. Henry Keene (brother of his friend and
> colleague on 'Punch,' Charles Keene), that gentleman offered
> to lend him some sketches he had made the year before at
> Whitby, which seemed fairly to resemble the descriptions of

[24] *Works,* VI, 24. There is a pertinent comment by Mrs. Chadwick
(*Mrs. Gaskell,* p. 264).

[25] *Works,* VI, 1. It is unclear whether Mrs. Gaskell regarded the
(Whitby) population as that of the parish, of the township, of the parliamentary borough (formed in 1832), or of the natural community (Whitby
township and Ruswarp); indeed each of her figures probably refers to a
differently defined population. Thus the 1801 Census put the parish at
10,974, the township at 7,483, and Ruswarp at 1,565; the comparable
1861 figures are 14,014, 8,142, 2,995 (with the parliamentary borough at
12,051): however the census returns are underestimates because they exclude mariners (in 1801 those both ashore and afloat, in 1861 those at
sea though not those on vessels in home ports). Relevant references include
William Page, ed. *The Victoria History of the County of York,* 3 vols.
and index, 1907-1925, III (London: Constable and Company Limited,
1913), 517, 523; Francis Kildill Robinson, *Whitby: Its Abbey, and the
Principal Parts of the Neighbourhood; Or A Sketch of the Place in Its
Former History and Present State, with the Topography and Antiquities
of the Surrounding Country,* Whitby: S. Reed, 1860, pp. 116-117; Young,
A History of Whitby, II, 514-523; and Young, *A Picture of Whitby and
Its Environs,* 1840, pp. 172-176.

[26] Elizabeth Cleghorn Gaskell, *Sylvia's Lovers,* Illus. edn, London:
Smith, Elder and Co., 1863. It was advertized on 5 December 1863 as a
new publication, and on 12 December as just ready, in *The Athenaeum
Journal of Literature, Science, and the Fine Arts,* No. 1884, p. 742, No.
1885, p. 788.

scenery in the novel. Hence it came about that the novel was illustrated, though the artist was unaware of it, from the picturesque seaport Mrs. Gaskell had in view.[27]

Mrs. Gaskell seems to have started thinking about 'The Specksioneer' (as she then called it) soon after her Whitby visit; for, in a letter to George Smith of 23 December [1859][28], she remarked that, though not far on, the story was very clear in her mind and what she wanted to write more than anything. Her own testimony suggests the book was begun on 8 April[29], and by early June 1860 she 'had nearly finished the first vol:'[30].

[27] Alfred Ainger's article on George Louis Palmella Busson Du Maurier (1834-1896) in *The Dictionary of National Biography*.

[28] Now in the archives of Sir John Murray. The date may be conjectured as 1859 from internal evidence—chiefly a reference to a story (almost certainly *A Dark Night's Work*) begun a year and a half before, and one to a second story (probably 'Curious, if True'), likely to occupy forty manuscript pages and destined for Smith's *Cornhill* by the author, who considered it good and only wrote at it during her 'best moments': this letter links with another in Sir John's archives, dated Tuesday 27 December [1859], where Mrs. Gaskell promises to try to send Smith one tale ('Curious, if True'?) for *The Cornhill Magazine* in a fortnight, and—very optimistically—to endeavour to let him have her three-volume novel in September (a date which, by 5 April [1860], seemed less of a possibility—*Gaskell-Norton Letters*, ed. Whitehill, p. 57). The letters providing these references occur respectively as *G.L.*, Nos. 451a, 452, 461. Her Monday [7 November 1859] letter (*G.L.*, No. 447a) to Marianne from Whitby (copies of which, once owned by Mr. J. T. Lancaster, belong to the present writer) contains a hint that she was then writing other things besides letters—possibly notes for the novel.

[29] According to a [(May) 1860] letter, written one Wednesday to Marianne (copies of which, once owned by Mr. J. T. Lancaster, belong to the present writer), in which she claimed to have finished a quarter of the book: this letter occurs as *G.L.*, No. 465a (dated [?Early May 1860] by Chapple and Pollard). Perhaps 8 April was when she began her final drafting; for Catherine Winkworth's 17 April letter to Mrs. Sandars states that, almost certainly during the previous month, 'Mrs. Gaskell read Emily and Will a good deal of her new story ["Sylvia's Lovers"] in London, and Will thinks it is going to be her best.'—*Letters and Memorials of Catherine Winkworth*, II ([ed. Susanna Winkworth and Margaret Josephine Shaen] 1886), 297: editors' square brackets; see too *G.L.*, No. 460.

[30] *Gaskell-Norton Letters*, ed. Whitehill, p. 62. Writing to Marianne one Sunday afternoon, Mrs. Gaskell remarked that she had '117 pages done of/ 570 *at least*'—this [(May) 1860] letter being in the collection of Mrs. Margaret Trevor Jones. Our quotation from the first letter (*G.L.*, No. 476), written on Monday 27 August [1860] and deposited in the Harvard University Library, is slightly differently punctuated by Chapple and Pollard; their dating for the second letter (*G.L.*, No. 465) is [?Early May 1860]. See too *G.L.*, No. 466.

The manuscript received little attention between then and 10 December 1860, when she informed Charles Eliot Norton of its being ' about one quarter done '[31]; on 28 August 1861, however, she could tell him it was ' above half-way done '[32]. In a letter of 1 February [1862] to W. S. Williams[33], she mentioned that Smith, from whom she had heard nothing, had had the first two volumes for a month[34], and offered to furnish Williams, if he had read these, with a sketch of the third, towards the events and crisis in which, she averred, everything else worked up; having confessed to thinking Smith no great literary critic, the novelist expressed her own extreme fondness for the work, perhaps (as she said) the result of having taken considerable pains with it and knowing the conclusion. After a rather adverse verdict from Williams, who may have read no more than the first volume, Mrs. Gaskell replied on 6 February[35], admitting she could not quite agree with his estimate, but acknowledging an author's partiality; she referred to having ' Philip's Idol ' in reserve as an alternative title. Her letter of 18 March [1862] informed Smith that, suspecting the third volume would prove the longest, she would " be/ very glad to move a little of/ the

[31] *Gaskell-Norton Letters*, ed. Whitehill, p. 74: *G.L.*, No. 480. In a letter (*G.L.*, No. 476a) of 29 August [1860] to W. S. Williams (copies of which, once owned by Mr. J. T. Lancaster, belong to the present writer), she stated that, because of domestic duties and Marianne's having been ill, the work was not getting on at all; however before early June, when news came of Marianne's suspected small-pox, Mrs. Gaskell had been going 'on famously, writing away', according to her 14 December 1860 letter to the Rev. Edward Everett Hale (owned by Miss Nancy Hale, and deposited in the Sophia Smith Collection at the Smith College Library).

[32] *Gaskell-Norton Letters*, ed. Whitehill, p. 94. In a letter to Mr. and Mrs. William Wetmore Story of 23 June 1861 (in the Texas University Library), she could report that she was ' getting on with/' her book. These letters appear respectively as *G.L.*, Nos. 493, 490; see too *G.L.*, No. 484b.

[33] A copy of this letter is to be found with Forster correspondence in the Gaskell Section, Brotherton Collection, Leeds University Library; part is fairly accurately quoted by Miss Rubenius (*The Woman Question in Mrs. Gaskell's Life and Works*, p. 35): Chapple and Pollard give its year (*G.L.*, No. 499) as [?1862] and the recipient as ?W. S. Williams.

[34] In a letter to George Smith of 9 December [1861]—now in the archives of Sir John Murray—Mrs. Gaskell wrote that two volumes were finished, and that he should get the third when he liked, provided the time was not so short as to hurry it at the expense of completeness. The year of this letter (*G.L.*, No. 495) Chapple and Pollard put at [?1861].

[35] A copy of this letter (*G.L.*, No. 499a), once owned by Mr. J. T. Lancaster, belongs to the present writer: its year is [1862].

second into the first, so/ as to leave "[36] room for such additions to the second as might be necessary. Five months or so later[37] she was returning revised proofs up to the end of the second volume, making a substitution for a passage on p. 63 of Vol. I, and providing an additional chapter for Vol. II (the printer having there wished for more material), noting also that many corrections remained to be made, nor would she specify that the book could be finished before the end of January. Writing from Eastbourne in the autumn[38], Mrs. Gaskell asked Smith how many of her pages would be required for the third volume, and implied she was hurrying over it; at the same time she told him she would be glad for the novel not to be published before February.

Although other commitments were partly responsible for its long period of composition[39], the historical nature of the work

[36] Quoted by Miss Hopkins (*Elizabeth Gaskell*, p. 266), whose transcript has been checked against the original letter, now in the archives of Sir John Murray: G.L., No. 501 (the year being given as [?1862] by Chapple and Pollard).

[37] According to her letters of 20 August 1862, 22 August and 14 September [1862] to W. S. Williams (the first and third being in the possession of Mrs. E. M. Gordon, Biddlesden Park, Brackley, Northants; a copy of the second being in Shorter and Symington, 'Correspondence, Articles and Notes Relating to Mrs. E. C. Gaskell. Transcripts', Vol. II, Section of Extracts from Letters Relating to Mrs. Gaskell and Her Work—a typescript in the Gaskell Section, Brotherton Collection, Leeds University Library), and that of 4 September [1862] to her publishers (in the possession of Mrs. E. M. Gordon). These letters appear respectively as G.L., Nos. 511, 511a (a copy, once owned by Mr. J. T. Lancaster and belonging to the present writer, was the source used by Chapple and Pollard, who give the year as [?1862]), 514 (to ?W.S. Williams), 512.

[38] Miss Hopkins (*Elizabeth Gaskell*, p. 265) pertinently quotes from the relevant fragment (now in the archives of Sir John Murray) of this [October 1862] letter—G.L., No. 517, dated [?Late September 1862] by Chapple and Pollard, whose transcript is more accurate.

[39] The letter (23 December [1859]) and the fragment ([October 1862]), both mentioned *supra,* written by Mrs. Gaskell to George Smith, show she was also engaged on (probably) *A Dark Night's Work* and a story, intended for *The Cornhill Magazine* (presumably 'Curious, if True'), which she thought would turn out well and which she did not want to hurry over. As we have noted, Mrs. Gaskell's letter to Smith of Tuesday 27 December [1859]—likewise in the archives of Sir John Murray—mentions her intention of sending a tale ('Curious, if True'?) in a fortnight as well as her hope (which had to be deferred) of letting him have her three-volume novel the following September; the same letter contains a reference to 'The Ghost in the Garden Room' (published in the 1859 Extra Christmas Number of *All the Year Round*). These letters appear respectively as G.L., Nos. 451a, 517 (dated [?Late September 1862] by Chapple and Pollard), 452.

must have made large demands on the author's time; for, as we have seen, she sought to be accurate. The result of this slow growth was not altogether happy, as the following letter indicates.

[page 1]

46 Plymouth Grove
Manchester
November 14 [1863]

Thank you very much/ for your corrections, which/ will be really useful/ to me in a fresh edi = / = tion of Sylvia's lovers/ which is to appear/ very soon. At least I/ hope they will be in//

[page 2]

time as I shall for = / = ward them to the pub = / = lisher by the same/ post as that which/ takes this letter. You/ are quite right in/ supposing that Whitby/ was the place I meant/ by Monkshaven; but/ I was only there once/ for a fortnight, about//

[page 3]

four years ago, in such/ cloudy November wea = / = ther that I might very/ easily be ignorant of/ the points of the com = / = pass if I did not look/ at a map: and I am/ afraid that I did not/ test my accuracy by/ so doing. I did not in = / = tend Haytersbank[40] for/ any particular place.//

[page 4]

or if I had some faint/ recollection of a farm house/ like it, it must have/ been a place near Sunder/ = land where I once stayed/ for a couple of nights./ I had forgotten that there/ was such a town as Kirby/ Moorside[41] until you/ named it. I am afraid/ that several of the mis/ = takes you are so kind/ as to point out appear/ very careless; but I lead//

---

[40] Haytersbank farm has been located (i) on the N.W. side of Whitby by Mrs. Chadwick (*Mrs. Gaskell,* p. 271) and Seccombe (pref. *Sylvia's Lovers,* by Mrs. Gaskell, pp. xxxi-xxxii); (ii) on the S.E. side of Whitby by Ward (ed. *Works,* VI, p. xiii, fn.). The novel seems to support both situations (e.g. *Works,* VI, 226, 381; 11-16, 396-399): however most Whitby-lovers have agreed in identifying Haytersbank with a particular farm, Du Maurier's letter to Ainger being typical in this respect (see the relevant extract in Edith Helen Sichel, *The Life and Letters of Alfred Ainger,* London: Archibald Constable and Company Limited, 1906, p. 280).

[41] In the early editions of *Sylvia's Lovers* (e.g. *Sylvia's Lovers,* 1st, 2nd, 3rd edns, 3 vols., London: Smith, Elder and Co., 1863, III, 31) Mrs. Gaskell had written that the Robsons were wont to worship at 'Kirby Moorside'; in later editions (e.g. Illus. edn, 1863, p. 357) this is changed to 'Scarby Moorside' (*Works,* VI, 379). We may note that both names contradict Philip's statement, made earlier in the novel, that his aunt always went to ' "Kirk Moorside " ' (found in all editions—e.g. 1st, 2nd, 3rd edns, I, 124; Illus. edn, 1863, p. 70; *Works,* VI, 75). Other references

[page 5]
   a busy life in many ways,/ and I have sometimes/ to put aside
   my MSS/ for weeks and even months;/ at others, just when I/
   have begun to write, some/ interruption comes, and/ I hastily
   finish off a/ sentence before leaving/ off writing.   /
   Thank you once more—/You will see I am/ only really obliged
   to/ you for your friendly//

[page 6]
   helpful letter.   /
   E. C. Gaskell.   //[42]

Without attempting to identify the particular mistakes this
correspondent pointed out, we may take Mrs. Gaskell's reply
as confirmation of what a close examination of *Sylvia's Lovers*
reveals—namely the piecemeal mode of composition. Although,
taken as a whole, the novel is structurally satisfying (except,
perhaps, for the Siege of Acre episode[43]), there are about a
score of errors of detail[44]. Some have been mentioned by Mrs.

---

to Kirk Moorside appear (1st, 2nd, 3rd edns, I, 138, II, 287; Illus. edn,
1863, pp. 78, 335; *Works,* VI, 83, 356). The second edition apparently
appeared between 28 March and 4 April 1863; the third edition, between
18 April and 25 April; the first illustrated edition (as has been noted) was
advertized as a new publication on 5 December and as just ready on 12
December—*The Athenaeum Journal of Literature, Science, and the Fine
Arts,* No. 1848, p. 413, No. 1849, p. 469; No. 1851, p. 533, No. 1852,
p. 564; No. 1884, p. 742, No. 1885, p. 788.
   [42] This letter, from Mrs. Gaskell to Dr. James Dixon, is in the
Cambridge University Library: MS. Add. 6604(5)—our transcript differs
slightly in punctuation from that (*G.L.,* No. 537) of Chapple and Pollard.
Dr. Dixon's points-of-the-compass remarks may have been prompted by
Mrs. Gaskell's ignorance of the peculiar geography of Whitby, situated on
the east and west banks of the northward-flowing Esk. For instance, there
are said to be ' on the south side of the stream . . . a few houses of more
pretension ' (*Works,* VI, 1) whereas the properties the novelist had in mind
lay on the east bank of the river.
   [43] *Works,* VI, 448-458: these pages make up the chapter entitled
' The Recognition '.
   [44] Miss ffrench is, therefore, incorrect in saying of Mrs. Gaskell, with
reference to *Sylvia's Lovers,* ' regarding details, she had taken great
care ' (*Mrs. Gaskell,* p. 102).

Chadwick[45] and Dr. Sanders[46]; but even they ignore more than half of them[47].

In writing a historical novel it was important for Mrs. Gaskell to make no blunders of a specifically factual sort. The ordinary reader, unless exceptionally acute, is only likely to attempt verification if his suspicions are aroused by an apparent error in general knowledge; otherwise he takes things on trust. Hence Judge Coleridge's correction of a slight legal point[48] could never have come from the common reader, who would not have checked that sort of technicality. However, Mrs. Gaskell was her father's daughter, as well as the biographer of Charlotte Brontë; and, as we have mentioned, she took trouble with her researches.

Much of Mrs. Gaskell's historical material was, it seems, gleaned from *The Annual Register*[49] (the greater part of which Mr. William Stevenson had for several years written and com-

---

[45] Esther Alice (Mrs. Ellis H.) Chadwick, intro. *Sylvia's Lovers,* by Mrs. Gaskell, London: J. M. Dent & Sons, Ltd.; New York: E. P. Dutton & Co. [1911], p. xii.

[46] *Elizabeth Gaskell,* pp. 114-115.

[47] Some hitherto unnoticed internal inconsistencies include (i) the day on which Sylvia's cloak was bought—*Works,* VI, 16: cont. 53; (ii) the number of men taken by the press-gang from the *Resolution*— *Works,* VI, 30: cont. 54; (iii) Molly's place in the order of birth of the Corney girls—*Works,* VI, 12: cont. 82, 124; (iv) the financial position of Kinraid—*Works,* VI, 76: cont. 207; (v) the Whitby market-day— *Works,* VI, 16, 418, 422: cont. 271-280; (vi) the date of Bell Robson's death—*Works,* VI, 414-422: cont. 425; (vii) the surname of Kester's widowed sister—*Works,* VI, 427: cont. 443: cont. 504; (viii) the Christian name of the domestic servant attached to Foster's shop— *Works,* VI, 34: cont. 313; (ix) the moral character of Alice Rose's husband—*Works,* VI, 85: cont. 254; (x) the misleading hint that Alice Rose may soon die—*Works,* VI, 438; (xi) the spelling of the surname of a leading landed family—*Works,* VI, 43: cont. 414; (xii) Sylvia's age, and that of her daughter, when Philip left them—*Works,* VI, 426: cont. 464; (xiii) there being at Monkshaven both a vicar and a rectory —*Works,* VI, 70: cont. 512; (xiv) the length of time the Robsons had been at Haytersbank—*Works,* VI, 14-15, 36-37, 126: cont. 27, 245. Certain annalistic anomalies are indicated in Graham Roderick Handley, 'The Chronology of "Sylvia's Lovers"', *Notes and Queries,* CCX (N.S. XII— August 1965), 302-303.

[48] Ward, ed. *Works,* VI, pp. xxvi-xxvii: *G.L.,* No. 521. The passage in question (*Sylvia's Lovers,* 1st, 2nd, 3rd edns, II, 237) was duly modified (*Sylvia's Lovers,* Illus. edn, 1863, p. 307; *Works,* VI, 326).

[49] Writing one Friday, Mrs. Gaskell asked Marianne to tell 'the Tutor not to trouble/ himself or his friends about the press-/ = gang

piled[50]); from this invaluable source of background information she probably went to such specialist works as the occasion demanded. Thus we find that in January 1796 subjects for conversation would have included, as the author says they did[51], the Seditious Meetings Act of the preceding year[52], the expected child of the Princess of Wales[53], the recent outrages to George III[54], and the high price of bread at 1/3 the quartern loaf[55]. In the same way, when Mrs. Gaskell came to describe the Siege of Acre[56], she had merely to look up the dispatches from Sir Sidney Smith quoted in *The Annual Register for* 1799[57], and supplement this reading by whatever further research she deemed necessary[58].

One might judge the artistic handling of such material as satisfactory, but no more. On occasions the novelist's descriptions of historical events appear to be rendered externally, almost from a text-book point of view: one inevitably finds oneself asking, Now what sources is she relying on for these

---

affair', *The Annual Register* having 'been *carefully* looked over *months*' previously; she further remarked that, with many people in Yorkshire at work for her, she would be sure to have her information sooner or later. This [(9 or 16) March 1860] letter is in the Yale University Library: MS Vault Sect. 16—it (*G.L.*, No. 457) is dated [March 1860] by Chapple and Pollard, in whose edition, by a printing error, '*carefully*' is not completely italicized.

[50] See his obituary notice—'William Stevenson, Esq., of the Records Office, in the Treasury', *The Annual Biography and Obituary*: 1830, XIV (London: Longman, Rees, Orme, Brown, and Green, 1830), 212. Mr. Stevenson, it seems also worth noting, 'completed [John] Campbell's "Lives of the British Admirals:" [1812-1817] . . . In 1824, he produced a valuable volume, entitled, "Historical Sketch of the Progress of Discovery, Navigation, and Commerce"' (*ibidem*).

[51] *Works*, VI, 177-178.

[52] *The Annual Register; or, A View of the History, Politics, and Literature, for the Year* 1796, London: F. C. & J. Rivington, 1813, ii, *172-*175.

[53] Charlotte Elizabeth, born 7 January 1796.

[54] *The Annual Register for* 1795, ii, *48-*49.

[55] *The Annual Register for* 1796, ii, *169.

[56] *Works*, VI, 448-458.

[57] ii, *110-*115, *132-*140; see too *op. cit.*, i, 151-159.

[58] Perhaps by consulting such works as [Edward Howard] *Memoirs of Admiral Sir Sidney Smith, K.C.B., &c.*, 2 vols., London: Richard Bentley, 1839, esp. I, 169-210; or, more probably, John Barrow, *The Life and Correspondence of Admiral Sir William Sidney Smith, G.C.B.*, 2 vols., London: Richard Bentley, 1848, esp. I, 261-336.

passages? A striking instance of fact and fiction being clumsily combined is afforded by the episode at Acre, where there seems something slightly incongruous about Philip and Kinraid rubbing shoulders, so to speak, with Sir Sidney Smith, Napoleon, Djezzar Pacha, and Hassan Bey. Seccombe, who notes several criticisms of this section[59], suggests that the Siege scene ' corresponds to a theatrical vision '[60]—and certainly ' stagey ' does come to mind as an appropriate epithet. He remarks, moreover, that perhaps the whole chapter is ' a little out of scale.'[61] As Miss Hopkins[62] indicates, its most important incident is later recounted to Sylvia by Kinraid's wife (where[63], by the way, Mrs. Gaskell is at her best), so the entire chapter could have been omitted with advantage. There is little doubt that in this part Mrs. Gaskell was padding to fill out the third volume[64]. Such a hypothesis receives support from the rather unnecessary inclusion, at the end of the chapter, of a little ghost story, put into the mouth of one of the sailors as an explanation for Kinraid's failure to have his mysterious rescuer traced. Very likely Mrs. Gaskell seized the opportunity to introduce one of her favourite anecdotes; when invention flagged, she had a ready repertoire on which to draw. Recalling how once at the George Smiths' Mrs. Gaskell delighted her listeners with legends of smugglers and ghosts[65], Lady Ritchie opined that this very story ' might have well been one of those that were recounted

---

[59] Seccombe, pref. *Sylvia's Lovers,* by Mrs. Gaskell, p. xxxix, fn. 1.
[60] Seccombe, pref. *Sylvia's Lovers,* by Mrs. Gaskell, p. xxxix, fn. 1.
[61] Seccombe, pref. *Sylvia's Lovers,* by Mrs. Gaskell, p. xxxix, fn. 1.
[62] *Elizabeth Gaskell,* p. 266.
[63] *Works,* VI, 473-476.
[64] On padding, see the opinion of Miss Hopkins (*Elizabeth Gaskell,* p. 265-266), who quotes from Mrs. Gaskell's correspondence to her publisher of, respectively, [October 1862] and 18 March [1862]—now in the archives of Sir John Murray—: *G.L.,* Nos. 517 (dated [?Late September 1862] by Chapple and Pollard), 501 (its year being given as [?1862] by Chapple and Pollard).
[65] Ritchie, ' Mrs. Gaskell ', *Blackstick Papers,* p. 213. For Whitby smuggling, mentioned in the novel (*Works,* VI, 24, 46, 54, 104), see Percy Shaw Jeffrey, collected and ed. *Whitby Lore and Legend,* 3rd and rev. edn, Whitby: Horne & Son, Ltd., 1952, pp. 4-8.

then.'[66] Certainly it was none of her devising, merely a slightly altered version of what had been told her as the truth[67].

There is yet one further source to which the author of *Sylvia's Lovers* was deeply indebted. Both Seccombe[68] and Professor Whitfield[69] have posited the influence on Mrs. Gaskell of the life of William Scoresby (1760-1829), the Whitby Arctic navigator, and the writings of his son, the Rev. William Scoresby (1789-1857), D.D., master-mariner and man of science. This contention can now be substantiated in two ways. Firstly, there is evidence that Mrs. Gaskell met Dr. Scoresby: not only does she mention, in her *Life of Charlotte Brontë*[70], conversing with him on the character of the inhabitants of the West Riding (he having at one time been Vicar of Bradford); she also refers more fully to their meeting, at Sir John Maxwell's, in a letter of 25 September [1855] to Ellen Nussey[71]. Hence,

[66] Ritchie, *Blackstick Papers,* p. 213. Lady Ritchie, mistakenly, attributes the anecdote to Sylvia's father (*ibidem*); the story-telling she places in Autumn 1864 (*op. cit.,* p. 214).

[67] Her original (manuscript) rendering of the ghost story, written down for an unknown friend at midnight on 5 October 1862, opens with the statement that she had learned about it the previous 'year from very good authority; from one/ who had heard it from the very person by whom/ the apparition was seen': Mrs. Gaskell then goes on to recount an anecdote very similar, albeit having a Yorkshire setting, to the Devon tale incorporated in her novel. This manuscript, in the Berg Collection at the New York Public Library, is noted by Miss Hopkins (*Elizabeth Gaskell,* p. 339), who, though giving a brief summary, fails to relate it to *Sylvia's Lovers* (*Works,* VI, 457-458).

[68] Pref. *Sylvia's Lovers,* by Mrs. Gaskell, pp. xxvi-xxvii.

[69] *Mrs Gaskell,* p. 164.

[70] *The Life of Charlotte Brontë,* 1st edn, 1857, I, 30.

[71] Copies of this letter (headed Dunoon, Argyleshire), once possessed by Mr. J. T. Lancaster, belong to the present writer: our dating and the subsequent, brief quotation follow a slightly more authoritative copy than that available to Chapple and Pollard, where (*G.L.,* No. 267a) the year is not enclosed within square brackets. We may also note that in it Mrs. Gaskell says she is staying with her 'unknown half-sister,' not seen for twenty-four years: this must be Catherine, the daughter of William Stevenson and his second wife, Catherine Thomson. In a letter to her sister-in-law, Eliza Gaskell, post-marked 16 December 1833, she refers to the approaching Christmas marriage of her 'little miss of a ½ sister/' (this letter—*G.L.,* No. 3, dated [c. 16 December 1833] by Chapple and Pollard—is owned by Mrs. Margaret Trevor Jones); the same letter mentions the young lady's being but seventeen that 8th of December. According to a conjecture in the family-tree supplied to Whitfield (*Mrs Gaskell,* p. ix) by (Professor Whitfield informs me) Bryan T. Holland, Catherine married a Mr. Robertson; however she is listed as having wed

knowing Dr. Scoresby, Mrs. Gaskell would, one supposes, naturally refer to his works when writing her Whitby story: this supposition is confirmed by the novel itself. Secondly, therefore, one can point to a series of Arctic anecdotes for which the author was directly obliged to the younger Scoresby. Thus Kinraid's example of the dangers of falling ice[72] comes straight out of his *Arctic Regions*[73]; and Robson's account of how he fell into the freezing sea[74] also closely follows this source[75], even to the extent of having the same latitude (81° North). Then

---

a Mr. Black (the marriage being without issue) in the family-trees of the late Mr. Walter Carter, the late Miss D. J. Harrison, and Dr. W. M. R. Henderson. There is a reference to Mrs. Gaskell's intention of going to Glasgow to see her 'step-mother & step/=sister whom', she claimed, not to have 'seen/ for 25 years & more' in a letter, written to 'dear Jane,' her cousin, one Tuesday [17 July 1855—rather than 30 August /55 (as dated by non-Gaskellian hands)], the property of Mr. S. Roscoe (Dunsmore, South Hill Avenue, Harrow, Middlesex): this letter (*G.L.*, No. 254) is dated [?17 July ?1855] by Chapple and Pollard. Doubtless memory-lapses explain the apparent chronological inconsistencies. That Mrs. Gaskell's half-brother (William) was dead by 5 March 1859 is shown by Mrs. Gaskell's letter of that date to John Blackwood, the publisher; it (*G.L.*, No. 415) refers to the help received in educating her half-brother, since deceased, from Mr. [William?] Blackwood—this letter being in the National Library of Scotland (MS. 4139, ff. 3-6; the relevant passage is on f. 4r).

[72] *Works*, VI, 105-106.

[73] William Scoresby, *An Account of the Arctic Regions, with a History and Description of the Northern Whale-Fishery,* 2 vols., Edinburgh: Archibald Constable and Co.; London: Hurst, Robinson and Co., 1820, II, 342. There was an [1849] abridgement of the second volume of this two-volume work—Captain Scoresby, *The Northern Whale-Fishery,* London: The Religious Tract Society. (The relevant reference to the present anecdote is *Northern Whale-Fishery,* pp. 130-131.) The abridgement contains the relevant Arctic anecdotes; but it omits the abstract of Parliamentary Acts and the account of affidavits and certificates, both appended to the fuller work (*Arctic Regions*, II, 491-505, 514-518), which may have helped Mrs. Gaskell with one of the legal citations in *Sylvia's Lovers* (*Works*, VI, 229: cf. *Arctic Regions*, II, 503, 516), though such is by no means certain, since there is another legal reference (*Works*, VI, 302) with which Scoresby could offer no assistance—for help with this the novelist probably applied to one of her numerous legal acquaintances. Perhaps we ought to note that Mrs. Gaskell specifically names the boat as the *John,* of Hull, whereas Scoresby only says it was a Hull whaler; doubtless her eye had travelled to the next section of Scoresby's anecdotes, where there appears the *John,* of Greenock.

[74] *Works*, VI, 106-107.

[75] Scoresby, *Arctic Regions*, II, 360-362; *Northern Whale-Fishery*, pp. 141-142.

Mrs. Gaskell introduces a typical sailor's yarn[76]—perhaps her own invention, or perhaps picked up during a conversation with an old tar[77]. After this she once more consults her reference book[78], and allows Robson to tell a *prima facie* tall story about how, in his harpooning days, he rode on a whale's back[79]. In such passages Mrs. Gaskell's reading bears ample fruit; she admirably incorporates into the dialogue what was borrowed from Scoresby. Much of this success seems due to her having dramatized the material. Since the anecdotes are interesting in themselves, they become doubly so when, rendered into Whitby dialect, they fall from the lips of the practising specksioneer, Charlie Kinraid, and the erstwhile specksioneer, Daniel Robson. Mrs. Gaskell had well observed the ways of seafaring men, doubtless stimulated by her own naval con-

[76] *Works,* VI, 107-108.

[77] Such as the loquacious sailor she once met at the Isle of Man (Seccombe, pref. *Sylvia's Lovers,* by Mrs. Gaskell, p. xxvi). Probably Meta Gaskell told Seccombe about this sailor; for she assisted his work and proof-read his Introduction—as is evidenced by (1910-11) letters from her to him, together with a list of her corrections, donated by Seccombe to Mrs. M. E. Miller (Fiery Beacon, Painswick, Gloucestershire), who allowed the present writer to purchase them. *Sylvia's Lovers* especially interested Meta. During its composition she wrote to Norton about the promised beauty of the story, concerning which, she said, her mother was pleased and hopeful; after publication she referred to Mrs. Gaskell's happiness at Norton's pleasure in the dedication (of the American edition to him), adding that she considered the book her mother's masterpiece: Meta's remarks appear respectively in her conclusion to Mrs. Gaskell's letter to Norton of 28 August 1861 (a conclusion not printed in Whitehill, ed. *Gaskell-Norton Letters,* p. 95: *G.L.,* No. 493) and in her own 7-17 April [1863] letter to him—both letters being in the Harvard University Library: bMS Am 1088 (2602, 2641).

[78] Scoresby, *Arctic Regions,* II, 365-367; *Northern Whale-Fishery,* pp. 143-145. It may be useful to mention (i) that the information about Kinraid's wages (*Works,* VI, 207) could owe something to Scoresby (*Arctic Regions,* II, 200-201; *Northern Whale-Fishery,* pp. 48-50); (ii) that the reference to whale-jaws used as arches (*Works,* VI, 5) is attested by Scoresby (*Arctic Regions,* II, 434-435; *Northern Whale-Fishery,* p. 172); (iii) that, with pardonable licence, the author has the *Resolution,* of Monkshaven, on the seas in October 1796 (*Works,* VI, 17, 11), although the *Resolution,* of Whitby, a ship once captained by Scoresby (*Arctic Regions,* II, 276; *Northern Whale-Fishery,* p. 100), was new in 1803 (*Arctic Regions,* II, 393; *Northern Whale-Fishery,* p. 155).

[79] *Works,* VI, 109-111.

nexions and by that love of the sea which made her remark:
"The blood of the Vikings still lingers in my veins."[80]

There is a sense in which it would be erroneous to consider
Sylvia's Lovers Mrs. Gaskell's first major venture into historical
fiction; as the author of *Mary Barton* she takes her place
among those novelists who ' have by design so treated the life
of their own period as to produce fiction that was historical
from the outset.'[81] Furthermore we must remember that *Ruth*
was set, if not ' vaguely about " a hundred years ago " '[82], then
at least during the early decades of the nineteenth century[83];
and the opening chapter of that novel affords ample proof
of its writer's historical sense. Indeed an appreciation of change,
a feeling for the romance of the past, was evident as early as
her sketch of Clopton Hall. Leaving aside the shorter stories,
many of which are placed in some not-too-distant past (well
evoked by the title of one of them—'Half a Lifetime Ago'), we
may also mention, as a forerunner of *Sylvia's Lovers, Lois the
Witch*. There too Mrs. Gaskell made use of source-books; and
she herself assumed the position of an enlightened Victorian,
looking back over the years[84]. Since this attitude is likewise
manifest in *Sylvia's Lovers*, it may be well to examine it further.

Authorial comments are of several sorts. Some are purely
factual, such as a reference to the light given by a scanty dip-
candle[85] (the chief luminant of those days being the fire[86]), and
serve usefully to convey the flavour of the period; they are, as
it were, let fall at random from a skilful pen. Others make
judgements on the actions of the characters, especially on those
of Philip. Yet others are unsubtle prognostications, inartistic

---

[80] Quoted by Mrs. Chadwick (*Mrs. Gaskell*, p. 255): cf. Ritchie,
pref. *Cranford*, by Mrs. Gaskell, p. x.

[81] Arthur Melville Clark, ' The Historical Novel ', *Studies in Literary Modes*, Edinburgh and London: Oliver and Boyd, 1946, p. 4.

[82] Miss Hopkins (*Elizabeth Gaskell*, p. 324) means a century before
the date of publication (1853), which is an erroneous reading.

[83] A careful perusal of the first chapter, especially of the first few
paragraphs, indicates that Mrs. Gaskell had in mind for the commencement of Ruth's history a time some fifty years previous to that of her
own writing; this is confirmed by what comes later in the tale, such
as, for instance, the reference to ' June of 18—' (*Works*, III, 61).

[84] E.g. *Works*, VII, 153.

[85] *Works*, VI, 100: cf. 522.

[86] *Works*, VI, 148.

hints at what will come next, like that which concludes the penultimate chapter[87]. Most interesting, however, are those meditative-reflective passages where the novelist, from a Victorian vantage-point, allows herself to pass historical verdicts. At the outset she displays this judicial tendency when, with regard to impressment, she says: 'Now all this tyranny (for I can use no other word) is marvellous to us; we cannot imagine how it is that a nation submitted to it for so long, even under any warlike enthusiasm, any panic of invasion, any amount of loyal subservience to the governing powers.'[88] Lest Mrs. Gaskell be charged with adopting too innocently a Whig interpretation of history, it will be well to quote the cogitations called forth by the Vicar of Monkshaven who, torn between respect for the law and natural sympathy for his gardener's bereavement, preached a wholly inadequate sermon at the funeral of Darley, killed while resisting the gang; the last (and saving) sentence suggests that its author was, perhaps, not quite such a complacent Macaulayan as one might at first suspect.

> In looking back to the last century, it appears curious to see how little our ancestors had the power of putting two things together, and perceiving either the discord or harmony thus produced. Is it because we are farther off from those times, and have, consequently, a greater range of vision? Will our descendants have a wonder about us, such as we have about the inconsistency of our forefathers, or a surprise at our blindness that we do not perceive that, holding such and such opinions, our course of action must be so and so, or that the logical consequence of particular opinions must be convictions which at present we hold in abhorrence? It seems puzzling to look back on men such as our vicar, who almost held the doctrine that the King could do no wrong, yet were ever ready to talk of the glorious Revolution, and to abuse the Stuarts for having entertained the same doctrine, and tried to put it in practice. But such discrepancies ran through good men's lives in those days. It is well for us that we live at the present time, when everybody is logical and consistent.[89]

Nonetheless Mrs. Gaskell was justly proud to remark, about the universal practice of smuggling, that 'one of the greatest signs of the real progress we have made since those times seems to be that our daily concerns of buying and selling, eating and

[87] *Works,* VI, 516.
[88] *Works,* VI, 7.
[89] *Works,* VI, 71-72.

drinking, whatsoever we do, are more tested by the real, practical standard of our religion than they were in the days of our grandfathers.'[90] Yet, having attacked the Government's financial policy for its demoralising effects, she wittily goes on to remark : ' It may seem curious to trace up the popular standard of truth to taxation; but I do not think the idea would be so very far-fetched.'[91]

Perhaps Mrs. Gaskell is most conspicuously of the mid-nineteenth century in her attitude to the mood of the times and the mentality of the people. Throughout *Sylvia's Lovers* there are references[92] to popular beliefs, traditions, and superstitious habits (subjects she always found fascinating) as well as to the forebodings of dreams; for she was aware that, in addition to the physical environment, a historical novelist should take account of the spiritual and intellectual atmosphere of the age. Among the most salient features of nearly all the characters are their simplicity and spontaneity : they feel rather than reflect; they act rather than think; they look outwards rather than turn inwards. Probably the first hint that this is how Mrs. Gaskell conceived of a past generation can be found in her meditations over the Whitby sailors who ' mostly slept through the sermons '[93], not discovering ' their daily faults or temptations under the grand aliases befitting their appearance from a preacher's mouth.'[94] A little further on she is more explicit.

In the agricultural counties, and among the class to which these four persons [Molly Corney, Hester Rose, Sylvia Robson (especially), and (though he is less typical) Philip Hepburn] belonged, there is little analysis of motive or comparison of characters and actions, even at this present day of enlightenment. Sixty or seventy years ago there was still less. I do not

---

90 *Works*, VI, 104.

91 *Works*, VI, 104.

92 *Works*, VI, 90, 293, 363, 364-365, 435-437, 457-458, 501. In effect the novel (*Works*, VI, 365) contains one of the verses which, according to the author, celebrated her own marriage, as is noted in Howitt, ' Stray Notes from Mrs. Gaskell ', *Good Words*, XXXVI (1895), 607, fn.: *G.L.*, No. 12, fn. 1. Virtually the same verse is quoted, again with reference to the Knutsford wedding-custom of sanding, by Mrs. Gaskell in her letter to W. S. Landor of 22 May 1854—now in the Forster Collection (F. MS. 215) at the Victoria & Albert Museum—: *G.L.*, No. 197.

93 *Works*, VI, 67.

94 *Works*, VI, 67.

mean that amongst thoughtful and serious people there was
not much reading of such books as Mason *On Self-Know-
ledge*, and Law's *Serious Call*, or that there were not the experiences of the Wesleyans, that were related at class-meeting
for the edification of the hearers. But, taken as a general rule,
it may be said that few knew what manner of men they were,
compared to the numbers now who are fully conscious of
their virtues, qualities, failings, and weaknesses, and who go
about comparing others with themselves—not in a spirit of
Pharisaism and arrogance, but with a vivid self-consciousness
that more than anything else deprives characters of freshness
and originality.[95]

Mrs. Gaskell returns to this theme later, where she claims that
intuition rather than ' reasoning or analytic processes '[96] guided
the conduct of such as Sylvia Robson.

Allied with these psychological comments are the author's
sociological *apperçus*. One comes upon a remark like the
following, given in explanation of the lack of intercourse between the sexes.

> Amongst uneducated people—whose range of subjects and in-
> terest do not extend beyond their daily life—it is natural that,
> when the first blush and hurry of youth is over, there should
> be no great pleasure in the conversation of the other sex. Men
> have plenty to say to men which in their estimation (gained
> from tradition and experience) women cannot understand; and
> farmers of a much later date than the one of which I am
> writing would have contemptuously considered it as a loss of
> time to talk to women; . . . [97]

The last words provide a clue as to how the novelist imagined
the folk of the period behaved. From personal experience
(including her Knutsford childhood and her Haworth investigations), she was acquainted with country-dwellers, not least
with those inhabiting the remoter regions of the British Isles.
Such observations, suitably modified, she seems to have transposed into the recent past of her tale.

Having considered how *Sylvia's Lovers* came to be written,
and having examined its specifically historical features, we must
now treat the novel as something more than an instance of a
particular *genre*. To range Mrs. Gaskell's publications in order
of merit appears an impossible task, they being so diverse in

[95] *Works,* VI, 78-79.
[96] *Works,* VI, 336.
[97] *Works,* VI, 93.

kind; yet one feels a strong temptation to agree with Canon
Ainger, who 'used to declare that the first two volumes of
" Sylvia's Lovers " were " the best thing Mrs. Gaskell had ever
done." ' [98] It was a chronic weakness of hers for the beginning
and middle of a work to surpass its end; but, even taken as a
whole—and that was how the author took it[99]—, *Sylvia's Lovers*
more than equals the other novels she completed. In its descriptive passages, it can rival *Ruth*; in its treatment of love, it
can compete with *North and South*; in its tragic colouring, it
can bear comparison with *Mary Barton*.

In the writer's estimation this was the saddest story she ever
composed[100], a story which, to Dr. Liddell's taste, seemed " like
a Greek tragedy, for power."[101] The ' tragic hero ', Philip
Hepburn, is the most complex character in the book. He
is also, one may hazard, the most successful full-length male
character in all Mrs. Gaskell's fiction; and it is with his
sentiments that the reader finds himself in greatest sympathy.   Although her treatment of Philip precludes complete
identification, one may surmise that the novelist found him the
most absorbing of her masculine creations, the one with whom
her own feelings most readily went.

Significantly Mrs. Gaskell at one time considered calling the
story ' Philip's Idol '[102]; and her letter to George Smith of 18
March [1862][103] indicates that, despite an awareness that such
a title would be open to punning, she was reluctant to lose the
word ' idol '. She also considered[104] ' The Specksioneer ', ' Too
Late ', and ' Monkshaven ', each of which (like the name
adopted) has something in its favour, though none signifies the

[98] Ward, ed. *Works*, VI, p. xiii.
[99] As is evidenced by her letter of 1 February [1862] to W. S. Williams
(a copy being with Forster correspondence in the Gaskell Section,
Brotherton Collection, Leeds University Library): *G.L.*, No. 499.
[100] Ward, ed. *Works*, VI, p. xii.
[101] Quoted in Ward, ed. *Works*, VI, p. xxvi, fn.
[102] *Gaskell-Norton Letters*, ed. Whitehill, p. 94: *G.L.*, No. 493—see
too *G.L.*, No. 499a.
[103] The relevant extract is quoted, with minor mistakes, by Miss
Hopkins (*Elizabeth Gaskell*, p. 219); this letter is now in the archives of
Sir John Murray, its year (*G.L.*, No. 501) being given as [?1862] by
Chapple and Pollard.
[104] Ward, ed. *Works*, VI, pp. xiv-xv; Sanders, *Elizabeth Gaskell*, p.
128; Hopkins, *Elizabeth Gaskell*, p. 219; and *G.L.*, Nos. 451a, 493, 499a,
501.

central theme—a theme made explicit at the end of the book in Philip's dying words to his wife.

> " Child," said he, once more. " I ha' made thee my idol; and, if I could live my life o'er again, I would love my God more, and thee less; and then I shouldn't ha' sinned this sin against thee. . . . "[105]

What these words should bring to mind is not so much Shakespeare as the authoress of *Ruth*. In *" My Diary "* Mrs. Gaskell had voiced the fear that she might make an idol of little Marianne[106]; in *Ruth* that fear found fictional expression in Miss Benson's warning to the heroine against idolizing her child (' " You must not make him into an idol, or God will, perhaps, punish you through him." '[107]). It was Philip's sin to break the First Commandment, a transgression from which every sorrow flowed. Although he also bordered on idolatry in his relations with his baby girl[108], and although Sylvia, very much like Ruth, resolved to be all in all to little Bella[109], Mrs. Gaskell gives no hint in this work that she saw such parental sentiments as potentially dangerous. What she stresses are the evil results of Philip's infatuation for his cousin, with the consequential clouding of his moral sense: only by deception could he succeed in wedding Sylvia. Nor did married life provide the conjugal felicity so fondly hoped for, even though he had the material means to carry out his heart's desire of ' placing his idol in a befitting shrine '[110]. It was his fate to fall in love with a not very remarkable girl[111], who could not return his affections; by devious methods he secured her acquiescence, only to find he had little but Dead Sea fruit to enjoy.

Before examining in more detail the author's treatment of the love triad—Philip, Kinraid, and Sylvia—, we may ask, What made Mrs. Gaskell so concerned with matrimony in general, and with unhappy love affairs in particular? Certainly

---

[105] *Works,* VI, 523.
[106] *" My Diary "*, pp. 11, 17.
[107] *Works,* III, 161.
[108] *Works,* VI, 371.
[109] *Works,* VI, 437.
[110] *Works,* VI, 360.
[111] A view which would not be endorsed by those critics who have applied to themselves the title of the novel: see Sanders, *Elizabeth Gaskell,* p. 128.

the love interest had not been absent from her earlier novels; but it had not usually held the centre of the stage. Even in *North and South,* middle-class romance though it was (at least the concluding scene provides the conventional happy ending), there is nothing about the married life of the hero and heroine. *Sylvia's Lovers* being thus the first full-length work to deal with the matrimonial theme, one wonders whether there could be a personal reason for its appearance at this time. Miss Rubenius, who might have considered the matter at length, as coming so completely within her terms of reference, is oddly silent. Having conjectured Mrs. Gaskell's marriage was not quite the ideal union Dr. Adolphus Ward took it to be[112], she ought surely to have examined *Sylvia's Lovers* in the light of that hypothesis. However, since the orthodox view concerning the ' mutual devotion '[113] of husband and wife appears unshaken, one's inclination is to look elsewhere. What suggests itself is their daughter's broken engagement with Captain Hill. About this affair the family seems to have been, quite rightly, rather reticent; it was, we recall, the reason for Mrs Gaskell's taking Meta to Heidelberg in 1858, a visit which helped her to forget the year's engagement[114]. Her mother, who knew that women

[112] Rubenius, *The Woman Question in Mrs. Gaskell's Life and Works,* pp. 20-30: cf. ' Il me semble que l'on sent dans toutes ses histoires qu'elle n'est pas heureuse dans son mariage, les parents de Sylvia, ceux de " Cousin Phillis ", et dans la nouvelle histoire " the squire and Mrs Hamley " ne se vont pas—ne se plaisent pas, tout en s'aimant bien.'— Mlle Ida Mohl in a letter of 23 November [1864] to Mme Mary Mohl (the relevant extract having been made by Miss Jane Revere Coolidge— subsequently Mrs. Whitehill—before the destruction of the Mohl letters during World War II).
[113] Hopkins, *Elizabeth Gaskell,* p. 376: cf. Chapple and Pollard, ed. *The Letters of Mrs Gaskell,* pp. xiii-xiv.
[114] Rubenius, *The Woman Question in Mrs. Gaskell's Life and Works,* p. 79. Other easily accessible references to Captain Hill or the engagement include *Gaskell-Norton Letters,* ed. Whitehill, pp. 5, 7, 17; Haldane, *Mrs. Gaskell and Her Friends,* p. 186; and *G.L.,* Nos. 350 (possible), 360, 362a-370, 374, 380, 382-384, 385a, 394, 414, 421, 421a, 451, 478, 480, 485, 495. The attachment may have been formed in Spring 1857 when Mrs. Gaskell, her two elder daughters, and Catherine Winkworth seemed to find the captain a pleasant travelling companion—*Letters and Memorials of Catherine Winkworth,* II ([ed. Susanna Winkworth and Margaret Josephine Shaen], 1886), 109-111, 120, 123, 137-141. Details about Hill and Meta occur in correspondence from Mrs. Gaskell to her daughter, Marianne (in the Gaskell Section, Brotherton Collection, Leeds University Library), to Eliza Fox (a copy being in the Gaskell Section,

'naturally yearn after children '[115], must have keenly appreciated her unhappiness, perhaps especially because, as this daughter showed more artistic talent and intellectual interests than the others[116], she must have been that much closer to the

---

Brotherton Collection, Leeds University Library), to Lord Hatherton (lodged in the Staffordshire County Record Office and owned by Edward Thomas Walhouse Littleton, the Fifth Baron Hatherton, Hatherton Hall, Cannock, Staffordshire), to Charles Eliot Norton (in the Harvard University Library: important passages are omitted, the omissions being indicated, in Whitehill, ed. *Gaskell-Norton Letters*, pp. 7, 17, 23, 73, 78), to John Malcolm Ludlow (her letter of 29 October [1857] being in the Cambridge University Library: MS. Add. 7348/10/126), to Miss Maria Martineau (in the Birmingham University Library, cited by kind permission of Lady Martineau), to Ellen Nussey (copies, once owned by Mr. J. T. Lancaster, belonging to the present writer), to Mrs. Nancy Robson (in the Yale University Library), and to George Smith (in the archives of Sir John Murray); and in that from Marianne Gaskell to Charles Eliot Norton—letters of Thursday 9 July [1857], 8 September [1857], and 25 January 1858, deposited in the Harvard University Library: bMS Am 1088 (3495, 3488, 3489). From these sources it would appear that Meta became engaged in late June or early July 1857 to Charles (Charlie) Hill, a widower with at least one child (Dudley); that an early wedding was envisaged because of Captain Hill's forthcoming return to India, but that it was later decided to defer matters till late the following year when one of her parents would accompany Meta to Egypt, Hill meeting her there for a (1858-9) winter wedding; that they should remain in India till May 1862, when Hill would retire with an annual pension of £200 and, if possible, secure a railway appointment at home; that the captain left the Gaskells c. 24 August, reaching Suez by 10 September; that, partly thanks to Mrs. Gaskell's efforts, he obtained the command of his regiment of sappers and miners (with £80 a month additional to his military pay) at Dowlaisheram; that a disturbing report from his sisters led Meta to suspect him of duplicity, and that, on receiving no explanation and on his not replying to her mother's enquiry about the arrangements for Meta's October departure, she broke off their relationship, a decision with which his brother, Captain Dudley Hill, concurred; that Hill, who had complained to his sisters about his prospective bride's lack of confidence in him, maintaining no union could be happy where the wife did not implicitly trust her husband, subsequently became engaged to Miss Matilda Wilson, whom he hoped to marry in April 1862; that, despite an initially favourable impression, Mrs. Gaskell probably came to hold the captain in little esteem; and that Charles Bosanquet restored some of the faith in *man*kind lost by Meta in consequence of Hill's character.

[115] *Gaskell-Norton Letters*, ed. Whitehill, p. 44: *G.L.*, No. 453.

[116] E.g. *Gaskell-Norton Letters*, ed. Whitehill, pp. 32, 64-65: *G.L.*, Nos. 418, 476—see too, for example, *G.L.*, Nos. 101, 126.

authoress[117]. Whether or not *Sylvia's Lovers* was written, among other things, to demonstrate that an unhappy marriage is worse than a broken engagement remains an open question, yet one worth posing.

Sylvia Robson, the object of Philip's devotion, was a simple country girl, at first hardly conscious of the nature of her cousin's attentions, which nonetheless she wished to avoid[118]. Mrs. Gaskell conveys Sylvia's maidenly coyness[119]; and, as the story proceeds, shows how she blossomed[120] into some one whom ' all the men under forty in Monkshaven '[121] found attractive. Like the heroine of ' The Doom of the Griffiths '[122], she aroused the most diverse responses in those around her.

> In fact, her peculiarity seemed to be this—that every one who knew her talked about her either in praise or blame; in church, or in market, she unconsciously attracted attention; they could not forget her presence, as they could that of other girls perhaps more personally attractive.[123]

With this gay, volatile, unthinking creature Philip was entirely out of keeping, his being, as Mrs. Robson told him, a very different nature.

> " I used to think as she and yo' might fancy one another; but thou'rt too old-fashioned like for her; ye would na' suit; . . . "[124]

The measure of this difference is shown by Philip's inability to comprehend ' in what way he was too " old-fashioned." '[125]

Mrs. Gaskell's success lay in making Philip, product as he was of self-help and self-denial, a wholly sympathetic character. There is, for example, the description of his reading aloud,

---

[117] In a letter of Saturday [(8?—pre 13—August) 1857] to George Smith (in the archives of Sir John Murray), Mrs. Gaskell described Meta as ' a most dear friend,/ more like a sister . . . than/ anything else '. This letter appears as *G.L.*, No. 365 (dated [?Early August 1857] by Chapple and Pollard).
[118] *Works*, VI, 26, 35, 82, 101, 125.
[119] *Works*, VI, 21-22.
[120] *Works*, VI, 120-121.
[121] *Works*, VI, 128.
[122] *Works*, V, 251-253.
[123] *Works*, VI, 128-129.
[124] *Works*, VI, 132: cf. 262.
[125] *Works*, VI, 133.

taking pleasure in what had with difficulty and labour been acquired[126]; then there is his devoted service to his master's interests, with 'his careful and punctual ministration to his absent mother's comforts, as long as she was living to benefit by his silent, frugal self-denial.'[127] There is too Mrs. Gaskell's fine insight when Philip is offered a partnership in the shop.

> Philip's voice quivered a little, as some remembrance passed across his mind; at this unusual moment of expansion out it came. "I wish mother could ha' seen this day."[128]

The author appreciated that such a sentiment would come naturally from a man like Philip, and took advantage of her perception to win readers to him. It is not, however, in these strokes that her greatest achievement resides, but rather in her making his fall from righteousness acceptable, psychologically and artistically.

The lie *motif* is a favourite ingredient in many of Mrs. Gaskell's compositions, most notably in *Ruth* and *North and South*. Yet, whereas in those earlier novels the deceptions could find some ethical justification, since they were committed from more or less altruistic motives, in *Sylvia's Lovers* it is self-interest alone which seems to dictate Philip's conduct. What reasonable excuses, the moralist might ask, could a man possibly have for keeping silent when, in addition to knowing his cousin's lover had been impressed, he had been expressly charged to tell her what had happened? Worse even than this appears his subsequent policy of allowing Sylvia to think Kinraid drowned and then marrying the girl himself, though quite aware that, had she not been fully convinced of her sweetheart's death, she could never have wed another. Moreover, not only does Philip keep silent about what actually befell Kinraid, he explicitly tells Sylvia he must be ' " dead and drowned " '[129], going on, by a neat piece of casuistry, to justify the untruth. Kinraid was, he told himself, very likely dead by that time: but, ' even if not, he was as good as dead to her; so that [he speciously reasoned] the word " dead " might be

[126] *Works,* VI, 100-101.
[127] *Works,* VI, 126.
[128] *Works,* VI, 184.
[129] *Works,* VI, 348.

used in all honest certainty, as in one of its meanings Kinraid
was dead for sure.'[130]

The cause of this deceit—deceit from one who (very much
as Margaret Hale or Ellinor Wilkins might have done) had
resolved, when all life lay before him, ' to show the world
" what a Christian might be " '[131], and who had once claimed
never to have told a lie[132]—was his infatuation for Sylvia, the
idolatry previously noticed. Mrs. Gaskell makes such a love
completely convincing. That having been established, the
motives for the deception become understandable, if not pardonable. Philip's jealousy had been early aroused by Kinraid's
intimacy with Sylvia[133], an intimacy not favoured by Mrs.
Robson who, indeed, later tried to warn her daughter against
the gallant specksioneer by means of an exemplary tale[134]. Nor
was Kinraid's behaviour such as, in the opinion of her devoted
cousin, could possibly be compatible with true love[135]. Furthermore Philip learned, from a most trustworthy source, that he
had already broken one girl's heart[136]. In this context Kinraid's
capture seemed providential[137]; yet Philip, on seeing his bravery
in fighting the gang, began to feel pity—until he noticed the
sailor was wearing a familiar ribbon[138], his own first present to
Sylvia[139]. Unsure whether or not he had explicitly pledged to
give Sylvia her lover's last message, Philip deferred making a
decision for the moment, only to overhear, at the end of the
day, a bar-room jest about Kinraid's light ways with women[140].
Thereafter he made himself believe that, for his failure to com-
municate to the Robsons the news of the impressment, impersonal forces were responsible[141]. However he might have reported what he had seen if, on his return from London to
Monkshaven, he had not discovered that Bessy Corney as well

---

[130] *Works*, VI, 348.
[131] *Works*, VI, 526: a minor typographical error has been corrected.
[132] *Works*, VI, 223.
[133] *Works*, VI, 117-118.
[134] *Works*, VI, 198-199.
[135] *Works*, VI, 175.
[136] *Works*, VI, 203.
[137] *Works*, VI, 228.
[138] *Works*, VI, 232.
[139] *Works*, VI, 141-142.
[140] *Works*, VI, 238.
[141] *Works*, VI, 239.

as Sylvia was grieving for the same missing sweet-heart[142].
Moreover there was Mrs. Robson's comforting declaration.

> "Lad! it's a' for t' best. He were noane good enough for her;
> and I misdoubt me he were only playin' wi' her as he'd done
> by others. Let her a-be, let her a-be; she'll come round to be
> thankful." [143]

Besides the factors which influenced Philip, Mrs. Gaskell
affords the reader additional evidence of Kinraid's 'gallantry'
with women. Before his rival does, we know of the conduct
which broke Coulson's sister's heart[144]; and, by virtue of our
privileged position, we can view those mental processes which
were hidden from Philip. There is, for example, the following
passage.

> After the Robsons had left, a blank fell upon both Charley
> and Philip. In a few minutes, however, the former, accustomed
> to prompt decision, resolved that she and no other should be
> his wife. Accustomed to popularity among women, and well
> versed in the incipient signs of their liking for him, he antici-
> pated no difficulty in winning her. Satisfied with the past, and
> pleasantly hopeful about the future, he found it easy to turn
> his attention to the next prettiest girl in the room, . . . [145]

There is too Sylvia's moment of insight on hearing that Kinraid, who had returned to Monkshaven to find her already
married, had subsequently wed an heiress. Kinraid had, one
recalls, virtually vowed he would have Sylvia or remain
single[146]; hence her invidious comparison is not without justification, since Philip, had he taken a similar oath, would not
so quickly have forgotten it[147].

> The idea was irresistibly forced upon her that Philip would
> not have acted so; it would have taken long years before he
> could have been induced to put another on the throne she had
> once occupied. For the first time in her life, she seemed to
> recognise the real nature of Philip's love.[148]

For the reader, however, the quality of that love had long been
evident. A final confirmation is Philip's moving declaration
when, confronted by Kinraid and accused of falsehood, he

[142] *Works*, VI, 246.
[143] *Works*, VI, 248.
[144] *Works*, VI, 88.
[145] *Works*, VI, 162.

[146] *Works*, VI, 207.
[147] *Works*, VI, 225.
[148] *Works*, VI, 461: cf. 500.

could yet testify with simple eloquence to the power of his devotion.

> " . . . He didn't love yo' as I did. He had loved other women. I, yo'—yo' alone. He loved other girls before yo', and had left off loving 'em. . . . How was I to know he would keep true to thee? It might be a sin in me, I cannot say; my heart and my sense are gone dead within me. I know this: I've loved yo', as no man but me ever loved before. . . . "[149]

Although Mrs. Gaskell succeeds in making Philip's conduct understandable, she is careful to underline its sinfulness, her moral condemnation being manifest[150]. Indeed Philip himself, on the death-bed, came to realize how he had succumbed to the devices of the devil, knowing then ' that the thoughts [planted by Satan] were illusions, the arguments false and hollow '[151]. In the Gaskellian ethic there was a difference of degree only between his deception and that of Thurstan Benson.

Of the other figures in the tragic triad less need be said. Kinraid has importance largely for the responses he calls forth from Philip and Sylvia. The author knew enough of the ways of such men with women to make him adequate for the *rôle* assigned. One notes, for instance, the ease with which, seeing his unexpected arrival had fluttered Sylvia, he engaged Kester in conversation so that she might regain her composure[152]. The contrast between Kinraid and Philip is neatly indicated by their different reactions to the hospitality of Sylvia's father.

> Pipes were soon produced. Philip disliked smoking. Possibly Kinraid did so too; but he took a pipe, at any rate, and lighted it, though he hardly used it at all, but kept talking to Farmer Robson on sea affairs.[153]

If Philip found an idol in Sylvia, she well-nigh hero-worshipped Kinraid, her attitude being astutely analyzed by Mrs. Robson.

> " . . . Thou sees, she thinks a deal on him for a spirited chap, as can do what he will. I belie' me she first began to think on him time o' t' fight aboard th' *Good Fortune*, when Darley were killed; and he would seem tame-like to her, if he couldn't conquer press-gangs and men-o'-war. . . . "[154]

---

[149] *Works*, VI, 403.
[150] E.g. *Works*, VI, 235, 238.
[151] *Works*, VI, 526.

[152] *Works*, VI, 189-190.
[153] *Works*, VI, 116.
[154] *Works*, VI, 268.

Mrs. Gaskell skilfully traces the development of Sylvia's love from the time when, fired by Kinraid's gallantry, she went for news of his health to Molly Corney[155], his sweet-heart as she then believed, and significantly changed her manner on Molly's suggestive remark that she was taking a great deal of interest in the sailor[156]. At Darley's funeral Sylvia eyed him for the first time, and thought him 'the nearest approach to a hero she had ever seen.'[157] Thereafter Mrs. Gaskell uses meaningful details to betoken Sylvia's progressive love—such as the girl's desire to wrap in a damask napkin some sausages her mother intended for the recuperating hero (foiled in this, she had to content herself with putting autumnal blossoms into the basket)[158]. A comparable technique had been employed in *North and South,* and in the present novel it is equally successful. Following 'her hero's apparent carelessness '[159] in not bidding farewell before leaving Monkshaven, Sylvia's incipient regard was quenched; yet his tales of marvels still lingered in the memory, and her eyes often fell ' on one spot in the map, not Northumberland, where Kinraid was spending the winter, but those wild northern seas about which he had told . . . such wonders.'[160] Subsequently Kinraid returned and her affections were renewed, the result being an unofficial engagement. Even when Kinraid was believed drowned, and she herself married to Philip, Sylvia still dreamt of him[161], and found solace in walks by the sea[162]. We recall that Mr. Robson had won his bride with tales of adventure[163]; and there was something of the same Othello strain in Kinraid's courtship of Sylvia.

We have often remarked upon Mrs. Gaskell's *penchant* for the disappearance *motif.* In *Sylvia's Lovers* this theme assumes its greatest importance. Firstly there is the strange disappearance of Kinraid (strange, that is, to all but Philip), which brings to mind that of the novelist's brother. Like Poor Peter in *Cranford,* Kinraid returns—but to precipitate a crisis, not bring about a happy ending. In ' The Manchester Marriage ' all moral difficulties had been shelved; for Mrs. Openshaw, the

---

[155] *Works,* VI, 60-63.
[156] *Works,* VI, 63.
[157] *Works,* VI, 75.
[158] *Works,* VI, 91.
[159] *Works,* VI, 120.
[160] *Works,* VI, 121.
[161] *Works,* VI, 373-374.
[162] *Works,* VI, 379-381, 389.
[163] *Works,* VI, 111, 138-139.

unwitting bigamist, was not required to face the conjugal
dilemma entailed by the re-appearance of her first husband.
No such difficulty could arise for Sylvia, who had never married
Kinraid; but, unlike Mrs. Openshaw, she had an ethical
decision to make, and the authoress renders plausible her refusal
to go off with Kinraid by showing that, when in conflict with
maternal feelings, all other sentiments lose their force[164].
Mrs. Gaskell's attitude may be that of the mother rather than
the moralist; yet it is artistically appropriate. She wrote the
scene more than once[165], and one can understand why she
should have found it difficult : she had to make convincing the
conflict within Sylvia herself, and at the same time prevent an
incident charged with potential melodrama from becoming
displeasingly theatrical. She succeeds because she dramatizes;
for the words of the participants have a saving realism, owing
largely to their dialectal vitality.

The home-coming and self-sacrifice of Philip Hepburn also
recalls ' The Manchester Marriage ', where Mrs. Openshaw's
first husband, doubtless realizing he could not morally resume
his marital rights, apparently drowned himself for the ultimate
happiness of his wife and child. In the novel a like ending is
made possible by Sylvia's refusal, at the time of Kinraid's
return, ever again to live as Philip's wife. Christian charity and
the law were on Philip's side; but Sylvia's character was hardly
such as to allow her in the future to accept him with all her
love and forgiveness, even though he might later save both
Kinraid and Bella from death, and even though (as illustrated
by her attitude towards the man who had testified against her
father[166]) Sylvia's vows never to forgive were less immutable
than Philip believed. As Dr. Sanders has said, ' If Philip had
lived, might not Sylvia have continued to remember deep
within herself that had Philip done his duty she might have
been the happy wife of Charles Kinraid?'[167] Mrs. Gaskell thus

---

[164] *Works,* VI, 404.
[165] Ward, ed. *Works,* VI, p. xii; and Seccombe, pref. *Sylvia's Lovers,*
by Mrs. Gaskell, p. xlv. The revision was undertaken at Meta Gaskell's
instigation, as she informed Thomas Seccombe in a letter of 13 September
1910 (a copy of which, once possessed by Mr. J. T. Lancaster, belongs
to the present writer; however, doubtless owing to a copyist's slip, it
begins ' Dear Mrs Seccombe ').
[166] *Works,* VI, 349-353.   [167] Sanders, *Elizabeth Gaskell,* p. 126.

showed wisdom in providing a tragic conclusion, while holding out the hope of perfect forgiveness and total reconciliation beyond the grave and '[b]ehind the veil '[168]. Nonetheless, despite its theoretical fitness, Mrs. Gaskell tends to handle the final scene rather like a stage-manager. Though the dialogue is adequate, the ' noises off ' are too much insisted upon. What one objects to is the frequency with which the waves are heard ' lapping up the shelving shore '[169]. However it would be ungenerous to carp at an unhappy repetition, especially when the author could so well convey Philip's awareness of the approach of death, his recognition of that ' new feeling—the last new feeling which we shall, any of us, experience in this world '[170].

Love and conjugal relationships extend beyond the three leading figures, and may further indicate that the problems of courtship and marriage bulked large for Mrs. Gaskell at this period. Whether or not Sylvia, Philip, and Kinraid owed much to her knowledge of particular individuals it is difficult to say. One feels she must be credited with considerable inventive excellence in the case of Philip, and, to a slightly less degree, in that of Sylvia also; yet these characters could have been created only by some one well acquainted with human nature. Concerning Hester Rose[171] we have the author's testimony that she was making use of a type she knew; for Hester's origins go back to the time of *North and South,* as the next quotation bears witness.

> . . . I have half won=/=dered whether another character might/ not be introduced into Margaret,—M^{rs}/ Thornton, the mother, to have taken as a/ sort of humble companion & young house=/=keeper the ∧orphan∧ daughter of an old friend/ in humble, retired country life on the/ borders of Lancashire,—& this girl to be/ in love with Mr Thornton

---

[168] Taken from the Tennysonian quotation on the title-page (*Works,* VI, p. v). This motto was of Meta Gaskell's choosing, according to her 13 September 1910 letter to Thomas Seccombe (a copy of which, once possessed by Mr. J. T. Lancaster, belongs to the present writer—see *supra,* fn. 165).

[169] This phrase—or variants thereof—occurs eight times in almost as many consecutive pages (*Works,* VI, 521, 522, 523, 524, 525, 527, 528, 529). Its forerunner appeared much earlier in the book (*Works,* VI, 74).

[170] *Works,* VI, 526.

[171] The surname brings to mind Mrs. Gaskell's Whitby landlady.

in a kind/ of passionate despairing way.—but/ both jealous
of Margaret, & yet angry/ that she gives Mr Thornton pain—/
I know the kind of wild wayward/ character that grows up
in lonesome/ places, which has a sort of Southern/ capacity
of hating & loving. She s^hd/ not be what people call
educated,/ but with strong sense.   /[172]

Hester's chief function is to contrast with Sylvia, her temperament being closer to that of Philip, with whom she is in love.
Philip, however, never suspects her feelings for him[173]—except
once when, a fleeting idea passing through his mind ('as tran-
sitory as a breath passes over a looking-glass '[174]), he immediately
' put away his thought as a piece of vain coxcombry, insulting
to Hester.'[175] She too, for her part, considered love-thoughts
mere wordliness[176]; and their being entertained towards one
who did not return them, shameful[177] : in this respect the
Quakerish Mrs. Rose could use her daughter's experience ' to
prove the vanity of setting the heart on anything earthly.'[178]
It was Hester's lot to appreciate all the merits in Philip which
Sylvia overlooked[179], her own love going unnoticed and unrequited[180]. Always ready to help others, whether it be sitting
with the bed-fast sister of Darley during that whaler's burial[181]
or helping the Robson family[182] when Daniel was taken to
prison, Hester seemed truly ' a star, the brightness of which was
only recognised in times of darkness.'[183]

To continue the examination of matrimony, we may note
that Hester, in her turn, had an unsuccessful lover, William
Coulson, Philip's fellow shopman. Whereas Philip, Sylvia,
Hester, and even Kinraid love in a more or less spiritual way,

---

[172] So wrote Mrs. Gaskell in a letter to John Forster of Sunday
[23 April 1854], now in the British Museum (Add. MS. 38794, ff. 263-
266; the passage quoted is on f. 265^v). The same passage (taken from
a slightly inaccurate copy in the Gaskell Section, Brotherton Collection,
Leeds University Library) may be found in Rubenius, *The Woman
Question in Mrs. Gaskell's Life and Works*, p. 258. The relevant part of
this letter (*G.L.*, No. 191) is slightly differently punctuated by Chapple
and Pollard.

[173] *Works*, VI, 167.   [179] *Works*, VI, 382.
[174] *Works*, VI, 358.   [180] *Works*, VI, 126.
[175] *Works*, VI, 358.   [181] *Works*, VI, 78-79, 87.
[176] *Works*, VI, 126-127.   [182] *Works*, VI, 306-314.
[177] *Works*, VI, 469.   [183] *Works*, VI, 382.
[178] *Works*, VI, 445.

the sentiments of Coulson are domestic rather than romantic. His nature is early diagnosed by Alice Rose.

" Thee'll marry," said Alice. " Thee likes to have thy victuals hot and comfortable; and there's noane many but a wife as'll look after that for t' please thee."[184]

Although he had Hester in view and, on being refused, asked Philip for help with his suit[185], Coulson was scarcely the man to mourn long as a rejected lover. Alice Rose's prediction that he would marry within a year proved correct[186]. Having used reason instead of fancy to direct his next proposal, he could henceforth enjoy a ' comfortable dinner at his well-ordered house, with his common-place wife.'[187]

Alice had professed, ' " I 'd liefer, by far, be i' that world wheere there's neither marrying nor giving in marriage, for it's all a moithering mess here " '[188]; yet hers was a wisdom born of bitter experience. She had been wooed by two men, the worthy John Foster and Jack Rose, the sailor whom against all advice she married and who turned out (in Jeremiah Foster's words) ' " a profligate sinner, and went after other women, and drank, and beat her." '[189] One can readily understand why Philip, on hearing this unhappy tale, should find in it parallels to Sylvia's situation[190].

Kinraid's ' betrayal ' of Sylvia by his marriage to an heiress has been noticed. We first learn of this when we read that, on believing himself about to die, 'tears came to his eyes as he thought of the newly-made wife in her English home, who might never know how he died thinking of her.'[191] That is all we are told of Kinraid's affection for his wife. She herself, when she arrives to thank Philip for rescuing her husband, seems a merely conventional figure beside Sylvia and Alice Rose[192]. We have also noticed the exemplary tale (of Nancy Hartley, driven mad by an unfaithful suitor) which Mrs. Robson related so that her daughter might take warning ' " again' thinking a man t' mean what he says when he's a-talking to a young woman." '[193]

[184] *Works*, VI, 85.
[185] *Works*, VI, 255-256.
[186] *Works*, VI, 259.
[187] *Works*, VI, 417: cf. 508-509.
[188] *Works*, VI, 258.
[189] *Works*, VI, 254.
[190] *Works*, VI, 254-255.
[191] *Works*, VI, 454.
[192] *Works*, VI, 471-476.
[193] *Works*, VI, 199.

Two further marriages remain for consideration: that between Sylvia's parents, and that between Molly Corney[194] and
Brunton, the Newcastle shop-keeper. Bell was won over by
Daniel's tall stories, his sailor's yarns[195]—her wedding being,
perhaps, the only rash thing she ever did[196]. However their
union proved happy, with Daniel's affecting to despise women's
ways in spite of being wholly dependent on Bell's care. His
wife's attitude was one of loving obedience, so that, for
example, when he claimed a point she had already made, 'Bell
did not answer, as she might have done, that this . . . had
been her own suggestion, set aside by her husband as utterly
unlikely.'[197]   Moreover Mrs. Robson expected, after her
daughter's marriage, that she too would put her husband's
comfort before everything else, and was deeply distressed to
find Sylvia apparently 'neglectful of those duties which she
herself had always regarded as paramount to all others'[198].

Molly Corney's attitude to men differed markedly from that
of Mrs. Robson, who found the former's casual talk of marriage
none to her liking[199]; to Sylvia her suggestive jokes on the same
subject were equally distasteful[200]. Molly, with an eye for
worldly advantage, viewed her marriage to the prosperous
Brunton with evident satisfaction[201]. Indeed when Sylvia later
saw her, after a separation of four years or more, 'each
secretly wondered how they had ever come to be friends.'[202]
With her extra thirty pounds of flesh[203], and her talk about the
luck of the matrimonial draw[204], Molly had coarsened both
physically and morally.   Her ill-natured treatment of little
Bella[205] was doubtless intended by the authoress to be the most
revealing part of her behaviour.

Mrs. Gaskell permits herself scarcely any explicit comment

---

[194] A common Whitby surname, e.g. John Corney, Mrs. Gaskell's
informant (Ward, ed. *Works*, VI, p. xxiii). Several proper names in this
story were seemingly not of the author's inventing—in which connexion
one may consult Chadwick, *Mrs. Gaskell*, pp. 267-268; and Young,
A History of Whitby, II, 524-527 (Whitby surnames), 945-953 (list of
subscribers).

[195] *Works*, VI, 109-111.
[196] *Works*, VI, 37.
[197] *Works*, VI, 39.
[198] *Works*, VI, 385.
[199] *Works*, VI, 121-122.
[200] *Works*, VI, 144-145.

[201] *Works*, VI, 122.
[202] *Works*, VI, 459.
[203] *Works*, VI, 460.
[204] *Works*, VI, 462.
[205] *Works*, VI, 464.

on marriage as such; but there is one passage in which she seems to speak from her own experience. It occurs in the following context. Sylvia entered into her union with Philip from motives far different from those which had bound her to Kinraid. She regarded Philip as a friend to her family in time of need, rather than as an ardent lover; hence she looked upon matrimony 'more as a change of home, as the leaving of Haytersbank, as it would affect her mother, than in any more directly personal way.'[206] Under such circumstances it was only to be expected that Philip should not enjoy the conjugal felicity he looked for.

> After all, and though he did not acknowledge it even to himself, the long-desired happiness was not so delicious and perfect as he had anticipated. Many have felt the same in their first year of married life; but the faithful, patient nature that still works on, striving to gain love, and capable itself of steady love all the while, is a gift not given to all.[207]

To this one may add the following wise words. They at least reveal that the author understood the masculine temperament better than those critics who, like Miss Rubenius[208], would find

[206] *Works,* VI, 354.

[207] *Works,* VI, 363.

[208] See especially the views expressed in her chapter entitled 'Mrs. Gaskell's Marriage' (*The Woman Question in Mrs. Gaskell's Life and Works,* pp. 19-37); she quotes Miss van Dullemen and Miss Haldane to support her thesis (*op. cit.,* p. 18, fn. 2). Significantly, however, neither our preceding, nor our subsequent, quotation from *Sylvia's Lovers* is to be found in her book—perhaps she likewise overlooked the fact that this novel was dedicated to Mr. Gaskell 'by her who best knows his value' (*Works,* VI, p. xxxv). As for Miss Haldane, she (*Mrs. Gaskell and Her Friends,* 1930, p. 301) felt that the couple 'never quite understood one another'; but these appear mild sentiments compared with the following, taken from Miss Margaret Josephine Shaen's letter to her of 23 November 1929 (now in the National Library of Scotland: MS. 6035, ff. 185-186, the passage quoted being on ff. 185v-186r). 'I wonder whether you/ will wish to say much/ about Mr Gaskell —I/ cd in talk tell you a/ good deal about him,/ more than I cd write./ Those sheets & sheets of/ love affairs are now all/ safely burnt—pitiful —/I shd have burnt them// on receipt! /' Miss Shaen's attitude towards Mr. Gaskell is further evidenced by her remark that his vanity led him to believe that Susanna Winkworth (whose niece she was) wanted to marry him, a remark made in her letter to Miss Haldane of 28 August 1930 (now in the National Library of Scotland: MS. 6036, ff. 53-54): perhaps for the novelist 'there was a slight jealousy of Susanna Winkworth' (Haldane, *op. cit.,* p. 254), though more probably she found Miss Winkworth's flirtatious appropriation of her husband rather amusing (*G.L.,*

Mr. Gaskell's keen absorption in his work slightly disconcerting, perhaps indicative that his marriage was not all it might have been.

> However, it is an old story, an ascertained fact, that, even in the most tender and stable masculine natures, at the supremest seasons of their lives, there is room for other thoughts and passions than such as are connected with love. Even with the most domestic and affectionate men, their emotions seem to be kept in a cell, distinct and away from their actual lives.[209]

One of the best things in *Sylvia's Lovers* is the tragi-comedy of Daniel Robson. This, besides its intrinsic value, directly ministers to the main plot; for Daniel's death is the major factor in bringing about Sylvia's marriage to Philip—a successful integration which illustrates the novelist's progress in constructional skill. The characters in the tragi-comedy are drawn with a confidence which bespeaks careful recording: they are, all of them, taken from humble life. In a sense, so is the tragic triad of the main plot; but here one seems less conscious of social status. Daniel Robson, his wife, Kester (their servant)[210], Donkin (the tailor)[211], John Hobbs (landlord of the ' Randyvowse ')[212], and Dick Simpson (his servant)[213] appear as part of a living sea-port community. Though they are less directly involved in Robson's calamity, the Foster brothers[214], Kester's sister[215], Ned Simpson (the butcher, Dick's prosperous brother)[216], William Darley (repairer of watches and chronometers)[217], Alice Rose[218], and the whole Corney family[219] are presented with the same convincing realism. One of Mrs. Gaskell's chief merits is her power of portraying people from the lower ranks of rural and industrial societies, without any exaggeration or distortion but with that sureness of touch which came from close obser-

---

No. 124; see too No. 108a). Similarly Mrs. Gaskell seemed amused rather than disquieted when William looked for a letter from the pretty Miss Louisa Shaen (Margaret Josephine's aunt) in consequence of his sitting beside her at the piano (Haldane, *op. cit.*, p. 239: cf. and cont. *G.L.*, No. 25a; see too No. 19).

[209] *Works*, VI, 377-378.

[210] *Works*, VI, 38 ff.
[211] *Works*, VI, 50 ff.
[212] *Works*, VI, 269 ff.
[213] *Works*, VI, 269 ff.
[214] *Works*, VI, 24 ff.

[215] *Works*, VI, 427 ff.
[216] *Works*, VI, 132 ff.
[217] *Works*, VI, 512 ff.
[218] *Works*, VI, 79 ff.
[219] *Works*, VI, 60 ff.

vation. She had a keen eye for their behaviour and an attentive ear for their speech, both of which could be demonstrated without difficulty from *Sylvia's Lovers*. Something of her method ought to emerge during a consideration of Robson's tragi-comic history.

As suggested by reference to his courtship and marriage, Sylvia's father lent himself to humorous treatment. Especially true for Mrs. Gaskell's delineation of Daniel is the remark of a discerning critic : ' At her best, it is impossible to separate her humour from her observation of character, so intimately is the one woven with the other.'[220] His obsession, in itself amusing yet having tragic consequences, is clearly conveyed in Bell's account of her husband's condition. Quotation here has the additional advantage of illustrating how the novelist, by employing a racy and idiomatic phraseology, could suggest Mrs. Robson's own vitality.

> " For good's sake, Philip, dunnot thee bring us talk about t' press-gang. It's a thing as has got hold on my measter, till thou'd think him possessed. He's speaking perpetual on it i' such a way, that thou'd think he were itching to kill 'em a', afore he tasted bread again. He really trembles wi' rage and passion; an' a' night it's just as bad. He starts up i' his sleep, swearing and cursing at 'em, till I'm sometimes afeard he'll mak' an end o' me by mistake. And what mun he do last night but open out on Charley Kinraid, and tell Sylvia he thought m'appen t' gang had got hold on him. It might mak' her cry a' her saut tears o'er again."[221]

Although Daniel had, for many years, borne a strong grudge against impressment, to avoid which, as he delighted to recount[222], he had mutilated thumb and fore-finger, in more recent days the subject had taken such a hold on his mind, now weakened by drink, that it seemed like ' a supernatural kind of possession, leading him to his doom.'[223] His was, however, but an extreme reaction against a tyrannous system generally abhorred. The precipitating cause of the tragedy was the gang's dastardly trick of ringing a fire-bell to ensnare the menfolk of

[220] Paul Beard, ed. *The Cage at Cranford and Other Stories*, by Mrs. Gaskell, London, Edinburgh, Paris, Melbourne, Toronto, and New York: Thomas Nelson & Sons Ltd [1937], p. 21.

[221] *Works*, VI, 267.

[222] *Works*, VI, 40, 55, 94.

[223] *Works*, VI, 268.

Monkshaven. For Daniel Robson this last assault of the gang proved too much to bear; and so, largely at his instigation, their rendezvous was stormed, the captives rescued, and the building razed to the ground. Here the novelist was elaborating on what actually happened at Whitby. As early as *Mary Barton,* in her handling of the fire at Carsons' mill[224], she had displayed a talent for crowd scenes: in *Sylvia's Lovers* she had lost none of this power, her vivid use of dialectal dialogue particularly deserving praise. She communicates the initial apprehension ('at the heart of the mystery . . . a silent blank '[225]) with the same success that she conveys the mounting anger of the people, with its outcome in violent action. She indicates too the slightly comic aspects of the situation— Daniel's summoning of his friends, 'old hands like himself, but "deep uns," also like himself, as he imagined '[226]; the poor, lean cow in the inn's outbuilding, who 'shifted herself on her legs, in an uneasy, restless manner, as her sleeping-place was invaded '[227]; Daniel's *naïve* pride in having been the man to lead the mob[228]; the inn-servant's laconic assessment of what the fire meant to himself and the landlord, Hobbs (' "He's had his sauce," said Simpson dolefully. "Him and me is ruined." '[229]). Details like the foregoing must have been of the author's inventing, included to render the episode graphic and realistic. Nonetheless once, according to Mrs. Chadwick[230], she incorporated the very words[231] of Atkinson (Robson's prototype). If indeed this were so[232], no reader could have detected them with-

---

224 *Works,* I, 53-61.
225 *Works,* VI, 272.
226 *Works,* VI, 274.
227 *Works,* VI, 275.
228 *Works,* VI, 278.
229 *Works,* VI, 278.
230 *Mrs. Gaskell,* p. 259.
231 *Works,* VI, 277.
232 Such a view is confirmed rather than invalidated by the slightly different version of Atkinson's inciting declaration found in 'The "Criminal Chronology of York Castle"', *The Whitby Repository, or Album of Local Literature,* N.S. II (February 1868), 288, fn. There we read that 'it was wont to be stated [forty years previously, by people who could remember his execution] that the old man called out to the rioters, "Well done my lads, if I was as young as you, I would soon make the highest stone the lowest." '

out special knowledge; for they seem of a piece with the rest of what the old man says.

Following this crisis, Mrs. Gaskell traces Robson's fate with equal dexterity. His inherent kindness is shown by his giving the penniless Simpson money for himself and the shelterless cow[233]—an act of charity which assumes tones of tragic irony when Simpson testifies against him[234]. Feeling flattered that 'his " world " looked upon him as a hero '[235], he returned to regale the household with the story of his bravery. Then follows an excellent evocation of the stormy night at the Robson farm-house, with significant hints from the superstitious fancies which assailed Sylvia as she anxiously awaited her father's homecoming[236]. Thereafter the humorous again mingles with the pathetic. One recalls Daniel's ingenuous conceit in suggesting the gang would never dare impress him[237]; the unwrapping of the warming pan, ' only used on state occasions,'[238] for the sorely-wearied old man; Kester's attentive listening to his tale of valour, ' his spoon . . . often arrested in its progress from the basin to his mouth '[239]; Sylvia's realization, from Philip's demeanour, that her father's actions could bear more than one interpretation[240]; Robson's slow recognition that he was in danger of prison, and his feeble attempts at jokes and sarcasm[241]. Daniel's capture ensues—itself tragi-comic, the aged farmer being detected in his ignominious hiding-place under the bed[242]. Later comes Sylvia's simple innocence in believing York Castle was only for ' " thieves and robbers " '[243], not for honest men like her father—who, with a comparable simplicity, under questioning ' always wandered off to accounts of previous outrages committed by the press-gang'[244], and, at his trial, as Philip reported in his pathetically hopeful letter, kept

[233] *Works*, VI, 279.
[234] *Works*, VI, 350-351.
[235] *Works*, VI, 280.
[236] *Works*, VI, 280-283.
[237] *Works*, VI, 284.
[238] *Works*, VI, 284.
[239] *Works*, VI, 285-286: cf. Sylvia's stance, with iron poised, while listening to Donkin (*Works*, VI, 57).
[240] *Works*, VI, 287.
[241] *Works*, VI, 288.
[242] *Works*, VI, 296.
[243] *Works*, VI, 312.
[244] *Works*, VI, 326.

on ' " saying he would do it over again, if he had the
chance " '[245]. In a scene which recalls a high-light from ' Half a
Lifetime Ago '[246], Sylvia and her mother make clap-bread, in
the fond belief that Daniel will return to eat it[247]. The tragi-
comedy draws to its close with the journey of Bell and her
daughter to York, there to see Robson for the last time[248]; with
Kester's night-walk, ' three halfpence in his pocket,'[249] on the
same sad errand; with Philip's impolitic returning of the money
which that typically Gaskellian faithful servant had contributed
towards his master's legal expenses[250]; and with the egg-pelting
of Simpson, who had testified against the old man[251]. Finally
occurs Bell's mental derangement (a blessing to herself, yet serving perpetually to renew Sylvia's grief) whereby, constantly
referring to her husband as being away from home, she ' had
always some plausible way of accounting for it which satisfied
her own mind '[252]. Thus it seems both ironic and fitting that,
as the tragi-comedy sprang from Daniel's abnormal preoccupation with impressment, so the consequences of that mania
should, by another distortion of reality, be providentially hidden
from his wife.

Irony, indeed, arises more than once in the novel, whose
ironic concluding passage was noticed at the outset. The writer,
as narrator, also employs her special knowledge to underline
the pathos of the tale, albeit suggesting its figures should be
viewed *sub specie aeternitatis*. Her tone in these places, one
could almost say, owes something to the author of *Vanity
Fair*[253], while remaining peculiarly her own. Such a manner is
entirely in keeping with this, her saddest story. Mellow, re-
flective, meditative, slightly nostalgic, it is the manner of some
one looking back over the years, telling of the old unhappy
far-off things.

[245] *Works*, VI, 327.
[246] *Works*, V, 311-312.
[247] *Works*, VI, 331-332.
[248] *Works*, VI, 334.
[249] *Works*, VI, 334.
[250] *Works*, VI, 335.
[251] *Works*, VI, 337.
[252] *Works*, VI, 339.
[253] The phrase ' " *vanitas vanitatum* " ' occurs in *Sylvia's Lovers*
(*Works*, VI, 153), though the characters are for Mrs. Gaskell not so
much puppets as ' actors ' (*Works*, VI, 141).

Dr. Sanders has 'A Note on Mrs. Gaskell's Use of Dialect'[254]; and Miss Hopkins has written wisely on the 'delicate gradations in the use of dialect'[255], pointing out, for instance, that Philip employs fewer rustic terms than Sylvia. Here we can do little more than stress how successfully the speech of North-East Yorkshire is rendered. Just as, in the industrial novels, the vigorous talk of working-class characters on occasions acts as a specific against sentimentality; so too, in *Sylvia's Lovers*, the provincial idiom lends substance to scenes which might otherwise have appeared slightly theatrical.

The dialect also works in a more general way, insinuating that the action is taking place in a particular locality and thereby subtly contributing to the historical realism. Furthermore Mrs. Gaskell was not unaware of the aesthetic effects she could produce. Keenly appreciative of the beauty of popular sayings and relishing the racy vitality of humble speech, she often introduces into her fiction memorable expressions encountered on the lips of common people. In this respect *Sylvia's Lovers* offers such a profusion of riches as to make illustration scarcely necessary. Perhaps, however, we may quote three passages not previously noted by critics[256].

" . . . It'd tax a parson t' say a' as a've getten i' my mind. It's like a heap o' woo' just after shearin'-time; it's worth a deal, but it tak's a vast o' combin', an' cardin', an' spinnin', afore it can be made use on. . . . "[257]

" A'll gang after 't, then, for a'm like a pair o' bellowses wi' t' wind out; just two flat sides wi' nowt betwixt."[258]

" The Lord is like a tender nurse as weans a child to look on, and to like, what it loathed once. He has sent me dreams as has prepared me for this, if so be it comes to pass."[259]

---

[254] *Elizabeth Gaskell*, pp. 145-155. See too Graham Roderick Handley, *Sylvia's Lovers* (*Mrs. Gaskell*), Notes on English Literature (ed. W. H. Mason), Oxford: Basil Blackwell, 1968, pp. 48-51. (Dr. Handley's study is the best critique of the novel known to the present writer.)

[255] Hopkins, *Elizabeth Gaskell*, p. 271.

[256] A gem (*Works*, VI, 13) is picked out by Seccombe (pref. *Sylvia's Lovers*, by Mrs. Gaskell, p. xliii) and by Handley—*Sylvia's Lovers* (*Mrs. Gaskell*), p. 48—, though both slightly misquote.

[257] *Works*, VI, 365: the speaker is Kester.

[258] *Works*, VI, 51: the speaker is Kester.

[259] *Works*, VI, 329: the speaker is Bell Robson.

Besides profiting from her own observations of Yorkshire speech—made not only during her Whitby holiday but also long before (for example, in the course of her Brontë researches) —Mrs. Gaskell benefited from the linguistic advice of General Perronet Thompson[260]. She took great care over this aspect of her work, as the most cursory collation of the first and second editions reveals[261]. One tribute to her accuracy is Wright's use of *Sylvia's Lovers* in compiling *The English Dialect Dictionary*[262]. Another is still more interesting. In 1855 a Whitby inhabitant published a local glossary[263] : although some of the words there listed can also be found in *Sylvia's Lovers*[264], it is gratifying to discover that, when, a couple of decades later, another Whitby glossary was put together by the same inhabitant (F. K. Robinson)[265], this included words and variants contained in the novel[266], but not given in his earlier compilation. At least one of Mrs. Gaskell's local phrases ('making marlocks

---

[260] Ward, ed. *Works*, VI, p. xxv, fn. There seem, however, to be no letters from Mrs. Gaskell among those Thompson MSS now deposited in the Hull University Library.

[261] See Appendix V.

[262] Sanders, *Elizabeth Gaskell*, p. 155. The relevant reference is Joseph Wright, ed. *The English Dialect Dictionary, Being the Complete Vocabulary of All Dialect Words Still in Use, or Known to Have Been in Use during the Last Two Hundred Years, Founded on the Publications of the English Dialect Society and on a Large Amount of Material Never Before Printed*, 6 vols., London: Henry Frowde; Oxford: 116 High Street; New York: G. P. Putnam's Sons, 1898-1905, VI (1905), 23 (Bibliography). Wright also lists *Mary Barton* in the Bibliography (*op. cit.*, VI, 12).

[263] *A Glossary of Yorkshire Words and Phrases, Collected in Whitby and the Neighbourhood. With Examples of Their Colloquial Use, and Allusions to Local Customs and Traditions*, by An Inhabitant [Francis Kildill Robinson], London: John Russell Smith, 1855.

[264] E.g. 'dree' *tedious* adj. (*Works*, VI, 48, 307); 'a gawby' *a dunce* n. (*Works*, VI, 412); 'kittle' *ticklish* adj. (*Works*, VI, 134); 'a lamiter' *a lame person* n. (*Works*, VI, 17); 'to redd . . . up' *to set . . . to rights* v. (*Works*, VI, 329).

[265] Francis Kildill Robinson, *A Glossary of Words Used in the Neighbourhood of Whitby*, Publications of The English Dialect Society, Nos. 9 and 13—Part of Series C (Original Glossaries, and Glossaries with Fresh Additions)—London: Trübner & Co. for The English Dialect Society, 1875-1876, p. i.

[266] E.g. 'fremd' *unknown* adj. (*Works*, VI, 299); 'hoast' n., hence 'hoasts' *mists* n. pl. (*Works*, VI, 282); 'mell' v., hence 'melling' *meddling* pres. part. (*Works*, VI, 256, 258, 284); 'nor' *than* conj. (*Works*, VI, 365).

. . . at'[267]) was completely neglected by Robinson, though it was later recognized by Wright[268] as a Yorkshire idiom; yet strangely enough even that distinguished philologist passed over the one dialectal expression[269] the novelist considered worth a gloss.

So far we have been chiefly concerned with those components of the novel peculiar to itself, though connexions with Mrs. Gaskell's earlier compositions have occasionally been noticed. At this stage there is scarcely any need to illustrate the concretion afforded by minutely observed domestic touches to scenes of humble life, such demonstration having been undertaken with regard to previous works. Nor have graphic passages of natural description been quoted, partly because the relevant quoting has been done elsewhere[270]. However it may be well to consider the interrelatedness of Mrs. Gaskell's publications by taking *Sylvia's Lovers* as a point of departure. We shall, therefore, turn our attention to those themes, incidents, and phrases which, to a reader familiar with the writer's total output, inevitably come to mind. Mrs. Gaskell's powers of invention were cyclical as well as progressive. Although she tried her hand as several *genres* and seldom attempted merely to repeat a success, her thoughts often turned to favourite *motifs,* and the same preoccupations occur again and again in her work.

---

[267] *Works,* VI, 323: it means *making eyes at.*

[268] Ed. *The English Dialect Dictionary,* IV (1903), 40: in fact Mrs. Gaskell is here quoted as an authority. The phrase 'main an'/and' *very, much* (*Works,* VI, 257, 314, 315) is also not mentioned by Robinson, though Mrs. Gaskell is again quoted by Wright (ed. *The English Dialect Dictionary,* IV, 13—*Works,* VI, 257). Other Yorkshire words omitted by Robinson, but employed by Mrs. Gaskell and listed by Wright, who often gives a Gaskell reference, include 'a coil' *a fuss* n. [*Works,* VI, 289—*The English Dialect Dictionary,* I (1898), 695]; 'dateless' *foolish* adj. [*Works,* VI, 403—*The English Dialect Dictionary,* II (1900), 29]; 'fause' *sly* adj. (*Works,* VI, 50, 500—*The English Dialect Dictionary,* II, 291: *Works,* VI, 50); 'fettle' *attend to* v. (*Works,* VI, 50: both this verb and its substantival derivatives are listed, though somewhat differently defined, in Robinson, *Glossary,* 1875-1876, pp. 65-66); 't' fettling' *the repairing* verb. n. (*Works,* VI, 52—*The English Dialect Dictionary,* II, 343); 'fuddled' *drunk* past part. (*Works,* VI, 281—*The English Dialect Dictionary,* II, 512); 'maskit' *infused* past part. (*Works,* VI, 315).

[269] ' "Well! yo' lasses will have your conks" (private talks) "a know; . . . " ' (*Works,* VI, 61). A Yorkshire provenance is not listed under the relevant entry in Wright, ed. *The English Dialect Dictionary,* I, 505.

[270] By Mrs. Chadwick (*Mrs. Gaskell,* pp. 256-257), Miss ffrench (*Mrs. Gaskell,* pp. 86-87), and Miss Hopkins (*Elizabeth Gaskell,* p. 272).

We have already hinted at the lie and disappearance themes, which form the skeleton of the story. We have also mentioned the importance of little Bella—the most valuable thing to come out of Philip's marriage with Sylvia[271]. Since Mrs. Gaskell was never more the mother than when an authoress, there is the inevitable reference to a woman's early loss of her baby[272], recalling the novelist's own bereavement. Mrs. Gaskell's stories frequently contain religious elements, and these have received attention from the Rev. George Andrew Payne[273]; however it is worth indicating the diversity in *Sylvia's Lovers*. One notes the earnest, Biblical, Calvinistic Quakerism of Alice Rose, who, holding that some were ' fore-doomed to condemnation '[274], believed ' the number of the elect was growing narrower and narrower every day '[275] yet trusted Sylvia might be ' rescued from the many cast-aways, with fervent prayer, or, as she phrased it, " wrestling with the Lord." '[276] Quite different is the pious eclecticism of her daughter; for Hester was, in Philip's words, ' " neither a Methodee, nor a Friend, nor a Church person " '[277] but had ' " a turn for serious things, choose wherever they're found." '[278] Philip himself, though in business matters manifesting the Puritan ethic, discovered, once he had risen by his own labours, that respectable church-going was socially profitable—yet he remained unaware that this was the main motive for his attendance.

> He believed that he went because he thought it right to attend public worship in the parish church whenever it was offered up; but it may be questioned of him, as of many others, how far he would have been as regular in attendance in a place where he was not known.[279]

For Sylvia and her family, on the other hand, ' worship . . . was only an occasional duty '[280]. Hence when, at a critical

271 E.g. *Works,* VI, 371, 386, 395-396, 408, 418-419, 427, 437, 470.
272 *Works,* VI, 46.
273 ' Mrs. Gaskell and Religion ', *Mrs. Gaskell: A Brief Biography,* Manchester: Sherratt & Hughes, 1929, pp. 75-81.
274 *Works,* VI, 441.
275 *Works,* VI, 441.
276 *Works,* VI, 441.
277 *Works,* VI, 140.
278 *Works,* VI, 140.
279 *Works,* VI, 378.
280 *Works,* VI, 287: cf. 378-379.

period, she and Mrs. Robson went to church, they did so ' with a strange, half-superstitious feeling, as if they could propitiate the Most High to order the events in their favour, by paying Him the compliment of attending to duties in their time of sorrow which they had too often neglected in their prosperous days.'[281] The Vicar of Monkshaven[282] brings to mind the easy-going Anglicanism of Mr. Mountford[283]; in politics a high Tory with a strong dislike of Dissenters, he was nonetheless ' a kindly, peaceable, old man, hating strife and troubled waters above everything.'[284] Mr. Mountford, we may notice in passing, bequeathed property to furnish the poor with an annual Christmas dinner that was to include a plum-pudding for which he left ' a very good receipt '[285]; similarly a receipt, though in this case for making beer, was provided in the legacy of Sir Simon Bray[286]. A further link with *My Lady Ludlow*[287] is the scientific farming attempted by Philip[288] and Kester[289].

We shall continue listing specific parallels between *Sylvia's Lovers* and Mrs. Gaskell's other works instead of lingering over correspondences of a more general nature or pointing to the direct use of autobiographic material in the book. One might, to be sure, suggest that Molly Corney recalls Mary Barton's coarse friend, Sally Leadbitter[290], though their *rôles* are not strictly the same; or one could remind oneself that Kester toasts Sylvia[291] with virtually one of the very verses used to

---

[281] *Works,* VI, 328. The general neglect of churches about this time is well demonstrated by Kenneth Stanley Inglis in the first section of his Oxford D. Phil. thesis (1956), ' English Churches and the Working Classes, 1880-1900, with an Introductory Survey of Tendencies Earlier in the Century ', pp. 1-101—the essence of this being contained in the Introduction to his *Churches and the Working Classes in Victorian England,* Studies in Social History (ed. Harold Perkin), No. 9, London: Routledge and Kegan Paul; Toronto: University of Toronto Press, 1963, pp. 1-20.

[282] *Works,* VI, 70 ff.
[283] *Works,* V, 20 ff.
[284] *Works,* VI, 70.
[285] *Works,* V, 25.
[286] *Works,* VI, 485.
[287] *Works,* V, 197-198.
[288] *Works,* VI, 321-322.
[289] *Works,* VI, 340.
[290] *Works,* I, 101 ff.
[291] *Works,* VI, 365.

celebrate the author's wedding[292] : but it should prove equally profitable to note particular literary echoes.

'Half a Lifetime Ago' has one or two affinities with *Sylvia's Lovers*, besides the clap-bread incident. Drinking bouts are mentioned in both as matters of course, receiving little moral censure from the men's wives[293]. There is too the epithet 'filmy'[294] applied to the eyes—though that was a favourite combination of the author's.

Two minor domestic items found in 'The Crooked Branch' recur in the present work: home-made shirts[295] and creepie stools[296]. On a similar plane, the Corneys' state-bedchamber[297] recalls that described in 'Cumberland Sheep-Shearers'[298]. The homely candle-economies of the novel[299] suggest Cranfordian carefulness[300]; another link with *Cranford*[301] is the hair-smoothing of the rustic Kester[302], with the hat-tidyings of Ned Simpson[303] and Philip[304] being comparable mannerisms.

Rather like the heroine of *Ruth*[305], Sylvia found solace in nature[306]; and, also like Ruth[307], nostalgically revisited her former, rural home[308]: in the first respect she resembles Maggie Browne[309]; in the second, Margaret Hale[310].

[292] Mrs. Gaskell reproduces these wedding verses in her letter of 18 August 1838 to Mrs. Mary Howitt, quoted in Howitt, 'Stray Notes from Mrs. Gaskell', *Good Words*, XXXVI (1895), 607—fairly accurately reprinted in Sanders, *Elizabeth Gaskell*, p. 38—: *G.L.*, No. 12; see too No. 197.

[293] *Works*, V, 280-281: cf. *Works*, VI, 46, 280-281.
[294] *Works*, V, 322: cf. *Works*, VI, 519.
[295] *Works*, VII, 218-219: cf. *Works*, VI, 215.
[296] *Works*, VII, 214, 219: cf. *Works*, VI, 16, 87.
[297] *Works*, VI, 142-143.
[298] *Works*, III, 457-458.
[299] *Works*, VI, 100, 102.
[300] *Works*, II, 50-51.
[301] *Works*, II, 19, 160.
[302] *Works*, VI, 99.
[303] *Works*, VI, 133.
[304] *Works*, VI, 299, 304.
[305] *Works*, III, 302.
[306] *Works*, VI, 389. Some astute remarks on Mrs. Gaskell's attitude to nature, especially relevant for the present context, appear in Marjory Amelia Bald, 'Mrs E. C. Gaskell', *Women-Writers of the Nineteenth Century*, Cambridge: The University Press, 1923, pp. 103-106.
[307] *Works*, III, 44-51.
[308] *Works*, VI, 396-398.
[309] *Works*, II, 293.
[310] *Works*, IV, 459-480.

North and South has some incidental parallels to *Sylvia's Lovers.* Mr. Hale's use of Margaret's fingers as sugar tongs[311] is only slightly varied to suit a different environment when Daniel Robson employs his daughter's little finger as a pipe-stopper[312]. Margaret's decision to tell her mother the shattering news of her father's intention to resign at the very moment when a certain bee should fly from its flower[313] has an affinity with Sylvia's resolution to speak to Philip about Kinraid just when she must stoop to pick up some empty milk cans[314]: in each instance the speaker sets the time at which to broach a difficult matter by reference to an external event.

If the foregoing similarities, doubtless trivial in themselves, have any cumulative force as evidence for a high degree of repetition, this is not necessarily a sign of incompetence. In the first place such correspondences would almost certainly escape the attention of the general reader as easily as they seem to have done that of the author. Moreover, even when they do come to one's notice, they do so more on account of their several contextual felicities than because of their repetitious nature; for usually the second appearance is entirely justified by its appropriateness to a new setting.

[311] *Works,* IV, 91.
[312] *Works,* VI, 42.
[313] *Works,* IV, 48.
[314] *Works,* VI, 346.

SECTION III

'An Italian Institution' (1863)

On 21 March 1863 'An Italian Institution' appeared in *All the Year Round*[1]. It was a sketch of the origin, methods, and history of the Camorra—a Neapolitan secret society whose concern was 'black-mail, so extended and organised as to apply to every walk in life, and every condition of human industry.'[2]

By its very nature such a subject would possess a certain appeal; yet Mrs. Gaskell succeeds in making the article entertaining as well as instructive. Garnishing a lucid exposition with illustrative anecdotes and narrating in the first person, she gives the impression of writing from direct observation of the Camorristi of Southern Italy. What might have been a merely factual account acquires added interest from this subjective colouring, though as usual the identity—even the sex—of the contributor remains concealed.

Mrs. Gaskell toured Italy in 1857 when, despite a lack of evidence to this effect, she may have visited Naples. She was again in Italy six years later; but her passport suggests she did not arrive at Civita Vecchia before 23 March 1863[3]. For the article she doubtless drew on what she had seen or (more likely) heard during her 1857 Roman holiday, probably supplemented by subsequent reading. No attempt has been made to ascertain what, if any, printed sources were used; but Lot 585[4] in the *Gaskell Sale Catalogue* is of interest.

[1] IX, 93-96.
[2] *Works*, VI, 531.
[3] Mrs. Gaskell's passport now forms part of the collection of her great grand-daughter, Mrs. Margaret Trevor Jones.
[4] This lot, for the sixth day's sale, is described in *Re the late Miss M. E. Gaskell, 84, Plymouth Grove, Manchester. Catalogue of the Valuable Contents of the Above House, Consisting of Furniture, Linen, Glass, China, Brass, Cutlery, Silver and Jewellery, Prints, Etchings, Engravings, Water Colours, Drawings, &c.; and about 4000 Vols. of Books, including many rare and valuable First Editions of the Works of Mrs. Gaskell, Charlotte Brontë, George Eliot, &c., &c. To be Sold by Auction, by Messrs. George H. Larmuth & Sons on the Premises as Above, Commencing on Monday, February 9th, 1914, and Tuesday,*

"La Camorra," by Mareo Mounier. 1862. The foundation of
Mrs. Gaskell's article on the Camorra.[5]

Nor must one forget Mrs. Gaskell's conversations and correspondence with those friends who, like herself, had taken Italy
to their hearts, friends such as William Wetmore Story, with
whom she hoped to stay while getting "a little initiated into
Roman ways"[6], and Charles Eliot Norton, whose *Notes of*

Wednesday, Thursday, Friday, and following Monday, 16*th February,*
p. 77. The address of the aforenamed Auctioneers is given as 10 St.
Ann's Square, Manchester; that of the Solicitors, Tatham, Worthington
& Co., as 1 St. James's Square, Manchester. (A copy of this catalogue
is deposited in Box 4 of the Gaskell Boxes, in the Manchester Central
Reference Library.) Other lots for the sixth day, of interest to readers
of *North and South* and *Sylvia's Lovers* respectively, are an edition of
Chorley's *Pomfret* (Lot 546) and a run of *The Annual Register, from*
1758 *to* 1838 (Lot 206); we may also note *Mémoires sur Madame de
Sévigné* (Lot 639), *Wither's Motto,* 1633 (Lot 467), *The Arabian Nights*
and similar romances (Lots 132, 319, 345, 422, 497), a first edition of
The Moorland Cottage inscribed by the author for her husband on 17
December 1850 (Lot 490), and a copy of Gray's *Works,* 1821, presented
on 2 August 1825 to E. C. Stevenson from her father (Lot 425—catalogued
incorrectly as from W. Gaskell: cont. 'The Gaskell Sale', *The Manchester
Guardian,* 18 February 1914, which reports that this presentation copy
from Mrs. Gaskell's father fetched £5-15-0).

[5] This description, at least as far as the author's name is concerned,
seems erroneous. However we will not pursue the matter, beyond
noting: *La Camorra, Notizie Storiche Raccolte e Documentate per
Cura M.M.,* Florence, 1862; and Marc Monnier, *La Camorra,
Mystères de Naples,* Paris: Michel-Lévy Frères, 1863—based on entries
in the General Catalogues of Printed Books of the British Museum and
the *Bibliothèque Nationale.*

[6] Quoted, from a [March 1857] letter by Mrs. Gaskell to W. W.
Story, in Henry James, *William Wetmore Story and His Friends, from
Letters, Diaries, and Recollections,* 2 vols., Edinburgh and London:
William Blackwood and Sons, 1903, I, 355: *G.L.,* No. 345 (to W. W.
and/or Emelyn Story, according to Chapple and Pollard, whose dating
is [?February 1857]). To help James in his biography of her father-in-law,
Mrs. Maud Waldo Story sent him all but one of Mrs. Gaskell's letters,
that not sent being unimportant; alarmed on hearing this, Mrs. Gaskell's
daughters urgently requested the letters be destroyed, which they were, 'on
account of their intimate character'—so wrote Mrs. M. W. Story in
a letter of 5 March [1929] to Miss Jane Revere Coolidge, subsequently
Mrs. Whitehill, who (ed. *Gaskell-Norton Letters,* pp. xviii-xix) published
(with very slight punctuation-changes) Mrs. Gaskell's unimportant letter
—of Monday 8 [9] February 1857 to Mrs. W. W. Story—from a copy
enclosed for her by Mrs. M. W. Story (*G.L.,* No. 342, Chapple and
Pollard misprinting 'Rue du Bac' as 'Rue de Bac'). The largest surviving
collection of Mrs. Gaskell's letters to W. W. Story and his wife is in the
Texas University Library.

Travel and Study in Italy (1860) she found it ' a pleasure to read '[7].

The only points requiring comment are, on the one hand, the writer's contempt for the ' organised intimidation '[8] and ' cruel tyranny '[9] of the corrupt Neapolitan Bourbons, and, on the other, her respect for the ' brave followers of Garibaldi '[10]. Like many English people, the Gaskells seem to have espoused the cause of Italian Unity[11]. Their friend, Mrs. William Shaen (*née* Emily Winkworth), was a fervent supporter of Mazzini[12], and strongly wished the novelist to know him[13]. Mrs. Gaskell's regard for Garibaldi, named more than once in the article[14], had been earlier evidenced by her Preface to *Garibaldi at Caprera*. Another admirer of the Liberator was the Rev. Patrick Brontë who, full of interest in Italian politics, had voiced his esteem for the patriot during Mrs. Gaskell's Haworth visit of November 1860[15].

It seems certain that Mrs. Gaskell composed a second piece on the Camorra (which never found its way into print, perhaps because her first had already appeared). Writing to Marianne

---

[7] *Gaskell-Norton Letters,* ed. Whitehill, p. 74: *G.L.,* No. 480.

[8] *Works,* VI, 532.

[9] *Works,* VI, 532.

[10] *Works,* VI, 539.

[11] It was Mr. Gaskell's custom at breakfast to read aloud the telegrams about Garibaldi which appeared in the daily paper: so Meta wrote to Charles Eliot Norton on Sunday 22 [23] September in a letter begun on Thursday 20 September 1860—now in the Harvard University Library: bMS Am 1088 (2601). Meta's letter includes her thanks for Norton's having sent a report of a speech of his on Garibaldi, enclosed with his letter to her of 19 August 1860 (also in the Harvard University Library: bMS Am 1088·2).

[12] Her impressions after first meeting him in the flesh are to be found in a letter to her sisters begun on 23 August 1850—quoted in Shaen, ed. *Memorials of Two Sisters,* pp. 59-60.

[13] Haldane, *Mrs. Gaskell and Her Friends,* pp. 251-252: cf. and cont. *G.L.,* No. 157.

[14] *Works,* VI, 537-539.

[15] Mrs. Gaskell mentions this visit and Mr. Brontë's admiration for Garibaldi's character in a fly-leaf inscription, dated 3 May 1861, to a copy, once owned by Richard Waugh Wright, of her *Life of Charlotte Brontë* (London: Smith, Elder and Co., 1860)—now in the Manchester Central Reference Library (Book No. B.R. 823.81 B160/1). Mr. Brontë's discussion of Italian politics with her mother, whose views accorded with his own, is mentioned also by Meta Gaskell in a letter to Emily Winkworth (Mrs. Shaen)—(quoted in Haldane, *Mrs. Gaskell and Her Friends,* p. 187).

from Florence on Wednesday 20 [May 1863], she enquired
whether the June number of *The Cornhill* contained ' an article
on *La Camorra* '[16]; it was, she said, hers, though not a word
must be breathed about its authorship. However, as is indicated
in the letter she composed at Venice for Marianne one Monday
evening [1 June 1863][17], Smith, finding the contribution un-
acceptable, had forwarded it to Froude, which infuriated the
author, who bade Froude return the manuscript to him with
directions for its immediate despatch to her (care of Mr.
Shaen). Smith was, Mrs. Gaskell wrote, quite right to refuse
the article, for, others having appeared on the subject, it no
longer possessed the recommendation of novelty—its probably
one great merit. What she objected to was his presumption in
deciding to whom she would wish it sent.   Another likely
reference to her rejected contribution occurs in a letter to
Smith of 20 September [1863]. There, speaking of the series
subsequently published as ' French Life ', Mrs. Gaskell wrote
interlinearly : " I thought of sending this to M[r] Froude/ to
make up for the/ ' Camorra '—that/ unlucky piece/ of work/"[18].
Froude's welcoming letter of 20 October [1863][19], with the
appearance of the travelogue in *Fraser's* the following year[20],
testifies that thought was translated into action, doubtless proving
an adequate compensation for any trouble the ' Camorra ' MS
may have caused.

[16] Copies of this letter (*G.L.*, No. 523a), once owned by Mr. J. T.
Lancaster, belong to the present writer.
[17] This letter is in the possession of Mrs. Margaret Trevor Jones:
G.L., No. 524.
[18] This letter (in the archives of Sir John Murray) is partly printed
by Miss Hopkins (*Elizabeth Gaskell*, p. 220), who, however, omits the
passage here quoted. The letter occurs as *G.L.*, No. 532.
[19] Waller, ed. *Letters Addressed to Mrs Gaskell by Celebrated Contemporaries*, p. 61. Mrs. Gaskell did not include the year when dating
this letter (in The John Rylands Library, Manchester: English MS. 730/
32); but its accompanying envelope is post-marked 21 October 1863.
[20] [Elizabeth Cleghorn Gaskell] ' French Life ', *Fraser's Magazine for
Town and Country*, LXIX (April-June 1864), 435-449, 575-585, 739-752.

SECTION IV

Cousin Phillis (1863-1864)

Possibly at one time intended for a Dickensian periodical,
'Cousin Phillis' 'escaped that fate'[1] by appearing, from
November 1863 to February 1864, in *The Cornhill Magazine*[2];
its leisurely manner better suited a monthly than a weekly form
of publication. As a book it came out initially in America[3],
then, illustrated by Du Maurier, in England[4].

By general concensus this novelette is ranked among the
highest achievements of its author's art; next to *Cranford,* it
is probably the most widely read of all her shorter works. To
indicate those features which have won favour among Gaskell
lovers, one can hardly do better than quote 'Q.'.

> I suppose its underlying sadness has kept it out of popular
> esteem—this tale of scarcely more than a hundred pages—a
> pale and shadowy sister of *Cranford*. It has none, or little of
> *Cranford*'s pawky fun: it has not *Cranford*'s factitious happy
> ending. But it beats me to guess how any true critic can pass
> it over and neglect a thing with all that is best in Theocritus
> moving in rustic English hearts. And it is not *invented*. It has
> in all its movements the suggestion of things actually seen
> —of small things that could not have occurred to any mind
> save that of an eye-witness—of small *recognitions,* each in its
> turn a little flash of light upon the steady background of rural
> England. It is England and yet pure Virgil . . . [5]

This idyllic quality is acknowledged by all who have written
on *Cousin Phillis*.

The rural background was provided by an intimate know-

[1] Hopkins, *Elizabeth Gaskell,* p. 221: cf. *G.L.,* No. 532.
[2] VIII (1863), 619-635, 688-706; IX (1864), 51-65, 187-209. Mrs. Gaskell
was still writing during publication (*G.L.,* No. 545), which doubtless
allowed little time for rereading—hence such slips as stating that Paul's
working-day began at eight o'clock and at eight-thirty (*Works,* VII, 3, 13).
[3] [Elizabeth Cleghorn Gaskell] *Cousin Phillis. A Tale,* New York:
Harper & Brothers, 1864.
[4] Elizabeth Cleghorn Gaskell, *Cousin Phillis. And Other Tales,* Illus.
edn, London: Smith, Elder and Co., 1865.
[5] Arthur Thomas Quiller-Couch, 'Mrs Gaskell', *Charles Dickens and
Other Victorians,* Cambridge: The University Press, 1925, p. 214.

ledge of Knutsford and its environs, particularly of Sandlebridge, the Holland farm. As both girl and married woman,
Mrs. Gaskell visited the traditional home of her maternal
relatives—' the/ old familiar place ' as she called it in an
ecstatic letter[6] on the pleasures of country life (birds, cattle,
lambs, honeysuckle, roses, bees and a host of other delightful
sights, scents, and sounds). She once confessed that, feeling un-
Manchester, she rejoiced in ' a smelling and singing world '[7];
this world, recaptured in the story, was enjoyed at Sandlebridge.

Sir Henry Holland remarked that his ' cousin, Mrs. Gaskell,
who knew Sandlebridge well, . . . pictured the place by some
short but very descriptive touches in one or two of her novels '[8] :
no doubt he had *Cousin Phillis* especially in mind. Sir Henry
also mentioned he could never revisit the picturesque old farm-
house without recalling his (and Mrs. Gaskell's) grandfather,
Samuel Holland, ' either as walking cheerfully over his fields,
or tranquilly smoking his pipe in an arm-chair coeval with
himself '[9]—Minister Holman, we may remember, likewise
smoked a pipe (presumably in his three-cornered chair)[10]. Even
though Elizabeth Stevenson was less than six when her
grandfather died, she could readily have supplemented her
recollections by what she heard about him from others[11].
Perhaps too, when creating the minister-farmer, Mrs. Gaskell
thought of her father, by turns preacher and agriculturalist before he found his true vocation as Keeper of Treasury Records.
Although both these identifications were denied by Meta
Gaskell (probably in a letter to Clement Shorter), Shorter's
comment on her denial seems reasonable enough.

> It is obvious that Mrs. Gaskell frequently went to people she
> had known for her characters. Every novelist does this, and
> every novelist repudiates doing so, and it may therefore be

---

[6] Post-marked 13 May 1836 and written from Sandlebridge to Eliza
Gaskell on the morning of Thursday [12 May 1836], this letter is in the
possession of Mrs. Margaret Trevor Jones: it occurs as *G.L.*, No. 4.

[7] *Gaskell-Norton Letters*, ed. Whitehill, p. 16: *G.L.*, No. 384.

[8] Holland, *Recollections of Past Life*, p. 7, fn.

[9] Holland, *Recollections of Past Life*, p. 7.

[10] *Works*, VII, 18-19.

[11] Mrs. Chadwick (*Mrs. Gaskell*, p. 50) states that, when her grandfather died on 26 May 1816, Elizabeth was only six; however, her birthdate
being 29 September 1810, she was in fact only five.

assumed that the likeness presented is unconsciously presented, and that in nine cases out of ten the portrait is a composite one, made from more than a single original.[12]

A similar comment would apply to claims that the author's girlhood experiences—for example her loneliness and solitary retreats[13]—went into the making of the heroine and that the narrator's father (John Manning) was based on James Nasmyth, both suggestions being likewise denied by Miss Gaskell[14]. In this last connexion, however, it is instructive to note, as does Mrs. Chadwick[15], two correspondences between the fictional character and his supposed prototype. The jokes enjoyed by Manning and Holdsworth about a gentleman-apprentice ' who used to set about his smith's work in white wash-leather gloves, for fear of spoiling his hands'[16], recall Nasmyth's contemptuous remarks concerning ' young engineers . . . addicted to wearing gloves'[17], then 'considered the genteel thing.'[18] The other feature that could well have been taken from life parallels an incident at which the writer was present. In order to demonstrate how his proposed turnip-cutting machine would work, Manning drew with a stick of charred wood on Mrs. Holman's wooden dresser (she, amusingly, making surreptitious attempts to discover whether the marks could easily be removed)[19]. About her visit to Nasmyth's works at Patricroft, where she was taken by Mrs. Gaskell in March 1856, Catherine Winkworth wrote as follows.

[12] Shorter, ed. *Novels and Tales,* VII (1911), pp. x-xi. Relevant here are some words Mrs. Gaskell wrote in a Wednesday 7 December [1859] letter (*G.L.,* No. 451++) to Miss Harriet Martineau (in the Birmingham University Library, quoted by kind permission of Lady Martineau): ' I . . . have been/ myself complimented or/ reproached, as the case/ might be, with having used/ such or such an incident,/ or described such & such/ a person, & never seem able/ to understand how one/ acquires one's materials/ unconsciously as it were./'

[13] For which see Conrad S. Sargisson, 'Mrs. Gaskell's Early Surroundings, and Their Influence on Her Writings', *The Bookman* (London), XXXVIII (1910), 246: cf. *Works,* VII, 72-73.

[14] Shorter, ed. *Novels and Tales,* VII, p. xi, fn. 1.

[15] *Mrs. Gaskell,* pp. 55-57.

[16] *Works,* VII, 32.

[17] *James Nasmyth, Engineer: An Autobiography,* ed. Smiles, p. 97.

[18] *James Nasmyth, Engineer: An Autobiography,* ed. Smiles, p. 97.

[19] *Works,* VII, 34. There is a comparable incident in *Sylvia's Lovers* where Philip draws with a piece of charred wood on his aunt's dresser when giving Sylvia her geography lesson (*Works,* VI, 115).

> I enjoyed it very much. Mr. Nasmyth showed us his room
> and models, and gave us a lesson in geology, illustrated by
> impromptu diagrams drawn on the wall, alternately with a
> piece of white chalk and a sooty fore-finger; . . . [20]

We may notice too that, like Nasmyth, who carried a ' Scheme
Book' in which to think out inventions[21], John Manning ' had
his little book that he used for mechanical memoranda and
measurements '[22].

It seems worth indicating some more correspondences, both
between fact and fiction and between *Cousin Phillis* and other
stories. The idyllic Hope Farm was almost certainly founded on
Sandlebridge. Not only, as we have seen, does Sir Henry's
evidence tend to support such a view, there is also testimony
from the author. Her reference, in mentioning the old Holland
home, to ' two pillars at the gate//way into the court, (a flight
of/ stone steps leading up to the/ said gateway,) which were/
surmounted by great stone/ balls about 6 or 7 feet apart '[23],
connects with her description of the frontage of Hope Farm[24].
Furthermore Sandlebridge came into the Holland family through
marriage[25]; in much the same way (by taking an heiress for
his wife) had Ebenezer Holman perhaps obtained Hope Farm[26].
The recent construction of the Knutsford railway (opened
on 12 May 1862[27]) may have caused Mrs. Gaskell to consider
what effects such an event would have on rural life; for, in a
sense, ' the little branch line from Eltham to Hornby '[28] brings
about Phillis's broken heart. Before the coming of Holdsworth
all was peaceful and serene; but the engineer, a strange and
an external factor, disrupts the pastoral harmony. Having
been on the Continent and wearing ' mustachios and whiskers

---

[20] *Memorials of Two Sisters,* ed. Shaen, p. 134.
[21] *James Nasmyth, Engineer: An Autobiography,* ed. Smiles, p. 240:
cf. Chadwick, *Mrs. Gaskell,* p. 57.
[22] *Works,* VII, 33.
[23] In a letter to Geraldine Jewsbury, quoted in T[heresa] C[oolidge],
' Mrs. Gaskell to Ruskin ', ' Library Notes ' Section, *More Books,* XXIII
(1948), 229—this quotation having been corrected against the original 2
April [1849] letter *(G.L.,* No. 43) in the Boston Public Library.
[24] *Works,* VII, 8: cf. Ward, ed. *Works,* VII, pp. xiv-xv.
[25] Ward, ed. *Works,* VII, p. xiv; and Chadwick, *Mrs. Gaskell,* p. 7.
[26] *Works,* VII, 5.
[27] Payne, *Mrs. Gaskell and Knutsford,* 1905, p. 12, fn. 1.
[28] *Works,* VII, 1.

of a somewhat foreign fashion '[29], he was naturally viewed
with distrust by the Cranfordesque Miss Dawsons, Eltham
ladies who, like Miss Matty[30] and Miss Pole[31], could find
no merits in France[32]. His foreign appearance was the first
thing which struck Phillis[33]; and her sober father found Hold-
worth's want of seriousness and lightness of talk alien[34] yet
fascinating[35]. At a different level the intrusion of the railways
is indicated by Mrs. Holman's fear of navvies[36]. Quite possibly
Mrs. Gaskell gained some knowledge of railway-building from
her first cousin, Samuel Holland, whose nephew (Charles Men-
zies Holland), 'brought up as a Mechanical Engineer'[37], had
helped with the line joining Blaenau and Ffestiniog village.
Samuel Holland had, moreover, taken an interest in the construction of the Menai Bridge[38], a project with which Robert
Stephenson, son of George (named in *Cousin Phillis*[39]), and
William Fairbairn (another engineer, well known to Mrs. Gaskell[40]) were both connected.

About those idyllic passages descriptive of the tranquillity at
Hope Farm much has been admirably written elsewhere[41]. It
suffices to say they were composed by some one intimately
acquainted with the English countryside. References to the
mundane tasks of farming[42] came naturally from a writer who,
even when a famous novelist in Manchester, 'was more proud
of her cows and poultry, pigs and vegetables, than of her
literary triumphs'[43]—at least in the opinion of Susanna Winkworth.

[29] *Works*, VII, 3.
[30] *Works*, II, 44.
[31] *Works*, II, 46-47.
[32] *Works*, VII, 4.
[33] *Works*, VII, 47.
[34] *Works*, VII, 53.
[35] *Works*, VII, 53, 58-59, 78-79.
[36] *Works*, VII, 55.
[37] *The Memoirs of Samuel Holland, One of the Pioneers of the
North Wales Slate Industry* [ed. Davies], p. 22.
[38] *The Memoirs of Samuel Holland* [ed. Davies], pp. 25-26.
[39] *Works*, VII, 32.
[40] Pole, ed. *The Life of Sir William Fairbairn*, pp. 451, 460-462.
[41] By, for example, Lord David Cecil (*Early Victorian Novelists*,
1948, pp. 174, 176), Miss ffrench (*Mrs. Gaskell*, pp. 94-95), Miss Hopkins
(*Elizabeth Gaskell*, p. 276), and Ward (ed. *Works*, VII, pp. xiv-xvi).
[42] *Works*, VII, 14-15.
[43] *Memorials of Two Sisters*, ed. Shaen, p. 24.

The presentation of intellectual life at Hope Farm likewise probably owed much to personal experience. One need not invoke a picture of Emily Brontë, studying German while kneading dough[44], as a counterpart to that of Phillis, reading Dante while peeling apples[45]; the authoress herself must often have had recourse to such devices, like any other woman with intellectual interests. We ought, perhaps, to notice the parallel with Margaret Hale: she was another student of Dante; and, just as Holdsworth saw the Italian word-list belonging to Phillis[46], so Lennox saw hers[47].

Other literary echoes include that fine scene, frequently praised, where the bare-headed Farmer Holman gives out a psalm to conclude the day's labour in the field[48]: this had its forerunner in 'Six Weeks at Heppenheim'[49]. Very likely Mrs. Gaskell observed similar incidents both at home and abroad. Minister Holman's inability, during his distress, to practise the precepts of resignation he was wont to preach[50] is reminiscent of similar failings in Fielding's Parson Adams and Goldsmith's Dr. Primrose. Here, if her experiences as a minister's wife did not provide sufficient examples, Mrs. Gaskell may have been influenced by *Rasselas,* a classic for her[51] as for Miss Debõrah Jenkyns[52]. We may note that one of the two fellow-ministers who came as Job's comforters to Holman enquired whether his affliction might not be due to his having made an idol of Phillis[53]. Holman's reply, that like Christ he held suffering was not sent as a punishment for sin, has some interest for its relevance to the author's general treatment of idolatry; but its immediate purpose is to allow a sly glance to be cast at theological rigidity (' "Is that orthodox, Brother Robinson?" asked the third minister, in a deferential tone of inquiry.'[54]).

[44] *The Life of Charlotte Brontë,* 1st edn, 1857, I, 150.
[45] *Works,* VII, 27.
[46] *Works,* VII, 48-49.
[47] *Works,* IV, 23.
[48] *Works,* VII, 15.
[49] *Works,* VII, 398.
[50] *Works,* VII, 104.
[51] Presumably—*Gaskell-Norton Letters,* ed. Whitehill, p. 12: *G.L.,* No. 384.
[52] *Works,* II, 10-11. For other Johnsonian citations and quotations, one may consult the admirable Appendix III of Rubenius, *The Woman Question in Mrs. Gaskell's Life and Works,* pp. 308-309.
[53] *Works,* VII, 105.　　　　　　　[54] *Works,* VII, 105.

References to Mrs. Holman's son[55] scarcely call for comment, being clearly autobiographical. When one reads about ' the aching sense of loss she would never get over in this world '[56], Mrs. Gaskell's words[57] about that wound which would never heal for her on earth immediately suggest themselves. Neither is there much need to comment on the scene where Phillis breaks her thread—were it not that in mentioning it Dr. Adolphus Ward makes one of his few mistakes[58], though one doubly erroneous. Having in a general sense remarked, fairly truthfully, that ' Mrs. Gaskell very rarely indeed merely repeated herself'[59], he added a rather misleading footnote.

> This applies even to details. Though she was not, in one sense of the word, a very careful writer, the rapidity of her imagination was always moving forward. The recurrence of such an incident as the snapping of the thread at the spinning-wheel, which, in not very different circumstances, marks the preoccupation of Cousin Phillis and of Faith Hickson in " Lois the Witch ", is quite exceptional.[60]

Certainly Faith's thread does snap on one occasion[61] (and, at another time, it significantly does not[62]); but Phillis was sewing, not spinning, when hers broke[63]. We may recall that Sylvia Robson used a spinning-wheel[64], and that the author considered its use set off a graceful figure in almost as becoming a manner as harp-playing[65]. However such references do little more than

[55] *Works*, VII, 10, 78, 89.
[56] *Works*, VII, 78.
[57] The relevant extracts from Mrs. Gaskell's letter of 24 April 1851 [1848] to Miss Annie Shaen are given in Haldane, *Mrs. Gaskell and Her Friends*, pp. 239-240; and Hopkins, *Elizabeth Gaskell*, p. 66. Pertinent quotations from a copy (in the Gaskell Section, Brotherton Collection, Leeds University Library) of part of Mrs. Gaskell's letter to Eliza Fox of 26 April 1850 appear in Rubenius, *The Woman Question in Mrs. Gaskell's Life and Works*, pp. 17, fn. 5 (slightly inaccurate), 198, fn. 3. These letters occur respectively as *G.L.*, Nos. 25a (dated [?24 April 1848] by Chapple and Pollard, who designate its recipient as ?Anne Shaen), 70.
[58] Others are noted in Pollard, *The Novels of Mrs. Gaskell*, p. 405.
[59] Ward, ed. *Works*, VII, p. xxv.
[60] Ward, ed. *Works*, VII, p. xxv, fn.
[61] *Works*, VII, 137.
[62] *Works*, VII, 150.
[63] *Works*, VII, 86.
[64] *Works*, VI, 44.
[65] *Works*, VI, 44.

suggest how Ward may have come to make the slip. Ironically his instance of what he considered quite exceptional was a bad example, one in which there was less repetition than he supposed.

We have pointed to the appearance in *Cousin Phillis* of elements found in earlier works; and, since Ward so stressed the the rarity of such recurrences, another illustration will not be out of place. ' Q.', as already noted, commends Mrs. Gaskell's first-hand observations. Of her meaningful *minutiae* there are two which especially attract the reader's attention, both being introduced at crucial points. One occurs at the moment of tension following the confession by Phillis of her love for Holdsworth : it serves to make vivid the narrator's mental state.

> . . . Then again a silence. I thought I saw Phillis's white lips moving, but it might be the flickering of the candle-light—a moth had flown in through the open casement, and was fluttering round the flame; I might have saved it, but I did not care to do so, my heart was too full of other things.[66]

The second, chronologically prior, echoes a similar incident in *Ruth* where[67], though in despair, the heroine was yet sufficiently conscious of the objective world to be acutely aware of a green beetle and a falling skylark, and to be able long afterwards to recall their features. Likewise in *Cousin Phillis* the narrator, having received word of Holdsworth's marriage and knowing this news would destroy his cousin's happiness, could nonetheless be affected by external nature.

> . . . I saw a chaffinch's nest on the lichen-covered trunk of an old apple-tree opposite my window, and saw the mother-bird come fluttering in to feed her brood—and yet I did not see it, although it seemed to me afterwards as if I could have drawn every fibre, every feather.[68]

Although Miss ffrench speaks of the effectiveness of Paul Manning as a narrator[69], some dissatisfaction has been expressed by Lord David Cecil[70], Miss Hopkins[71], and Elizabeth Jenkins. The last considers ' the effect on the reader is to make him

---

[66] *Works,* VII, 99.
[67] *Works,* III, 93.
[68] *Works,* VII, 82.
[69] ffrench, *Mrs. Gaskell,* p. 75; see too pp. 95-96.
[70] *Early Victorian Novelists,* 1948, p. 184.
[71] *Elizabeth Gaskell,* pp. 276-277.

say: " What an excellent imitation of a young man !" rather than to surrender to absolute conviction, as in *Cranford*.[72] Instead of this invidious comparison with Mary Smith, a reference to the narrator of ' Mr. Harrison's Confessions' might have been more pertinent, particularly as the latter's response to Duncombe recalls, albeit at a slightly more mature level, that of young Manning to Eltham. Moreover the incongruity Miss Hopkins[73] detects in his character seems due to swift maturity rather than, as she suggests, to the unnatural fact that he himself did not fall in love with Phillis—for he half did so[74]; but, treated like a younger brother[75] by a girl nearly two years his junior[76], he sought consolation in thinking the grapes were sour[77]. At the beginning of the story Paul was seventeen[78], and his reactions to the Eltham *milieu* were appropriately those of a callow youth. This is clearly brought out by his distaste for the Dissenting way of life to which he was expected to ' conform '. We have noticed how Mrs. Gaskell liked to indulge her sly humour by poking fun at certain aspects of Nonconformity. Here she has some rich remarks about Paul's boredom with ' droning hymns, and long prayers, and a still longer sermon, preached to a small congregation'[79]. There is an admirable thumb-nail sketch of Mr. Peters who, after being dutifully ministerial all day, did over supper ' unbend a little into one or two ponderous jokes, as if to show . . . that ministers were men, after all.'[80]

The main events of the novelette take place over a year later, Paul then being nearly nineteen[81], and in the summer following.

[72] Elizabeth Jenkins, intro. *Cranford* [and] *Cousin Phillis*, London: John Lehmann, 1947, p. xi.
[73] *Elizabeth Gaskell*, p. 276.
[74] *Works*, VII, 13, 28-29.
[75] *Works*, VII, 37.
[76] *Works*, VII, 10, 25.
[77] *Works*, VII, 28.
[78] *Works*, VII, 1.
[79] *Works*, VII, 3. A small congregation would certainly have been found in the eighteen-forties—the new penny-postal system having just come in (*Works*, VII, 90)—at Brook Street Chapel, Knutsford, where in 1827 it numbered about forty adults, dropping to a score by the middle of the century (George Andrew Payne, *An Ancient Chapel*: *Brook Street Chapel, Knutsford, with Allostock Chapel, Nr. Knutsford*, Banbury: " The Banbury Guardian " Office, 1934, p. 27).
[80] *Works*, VII, 4.   [81] *Works*, VII, 5.

Hence, though not without his awkward moments, he appears a far more responsible and sympathetic narrator during the greater part of the tale than he had shown himself at its outset. Perhaps his attitude to Minister Holman affords a good indication of the change. Though somewhat apprehensive about the minister[82], he grows to value the intellectual prowess of the man[83], to appreciate his eminently practical type of religion[84], and to comprehend the difficulties he encountered in reaching the people[85]. Mrs. Gaskell was doubtless drawing, to some degree at least, on her personal knowledge of ministerial life; yet there is nothing disconcertingly out of character in this part of Paul Manning's narrative. Perhaps it is symptomatic of the alteration in his function that, when two unctious brother-preachers are lightly satirized, the work is done through Betty, that racy, vigorous, down-to-earth servant of the Holmans.

> " 'Od rot 'em!" said she; "they're always a-coming at ill-convenient times; . . . but I'll do some ham and eggs, and that'll rout 'em from worrying the minister. They're a deal quieter after they've had their victual. Last time as old Robinson came, he was very reprehensible upon master's learning, which he couldn't compass to save his life, so he needn't have been afeared of that temptation, and used words long enough to have knocked a body down; but after me and missus had given him his fill of victual, and he'd had some good ale and a pipe, he spoke just like any other man, and could crack a joke with me."[86]

In *Cousin Phillis* there is nothing (except a redundant rhetorical apostrophe[87]) one would wish omitted; and many incidental felicities could be mentioned which, admirable in themselves, serve to give substance to the plot and body to the characters. Examples include the narrator's passing comment on Holdsworth's initial encounter with Holman ('Men have always a little natural antipathy to get over when they first meet as strangers.'[88]); his remarks both on the isolation occasionally felt by Mrs. Holman when her husband and daughter en-

82 *Works*, VII, 11.
83 *Works*, VII, 20, 76.
84 *Works*, VII, 15-16, (esp.) 24.
85 *Works*, VII, 29.
86 *Works*, VII, 105.
87 *Works*, VII, 53.
88 *Works*, VII, 49.

gaged in intellectual conversation[89] and on her slight signs of
jealousy at their having interests from which she was excluded[90];
and his manner of dating events at Hope Farm by reference to
seasonal occupations[91]. There is, too, the wonderful evocation
of the timeless quality at the farm : thus, after a week away,
Paul found Phillis still at her knitting[92]; and, when reading to
her and Mrs. Holman in a quiet hour, he felt as if he ' had
lived for ever, and should live for ever, droning out paragraphs
in that warm sunny room, . . . the curled-up pussy-cat sleeping
on the hearthrug, and the clock on the house-stairs perpetually
clicking out the passage of the moments.'[93]

Rather than dilate on details like these, however, we may
find it more instructive to attempt an explanation of the peculiar
charm of *Cousin Phillis* in terms of its general thematic structure. One of the grounds for excluding Mrs. Gaskell from the
very first rank of novelists is the absence in her work of univer-
sally significant concerns. Often defective in the mere framework of their construction, her novels and tales also lack
patterns at deeper levels; instead they rather touch the surfaces
of life, treating manners and social conditions, sometimes seri-
ously, sometimes humorously, yet always with kindly understanding. Mrs. Gaskell was a good, charming, humane, tolerant,
sensitive lady, attractive in every respect; but she was neither
original nor profound. Her talents were diverse, her gaze extended beyond the Midland counties, and her observations
were not confined to the middle classes; nevertheless she had
limitations. Her range, if in one sense wide, was, in another,
not wide enough : it lacked comprehension. Although most
Victorian novelists were somewhat constricted by their age,
Mrs. Gaskell's fiction was circumscribed by the position and
personality of its authoress as well as by the social and moral
pressures of the period.

One is tempted to summarize this sort of criticism by
saying that there is nothing archetypal in her writings; but
such a statement could prove a little misleading. On occasions

---

[89] *Works*, VII, 34-35.
[90] *Works*, VII, 58.
[91] *Works*, VII, 54.
[92] *Works*, VII, 12.
[93] *Works*, VII, 26.

one does come across incidents which seem to have significance
beyond their individual contexts. Thus, from *Sylvia's Lovers,*
there comes to mind a picture the heroine herself often recalled,
that of ' the straight, upright figure of her mother, fronting the
setting sun, but searching through its blinding rays for a sight
of her child '[94]—surely here Mrs. Robson seems to represent the
eternal mother seeking for her young at the close of the day.
Albeit in a weak and modified form, this picture first appeared
in *Mary Barton,* where Alice's last memory of her mother was
of Mrs. Wilson's shading her eyes to watch the girl's leaving
home[95]; again somewhat changed, it reappears in the present
tale when Mrs. Holman bids Paul come again as she stands
' at the curate-door, shading her eyes from the sinking sun '[96].
Another variation is to be found in *Wives and Daughters;* for
Molly sees the departing Roger Hamley, hoping to catch a last
glimpse of Cynthia, ' turn round and shade his eyes from the
level rays of the westering sun, and rake the house with his
glances '[97].

Apart, however, from such universally-meaningful images,
one would be at a loss to indicate anything archetypal in the
Gaskell canon, were it not for *Cousin Phillis*—and even here
we may be reading into the story more than the text will
warrant.

If, in Seccombe's words, *Cousin Phillis* is no mere ' mosaic
of accurately-observed pieces, but a faithful impression of a
shadow cast by Life as a whole '[98], then possibly the universality
of its appeal can be accounted for in the following fashion.
Hope Farm signifies an Eden of Innocence into which a foreign
element (Holdsworth) intrudes; discord results; but, through
suffering, harmony is again established, though of a sort different from before : the movement of the narrative could thus be
viewed in terms of Hegel's triad (thesis, anti-thesis, and synthesis).
' Q.', with Shakespeare in mind, detects in Mrs. Gaskell too ' a
certain sunset softness—a haze . . . —in which many hard

[94] *Works,* VI, 64-65.
[95] *Works,* I, 33.
[96] *Works,* VII, 11.
[97] *Works,* VIII, 436.
[98] Thomas Seccombe, pref. *Cousin Phillis,* by Mrs. Gaskell, London :
George Bell & Sons, 1908, p. xxviii.

experiences are reconciled '[99]; and perhaps a comparison with the Final Plays is not entirely out of place. Yet, should one reject an interpretation which suggests an Age of Experience growing painfully out of an Age of Innocence, there seems at least one area where the particular extends to the general, namely that of the heroine's sexual development. Certainly the stress laid on the pinafore[100] and Phillis's discarding of it[101] gives some cause for taking this symbolically as betokening a laying aside of childish things and an acceptance of womanhood. Her parents fail to recognize the change, Mr. Holman's cry being the perennial lamentation of a father losing his offspring to the world at large—' " Phillis! did we not make you happy here? Have we not loved you enough?" '[102] Betty, on the other hand, represents by her commonsense acceptance of reality the wisdom of the ages: not only does she exhort the languishing and broken-hearted Phillis to face the world[103], she also offers an astute diagnosis of the Holmans' parental blindness to their daughter's attraction for men.

> " . . . They've called her ' the child ' so long—' the child ' is always their name for her when they talk on her between themselves, . . . —that she's grown up to be a woman under their very eyes, and they look on her still as if she were in her long-clothes. And you ne'er heard on a man falling in love wi' a babby in long-clothes!"[104]

Even if every sort of symbolic interpretation be dismissed as fanciful, *Cousin Phillis* can still be enjoyed and admired as the delicately-rendered story of a young girl's first love[105]. In its quiet way this tale enters a plea for the recognition that, like men, women have their affections, and that these may legitimately be aroused before they have received any formal declaration. Possibly Mrs. Gaskell's concern with a girl's disappointment in love can be related to Meta's broken engagement

[99] Quiller-Couch, *Charles Dickens and Other Victorians,* p. 217.
[100] *Works,* VII, 9, 48, 98.
[101] *Works,* VII, 32.
[102] *Works,* VII, 99.
[103] *Works,* VII, 108.
[104] *Works,* VII, 88: cf. the Robsons' attitude to Sylvia (*Works,* VI, 128).
[105] The reasons for such admiration can be found in the praises of former critics, notably Seccombe (pref. *Cousin Phillis,* by Mrs. Gaskell, pp. xxv-xxxii).

(already mentioned in our discussion of *Sylvia's Lovers*); and, incidentally, it is worth noting that, like Meta, Phillis had scholarly interests. Although Holdsworth, unlike Captain Hill, never actually proposed, each gentleman left his beloved to go abroad, and in both cases the expected marriage did not take place[106].

---

[106] Is there an oblique reference to Meta in Shorter's remark that Phillis's romantic disappointment 'had some slight counterpart in the experience of a charming girl of Mrs. Gaskell's acquaintance' (Shorter, ed. *Novels and Tales*, VII, p. xi)? Certainly he had once handed to Meta a number of her mother's letters telling 'an old love story of which' this daughter 'was the heroine.'—C.K.S., 'A Literary Letter: The late Miss "Meta" Gaskell', *The Sphere*, Vol. LV, No. 720 (8 November 1913), p. 154.

SECTION V

' The Cage at Cranford ' (1863)

On 28 November 1863 ' The Cage at Cranford ' appeared
in *All the Year Round*[1]. It was never reprinted during Mrs.
Gaskell's lifetime; nor did Dr. Adolphus Ward include it in the
Knutsford Edition—doubtless, as Mrs. Chadwick says[2], because
the author disliked the piece, and so her daughters would not
wish to see it ' in a " definitive " edition of her writings.'[3]

Just as ' Mr. Harrison's Confessions ' was a sort of prelude to
Cranford, so this episode forms a kind of postscript to that
series. As an extraordinarily clever *pastiche,* it might have come
from the pen of a parodist of genius. ' The Cage at Cranford '
has everything, except ' the spirit that made the earlier sketches
real literature'[4].

The familiar figures take part—although, perhaps significantly, Miss Matty makes only a brief appearance (the chief
personage, other than the narrator, being Miss Pole). The
incident of the cage itself is typically Cranfordesque : Mary
having asked Mrs. Gordon (*née* Brown) to send Miss Pole, on
her behalf, a fashionable present from Paris, a ' cage ' arrives
which, despite her maid's objections, is prepared as a bird-cage
for Miss Pole's parrot; Mr. Hoggins confounds the ladies—but
not the maid—by demonstrating that the mysterious framework
is a new invention for holding out gowns; and Mr. Peter
characteristically effects a happy ending.

> " It is a cage," said he, bowing to Miss Pole; " but it is a
> cage for an angel, instead of a bird! . . . "[5]

Many reminiscences of *Cranford* occur. Mr. Hoggins still eats

---

[1] X, 332-336. It is reprinted in *Novels and Tales,* III (1907), 197-209.
[2] Chadwick, *Mrs. Gaskell,* p. 296.
[3] Ward, ed. *Works,* I, p. xiii.
[4] Sanders, *Elizabeth Gaskell,* p. 112: a minor typographical error has
been corrected.
[5] *Novels and Tales,* III, 209.

bread and cheese[6]; money is still a delicate subject[7]; turban-style caps are still considered fashionable head-gear[8]; calashes are still worn[9]; candle-economies are still in favour[10]; men are still held to be encumbrances[11]; and maids still come from the charity school[12]. More important, however, are the Cranfordian witticisms and paradoxical turns of phrase. For instance, Miss Pole remarks: ' " Now there is no anticipation in a surprise; that's the worst of it." '[13] A little later she delivers the following rebuke.

> " Mr. Hoggins! you may be a surgeon, and a very clever one, but nothing—not even your profession—gives you a right to be indecent."[14]

In rather the same eccentrically apposite manner is the narrator's comment that it was just because a criticism of Miss Pole's seemed like the truth that she minded its being said[15].

Another correspondence with *Cranford* is suggested by the mode of narrating, there being the same *naïve* assumption on Mary's part that everyone shares her social values. Thus she naturally supposes Mr. Hoggins must have escaped ' in shame '[16] after insulting Miss Pole with his remark that the cage was meant for her and not for her parrot, whereas he had merely gone to fetch his wife's fashion-book to prove his point.

Although, as may be gathered from such illustrations, ' The Cage at Cranford ' contains some good things, one finishes the

---

6 *Novels and Tales*, III, 204: cf. *Works*, II, 137.

7 *Novels and Tales*, III, 197, 207: cf. *Works*, II, 4, 164-168.

8 *Novels and Tales*, III, 198: cf. *Works*, II, 97-99, 102-104.

9 *Novels and Tales*, III, 209: cf. *Works*, II, 41, 78, 83.

10 *Novels and Tales*, III, 201: cf. *Works*, II, 8, 50-52, 56, 62, 186. See too *Works*, III, 378.

11 *Novels and Tales*, III, 204: cf. *Works*, II, 1.

12 *Novels and Tales*, III, 204: cf. *Works*, II, 3, 94. However Miss Pole's maid is here (*Novels and Tales*, III, 202) called Fanny—the name of one of Miss Matty's maids in *Cranford* (*Works*, II, 29), where Miss Pole's servant is Betty (*Works*, II, 99).

13 *Novels and Tales*, III, 201.

14 *Novels and Tales*, III, 208.

15 *Novels and Tales*, III, 199. This insightful remark, albeit in a far less sombre context, recalls the authorial comment in *Mary Barton* that it is just because a woe has no remedy that one mourns (*Works*, I, 284) and the heroine's statement in *Ruth* that her very reason for crying was that the dead could not be restored (*Works*, III, 48).

16 *Novels and Tales*, III, 209.

piece feeling slightly disappointed. Literary successes can rarely be repeated, and Mrs. Gaskell rarely endeavoured to do so. An attempt which fails is a tarnished reflexion of the initial achievement. Therefore the decision not to sanction republication was doubtless wise, since it seems better for most lovers of *Cranford* not to know its author failed to strike the pure gold of that vein again, a decade later[17].

[17] The opening words of the sketch suggest no Cranford news had been related ' since the year 1856 ' (*Novels and Tales,* III, 197): actually 21 May 1853 was when the final ' Cranford ' instalment appeared in *Household Words* (VII, 277-285).

SECTION VI

'Robert Gould Shaw' (1863)

In December 1863 Mrs. Gaskell's appreciative and signed obituary, 'Robert Gould Shaw', appeared in *Macmillan's Magazine*[1]; it seems to have been her only contribution to that periodical, though at its inception she was approached by David Masson[2]. Having known the Shaw family since 1855[3], she had private reasons for writing the notice; yet these were subordinate to her public intentions.

Troubled by reports in English newspapers that Northerners of standing avoided suffering and sacrifice (they being content for foreign mercenaries to fight the Confederates)[4], Mrs. Gaskell felt obliged to vindicate the honour of wealthy Federal

---

[1] IX, 113-117. In a letter (*G.L.*, No. 547) of Saturday 6 February [1864]—in the Fitzwilliam Museum, Cambridge (Ashcombe Collection II, 118)—Mrs. Gaskell gave permission for a friend of the recipient to translate into German her 'little notice of Colonel/ Shaw'.

[2] Mrs. Gaskell's letter to George Smith of Monday 19 September [1859] mentions Masson's having 'written to ask/ for things for a Mag./ or something' that Macmillan was going to establish. In her letter of Saturday [late September or early October—probably 1 October—1859], Mrs. Gaskell told Smith she had replied in the negative to Masson's request. Both letters are in the archives of Sir John Murray; a relevant quotation from the second is given by Miss Hopkins (*Elizabeth Gaskell*, p. 206), though she has Mason for Masson: they appear respectively as *G.L.*, Nos. 440, 442 (dated [?1 October 1859] by Chapple and Pollard). Also relevant may be an undated letter to (most probably) Frederick James Furnivall (in the British Museum: Add. MS. 43798A, ff. 26-27): here Mrs. Gaskell remarked that she was much obliged to Mr. Macmillan and her correspondent, but that she then had nothing to say and doubted whether she would again write for publication; nevertheless she added that her correspondent's kindness and Macmillan's proposal would be borne in mind against the future. This letter (*G.L.*, No. 237, to ?F. J. Furnivall) is (doubtfully) dated [?May ?1855] by Chapple and Pollard, partly because of the similarity of its paper to *G.L.*, No. 236 (which they date 3 May [?1855]); yet both letters may have been written in 1860—the Mme Mohl reference in *G.L.*, No. 236 linking with those in *G.L.*, Nos. 454, 455; the Macmillan reference in *G.L.*, No. 237 with that in *G.L.*, No. 440.

[3] *Macmillan's Magazine*, IX, 113.

[4] *Macmillan's Magazine*, IX, 115—cf. *Gaskell-Norton Letters*, ed. Whitehill, p. 114: *G.L.*, No. 551.

families. From her ' own personal knowledge '[5] she could testify that three sons of rich parents had died for the cause; but the example she treats at length is that of Robert Gould Shaw. With his mother she appears to have corresponded with intimacy[6], so she was peculiarly well placed to present the Northern stand-point to English readers.

The introductory passage, mentioning the writer's acquaintance with, and high opinion of, the Shaws, gives force and pathos to her subsequent account of the colonel's bravery and gallant death. The reader is made aware of what was relinquished when he took charge of his black volunteers.

Mrs. Gaskell does not attempt any political justification of the Civil War—such politics she ' could *not* understand '[7]. Her concern was rather ethical and religious, opposed alike to the fanaticism of Anti-Slavery converts[8] and to the protestations of

---

[5] *Macmillan's Magazine,* IX, 115.

[6] Mrs. Gaskell quotes from one of her letters in the article (*Macmillan's Magazine,* IX, 115-116); and, writing to Norton on 28 August 1861 (*Gaskell-Norton Letters,* ed. Whitehill, p. 91: *G.L.,* No. 493), she refers to having just received a letter from Mrs. Shaw (probably the affectionate one of 10 August 1861, signed S[arah] B[lake] S[haw]—which, I am informed by Mrs. Whitehill, who has generously lent me her photostat, was among the MSS deposited by Miss Elizabeth Gaskell Norton at Harvard University, though the Houghton Library staff cannot trace its present location). Furthermore, in a letter of 23 April 1863, Norton speaks of ' the son of your correspondent Mrs. Shaw ' when praising Robert's command over a black regiment (*Gaskell-Norton Letters,* ed. Whitehill, p. 101). After receiving confirmation of the colonel's death, Mrs. Gaskell sent Mrs. Shaw a note of sympathy and consolation; in it she says that, knowing what the loss of a child meant, she could feel for her, adding she would rather be the mother of Mrs. Shaw's dead son than of any living man of her acquaintance: this 29 August [1863] letter appears in *Memorial:RGS,* Cambridge [Mass.]: University Press, 1864, pp. 149-150 —an accurate copy (*G.L.,* No. 530) being in the Gaskell Section, Brotherton Collection, Leeds University Library.

[7] *Gaskell-Norton Letters,* ed. Whitehill, p. 82: *G.L..,* No. 488—cf. No. 490.

[8] *Macmillan's Magazine,* IX, 114. Relevant here is Mrs. Gaskell's vehemence against those who attended Anti-Slavery lectures only to have stirred up feelings which could find no natural outlet in simple action: her anger against such emotional indulgence is voiced in a [Sunday (post 5—possibly 6—February) 1859] letter to Mrs. Nancy Robson (*G.L.,* No. 414, dated [February 1859] by Chapple and Pollard), now in the Yale University Library (MS Vault Sect. 16)—the pertinent passage being quoted by Miss Rubenius (*The Woman Question in Mrs. Gaskell's Life and Works,* pp. 221-222) from a slightly inaccurate copy in the Gaskell Section, Brotherton Collection, Leeds University Library.

those who took 'up a great moral question as a party cry.'[9]
Throughout the article one is as conscious of the humanity of
its author as of the virtues of its subject.

[9] *Macmillan's Magazine*, IX, 114.

SECTION VII

' Crowley Castle ' (1863 : 1906)

In *Mrs. Lirriper's Lodgings*[1], the 1863 Extra Christmas Number of *All the Year Round,* there appeared, as one of the seven stories making up that series, ' How the First Floor Went to Crowley Castle '[2]. During the compilation of the Knutsford Edition it was discovered that something over the first two-thirds of this tale corresponded, except for a few ' signs of compression '[3], to a hitherto unidentified Gaskell manuscript[4] which Ward had already had put into type. He decided, therefore, to publish a composite version which, following in the main the *All the Year Round* text, was entitled ' Crowley Castle '. To this we now turn.

In 1862, fatigued by her exertions to alleviate suffering during the Manchester cotton famine[5], Mrs. Gaskell went to recuperate at Eastbourne; while there she very likely obtained material for ' Crowley Castle '. It would be gratifying if one could find a historical basis for the leading events of the plot; but, though there may well be one, research has not yet revealed it. Nonetheless suggestions are possible. There is, firstly, the author's explicit statement that in the previous year she had visited the ruins of a Norman Castle, the show-excursion

[1] Pp. 12-25.
[2] Reprinted in *Novels and Tales,* X, 477-518.
[3] Ward, ed. *Works,* VII, p. xxxix.
[4] This manuscript (45 folios) is now in the Manchester Central Reference Library—MS. F. 823.894 Z1. Apparently, the complete MS having been bound, the concluding folios were subsequently cut out; the evidence of stubs and mountings suggests that about a score of leaves may have been so removed. It is interesting that in this manuscript the Crowley residence is initially (f. 1) called Crowe Castle.
[5] This work is described by Ward (ed. *Works,* I, pp. xxxvii-xxxviii), who quotes what Mrs. Gaskell wrote to George Smith from Eastbourne in October 1862 (*G.L.,* No. 517, dated [?Late September 1862] by Chapple and Pollard). Mrs. Gaskell and Meta stayed at Eastbourne for a month, according to what the latter wrote to Charles Eliot Norton on 30 or 31 October in a letter begun on Monday 21 [20] October [1862] —now in the Harvard University Library: bMS Am 1088 (2604)—; probably they went there in mid-September (*G.L.,* Nos. 514, 515).

449

of 'the little sea-bathing place in Sussex'[6] where she was apparently staying; this resort can fairly confidently be identified as Eastbourne. Furthermore the castle is, towards the end of the narrative[7], shown to be within easy travelling distance of Brighton. Such considerations have led Professor Whitfield to postulate that Crowley 'appears to be founded on Pevensey Castle'[8]. Since, during her holiday, Mrs. Gaskell must surely have paid a visit to this castle, which figures quite prominently in Eastbourne hand-books, such a supposition seems highly plausible. Moreover the author's reference to the old man who acted as guide[9] fits in with what a contemporary tourists' manual says about 'a cottager, whose children run out to open the gate for the visitor, proffering small fragments of tile as precious relics of the place, while the seniors undertake the office of *cicerone* for those who may desire their service.'[10]

However Mrs. Gaskell's remarks about 'the neighbouring church, where the knightly Crowleys lie buried: some commemorated by ancient brasses, some by altar-tombs, some by fine Latin epitaphs'[11] apply less appropriately to the monuments in Pevensey Church[12], or even to those in the neighbouring Westham Church[13], than to the Dacre altar-tombs and brasses[14] found at Hurstmonceux. Hurstmonceux, we may notice, also had its castle—albeit not Norman—which, demolished in the later eighteenth century, would in this respect correspond to that at Crowley, inhabited as late as 1772[15]. Mrs. Gaskell must almost certainly have gone to Hurstmonceux since, as well as its historical interest, it possessed an additional

  6 *Works,* VII, 681.
  7 *Works,* VII, 716-718.
  8 Whitfield, *Mrs Gaskell,* p. 75.
  9 *Works,* VII, 681-682.
  10 *The Guide to East Bourne and Its Environs. A Descriptive Account of That Beautiful Watering-Place, and the Objects of Interest in its Vicinity,* New edn, East Bourne: E. M. & E. Hopkins [1856], p. 41: repeated in T. S. Gowland, *The Guide to Eastbourne and its Environs, with a Map, and Illustrations, and a Descriptive Account of the Objects of Interest in Its Vicinity,* 6th edn, Eastbourne: T. S. Gowland, 1863, pp. 40-41.
  11 *Works,* VII, 681-682.
  12 See Mark Antony Lower, *Chronicles of Pevensey, with Notices Biographical, Topographical, and Antiquarian; for Visitors,* Lewes: R. W. Lower; London: J. R. Smith, 1846, pp. 48-49.
  13 Lower, *Chronicles of Pevensey,* pp. 50-51.
  14 Mentioned in all guide-books.   15 *Works,* VII, 682.

attraction in that Archdeacon Hare, whose family held the living, had been rector there, John Sterling for a time being his curate. Moreover Baron Bunsen, a friend of the Gaskells, may well have mentioned the place; for he too had once resided in the district[16]. Finally we may note that, according to her own testimony[17], Susanna Winkworth was there in October 1855, when she visited Mrs. Augustus Hare while her sister and her husband (Mr. and Mrs. William Shaen) went to look at the castle; later she herself saw the church and castle-ruins. The Shaens, intimate acquaintances of the novelist, often spent holidays at Eastbourne—indeed they did so in 1862[18]. Here, then, we have one more reason why Mrs. Gaskell may have paid Hurstmonceux a visit.

Unfortunately neither Pevensey nor Hurstmonceux appears to provide suitable genealogical material for ' Crowley Castle '. However Mrs. Gaskell could easily have heard elsewhere a family tradition, similar to that recounted in the tale, and transposed this material to give it a Sussex setting.

It would be possible to sum up one's reactions to ' Crowley Castle ' by commending the characterization but not the plot. Even if Mrs. Gaskell did not devise the main outlines of the latter, one may legitimately criticize her handling of the sensational scenes; here her capacity for invention seems small, probably indicating she was not deeply absorbed in the task. This lack of interest betrays itself in stock phraseology: one comes across such combinations as ' an old, querulous, grey-haired man '[19] (applied to Sir Mark); ' that grim visitant '[20] (poverty); ' the mocking smile '[21] of a villain whose ' eyes flashed lurid fire '[22]; ' a fearful threat '[23] from a servant with ' a deadly smile '[24]; and so forth. Only occasionally is the reader compensated by an effectively gruesome detail, as when

---

[16] This information on Hurstmonceaux (an alternative spelling) can conveniently be found in Augustus J. C. Hare's article on Julius Charles Hare (1795-1855) in *The Dictionary of National Biography*.

[17] Her Sister [Susanna Winkworth], ed. *Letters and Memorials of Catherine Winkworth*, I (1883), 507-508.

[18] [Susanna Winkworth and Margaret Josephine Shaen, ed.] *Letters and Memorials of Catherine Winkworth*, II (1886), 377-379; and *G.L.*, No. 514

[19] *Works*, VII, 694.   [22] *Works*, VII, 701.

[20] *Works*, VII, 698.   [23] *Works*, VII, 702.

[21] *Works*, VII, 701.   [24] *Works*, VII, 702.

Victorine speaks of a building's being ' " secure against wind
and storm and all the ravages of time, if the first mortar used
has been tempered with human blood." '[25]

Instead of lingering over the melodramatic and horrific
elements, it will be better to notice how well, by comparison,
the author manages the domestic parts; for the opening pages,
which introduce the major characters, are certainly not below
Mrs. Gaskell's habitual standard. Four of these characters seem
somehow familiar. Victorine, the devoted but passionate French
bonne, recalls Bridget Fitzgerald from ' The Poor Clare '; both
act wickedly, thereby causing suffering to her whom each loves
most in the world. The two girls—Theresa Crowley, exotic,
sensual, wayward[26]; Bessy Hawtrey, gentle, sweet, sensible[27]
(in fact ' a daisy of an English maiden '[28])—are reminiscent of
the constrasted couple[29], Erminia Harvey and Maggie Browne,
of *The Moorland Cottage*; in addition they connect with the
similarly contrasted figures[30] of Molly Gibson and Cynthia
Kirkpatrick in *Wives and Daughters.* That novel also contains
Roger Hamley, to some extent foreshadowed by Duke Brown-
low who, in turn, has Frank Buxton as his forerunner in *The
Moorland Cottage.* Duke, expected by his uncle to marry
Theresa[31], did indeed marry his cousin[32], but only after Bessy's

[25] *Works,* VII, 712.
[26] *Works,* VII, 682-683.
[27] *Works,* VII, 684.
[28] *Works,* VII, 697. Perhaps this is the place to note that Miss
Rubenius has an unfortunate misinterpretation which leads her to remark that when Mrs. Gaskell ' wrote *Crowley Castle* she had nothing
but pity, condescension, contempt almost, for the " innocent virtues "
of Bessy, whereas the sparkling, intelligent passionate Theresa had all
her sympathy.'—*The Woman Question in Mrs. Gaskell's Life and
Works,* p. 86. Comment seems almost superfluous for those who both
have read the story and know something of its author: Mrs. Gaskell
would never have despised ' innocent virtues ', though she may have
done Theresa's failure to keep a promise (*Works,* VII, 690-691). There
is a significant incident where Theresa's maid, in order to make a
cosmetic for her mistress, unwittingly used the very cream laid aside
for Bessy's ailing child (*Works,* VII, 709). Who, one wonders, had
the sympathies of the authoress in that instance?
[29] *Works,* II, 285.
[30] *Works,* VIII, 251-252, 254-255, 277, 313, 371-372, 377-378, 381,
400, 402, 437, 454-455, 466-467, 485, 487-488, 542, 621.
[31] *Works,* VII, 682.
[32] *Works,* VII, 711.

death had left him a widower[33]; Frank was likewise expected
to marry his cousin[34], yet he took as his first (and, for him,
only) wife not Erminia, whom his father favoured, but the
homely Maggie. Furthermore the relations of the three young
people to one another are not dissimilar. Theresa[35] and
Erminia[36] patronized (though both were fundamentally generous
girls), and Duke[37] and Frank[38] befriended, Bessy and Maggie
respectively.

There is one other, albeit a minor, character in ' Crowley
Castle ' who looks back to *The Moorland Cottage* and forward
to *Wives and Daughters*; for the ' silky manner '[39] of Madam
Hawtrey, Bessy's mother, suggests the ways of Mrs. Browne as
well as those of the second Mrs. Gibson. Like them she married
a clergyman[40], and like them she knew how to scheme and
angle[41]. She is the only person to any extent humorously treated
in a work which, as Dr. Adolphus Ward[42] has remarked, is
conspicuous among Mrs. Gaskell's later writings for its lack
of humour. Perhaps the following is as near the author comes
to indulging her favourite propensity.

> There were two people strongly affected by this news [of
> Duke's betrothal to Theresa] when it was promulgated; one—
> and this was natural under the circumstances—was Madam
> Hawtrey; who chose to resent the marriage as a deep personal
> offence to herself as well as to her daughter's memory, . . . [43]

Little else deserves comment. There are truthful touches, such
as the remark that, whatever the theoretical position, ' she to
whom the housekeeper takes her accounts, she in whose hands
the power of conferring favours and privileges remains *de facto*,
will always be held by servants as the mistress '[44]. There are
also telling observations whereby character is indicated, as

[33] *Works*, VII, 710.
[34] *Works*, II, 307.
[35] *Works*, VII, 684.
[36] *Works*, II, 283.
[37] *Works*, VII, 684.
[38] *Works*, II, 283.
[39] *Works*, VII, 686.
[40] *Works*, VII, 684.
[41] *Works*, VII, 696-697.
[42] Ed. *Works*, VII, p. xxxix.
[43] *Works*, VII, 711.
[44] *Works*, VII, 704.

when Theresa, having asked Bessy what she intended to do with some gooseberries, 'lazily picked the ripest out of the basket, and ate them.'[45] One may note too the vivid description of how Victorine arrayed Theresa for her Parisian conquests[46]. Having drawn attention to these felicities, we may conclude our discussion of ' Crowley Castle '.

[45] *Works,* VII, 687.
[46] *Works,* VII, 692-693.

CHAPTER IX

' FRENCH LIFE ' (1864) TO
' TWO FRAGMENTS OF GHOST STORIES ' (1906)

SECTION I

'French Life' (1864)

'French Life' came out anonymously in *Fraser's Magazine*[1] between April and June 1864; a letter[2] to Mrs. Gaskell from its editor, J. A. Froude, indicates that she had proposed the subject

[1] *Fraser's Magazine for Town and Country*, LXIX, 435-449, 575-585, 739-752.

[2] Cited in Waller, ed. *Letters Addressed to Mrs Gaskell by Celebrated Contemporaries*, p. 61. As far as is known, 'French Life' was the author's sole contribution to *Fraser's Magazine*. However, in her letter of Monday [1 June 1863], written to Marianne from Venice, Mrs. Gaskell speaks with annoyance of George Smith's having forwarded to Froude a manuscript he himself did not want; and mentions having taken steps to recover it, since she did not wish Froude for old friendship's sake to take one of Smith's rejects. She confessed that, as previous articles had appeared on the same subject, her piece no longer possessed the recommendation of novelty; but added that Smith should never have presumed to decide to whom she wanted the manuscript sent. Indeed his presumption, she said, had settled her in her resolve never again to publish with him—a resolve formed when he went against her distinct desire and retained 'dark' in the title of *A Dark Night's Work* (the book-form publication in 1863 of Mrs. Gaskell's *All the Year Round* serial story). The letter containing this information is in the possession of Mrs. Margaret Trevor Jones. It seems possible that the MS Smith despatched to Froude was in some way related to 'An Italian Institution', which appeared on 21 March 1863 in *All the Year Round* (IX, 93-96). It may well have been a second article about the Camorra; for in her letter to Smith of 20 September [1863]—now in the archives of Sir John Murray—Mrs. Gaskell, having referred to 'Notes of a Wanderer' (the origin of 'French Life'), wrote interlinearly "I thought of sending this to Mr Froude/ to make up for the/ 'Camorra'—that/ unlucky piece/ of work/". This afterthought is not to be found in the transcript by Miss Hopkins (*Elizabeth Gaskell*, p. 220) from which we quote *infra*, though it is very relevant to her equation of 'Notes of a Wanderer' with 'French Life'. (Mrs. Gaskell's letters appear respectively as *G.L.*, Nos. 524, 532.) On 20 October [1863] Froude wrote to welcome Mrs. Gaskell's proposal for travel notes, feeling their desultory variety fitted them well for periodical publication, and he asked when she would begin; his 5 March [1864] note indicates he was then sending her proof-sheets; and in a 20 March [1864] letter he enquired whether she wished her *name* to appear and gave instructions about the despatch of further material, when ready, as another number could not be made out of what had originally been sent—Froude's letters are in The John Rylands Library, Manchester (English MS. 730/32, 33, 34); Waller (*op. cit.*, p. 61) cites, and slightly misquotes, only the first, whose accompanying envelope is post-marked 21 October 1863.

of these articles by 20 October 1863. Miss Hopkins[3] plausibly
suggests they grew out of what Mrs. Gaskell had on hand when
on 20 September [1863] she wrote to George Smith as follows.

> " Notes of a wanderer "—all/ sorts of odd bits, scenes,//
> conversations ∧with rather famous people in Paris∧, small
> ad = / = ventures, descriptions &c &c/ met with during our
> two/ last journeys abroad in Brittany/ Paris, Rome, Flor-
> ence—/50 pages written—[4]

The first visit, comprising a week in Paris and ten days in
Brittany and Normandy[5], probably lasted from 17 May to
early June 1862[6]; on it Mrs. Gaskell was accompanied by Meta
and Meta's friend, Miss Isabel Thompson[7], they appearing in
the narrative as Mary and Irene respectively[8]. The second
Continental sojourn began in February 1863, when Julia Gaskell

---

[3] *Elizabeth Gaskell,* p. 221.

[4] Quoted by Miss Hopkins (*Elizabeth Gaskell,* p. 220), whose trans-
script has been slightly emended by reference to the original letter (now
in the archives of Sir John Murray). For the interlinear afterthought
which immediately follows, see our penultimate footnote. This letter
occurs as *G.L.,* No. 532.

[5] So Meta Gaskell informed Charles Eliot Norton when writing on
30 or 31 October in a letter, begun on Monday 21 [20] October [1862],
now in the Harvard University Library: bMS Am 1088 (2604).

[6] A period suggested by the letter Mrs. Gaskell wrote to Marianne one
Friday morning [16 May 1862] and by her Friday-evening postscript—the
postscript is in the Gaskell Section, Brotherton Collection, Leeds University
Library; and copies of both, once owned by Mr. J. T. Lancaster, belong to
the present writer: they appear as *G.L.,* No. 509 (dated [?16 May 1862]
by Chapple and Pollard); see too No. 506a. The latter part of this French
sojourn (from the day before Saturday [24 May] till Tuesday 3 June) is
narrated on a daily basis in a [1862] fragment by Mrs. Gaskell (in the
National Library of Scotland: MS. 6044, ff. 191-198), by non-Gaskellian
hands both endorsed 23 July 1861 and headed Mrs. Gaskell to Miss
Winkworth: *G.L.,* No. 509b (the recipient being ?Catherine Winkworth
and the year [1862], according to Chapple and Pollard, whose appropriate
footnote might have stated that Derby Day in 1862 fell on Wednesday
4 June.

[7] Whose decision to go was a last-minute one, as is evidenced both by
Mrs. Gaskell's Friday-evening postscript (in the Gaskell Section, Brotherton
Collection, Leeds University Library) to her letter to Marianne begun
Friday morning [16 May 1862] and by the note Meta wrote as a tail-piece
to that letter—copies of all these communications, once owned by Mr.
J. T. Lancaster, belong to the present writer. Mrs. Gaskell's letter occurs
as *G.L.,* No. 509 (dated [?16 May 1862] by Chapple and Pollard). See
too Ward, ed. *Works,* I, p. xl; VII, p. xxxv; and Shorter, ed. *Novels and
Tales,* VII (1911), p. xvi.

[8] *Works,* VII, 627.

and her mother went to stay with Mme Mohl in Paris[9]; having been joined five weeks later by Florence and Meta[10], they sailed from France for Italy in mid-March[11].

Although overtly cast in diary-form[12], the articles are far from being *verbatim* extracts from an actual travel-journal, even supposing their author kept one. For instance, the dating of the 1862 tour not only fails to tally with the time Mrs. Gaskell and her two companions were in France but also lacks internal consistency (the entry of ' *May 4th.*'[13] being manifestly misdated). Moreover the travelogue clearly implies both Mary and Irene were with the writer in 1863[14] as well as in 1862; yet for their prototypes such was by no means the case. Nevertheless Mrs. Gaskell may have refreshed her memory or stimlated her imagination by consulting something composed while she was abroad—perhaps a now-lost diary.

As in ' Company Manners ', what is most striking in these sketches is the personality of their author, a personality easily recognized by at least one of Mrs. Gaskell's acquaintances, Henry Bright.

[9] Sanders, *Elizabeth Gaskell*, p. 111. Their presence is mentioned in a 3 March 1863 letter from Mme Mohl, quoted by Mrs. Simpson (*Letters and Recollections of Julius and Mary Mohl*, p. 201).

[10] According to what Meta wrote to Charles Eliot Norton on Wednesday [8 April] in a letter, headed 7 April and finished on 17 April [1863], now in the Harvard University Library: bMS Am 1088 (2641). See too *Gaskell-Norton Letters*, ed. Whitehill, p. 105: *G.L.*, No. 526.

[11] This seems consistent with a 16 March 1863 *Cranford* receipt from Paris (owned by Mrs. E. M. Gordon: *G.L.*, No. 539, fn.) and with data on Mrs. Gaskell's passport (owned by Mrs. Trevor Jones): cf. and cont. *Works*, VII, 678-680.

[12] *Works,* VII, 644—despite an incongruous 1864 reference (p. 659).

[13] *Works*, VII, 641; *Fraser's Magazine for Town and Country*, LXIX, 579. The slip may have been compositorial; the appropriate reading would be '*May 14th.*' However '*May 13th.*' might prove even more suitable; for the two previous entries appear rather confused in their chronology: that headed '*May 12th.—Vitré.*' (*Works*, VII, 634-637) seems to deal wholly with events of the preceding day (11 May); so the one headed '*May 13th.*' would logically concern 12 May happenings. Albeit antedated by a fortnight, the entire Paris-to-Rouen section (*Works*, VII, 632-641), commencing with the '*Chartres, May 10th, 1862.*' entry, parallels extremely closely the Paris-Rouen itinerary, begun on Saturday [24 May 1862], recorded by Mrs. Gaskell in the [1862] fragment in the National Library of Scotland (MS. 6044, ff. 191-198)—so much so that the latter (*G.L.*, No. 509b) may well have provided the basis for this part of ' French Life ', and indeed also for the visit to St. Germain on the day before the journey started (*Works*, VII, 626-632).

[14] *Works*, VII, 662, 678.

By the way [he writes in 1864] have you seen Mrs. Gaskell's
pleasant articles on 'French Life' in Fraser?—I felt sure they
were hers, & taxed her with it the other day at Manchester,
when we were helping Mr. Stansfield to lay the stone of our
heretic 'Memorial Hall.'[15]

The articles instruct as well as entertain, and one is constantly made aware that their composer had English readers
in mind; for, whenever possible, to help clarify a French custom
she draws a comparison or contrast with something already
familiar. Thus we learn that on 'receiving' days the hostess
and her family 'have generally much the same sort of dinner
that in England we associate with the idea of washing-days'[16],
and that under the first-floors of houses at Vitré there are
colonnades beneath which people may walk—'something like
Chester'[17]. On the other hand we are told that, to one living
with a French middle-class family, daily habits seem very 'different from those of England'[18]; and we are informed in what
respects marriage arrangements in France vary from those on
this side of the Channel[19]. However Mrs. Gaskell is not afraid
to provide the requisite information more directly when the
occasion requires, be it a definition of the *guéridon*[20] or an
account of the Paris omnibus system[21], be it a paragraph on
prices and provisions[22] or a discourse on the duties of a *con-
cierge*[23]. All these observations and explanations enter unobtrusively into the narrative, and are made with their author's
habitual courtesy; there is no 'writing down' to the reader,
only a fine display of literary good manners. Dr. Adolphus Ward
puts the matter well.

Of Mrs. Gaskell it may be asserted that, while she observed
with quick insight, she chronicled with unfailing tact. For the
things she noted, whether in Madame A——'s hospitable bed-room
[*Works*, VII, 605-606], or in the silken chamber of the condescending *lionne* [*Works*, VII, 617-618], or in the ample
drawing-room where Madame E—— dispensed tea at a guinea a
pound to those who cared for the beverage [*Works*, VII,

---

[15] Quoted, from a letter to Lord Houghton, in James Pope-Hennessy,
Monckton Milnes [Vol. II]. *The Flight of Youth*: 1851-1885, London:
Constable, 1951, p. 193: the parenthesis within square brackets in the
quotation is by Pope-Hennessy.

[16] *Works*, VII, 613.   [20] *Works*, VII, 605.
[17] *Works*, VII, 637.   [21] *Works*, VII, 612.
[18] *Works*, VII, 608.   [22] *Works*, VII, 615-616.
[19] *Works*, VII, 651-653.   [23] *Works*, VII, 609-610.

620-621[24]], were always things distinctive and things possessed of a human interest.[25]

Interwoven with the more specifically informative parts are passages where the writer speaks of the people (famous and ordinary) she has seen, relates anecdotes, and tells of the itinerary and doings of herself and her companions. Such passages can, perhaps, be distinguished only in theory from the others; for they frequently blend together. Nevertheless it may be broadly stated that in the earlier pages Mrs. Gaskell introduces her readers to French life, and then continues with a more personal narrative—beginning with the entry for 10 May[26], when she describes St. Germain and her sketching friends are named as Mary and Irene.

The personality of the narrator is of a piece with that displayed in Mrs. Gaskell's life and letters. We may note especially how, in the articles, she shows herself interested in common folk, eager to engage them in conversation at the slightest opportunity—and, as has been earlier indicated, her public writings often incorporate what she learnt from such encounters. For instance, she remarks that in the older parts of Paris the people 'have so much more originality of character about them;'[27] readily strikes up an acquaintanceship at Versailles ' with one of the gardeners, and with a hackney-coachman '[28] who was also there; gossips with the *Dame du Comptoir* of a St. Germain restaurant[29]; asks the driver taking her party to Les Rochers ' various questions about Breton cows '[30]; and, once arrived, is soon hearing from an impoverished old man how ' he was a De la Roux, and had relations " in London." '[31]

---

[24] Tea-prices were important for the genteel ladies of *Wives and Daughters* (*Works*, VIII, 195); however a more appropriate comparison would be with that passage in *Ruth* (*Works*, III, 262) where Mr. Bradshaw speaks about the exorbitant cost of pine-apples. That Mrs. Gaskell was only too familiar with a similar vulgarity on the part of ' rich Manchesterians ' is exemplified by her letter of Saturday 21 July [1855] to Miss Parthenope Nightingale, now in the collection of Sir Harry Calvert Williams Verney, Bart. (Ballams, Middle Claydon, Bletchley, Bucks.)—a relevant extract from which is given in Pollard, *The Novels of Mrs. Gaskell*, p. 416—: *G.L.*, No. 255.

[25] Ward, ed. *Works*, VII, p. xxxv.

[26] *Works*, VII, 626-632.   [29] *Works*, VII, 629, 631-632.

[27] *Works*, VII, 622.   [30] *Works*, VII, 638.

[28] *Works*, VII, 629.   [31] *Works*, VII, 639.

In addition we are introduced to celebrities the narrator professes to have met. We hear of Madame de Circourt, whose death in February 1863 came with such grief[32]; there follows an anecdote by her husband[33], who was accustomed to supply Mrs. Gaskell with historical information[34]; then come tales of Revolutionary France, related by other friends[35]—in which respect 'French Life' suggests how the author probably obtained her material for the Clément-and-Virginie episode in *My Lady Ludlow*.

Madame Récamier, here[36] as in 'Company Manners'[37], is praised for possessing the qualities of a perfect hostess. Doubtless Mrs. Gaskell heard a great deal about her talents from Madame Mohl, whose own *salon* owed much of its success to her years of 'intimacy with Madame Récamier.'[38] Guizot, who had once praised *Ruth*[39], is mentioned as a social bait[40]; and 'the gracious figure of Montalembert . . . flits across the

[32] *Works*, VII, 644-645.
[33] *Works*, VII, 645-646.
[34] Dated 27 August 1861, 23 March 1862, and 15 April 1862, three such informative letters from him are in The John Rylands Library, Manchester (English MS. 730/18-20); each indicates his wife's regard for Mrs. Gaskell. Waller (ed. *Letters Addressed to Mrs Gaskell by Celebrated Contemporaries*, pp. 67-68), who corrects Ward's misdating of the second letter (also slightly misquoted, in Ward, ed. *Works*, VIII, p. xxix), himself misdates the first. Mrs. Gaskell refers to having called on the de Circourts in a [Friday 23 February 1855] Paris letter, part of which is in the Yale University Library (MS Vault File): this fragment appears as *G.L.*, No. 230 (to ?Marianne Gaskell and dated [February 1855], according to Chapple and Pollard); and contains remarks on eating-habits at Mme Mohl's, not unlike those in 'French Life' (*Works*, VII, 611-615). 'French Life', incidentally, contains occasional references to pre-1862 Paris visits (*Works*, VII, 604, 617-619, 653); and we may note that, although, contrary to the dates given in the first article, Mrs. Gaskell was apparently not in France during February (or March or April) 1862, she was there, not only in February 1855, but also in February 1857—Shaen, ed. *Memorials of Two Sisters*, p. 170; and *Gaskell-Norton Letters*, ed. Whitehill, pp. xviii-xix: cf. and cont. *G.L.*, No. 342.
[35] *Works*, VII, 646-651.
[36] *Works*, VII, 642.
[37] *Works*, III, 494-495.
[38] Simpson, *Letters and Recollections of Julius and Mary Mohl*, p. 19; see too p. 27.
[39] Quotations from his eulogistic letter of 23 May 1862 are given by Ward (ed. *Works*, III, p. xi) and Waller (ed. *Letters Addressed to Mrs Gaskell by Celebrated Contemporaries*, pp. 68-69).
[40] *Works*, VII, 642.

scene '41. The introduction of this last affords an excellent illustration of how to mix the *utile* with the *dulce*; for he gives advice about a charming *détour* for those travelling from Paris to Rome[42] which many readers must have appreciated when they next visited the Continent. One hopes, however, they made sense of the slightly misleading reference to ' " Ed. Joanne's *Guide du Voyageur. Est-et-Mur.*" '43

Since there is considerable similarity in tone and atmosphere between ' Company Manners ' and ' French Life ', it is not surprising to find a passage from the latter (dealing with the preparation of salads)[44] is almost the same as one from the former[45]. In each instance a touch of humour colours the description of what was, to the exacting French taste, little less than a fine art. Humour indeed, as one would expect, enlivens the travelogue. Sometimes it has a personal reference, as when the narrator confesses that, though converted to drinking *eau sucrée,* she does not ' tipple at it in private.'[46] Sometimes the situation itself is slightly comic : as at Chartres, where she was given a bed-room within leaping-distance of a fair-booth lion[47]; or as at Avignon, where the travellers, seized by the *mistral,* could only shut their eyes, try to keep on the ground, and wonder where their petticoats were[48]. At other times one finds the smiling feminine commonsense of a remark like that upon

---

[41] Ward, ed. *Works,* VII, p. xxxvi. Guizot and Montalembert were among the notables Mrs. Gaskell must often have met when visiting Mme Mohl: for example, she mentions their having called, during her Spring 1865 visit, in a letter of 27 March to Mrs. Emily Shaen (*née* Winkworth)—quoted by Miss Haldane (*Mrs. Gaskell and Her Friends,* pp. 296-300, see esp. pp. 298-300), who, however, has the year as 1863, although such internal evidence as a reference to *Wives and Daughters* unmistakably puts the letter in 1865—: G.L., No. 564 (the year being given as [?1865] by Chapple and Pollard). This letter contains an account of Mme Mohl's appartment in the Rue du Bac (cf. Simpson, *Letters and Recollections of Julius and Mary Mohl,* pp. 26-27), recalling the appartment described in ' French Life ' (*Works,* VII, 608-611).

[42] *Works,* VII, 657-658.

[43] *Works,* VII, 657. Mrs. Gaskell (or Montalembert) must have had in mind one of the guides brought out under the general supervision of Adolphe-Laurent Joanne, possibly the relevant section in *Guide du Voyageur en France,* by Richard [Jean-Marie-Vincent Audin], 25th edn, Paris: L. Hachette, 1861 (based on an entry in the *Catalogue Général des Livres Imprimés de la Bibliothèque Nationale*).

[44] *Works,* VII, 614-615.   [47] *Works,* VII, 633-634.
[45] *Works,* III, 511.   [48] *Works,* VII, 660.
[46] *Works,* VII, 621.

certain Protestant charitable organizations in Paris: 'The worst that can be said is, that *Dizaines* (like all ladies' committees I ever knew) are the better for having one or two men amongst them.'[49]

Only once is there a trace of irony. Having recounted the anecdote supplied by M. de Circourt (how an aristocratic Montmorenci had objected to sleeping in a room that had once belonged to the Jansenist, Madame de Sévigné), Mrs. Gaskell includes the following paragraph.

> The young man was afraid of the contamination of heresy that might be lingering in the air of the room. There are old rooms in certain houses shut up since the days of the Great Plague, which are not to be opened for the world. I hope that certain Fellows' rooms in Balliol may be hermetically sealed, when their present occupants leave them, lest a worse thing than the plague may infect the place.[50]

Herself a devotee of Mme de Sévigné, whose life she considered writing[51], Mrs. Gaskell records in 'French Life' her

[49] *Works,* VII, 656.
[50] *Works,* VII, 646.
[51] See the statements, sometimes with relevant quotations, made by Ward (ed. *Works,* I, p. xl; VII, p. xxxvi), Shorter (ed. *Novels and Tales,* VII, p. xvii), Mrs. Chadwick (*Mrs. Gaskell,* pp. 241, 281), and Miss Hopkins (*Elizabeth Gaskell,* pp. 220-221). Mrs. Gaskell's letter of 1 February [1862] to W. S. Williams (a copy being with Forster correspondence in the Gaskell Section, Brotherton Collection, Leeds University Library) indicates that, with *All the Year Round* initially in mind, she had begun a series of articles, illustrative of Parisian and Provincial life in seventeenth-century France, which centred on Mme de Sévigné; that she was seeking to discover whether this field had recently been traversed; and that, if not, she wished to know whether Williams thought Smith might bring out such a study in one volume, she preferring book-form to serial publication. From her letter to Smith of 28 March [1862] it seems that he was considering this Mme de Sévigné memoir, of which in a letter of 18 March she had informed him she had written the first chapter, for *The Cornhill Magazine*; but her letter to him of 20 September [1863] suggests that, though still interested in the work, she had added little more on paper —these letters (the last being relevantly and quite accurately quoted in Hopkins, *Elizabeth Gaskell,* p. 220) are now in the archives of Sir John Murray. The aforementioned letters appear respectively as *G.L.,* Nos. 499 (to ?W. S. Williams with the year as [?1862], according to Chapple and Pollard, who, not emending their source, retain readings which suggest Mme de Sévigné lived in 19th-century—not 17th-century— France), 502 (the year, like that of No. 501, being [?1862] according to Chapple and Pollard), 501, 532; see too No. 509b.

pilgrimage to Les Rochers[52]. Hence the author's manifest affection for the Jansenist ought to indicate where her own sympathies would lie, especially when one remembers that she too was 'heretical', being a Unitarian. It seems plausible, therefore, to take her reference—if such it be—to the contributors to *Essays and Reviews*[53] as a protest against the hostile reception their work received. Mrs. Gaskell's habitual gentleness makes her ridicule the more noteworthy, it being quite out of keeping with the general tone of the articles.

A narrator who could find poetry in the ruins at Marly[54] must surely have had her own faculty in view when she spoke of 'that kind of imagination which loves to repeople places'[55]; she was always ready to remind her readers of historical associations, to link present observations with memories of the past. Thus, with reference to the Place Royale, she mentions[56] the old Palace des Tournelles, the masque there that ended in flames, and the ensuing madness of Charles VI, which led to the invention of playing-cards. A little later, in connexion with Marly, we are told how our military salute may have resulted from the eye-shading salutation of the courtiers of *le roi soleil*[57].

Avignon provides Mrs. Gaskell with historical material in abundance, ranging from the statue of Jean Althen[58] (the in-

---

[52] *Works*, VII, 635-640. Meta Gaskell mentioned this pilgrimage to the *château* of Mme de Sévigné when writing to Charles Eliot Norton on 30 or 31 October in a letter, begun on Monday 21 [20] October [1862], now in the Harvard University Library: bMS Am 1088 (2604). Another reference to it occurs in Mrs. Gaskell's [1862] fragment (*G.L.*, No. 509b) in the National Library of Scotland (MS. 6044, ff. 191-198), where (f. 191r) one also reads that her Paris researches 'laid a good foundation/ for future work at Mme de Sévigné'.

[53] *Essays and Reviews* [ed. J. Parker], London: John W. Parker and Son, 1860. Mrs. Gaskell's pointed remark about 'certain Fellows' rooms in Balliol' is slightly erroneous. Of the seven contributors only Benjamin Jowett was at that time a Fellow; Frederick Temple had once been one, but the others were not Balliol men. Mrs. Gaskell was naturally most attracted to that liberal section of the Church of England which included Stanley, Maurice, Kingsley, Pattison, and Jowett.

[54] *Works*, VII, 631.

[55] *Works*, VII, 604.

[56] *Works*, VII, 625.

[57] *Works*, VII, 630.

[58] *Works*, VII, 660-661.

troducer of madder to Southern France) to the Palace of the
Popes, where once lived ' John XXII. (that most infamous
believer)'[59]. Gazing at the short-lived sparks of an inn-fire brings
Mrs. Gaskell, somewhat incongruously, to recall how, when
once in Ramsay[60], she had talked with an old fisherman's wife
whose brother had unwittingly killed the last of the fairies[61].
With a little more excuse, as her hostess possessed an account
of the murder trial, she then relates the tragic history of
Madame la Marquise de Gange[62]—which proves a not displeasing device for filling out the last article. Nothing need be
said about the tale—just the sort of thing Mrs. Gaskell might
have developed into a short story—beyond noting how, wherever appropriate, she stressed those aspects of the narrative
which afforded ' curious glimpses of the manners of the period,
as well as of the state of society.'[63]

Concerning the source of this digression, it will suffice to remark that comparisons do not suggest Mrs. Gaskell consulted
the story of the ' Marchioness de Ganges ' contained in an

---

[59] *Works,* VII, 661.

[60] Perhaps during that stay in the Isle of Man when, one Saturday
[2 September 1854], she wrote Julia a birthday letter (now in the
possession of Mrs. Margaret Trevor Jones)—this probably being the
same time as she and Meta sent Marianne from the Isle of Man a
joint but undated letter (now in the Gaskell Section, Brotherton Collection, Leeds University Library). See too, in this connexion, Seccombe,
pref. *Sylvia's Lovers,* by Mrs. Gaskell, p. xxvi. Mrs. Gaskell's letters
appear respectively as *G.L.,* Nos. 208, 209 (dated [?Early September 1854]
by Chapple and Pollard).

[61] *Works,* VII, 663. In her letter to Mrs. Mary Howitt of 18 August 1838
Mrs. Gaskell remarked that she knew a man who had "seen the
Fairies"—quoted in Howitt, ' Stray Notes from Mrs. Gaskell ', *Good
Words,* XXXVI (1895), 610: *G.L.,* No. 12.

[62] *Works,* VII, 664-680.

[63] *Works,* VII, 668. Such aspects include the perils to which an un-
protected young woman was then exposed (*Works,* VII, 667), the
carrying of an antidote to poison as a matter of course (*Works,* VII,
671), and the mode of addressing a married woman appropriate to her rank
in society (*Works,* VII, 670-671). In this last connexion there is a
curious (compositorial?) mistake; for ' the *Traité sur la manière d'Ecrire
des Lettres,* par [Jean-Léonor Le Gallois, sieur de] Grimarest, 1667,'
(*Works,* VII, 670) actually appeared in 1709 (Paris: J. Estienne),
according to the *Catalogue Général des Livres Imprimés de la Bibliothèque Nationale.*

English translation[64] of a selection from Dumas' *Crimes Célèbres*[65]; but that she may have had recourse to Gayot's *Causes Célèbres*[66] and/or some other authority which used the form ' Gange ' rather than ' Ganges '.

Before leaving the account of Madame de Gange, and indeed ' French Life ' itself, we may note three minor matters. By an error, almost certainly compositorial, ' Rossau '[67] appears for ' Rossan '[68]; Mrs. Gaskell introduces some favourite lines of hers about Jess MacFarlane[69], presumably prompted by

[64] Alexander Dumas, *Celebrated Crimes,* London: Chapman and Hall, 1843.

[65] *Crimes Célèbres,* Vols. I-VI by Alexandre Dumas the elder, Vols. VII-VIII by Alex. Dumas, Auguste Arnould, Narcisse Fournier, Pier-Angelo Fiorentino, and Pierre-Jean-Félicien Mallefille, 8 vols., Paris: Administration de Librairie, 1839-1840. Vols. II-III contain the story of ' La Marquise de Ganges [*sic*] ' (based on entries in the General Catalogues of Printed Books of the British Museum and the *Bibliothèque Nationale*).

[66] [François Gayot de Pitaval] *Causes Célèbres et Intéressantes, avec les Jugements qui les ont decidées. Recueillies par* M^xxx [Gayot], 20 vols., Paris: G. Cavelier (Le Gras, Vve Delaulne, C.-N. Poirion, and J. de Nully), 1734-1743 (inferential expansion of an entry in the *Catalogue Général des Livres Imprimés de la Bibliothèque Nationale*). It seems worth commenting that Mrs. Gaskell is hardly likely to have used a collection of tales, freely based on *Causes Célèbres,* brought out by Mrs. Charlotte Smith (*The Romance of Real Life,* 3 vols., London: T. Cadell, 1787); although a somewhat romanticized version of the story of ' The Marchioness de Gange ' appears in Mrs. Smith's first volume (pp. 1-84), it does not contain, for example, the precise date of the murder—recorded by Mrs. Gaskell (*Works,* VII, 668)—as does [François Gayot de Pitaval] *Causes Célèbres et Intéressantes, avec les Jugemens qui les ont decidées,* V (New edn, Paris: Théodore Legras. 1738), 396, 430. This last edition of *Causes Célèbres,* consulted in the Bodleian Library, consists of twenty volumes (Vols. I-XII, XV-XX, Paris: Théodore Legras, 1738-1743; Vols. XIII-XIV, Paris: Guillaume Desprez and Pierre-Guillaume Cavelier fils, 1747).

[67] *Works,* VII, 664.

[68] This form is found in [Gayot] *Causes Célèbres,* V, 368.

[69] *Works,* VII, 665. Jess is mentioned in *Sylvia's Lovers* (*Works,* VI, 99), where are quoted three more lines of the song; a phrase is found in ' Mr. Harrison's Confessions ' (*Works,* V, 459)—see Rubenius, *The Woman Question in Mrs. Gaskell's Life and Works,* pp. 364-365. Both verses (that in ' French Life ' and that in *Sylvia's Lovers*) occur, with minor variants, in Mrs. Gaskell's letter (*G.L.,* No. 195) to John Forster of Wednesday night [17 May 1854], in the National Library of Scotland (MS. 2262, ff. 34-40; the lines appear on ff. 34^r-34^v).

the verses with which Gayot garnishes his narrative[70]; and Stanley's description of Palestine[71] is mentioned for comparison's sake[72].

[70] [Gayot] *Causes Célèbres,* V, 368, 374, 447.

[71] To be found in Arthur Penrhyn Stanley, *Sinai and Palestine in Connection with Their History,* London: John Murray, 1856, esp. pp. 99-155. Part of the account, which Mrs. Gaskell may have read to her Sunday-School pupils, is printed in *The Bible in the Holy Land. Being Extracts from Canon Stanley's "Sinai and Palestine." For the Use of Schools, Village Clubs, Etc.,* London: John Murray, 1862, pp. 11-17. Perhaps the appearance of this abridged edition explains Mrs. Gaskell's topographical reference. It is worth while suggesting that Mrs. Gaskell possibly consulted Stanley's book in general, and in particular his description of the Plain and Bay of Acre (*Sinai and Palestine,* pp. 259-262), during her researches for the Siege of Acre episode in *Sylvia's Lovers* (*Works,* VI, 448-458, esp. 448-450).

[72] *Works,* VII, 678.

SECTION II

Wives and Daughters (1864-1866)

Between August 1864 and January 1866 'Wives and Daughters. An Every-Day Story' appeared in *The Cornhill Magazine*[1]; it was published in book-form[2] soon afterwards. Because of its author's death on 12 November 1865, the novel was never completed. Frederick Greenwood, having learnt something of her mother's intentions from one of the Miss Gaskells[3] (most probably Meta[4]), supplied the conclusion[5]—not a difficult

[1] X (1864), 129-153, 355-384, 385-408, 583-608, 695-721; XI (1865), 65-87, 197-222, 320-345, 434-460, 564-590, 682-705; XII (1865), 1-29, 129-164, 257-295, 385-425, 513-546, 641-678; XIII (1866), 1-15—1-11 [by Mrs. Gaskell], 11-15 (Concluding Remarks) by Ed. C. M. [Frederick Greenwood]. It opened the numbers for August and October 1864, and those from July 1865 to January 1866.
[2] Elizabeth Cleghorn Gaskell, *Wives and Daughters. An Every-Day Story*, 2 vols., London: Smith, Elder and Co., 1866. It was published in February, according to Sadleir (*Excursions in Victorian Bibliography*, p. 211).
[3] Shorter, ed. *Novels and Tales*, VI (1910), pp. viii-ix.
[4] William Shaen wrote to Catherine Winkworth on 15 November [1865] as follows: 'The *Cornhill* story is left unfinished. The part for December is all written, and it was to have ended in January, but that part is not even begun; [but] Meta knows what her general intention was, and will I think put a note at the end of the December part, just stating the end of the story.'—Quoted in [Susanna Winkworth and Margaret Josephine Shaen, ed.] *Letters and Memorials of Catherine Winkworth*, II (1886), 429: the parenthesis within square brackets is editorial.
[5] Incorporated in the January 1866 instalment (*The Cornhill Magazine*, XIII, 11-15), immediately after Mrs. Gaskell's own words. Whether the serial was initially intended to end in December or January appears uncertain; for there seems some ambiguity about the author's statements (quoted fairly accurately in Hopkins, *Elizabeth Gaskell*, p. 294) made in a letter to Mrs. Nancy Robson of Wednesday [10 May 1865 (not 10 January 1865, as is given in Hopkins, *op. cit.*, p. 293)]— now in the Gaskell Section, Brotherton Collection, Leeds University Library. Having expressed a wish that the story were finished and said that it was to last till after the December number, Mrs. Gaskell remarked that, with the August instalment already composed, she had four more numbers to write and a great deal to get in. Mrs. Gaskell's letter occurs as *G.L.*, No. 570 (dated [?10 May 1865] by Chapple and Pollard).

task since, though Mrs. Gaskell had left the last two chapters unwritten, ' nothing really remained to be said '[6].

On 3 May [1864][7] Mrs. Gaskell informed George Smith that, having jettisoned a story—her ' Two Mothers '[8]—which, she felt, had not altogether pleased him, she had devised a tale of country-town life, set forty years in the past. She then furnished a sketch of *Wives and Daughters*. This possesses a two-fold value, both as further evidence of the author's prior planning of her major works[9] and as proof that her inventive faculty was, during composition, flexible enough to diverge from what she had originally intended. It may be well, therefore, to summarize her outline, especially with a view to noting any differences between it and the written novel.

Mrs. Gaskell conceived of a widowed doctor who, when his only daughter (Molly) was about sixteen[10], would marry again, his wife being a widow, also with one girl (Cynthia); the two girls, contrasted characters[11], not sisters[12] but living as such in

[6] Thomas Seccombe, pref. *Wives and Daughters. An Every-Day Story,* by Mrs. Gaskell, London: Herbert & Daniel, 1912, p. ix.

[7] Mrs. Gaskell's letter of this date to George Smith is now in the archives of Sir John Murray. The relevant passage is quite accurately quoted by Miss Hopkins (*Elizabeth Gaskell,* p. 293), though she does not print the outline of *Wives and Daughters.* The letter appears as *G.L.,* No. 550.

[8] This is the story which, in a letter of 20 September [1863] to George Smith (now in the archives of Sir John Murray), Mrs. Gaskell said was in her ' head/ very clear '—the relevant quotation being in Hopkins, *Elizabeth Gaskell,* p. 220: *G.L.,* No. 532.

[9] Cont. Mrs. Marianne Holland's words, as quoted by Edna Lyall [Ada Ellen Bayly] (' Mrs. Gaskell ', in *Women Novelists of Queen Victoria's Reign: A Book of Appreciations,* p. 144): " Sometimes she planned her novels more or less beforehand, but in many cases, certainly in that of ' Wives and Daughters,' she had very little plot made beforehand, but planned her story as she wrote. She generally wrote in the morning, but sometimes late at night, when the house was quiet." This may, of course, apply to those elements in the novel not mentioned in the scheme sent to Smith.

[10] In the novel she is seventeen when her father remarries (*Works,* VIII, 149, 154, 161). We find her in the first chapter aged twelve (*Works,* VIII, 2); yet by the opening of the story proper she is sixteen and three-quarters (*Works,* VIII, 53).

[11] E.g. *Works,* VIII, 251-252, 254-255, 277, 313, 371-372, 377-378, 381, 400, 402, 437, 454-455, 466-467, 485, 487-488, 542, 621.

[12] Molly thought of Cynthia as her sister (*Works,* VIII, 249); but she disliked it when *Roger* spoke of her as Molly's sister (*Works,* VIII, 362). See too *Works,* VIII, 411.

the same house, were to be unconscious rivals for the love of Roger Newton[13], the second son of a neighbouring squire—or, rather, yeoman[14]. She intended that Roger should be taken with Cynthia, who would not care for him[15], though Molly would. Roger's elder brother was to have formed a clandestine marriage at Cambridge[16]; supposedly clever before going there, albeit morally weak, he would have disappointed his father so much as to make the old squire refuse to send Roger, almost denying him an education[17]. The elder son would live at home, out of health, in debt, and afraid to inform his angry father of the wedding. Roger was to act as his sole confidant, and give him money to support his inferior (if not disreputable[18]) wife and child, no one else knowing about the union[19]. Roger the author envisaged as rough and unpolished, yet making a name for himself in natural science; tempted by a large sum, he would, like Charles Darwin, go round the world as a naturalist—with the stipulation that half his money for the three-year voyage[20] should be paid in advance, so that he might thus help his brother[21]. Mrs. Gaskell's plan was for him to leave with a sort of fast and loose engagement to Cynthia; after his

[13] Roger Hamley in the novel (*Works*, VIII, 48).

[14] In the novel, despite his ancient ancestry, the squire's yeoman-like habits are stressed (*Works*, VIII, 43-45).

[15] Although Cynthia enjoyed his attentions, 'she did not care for Roger one thousandth part of what he did for her' (*Works*, VIII, 410).

[16] Actually Osborne, though a Cambridge undergraduate, met Aimée in London (*Works*, VIII, 351), followed her to Metz (*Works*, VIII, 352), and married her in Carlsruhe (*Works*, VIII, 408).

[17] In the novel Squire Hamley, himself denied an education befitting his station (*Works*, VIII, 44), nevertheless sent both his sons to Trinity (*Works*, VIII, 46-47). Osborne fell into disgrace, because of academic failure, only after Roger had gone up to Cambridge (*Works*, VIII, 217).

[18] She is, in the novel, an innocent French *bonne* (*Works*, VIII, 351-352, 574); yet her humble birth is unfavourably commented on by Squire Hamley and the second Mrs. Gibson (*Works*, VIII, 735-736, 743).

[19] In the novel Molly accidentally discovers that Osborne is married, but is sworn to secrecy (*Works*, VIII, 240-242); Osborne later confides in her, giving the address of his wife and child (*Works*, VIII, 574).

[20] In the novel his journey was to last two years (*Works*, VIII, 422, 425, 441, 447, 454).

[21] In the novel Roger lent Osborne most of his Fellowship money to help maintain Aimée (*Works*, VIII, 403, 409). He borrowed on the expectation of his future remuneration from the voyage, insuring his life as a safeguard; this money he intended his father to use so that the squire's drainage-scheme could be recommenced (*Works*, VIII, 425).

departure his brother would break a blood vessel and die[22]. Cynthia's mother was then to confirm and broadcast the engagement[23]; but her daughter would have taken a fancy to another man, making Molly her confidante[24]. Mrs. Gaskell concluded by remarking that Smith could see the nature of the story, whose title she left to him as she was unable to find one. Although confessing she could never really tell beforehand, she anticipated the novel would fill three volumes[25].

The most conspicuous omissions from Mrs. Gaskell's sketch are the Cumnor set, the Cranfordesque ladies of Hollingford, Mrs. Hamley, and Mr. Preston. Otherwise this is a fair summary of the story. There seems, however, little indication of how the important characters of the doctor, his wife, daughter, and step-daughter will be developed; indeed Mrs. Gaskell may have intended the Newton (i.e. Hamley) family to be at least equally prominent.

As regards the personal background to the novel, not a great deal need be said. Hollingford is by all commentators taken to be Knutsford, the identification being self-evident. One ought to add that it is Knutsford transposed to a Midland setting, having its station on the London-Birmingham line[26] and not being far from Feversham[27]: doubtless Mrs. Gaskell was recalling her time at Stratford-on-Avon[28]. The nearest literary

---

[22] Although the cause of death is not given when Osborne is found in the grass (*Works,* VIII, 641), his decease was the result of some heart disease (*Works,* VIII, 645, 659-660), presumably aneurism of the aorta, earlier diagnosed by Mr. Gibson (*Works,* VIII, 443).

[23] The second Mrs. Gibson did not in fact do this, since before the news of Osborne's death reached the family Cynthia had already written to the squire and Roger, saying she was breaking off her engagement (*Works,* VIII, 637).

[24] Molly became Cynthia's confidante in her attempt to rid herself of the long-drawn-out affair with Preston (*Works,* VIII, 541 ff.).

[25] The first edition (1866) occupied two volumes.

[26] *Works,* VIII, 705.

[27] *Works,* VIII, 665. This applies more especially to Hamley, a village some seven miles from Hollingford (*Works,* VIII, 68).

[28] The Hollingford church, for instance, unlike that at Knutsford but like the Stratford parish church attended by Elizabeth Stevenson, has a spire (*Works,* VIII, 654, 714: see Hicks, *A Quest of Ladies,* p. 81). Mrs. Gaskell even employs the Warwickshire dialect word ' unked ' (*Works,* VIII, 196), a vague definition of which she gave to W. S. Landor in the very letter where she speaks of her five years' schooling in Warwickshire (this letter of 22 May 1854 is in the Forster Collection —F. MS. 215—at the Victoria and Albert Museum): *G.L.,* No. 197.

parallel to Hollingford is probably Hamley, in *A Dark Night's Work*; and, interestingly, this name occurs in the present story with the family of ' " Hamley of Hamley " '[29]. The description of Hamley assemblies[30] relates more closely to that of the Hollingford charity ball[31] than does the latter to what is found in *Cranford,* where the Assembly Room at the *George* receives only passing mention[32]. There is, nonetheless, a Cranfordian aspect to the Hollingford *milieu,* indicating a debt to Knutsford. This is conspicuously illustrated by such ladies as the Browning sisters (' " Pecksy and Flapsy " '[33] to Lady Harriet), Mrs. Goodenough, and Mrs. Dawes. A few examples must suffice. As a characteristic Cranfordism, Mrs. Goodenough's comment on the squire's lineage deserves to be quoted.

> " I have always heerd," said she, with all the slow authority of an oldest inhabitant, " that there was Hamleys of Hamley afore the time of the pagans."[34]

More genteel than Mrs. Goodenough, as befitted their position as daughters of the late incumbent[35], are the Miss Brownings. An appropriate instance of Cranfordesque conduct is their behaviour when Lady Harriet called[36]. Taken unawares, Miss Phoebe was wearing only her black skull-cap as she sat, feet on fender, her gown above her knees, pulling out the—inevitable—old lace[37] she had just been washing; her sister was snoozing, and did not wake upon her ladyship's entrance. After some time the conversational buzz aroused Miss Browning, making her protest that she had been unable to sleep because of (what she supposed to be) the chatter of Phoebe and the maid. The reply she evoked made things even worse.

[29] *Works,* VIII, 45.
[30] *Works,* VII, 406-408.
[31] *Works,* VIII, 325-345.
[32] *Works,* II, 98-100, 102-103, 191.
[33] *Works,* VIII, 184, 186, 212, 420.
[34] *Works,* VIII, 43: cf. the origin of the Cranworths in *Ruth* (*Works,* III, 251).
[35] *Works,* VIII, 29. The Misses Jenkyns of Cranford had the same status (*Works,* II, 10, 31, 35, 52-71, 85, 88, 179). It seems scarcely worth noting the anomaly whereby Mr. Browning, the vicar (*Works,* VIII, 29), lived in the Rectory (*Works,* VIII, 581).
[36] *Works,* VIII, 193-195.
[37] Cf. Cranford lace (*Works,* II, 74, 94-95); see too *Works,* VIII, 325

" ' Sister, it's her ladyship and me that has been conversing.'
" ' Ladyship here, ladyship there! have you lost your wits,
Phoebe, that you talk such nonsense—and in your skull-cap,
too!' "[38]

About the consummately-conceived character of the second
Mrs. Gibson every critic has found something to say, yet no
one seems to have noticed that she too has not a little of Cranford about her. Recalling how Miss Debōrah Jenkyns delighted
in wine and dessert, as much for show as for consumption[39],
and how the Miss Hollands of Knutsford put out ginger wine
for display rather than for drinking[40], we may find an echo of
such genteel economy in Clare's having set out for herself and
Molly almonds, raisins, and dates—no extravagance, since
neither ate them[41]. We may also note that she professed to
aim at simple elegance[42] and esteemed refinement[43].

Strongly reminiscent of the Cranfordesque habit of Miss
Galindo, who avowedly wore her muslin apron crookedly in
order to conceal a lemon stain[44], is Mrs. Goodenough's amusing
trick for hiding marks.

" . . . I remember, speaking o' breadths, how I've undone my
skirts, many a time and oft, to put a stain or a grease spot
next to poor Mr. Goodenough. He'd a soft kind of heart, when
first we was married; and he said, says he, ' Patty, link thy
right arm into my left one, then thou'lt be nearer to my
heart;' . . . "[45]

Cranfordian[46] too is the delicacy of the Hollingford ladies in
declining to call a spade a spade. Thus Mr. Preston's tendency
to drink must never be termed drunkenness. As Miss Browning
remarked to Miss Phoebe, who had committed this *faux pas*,
' " A man may take too much wine occasionally, without being

[38] *Works,* VIII, 194.

[39] *Works,* II, 31.

[40] The relevant extract from a letter by their niece, Mary Sibylla
Holland, is conveniently quoted by Ward (ed. *Works,* II, pp. xx-xxi)—his
source being *Letters of Mary Sibylla Holland,* selected and ed. Bernard
Henry Holland, London: Edward Arnold, 1898, pp. 21-23.

[41] *Works,* VIII, 579.

[42] *Works,* VIII, 414. We think of Cranford, where ' economy was
always " elegant " ' (*Works,* II, 4).

[43] *Works,* VIII, 570, 742.

[44] In *My Lady Ludlow* (*Works,* V, 134).

[45] *Works,* VIII, 484.

[46] Cf. *Works,* II, 41, 81, 101, 124, 137.

a drunkard. Don't let me hear you using such coarse words, Phoebe!" [47] Having learnt her lesson, Miss Phoebe was later able to add a contribution of her own to her sister's stock of euphemisms.

> "Oh, don't call them 'lies', sister; it's such a strong, ugly word. Please call them tarradiddles, for I don't believe she meant any harm. ..." [48]

There is, similarly, the second Mrs. Gibson's reluctance to designate the relationship between Cynthia and Roger an engagement [49], as well as her avoidance of the word 'mess' in describing Cynthia's entanglement with Preston [50]. On another occasion she had cause to reprimand her step-daughter for a lack of linguistic refinement.

> "Molly! Molly! pray don't let me hear you using such vulgar expressions. When shall I teach you true refinement—that refinement which consists in never even thinking a vulgar, commonplace thing! Proverbs and idioms are never used by people of education. 'Apple of his eye!' I am really shocked." [51]

Even Mrs. Gibson's use of ' "leetle" ' [52] is instructive; it may be compared with that of Cranford's Miss Betsy Barker [53], and with that of the author's friend, Mme Mohl [54].

How much of such phraseology was invented by Mrs. Gaskell [55] and how much had been heard at Knutsford (or elsewhere) is difficult to decide, though *prima facie* it seems likely that a great deal came from actual conversation. In this context

---

[47] *Works,* VIII, 516.

[48] *Works,* VIII, 592. Mrs. Gaskell once asked Mrs. Charles Holland (Eliza Gaskell) whether she had told 'a tally diddle'—this question appearing in a letter written one Sunday morning [1844 or 1845], copies of which, once owned by Mr. J. T. Lancaster, belong to the present writer: *G.L.,* No. 16a (dated [Summer 1845] by Chapple and Pollard).

[49] *Works,* VIII, 570.

[50] *Works,* VIII, 631.

[51] *Works,* VIII, 743-744.

[52] *Works,* VIII, 210.

[53] *Works,* II, 81.

[54] Who apparently underlined the word in one of her letters, quoted in Simpson, *Letters and Recollections of Julius and Mary Mohl,* p. 208.

[55] Who could remark, for example, that her 'ancles ached with talking'—in a letter to Eliza Fox of Monday [Tuesday] 29 May 1849, a copy of part of which is in the Gaskell Section, Brotherton Collection, Leeds University Library: *G.L.,* No. 48.

the following Cranfordian anecdote, recounted by one of the
novelist's daughters, seems relevant.

> . . . Some/ cousins of Mama's very often had an old/ lady stay-
> ing with them who was most in = /quisitive and if the cousins
> went out of/ the room or were away from her for some/
> time, on their return this old lady/ would make a point of say-
> ing " Well Mary/ and what have you been doing[?]" Mary/
> told her, but in time this grew very/ tiresome, so they deter-
> mined to invent/ a word which was to mean anything/ they
> chose. So the next time the old/ lady asked her everlasting
> question/ of " Well Mary and what have you been/ doing[?]"
> Oh said Mary I have been// " Scrattling ". The old lady never
> liked/ to betray her ignorance of this word/ so she said " Oh
> Scrattling have/ you and a very nice employment it/ is for
> you " . . . 56

Of the Cranfordesque elements in *Wives and Daughters* further examples, often having obvious parallels in *Cranford* itself, can readily be given. Such quaint turns of phrase[57], eccen-
tricities of thought[58], and odd modes of behaviour[59] were the
author's literary responses to the visual and auditory stimulation
received at Knutsford.

56 So wrote Marianne Gaskell to Charles Eliot Norton on 25 January
1858 in a letter, begun then and finished a fortnight later, now in the
Harvard University Library: bMS Am 1088 (3489). The cousins of the
novelist mentioned in this passage were almost certainly Miss Mary and
Miss Lucy Holland, daughters of the Knutsford surgeon.

57 E.g. Mr. Gibson was, ' as one good lady observed, " so very trite
in his conversation," by which she meant sarcastic ' (*Works*, VIII, 30);
his apprentices were in a position which was, ' as Miss Browning called
it with some truth, " amphibious " ' (*Works*, VIII, 34); Lord Hollingford
was pointed out ' as " That's Lord Hollingford—the famous Lord
Hollingford, you know; you must have heard of him, he is so scientific." '
(*Works*, VIII, 39); travelling by rail was, Mr. Gibson told Molly,
' " . . . ' sitting on tea-kettles,' as Phoebe Browning calls it." ' (*Works*,
VIII, 654).

58 E.g. Miss Browning confessed that arguing always gave her a head-
ache (*Works*, VIII, 165: cf. *Works*, II, 1, 155); she praised the sedan-
chair as a means of transport which, filled with hot air from the parlour, carried one into another warm room without the need ever to
show one's legs (*Works*, VIII, 325-326: cf. *Works*, II, 5, 82, 116-117,
120-121, 124); Mrs. Goodenough wished she could get a judge's robes
second-hand out of which to make a winter-cloak (*Works*, VIII, 483);
like Clare's Methodist cook, she viewed things French with little
pleasure (*Works*, VIII, 203-204; 484-485: cf. *Works*, II, 44, 46-47;
Novels and Tales, III, 206); Miss Browning, who also had no high
opinion of France, displayed a similar dislike for London (*Works*, VIII,
516; 525-526); Miss Phoebe Browning considered it unmaidenly to be

Mrs. Gaskell's observations of Cheshire life, however, have a far wider applicability to *Wives and Daughters* than the foregoing humorous illustrations may suggest. In this work more than in any other she exhibits a social panorama, enabling her readers to comprehend what it was like to live in a country-town during the second quarter of the nineteenth century. Despite occasional chronological anomalies[60], there is a Trollopean fidelity about the novel, one of whose major achievements lies in the convincing presentation of ordinary events, as promised by its sub-title (*An Every-Day Story*). Very little 'happens'

---

in close proximity to a gentleman (*Works*, VIII, 577: cf. *Works*, II, 37, 40-41); in her sister's eyes, matrimony was a weakness to which some worthy people were prone (*Works*, VIII, 581: cf. *Works*, II, 15, 127, 137, 140, 163); Miss Phoebe wondered whether blue would look green in candlelight (*Works*, VIII, 592: cf. *Works*, II, 145-147; *Novels and Tales*, III, 198); Miss Browning warned against speaking lightly of Satan, for one never knew what might happen if one did (*Works*, VIII, 598); her advice to Miss Hornblower was never to sit on the boiler if she travelled by train (*Works*, VIII, 654).

[59] E.g. Miss Phoebe Browning should have pretended that Lady Harriet was imbibing the expensive company-tea, even though she was drinking a much cheaper brand (*Works*, VIII, 195: cf. *Works*, II, 145-146, 175-176); as a compliment to the Menteith diamonds, Miss Phoebe wore her miniature, usually locked away in a safe hiding-place, known only to her sister, since Phoebe could not be trusted to keep silent in face of a burglar's loaded pistol (*Works*, VIII, 329: cf. *Works*, II, 107-127; V, 433—this last being a reference in the Cranfordesque 'Mr. Harrison's Confessions'); Mrs. Goodenough learnt economies, even where colds were concerned (*Works*, VIII, 336: cf. *Works*, II, 4-5, 8, 12, 31, 49-52, 56, 62, 87, 93, 186; *Novels and Tales*, III, 201); Miss Phoebe's drawer-tidying was a sign of impending misfortune, possibly the failure of the Highchester bank, thought her sister (*Works*, VIII, 591: cf. *Works*, II, 49, 143-153).

[60] Some of which are noted by Mrs. Tillotson (*Novels of the Eighteen-Forties*, 1956, p. 105, fn. 4) and Miss ffrench (*Mrs. Gaskell*, pp. 102-103). To illustrate further, one may mention that, during the decade after the Continental War and 'before railroads were,' we hear of the spread of trains and of the newly-built Birmingham-London line (*Works*, VIII, 40, 325: cont. 654, 705); that Catholic Emancipation was only just being talked about, yet the time was the eighteen-thirties (*Works*, VIII, 300: cont. 660); and that when Molly was twelve the date was some forty-five years prior to that of the novel's composition, whereas when she was eight the period was only forty years previous to the mid-eighteen-sixties (*Works*, VIII, 2: cont. 34-35). As in many of her stories, Mrs. Gaskell envisaged the action of *Wives and Daughters* taking place about half a lifetime before—when the authoress would have been a contemporary of Molly and Cynthia. Some temporal aspects of the novel are usefully discussed in Wright, *Mrs. Gaskell*, pp. 194-195, 207-215.

in the usual sense of the word : neither murder, nor seduction, nor impressment—nothing at all 'sensational'. According to Seccombe, the plot was suggested to Mrs. Gaskell 'by one of her own daughters in the Hôtel de Flandres at Brussels.'[61] The value of the book, however, resides less in the plot than in the characters; and the characters are firmly placed in their social setting.

To begin with the highest stratum, one must first mention the Cumnors, the aristocratic family to whom all Hollingford owed feudal allegiance[62]. The story opens with a knowledgeable account of that great annual event when the lady-visitors to the countess's school were received at the Towers by Lord and Lady Cumnor. Here at least fiction went hand in hand with Knutsford history, as the testimony of the Hon. Mrs. Lionel Tollemache bears witness.

> I have heard my mother say that the chapter at the beginning of *Wives and Daughters*, describing the garden-party, is an exact account of the parties at Tatton which my grandmother [Mrs. Wilbraham Egerton] used to give to the ladies of the town who helped as teachers in the Sunday-school. The garden, where Molly (in the novel) fell asleep on that hot afternoon, and which was the Paradise of our childhood, still charms a younger generation; and Cranford, though the quaint old folk are gone, is a flourishing and growing town.[63]

[61] Seccombe, pref. *Wives and Daughters,* by Mrs. Gaskell, p. xviii, fn. —presumably his informant was Meta Gaskell (who had helped him with his Preface to Mrs. Gaskell's *Sylvia's Lovers,* as is evidenced by letters from her to Seccombe in the possession of the present writer). The footnote, incidentally, seems designed to explode the 'remarkable discovery . . . that the plot of *Wives and Daughters* was derived from Miss Bremer's *A Diary*' (*op. cit.,* p. xviii)—a discovery (supposedly) made by an anonymous reviewer in *The Athenaeum Journal of Literature, Science, and the Fine Arts,* No. 2001 (3 March 1866), p. 295. This ingenious theory is resuscitated and documented at length by Miss Rubenius (*The Women Question in Mrs. Gaskell's Life and Works,* pp. 260-268), who identifies the anonymous *Athenaeum* reviewer as Henry Fothergill Chorley (*op. cit.,* p. 251, fn. 5). In fairness one must state that all the reviewer intended was to indicate a similarity, *not* to charge Mrs. Gaskell with plagiarism.

[62] *Works,* VIII, 2, 342.

[63] Tollemache, *Cranford Souvenirs and Other Sketches,* pp. 6-7. This identification is repeated in Lionel A. Tollemache, 'Lady Cumnor in "Wives and Daughters"', *The Spectator. A Weekly Review of Politics, Literature, Theology, and Art,* XCVII (1906), 490—where one may find an amusing anecdote about 'the lady who was, so to say, officially the original of Lady Cumnor'.

The sketch of Lord Cumnor, taking part, when the fancy moved him, in the management of his estates—' " pottering " (as the agent irreverently expressed it in the sanctuary of his own home)'[64]—had its basis in fact.

A steward of Lord Egerton of the Cranford days was fond of talking about his master and mistress, Lord and Lady Egerton, the earl and countess of Mrs. Gaskell's story: how his lordship would go " pottering " round his farms, criticising and advising, and—what was more difficult to put up with—altering the steward's arrangements, and substituting his own eccentric plans, and how "My Lady" was the authority over the woman's kingdom at Knutsford. She claimed the right, as the lady of the manor, to know the gossip of the little town, and to advise and interfere if need be, just as Mrs. Gaskell gives it in her story.[65]

Well conveyed is the aristocratic *hauteur* of Lady Cumnor— now proposing that Clare's wedding be held at Christmas as ' " a nice amusement for the children " '[66]; now admonishing Cynthia about domestic economy and conjugal obedience, displeased that her nuptials were not to take place in the parish church[67]. Characteristic is the dismissal of her husband's comment on the good-looks of Mr. Preston.

" I never think whether a land-agent is handsome or not. They don't belong to the class of people whose appearance I notice."[68]

In the same vein she later disclaimed any obligation to regard Preston's wishes[69]—as for his feelings, she was unaware of their existence[70]. This disregard for the lower orders comes out in

[64] *Works*, VIII, 4.

[65] Chadwick, *Mrs. Gaskell*, p. 48: a minor typographical error has been corrected. The deference of Cranford is suggested by the reverential styles of address used in speaking of or to ' " the earl " and " the countess " ' (*Works*, VIII, 2, 210; 3-4, 25, 147, 184, 193-195, 339: cf. *Works*, II, 84, 94-96, 108). It was the mother (Mrs. Wilbraham Egerton) of this Lord Egerton (the First Baron—created 1859) who gave the garden-parties mentioned by the Tollemaches (see *supra*). Apparently Mrs. Gaskell drew on more than one generation for her picture of life at the Towers (*aliter* Tatton Park). Ironically she anticipated the Earldom, which was conferred in 1897 on the Second Baron.

[66] *Works*, VIII, 139: cf. 157.

[67] *Works*, VIII, 705-708.

[68] *Works*, VIII, 106.

[69] *Works*, VIII, 626.

[70] *Works*, VIII, 627.

less obvious ways, such as her slight annoyance because, her
toilette being completed earlier than usual, ' Clare had not
been aware by instinct of the fact, and so had not brought
Molly Gibson for inspection a quarter of an hour before.'[71] As
we should expect, Lady Cumnor was not in the habit of
studying her interlocutors, ' of observing the revelations made
by other people's tones and voices '[72]; however she liked
' " everybody to have an opinion of their own " '[73]—provided
they would always ' " allow themselves to be convinced " '[74] by
her ladyship's greater thought and experience. Even so she was
not wholly bereft of humanity, being able to appreciate that for
Molly a new step-mother would prove a trial[75].

Equally successful is the portrait of Lady Harriet, the youngest of the Cumnor girls. One of Mrs. Gaskell's commendable
achievements in this work is her treatment of different members
of a family in such a manner as to suggest resemblances and
contrasts. Lady Harriet is certainly her mother's daughter in
her remarks about the Miss Brownings, whose *ménage* she
expected to find interesting[76]; and in her talk of separating
Molly off ' " from all these Hollingford people." '[77] She likewise
displayed at times the same lack of feeling, as when she described Aimée's fatherless child as ' " this tiresome little heir,
that nobody wanted " '[78]. Nonetheless Lady Harriet, with kindly
patronage, took Molly under her wing and, when the latter
had fallen beneath a cloud, dispersed all scandal by accompanying her round the town[79]; moreover, oblivious to the
danger of appearing ' to " make herself common " (as Mrs.
Gibson expressed it) '[80], she graced the Miss Brownings with a
visit, subsequently recounted by Miss Phoebe as the highest of
honours[81]. Unlike Lady Cumnor, her daughter did spare some

71 *Works,* VIII, 146.
72 *Works,* VIII, 626.
73 *Works,* VIII, 708.
74 *Works,* VIII, 708.
75 *Works,* VIII, 149.
76 *Works,* VIII, 184.
77 *Works,* VIII, 185.
78 *Works,* VIII, 722.
79 *Works,* VIII, 619-620.
80 *Works,* VIII, 420: this phrase is used of her second visit.
81 *Works,* VIII, 193-195.

thought for Mr. Preston, although the opinion formed was
scarcely more favourable.

> " I cannot bear that sort of person, . . . giving himself airs of
> gallantry towards one to whom his simple respect is all his
> duty. I can talk to one of my father's labourers with pleasure,
> while with a man like that underbred fop I am all over thorns
> and nettles. . . . "[82]

Significantly, shortly afterwards, she speaks of an aristocratic
aunt who referred to those who worked for a living as ' persons ', and appropriated all and sundry by calling them ' my
woman ', ' my people ', and so forth[83]. Somewhat similarly both
Lady Harriet and her mother, well-intentioned though they
were, tended to take possession of Molly and make plans for
her welfare, very much as if she were ' an inanimate chattel '[84].

Over against the Cumnors, ' " mere muck of yesterday " '[85]
as he racily termed them, stands Squire Hamley of Hamley,
one of Mrs. Gaskell's richest creations. An old Tory, dogmatic,
insular, strongly anti-Catholic, proud of his ancestry but (like
Mr. Buxton[86]) sensitive about his educational deficiencies, the
squire is a traditional English figure who emerges full of vitality
from the pages of the novel[87]. *Wives and Daughters* indicates
Mrs. Gaskell's kinship with, rather than her indebtedness to,
Trollope; and nowhere is this more manifest than in her picture
of old Roger Hamley, both in himself and in his relations with
others. Her insight into the nature of a man of his kidney
comes out in little touches, such as the fact that he, unlike
Lord Cumnor, could speak to his men ' in their own strong,
nervous country dialect '[88]. There is one scene[89] which is especially important for demonstrating Mrs. Gaskell's Trollopean
Englishness: it takes place when the squire is asked to visit old

[82] *Works,* VIII, 183.
[83] *Works,* VIII, 184-185.
[84] *Works,* VIII, 619, 711.
[85] *Works,* VIII, 82: cf. Lady Harriet's own remarks on her tobacco-
selling ancestor (*Works,* VIII, 707).
[86] In *The Moorland Cottage*—there being closely parallel passages
in both books (*Works,* II, 323: cf. *Works,* VIII, 288-289, 499).
[87] Some key references are: *Works,* VIII, 43-48, 81-82, 284-296,
299-300, 349-355, 390-395, 405, 425, 655, 735, 743.
[88] *Works,* VIII, 286.
[89] *Works,* VIII, 386-395.

Silas, his former gamekeeper, then on the point of death. The man's cottage was near Squire Hamley's drainage-works, unfortunately abandoned through lack of money, and not far from the land Lord Cumnor was reclaiming (a pathetic contrast for the squire). Having reached the cottage, he went to the gamekeeper's death-bed, just as his father had done when Silas's father had died; there he learnt his foxes were being endangered because of indiscriminate gorse-removal by Lord Cumnor's workmen. A brush with Preston ensued, the Whig agent treating the old Tory with cool contempt; however Roger intervened, and led his father away. Simple though it seems in bald summary, this episode is one of the most memorable in the book, betokening its author's deep appreciation of, and feeling for, a traditional, and typically English, way of life. Few other major Victorian novelists could have written it. Moreover, as a character in his own right, the squire comes convincingly to life, often as a result of Mrs. Gaskell's inclusion of significant details; for she created an individual as well as a representative figure. An example—in its way a stroke of genius —occurs when Osborne calls in question the accuracy of his father's timepiece.

> Now, impugning that old steady, turnip-shaped watch of the Squire's was one of the insults which, as it could not reasonably be resented, was not to be forgiven. That watch had been given him by his father, when watches were watches, long ago. It had given the law to house-clocks, stable-clocks, kitchen-clocks—nay, even to Hamley Church-clock in its day; and was it now, in its respectable old age, to be looked down upon by a little whipper-snapper of a French watch which could go into a man's waistcoat pocket, instead of having to be extricated with due efforts, like a respectable watch of size and position, from a fob in the waistband![90]

The chief personages from the professional classes are Mr. Gibson (the Hollingford medical man) and Mr. Ashton (the vicar), though others receive passing mention, such as Mr. Goodenough (' " a very clever attorney, with strong local interests and not a thought beyond " '[91]), Mr. Sheepshanks (Lord Cumnor's agent, ' " a hardish man of business " '[92]), Mr. Roscoe

[90] *Works,* VIII, 291.
[91] *Works,* VIII, 165.
[92] *Works,* VIII, 6.

(the young Ashcombe doctor[93]), Dr. Nicholls (' the skilful old
physician '[94]), and Mr. Hall (Mr. Gibson's predecessor, also a
'skilful doctor'[95]). Of the vicar we learn much less than of Mr.
Gibson, whose delight it was to lead him to the brink of heresy[96].
Having some kinship with Mr. Mountford, who knew his Hanbury parishioners preferred good food to calls from their pastor[97],
Mr. Ashton, though rarely visiting the poorer members of his
flock, ' was always willing to relieve their wants in the most
liberal, and, considering his habits, occasionally in the most
self-denying, manner, whenever Mr. Gibson, or any one else,
made them clearly known to him.'[98]

In Mr. Gibson Mrs. Gaskell's earlier fictional doctors find
their consummation. His origins almost certainly go back to the
author's girlhood, when she accompanied the Knutsford surgeon
on his daily rounds. Although Meta Gaskell averred " No two
people could be more unlike than Dr. Gibson and Mr.
Holland "[99], most scholars refer to the writer's uncle as the
main source for all her medical men. The historian of the
Hollands, for instance, remarks that Knutsford was " the model
of the town in her novels, ' Cranford,' and ' Wives and Daughters,' and [that] her uncle, Dr. Peter Holland, and his family
can be recognised among the characters in her stories."[100] We
have mentioned that Mrs. Gaskell had other relatives in the
profession—for example, her cousin (Henry Holland) and her
brother-in-law (Sam Gaskell[101])—; but, since *Wives and
Daughters* patently looks back to the time of her girlhood, her

[93] *Works,* VIII, 326.
[94] *Works,* VIII, 377.
[95] *Works,* VIII, 29.
[96] *Works,* VIII, 41-42.
[97] In *My Lady Ludlow* (*Works,* V, 22-24).
[98] *Works,* VIII, 42.
[99] Quoted by Payne (*Mrs. Gaskell and Knutsford,* 1905, p. 37), who, of
course, knew Miss Gaskell.
[100] Bernard Henry Holland, *The Lancashire Hollands,* London: John
Murray, 1917, p. 300—in a footnote he adds: ' The two Misses Browning in *Wives and Daughters* are the images of two old daughters of
Peter Holland, who lived at Knutsford, and the two old sisters in *Cranford*
have also a strong resemblance.'
[101] A ' dry [and] practical ' man, as Mrs. William Shaen (Emily
Winkworth) once called him—Shaen, ed. *Memorials of Two Sisters,* p.
122: our square brackets. This description would fit Mr. Gibson (*Works,*
VIII, 33, 40, 50-52, 464, 476).

youthful observations of Peter Holland's practices may reasonably be supposed of greatest importance. Nevertheless it should not be forgotten that in later life Mrs. Gaskell used to stay with the Miss Hollands[102] (whose father did not die till 1855[103]): nor that, according to Lady Ritchie, Knutsford people spoke ' *of her long country drives with an old friend, a doctor, going his rounds, twenty and thirty miles at a time; of her talk and interest in all the details along the way.*'[104]

Mr. Gibson's professional relations with the Cumnors are nicely contrasted with those of his predecessor. Mr. Hall was ' received with friendly condescension '[105]; and he took his meals ' in the housekeeper's room, not *with* the housekeeper, *bien entendu.*'[106] On privileged occasions he was admitted to the ceremony of dinner, there to meet some distinguished medical man who was advising at the Towers (it sounded well to mention such visits to the neighbouring squires)[107]. Mr. Gibson, on the other hand, having a Scottish accent not a provincial one and possessing a dignified bearing, found a readier access to Cumnor dinners, though he regarded them as professional duties rather than as pleasurable events[108]. This aristocratic recognition of Mr. Gibson as a man as well as a surgeon apparently paid handsome dividends as far as his general practice was concerned[109]; hence a low rate of payment seemed justified, it being supplemented by the prestige of attending at the Towers[110]. If the countess took a (slightly unfair) pecuniary advantage from her position with regard to Mr. Gibson, his second wife rather enjoyed being made use of—as her ladyship's agent in carrying out small commissions[111]. These, involving as they did bills for flys and cars, scarcely pleased her

---

102 Ritchie, pref. *Cranford,* by Mrs. Gaskell, p. xxi.
103 Holland, *The Lancashire Hollands,* p. 298.
104 Ritchie, pref. *Cranford,* by Mrs. Gaskell, p. xxii. The Cranford surgeon had a 'round of thirty miles' (*Works,* II, 1); Mr. Gibson also had an extensive practice, which included ' all the gentry within a circle of fifteen miles round Hollingford ' (*Works,* VIII, 60).
105 *Works,* VIII, 39.
106 *Works,* VIII, 39.
107 *Works,* VIII, 39-40.
108 *Works,* VIII, 40-41.
109 *Works,* VIII, 60.
110 *Works,* VIII, 372.
111 *Works,* VIII, 211.

husband; yet he found the subsequent presents of game no less distasteful, albeit for a different reason[112].

With the Hamleys Mr. Gibson was socially more at ease. Except for the scientific Lord Hollingford, the squire was the man to whom he took most kindly[113]; but there was still that difference in rank which prevented Squire Hamley from viewing with favour any connexion by marriage with the local surgeon[114].

Mrs. Gaskell astutely suggests the cultural isolation to which men like Mr. Gibson were prone. If he remarried, he would hardly favour a bride from a farming family, a woman without refinement or education; nor could he, a mere country practitioner, presume to court a squire's daughter[115]. He was little better off in male company; for 'there was no one equal to himself among the men with whom he associated, and this he had felt as a depressing influence, although he never recognised the cause of his depression.'[116] Such isolation made a visit from Mr. Kirkpatrick, Q.C., very welcome: from the outset the attraction was mutual[117].

What also requires notice is the way Mrs. Gaskell, often through Molly, keeps her readers conscious of Mr. Gibson's professional habits and qualities (Molly, one feels, standing somewhat in the same relation to her father as Elizabeth Stevenson did to her uncle). Thus we learn that Mr. Gibson's contempt for demonstrative people arose 'from his medical insight into the consequences to health of uncontrolled feeling'[118] —he himself 'rarely betrayed what was passing in his heart'[119]. Minor matters include such things as the surgeon's need for punctual meals[120], with his liking for bread and cheese[121] (to

---

[112] *Works*, VIII, 211.
[113] *Works*, VIII, 43.
[114] *Works*, VIII, 61-62, 242, 426-428, 452-455, 501-503: cf. Mr. Buxton's opposition to his son's marriage to Maggie, not for personal reasons but because of her social position (*Works*, II, 324-325).
[115] *Works*, VIII, 114.
[116] *Works*, VIII, 41.
[117] *Works*, VIII, 487.
[118] *Works*, VIII, 33.
[119] *Works*, VIII, 58: cf. 67, 152, 463-464.
[120] *Works*, VIII, 144.
[121] *Works*, VIII, 145, 203, 507, 510.

which Cranford's Mr. Hoggins was also partial[122]), and his habit of leaving word concerning his whereabouts in case of urgent calls[123]. One finds too an awareness of what death means for a medical man[124] and an appreciation of the ethics of the profession[125], both of which bespeak special knowledge on the part of the author. There are, in addition, telling remarks by Molly, as when she says to her step-mother, ' " Papa enjoys a joke at everything, you know. It is a relief after all the sorrow he sees." '[126]

The humorous side to the ladies of Hollingford has already been noticed. However their other aspects deserve attention; for, like *Cranford, Wives and Daughters* evinces an acute observation of how a group of spinsters and widows conduct themselves in their intercourse with one another and with the outside world. Mrs. Gaskell admirably conveys the life of that ' selectest circle of the little town '[127], whose law-giving and representative figure *par excellence* was Miss Browning (by virtue ' of being a deceased rector's daughter '[128]). This circumscribed world is both knowingly and lovingly depicted—a world of card-parties[129], invitation notes[130], and pretty serving maids (whose real function, like a subscription to the Hollingford Book Society, was to act ' as a mark of station '[131]). As in *Cranford,* the author takes considerable trouble to describe dress and manners—so much so, in fact, that since the supposed models of the Miss Brownings ' did wear white satin shoes when they took their luncheon at the great house, . . . there was natural

---

[122] *Works,* II, 137; *Novels and Tales,* III, 204.
[123] *Works,* VIII, 641.
[124] *Works,* VIII, 198, 251.
[125] *Works,* VIII, 269, 445, 609, 645.
[126] *Works,* VIII, 573.
[127] *Works,* VIII, 582.
[128] *Works,* VIII, 582. Miss Jenkyns, Cranford's arbiter in literature as well as in life, was also the ' daughter of a deceased rector ' (*Works,* II, 10).
[129] *Works,* VIII, 272-279, 580: cf. Cranford card-parties (*Works,* II, 8-10, 75, 80-83, 94, 101-103, 106, 116-117).
[130] *Works,* VIII, 398-399, 511: cf. Cranford rules of calling (*Works,* II, 2-3).
[131] *Works,* VIII, 577: cf. the similar Cranford status-symbols (*Works,* II, 1, 3, 8-9, 12, 14, 29-30, 39, 71, 73, 78, 82, 112, 114-115, 117, 138-139, 163; *Novels and Tales,* III, 202).

resentment at the account of the fact!'[132] A pleasing nostalgia is, moreover, evoked by such things as 'formal dipping curtseys,'[133] old-style worsted work[134], by-gone fashions in gowns[135], and the wearing of a turban[136]. Lord David Cecil, who praises Mrs. Gaskell's world for 'the reality of its social structure'[137], comments on that 'power of observation [which] enabled her to make the most uneventful scenes interesting'[138], an excellent illustration being the disappointment experienced at the charity ball by Hollingford gentlefolk when the aristocracy failed to fulfil their expectations—for the Duchess of Menteith arrived both very late and without her diamonds[139].

The novelist gives depth to her treatment of Hollingford gentility by revealing its less pleasant features. Lady Harriet's supposition that the good ladies probably spoke of the poor in a way they would dislike[140] was soon borne out by Miss Browning's passing reference to ' "the common people " '[141]. A further instance of genteel snobbery is provided by the second Mrs. Gibson's disapproval when Cynthia and Molly had for their respective partners an attorney's clerk and a Coreham bookseller: one ought not to dance with some one from, so to speak, the wrong side of the counter[142].

---

[132] Haldane, *Mrs. Gaskell and Her Friends*, p. 278: the reference in *Wives and Daughters* is *Works*, VIII, 10. See too Montgomery, 'Elizabeth Cleghorn Gaskell', *The Fortnightly Review*, XCIV (N.S. LXXXVIII—1910), 454: here only one Knutsford lady is mentioned as having been so shod.

[133] *Works*, VIII, 585: cf. *Works*, II, 48, 78, 100.

[134] *Works*, VIII, 750: cf. Cranford worsted-work (*Works*, II, 14, 157).

[135] *Works*, VIII, 317: cf. Cranford fashions (*Works*, II, 2, 16, 89).

[136] *Works*, VIII, 328: cf. turbans in Cranford (*Works*, II, 97-99, 104; *Novels and Tales*, III, 198).

[137] Cecil, *Early Victorian Novelists*, 1948, p. 162.

[138] Cecil, *Early Victorian Novelists*, 1948, p. 158.

[139] *Works*, VIII, 336: cf. the way Lady Glenmire disappoints Cranfordian expectations (*Works*, II, 91-92).

[140] *Works*, VIII, 184.

[141] *Works*, VIII, 189.

[142] *Works*, VIII, 333: cf. the situation at Cranford, where the Hon. Mrs. Jamieson must never know she had been in the same room as a shopkeeper's niece, and where on social occasions the shopkeepers kept a respectful distance from the gentlefolk (*Works*, II, 9, 103). Mrs. Gaskell in one of her letters implied that it was much better to marry a governess than 'an uneducated girl, a daughter of a rich *trades*person' (*Gaskell-Norton Letters*, ed. Whitehill, p. 11: *G.L.*, No. 384).

As could be expected in ' " such a tittle-tattle place as
Hollingford " '[143], gossip among high and low[144] was a natural
by-product of social intercourse; but the consequences of scandal
nearly proved disastrous for Molly[145]. Mrs. Gaskell's shrewd
analysis of irresponsible small-talk indicates how sensitive had
been the registration, with eye and ear, of the comparable side
of Knutsford life.

> Scandal sleeps in the summer, comparatively speaking. Its
> nature is the reverse of that of the dormouse. Warm ambient
> air, loiterings abroad, gardenings, flowers to talk about, and
> preserves to make, soothed the wicked imp to slumber in the
> parish of Hollingford in summer-time. But when evenings grew
> short, and people gathered round the fires, and put their feet
> in a circle—not on the fenders, that was not allowed [146]—
> then was the time for confidential conversation! Or, in the
> pauses allowed for the tea-trays to circulate among the card-
> tables—when those who were peaceably inclined tried to stop
> the warm discussions about " the odd trick," and the rather
> wearisome feminine way of " shouldering the crutch, and show-
> ing how fields were won "—small crumbs and scraps of daily
> news came up to the surface, such as " Martindale has raised
> the price of his best joints a halfpenny in the pound;" or,
> " It's a shame of Sir Harry to order in another book on
> farriery into the Book Society; Phoebe and I tried to read it,
> but really there is no general interest in it;" or, " I wonder
> what Mr. Ashton will do, now Nancy is going to be married!
> Why, she's been with him these seventeen years! It's a very
> foolish thing for a woman of her age to be thinking of matri-
> mony; and so I told her, when I met her in the market-place
> this morning!"[147]

In *Wives and Daughters* Mrs. Gaskell for the first time treats
governesses at any length. Molly has one (appropriately called
Miss Eyre), whose status in the Hollingford hierarchy is not
high, she being, though respectable, only ' the daughter of a

[143] *Works,* VIII, 210.
[144] E.g. *Works,* VIII, 29-32, 40, 281, 420, 513-514, 580-582, 610-
613, 633.
[145] *Works,* VIII, 582-583, 599-607, 612-619.
[146] Except, of course, to the aristocracy (*Works,* VIII, 414)—Miss
Phoebe also indulged, but in private (*Works,* VIII, 194). It is worth
noting that Mme Mohl, Mrs. Gaskell's friend, used to put her feet
on the fender (see the remarks of Mrs. Story, quoted in James, *William
Wetmore Story and His Friends, from Letters, Diaries, and Recollections,* I, 365).
[147] *Works,* VIII, 579-580.

shop-keeper '[148]. Inevitably she suffered ill-usage at the hands of Betty, the Gibsons' termagant domestic[149]. Another governess— a charming person for ' " any one who wasn't particular about education " '[150]—is Mrs. Kirkpatrick (*née* Clare), subsequently the second Mrs. Gibson. Clare's difficulties, as both school-mistress[151] and governess[152], do something to win the reader's sympathy. Although Mrs. Gaskell, unlike many nineteenth-century authoresses, made comparatively little of the governess question, she was nevertheless, as this brief treatment shows, well aware of the problems of spinsters and widows who had reluctantly to teach.

Hand in hand with the portrayal of a country-town community went a keen appreciation of the surrounding landscape : for both reasons *Wives and Daughters* appears a very English novel. Mrs. Gaskell, as befitted the daughter of a scientific farmer, had an observant eye for features like ' pretty lanes, with grassy sides and high-hedge banks not at all in the style of modern agriculture.'[153] In addition she possessed what Lord David Cecil has termed ' a Morland-like sensibility to the modest beauty of the English rural scene '[154], a sensibility which had already received felicitous expression in such compositions as *Cousin Phillis*. Throughout the present work one finds fine passages of natural description[155], exquisitely evoking the seasonal background against which the characters act their leisurely parts—for *Wives and Daughters* is a leisurely story, albeit written under pressure[156].

The slowness of the action seems wholly in keeping with the gradual passing of the years in a locality little touched by time. Thus, although the watchful scholar may discover incon-

---

[148] *Works,* VIII, 34.
[149] *Works,* VIII, 36-37.
[150] *Works,* VIII, 102.
[151] *Works,* VIII, 138-139, 142.
[152] *Works,* VIII, 141-142.
[153] *Works,* VIII, 420.
[154] Cecil, *Early Victorian Novelists,* 1948, p. 175.
[155] *Works,* VIII, 92-93, 123, 190, 217-218, 239, 422-423, 432-433, 531.
[156] See, for instance, *G.L.,* Nos. 336 (possibly), 561, 563-565, 570, 572, 575a, 576, 582, 588; also relevant is Mrs. Gaskell's Tuesday [11 April 1865] letter to Mme Schérer (in the Parrish Collection at the Princeton University Library).

sistencies in the narrative[157], these scarcely appear important.
The novel is so long, and the plot so loosely constructed, that
such anomalies are soon forgotten. The form is admirably suited
to its content; events follow one another chronologically rather
than logically, there being nothing taut or closely knit in the
structure. One feels that Mrs. Gaskell could have gone on
writing almost *ad infinitum*. All she had to do was to enlarge
the story with the help of those hundred and fifty or more
characters who are mentioned but not developed; the novel

[157] Sanders (*Elizabeth Gaskell*, p. 137), Miss Malcolm-Hayes ['Notes
on the Gaskell Collection in the Central Library', *Memoirs and Proceedings of the Manchester Literary & Philosophical Society* (*Manchester Memoirs*), LXXXVII (1945-1946), 172-173], Miss ffrench (*Mrs.
Gaskell*, p. 103), and Miss Rubenius (*The Woman Question in Mrs.
Gaskell's Life and Works*, p. 137, fn. 3) point out that the elder Miss
Browning is variously called Sally, Clarinda, and Dorothy—*Works*, VIII,
10: cont. 170: cont. 329, 591. It may be well to list other *prima
facie* contradictions. (i) In c. 1820 Mrs. Kirkpatrick had been a widow
for seven months; but some five years later her daughter, aged about
eighteen, implied that her father had died when she was four—*Works*,
VIII, 19: cont. 252-253, 453. (ii) The *Cumnor Arms* seems to change
its name to the *George*—*Works*, VIII, 35, 40: cont. 193, 211, 436,
464, 467, 575. (iii) Squire Stephen Hamley was 'plucked at Oxford'—
Works, VIII, 44 (doubtless one of those things 'viewed from the wrong
side of college windows'—Ward, ed. *Works*, VIII, p. xxvi). (iv) Though
she got her building rent-free, Clare could scarcely 'pay for house-rent'
—*Works*, VIII, 101: cont. 138. (v) In spite of having previously met
Osborne, the second Mrs. Gibson seemingly forgot their encounter
—*Works*, VIII, 206: cont. 266. (vi) In one place Osborne and Roger
receive £250 and £200 while at Trinity; in another their respective
allowances are £300 and £200—*Works*, VIII, 220: cont. 297. (vii)
Although comparatively young women some five years before, the Miss
Brownings at the time of the charity ball had been non-dancers for
twenty-five years—*Works*, VIII, 9, 14: cont. 325. (viii) Apparently
without a ridable horse, Squire Hamley was still able to order one—
Works, VIII, 302: cont. 387. (ix) When twelve Molly could not understand French; yet she had been learning the language since she was
eight—*Works*, VIII, 21: cont 35. (x) At variance with his former
ignorance on the matter is Roger Hamley's decision to insure his life—
Works, VIII, 406: cont. 425. (xi) Albeit usually fond of exercise,
Cynthia, unlike Molly, did not find a daily walk a necessity—*Works*,
VIII, 360: cont. 430. (xii) Mrs. Gaskell omitted to kill off Mr.
Goodenough—*Works*, VIII, 165: cont. 484. (xiii) Cynthia's yearly income mysteriously shrinks from £30 to £20—*Works*, VIII, 158, 453:
cont. 490. (xiv) Mr. Gibson's stableman is now Dick, then James—
Works, VIII, 26: cont. 641. (xv) A non-existent carriage was at Squire
Hamley's disposal—*Works*, VIII, 288: cont. 652. (xvi) Cynthia's Boulogne
boarding-school was kept by a lady whose surname changed from Lefèvre
to Lefèbre—*Works*, VIII, 159: cont. 257, 474, 548-549.

teems with proper names, only space was lacking for their translation into full-blooded people.

Wives and Daughters is the most feminine of Mrs. Gaskell's longer works, just as it is the most English. Everything is quiet, peaceful, serene; there are no causes to be pleaded, no tears to be shed. The authoress explores the domestic lives of ordinary people—nothing more. To many this might seem an unexciting, even an unpromising, theme: for how could the reader's attention be held by the common or garden affairs of a country surgeon or by those of his relatives and acquaintances? Moreover the scene never changes. Though places like London, Winchester, and Worcester are mentioned, happenings[158] outside Hollingford are known only by report.

Even in the mid-Victorian age, however, uneventful lives held a certain attraction for those who looked back with nostalgia to the ' days before railways '[159] and ' their consequences, the excursion-trains '[160]. Hollingford has, to be sure, its new Birmingham to London line; but this is mentioned as a new thing towards the end of the book[161], the traditional means of travel still being the horse. Like many of her contemporaries, Mrs. Gaskell is writing of what she had known in her youth, ' before the passing of the Reform Bill '[162] and ' before muscular Christianity had come into vogue '[163] : from the standpoint of the mid-sixties, the story is set, like not a few of her tales, half a lifetime ago. Though relatively free from disasters, her married years were very busy and full, an untimely death from heart-failure being not without significance. Reading Mrs. Gaskell's correspondence gives the impression of some one frequently overtaxing her strength, fleeing to the Continent for recuperation, yet constantly burdened by domestic and social commitments. Perhaps she would not have wished it otherwise; nevertheless, in such circumstances, the period before her marriage

[158] E.g. Cynthia's first visit to her uncle in London (*Works,* VIII, 253); the life led by Osborne's wife at Winchester (*Works,* VIII, 351, 353); Cynthia's involvement with Mr. Preston during the Worcester Festival (*Works,* VIII, 543-547).

[159] *Works,* VIII, 3.

[160] *Works,* VIII, 325.

[161] *Works,* VIII, 705.

[162] *Works,* VIII, 3.

[163] *Works,* VIII, 30.

must have appeared one of blessed tranquillity, and Knutsford the embodiment of gracious and quiet living. What could be more natural, therefore, than that in middle-age she should again return to ' Cranford ', to recreate in fiction what could seldom be enjoyed in reality? Although Marianne Gaskell might still find at Knutsford in 1857 ' a/ regular Cranfordian party of old/ ladies and hardly any gentlemen// and the Sedan Chair, and lantern/'[164], her mother had few opportunities for experiencing such delights.

Whatever its socio-historical value as a picture of a by-gone age, *Wives and Daughters* will always be most highly esteemed for its characters. By universal consent, the portraits of Mr. Gibson, his second wife, his daughter, and his step-daughter are among—some would doubtless say are in fact—the best things Mrs. Gaskell ever did. It is these characters, and their relations among themselves, which provide the core of the book. Love interest as such is remarkably rare; and, when examined critically, seems not very successfully rendered. From the outset one knows that Molly is destined, whatever the hazards, to marry Roger; but mutual affections of a specifically amorous nature are scarcely mentioned. Cynthia's attachments have, at least on her part, little passion about them. Indeed the only person who suggests with any plausibility that love can be an overwhelming and bitter experience is, oddly enough, Mr. Preston[165] (who, distantly related to Kinraid and Holdsworth, is one of the author's minor villains). Moreover it is he who hints, however mildly, that there might be a sexual side to matrimony—such, at any rate, is one possible inference from his remarks about making Cynthia love him after they are married[166].

The character of Molly Gibson was, for the nineteenth

---

[164] Extract from Marianne's Knutsford letter to Charles Eliot Norton of 8 September [1857], now in the Harvard University Library: bMS Am 1088 (3488). In the same letter she remarks: ' Knutsford you know/ is Cranford, only the people here don't/ at all approve of its being called/ Cranford '. Marianne uses the phrase ' Knutsford (alias/ Cranford)' in another letter to Norton—that of 13 October 1859, also in the Harvard University Library: bMS Am 1088 (3490).

[165] See especially *Works*, VIII, 558-560, 589.

[166] *Works*, VIII, 538, 551.

century, of greatest importance. Typical were the reactions of
Austin Dobson's young lady.

> She thought " Wives and Daughters " " *so* jolly ";
> " Had I read it?" She knew when I had,
> Like the rest, I should dote upon " Molly ";
> And " poor Mrs. Gaskell—how sad!"[167]

Similarly when a book of *Great Characters of Fiction* came to
be compiled in the last decade of that century, it was Molly
Gibson whom Christabel Coleridge chose to extol[168]—not
Cynthia Kirkpatrick, nor the second Mrs. Gibson. Today
estimates have changed; and, according to Rosamond Lehmann, Molly appears very much a period piece, however delightful.

> She is a dear, a sweet girl, whose strength of character we
> admire, but we do not tremendously long to know her; and
> even if we did, we could not. She sleeps in her Victorian
> tomb, flower-planted; we linger to read her touching epitaph,
> and wish her back; but she cannot come again. It is partly
> the Women's Revolution, partly the Freudian . . . One can
> hear the deafening chorus: "emotional blackmail," "infantilism,"
> " atavism," " father-fixation "; and poor Molly going down
> defenceless, drowned, beneath it.[169]

In Molly Gibson Mrs. Gaskell makes goodness attractive. To
find fictional prototypes is not difficult. As early as *The Moorland Cottage* she had conceived Maggie Browne[170] along such
lines; and the figure of Bessy Hawtrey[171] shows that, when
writing ' Crowley Castle ', she still had the type in mind.
Molly's personality, as it struck Squire Hamley, emerges from
his questions about Cynthia.

> " Is she—well, is she like your Molly?—sweet-tempered
> and sensible—with her gloves always mended, and neat about

[167] Quoted, with minor variants, in Shorter, ed. *Novels and Tales,*
VI, p. v. The *vers de société,* ' Incognita', from which these lines are
taken may be found in, e.g., Henry Austin Dobson, *Collected Poems,*
London: Kegan Paul, Trench, Trübner & Co. Ltd, 1897, pp. 383-386.

[168] Christabel Rose Coleridge, ' Molly Gibson ', in *Great Characters
of Fiction,* ed. Mary Elizabeth Townsend, London: Wells Gardner,
Darton, & Co., 1893, pp. 209-218.

[169] Rosamond Nina Lehmann, intro. *Wives and Daughters,* by Mrs.
Gaskell, London: John Lehmann, 1948, pp. 12-13.

[170] *Works,* II, 268 ff.

[171] *Works,* VII, 684 ff.

the feet, and ready to do anything one asks her, just as if
doing it was the very thing she liked best in the world?"

Mr. Gibson's face relaxed now, and he could understand
all the Squire's broken sentences and unexplained meanings.

"She's much prettier than Molly to begin with, and has very
winning ways. She's always well-dressed and smart-looking,
and I know she hasn't much to spend on her clothes, and
always does what she's asked to do, and is ready enough with
her pretty, lively answers. I don't think I ever saw her out
of temper; but then I'm not sure if she takes things keenly
to heart, and a certain obtuseness of feeling goes a great way
towards a character for good temper, I've noticed. Altogether
I think Cynthia is one in a hundred."

The Squire meditated a little. "Your Molly is one in a thousand, to my mind. ... "[172]

Molly is the character to whom we feel closest : her thoughts,
emotions, decisions, problems, and resolutions are ours. All the
other figures are, however convincingly depicted, portrayed
from the outside. About them one forms opinions and makes
moral assessments; but as regards Molly no such appraisals are
required. Notwithstanding the consummate inventive skill which
created Cynthia and Clare, Mrs. Gaskell would never have
chosen either as the standpoint from which to view the story.
They were figures whom she sought to present with varying
degrees of humour, satire, kindness, and criticism; they were
not persons with whom more intimate contact was possible, or
with whom all our sympathies were meant to go. Molly, on the
contrary, the novelist allows us to observe from the inside.
Hence it is not surprising to find scholars drawing parallels
between Elizabeth Stevenson's early life and that of the heroine.
Dr. Sanders, for instance, remarks that 'Molly's grief when she
heard of her father's engagement is one of the most realistic
scenes of the book[173], and her griefs are told with such sympathy as to indicate that the author herself had gone through
much that Molly felt and knew.'[174] Since Elizabeth was only
four at the time her father married again[175], perhaps one ought

172 *Works,* VIII, 454-455: cont. 'Would not we sacrifice twenty
Mollys for a single Cynthia?'—Cecil, *Early Victorian Novelists,* 1948, p.
168. ' " I'm not sure if I don't think she's worth half-a-dozen Cynthias" '
was the opinion of Miss Browning (*Works,* VIII, 485).

173 *Works,* VIII, 125-138.

174 Sanders, *Elizabeth Gaskell,* p. 136.

175 Rubenius, *The Woman Question in Mrs. Gaskell's Life and
Works,* p. 261.

rather to stress the correspondence between Molly's reactions to her new step-mother and those of the young Miss Stevenson to her father's second wife when she visited the family in London during the late eighteen-twenties[176]. In support of Sanders' main point, however, it is interesting to notice that the grief-stricken Molly sought solitude among the trees and greenery of the Hamley grounds[177]—somewhat in the way that, so Anne Thackeray Ritchie heard, Elizabeth Stevenson '*in her hours of childish sorrow and trouble . . . used to run away from her aunt's house across the Heath and hide herself in one of its many green hollows, finding comfort in the silence, and in the company of birds and insects and natural things.*'[178] Yet Molly's girlhood was on the whole a very happy one[179] like, presumably, the author's own; and one may confidently postulate that such carefree activities as the heroine's reprehensible cherry-tree sitting[180] had their equivalents in similar tom-boy habits of Elizabeth Stevenson's.

Three aspects of Molly's characterization call for special consideration. Firstly one must commend the perceptiveness lying behind the accounts of the heroine's early experiences; such insights into a child's world almost certainly had their origin in the novelist's recollections of her own childhood, supplemented by a careful observation of the development of four daughters. Particularly noteworthy are the telling psychological details— as when Molly's eyes opened wide at the approach ' of " the earl;" for to her little imagination the grey-haired, red-faced, somewhat clumsy man, was a cross between an archangel and a king.'[181] Another example of Mrs. Gaskell's knowledge of non-adult behaviour can be found in Molly's mental and emotional responses to Lord Cumnor's laboured jocularity[182].

The second important feature in Molly's portrayal is the rendering of the paternal-filial relationship. When one recalls

[176] Chadwick, *Mrs. Gaskell,* p. 94; and Whitfield, *Mrs Gaskell,* p. 5.
[177] *Works,* VIII, 127-128.
[178] Ritchie, pref. *Cranford,* by Mrs. Gaskell, p. xii. Maggie Browne was another Gaskellian heroine who sought solace in nature (*Works,* II, 292-294, 326-327, 334).
[179] *Works,* VIII, 37, 544.
[180] *Works,* VIII, 28, 36, 273.
[181] *Works,* VIII, 6.
[182] *Works,* VIII, 21-22.

that during her formative years Elizabeth Stevenson was virtually fatherless, the extent of this achievement becomes apparent.
By deft touches[183] and without the least trace of mawkish
sentimentality, the author admirably suggests the strong mutual
bond existing between Molly and the affectionate, slightly
possessive, undemonstrative Mr. Gibson. The only false note,
struck but briefly, occurs when Mr. Gibson is informed of the
rumours surrounding Molly and Mr. Preston—that scene[184]
and its sequel[185] have a melodramatic ring about them. At the
beginning of the story the heroine is still very much a daughter;
at the end she is on the verge of becoming a wife, as her father
reluctantly acknowledges (' " Lover *versus* father !" thought he,
half sadly. " Lover wins." '[186]). As earlier indicated, family likenesses are common in *Wives and Daughters*. Molly possessed,
through heredity or imitation, her mother's characteristic ' mode
of caressing '[187]; in serious conversation she talked ' in the quiet
sensible manner which she inherited from her father'[188], whom
she also resembled (according to her step-mother) in her lack of
poetic spirit[189]. Such affinities contribute considerably to the
domestic verity of the novel.

Thirdly, Mrs. Gaskell's depiction of Molly's adolescent attitudes requires brief attention. The reader, as the author intended, smiles a little at Molly's realization that she might be
pretty[190] as she made her first objective assessments of her
physical appearance; he too, like the novelist, appreciates the
girl's consciousness of guilt when her growing critical sense became aware of the defects of the Miss Brownings—' the coarser
and louder tones in which they spoke, the provincialism of their
pronunciation, the absence of interest in things, and their
greediness of details about persons.'[191] There is, moreover, the
fine stroke whereby Molly's penitence for having been im-
pertinent to the elder sister was deepened when she found her-

[183] E.g. *Works*, VIII, 26, 33, 35, 48, 59, 63, 66-67, 76, 87, 123-124,
128, 431, 463-464, 510, 605, 634, 644, 676-677.
[184] *Works*, VIII, 596-598.
[185] *Works*, VIII, 599-605, esp. 599-600.
[186] *Works*, VIII, 750.
[187] *Works*, VIII, 381.
[188] *Works*, VIII, 733.
[189] *Works*, VIII, 520: cf. 119, 145.
[190] *Works*, VIII, 72-73, 173.
[191] *Works*, VIII, 168.

self a guest in that neat little bed-room of theirs which in childhood days had appeared the height of luxury[192]. Molly's
romanticizing, her envisaging Osborne as a troubadour or a
knight in armour[193], is well contrasted with the dawning of a
more mature kind of love, that for Roger Hamley, even though
Molly herself believed her feelings towards him were rather
those of a sister[194]. Hence, when the ' unacknowledged hope '[195]
was explicitly and bluntly voiced by Mrs. Goodenough, her
maidenly modesty was troubled, and her conduct towards
Roger changed in consequence[196]. The author permits us to be
amused at this, while recognizing how very real youth's miseries
could be[197]. However perhaps Mrs. Gaskell's greatest success
lies in her treatment of adolescent morality. She stresses Molly's
anxiety about her step-mother's distortions of truth, at the same
time indicating the ' girl's want of toleration, and want of experience to teach her the force of circumstances, and of temptation '[198]; yet to Molly it seemed that she was faced with a
major ethical problem—whether or not to turn a blind eye to
Mrs. Gibson's little deceptions for the sake of peace at home[199].
Although the novelist, like Molly, probably held goodness ' to
be the only enduring thing in the world '[200], she avoids the pit-
fall of making her heroine the mouthpiece for irreproachable
moral sentiments. How she used her artistic invention to do so
is illustrated by the following extract. Mrs. Gibson's view of
human nature, like that of Mr. Henry[201], must have been completely antipathetic to her own; nevertheless she gives the devil
some good lines.

> "I don't wonder at your indignation, my dear!" said Mrs.
> Gibson [having wholly misinterpreted her step-daughter's pre-
> ceding remarks]. "It is just what I should have felt at your
> age. But one learns the baseness of human nature with advan-
> cing years. I was wrong, though, to undeceive you so early—

192 *Works*, VIII, 170-171.
193 *Works*, VIII, 167, 188.
194 *Works*, VIII, 311, 411, 433, 436, 438, 676, 721, 732.
195 *Works*, VIII, 723.
196 *Works*, VIII, 729-739.
197 *Works*, VIII, 730.
198 *Works*, VIII, 420.
199 *Works*, VIII, 430-431.
200 *Works*, VIII, 253.
201 In *The Moorland Cottage* (*Works*, II, 338).

but, depend upon it, the thought I alluded to has crossed
Roger Hamley's mind!"
   "All sorts of thoughts cross one's mind—it depends upon
whether one gives them harbour and encouragement," said
Molly.
   "My dear, if you must have the last word, don't let it be a
truism. ... "202

The other daughter of the title is that fascinating creature,
Cynthia Kirkpatrick. How did Mrs. Gaskell come to conceive
of such a character? Certainly she was no late product of the
author's invention; for as early as 1850 we have her precursor,
Erminia203, in *The Moorland Cottage*. The contrasted friends
of that book, Maggie and Erminia, prefigure the contrasted
step-sisters of *Wives and Daughters* (even their Christian names
suggest the parallel). In looks and attire each girl acts as a foil
to the other204. Their education and accomplishments continue
the correspondence. Thus Erminia's schooling on the Con-
tinent205 and such social graces as her elegant singing of some
' newest and choicest French airs '206 respectively bring to mind
Cynthia's Boulogne boarding-school207 and her charming rendering of a ' " little French ballad " '208. It would form an interesting study to consider how much of Cynthia's personality was
foreshadowed by Erminia's; but we must content ourselves with
two quotations, striking in their verbal similarity. The repetition
of a particular image surely indicates, better than more general
affinities, the kinship between these characters.

   The gay, volatile, wilful, warm-hearted Erminia was less
   earnest [than Maggie] in all things. . . . Her life was a
   shattered mirror; every part dazzling and brilliant, but wanting
   the coherency and perfection of a whole.209

   If Molly had not been so entirely loyal to her friend, she might
   have thought this constant brilliancy [of Cynthia's] a little tiresome, when brought into everyday life; it was not the sun-
   shiny rest of a placid lake—it was rather the glitter of the
   pieces of a broken mirror, which confuses and bewilders.210

Pertinently we may enquire whether, like so many figures in
Mrs. Gaskell's fiction, Cynthia was based on the author's obser-

202 *Works,* VIII, 744.
203 *Works,* II, 282 ff.
204 *Works,* II, 285.
205 *Works,* II, 299, 305.
206 *Works,* II, 309.

207 *Works,* VIII, 118, 158-159.
208 *Works,* VIII, 311.
209 *Works,* II, 295.
210 *Works,* VIII, 400.

vation of folk she knew. When discussing her novels, she always talked ' of her personages as if they were real people '[211]; and she certainly had clear-cut ideas about what her characters would be likely to do—as when, for example, she decided that Molly, not Cynthia, would describe Roger as ' " a prince amongst men." '[212] If she did model Cynthia on one of her acquaintances, she would necessarily have strong views on what would be in keeping with her temperament. One must, none-theless, admit there is no incontrovertible evidence that Mrs. Gaskell was drawing from life, though there is some that she may have been.

The only internal clue is a sentence in the initial analysis of Cynthia.

> A school-girl may be found in every school who attracts and influences all the others, not by her virtues, nor her beauty, nor her sweetness, nor her cleverness, but by something that can neither be described nor reasoned upon.[213]

The Gaskell material in the National Library of Scotland points to two possible candidates.

In a letter to John Forster of Wednesday night [17 May 1854][214], Mrs. Gaskell, referring to Ruskin's matrimonial diffi-culties, says that she went to the same school (almost certainly Avonbank) as Mrs. Ruskin[215], and that, though Effie Grey[216]

---

[211] According to Catherine Winkworth—*Letters and Memorials of Catherine Winkworth*, I (ed. Her Sister [Susanna Winkworth], 1883), 383.

[212] *Works*, VIII, 438. In her manuscript Mrs. Gaskell had originally given virtually the same phrase to Cynthia, though on second thoughts she realized it would be '*extreme/=ly* out of character' (the relevant extract from Mrs. Gaskell's letter of 5 March [1865] to George Smith —now in the archives of Sir John Murray—is quoted in Hopkins, *Elizabeth Gaskell*, p. 295: *G.L.*, No. 563).

[213] *Works*, VIII, 249.

[214] National Library of Scotland: MS. 2262, ff. 34-40—*G.L.*, No. 195.

[215] Admiral Sir William Milburne James, G.C.B. (Wynd House, Elie, Fife) cannot confirm this. In a letter of 7 November [1962] he kindly informed me that he had always thought Effie went to school in London since, when in October 1846 she left school for the last time, she stayed with the Ruskins until her father arrived from Perth to take her home; moreover he reminded me that she first met John Ruskin ' when she was twelve and stopping with his parents for a few days on her way to school' (cf. William Milburne James, ed. *The Order of Release: The Story of John Ruskin, Effie Gray and John Everett Millais, Told for the First Time in Their Unpublished Letters*, London: John Murray, 1947 [1948], pp. 19, 17). However in her helpful letters of

was much younger than herself, they had many school-fellows in common. She comments on Effie's beauty[217], and on her only serious faults (vanity and—except to her own relatives—coldheartedness); mentions the girl's delight in adding new offers to a long list of proposals; remarks that she was already engaged when she accepted Ruskin, who knew nothing about it till after their wedding; and recalls that four years previously her old schoolmistress (Miss—Mary(?)—Ainsworth[218]) had prophesied that some one with her high temper and love of admiration would never submit to strict rules. Although, like Cynthia, Effie got into 'many scrapes'[219], Mrs. Gaskell's final judgement seems not entirely unfavourable.

---

8 November 1967 and 22 May 1968 Mary Lutyens (Mrs. J. G. Links, 2 Hyde Park Street, London W.2) informed me that according to the Bowerswell Papers (the basis of Sir William's book and now in the Pierpont Morgan Library) Effie did indeed go to Avonbank—initially in August 1840, remaining there till July 1841, during which period the Miss Byerleys handed over their establishment to the Miss Ainsworths; and again from January to June 1844, when she left school for the last time (cf. Mary Lutyens, ed. *Effie in Venice: Unpublished Letters of Mrs John Ruskin written from Venice between* 1849-1852, London: John Murray, 1965, pp. 4-5).

[216] Mrs. Gaskell spells the surname incorrectly. Euphemia Chalmers Gray, born 7 May 1828, married Ruskin on 10 April 1848 (James, ed. *The Order of Release,* pp. 12, 95).

[217] Graphically illustrated by the reproductions in James, ed. *The Order of Release.* Like Cynthia's (*Works,* VIII, 146, 248), her hair was 'a golden auburn' (according to her son, as quoted in James, ed. *The Order of Release,* p. 198); Cynthia had grey eyes (*Works,* VIII, 248), Effie's were grey-blue (Lutyens, ed. *Effie in Venice,* p. 23).

[218] Her informant, Mrs. Gaskell remarked, had been staying with the Ruskins that Christmas: Miss (doubtless Mary) Ainsworth was at Denmark Hill in January 1854—Mary Lutyens, *Millais and the Ruskins,* London: John Murray, 1967, p. 129.

[219] National Library of Scotland: MS. 2262, f. 37r—*G.L.,* No. 195. Cf. Cynthia's ' " I do sometimes believe I shall always be in scrapes " ' (*Works,* VIII, 524). A Letter from Mary Lutyens to the Editor of *The Times Literary Supplement* (No. 3395, 23 March 1967, p. 243)—following its Review of *The Letters of Mrs Gaskell,* ed. Chapple and Pollard, on 16 March 1967 (No. 3394, pp. 209-210)—stressed the groundlessness of Mrs. Gaskell's allegations that Effie was already engaged when she accepted Ruskin and that she got into many scrapes at Venice; yet the first denial at least proved controversial, evoking further correspondence during the subsequent six weeks (Nos. 3396-3401). However such matters are strictly irrelevant to a consideration of how far the novelist's conception of Effie influenced her portrayal of Cynthia.

> . . . She really is very close to a/ charming character; if she had had the/ small pox she would have been so. . . . [220]

Mrs. Gaskell may have had Effie's *liaisons* in mind when she described not only Cynthia's entanglements with Mr. Preston[221] and Mr. Coxe[222] but also her virtual acceptance of Roger Hamley[223] before being free from Preston; added to which Mr. Henderson, whom she eventually married, made his initial proposal[224] in complete ignorance ' " of this clandestine engagement " '[225] with Roger. Moreover Effie's manifest power over men is easily matched by Cynthia's influence over the male sex, as represented by Mr. Gibson[226]; his gardener[227]; Osborne Hamley[228]; the schoolboy, William Orford[229]; her uncle, Mr. Kirkpatrick[230]; and Squire Hamley[231]. Although Cynthia was, like Effie, very beautiful, she differed from her in that ' no one with such loveliness ever appeared so little conscious of it.'[232] Nevertheless she resembled Effie both in her appetite for admiration[233] and in her lack of consideration for the feelings of others[234].

On 27 September 1942 Miss Maria I. Steuart wrote ' A Lengthening Chain ' for Florence Peck (*née* Campbell) and her son, Dennis—the typescript is now deposited in the National Library of Scotland[235]. According to Miss Steuart, her grandmother, Elizabeth Scott, and her grand-aunt, Jessy, attended Avonbank between 1820 and 1825; subsequently a third sister, Catherine Scott (Mrs. Florence Peck's grandmother), went to

[220] National Library of Scotland: MS. 2262, f. 38r—*G.L.*, No. 195.
[221] *Works*, VIII, 534-552.
[222] *Works*, VIII, 466-475.
[223] *Works*, VIII, 434.
[224] *Works*, VIII, 622-623.
[225] *Works*, VIII, 633.
[226] *Works*, VIII, 263-264, 540.
[227] *Works*, VIII, 264.
[228] *Works*, VIII, 264.
[229] *Works*, VIII, 276.
[230] *Works*, VIII, 488.
[231] *Works*, VIII, 497-498.
[232] *Works*, VIII, 250.
[233] *Works*, VIII, 384, 472, 586, 636-637.
[234] *Works*, VIII, 470-471, 748.
[235] MS. 3109, ff. 233-243. The date (presumably of composition)—
' 27 Sept. 1942 '—appears in ink within square brackets at the end (f. 243) of the typescript.

the same school: as we should expect, 'a fellow-pupil of the
little Scotts was none other than Elizabeth Cleghorn Stevenson '[236]. Miss Steuart, after stressing the Scottish influences
detectable in *Round the Sofa* and *Cranford*, turns to the
present novel.

> It is . . . when we get to "Wives and Daughters" that
> the links with the School at Stratford-on-Avon and Scotland
> become closer.
>   Whether that delightful elderly hero Dr. Gibson was taken
> from any Edinburgh friend of Mrs Gaskell's I cannot tell,
> but we were always told that Molly Gibson was drawn as to her
> disposition and character from my Grandmother, Elizabeth
> Steuart[[237]], née Scott, but that her looks were given to
> Cynthia Kirkpatrick.
>   Certainly the description we had of our grandmother with
> her brilliant fair colouring (none of us ever saw her, for she
> died very young—before any of her children even were grown-
> up) tallied with that of Cynthia. The dark soft curling hair
> Molly is given belonged to her sister Jessy.[238]

Miss Steuart goes on to mention that Mrs. Gaskell wrote 'a
charming letter about her visit to Auchencairn shortly before
she began to write *Wives and Daughters* '[239], opining that this
visit may have suggested the name and baronetcy of Kirkpatrick, there being ' a Baronetcy in the family of Kirkpatricks

[236] National Library of Scotland: MS. 3109, f. 234.

[237] Miss Steuart records in a footnote: 'Elizabeth Scott's brother-
in-law Colonel Thomas Ruddiman Steuart married secondly a Mrs
Atkin née *Ruck*—a Welsh woman. Her son by her first marriage who is
now Lord Atkin of Aberdovey and his brothers counted us as "cousins".
Now a *Ruck* married a Darwin and it is thought that the career of Roger
Hamley one of the Heroes in "Wives and Daughters" with his scientific travels and successes is supposed to have been suggested by the great
Charles Darwin.' That it probably was so suggested Mrs. Gaskell's
outline of the story makes clear.

[238] National Library of Scotland: MS. 3109, ff. 240-241.

[239] National Library of Scotland: MS. 3109, f. 242. The letter
mentioned by Miss Steuart may be that of 25-30 October [1859] to
Charles Eliot Norton (*Gaskell-Norton Letters*, ed. Whitehill, pp. 36-40);
but it is more probably the one Mrs. Gaskell wrote to George Smith
from Auchencairn on Wednesday 29 June [1859]—now in the archives
of Sir John Murray—from which extracts are (fairly accurately) quoted
by Ward (ed. *Works*, I, p. xxxix-xl) and Miss Hopkins (*Elizabeth Gaskell*,
p. 211)—: respectively *G.L.*, Nos. 444, 434.

of Closeburn '[240]. Finally, having noted that the Empress Eugénie's mother was a Kirkpatrick, she remarks:

> It would be delightful to think the description in contemporary memoirs dealing with the Empress and her "liquid swaying grace" are just what correspond to Cynthia "with the beautiful free stately step of a wild animal in the forest—moving always as it were to the continual sound of music."[241]

To decide how far Miss Steuart's identifications are plausible is no easy task: perhaps the Scottish verdict of 'Not proven' is appropriate. However there seems no doubt Miss Stevenson was a friend of Elizabeth and Jessy Scott, since her name appears among those inscribed on a copy of Beattie's *Minstrel* presented to the sisters on 15 June 1824; this is the one piece of written evidence Miss Steuart adduces in support of her case[242].

There was at Avonbank yet another schoolgirl who may have contributed, albeit unconsciously, to the conception of Cynthia Kirkpatrick—namely the authoress herself, who certainly had something 'of the sprightliness of Cynthia in her make-up.'[243] Like Cynthia[244], she could hardly help being agreeable in the company of men.

> "I wish," she writes to Miss Winkworth, in her attempt at puritanical modesty, "I could help taking to men so much more than to women (always excepting the present company, my dear!) and I wish I could help men taking to me; but I believe we've a mutual attraction of which Satan is the originator."[245]

It is worth noting a further possible resemblance, albeit a slight

---

[240] National Library of Scotland: MS. 3109, f. 242. The old Kirkpatrick baronetcy is mentioned more than once in the novel (*Works*, VIII, 20, 142, 453): that referred to by Miss Steuart dates from 1685. Perhaps one should state that the description of Cynthia is slightly misquoted: according to the novel (*Works*, VIII, 250) she walked 'with the free stately step of some wild animal of the forest—moving almost, as it were, to the continual sound of music.'

[241] National Library of Scotland: MS. 3109, f. 242.

[242] National Library of Scotland: MS. 3109, f. 243—cf. Chadwick, *Mrs. Gaskell*, p. 81.

[243] Haldane, *Mrs. Gaskell and Her Friends*, p. 278.

[244] *Works*, VIII, 471, 540.

[245] Haldane, *Mrs. Gaskell and Her Friends*, p. 285: Mrs. Gaskell's words appear as *G.L.*, No. 633 (the addressee being ?Catherine Winkworth).

one. When her father died, the question of a future career probably crossed Elizabeth's mind. Mr. Stevenson had once been offered the Professorship of Technology at Charkov—a fact only known to his family after his death[246]. This may have given his daughter fleeting thoughts about going as a governess to Russia, in the way that Cynthia entertained comparable ideas at a time of crisis[247].

One feels inclined to look to Mrs. Gaskell's daughters in seeking models for Cynthia, yet to do so is not very fruitful. All one can say is that Florence (Flossy), the only one to wed during her mother's lifetime, like Cynthia married a barrister; the marriage proved a happy one, and the couple often stayed at Plymouth Grove[248]—just as Mrs. Gaskell apparently intended Cynthia and her husband to be frequent visitors at the house of Mr. Gibson[249]. There is, however, one curiosity worth recording with regard to Marianne (Polly) and the two daughters of the novel: when writing to Marianne, Mrs. Gaskell once addressed her as Molly[250] and twice as Cynthia[251]. Both letters were sent several years before *Wives and Daughters* was begun; but the use of these proper names gives food for speculation.

All who have written on Cynthia have praised her portrayal; and there seems little to add to such fine appreciations as those by Lord David Cecil[252] and Rosamond Lehmann[253], each of whom regards her as unique in Victorian fiction. However, partly owing to this uniqueness, her qualities are peculiarly difficult to define. Molly recognized Cynthia's ' real self was shrouded in mystery '[254]; and confessed she did not ' " quite

---

[246] 'William Stevenson, Esq., of the Records Office, in the Treasury', *The Annual Biography and Obituary*: 1830, XIV (1830), 211-212.
[247] *Works*, VIII, 474, 551, 637, 674, 693-694, 696, 702.
[248] *Gaskell-Norton Letters*, ed. Whitehill, p. 120: *G.L.*, No. 560.
[249] *Works*, VIII, 754, 757.
[250] In a letter, written one Saturday noon [1860], now in the Gaskell Section, Brotherton Collection, Leeds University Library: *G.L.*, No. 479 (dated [?Late 1860] by Chapple and Pollard).
[251] In letters of Thursday [3 November 1859] and Tuesday [8 November 1859], the former being in the possession of Mrs. Margaret Trevor Jones and copies of the latter, once owned by Mr. J. T. Lancaster, in that of the present writer: respectively *G.L.*, Nos. 447 (to ?Marianne Gaskell and dated [November 1859], according to Chapple and Pollard), 447b (to ?Marianne Gaskell, according to Chapple and Pollard).
[252] *Early Victorian Novelists*, 1948, pp. 166-168.
[253] Intro. *Wives and Daughters*, by Mrs. Gaskell, p. 13.
[254] *Works*, VIII, 481.

understand her " '²⁵⁵. Moreover her father, though he found Cynthia fascinating, admitted that he too did not ' " quite understand her " '²⁵⁶—but to women, Mr. Gibson realized, understanding was not necessary²⁵⁷—(nor was Cynthia one to express, even if she felt, any emotion expected of her²⁵⁸). Many readers, similarly perplexed, may therefore feel like agreeing with Mrs. Chadwick's interpretation²⁵⁹ of Mme Mohl's remark about not being ' up to Cynthia yet '²⁶⁰ (even though what she really meant was probably not that she found Cynthia a puzzling character but that she had only read the first fourteen chapters of ' Wives and Daughters '²⁶¹).

In lesser hands Cynthia might have been little more than a flirt and a jilter—or merely the ' " heroine of genteel comedy " '²⁶² she seemed to Lady Harriet. There was indeed something of a potential heroine about Cynthia, as she herself owned²⁶³; yet she was nearer the truth in describing herself as ' " a moral kangaroo " '²⁶⁴, capable of ethical jerks but not of ' " every-day goodness " '²⁶⁵. Of all Gaskellian characters she possesses the most chequered nature. Very much a creature of impulse, Cynthia is neither wholly good nor wholly bad, which explains part of her charm. With some justice Squire Hamley,

²⁵⁵ *Works,* VIII, 462.
²⁵⁶ *Works,* VIII, 400, 462: cf. Duke Crowley's realization, with special reference to the Cynthia-like Theresa, that women were beyond his comprehension—' Crowley Castle ' (*Works,* VII, 687).
²⁵⁷ *Works,* VIII, 462.
²⁵⁸ *Works,* VIII, 522-523.
²⁵⁹ Chadwick, *Mrs. Gaskell,* p. 46.
²⁶⁰ 'I have this very evening read the last number of the *Cornhill,* and am as pleased as ever. The Hamleys are delightful, and Mrs. Gibson!—oh, the tricks are delicious; but I am not up to Cynthia yet. Molly is the best heroine you have had yet. Every one says it's the best thing you ever did. Don't hurry it up at the last; that's a rock you must not split on.'—so wrote Mme Mohl to the author in a letter of 28 December 1864. The whole extract may be found in Simpson, *Letters and Recollections of Julius and Mary Mohl,* pp. 217-218.
²⁶¹ The section of the novel included in the December number of *The Cornhill Magazine* (X, 695-721) took the story as far as the end of Chapter XIV (*Works,* VIII, 195): Cynthia arrives in Chapter XIX, contained in the following-February number (*The Cornhill Magazine,* XI, 207-215).
²⁶² *Works,* VIII, 612.
²⁶³ *Works,* VIII, 254.
²⁶⁴ *Works,* VIII, 254.
²⁶⁵ *Works,* VIII, 254.

in the same breath as he acknowledged her prettiness, referred
to her as ' " the baggage " '[266]; but she had already confessed to
having given herself ' " up a long time ago as a heartless baggage!" '[267] On the other hand this ' " very fascinating, faulty
creature " '[268], as Mr. Gibson called her, wins the reader's heart
by little acts of spontaneous generosity—plucking artificial
flowers from her own best bonnet to adorn Molly's[269]; spoiling
her bouquet to make a coronet for her step-sister[270]; giving
roses to Roger on the impulse of a moment[271]. One can scarcely
judge Cynthia morally, especially since her standards were more
aesthetic than ethical : she obeyed, albeit often unawares, the
dictates of taste[272] rather than those of conscience. One must
accept Cynthia on her own (non-moral) terms[273].

Mrs. Gaskell displayed literary wisdom in making Cynthia
Clare's daughter; for she thus both afforded some explanation
of the girl's personality and extended the network of family
likenesses. Not only was Cynthia in Christian name[274] and
prettiness of complexion[275] akin to her mother, there were more
significant similarities. Both shared a desire for admiration,
wanting to be liked[276]; both enjoyed flirting, and employed the
same means of attracting men[277]. Each lacked emotional depth :
Cynthia's deficiency amounted to ' " a certain obtuseness of
feeling " '[278]; and Clare, despite her own ' affectation and false
sentiment '[279], called ' " making a scene " . . . showing any
signs of warm feeling '[280]. One can appreciate Mrs. Gaskell's
irony in attributing to Clare the thought that her daughter, not

[266] *Works,* VIII, 735.
[267] *Works,* VIII, 382.
[268] *Works,* VIII, 748.
[269] *Works,* VIII, 255.
[270] *Works,* VIII, 321-322.
[271] *Works,* VIII, 367-368.
[272] E.g. *Works,* VIII, 436.
[273] *Works,* VIII, 257.
[274] *Works,* VIII, 119.
[275] *Works,* VIII, 146, 248, 753.
[276] *Works,* VIII, 477.
[277] *Works,* VIII, 628.
[278] *Works,* VIII, 455.
[279] *Works,* VIII, 461.
[280] *Works,* VIII, 369.

having inherited her barometrical sensitivity, would not be ' " easily affected in any way " '[281].

If having Clare as a mother partly accounts for Cynthia's innate temperament, it also sheds light on her acquired characteristics. The adult personality owes much to an individual's early life, the child being father of the man (or mother of the woman). Mrs. Gaskell had been conscious of this truism at least thirty years before, when she began watching for baby Marianne's ' many little indications of disposition '[282]; and, as her letters testify[283], she continued to observe the dispositions of her offspring for the rest of her days. *Wives and Daughters* reveals a similar awareness of the importance of childhood experiences. At an early age each girl had lost one parent, though the effect (both short- and long-term) on Molly[284] was much less than that on Cynthia[285], the latter's trying time with her mother being in marked contrast[286] to Molly's happiness with Mr. Gibson. Clare's plaintive references to her ' " poor fatherless girl " '[287] tell us something about the mother as well as about the daughter. When young, Cynthia had lacked the opportunity to establish those strong and intimate bonds necessary for emotional maturity, her subsequent inability to love passionately and deeply[288] being consonant with the maternal indifference from which she had suffered[289]; for, as Cynthia acknowledged, she had always been an encumbrance to her mother[290], passed on from one school to the next since the age of four[291]. With such a background, her antipathy to people

---

[281] *Works,* VIII, 569. Molly agreed that she was not easily—or, rather, not deeply—affected (*Works,* VIII, 569).

[282] " *My Diary* ", p. 5.

[283] *The Letters of Mrs Gaskell,* ed. Chapple and Pollard, *passim.* The editors devote part of their Introduction (*op. cit.,* pp. xiv-xvi) to Mrs. Gaskell's relations with her children.

[284] *Works,* VIII, 2.

[285] *Works,* VIII, 252-253.

[286] *Works,* VIII, 543-545.

[287] *Works,* VIII, 444, 491: variants include ' " A fatherless girl— you know one always does call them ' poor dears.' " ' (*Works,* VIII, 246); ' " my poor fatherless child " ' (*Works,* VIII, 634); ' " Poor Cynthia! My poor child! " ' (*Works,* VIII, 688).

[288] *Works,* VIII, 384, 437-438, 474.

[289] *Works,* VIII, 257, 410, 521, 537.

[290] *Works,* VIII, 693.

[291] *Works,* VIII, 253.

with deep feelings[292] and her preference for diffused rather than concentrated affection[293] become understandable. Cynthia herself realized that, if her upbringing had been otherwise, her moral and natural sentiments would also have been different[294] : if only she had known the Gibsons earlier![295] Under these circumstances it was only to be expected that, when she came into daily contact with Mr. Gibson, he should become for her a parent-surrogate. This at least is one explanation of Cynthia's attraction to Molly's father[296].

Although one may find hints of Cynthia's mother in Mrs. Shaw's plaintive ways[297] and 'Madam Hawtrey's silky manner'[298], Clare is most distinctly foreshadowed by Mrs. Browne of *The Moorland Cottage* (1850). Perhaps their temperamental similarity may best be demonstrated by juxtaposing two quotations. It will be recalled that Mrs. Browne, like Mrs. Kirkpatrick[299] a curate's widow[300], used to cry over her husband's grave[301]; yet for both ladies bereavement brought sartorial consolations.

> Mrs. Browne remembered having heard the rector say, "A woman never looked so lady-like as when she wore black satin," and kept her spirits up with that observation; ...[302]

> ... it was her taste, more than any depth of feeling, that had made her persevere in wearing all the delicate tints—the violets and greys—which, with a certain admixture of black, constitute half-mourning. This style of becoming dress she was supposed to wear in memory of Mr. Kirkpatrick; in reality, because it was both lady-like and economical.[303]

If Mrs. Gaskell modelled Mrs. Browne on a real person, it could scarcely have been the Mrs. Erskine whose Clare-like qualities she delightfully recounted in a [1855] letter to her

---

[292] *Works,* VIII, 700.
[293] *Works,* VIII, 657.
[294] *Works,* VIII, 638.
[295] *Works,* VIII, 493.
[296] *Works,* VIII, 248, 263, 450, 471, 474, 494, 542, 637-638.
[297] In *North and South* (*Works,* IV, 11).
[298] In 'Crowley Castle' (*Works,* VII, 686).
[299] *Works,* VIII, 19.
[300] *Works,* II, 268.
[301] *Works,* II, 268.
[302] *Works,* II, 278.
[303] *Works,* VIII, 107-108.

girls[304]. Nevertheless what she heard about this lady may have influenced her conception of the second Mrs. Gibson. If so, ' it is a good instance of how she captured the essence of an actual personality without direct imitation. For certainly the whole character was not drawn from Mrs. Erskine, who was said to drink like a fish and to be shunned by most people.'[305] Bearing all this in mind, we could slightly modify a view of Rosamond Lehmann's, and surmise that, in addition, some at least (though not all) of Mrs. Gibson's traits the novelist probably ' derived from memories of the detested stepmother of her own youth.'[306]

Undoubtedly Clare is a Gaskellian masterpiece. To have drawn a caricature would have been easy, to have presented her as purely an object of irony or ridicule would not have been difficult; yet Mrs. Gaskell did neither. Instead she painted ' one of the most brilliantly effective and subtle portraits in English fiction.'[307] If any governing principle can render intelligible the behaviour of this ' superficial and flimsy '[308] creature, then it must be egotism : not mere selfishness, she seeming scarcely conscious of the main-spring of her conduct, but rather an egocentricity which ' took up the points of every word or action where they touched her own self (and called it sensitiveness)'[309]. Clare was, as she virtually acknowledged, as sensitive as a thermometer[310]—though only to whatever might directly refer to herself. Thus, when Lady Cumnor held forth, she ' was always apt to consider these remarks as addressed with a personal direction at some error of her own, and defended the fault in question with a feeling of property in it, whatever it might happen to be.'[311] On the other hand, she

---

[304] Now in the Gaskell Section, Brotherton Collection, Leeds University Library. A summary of the relevant parts of this letter, written one Saturday morning, is given by Miss Hopkins (*Elizabeth Gaskell,* p. 366), who, however, (mis)dates it as late in 1854 from internal evidence— presumably an attack on Sebastopol, though in fact this occurred on 8 September 1855. The recipients were probably Marianne and Meta. The letter occurs as *G.L.,* No. 273 (to Marianne and Margaret Emily Gaskell and dated [?Late 1855], according to Chapple and Pollard).

[305] Hopkins, *Elizabeth Gaskell,* p. 366.

[306] Lehmann, intro. *Wives and Daughters,* by Mrs. Gaskell, pp. 13-14.

[307] ffrench, *Mrs. Gaskell,* p. 99.

[308] *Works,* VIII, 159.

[309] *Works,* VIII, 527.

[310] *Works,* VIII, 506: cf. 569.

[311] *Works,* VIII, 625.

took little account of the feelings of others, being naturally ' an unperceptive person, except when her own interests were dependent upon another person's humour'[312].

Of Clare's self-regarding disposition many instances could be found. It lies behind her inability to comprehend individual differences, with a consequential failure in communication; for ' her own words so seldom expressed her meaning, or, if they did, she held to her opinions so loosely, that she had no idea but that it was the same with other people.'[313] It explains her attempts to prevent others from enjoying pleasures which she had no mind for[314] or which might involve her in the slightest inconvenience[315]; and it accounts for the apparent callousness of her remark that Molly's was ' " more a tedious, than an interesting illness." '[316]

Complementary to this egotism is a lack of sensitivity, verbally betrayed by phrases which ' were always like ready-made clothes, and never fitted individual thoughts. Anybody might have used them '[317]. Even where her daughter was concerned, Clare ' was not one to notice slight shades or differences in manner '[318]; nor was she likely ' to probe beneath the surface.'[319] Indeed she reveals her obtuseness early in the novel by failing to understand the perplexities and fears of the twelve-year-old Molly, lost among strangers[320] during that ' unlucky detention at the Towers ' [321]—although, rather ironically, Mr. Gibson felt ' at the time as if Mrs. Kirkpatrick had behaved very kindly to his little girl.'[322]

Clare's mind was at once shallow and ' mirror-like '[323]. Her second husband easily ' perceived of how flimsy a nature were all her fine sentiments '[324]; and her daughter delighted in

[312] *Works*, VIII, 204.
[313] *Works*, VIII, 465.
[314] *Works*, VIII, 431, 440.
[315] *Works*, VIII, 213-216, 725.
[316] *Works*, VIII, 681. In most things Clare was ' amiably callous ' (*Works*, VIII, 456).
[317] *Works*, VIII, 355.
[318] *Works*, VIII, 540.
[319] *Works*, VIII, 692.
[320] *Works*, VIII, 14-29.
[321] *Works*, VIII, 115.
[322] *Works*, VIII, 115.
[323] *Works*, VIII, 152.
[324] *Works*, VIII, 372.

counterventing her ' affectation and false sentiment.'[325] To Molly her ' sweet, false tone '[326] was ' like the scraping of a slate-pencil on a slate '[327], though Osborne Hamley found ' the soothing syrup of . . . [her] speeches '[328] in no way disagreeable. By thus suggesting the reactions of others, as well as by more explicit means, Mrs. Gaskell makes Clare an entirely convincing figure. However her personality is perhaps best manifested through the words she uses. Doubtless Mrs. Gaskell's memory for dialogue provided one or two phrases; but she must have invented many more. Everything Clare says is in keeping with her character. She was incapable of an original thought; yet her manner and style are all her own. Being well versed in the art of light conversation[329], she possessed ' skill in the choice and arrangement of her words, so as to make it appear as if the opinions that were in reality quotations were formed by herself from actual experience or personal observation '[330]. Since most scholars who have examined *Wives and Daughters* have quoted at length—sometimes taking the same extracts[331]—there appears little need to demonstrate how revealing Clare's conversation can be. One may, nonetheless, draw attention to the frequency[332] with which the word ' plaintive ', or some variant thereof, is employed to describe her tone of voice and way of speaking.

Mrs. Gaskell's eye for significant detail is put to good service. There is Clare's trick of hand-kissing[333]; and there is her indul-

---

[325] *Works*, VIII, 461.

[326] *Works*, VIII, 366.

[327] *Works*, VIII, 366. In a letter to Marianne (only the last part of which is in the Gaskell Section, Brotherton Collection, Leeds University Library), Mrs. Gaskell mentions a similar phrase—' like a slate-pencil on/ slate '—being employed by Catherine Winkworth to describe the effect Annie Shaen's singing used to have on her. The relevant passage is quoted, though rather inaccurately, by Miss Hopkins (*Elizabeth Gaskell*, pp. 307-308). This [February or March 1851] letter occurs as *G.L.*, No. 116 (in a footnote Chapple and Pollard indicate that their [?February 1852] dating is probably incorrect).

[328] *Works*, VIII, 358.

[329] *Works*, VIII, 108.

[330] *Works*, VIII, 207 : a minor typographical error has been corrected.

[331] E.g. Whitfield, *Mrs Gaskell*, pp. 183-184: cf. ffrench, *Mrs. Gaskell*, p 99: cf. Hopkins, *Elizabeth Gaskell*, p. 287. Hopkins, *Elizabeth Gaskell*, p. 286: cf. Allott, *Elizabeth Gaskell*, pp. 34-35.

[332] E.g. *Works*, VIII, 14, 119, 372, 496, 527, 621.

[333] *Works*, VIII, 17, 751.

gence in ' the dirty, dog's-eared delightful novel from the Ashcombe circulating library, the leaves of which she turned over
with a pair of scissors '[334]. Like Squire Hamley, she had a
characteristic watch—a ' little foreign elegance that had hung
at her side so long, and misled her so often.'[335] Typical also
of Clare is her remark, on hearing about Lady Cumnor's illness, that she was glad she had already breakfasted as otherwise she would have been unable to eat a thing[336]. We may
note too her social hedonism, a quick calculation in snobbish
terms of the probable advantages and inconveniences of any
suggestion[337]. How ironical yet how fitting that this lover of
the artificial, this ' pretty, faded, elegant-looking woman,'[338]
should have, as she said, a sentimental feeling—or prejudice—
' " against bought flowers." '[339]

Despite her failings, the second Mrs. Gibson possessed re-
deeming features—features so much of a piece with her deficiencies as to render the portrait even more convincing. She was
usually placid, so rarely rude[340]; sarcasm never embittered her,
for she had difficulty in comprehending it[341]; nor was she one
to retain angry feelings or actively retaliate[342]. Her experience
of widowhood made her unwilling to expose Cynthia to a
similar fate[343]; and she confessed that her heart would be
broken if her girl ever ended up as an old maid[344]. Always
priding herself on being an affectionate and impartial step-
mother[345], she was, after her fashion, kind to Molly[346]—especially if Cynthia displeased her[347]. Among Clare's other good
points may be reckoned kindness to the poor[348] and assiduity

[334] *Works*, VIII, 148.
[335] *Works*, VIII, 160.
[336] *Works*, VIII, 565.
[337] *Works*, VIII, 553, 710-711.
[338] *Works*, VIII, 319.
[339] *Works*, VIII, 357.
[340] *Works*, VIII, 364.
[341] *Works*, VIII, 477.
[342] *Works*, VIII, 315.
[343] *Works*, VIII, 456.
[344] *Works*, VIII, 631.
[345] *Works*, VIII, 140, 142, 210, 280, 373, 444, 448, 527-529, 754.
[346] *Works*, VIII, 421, 607.
[347] *Works*, VIII, 400, 654.
[348] *Works*, VIII, 530.

in paying debts[349]. Probably her most distinctive virtue was
scrupulosity in minor matters, since she attached ' infinite importance to fulfilling small resolutions, made about indifferent
trifles without any reason whatever.'[350]

A consideration of the second Mrs. Gibson leads naturally to
a brief examination of two major themes : matrimony and deception. At the outset we remarked that *Wives and Daughters*
was not primarily a love-story. As with many authoresses, Mrs.
Gaskell's interest lay less in love for its own sake than in its
outcome, marriage; and almost certainly she intended the novel
to conclude with Molly's wedding to Roger Hamley.

When the tale opens, the Hamleys, a happily if incongruously matched couple, have been together for many years. In
not a few ways they recall the Buxtons of *The Moorland
Cottage*; for the ' " delicate and weakly " '[351] Mrs. Buxton pre-
figures the 'tender and good'[352] Mrs. Hamley, and each invalid
has a devoted husband[353]. Furthermore, themselves daughter-
less, both wives establish quasi-maternal relations with young
girls (Maggie and Molly), upon whom from the first their sweet
gentleness makes a deep impression[354]. Each dies in the course
of the novel[355]; but of Mrs. Hamley no less than of Mrs. Buxton would it be true to say that the memory of her patience
and contentment in suffering ' broods like a dove '[356] over those
left alive. Maggie, in remembering Mrs. Buxton, might well
have used the same lines as came into Molly's mind.

> . . . She was thinking again of Mrs. Hamley—
> > " Only the actions of the just
> > Smell sweet and blossom in the dust;"
> and " goodness," just then, seemed to her to be the only en-
> during thing in the world.[357]

The reader is told little of the union between Cynthia and
Mr. Henderson beyond the domestic details (which appeared so

---

[349] *Works*, VIII, 159.
[350] *Works*, VIII, 365.
[351] *Works*, II, 278.
[352] *Works*, VIII, 45.
[353] *Works*, II, 287-288; VIII, 46.
[354] *Works*, II, 285; VIII, 68.
[355] *Works*, II, 303; VIII, 251.
[356] *Works*, II, 383.
[357] *Works*, VIII, 253.

important to Cynthia's mother[358]) and the slightest hint that its
final outcome left something to be desired[359]. Indeed the most
memorable incident occasioned by the wedding concerns not
so much the couple themselves as Lady Cumnor. It is the scene
in which her ladyship instructs the future Mrs. Henderson on
the deference and obedience due to one's husband[360]—advice
she herself conspicuously failed to follow. Mr. Henderson was,
we may note, a barrister. Personable, well-mannered, even-
tempered, and kind, he was yet ' not without some of the cheerful flippancy of repartee which belonged to his age and profession, and which his age and profession are apt to take for
wit.'[361] Mrs. Gaskell's literary antipathy to lawyers doubtless
explains why, in her heroine's eyes, Mr. Henderson should have
been found slightly wanting[362].

Osborne's clandestine marriage combines the themes of
matrimony and deception. A recent critic may be right in remarking that ' [t]his secret marriage, and indeed the whole of
Osborne's character is . . . the most unsatisfactory part of the
book '[363]; nevertheless he is of interest as being the unfortunate
product of maternal idolization[364], thereby affording another
example of one of the authoress's favourite concerns. The affair
itself illustrates something Mrs. Gaskell often emphasized[365]—
the dangers of concealment. It also has its humorous aspect.
We smile at Molly's simplicity in thinking Osborne did not
look like a married man[366]; and we can, with Roger, appreciate
the irony of Osborne's listening to Cynthia's singing of a

---

[358] *Works,* VIII, 724, 752-754.
[359] *Works,* VIII, 638.
[360] *Works,* VIII, 705-706.
[361] *Works,* VIII, 701.
[362] *Works,* VIII, 701. On 8 September 1863 Mrs. Gaskell's daughter,
Florence, married Charles Crompton, Q.C.; but he had not the flippancy
typical of a clever young barrister, as Meta, writing on Wednesday
[8 April], informed Charles Eliot Norton in a letter, headed 7 April and
finished on 17 April [1863], now in the Harvard University Library:
bMS Am 1088 (2641).
[363] Pollard, *The Novels of Mrs. Gaskell,* p. 422: cont. Frederick
Greenwood's esteem for the delineation of Osborne, voiced in his
Concluding Remarks to *Wives and Daughters (Works,* VIII, 760).
[364] *Works,* VIII, 222.
[365] Even in *Cranford (Works,* II, 175).
[366] *Works,* VIII, 243-244: cf. 268.

pretty French ditty, playfully warning against matrimony[367]. We may even find it pleasantly ironical that, at the very time Squire Hamley was voicing his ambitious hopes about 'the grand, the high, and the wealthy marriage which Hamley of Hamley, as represented by his clever, brilliant, handsome son Osborne, might be expected to make'[368], that self-same son should be united to a quondam *bonne*. On the other hand the potential danger as well as the inherent irony of the situation comes out in a remark made by Clare (of all people—but then duplicity was the one thing which revolted her![369]).

> "Osborne married!" exclaimed Cynthia. "If ever a man looked a bachelor, he did. Poor Osborne! with his fair delicate elegance—he looked so young and boyish!"
> "Yes! it was a great piece of deceit, and I can't easily forgive him for it. Only think! If he had paid either of you any particular attention, and you had fallen in love with him! Why, he might have broken your heart, or Molly's either. I can't forgive him, even though he is dead, poor fellow!"[370]

Matrimony and deception are, as previously hinted, most conspicuously conjoined in the union of Clare and Mr. Gibson. The latter's first marriage was marred only by the early death of his wife, though he kept his grief to himself[371]. Mrs. Gaskell may have learnt something about second alliances from those of both her father and her uncle, the Knutsford surgeon[372]. Possibly even more important were her worries about what might happen if she were to die and her husband, who (like Mr. Gibson) was reserved in expressions of affection and sym-

---

[367] *Works*, VIII, 311.
[368] *Works*, VIII, 242: cf. 61-62, 287, 502.
[369] *Works*, VIII, 655.
[370] *Works*, VIII, 656.
[371] *Works*, VIII, 32-33.
[372] Peter Holland (1766-1855) married twice: his first wife was Mary Willetts; his second, Mary Whittaker (Holland, *The Lancashire Hollands*, p. 298). Dr. Holland's first wife died in 1803, and his second marriage took place at Bath in 1808, according to Hall (ed. "'Cranford' again: The Knutsford Letters, 1809-1824", Footnotes, p. i) and the Knutsford antiquarian, Alderman Thomas Beswick (as reported in "'Old Knutsford' recalled on author's birthdate", *Knutsford Guardian*, 28 September 1956). It is worth noting that some Holland-Whittaker letters (copies and originals), descriptive of Knutsford life in the early nineteenth century, are in the possession of Alderman Beswick (The Croft, Legh Road, Knutsford)

pathy towards his offspring, should marry again[373]. Quite likely
Miss Browning was voicing the novelist's own views about
widowers and their ways when she astutely explained that
utility rather than sentiment governed the choice of a second
spouse.

> " . . . Did you ever know a widower marry again for such
> trifles as those [elegance and prettiness]? It's always from a
> sense of duty of one kind or another—isn't it, Mr. Gibson?
> They want a housekeeper; or they want a mother for their
> children; or they think their last wife would have liked it."[374]

In the case of Molly's father the first two reasons held good :
he wanted a chaperone for his daughter[375]; and he had experienced domestic difficulties[376] which the presence of a wife might
have obviated. Hence he found himself ' drifting into matrimony.'[377] He was not, however, indifferent to the more personal
considerations rejected by the spinster : Clare's agreeable voice,
her tasteful clothes, and her graceful manner made him think
' he should be fortunate if he could win her, for his own sake.'[378]
If on the whole Mr. Gibson's approach to marriage was
rational rather than romantic, his motives were far from selfish.
Clare was equally calculating; yet she had in view only herself.
In the past, like Mr. Gibson[379], she had had love-affairs[380]; but
she subsequently came to look upon marriage mainly as a way
of escape from minor discomforts[381], a means to end all her

---

[373] These fears she insinuated when writing one Wednesday evening
[23 December 1840] to Mrs. Nancy Robson, her sister-in-law. The
original letter, whose dating presents problems, is in the Gaskell
Section, Brotherton Collection, Leeds University Library; but relevant
quotations are given, more or less accurately, by Miss Rubenius (*The
Woman Question in Mrs. Gaskell's Life and Works,* pp. 25, 27) and
Miss Hopkins (*Elizabeth Gaskell,* p. 309): it occurs as *G.L.,* No. 16 (to
?Anne Robson and dated [23 December 1841], according to Chapple and
Pollard).

[374] *Works,* VIII, 164. Miss Browning, we may recall, regarded
' " matrimony as a weakness to which some very worthy people are
prone " ' (*Works,* VIII, 581).

[375] *Works,* VIII, 83-84, 125-127, 151-152.

[376] *Works,* VIII, 83-84, 100, 113-114, 126.

[377] *Works,* VIII, 99.

[378] *Works,* VIII, 118.

[379] *Works,* VIII, 53-54, 58, 162: cf. Mr. Manning (*Works,* VII, 36-38)

[380] *Works,* VIII, 104, 752.

[381] *Works,* VIII, 159-160.

struggles[382]. Conjugal bliss, to her mind, meant that the husband
should do all the dirty work while his wife sat lady-like in
the drawing-room[383]. Nonetheless, though Mr. Gibson was of
greatest use in releasing her from toil, she did not dislike ' him
personally—nay, she even loved him in her torpid way '[384].
Like her husband's, Clare's first marriage had been one of the
heart[385]; her second was one of convenience—indeed, according
to Miss Hornblower, she would even ' " have been glad enough
to marry Mr. Preston " '[386], towards whom she had apparently
once made advances[387].

Matrimony provided Clare with what she wanted : ' a man
whom she liked, and who would be bound to support her
without any exertion of her own '[388]. Despite a few complaints
about the solitary life of a doctor's wife[389] and the limitations
of the medical as opposed to the legal profession[390], she did
' very well for herself.'[391] With Mr. Gibson things were much
less satisfactory. At the outset he spoke to Molly of the need
to establish a firm family bond[392]; yet such was never really
effected, partly because his wife's sentimental ideas on family
affection[393] were far from being his own, but chiefly because
Clare's moral code differed markedly from that of her husband[394]. This ethical incompatibility led not only to those petty
annoyances, deceptions, and subterfuges which so troubled
Molly, but also to Clare's much graver offence of trying to
profit from one of the surgeon's professional secrets. As regards
the former, Mr. Gibson could find comfort in ignoring her
faults and thinking rather of the advantages of the match[395];
experience taught him that silence acted ' as a great preserva-

[382] *Works,* VIII, 120.
[383] *Works,* VIII, 110.
[384] *Works,* VIII, 142.
[385] *Works,* VIII, 19-20, 104, 216, 258, 519-520, 607, 752.
[386] *Works,* VIII, 328.
[387] *Works,* VIII, 548.
[388] *Works,* VIII, 181.
[389] *Works,* VIII, 258.
[390] *Works,* VIII, 695, 753.
[391] *Works,* VIII, 418: cf. 487.
[392] *Works,* VIII, 199-200.
[393] *Works,* VIII, 487.
[394] *Works,* VIII, 448.
[395] *Works,* VIII, 204, 372-373.

tive against long inconsequential arguments '[396], and he was content enough if he got food, peace, and quiet[397]. It was when he discovered his spouse had abused her position as a doctor's wife[398] that the domestic situation distinctly deteriorated. Now acutely sensitive to her defects, Mr. Gibson became dry and sarcastic in manner[399], and a state of ' dumb discordancy '[400] arose between the pair.

The deception *motif* is further illustrated by Cynthia's concealment of her past with Mr. Preston[401], and even by her unwillingness to have the quasi-engagement with Roger noised abroad[402]. We have often drawn attention to Mrs. Gaskell's preoccupation with lies and evasions; so, rather than enumerate Cynthia's duplicities and reservations, we may point to a little incident typical both of her character and of her creator's artistic method. It is the response elicited by Mr. Gibson's promise to sugar the medical pill for his step-daughter.

> " Please don't! If you but knew how I dislike emulsions and disguises! I do want bitters—and if I sometimes—if I'm obliged to—if I'm not truthful myself, I do like truth in others—at least, sometimes!" She ended her sentence with another smile; but it was rather faint and watery.[403]

Besides Molly, the one to suffer most from Cynthia's devious ways is Roger Hamley, with whom she should never have entered into any sort of engagement, as Molly implied[404]. Moreover, not only did Cynthia fail to be frank about her ' underhand work '[405] with Mr. Preston, she felt no obligation to mention Mr. Coxe's previous offer[406]—nor, for that matter, did the author envisage she would inform Mr. Henderson about her quondam connexion with Roger[407]. Mrs. Gaskell's treatment of this—the amorous—side of Roger is, incidentally, among the less satisfactory aspects of *Wives and Daughters*. His relations with his father and his brother are much more convincing. In Frederick Greenwood's opinion, for example, the genius which put Mrs. Gaskell's later novels on a level with the finest ' works

[396] *Works*, VIII, 256.
[397] *Works*, VIII, 229.
[398] *Works*, VIII, 442-446.
[399] *Works*, VIII, 476-477.
[400] *Works*, VIII, 478.
[401] *Works*, VIII, 260-634.

[402] *Works*, VIII, 435, 448-451.
[403] *Works*, VIII, 361.
[404] *Works*, VIII, 549.
[405] *Works*, VIII, 552.
[406] *Works*, VIII, 472-473.
[407] *Works*, VIII, 757-758.

of art and observation '[408] of the time found unequalled expression in scenes like the one where Roger smokes a pipe with his father[409]. Certainly that episode is admirably executed, albeit, on a second reading, it may seem just a trifle contrived—perhaps because it came from the pen of a lady-novelist.

Roger Hamley affords another instance of a character drawn partly from life; for her outline of the plot suggests that Charles Darwin's exploits were at the back of the author's mind. Mrs. Gaskell was distantly connected to the Darwins[410]; and one of her daughters (Meta) had had Charles' sister as a travelling companion[411]. Both Dr. Sanders[412] and Miss Haldane[413] mention that Roger was supposed to have been modelled on Darwin. Indeed the novelist may even have sought his professional advice, since at the time of her death she was, according to Ward, trying ' to inform herself precisely through a scientific friend of the kind of public acknowledgment or appointment which Roger Hamley might have been likely to obtain on his return from his brilliantly successful biological expedition.'[414] On the other hand, although she (erroneously) rejects the Darwin parallel, Miss Rubenius is assuredly wise in stressing the striking resemblance between the picture of Roger given in the novel and the thumbnail sketch of her future son-in-law, Charles

---

[408] Concluding Remarks to *Wives and Daughters* (*Works,* VIII, 759).
[409] *Works,* VIII, 303-306.
[410] Chadwick, *Mrs. Gaskell,* p. 8; Haldane, *Mrs. Gaskell and Her Friends,* p. 17; and Hopkins, *Elizabeth Gaskell,* p. 19. Members of the Darwin family are mentioned more than once in the novelist's correspondence, the most relevant passage occurring in a letter to Eliza Fox written (apparently) one Friday evening, a copy of which is in the Gaskell Section, Brotherton Collection, Leeds University Library. There Mrs. Gaskell speaks of a forthcoming dinner-engagement at which she would meet Charles Darwin, a cousin of hers whom she had ' not seen for years,' since when he had ' been round the world ', he having ' volunteered to come up 15 miles [presumably from Down] to see ' her ' and dine at the Wedgwoods '. This [(possibly) 4 July 1851] letter occurs as *G.L.,* No. 99 (dated [?10 July ?1851] by Chapple and Pollard, who postulate an association with *G.L.,* No. 100 [13 July 1851]; if so, internal evidence suggests a date some six days prior to the one they conjecture).
[411] *Gaskell-Norton Letters,* ed. Whitehill, p. 62: *G.L.,* No. 476—see too Nos. 461, 553.
[412] *Elizabeth Gaskell,* p. 133.
[413] *Mrs. Gaskell and Her Friends,* p. 277.
[414] Ward, ed. *Works,* VIII, p. xvii.

Crompton, found in Mrs. Gaskell's letter of 13 July 1863 to Charles Eliot Norton[415].

In many works one discovers arresting observations which outlast their immediate contexts; nor does *Wives and Daughters* here disappoint. We have mentioned its fine passages of natural description; but there is also an inwardness of feeling for the living world, well exemplified by Molly's pity for the dying leaf[416]. Truths which only require stating to be recognized as such may be illustrated by the squire's remark that, though he had already lived longer than his father, he still thought of him as a very old man[417]. One thinks too of the psychological commonsense lying behind the novelist's comment that caution is the product of education[418]; or of her astute remark that people with great responsibilities are, on occasions, especially glad to submit to externally imposed decisions, much to the benefit of their mental health[419].

Such authorial *apperçus* merge into insights of a more autobiographical significance. Thus Molly's powerful affirmation of present living[420] and her father's stoical acceptance of somehow getting through one's troubles[421] indicate how Mrs. Gaskell probably responded in times of anguish, such as that following the appearance of her *Life of Charlotte Brontë*[422] or that occasioned by the death of her son. In passing we may note that Mrs. Hamley loses a child[423] and, more importantly, that scarlet fever twice strikes young children[424].

---

[415] The relevant extracts (from *Gaskell-Norton Letters,* ed. Whitehill, pp. 105-106) are given, more or less accurately, by Miss Rubenius (*The Woman Question in Mrs. Gaskell's Life and Works,* p. 269). The letter occurs as *G.L.,* No. 526.

[416] *Works,* VIII, 438-439.

[417] *Works,* VIII, 660: cf. Sylvia Robson's belief that her parents would live for ever (*Works,* VI, 137-138).

[418] *Works,* VIII, 664.

[419] *Works,* VIII, 116.

[420] *Works,* VIII, 154.

[421] *Works,* VIII, 663.

[422] During the Manchester Art Exhibition, towards the end of that stressful summer of 1857, Charlotte Brontë's biographer, despite sorrow and fatigue, strove to ' live in the present,' lashing herself ' up into being active '—as she informed Ellen Nussey in a letter of 30 December 1857, copies of which, once owned by Mr. J. T. Lancaster, belong to the present writer: *G.L.,* No. 385a.

[423] *Works,* VIII, 232.

[424] *Works,* VIII, 83-85, 744, 747.

It merely remains to stress how well *Wives and Daughters*
displays its author's fondness for repetition. We have already
indicated correspondences between the novel and such earlier
books as *The Moorland Cottage* and *Cranford*. With the latter
especially there are several minor links: for example, Hollingford[425] and Cranford[426] have, like Knutsford itself, their *Angel*
inns; in each work the same blotting-paper comparison is used
of verbal communication[427]; and in both macaroons appear as
card-party delicacies[428]. However it seems more pertinent to
emphasize how the Cranford spirit of kindness[429] is echoed
in *Wives and Daughters*. At one level such charitableness is
manifested in Hollingford's care for the invalid Molly[430], which
closely parallels what the sick Miss Brown experienced in Cranford[431] (not to mention the concern shown for Phillis in her
illness[432]). At another level, suggestive of Miss Matty's trust
and kindliness[433], it reveals itself in Miss Browning's admonition
never to repeat evil reports unless good could come thereby[434].

'Mr. Harrison's Confessions' has something Cranfordesque
about it; its very opening, like that of *Wives and Daughters*,
promises old-fashioned story-telling and evokes the atmosphere
of a by-gone world. Appropriately enough, all three contain
references to home-made wine; but there are differences of
emphasis. In two it provides an occasion for amusement, since
Jack Marshland's reactions to black-currant wine[435] explain
why Mr. Sheepshanks shuddered at the memory of what he
had tasted at Hollingford parties[436]. At Cranford too home-
made wine was tasted[437], though one cannot help recalling the

---

[425] *Works*, VIII, 246, 259.
[426] *Works*, II, 15.
[427] *Works*, VIII, 30; II, 97.
[428] *Works*, VIII, 278; II, 81.
[429] *Works*, II, 1.
[430] *Works*, VIII, 683.
[431] *Works*, II, 18-19.
[432] In *Cousin Phillis* (*Works*, VII, 102-107).
[433] *Works*, II, 173-174, 192.
[434] *Works*, VIII, 595.
[435] *Works*, V, 442.
[436] *Works*, VIII, 399. Captain Brown—in *Cranford* (*Works*, II, 31)—
apparently suffered in a similar way, though the wine he tasted was
not home-made.
[437] *Works*, II, 120, 163, 165.

sad associations cowslip held for Miss Matty[438]. In its medical
aspect also, ' Mr. Harrison's Confessions' has a slight affinity
with *Wives and Daughters,* since both Mr. Harrison[439] and Mr.
Gibson[440] began their careers as junior partners—and, in
addition, both unwittingly caused expectations of imminent
proposals to arise in female breasts[441].

Some links with *My Lady Ludlow* have earlier been suggested. Lady Ludlow herself is of a different nature from Lady
Cumnor, as Miss ffrench points out[442]. Nevertheless the two
peeresses shared an aristocratic disdain for physical comfort[443]
—and, incidentally, both lived at a time when bedrooms were
fitted out as bedrooms, not as sitting-rooms[444]. Molly's arrival
at Hamley Hall and the picture of its interior[445] recall the
coming of Margaret Dawson to Hanbury Court and the
description of the furnishings there[446] (though the Virginian
creeper becomes in the present novel a feature of Ashcombe
Manor-house[447], whose larger drawing-room reminded Molly of
Hamley[448]—and reminds us of Hanbury[449]).

We may conclude with a hotch-potch of similarities. Miss
Browning rejoiced in the power conferred by money[450], very
much as did Mary Barton[451]. Mrs. Gibson's admonitory anec-

[438] *Works,* II, 64.
[439] *Works,* V, 406.
[440] *Works,* VIII, 29-32.
[441] *Works,* V, 468-473; VIII, 163.
[442] ffrench, *Mrs. Gaskell,* pp. 74-75.
[443] *Works,* V, 43; VIII, 111.
[444] *Works,* V, 17; VIII, 172-173.
[445] *Works,* VIII, 67-74.
[446] *Works,* V, 13-18.
[447] *Works,* VIII, 174. Possibly the author was recalling what she
once saw at Lea Hurst: 'Virginian Creeper as gorgeous/ as can be '—
as Mrs. Gaskell described it one Saturday evening [14 October 1854]
to Catherine Winkworth (in a letter, apparently begun on Wednesday
evening [11 October], post-marked 15 and 16 October 1854, now in
the Gaskell Section, Brotherton Collection, Leeds University Library).
Relevant too, in the present context, are her comments on the austere
furnishings of the Miss Nightingales' bedrooms, found in the same
passage. This letter is quoted, though not fully nor wholly accurately,
by Miss Haldane (*Mrs. Gaskell and Her Friends,* pp. 98-104), whose
dating is erroneous; it occurs as *G.L.,* No. 211.
[448] *Works,* VIII, 176.
[449] *Works,* V, 45-46.
[450] *Works,* VIII, 166.
[451] *Works,* I, 16.

dote about the young lady who assumed mourning on the reported death of a man to whom she was never engaged[452]
brings to mind Bessy Corney's conduct[453], with distant echoes
of the story of Phillis Holman. A second link between *Wives
and Daughters* and both *Sylvia's Lovers* and *Cousin Phillis* is
provided by Mr. Preston, whose ways with women[454] seem not
unlike those of Kinraid[455] and those believed about Holdsworth[456]. *A Dark Night's Work*, besides its Knutsford background, has two minor points in common with *Wives and
Daughters*: in touching a letter from Roger, Molly's emotion[457]
parallels (though in the reverse direction, so to speak) that of
Ellinor who, while preparing a parcel for Mr. Corbet, thought
that *he* (her former suitor) might be the very person to untie
the knot[458]; secondly, Ellinor's feeling that the murder of
Dunster made all that had gone before part of ' the old life of
yesterday '[459] connects with Molly's experience on seeing the
letter to Squire Hamley which Cynthia had written before
Osborne's death[460]—Mr. Hale's decision to resign affected Margaret in a similar way[461].

The penultimate affinity in this medley is that between Margaret Hale's merely bowing in response to Mr. Thornton's unexpectedly proffered hand[462] and Roger Hamley's reaction to a
similar gesture of friendship[463]. The final similarity, reserved
till now since with it we virtually come full circle, is made

[452] *Works*, VIII, 435.
[453] *Works*, VI, 246, 249, 260-261, 349, 460-461.
[454] *Works*, VIII, 514-515, 548, 558.
[455] *Works*, VI, 88-89, 174, 217-218, 222-223, 238, 244, 461.
[456] *Works*, VII, 89, 96.
[457] *Works*, VIII, 479-480.
[458] *Works*, VII, 541. Mrs. Gaskell expressed a comparable sentiment in
her letter to Norton of 5 February 1865 (*Gaskell-Norton Letters*, ed.
Whitehill, p. 119: *G.L.*, No. 560).
[459] *Works*, VII, 467.
[460] *Works*, VIII, 648.
[461] *Works*, IV, 46.
[462] *Works*, IV, 98-99.
[463] *Works*, VIII, 95-96. Mrs. Gaskell was herself unsure about when
—' in what stage of intimacy '—to begin shaking hands, and so, on her
meeting Macready, there had been a ' backwards and forwards ' of
hands which had ' ended by [their] not shaking at all ' (as she told
Eliza Fox in a letter of 26 November 1849, a copy of part of which
—*G.L.*, No. 55—is in the Gaskell Section, Brotherton Collection, Leeds
University Library).

possible by a phrase of Mr. Gibson's, occurring among the last paragraphs ever written by the novelist.

> "Come, come! Remember, I belong to the last generation," said Mr. Gibson.[464]

What we remember is that one of Mrs. Gaskell's earliest articles, the forerunner of *Cranford* and of all things Cranfordian, was entitled 'The Last Generation in England'[465].

We have noticed detailed correspondences between other stories and *Wives and Daughters*. Does the author repeat herself within the novel? In some respects she does. To increase the verisimilitude of the dialogue, she uses a certain stylistic device three or more times—that of making the speaker break off what he was saying rather than mention something which had just come into his mind[466]. At least twice she employs metaphorically an expression about seeing 'the wrong side of the tapestry'[467]. Both Osborne[468] and Squire Hamley[469] adopted the same posture at the fireplace. Mr. Gibson's soft whistling signified contentment[470]; the squire's, on the other hand, indicated annoyance[471] (we recall that another Gaskellian whistler, Faith Benson, did so 'when surprised or displeased'[472]). Finally there is Mrs. Gaskell's reiteration of the notion that sentiments are defined when verbalized[473]: she herself once preferred not to shape her thoughts and feelings by putting them into words —for 'after all words are coarse things.'[474]

---

[464] *Works*, VIII, 754.

[465] *Sartain's Union Magazine*, V (1849), 45-48.

[466] *Works*, VIII, 233, 560, 651. One might include an interrupted speech of Mr. Gibson's (*Works*, VIII, 702).

[467] *Works*, VIII, 401, 525.

[468] *Works*, VIII, 238.

[469] *Works*, VIII, 227.

[470] *Works*, VIII, 458.

[471] *Works*, VIII, 214.

[472] *Works*, III, 111. We may note that Miss Galindo—in *My Lady Ludlow* (*Works*, V, 143-144)—whistled so that her femininity might be forgotten. However Mr. Bell—of *North and South*—was a silent whistler (*Works*, IV, 420); so was Dr. Morgan, from *Sylvia's Lovers* (*Works*, VI, 416).

[473] *Works*, VIII, 152, 346. Other references to defining mentally and emotionally include *Works*, VIII, 356, 373, 423.

[474] So, referring to the reactions evoked by some Pre-Raphaelite paintings, Mrs. Gaskell informed Norton in a letter of 25-30 October [1859]—*Gaskell-Norton Letters*, ed. Whitehill, p. 38: *G.L.*, No. 444.

It seems fitting that Mrs. Gaskell's last novel should illustrate in miniature elements of observation and invention writ large in the whole corpus: a heavy debt to personal experience; thematic repetitions; the recurrence of certain character-types; favourite turns of style. By concentrating on this aspect of the work, one can easily forget that *Wives and Daughters* was, and probably still is, regarded by most Gaskell devotees ' as the most artistically perfect of all her productions '[475]. Nevertheless perhaps something has been accomplished, at least by way of quotation, to support such a judgement.

---

[475] Ward, ed. *Works,* VIII, p. xiii.

SECTION III

Columns of Gossip from Paris
in *The Pall Mall Gazette* (1865)

Whilst engaged on *Wives and Daughters,* Mrs. Gaskell contributed two series (one anonymous, the other pseudonymous) to George Smith's newly founded *Pall Mall Gazette.* These form an appropriate conclusion to the writer's canon, if only because the first reveals primarily her keen observation whereas the second shows rather her lively invention.

Dr. Sanders mentioned that Mrs. Gaskell 'gathered bits of Paris news and wrote it up in a gossipy form for *The Pall Mall,* going, her daughter said, from her room at the very top of a very high house to a mail box some distance away after midnight each day to post her articles.'[1] However he did not attempt an identification. Apparently the only person to do so was Graham Owens, who lists[2] three articles of Paris gossip[3] among the doubtful works of the author, albeit advancing no reasons for this dubious attribution.

The articles are ephemeral in nature, though they evidently

---

[1] Sanders, *Elizabeth Gaskell,* p. 140. Professor Whitfield is (erroneously) given as the source of this statement by Miss Haldane (*Mrs. Gaskell and Her Friends,* p. 294, fn.). The house would be the hotel whose top storeys accommodated Mme Mohl, with whom the author was then staying; Mrs. Gaskell's account of this visit is given in her letter of 27 March to Mrs. Emily Shaen (*née* Winkworth)—quoted by Miss Haldane (*Mrs. Gaskell and Her Friends,* pp. 296-300, see esp. pp. 296-297), who, however, has the year as 1863 although such internal evidence as a reference to *Wives and Daughters* unmistakably puts the letter in 1865—: *G.L.,* No. 564 (the year being given as [?1865] by Chapple and Pollard).

[2] In the Bibliography of Graham Owens, 'Town and Country in the Life and Work of Mrs. Gaskell and Mary Russell Mitford', M.A. thesis, University College of North Wales, Bangor, 1953, pp. 400, 402.

[3] 'A Column of Gossip from Paris', *The Pall Mall Gazette: An Evening Newspaper and Review,* Saturday 25 March 1865, p. 4 (Vol. I, No. 41, p. 388 of the bound edition). 'A Column of Gossip from Paris', *The Pall Mall Gazette,* Tuesday 28 March 1865, p. 9 (Vol. I, No. 43, p. 417 of the bound edition). 'A Letter of Gossip from Paris', *The Pall Mall Gazette,* Tuesday 25 April 1865, p. 11 (Vol. I, No. 66, p. 695 of the bound edition).

came from the pen of an observant person possessing a fair knowledge of the French social, political, and literary scene at the time of the Second Empire. Probably the most profitable thing to do will be to endeavour to say why this journalism can confidently be assigned to Mrs. Gaskell.

According to Mme Mohl[4], Mrs. Gaskell stayed with her in Paris from 12 March to 20 April. This period covers that of the first two articles; the third, dated ' Paris, *Monday* [24 or, perhaps, 17 April 1865]', could easily have been despatched after Mrs. Gaskell left her friend's yet largely composed before she quit the French capital. Internal evidence clinches the matter.

There are, firstly, links with *Wives and Daughters,* much of which the author wrote in Mme Mohl's ' larger *salon*, standing up before the mantelpiece '[5]. In the articles of 25 March and 28 March, the columnist respectively refers to Sir Charles Grandison and quotes the first verse of a Paris street-song dealing with M. de la Palisse; the novel contains Mrs. Gaskell's only other literary reference to Grandison[6] and her only other poetical quotation (the same lines) on the subject of M. de la

---

[4] Whose statement to this effect may be found in a letter of 18 May 1865, quoted in Simpson, *Letters and Recollections of Julius and Mary Mohl,* p. 219.

[5] Simpson, *Letters and Recollections of Julius and Mary Mohl,* p. 126. As early as 1854 the author had already been acquainted with Mme Mohl for many years, according to Mrs. Gaskell's letter to Eliza Fox of Monday 24 [25] December 1854—quoted by Miss Haldane (*Mrs. Gaskell and Her Friends,* pp. 245-247, esp. p. 246) and briefly by Miss Rubenius (*The Woman Question in Mrs. Gaskell's Life and Works,* p. 41, fn. 3), though their transcripts fail to tally exactly both with each other and with the copy of part of this letter in the Gaskell Section, Brotherton Collection, Leeds University Library—: *G.L.,* No. 222 (the day being given as [?25] by Chapple and Pollard).

[6] *Works,* VIII, 28. When tracing Mrs. Gaskell's quotations and citations, one should consult the invaluable Appendix III of Rubenius, *The Woman Question in Mrs. Gaskell's Life and Works,* pp. 284-370. Mr. Charles B. P. Bosanquet is described as having ' manners à la Sir/ Charles Grandison ' in Mrs. Gaskell's letter to Thurston Holland of Saturday 5 February [1859], now in the Rutgers University Library (MS A Symington Collection ·G2535); she also mentions ' his grave Sir-Charles-Grandeson [*sic*] manner/' in her letter of 16 April 1861 to Charles Eliot Norton—deposited in the Harvard University Library (the relevant phrase being slightly misquoted in Whitehill, ed. *Gaskell-Norton Letters,* p. 81). These letters respectively appear as *G.L.,* Nos. 411, 485.

Palisse[7]. Secondly, we may remark that the first article contrasts the widowed Duchess di Colonna (formerly Mlle d'Affry), a well-known sculptress, with the Princess Metternich, notorious for her fast way of life; that the second names M. Jules Simon; and that the third speaks of Mlle Patti, the famous singer. All these celebrities are mentioned, for the most part in very similar terms, in various contemporary letters by Mme Mohl[8], a likely source for much of the gossip. She once commented on Mrs. Gaskell's apparent habit of " scenting clever *mots* "[9] : several appear in the *Pall Mall Gazette* pieces; but possibly Mme Mohl was herself responsible for gathering some of them. Finally, we should note that the second paragraph of the 25 March contribution concerns the *Labienus* satire : significantly a transcript of this same pamphlet was made by Mrs. Gaskell for her publisher[10].

---

[7] *Works,* VIII, 494-495.

[8] Simpson, *Letters and Recollections of Julius and Mary Mohl,* pp. 220; 208; 208, 209, 222-223; 223. The letters range from 8 March 1864 to 8 April 1866.

[9] Quoted in Chadwick, *Mrs. Gaskell,* p. 312.

[10] The relevant extract from Smith's Reminiscences (in [Huxley] *The House of Smith Elder,* pp. 76-78) may be found in Hopkins, *Elizabeth Gaskell,* pp. 222-223. There are references to the satire and to M. Mohl in an undated letter from Mrs. Gaskell to George Smith, written (probably from London in April 1865) after her return from Paris; this letter is now in the archives of Sir John Murray, and appears as *G.L.,* No. 565 (located [London] and dated [?April 1865] by Chapple and Pollard).

SECTION IV

'A Parson's Holiday':
Letters to the Editor in *The Pall Mall Gazette* (1865)

The second *Pall Mall Gazette* series, hitherto undiscovered, came out between 11 August and 5 September 1865. Five in number, these contributions appear in the 'Correspondence' section under the title of 'A Parson's Holiday'[1]; all but the penultimate (which is unsigned) bear the initials M.N. The letters, purportedly written to the Editor by a Dissenting minister, Mark N., tell of the correspondent's difficulties and adventures in attempting to escape from his congregation for one month's holiday in the year. Throughout the manner is humorous, and the treatment of Nonconformity benevolently ironical.

The external evidence for adding these short pieces to the canon consists of a letter by Mrs. Gaskell to her daughter, Marianne, written from Manchester one Saturday morning (almost certainly 2 September 1865) in which she mentions Smith's request 'for another letter article/ for Pall Mall Gaz *by return*/ of post'[2]. On the following Tuesday (5 September) the 'Correspondence' columns of *The Pall Mall Gazette* contained what was to be the last communication from M.N.

Mrs. Gaskell's letter to Marianne indicates that she was be-

[1] M.N., 'A Parson's Holiday', *The Pall Mall Gazette*, Friday 11 August 1865, p. 3 (Vol. II, No. 159, p. 51 of the bound edition). M.N., 'A Parson's Holiday', *The Pall Mall Gazette*, Tuesday 15 August 1865, pp. 3-4 (Vol. II, No. 162, pp. 87-88 of the bound edition). M.N., 'A Parson's Holiday', *The Pall Mall Gazette*, Thursday 17 August 1865, pp. 3-4 (Vol. II, No. 164, pp. 111-112 of the bound edition). [M.N.] 'A Parson's Holiday', *The Pall Mall Gazette*, Monday 21 August 1865, pp. 3-4 (Vol. II, No. 167, pp. 147-148 of the bound edition). M.N., 'A Parson's Holiday', *The Pall Mall Gazette*, Tuesday 5 September 1865, pp. 3-4 (Vol. II, No. 180, pp. 303-304 of the bound edition).
[2] This letter is in the collection of Mrs. Margaret Trevor Jones. Its exact dating depends on the rather complicated chronological relationships among several letters dealing with Mrs. Gaskell's newly-acquired house at Alton. The visit to London from Wednesday to Friday, mentioned in the present letter, can fairly confidently be placed as being from 30 August to 1 September 1865; Chapple and Pollard, whose dating (*G.L.*, No. 582) concurs with ours, punctuate slightly differently.

hindhand with *Wives and Daughters,* and many others[3] of this period show the strain under which the author was working. In such circumstances it would be unjust to carp at the quality of journalism composed more or less at a moment's notice. The novel, obviously, made the greatest demands on her artistic powers; the articles at best only called for inventive competence. Nevertheless one of Mrs. Gaskell's characteristics is that of rarely disappointing: with her ' one can be sure of . . . pleasure '[4]. Even here this holds good. One cannot, of course, expect consistency in minor details—she forgot trifles[5]—; yet the manner is delightful. The nearest parallel appears to be ' Mr. Harrison's Confessions'; for the humour depends on situation rather than on character, though to some one acquainted with Mrs. Gaskell's other works the characters are familiar enough to acquire overtones (so to speak) from their previous appearances.

Probably the best way to confirm that Mrs. Gaskell did indeed write what on external grounds we have ascribed to her will be to examine these articles in the light of her earlier publications. This will also serve to demonstrate once more how her invention produced and repeated distinctive incidents and characters.

We can begin by noticing the proper name of Donkin[6]; this

³ See, for instance, *G.L.,* Nos. 336 (possible), 561, 563-565, 570, 572, 575a, 576, 588; also relevant is Mrs. Gaskell's Tuesday [11 April 1865] letter to Mme Schérer (in the Parrish Collection at the Princeton University Library).

⁴ Marghanita Laski, ' Words from Mrs. Gaskell—I ', *Notes and Queries,* CCVI (N.S. VIII—September 1961), 339.

⁵ E.g. (i) Unless the minister's wife had borne three more offspring within six years, it is difficult to reconcile the six children of the first letter with the three mentioned in the second and third. (ii) In the second article Jemmy is one of the three children; but these are called Mary, Bessy, and Bob in the third; and the fourth tells of the birth of Johnny, the second child. (iii) The third contribution refers to Boscombe as if we had already met the name, which we had not, in the second letter. (iv) Mrs. Woodhouse's sister is Miss Donkin, according to the second article; yet the third gives her brother as Mr. Mappin. (v) Although the third missive speaks of the parson's wife's qualms on having to leave her children in England for three weeks, the foreign holiday lasted for a month, according to the fifth letter. (vi) In the fourth article the author seems to have forgotten the name of the Dissenting minister's town, mentioned in the first three letters—at any rate she skilfully avoids using it.

⁶ *The Pall Mall Gazette,* 15 August 1865, p. 3.

also occurs in ' Morton Hall '[7], *North and South*[8], *My Lady Ludlow*[9], *Sylvia's Lovers*[10], and (perhaps most significantly) in *Wives and Daughters*[11]. Although Brown and Jones, both contained in the third article[12], are found much more often than Donkin in the rest of the Gaskell canon (each likewise appearing in *Wives and Daughters*[13]), they are names which any writer might employ. Higgins, rarer than Brown or Jones, but less so than Donkin, is used in ' The Squire's Story '[14], *North and South*[15], and *Sylvia's Lovers*[16] as well as in the present series[17].

The opening paragraphs of the first article strongly recall the little Nonconformist world discovered at Eltham by Paul Manning[18]; their gentle irony is enhanced for those who know that the writer was, if not a minister, then at least a minister's wife. They also, albeit to a slighter degree, recall Cranford and Duncombe; so it is fitting that the second letter should introduce us to Mrs. Woodhouse and Miss Donkin. These sisters, though they have something in common with all other Cranford-style ladies, are most nearly akin, by virtue of their more undesirable attributes, to the Duncombe couple—the Misses Tomkinson— of ' Mr. Harrison's Confessions '.

Mrs. Dunne, the nurse in the fourth article, might well be sister to the incomparable Sally of *Ruth*. Like her[19], she considered that, as a Churchwoman, she was bestowing a great favour by working for Dissenters; and, also like her, she readily evokes a smile—in proof whereof one may quote the following extract.

" . . . My ladies never reads, and never is read to, except out of the Holy Bible on a Sunday, which does not try the head.

[7] *Works*, II, 465.
[8] *Works*, IV, 68.
[9] *Works*, V, 215.
[10] *Works*, VI, 50, 229, 301.
[11] *Works*, VIII, 37.
[12] *The Pall Mall Gazette*, 17 August 1865, pp. 3-4.
[13] *Works*, VIII, 26, 187, 319, 328, 754; 42, 237, 520.
[14] *Works*, II, 534, 539.
[15] *Works*, IV, 83, 115.
[16] *Works*, VI, 364.
[17] *The Pall Mall Gazette*, 17 August 1865, p. 4.
[18] *Works*, VII, 1-6.
[19] *Works*, III, 165.

You may be sure, sir, if you've got a life of Mrs. Anybody it
will end in a death; and deaths is pathetic; and my ladies
must not have their feelings touched, because of the milk. ... "[20]

Besides exemplifying Mrs. Dunne's amusing forthrightness,
this passage illustrates Mrs. Gaskell's capacity for being humorous at her own expense. She too had written a biography which
ended, inevitably, with the death of her subject. More importantly, she had written *Mary Barton*; and had not Maria
Edgeworth complained to the novelist's cousin[21] about the
numerous death-bed scenes contained in that book?

If we turn from the characters to the situations in our search
for correspondences, what could be more farcical *à la* ' Mr.
Harrison's Confessions' than an incident recounted in the fourth
article? There the pastor tells how he unsuccessfully attempted
to hide from the eyes of his chapel-warden a pack of cards
with which he and his wife had been sinfully indulging in
beggar-my-neighbour—an episode, incidentally, that recalls the
confusion of Squire Hamley when caught playing cards before
family prayers[22].

Also suggesting a Gaskellian origin is the fact that these *Pall
Mall Gazette* contributions contain a number of witticisms—

---

[20] *The Pall Mall Gazette,* 21 August 1865, p. 3.
[21] Maria Edgeworth's letter of 27 December 1848 to Miss Mary
Holland is fully, and more or less accurately, quoted in Waller, ed.
Letters Addressed to Mrs Gaskell by Celebrated Contemporaries, pp. 9-12.
In an undated letter to her sister, Lady Beaufort, probably written in
December 1848 or early in 1849, Maria Edgeworth remarks: ' There
are about a dozen too many deaths—and death is unavoidable and
deathbed scenes in my opinion very objectionable in a moral and social
point of view. Deathbed spies are hateful moralists—But after boring
you with all this I advise you to read the book and you will do it
more justice than I have done. It is written by Mrs. Gaskell a friend
and I believe a relation of the Hollands.'—Extract from a copy of a
copy, most kindly furnished by Mr. J. A. V. Chapple (Dept. of English,
Manchester University), and quoted by his permission. Mr. Chapple's
brother-in-law, Mr. James L. Bolton, who supplied this copy of a copy,
remarks that there is some indication that Maria Edgeworth wrote to
Mrs. Gaskell, though there were none of the latter's letters among the
Edgeworth papers he was examining in connection with work for the
Victoria County History Series. Miss Edgeworth also mentions *Mary
Barton* death-beds in a letter of 2 February 1849 to Mme Belloc (quoted
by Louise Swanton Belloc in her prefatory Notice to *Cousine Phillis,
L'Oeuvre d'une Nuit de Mai, Le Héros du Fossoyeur,* by Mrs. Gaskell,
trans. E.-D. Forgues, Paris: Librairie de L. Hachette et Cie, 1867, p. 9).
[22] *Works,* VIII, 76-77.

or rather Cranfordisms. Thus the minister says of his wife's speech that it ' was not argumentative, but it was convincing, which argument is not always.'[23] They have too a few sentiments that would have been familiar to Miss Matty[24], as when the pastor's wife begins to wonder what forbidden pleasures are like[25].

No small measure of Mrs. Gaskell's success in first-person narratives derives from the slightly ironical treatment of a *naïve* story-teller. In the present articles one finds instances of this. For example, the minister is made to call, with engaging simplicity, the placing of bets a scientific experiment—until he loses, when he sees it to be ' " regular gambling after all " '[26].

To complete our examination of the internal indications of authorship, we may note that in the third letter there is a reference to *The Arabian Nights*. Mrs. Gaskell was obviously fond of this compilation; for she frequently[27] makes allusions to its contents.

It is interesting to speculate how much the articles owe to personal experience. As a minister's wife, Mrs. Gaskell knew almost all there was to know about ministerial duties; yet, at the same time, she had the advantage of a degree of detachment. She never considered that, by virtue of being married to the *Rev.* William Gaskell, she had any obligations to his Unitarian congregation, even though in fact she did much good work among the poor and with Sunday-School pupils[28]. Doubt-

---

[23] *The Pall Mall Gazette*, 17 August 1865, p. 3: cf. the Cranfordesque opinions about rational arguments expressed in *Cranford* (*Works*, II, 1, 155), ' Morton Hall ' (*Works*, II, 484), and *Wives and Daughters* (*Works*, VIII, 165).

[24] Who said of her visit to an old bachelor, ' " I only hope it is not improper; so many pleasant things are! " ' (*Works*, II, 41).

[25] *The Pall Mall Gazette*, 21 August 1865, p. 3.

[26] *The Pall Mall Gazette*, 17 August 1865, p. 3.

[27] Miss Rubenius (*The Woman Question in Mrs. Gaskell's Life and Works*, p. 359) remarks upon these allusions; but she supplies no references: a few examples may be found in *Cranford, The Moorland Cottage, North and South*, and *Wives and Daughters* (*Works*, II, 40, 185; 288; IV, 92-93; VIII, 163). Mrs. Gaskell also mentions *The Arabian Nights* in her letters: e.g. *G.L.*, Nos. 195, 476.

[28] An appropriate source for these remarks is one of her obituaries— M[ary Jane Robberds (Mrs. Charles James Herford)], ' The late Mrs. Gaskell ', *The Unitarian Herald*, Vol. V, No. 238 (Friday 17 November 1865), pp. 366-367, esp. p. 366.

less too, being a feminine onlooker, she would appreciate the
humour of situations in a way denied to her husband. The parson's initial letter was occasioned by his difficulties in fleeing
from his flock; significantly Mr. Gaskell tried to escape not
only from his flock but also from his family in his search for
freedom from responsibility[29].

The minister's point about the effect of railways in spreading
respectability has only to be stated to be accepted. In one sense
the Victorian Age began with the Railway Era. Like her fellow-
novelists[30], Mrs. Gaskell was aware of the changes which came
over English life with the advent of the train; and many of
her stories take place ' before railroads were, and before their
consequences, the excursion-trains,'[31] were felt. Her honeymoon
had been spent touring North Wales by coach[32]; but nearly a
quarter of a century later it appeared impossible for the pastor
to find ' retired nooks in England and Wales, where the cheap-
ness of provisions was extraordinary, and where the inhabitants
were too rustic and too busy to spy much after the affairs of
others '[33]—because, by then, the railways had already 'ploughed
up the village mind '[34].

The second article recounts the minister's adventures some
seven years before at ' a little primitive village, situated on a
lovely bay '[35]. It seems not entirely fortuitous that this description should fit Mrs. Gaskell's favourite retreat, Silverdale[36],
where she had spent a summer holiday in 1858[37].

The third and subsequent letters tell of the Continental tour

[29] The evidence is ably marshalled by Miss Rubenius (*The Woman
Question in Mrs. Gaskell's Life and Works*, pp. 26-27).

[30] The importance of railway-building for Victorian novelists is well
indicated in Tillotson, *Novels of the Eighteen-Forties*, 1956, pp. 105-
109.

[31] *Wives and Daughters* (*Works*, VIII, 325).

[32] The best account of this honeymoon may be found in Hopkins,
Elizabeth Gaskell, pp. 51-52.

[33] *The Pall Mall Gazette*, 11 August 1865, p. 3.

[34] *The Pall Mall Gazette*, 11 August 1865, p. 3.

[35] *The Pall Mall Gazette*, 15 August 1865, p. 3.

[36] What Silverdale looked like in 1861 can be seen from the reproduction of Meta Gaskell's water-colour, which forms the frontispiece to
Vol. III (*Ruth and Other Tales, &c.*) of the Knutsford Edition.

[37] Mrs. Gaskell was, as she told Norton in her letter of 25 July
[1858], ' never . . . disappointed in coming back to Silverdale.'—
Gaskell-Norton Letters, ed. Whitehill, p. 28: *G.L.*, No. 401.

on which the minster and his wife embarked the following year. Mrs. Gaskell often travelled abroad; and in this connexion probably most relevant are the Rhine trip she made with her husband in 1841[38] and her visit to Pontresina of August 1864[39]: the latter is especially important, since there can be little doubt memories of that visit[40] went into the fifth article.

Recollections of other holidays may well have stimulated the composition of these pieces. There was, for example, the time spent at Auchencairn, " far away from newspapers or railways or shops, or any sign of the world "[41]. As was Silverdale to London, so was Auchencairn to Silverdale[42]; yet places as secluded as Auchencairn (itself in North Britain) became increasingly difficult to discover as the Age of Steam progressed. The spread of railways, with the consequential growth of 'respectability', had to be paid for, these articles remind us, in terms

[38] See Hopkins, *Elizabeth Gaskell,* pp. 63-65.

[39] See Chadwick, *Mrs. Gaskell,* p. 298.

[40] With her four daughters, Thurstan Holland, and Charlie Crompton. Mrs. Gaskell subsequently described Pontresina as 'primitive, cheap & bracing' (in her letter to Norton of 5 February 1865, deposited in the Harvard University Library—the relevant passage being unprinted, though the omission is indicated, in Whitehill, ed. *Gaskell-Norton Letters,* p. 120). In a letter to George Smith of Monday 25 July [1864]—now in the archives of Sir John Murray—the author had spoken of planning to go to Pontresina, 'a cheap, unknown-*ish* place', with the intention of living quietly there. Similar reasons caused the parson and his wife to pay their visit. Perhaps, like them, Mrs. Gaskell's party found the spot less secluded than had been expected, though there are no complaints about Pontresina in her letter to Mrs. Nancy Robson of 2 January 1865 (a copy of which is in the Gaskell Section, Brotherton Collection, Leeds University Library). The novelist took 'a quiet room outside the village to work in peacefully. There she finished a great part of her last story, *Wives and Daughters.* She was', we are also told, 'very beautiful and gentle, with a sweet-toned voice, and a particularly well-formed hand.'—*Recollections of a Happy Life, Being the Autobiography of Marianne North,* ed. Mrs. John Addington Symonds, 2 vols., London and New York: Macmillan and Co., 1892, I, 34. Mrs. Gaskell's letters occur as *G.L.,* Nos. 560, 553, 558.

[41] Quoted by Ward (ed. *Works,* I, p. xxxix) from Mrs. Gaskell's Auchencairn letter to George Smith of Wednesday 29 June [1859], now in the archives of Sir John Murray. A fairly accurate quotation from the same letter (*G.L.,* No. 434) also appears in Hopkins, *Elizabeth Gaskell,* p. 211.

[42] A comparison made by Mrs. Gaskell in a [Summer 1859] letter from 'Mr Turnbull's/ Auchencairn/ *By* Dumfries/ N B/' to 'dear Harriette'; this letter is in the Parrish Collection at the Princeton University Library, and occurs as *G.L.,* No. 436 (dated [c.July 1859] by Chapple and Pollard, who punctuate the heading slightly differently).

of less privacy, less solitude, even less personal (if more efficient[43]) postal services.

Improved communications influence social behaviour, though not necessarily for the better. As a (historical) novelist, Mrs. Gaskell was a sensitive observer of change, keenly conscious of the contrast between past and present. Here this awareness is finely expressed when, looking back over the years, the parson recalls the mentality of an earlier generation of rustics.

> Sometimes a slow wonder stole into their minds as to the inducement which brought strangers to the place; but an instinct told them that, if they began to try to account for other folks' actions, it might prove to be an interminable trouble, and so they solemnly let them alone.[44]

It is apposite that we should close with a quotation suggestive of an idyllic age; for much of Mrs. Gaskell's work has that flavour about it. To Rosamond Lehmann, indeed, the author was typified by an ' orchard, sheltered, fragrant, sweet and wholesome to taste.'[45]

---

[43] Besides the unlettered postman mentioned in the first article (*The Pall Mall Gazette,* 11 August 1865, p. 3), we may notice his irresponsible counterpart in *Cousin Phillis* (*Works,* VII, 90-91); at Cranford also the postal services left much to be desired (*Works,* II, 142-143). It is interesting that the Silverdale postman could not be trusted; for, given to drinking, he was inclined to drop or mislay his letters—as Mrs. Gaskell told ' dear Edward,' (probably) a (Holland) cousin, in a letter from Silverdale of Monday 29 July [1861], now in the collection of Mrs. Margaret Trevor Jones: *G.L.,* No. 492 (the recipient being identified as Edward Holland by Chapple and Pollard).

[44] *The Pall Mall Gazette,* 11 August 1865, p. 3.

[45] Lehmann, intro. *Wives and Daughters,* by Mrs. Gaskell, p. 5.

SECTION V

'Two Fragments of Ghost Stories' (1906)

In examining Mrs. Gaskell's literary output, our approach has been to consider her writings in their published order; when a work was not printed till after the author's death, then the date of composition determined its place in our study. Such a procedure is not possible with 'Two Fragments of Ghost Stories', pieces which first appeared in the penultimate volume of Ward's Knutsford Edition (1906)[1]. Found among Mrs. Gaskell's papers, they bore no 'date or other clue to the period of their production'[2].

These fragments seem to have been headed 'Ghost Stories' by their composer[3]. Such a designation certainly indicates the nature of the existing portion of one of the tales; for the first piece, from its outset, arouses interest in what the avowedly rational narrator terms 'an unexplained circumstance'[4]—the subsequently related appearance (or apparition) of a woman and child[5]. The second, on the other hand, contains no hint of the supernatural, its most marked feature being the contrast afforded to 'smoky rooms in Manchester'[6] by Lorton Grange, apparently set among the hills and dales of North Lancashire[7].

The presentation, in the first fragment, of an uncanny occurrence follows Mrs. Gaskell's accustomed (Defoesque) manner of setting the strange squarely within a prosaic framework. Only after one has learnt the date[8], been told about red-brick houses[9], and read of night-wear being aired[10] are the out-of-the-ordinary figures introduced[11]. As befits this everyday context, the tone is

[1] *Works,* VII, 721-727.
[2] Ward, ed. *Works,* VII, p. xl.
[3] Ward, ed. *Works,* VII, p. xl.
[4] *Works,* VII, 721.
[5] *Works,* VII, 724-725.
[6] *Works,* VII, 725.
[7] Ward, ed. *Works,* VII, p. xl.
[8] *Works,* VII, 721.
[9] *Works,* VII, 722.
[10] *Works,* VII, 723.
[11] *Works,* VII, 724.

far from serious; and its informality is enlivened with touches of humour (largely at the expense of Quakerish sobriety). The other piece is similarly colloquial in style, and matter-of-fact in content. Both, being couched in epistolary form, favour ease of expression, the very casualness of their narrators conferring plausibility on the events recounted.

By their intrinsic nature, stories savouring of the unusual appealed to Mrs. Gaskell who, not long before her death, had ensured that, were she not spared to write it, one such would not perish with her[12]. Further Gaskellian characteristics are suggested by the correspondents themselves. The first is Hannah Johnson, who recalls what once befell during a journey from her home (near Chester[13]) to her school (past Birmingham[14]) at a time when the slave-trade was causing concern[15]. Elizabeth Stevenson too, one remembers, must have travelled by coach from Cheshire when, before Emancipation, she attended a Warwickshire school. Whether the strange incident described in the fragment was invented, heard from another person, or even ' observed ' around the eighteen-twenties by the author herself (possibly in a dream or during a hypnopompic hallucination[16]) remains a matter for speculation. The other letter-writer, though a man, also brings Mrs. Gaskell to mind. Like her, he knew his Manchester well, being able to compile ' an inventory of the

---

[12] See Hare, *The Story of My Life*, III (1896), 117-123. Clearly it was to this story that Mrs. Gaskell was referring when, apparently in a letter to Eliza Fox begun one Monday [17 November 1851 (?)], she wrote: ' How are the Dickens? wretch that he is to go and write MY story of the lady haunted by the face; I shall have nothing to talk about now at dull parties.' Although her dating is erroneous, the version printed by Miss Haldane (*Mrs. Gaskell and Her Friends*, pp. 252-254) agrees quite well with the copy of part of this letter in the Gaskell Section, Brotherton Collection, Leeds University Library: *G.L.*, No. 108a (to ?Eliza Fox and dated [?17 November 1851], according to Chapple and Pollard, who small-capitalize ' MY '). Dickens' relation of the face story, thematically similar to that recorded by Hare, occurs in his ' To Be Read at Dusk ', *The Keepsake*, 1852, ed. Margaret A. Power, pp. 119-128; that Mrs. Gaskell complained to Dickens about this plagiarism is suggested by his jocular rejoinder to her of 25 November 1851 (*The Letters of Charles Dickens*, ed. Dexter, II, 360).

[13] *Works*, VII, 721.
[14] *Works*, VII, 721.
[15] *Works*, VII, 722.
[16] A hallucination occurring in the semi-conscious state between sleep and waking: we are informed that the lady awoke—but (if her memory proved correct) to full consciousness (*Works*, VII, 723).

furniture . . . of any room in a lodging-house '[17] there. Feeling slightly sad to be severing his ties with the town, prior to a holiday in the country, he nevertheless preferred seven days in the wilds to ' the delights of a railway excursion every day during Whitsun-week '[18], and soon discovered that 'the delicious mountain-air blew away melancholy '[19]. Early in her literary career—indeed when composing the Whitsuntide section of *Libbie Marsh's Three Eras*—the author had expressed a comparable ambivalence about ' Manchester—ugly, smoky Manchester; dear busy, earnest, noble-working Manchester '[20]. A decade later, in one of her letters to Charles Eliot Norton, similar sentiments appeared. Then, though manifestly not without affection for ' dear old dull ugly smoky grim grey Manchester '[21], she confessed to being ' *un* Manchester '[22] and to liking ' a smelling and singing world.'[23]

A ' singing world '—that, perhaps, is not an altogether unsuitable phrase with which to conclude a study of Mrs. Gaskell's non-biographic compositions.

[17] *Works*, VII, 727.
[18] *Works*, VII, 725.
[19] *Works*, VII, 725.
[20] *Works*, I, 477.
[21] *Gaskell-Norton Letters*, ed. Whitehill, p. 12: *G.L.*, No. 384.
[22] *Gaskell-Norton Letters*, ed. Whitehill, p. 16: *G.L.*, No. 384.
[23] *Gaskell-Norton Letters*, ed. Whitehill, p. 16: *G.L.*, No. 384.

CHAPTER X

EPILOGUE

More more, he cried, ere Phillis breath'd her last,
Three Volumes more, I want them quick and fast
Trollope's too long; Macdonald slow and tame
There's only you can raise the Cornhill's fame.

Müti has charms, no doubt, and Elsie too
But listen to your Smith and Elder—do
March is upon us; Copy's wanted sore.
Oh! be our Valentine, and send us more.

St Valentine's Day.
1864.

Dr. Winifred Lamb

Valentine sent to Mrs. Gaskell by her Publishers, 1864.

EPILOGUE

Aged fifty-five, Mrs. Gaskell died on 12 November 1865 at the height of her powers[1]. Her productive period had been relatively brief; for she was in her late thirties before her fiction began to be published. Then fame came, and remained to the end.

With 'observation' and 'invention' as its key terms, the present study sought connexions between Mrs. Gaskell's life and writings, and inter-relations among the works themselves. At the same time some attempt was made at critical assessment, with every known (non-biographic) publication receiving attention. Partly because of the diversity of her output, one can here do little more than touch on a few of the topics considered.

Clearly personal experience supplied much material. The importance of years in Knutsford ('Cranford') and Manchester ('Drumble') is commonly acknowledged; yet one should not

---

[1] With this in mind, Meta Gaskell remarked to Charles Eliot Norton upon the element of beauty 'about people dying at their very best—/ before there is any falling away from/ their highest life & effort.' She went on to mention that her mother 'had/ never written so easily; nor', according to most people, 'so well'. This passage, composed on 6 April, occurs in a letter Meta began on 27 March [1866]—now in the Harvard University Library: bMS Am 1088 (2608). As a slight qualification to Meta's words about her mother's literary facility, it should be noted that, according to Mrs. Gaskell's letter of Tuesday [22 August 1865] to Marianne (copies of which, once owned by Mr. J. T. Lancaster, belong to the present writer), worries about the house she had bought at Alton were telling on her powers of composition, she being behindhand with *Wives and Daughters* in consequence; yet the novelist realized that only by writing could she free herself from debt: the letter occurs as *G.L.*, No. 575a. Other correspondence describing Mrs. Gaskell's death (at her Hampshire house) includes Edward Thurstan Holland's letter of 18 November 1865 and Meta's of 24 November [1865], both to Norton and in the Harvard University Library—bMS Am 1088 (3484, 2607)—; and that of 22 January [1866] from Meta to Ellen Nussey (in the Rutgers University Library: MS A Symington Collection ·G2535): most of the first letter, based on a fairly faithful copy, appears in *G.L.*, Appendix F; the second indicates that Mrs. Gaskell, who expired in Meta's arms, had always wished for a sudden death; and the third (much of which is quite accurately quoted in Hopkins, *Elizabeth Gaskell*, p. 319) ends with Meta's mentioning the sunset beauty of her 'noble beyond words' mother.

forget frequent holidays at Silverdale, numerous Continental tours, or even a fortnight at Whitby, all of which provided grist for the author's mill. Nor was observation of people less fruitful than that of places. Mrs. Gaskell had " so many friends, —so large a circle of acquaintance,"[2] that prototypes for fictional figures were never lacking.

In many ways her literary technique lent itself well to a more or less direct reliance on past observation. Something of her method was early indicated by Henry James when, with reference to *Wives and Daughters,* he stressed the importance of domestic *minutiae* for Mrs. Gaskell's ' " realization " of her central idea, *i.e.,* Molly Gibson, a product, to a certain extent, of clean frocks and French lessons '[3]. What he said about the novelist's treatment of the other ' heroine ' is even more relevant.

> She had probably known a Cynthia Kirkpatrick, a résumé of whose character she had given up as hopeless; . . . She contents herself with a simple record of the innumerable small facts of the young girl's daily life, and leaves the reader to draw his conclusions.[4]

Themes were frequently suggested by both public and private events. Being a sensitive Victorian, Mrs. Gaskell was, quite naturally, led to write about the struggles of masters and men, and about the tribulations of fallen women. As a historian's daughter, she was attracted by accounts of press-gangs, and by country traditions and legends. Because of her family background, she composed stories featuring disappearing (and returning) sailors, motherless daughters, unsympathetic stepparents, and kindly doctors.

An examination of the entire corpus reveals a fondness for ringing literary changes on favourite *motifs,* characters, and *milieux.* Mrs. Gaskell's success lay in the subtlety with which this was accomplished; for even her closest student would not tax her with laziness of invention[5]—except, possibly, in the

[2] Quoted, from a letter Charlotte Brontë sent her, by Mrs. Gaskell (*The Life of Charlotte Brontë*, 1st edn, 1857, II, 295).

[3] Henry James, Review of *Wives and Daughters*, in *The Nation*, II (22 February 1866), 247.

[4] James, Review of *Wives and Daughters*, in *The Nation*, II, 247.

[5] As Meta Gaskell implied in a letter to Thomas Seccombe of 13 September 1910 (a copy of which, once owned by Mr. J. T. Lancaster,

matter of proper names⁶. If one were to make any adverse criticisms, these would concern the lack of grand designs and the absence of a pervasive philosophy: Mrs. Gaskell possessed little architectonic power; nor did she see into the life of things.

Whenever the opportunity arose, attention was called to those aspects of her fiction which betoken the pen of a lady-novelist; on such occasions the term 'authoress' appeared appropriate. Being both wife and mother, Mrs. Gaskell was qualified to treat family relationships; as the manager of a busy household, she could present a convincing picture of domestic life—which explains why her servants seem such vital creations. She had, moreover, a woman's concern for the significant trivialities of daily intercourse, and could depict the manners of Lancashire operatives with the same vividness as she portrayed those of Knutsford ladies. This careful recording contributes in no small measure to the reality of the widely differing social groups encountered in her novels. Even when she turned to the macabre, the gothick, or the fantastic, she always retained a feminine eye for the telling detail.

It is pleasant to pay tribute to the lady as well as to the novelist; for her life exemplifies the finest qualities of Victorian womanhood. Lord David Cecil has compared her to a dove⁷: and in Professor Whitfield's estimation she possessed those virtues which made 'a devoted, careful and tender wife; an honest, friendly, and affectionate mother.'⁸

It is also pleasant to mention a characteristic few would deny, that of moral excellence. This attribute, which shines forth from her letters no less than from her fiction, secures for Mrs. Gaskell a unique place among her contemporaries. In a letter to Lady Kay-Shuttleworth⁹ she confessed that, in contrast to Charlotte Brontë, she put all her goodness into her works which were, in consequence, much better than herself. She need not have done so. No one who has studied her life

---

belongs to the present writer), her mother's writings were far from being mere 'compilations of experience' nor was each character just 'a photograph of some living person.'

⁶ See Appendix VII.

⁷ Cecil, *Early Victorian Novelists*, 1948, p. 152.

⁸ Whitfield, *Mrs Gaskell*, p. 89.

⁹ This letter of 7 April [1853] is in the possession of Lord Shuttleworth, and appears as *G.L.*, No. 154.

and correspondence would ever think of charging the author of
(say) *Ruth* with literary hypocrisy—though to be sure she
found it possible to say things in her social-purpose novels
which she could not have said in public[10]. Her intimate friends,
however, would have agreed with Frederick Greenwood that
the writer ' was herself what her works show her to have been
—a wise, good woman.'[11] Similarly T. S. Eliot recognized both
her aesthetic and her ethical merits when he praised Mrs. Gaskell for knowing ' how to make a literary virtue out of . . .
simple goodness.'[12]

Mrs. Gaskell tried her hand at many *genres,* in most of
which she attained distinction; yet, reviewing the range of her
achievement, one feels that recent criticism has done her less
than justice. E. M. Forster called her ' a great Victorian novelist '[13]; but few have concurred with his verdict. Even Mr. Arthur
Pollard, after an appreciative critique, is content to conclude
that, ' although she may not be a major novelist, she is certainly a major minor novelist '[14] : and Dr. Miriam Allott states
with assurance that ' Mrs. Gaskell is not one of our major
novelists.'[15]

Against such modern assessments should be set the judgements
of a former generation. Henry James acknowledged her genius[16]; Clement Shorter, a devotee of long standing, confidently
placed ' Mrs. Gaskell among the unquestionably great prose
authors of our latter-day literature '[17]. ' Q.' was even more
eulogistic :

[10] As she told Frederick James Furnivall, with reference to *Mary
Barton* and *Ruth,* in a letter, written one Tuesday evening [6 December
1853], now in the Henry E. Huntington Library and Art Gallery—MSS
Catalogue FU 312. This letter occurs as *G.L.,* No. 171.

[11] Concluding Remarks to *Wives and Daughters* (*Works,* VIII, 761).

[12] Thomas Stearns Eliot, Review of *Letters of Mrs. Gaskell and
Charles Eliot Norton,* 1855-1865, ed. Jane Whitehill, in *The New England
Quarterly,* VI (1933), 628.

[13] Edward Morgan Forster, ' The Charm and Strength of Mrs. Gaskell ', *The Sunday Times,* 7 April 1957, p. 10.

[14] Pollard, *The Novels of Mrs. Gaskell,* p. 423 : cf. and cont. *Mrs
Gaskell: Novelist and Biographer,* pp. 8-9.

[15] Allott, *Elizabeth Gaskell,* p. 40.

[16] James, Review of *Wives and Daughters,* in *The Nation,* II, 247.

[17] Shorter, intro. *"My Diary"*: *The early years of my daughter
Marianne,* by Elizabeth Cleghorn Gaskell, p. 4.

The Victorian Age lent itself to excess; and its excessive figures are our statues for some to deface or bedaub. But I, who have purposely compared Elizabeth Gaskell with her most ornate contemporary [Disraeli], dare to prophesy that when criticism has sifted all out, she will come to her own, as a woman of genius, sweetly proportioned as a statue, yet breathing; one of these writers we call by that vain word—'so vain, so pathetic even when used of the greatest poet—' immortal.'[18]

We shall be more than satisfied if the present study, albeit inadequately, does a little to help fulfil this prediction, at least by directing attention to the works themselves. Frequent—perhaps over-frequent—use has been made of quotations, partly because Mrs. Gaskell lends herself to being quoted, partly because one cannot expect that familiarity with her writings which a critic of (say) Charlotte Brontë would take for granted. However we may hope that the centenary of the author's death (marked by two worthy rehabilitations[19]) has heralded a new era—an era when, as ' Q.' prognosticated, Mrs. Gaskell will come to her own.

[18] Quiller-Couch, *Charles Dickens and Other Victorians,* p. 218.
[19] Pollard, *Mrs Gaskell: Novelist and Biographer*; and Wright, *Mrs. Gaskell: The Basis for Reassessment.*

APPENDIX I

THE GENESIS OF *MARY BARTON*

Mrs. Gaskell affirmed that the tale was conceived, " and the greater part of the first volume . . . written "[1], at a time when she " took refuge in the invention to exclude the memory of painful scenes "[2]—presumably those connected with the fatal illness of her son, who died in Wales on 10 August 1845[3]. She probably sent the manuscript of this first volume to William Howitt shortly after its completion; for his wife remarked that a few months separated its arrival from their receipt of the

[1] Quoted, from the draft of Mrs. Gaskell's letter to Mrs. Sam Greg, by Ward (ed. *Works*, I, p. lxiii): *G.L.*, No. 42 (dated [?Early 1849] by Chapple and Pollard).

[2] Quoted, from the draft of Mrs. Gaskell's letter to Mrs. Sam Greg, by Ward (ed. *Works*, I, p. lxiii): *G.L.*, No. 42—cf. Mrs. Gaskell's opening words in her Preface to *Mary Barton* (*Works*, I, p. lxxiii).

[3] Sanders, *Elizabeth Gaskell*, p. 17, fn. 2. The novel was begun ' in the spring or summer of 1846 ' according to an anonymous review of Esther Alice (Mrs. Ellis H.) Chadwick, *Mrs. Gaskell: Haunts, Homes, and Stories*, London: Sir Isaac Pitman and Sons, Ltd., 1910—' Biographical Guesswork ', ' New Books ' Section, *The Manchester Guardian*, 26 September 1910, p. 5—; and it ' was chiefly written . . . after the birth [3 September 1846] of the novelist's youngest daughter ' (*ibidem*). According to G. A. Payne's holograph note on a cutting of this critique, inserted in the late Mr. J. T. Lancaster's annotated first edition of Mrs. Chadwick's book (now owned by the present writer), Meta Gaskell was the reviewer: certainly her letter—' Mrs. Gaskell's Life '—to the Editor of *The Guardian* (30 September 1910, p. 1337) repudiated co-operation with Mrs. Chadwick, who (she affirmed) had most inaccurately reported what Meta had told her in private; but probably Meta, rather than herself contributing the review, merely supplied corrections for the reviewer—much as she did for Clement King Shorter (C.K.S., ' A Literary Letter: The late Miss " Meta " Gaskell ', *The Sphere*, 8 November 1913, p. 154; and Shorter, intro. *" My Diary "*, by E. C. Gaskell, p. 3) and for Thomas Seccombe (whose copy of Mrs. Chadwick's biography, with notes therein, ' presumably Meta's ', was, Mr. Lancaster records on his copy's fly-leaf, a source for his own annotations). Although many of these corrections seem justified, each must be taken on its merits.

rest of the novel[4]. According to an extract[5] from William Howitt's letter to Mrs. Gaskell of 17 November 1847, negotiations were then in process between himself (acting for ' Cotton Mather Mills') and the firm of Chapman & Hall[6]. An extract[7] from Mary Howitt's letter of 9 January 1848 mentions that, having read the conclusion of the story, she and her husband immediately sent it to the publishers. In January Mrs. Gaskell was herself introduced to Chapman, an agreement being arrived at between him and Howitt (on the author's behalf); Chapman, however, showed little inclination to fulfil his promise of publishing in the spring[8]. After the bulk of the manuscript had

[4] *Mary Howitt: An Autobiography,* ed. Howitt, II, 28. Mary Howitt's remark *(ibidem)* that Mrs. Gaskell acknowledged her story to be the result of William Howitt's advice is confirmed by William's claim that the book was written at his suggestion and disposed of by him (made in a letter quoted by a correspondent to *The Manchester Guardian,* the relevant cutting therefrom—sent by Clement Shorter to Dr. W. E. A. Axon—being in Box 1 of the Gaskell Boxes in the Manchester Central Reference Library). However many influences caused *Mary Barton* to be written.

[5] To be found in Shorter and Symington, ' Correspondence, Articles & Notes Relating to Mrs. E. C. Gaskell. Transcripts ', Vol. II, Section on *Mary Barton*—a typescript in the Gaskell Section, Brotherton Collection, Leeds University Library. Although Howitt *(ibidem)* may well have introduced the novelist under the guise of Cotton Mather Mills, Mrs. Gaskell (whose Stevenson forbears lived at Berwick) suggested Stephen Berwick as a *nom de guerre* in a 19 October [1848] letter *(G.L.,* No. 28) to her publisher (now in the Pierpont Morgan Library: Autographs-Miscellaneous-English); but this suggestion came too late, according to Chapman's 23 October 1848 reply—quite accurately quoted by Miss Hopkins (' " Mary Barton ": A Victorian Best Seller ', *The Trollopian,* III, 2-3) from the copy of part of this letter in Shorter and Symington, *op. cit.,* Vol. II, Section on *Mary Barton.*

[6] Though refused ' as a *gift* ' by Moxon (the author told Richard Bentley in a 29 September [1853] letter—*G.L.,* No. 167a—, now in the Illinois University Library), the story when published brought £100 (according to the 11 December 1848 receipt—*G.L.,* Appendix F—in the Pierpont Morgan Library; see too *G.L.,* Nos. 34, 81): another (gratuitous) £100 apparently came from Chapman & Hall with the printing of the second edition *(The Letters of Elizabeth Barrett Browning, with Biographical Additions,* ed. Frederic George Kenyon, 2 vols., London: Smith, Elder, & Co., 1897, I, 471). See too Ward, ed. *Works,* I, pp. l-li.

[7] To be found in Shorter and Symington, ' Correspondence, Articles & Notes Relating to Mrs. E. C. Gaskell. Transcripts ', Vol. II, Section on *Mary Barton.* There it is (erroneously) attributed to William Howitt; but internal evidence strongly suggests that the original letter was written by Mrs. Howitt to Mr. Gaskell.

[8] The evidence for the statements in this sentence may be culled from Mrs. Gaskell's [1848] letters to Chapman of 21 March, 2 April, and

been in his hands for some fourteen months, and after most of the tale had been printed, the novelist was asked for extra material, seemingly to bring the second volume to its requisite length; she reluctantly complied with an interpolation (especially the penultimate chapter) between the death of John Barton and that of Esther[9].

Reproduced below are a rough sketch for the novel and an outline of its proposed conclusion. A copy of the former occurs in the *Mary Barton* section of the second volume of the Shorter-Symington typescript, ' Correspondence, Articles & Notes Relating to Mrs. E. C. Gaskell. Transcripts' (lodged in the Gaskell Section, Brotherton Collection, Leeds University Library): whether or not the original is extant remains unknown; it may

---

13 April—now in the Pierpont Morgan Library (Autographs-Miscellaneous-English)—: *G.L.*, Nos. 22-24.

[9] The evidence for the statements in this sentence may be found in the quotation from the draft of Mrs. Gaskell's letter to Mrs. Sam Greg given by Ward (ed. *Works*, I, p. lxiv): there Mrs. Gaskell implies the whole MS (excluding the last-minute interpolation) was in Chapman's hands more than fourteen months before publication; yet the extract from Mary Howitt's letter of 9 January 1848 (see our penultimate footnote) shows that such could not have been the case. According to Thomas Seccombe (intro. *Mary Barton,* by Mrs. Gaskell, London: J. M. Dent & Sons, Ltd.; New York: E. P. Dutton & Co. [1911], p. xii), the publishers demanded an extra six thousand words, which resulted in padding in the thirty-third, thirty-fourth, and (especially) thirty-seventh chapters: Seccombe does not give his source for this statement; but it was probably Meta Gaskell, for she had helped with his Preface to Mrs. Gaskell's *Sylvia's Lovers,* as is evidenced by letters from her to Seccombe now in the possession of the present writer. Mrs. Gaskell herself, in the draft letter to Mrs. Sam Greg—*G.L.*, No. 42 (dated [?Early 1849] by Chapple and Pollard)—, stated that the novel "was originally complete without the part which intervenes between John Barton's death and Esther's; about 3 pages, ... including that conversation between Job Legh, and Mr. Carson, and Jem Wilson " (quoted in Ward, ed. *Works,* I, p. lxiv): such ' an addition ... extends to considerably more than three pages ' (Ward, ed. *Works,* I, p. lxii); but perhaps Mrs. Gaskell actually wrote, or meant to write, ' 33 pages '—the approximate distance in terms of full pages of first-edition type between John Barton's death and Esther's (*Mary Barton,* 1st edn, 1848, II, 276-311). We may perhaps note that, if Mrs. Elizabeth Barrett Browning's informant was trustworthy, then the author had already altered her manuscript, before any publishers had seen it, in deference to criticisms from Mrs. A. T. Thompson, a relative by marriage (*The Letters of Elizabeth Barrett Browning, with Biographical Additions,* ed. Kenyon, I, 471).

once have been in the possession of the Howitts[10] and, later, of Meta Gaskell[11]. The manuscript of the latter (almost certainly the author's holograph) forms part of the Forster Collection at the Victoria & Albert Museum : possibly it came into Forster's hands when, as ' a reader for Chapman & Hall, . . . he recommended '[12] the novel for publication. Whereas in many places the first edition is at odds with the rough sketch, divergencies from the outlined conclusion are minor and few; but, not unnaturally, much appears in the printed version of which there is no suggestion in either. As regards the intended ending, it will be recalled that Mrs. Gaskell was required to supply additional material when the presses were already at work.

GASKELL (MRS. E. C.)
COPY OF THE ROUGH SKETCH MADE BEFORE BEGINNING TO WRITE " MARY BARTON " [[13]]

" MARY BARTON "
First Chap.

Scene in G. H.—Spring Evening—Wilsons & Bartons—The Wilsons speak of Esther's disappearance—are joined by the Bartons, &c.

---

[10] This surmise is suggested by a letter from Mary Howitt to Mrs. Gaskell, an undated extract from which appears in Shorter and Symington, ' Correspondence, Articles & Notes Relating to Mrs. E. C. Gaskell. Transcripts', Vol. II, Section on *Mary Barton.* Mrs. Howitt there speaks of her husband and herself reading the novel; she enquires how much more remains to be written, yet in such terms as show her aware of the happy ending. On the other hand, one could argue that the Howitts did not have the rough sketch, but rather the MS of the proposed conclusion or even a brief note from the author about her intended outcome.

[11] ' Miss Gaskell tells me that her mother thought out the scheme of the book [*Mary Barton*], and even the subjects of the chapters, before starting to write it, and that she kept to her original plan precisely.'— Sarah A. Tooley, ' The Centenary of Mrs. Gaskell ', *The Cornhill Magazine,* N.S. XXIX (1910), 322. We may also note that among items offered as help with preparing the Knutsford Edition the Miss Gaskells ' named " a rough sketch of the plot of ' Mary Barton,' drawn out before a word of the book was written, but strangely adhered to in the writing " ' ([Huxley] *The House of Smith Elder,* p. 206)—see too Wright, *Mrs. Gaskell,* pp. ix, 265-268.

[12] Sanders, *Elizabeth Gaskell,* p. 18.

[13] Although the general lay-out of the Brotherton typescript has been followed, exact reproduction has not been sought.

Second Chap.

4 years passed away. Changes. The strong Alice Wilson and
healthy Thomas Barton dead—while the feeble and less
healthy remain behind—No news yet of Esther.

Good times—How flourishing Wilson is—How he joins a Chartist
Club at the instigation of Job Leigh—How he apprentices
Mary to a dress-maker. How Widow Barton strives on to
keep her delicate twins with the help of her son Thomas and
succeeds.

How Thomas Barton in his way to his work always meets
Mary, and what arises therefrom.

How Mr. Chadwick Junior on his way home to dinner always
meets Mary and what arises therefrom.

A Father and daughter's talk over the fire; Past life—gone
and dead. The old always homing to the past, the young
looking to the future. Plans for a day at Dunham next
Whitsun week.

The day at Dunham.

Rumours of Bad times—Bad times.

Bradshaw & Co. fail. Wilson dismissed.

Mrs. Barton's sorrows.

Wilson engaged at Chadwick & Co's Mill.

How Charterism from a theory becomes an action in bad times.

END OF VOL. I.

How Mary suffers from the bad times.

Margaret Clegg and Mary have mourning to make.

Death at the Bartons'   Mary and Aunt Esther sit up by turns.

———

Mary's first love.

———

How in the midst of much sorrow, Mary is happy in her own individual world of love.

———

Poor Thomas Barton.

———

Thomas and Mary quarrel. His despair.

———

Mary's bliss. Her conscience-struck visit to poor Widow Barton. Aunt Esther.

———

Mary's downfall of heart. Mr. Chadwick's threat.

———

Fanny's first visit to Wilson—her tale—her warning regarding Mary.

———

Mary undeceived. Who was listening.

———

Trades Unions, and desperation.

———

Mr. Chadwick murdered.

———

VOL. III

The police on the scent.

———

Barton arrested.

———

Mary's revulsion of feeling. Goes to see Widow Barton. Accompanies her to prison.

———

Barton in prison.

———

Mary's determination to prove Barton's innocence.

———

Discovers the Murderer.

———

Fanny.

———————

Agony.

———————

Visits Widow Barton. Aunt Hester's childishness.

———————

A sympathizing and advising friend, Job Leigh.

———————

How she proves an alibi by Margaret Clegg's help.

———————

Interview with Barton. *He* knew too.

———————

Father's death of remorse—Widow Barton's.

———————

Aunt Hester's death.

———————

Marriage—Sail for America.

————oOo————

NOTES

G.H. is for Green Heys.
The names are different in the novel :—
    Wilson and Barton being interchanged there, and Jem sub-
    stituted for Thomas—and Carson for Chadwick.

Notes on Divergencies between the
Rough Sketch and the First Edition

It may be well to supplement the notes in the Brotherton
typescript by summarizing some main points of difference between the sketch and the book. The following list does not
claim to be exhaustive; nor are the numerous additions in the
printed version noticed.

  1. Many names are altered. For example :
      (i)   Wilsons and Bartons are interchanged;
      (ii) Chadwick becomes Carson;
      (iii) Job Leigh becomes Job Legh;
      (iv) Esther/Fanny is apparently the Esther of the novel;
      (v)   Margaret Clegg becomes Margaret Jennings.

2. The Wilsons (= Bartons) are not joined by the Bartons (= Wilsons) after they have spoken of Esther's disappearance.

3. There is no four-year gap between the first and second chapter.

4. The death of healthy Thomas Barton (= George Wilson) does not occur till quite late in the story, after that of his twins.

5. Job Leigh (= Legh) is not an active Chartist, only a reluctant Unionist; nor does he introduce Wilson (= Barton) to Chartism.

6. Strictly speaking, one would say that Mary apprenticed herself to a dress-maker.

7. Thomas Barton (= Jem Wilson) does not always meet Mary as he goes to work.

8. There is no father-daughter fireside talk about the past and the future.

9. The day at Dunham occurs in ' Era II ' of *Libbie Marsh's Three Eras*, not in *Mary Barton*.

10. There is no failure of Bradshaw & Co.; Wilson (= Barton) once had to be turned off when work at Mr. Hunter's stopped (*Works*, I, 24).

11. Wilson (= Barton) is never engaged at Chadwick & Co.'s (=Carsons') Mill.

12. Mary and Aunt Esther (? = Aunt Alice Wilson) never sit up by turns.

13. There is no real threat by Mr. Chadwick (= Carson), senior or junior.

14. The suggestion in the sketch that perhaps the murderer of Chadwick (= Carson) listens when Mary is undeceived is not borne out by the novel.

15. It is not quite clear in the sketch whether it is Mr. Chadwick (= Carson) senior or his son who is murdered.

16. Mary does not accompany Mrs. Barton (= Wilson) to prison; indeed neither visits there.

17. The help given by Margaret Clegg (= Jennings) in proving the alibi is slight compared with that of Will, the sailor.

18. Widow Barton (= Wilson) does not die, but emigrates to America with her son and daughter-in-law.

19. The sequence of events set out in the sketch differs in several ways from that found in the book.
20. The novel came out in two, not three, volumes.
   [page 1]

Conclusion yet to be written.[14]

Mary had a brain fever, and knew not the/
end of the trial; how Will had proved an alibi,/
if not to the satisfaction of all, at any rate sufficiently/
to make the jury give Jem the benefit of the doubt/
how Will snapped his fingers at the lawyers, and/
how Ben Sturgis & the pilot proved that he *had*/
been summoned back from sea. For many days/
Mary knew nothing,—she was nursed by M^{rs}/
Sturgis, and by Jem; at least by Jem after he had/
taken his mother home; accompanied by Will/
who hastened to see Aunt Alice once more;—she,/
blessed with a veiled blessing, (with second childhood,)/
sang her canticle of departure, believing her-/
self to be once more in the happy happy realms/
of childhood, once more dwelling in the lovely/
scenes where she had so often longed to be—un = /
changed, & in the old radiant hues—and death/
came to her as Evening comes to the wearied child//

   [page 2]
But leaving Will & Margaret plighting their faith/
⟨b⟩ y [Alice's death bed, *deleted*] Alice's grave; leaving his
                                              mother/
⟨in⟩ Margaret's care, Jem returned to Mary, and/
⟨w⟩ hen her reason returned his was the first face she/
⟨s⟩ aw.—They came back to Manchester as soon as/
⟨h⟩ er strength would admit, with a heavy weight on/
their hearts, (although no word on the subject had/
⟨p⟩ assed between them,—) in regard to John Barton, about/
⟨w⟩ hom they had heard nothing, & durst make no/

---

[14] This manuscript (a single sheet, folded to make four pages), almost certainly Mrs. Gaskell's holograph, is in the Forster Collection—F. MS. 215* (pressmark: F. 48. E. 23, No. 138)—at the Victoria & Albert Museum. At the top right-hand corner of the first page is written, in a different hand, ' (Mrs Gaskell) '.

⟨e⟩ nquiries. But when Mary opened the apparently/
⟨s⟩ hut up house there was her father sitting motion=/
⟨le⟩ ss by the cold grey ashes of his hearth. His appearance/
⟨a⟩ ll anguish-stricken by remorse made Mary for-/
⟨ge⟩ t every thing but her love towards him—she forgot/
⟨th⟩ e crime in her endeavours to soothe,—But he was/
⟨s⟩ tony,—speechless—Do you remember the bit/
in Fuller's Worthies   /
⟨'⟩ 'I have read of a bird which hath a face like, &/
yet will prey upon a man,—who coming to the/
water to drink, and finding there by reflection/
⟨h⟩ e hath killed one like himself pineth away by/
degrees."[15] And do you also remember an exquisite//
     [page 3]
piece of Wither ending with   /

                    But this I know full well/
     My Father who above the Heavens doth dwell,/
     An eye upon his wandering child will cast/
     And he will bring me to [his *deleted*] ∧my∧ home at last./[16]
And [th *deleted*] such was the beginning & ending of poor John/
Barton's last scene. His sin had found him out. His/
temptation was suicide. Death seemed as if it w^d/
take him to the Father whose judgments are more/
merciful than those of men, & who would teach him/
the right way which he had so wandered from here./
But he resisted that temptation, [though he longed to *deleted*]
                              ∧no he would not∧/
[escape from his remorse. *deleted*] ∧escape∧ He had not heard
                                                         of Jem's/
arrest or trial till it was over, & then he had reached/
home he knew not how. But he told Mary nothing,/
but sank day by day, conscience-stricken. Still he/
saw a duty;—unknown to Mary or to Jem (who/

---

[15] The passage occurs in Thomas Fuller's sketch of Sir Edward Har-
wood (which appears under the heading of Soldiers, in the section on
Lincolnshire) in his *History of the Worthies of England* (1662). Besides
modifying the spelling and punctuation, Mrs. Gaskell apparently omitted
'that' ('by reflexion, that he had') from this quotation.
[16] These lines by George Wither, here slightly misquoted, come from
the 'Nec Careo' section of *Wither's Motto* (1621).

avoided coming to the house from delicacy,) he sent/
for [a po *deleted*] Mr Carson, and to him he told his guilt &/
exculpated Jem fully; he was then dying, & told/
Mr Carson how thankful he would have been to be/
hanged, how infinitely more awful was a life of remorse/
But Mr C. did not understand him, & dying as he wa ⟨s⟩ /
gave him in charge to the police that night. But un ⟨able⟩ //

[page 4]
like King Darius[17] to rest upon his bed, he went/
early the next morning to John Barton's house, and/
found the police, who had watched him through the/
night, taking him to prison in spite of Mary's entreaties/
He [by his *deleted*] ∧with a∧ last penitent cry to God for
                                        pardon, died, &/
as the breath fled, the stern Mr Carson joined in the/
prayer, and, softened by the agony which ended in Death,/
forgave him.   /
Then Jem & Mary talked over things, & told each other/
about Esther, & Jem resolved to find her out. By the/
help of the police he tracked her to a lodging house/
where all the outcasts sleep that have a penny to pay/
for a roof. He went in, early one morning and/
found her on her miserable couch ∧of straw∧ among twenty/
other men women & children—dead;—with a little/
lock of a child's yellow hair clenched in her hand./
Then I suppose Will & Margaret were married/
only I dare say she was couched first[18],—but/
Jem & Mary, & his mother, weary & sick of Manches/
=ter, resolved to go to America, & so, sailing along the/
path of the setting sun, they fade from my sight,/
& darkness mantles over their future, & shrouds/
it from my vision.   //

Notes on Divergencies between the Proposed Conclusion and the Ending of the First Edition

Below are listed the chief differences between the MS plan
and the ending as printed; no account is taken of events found
in the first edition but not mentioned in the manuscript.

---

[17] Daniel 6[19].   [18] Cf. *Works*, I, 458.

1. Will and Margaret do not plight their troth by Alice's deathbed or grave.
2. Strictly speaking, one must say that the face of Mrs. Sturgis, not that of Jem, was the first seen by Mary on her recovery (*Works*, I, 404).
3. Mr. Carson did not give John Barton in charge to the police; nor, on his return the following morning, did he find them taking Barton to prison.
4. Jem did not find Esther dead in a lodging-house.

APPENDIX II

THE PLOT OF *NORTH AND SOUTH*

It seems worth examining the difference between the way Charles Dickens proposed the first part of the novel should be serialized and how it eventually appeared in *Household Words*. The approximate column-space occupied by each instalment is indicated.

Dickens Proposed Divisions[1]	*Household Words* Instalments[2]
No. 1 ... the announcement of Mr Lennox at the parsonage.	*... the announcement of Mr Lennox at the parsonage.* (H.W., X, 61-68 : 14¾ cols.[3])
No. 2 ... Lennox's proposal ... the father's communication to his daughter of his leaving the church ... Mr. Hale's announcement to Margaret, that Milton-Northern is the place they are going to.	*... Lennox's proposal ... the father's communication to his daughter of his leaving the church ... Mr. Hale's announcement to Margaret, that Milton-Northern is the place they are going to ...* her promise to tell Mrs. Hale how things stand. (H.W., X, 85-92 : 15⅔ cols.)
No. 3 ... their fixing on the watering-place as their temporary sojourn.	*... their fixing on the watering-place* [Heston] *as their temporary sojourn.* (H.W., X, 109-113 : 9⅔ cols.)

[1] A schema derived from *The Letters of Charles Dickens,* ed. Dexter, II, 562, 571: letters to Mrs. Gaskell of Thursday 16 [15] (to Saturday 17) June 1854, 26 July 1854.

[2] In this column whatever also occurs in the first column is in italics. The parenthetic words within square brackets are used solely to clarify, and do not necessarily correspond in both columns.

[3] These are only approximate estimates.

No. 4   ... the account of
        Milton, and the new
        house ... the Mill
        Owner's first visit
        ... Margaret's sitting
        down at night in their
        new house, to read
        Edith's letter.

*... the account of Milton,
and the new house ... the Mill
Owner's* [Thornton's] *first
visit* ... the actual removal
to the new house.
(*H.W.*, X, 133-138 : 11 cols.)

No. 5   ... the introduction
        of the working father
        and daughter—the
        Higgins family ...
        [and] of his [the Mill-
        Owner's] mother ...
        the Mill-Owner's
        leaving the house
        after the tea-visit.

*... Margaret's sitting down
at night in their new house,
to read Edith's letter ...
the introduction of the
working father and daughter—
the Higgins family ...* [and]
of his [Thornton's] *mother ...*
who remarks that she hates
Margaret for despising her son.
(*H.W.*, X, 157-162 : 11 cols.)

No. 6   ... Margaret leaving
        their [the Higginses']
        dwelling, after the
        interview with Bessy
        when she is lying
        down.

*... the Mill-Owner's leaving
the* [Hales'] *house after the
tea-visit ...* Margaret meets
Bessy in the street and
accompanies her home ...
Mr. Hale tells his wife and
Margaret that Mrs. Thornton
will call.
(*H.W.*, X, 181-187 : 13 cols.)

No. 7   ... the end of the
        strike conversation
        held by Margaret and
        her father with
        Mr Thornton.

*... Margaret leaving their
[the Higginses'] dwelling, after
the interview with Bessy when
she is lying down ...* Mr. Hale
paces about when he begins to
suspect that his wife is unwell.
(*H.W.*, X, 205-209 : 9⅔ cols.)

No. 8   ... the receipt of the
        dinner Invitation
        [from Mrs. Thornton
        by the Hales].

*... the end of the strike
conversation held by Margaret
and her father with Mr
Thornton.*
(*H.W.*, X, 229-237 : 17 cols.)

No. 9   ... Margaret's leaving Higgins's house after Boucher has charged his miseries upon Higgins and the Union.

... Margaret's conversation with Bessy, who cherishes the promise of the life to come. (*H.W.*, X, 253-259 : 12¼ cols.)

No. 10   ... her [Margaret's] being admitted into the Mill on the day of the Riot, and the porter's shutting the gate.

... the receipt of the dinner Invitation ... Margaret's leaving Higgins's house after Boucher has charged his miseries upon Higgins and the Union.[4]
(*H.W.*, X, 277-284 : 15¼ cols.)

No. 11   ... the end of the Thornton declaration scene.

... her [Margaret's] being admitted into the Mill on the day of the Riot, and the porter's shutting the gate.
(*H.W.*, X, 301-307 : 13⅔ cols.)

No. 12   ... Margaret sleeps fitfully, exhausted after the events of the riot.
(*H.W.*, X, 325-333 : 16¼ cols.)

No. 13   *... the end of the Thornton declaration scene* ... Thornton, after telling his mother Margaret has refused his proposal, mentions that warrants are out against the leading rioters.
(*H.W.*, X, 349-357 : 16¼ cols.)

[4] This instalment actually closes with Bessy's words of farewell; the subsequent one opens with Margaret's journeying home (*Household Words*, X, 301).

The foregoing comparison is largely self-explanatory. Dickens had initially misjudged the amount of *Household Words* space his divisions would require, no better estimate being made, as it should have been, by the printers[5]. He intended the serialized sections of ' North and South ' to follow the pattern of ' Hard Times '[6], its immediate predecessor, which had usually taken up from nine to eleven columns of print. Originally given *carte blanche* to write the story in her own way[7], Mrs. Gaskell found herself, four months later, receiving advice about the need for careful division; for on [15] June 1854 Dickens wrote:

> . . . I do not apologize to you for laying so much stress on the necessity of its dividing well, because I am bound to put before you my perfect conviction that if it did not, the story would be wasted—would miss its effect as it went on—*and would not recover it when published complete*. . . . [8]

Despite pressure from Dickens, partly due perhaps to his apprehension (which was confirmed[9]) that sales would fall, Mrs. Gaskell remained on the whole resolute not to allow cutting[10], although she may have rewritten the scene in which Mr. Hale expresses his doubts to Margaret, in response to Dickens' pleas for brevity[11]. What Mrs. Gaskell undoubtedly did do was to

[5] *The Letters of Charles Dickens,* ed. Dexter, II, 562-563; 580-581, 583, 598: letter to Mrs. Gaskell of Thursday 16 [15] (to Saturday 17) June 1854; letters to W. H. Wills of 19 August 1854, 24 August 1854, 14 October 1854.

[6] *The Letters of Charles Dickens,* ed. Dexter, II, 581, 584: letters to Wills of 20 August 1854, 24 August 1854.

[7] *The Letters of Charles Dickens,* ed. Dexter, II, 542: letter to Mrs. Gaskell of 18 February 1854.

[8] *The Letters of Charles Dickens,* ed. Dexter, II, 562.

[9] *The Letters of Charles Dickens,* ed. Dexter, II, 598: letter to Wills of 14 October 1854.

[10] *The Letters of Charles Dickens,* ed. Dexter, II, 646: letter to Wilkie Collins of 24 March 1855.

[11] *The Letters of Charles Dickens,* ed. Dexter, II, 562, 581-583 (Dickens advised compression of dialogue elsewhere—*Letters,* II, 571). Perhaps here Mrs. Gaskell herself felt the need for excision. In a letter to tell Forster she had sent him seventy-six pages of her ' Margaret Hale ' manuscript (probably the first section), she remarked that she had ' got the/ people well on,—but . . . in too/ lengthy a way ', and confessed she had ' never/ had time to prune '. This letter, written one Wednesday night [17 May 1854], is in the National Library of Scotland (MS. 2262, ff. 34-40; the passage quoted being on f. 40ʳ). During the course of another (apparently earlier) letter to John Forster, Mrs. Gaskell mentioned a criticism by her friend, Mrs. Shaen, that what she had

hurry over the last numbers of the serial. Moreover in at least
one of these—that for 20 January 1855[12]—she was prepared to
permit editorial abridgement: realizing that the thirty-three
MS pages she sent as the penultimate instalment would have
to be curtailed, she sanctioned such shortening as might be
thought ' best for H W./'[13]. In her Preface to the first edition,
echoing Dickens' words to Wills (for him to pass on to Mr.
Gaskell) about " the vital importance of faith being kept with
the public "[14], she put her difficulties before the reader.

> On its first appearance in " Household Words," this tale was
> obliged to conform to the conditions imposed by the require-
> ments of a weekly publication, and likewise to confine itself
> within certain advertised limits, in order that faith might be
> kept with the public. Although these conditions were made
> as light as they well could be, the author found it impossible
> to develop the story in the manner originally intended, and,
> more especially, was compelled to hurry on events with an
> improbable rapidity toward the close. In some degree to remedy
> this obvious defect, various short passages have been inserted,
> and several new chapters added. ... [15]

Mrs. Gaskell made no attempt to conceal her dislike of her

---

written was ' out of pro = / = portion to the length of the/ planned
story '—this part of Mrs. Gaskell's [(pre 15) May 1854] letter is in
the British Museum (Add. MS. 38794, ff. 267-268; the passage quoted
being on f. 268ᵛ); relevant quotations are given by Miss Rubenius (The
Woman Question in Mrs. Gaskell's Life and Works, pp. 35-36) and,
less accurately, by Miss Haldane (Mrs. Gaskell and Her Friends, p. 154):
the immediately-succeeding portion of the same letter is in the National
Library of Scotland (MS. 2262, f. 132). Mrs. Gaskell's letters appear
respectively as G.L., Nos. 195, 192 (dated [?8-14 May 1854] by Chapple
and Pollard); the relevant letters by Dickens are those to Mrs. Gaskell of
Thursday 16 [15] (to Saturday 17) June 1854, 26 July 1854, 20 August
1854, and those to Wills of 20 August 1854, 23 August 1854, 24 August
1854.

[12] Household Words, X, 540-551.

[13] In a letter to (almost certainly) Dickens of Sunday [(post 14) December 1854], now in the Library of the University of California, Los
Angeles: G.L., No. 220 (the recipient being ?Charles Dickens and the
date [?17 December 1854], according to Chapple and Pollard).

[14] Quoted (from a letter of 29 October 1854 by Dickens to Wills,
now in the Huntington Library) in Hopkins, ' Dickens and Mrs. Gaskell',
The Huntington Library Quarterly, IX (1946), 372; Elizabeth Gaskell,
p. 148. Wills was also to inform Mr. Gaskell that the quantity would be
increased—perhaps in length, not number, of instalments.

[15] Works, IV, p. xxix.

treatment by Dickens. She informed Mrs. Jameson[16] that she had been led (in fact, probably quite unintentionally) to suppose twenty-two, not twenty, numbers would be her allowance; and remarked that every page had been grudged at the very last when, she nevertheless admitted, though forced to compress desperately, she had certainly exceeded the amount prescribed (presumably by two numbers). For publication in book-form, therefore, she felt it necessary—so the Preface suggests—to expand the final sections. Since these alterations have been analysed elsewhere[17], there is little here to notice, except to mention that the dovetailing occasioned by the additions was not very expertly managed[18].

A few notes may be appropriate regarding the changed ending:

1. The divergency begins in the paragraph whose opening words are ' Margaret did not feel . . . '; the second sentence of this paragraph differs in the first edition (*North and South*, II, 262) from what is found in *Household Words* (X, 548).

2. Although the last words of the preceding chapter are the same in both *Household Words* (X, 551) and the first edition (II, 322), the narratives only truly become parallel again with that chapter whose initial paragraph begins ' " Is not Margaret the heiress?" . . . ' (*Household Words*, X, 561; *North and South*, 1st edn, II, 323): thereafter an extra paragraph ('Among other hopes . . . best of that.') and a long extension (' " I have arrived . . . each other more." ') to an existing paragraph (' " Because I believe . . . to be tried." ') provide the only major departures in the first

[16] In a letter, written one Sunday evening [January 1855], now in the Yale University Library (MS Vault Sect. 16). It is quoted, fairly accurately, in Erskine, ed. *Anna Jameson: Letters and Friendships* (1812-1860), pp. 296-297; and appears as *G.L.*, No. 225.

[17] Whitfield, *Mrs Gaskell*, p. 219; Hopkins, ' Dickens and Mrs. Gaskell ', *The Huntington Library Quarterly*, IX, 375, *Elizabeth Gaskell*, p. 151; and John Alfred Victor Chapple, ed. *North and South*, by Mrs. Gaskell (New English Library forthcoming publication).

[18] Shorter [ed. *Novels and Tales*, IV (1908), p. vii] remarked upon some sentence-repetitions, but without, apparently, seeing their significance as examples of careless knitting together, where new material had been inserted.

edition (II, 325-326, 353-354) from *Household Words* (X, 561, 568).

3. During the divergency-period the difference is due on the whole to additions to the old (*Household Words*) material rather than to changes in that material. Mrs. Gaskell did not attempt any large-scale refashioning—possibly bearing in mind Mrs. Jameson's advice that 'what has been once thrown warm off the mind and has run into the mould seldom bears alteration'[19]. She attempted the alternative method of welding onto her existing material something new.

4. The lengthiest addition ('Helstone Revisited' we have called it) consists of Margaret's return to Helstone in the company of Mr. Bell; but this addition is virtually self-contained, and it in no way changes the abrupt conclusion of the Margaret-Thornton love-plot. Perhaps, however, the opinion of Mrs. Gaskell herself, contained in a letter to Mrs. Jameson, ought to be quoted for the sake of putting the author's own position fairly. After having referred to Dickens' parsimony about space, she says:

. . . / But now I am not sure if, when/ ⋏the barrier gives way between⋏/ 2 such characters as Mr Thornton/ and Margaret it would not go/ all smash in a moment,—and/ I don't feel quite certain that/ I dislike the end as it now/ stands. But, it is being re-published/ as a whole, in two vols;—and/ the question is shall I alter &/ enlarge what is already written,/ bad & hurried-up though it be?// I can not insert small pieces/ here & there—I feel as if I must/ throw myself back a certain/ distance in the story, & re-write/ it from there; retaining the present/ incidents, but filling up intervals/ of time &c &c. Would you give me/ your *very* valuable opinion as/ to this? . . . /[20]

[19] Quoted in Haldane, *Mrs. Gaskell and Her Friends,* p. 113. Miss Haldane marks her quotations by italics, but we have not followed this convention when repeating what she quotes. Even the revision was done in a hurry, as is evidenced by Mrs. Gaskell's reply to Mrs. Jameson of Tuesday 30 January [1855], now in the Berg Collection at the New York Public Library, which is more or less accurately quoted in Erskine, ed. *Anna Jameson: Letters and Friendships* (1812-1860), pp. 297-298: this letter occurs as *G.L.,* No. 227; see too Nos. 226, 229.

[20] Quoted in Erskine, ed. *Anna Jameson: Letters and Friendships* (1812-1860), pp. 296-297. Mrs. Erskine's transcript has been corrected against Mrs. Gaskell's original letter, written one Sunday evening [January 1855], now in the Yale University Library—MS Vault Sect. 16—: *G.L.,* No. 225.

It was in response to this request that Mrs. Jameson gave the advice mentioned in the third note.

North and South contains certain (perhaps inevitable) oversights attendant upon its mode of production and publication. Captain Lennox, for example, at one time[21] has the Christian name of Cosmo, at another[22] that of Sholto. Similarly Mrs. Hale praised a water-bed[23] at a time when she could not have experienced its virtues[24]. Probably it was nothing of this sort which Sir William Fairbairn pointed out to Mrs. Gaskell; but her reaction to his criticism is especially interesting, since it shows how ready she was to improve her work for later editions[25].

> Your kind and racy critiques both give me pleasure and do me good; that is to say, your praise gives me pleasure because it is so sincere and judicious that I value it; and your fault-finding does me good, because it always makes me *think*, and very often it convinces me that I am in error. This time I believe you have hit upon a capital blunder . . . I don't think a second edition will be called for; but if it should be, you may depend upon it I shall gladly and thoughtfully make use of your suggestion.
>
> I agree with you that there are a certain set of characters in 'North and South,' of no particular interest to any one in the tale, any more than such people would be in real life; but they were wanted to fill up unimportant places in the story, when otherwise there would have been unsightly gaps.[26]

A cursory collation suggests that one slip Sir William may have noticed was that Mrs. Gaskell had virtually repeated herself twice when revising the *Household Words* instalments for the first (separately printed) edition; in other words, it is conceivable that he drew attention to the imperfect dovetailing

---

[21] *Works,* IV, 278.

[22] *Works,* IV, 423.

[23] *Works,* IV, 239.

[24] *Works,* IV, 226.

[25] The inconsistencies noted in this paragraph appeared unchanged in [Elizabeth Cleghorn Gaskell] *North and South,* 2nd edn, 2 vols., London: Chapman and Hall, 1857, II, 46, 233; I, 313, 296.

[26] Quoted in Pole, ed. *The Life of Sir William Fairbairn, Bart.,* p. 461; and probably written soon after the March publication of the book (the second edition appearing some three months later—*G.L.*, No. 382). [The first edition was advertized for 26 March, the second for shortly after 9 June, in *The Athenaeum Journal of Literature, Science, and the Fine Arts,* No. 1430 (24 March 1855), p. 356; No. 1441 (9 June 1855), p. 682.] Pole's complete extract occurs as *G.L.*, No. 249 (dated [?Summer 1855] by Chapple and Pollard, who omit ' that ' from our second quoted paragraph).

upon which we have already remarked. When the book was reprinted it did not include these two redundant (because repetitious) paragraphs[27]; however, perhaps partly to compensate compositorially for the omissions, Mrs. Gaskell appended a long, meditative paragraph to the chapter entitled ' " Ne'er to Be Found Again " '. Since copies of the second edition are difficult to come by, and because of the intrinsic interest of a passage which provides yet another illustration of the author's concern with the lie *motif*, we shall quote this addition *in extenso*.

[page 321]
But when night came—solemn night, and all the/
house was quiet, Margaret still sate watching the/
beauty of a London sky at such an hour, on such a/
summer evening; the faint pink reflection of earthly/
lights on the soft clouds that float tranquilly into the/
white moonlight, out of the warm gloom which lies/
motionless around the horizon. Margaret's room/
had been the day nursery of her childhood, just when/
it merged into girlhood, and when the feelings and/
conscience had been first awakened into full activity./
On some such night as this she remembered pro-/
mising to herself to live as brave and noble a life as/
any heroine she ever read or heard of in romance, a/

[27] ' The course of Margaret's day . . . spirits and delicate health.' and ' Edith piqued herself . . . expressing her feelings.'—*North and South*, 1st edn, II, 311-313: cf. II, 263, 262-263; cont. *North and South*, 2nd edn, II, 311-312. Apparently Mrs. Gaskell was referring to only one ('Edith piqued herself . . . expressing her feelings.') of the passages when she informed her publisher in a 25 April [1855] letter (*G.L.*, No. 235)—in the Pierpont Morgan Library (Autographs-Miscellaneous-English)—that the book (1st edn, March 1855) contained a piece of sixteen lines printed twice, on pages 262 [- 263] and 312 [- 313], and reminded him that her husband, on returning one of the proofs, had asked him to enquire from the printer whether there were not a repetition. In fact of the two repeated passages all three versions—that in *Household Words* (X, 549) and both those in the first edition—differ among themselves, thus suggesting that the initial mistake lay with the author, and that she had unwittingly re-written the original (*Household Words*) passages twice when preparing the second volume. The variations are tabulated below. (Some interesting minor variants, found by collating the first three editions—*Household Words*, 1st and 2nd book-form editions—, will appear in Chapple, ed. *North and South*, by Mrs. Gaskell, New English Library forthcoming publication.)

life sans peur et sans reproche; it had seemed to/
her then that she had only to will, and such a life/
would be accomplished. And now she had learnt/
that not only to will, but also to pray, was a neces-/
sary condition in the truly heroic. Trusting to/
herself, she had fallen. It was a just consequence/
of her sin, that all excuses for it, all temptation to it,/
should remain for ever unknown to the person in/
whose opinion it had sunk her lowest. She stood//

H.W., X, 549	1st Edn, II, 263	1st Edn, II, 311-312
The course of Margaret's day	The course of Margaret's day	The course of Margaret's day
this: a	this; a	this: a
breakfast; an endless discussion of plans at which, although	breakfast; an unpunctual meal, lazily eaten by weary and half-awake people, but yet at which, in all its dragged-out length, she was expected to be present, because, directly afterwards, came a discussion of plans, at which, although	breakfast; an endless discussion of plans, at which, although
expected to be present, to give	expected to give	expected to be present to give
her with	her, with	her with
the éloquence du billet	her eloquence du billet	her eloquence du billet
Sholto, as	Sholto as	Sholto, as
his walk; lunch; the care	his morning's walk; besides the care	his walk; lunch; the care
the servants' dinner	the servants' dinner	the servant's dinner

[page 322]
face to face at last with her sin. She knew it for/
what it was; Mr. Bell's kindly sophistry that nearly/
all men were guilty of equivocal actions, and that/
the motive ennobled the evil, had never had much/
real weight with her. Her own first thought of/
how, if she had known all, she might have fearlessly/
told the truth, seemed low and poor. Nay, even now,/
her anxiety to have her character for truth partially/
excused in Mr. Thornton's eyes, as Mr. Bell had/
promised to do, was a very small and petty consi-/

evening engagement	morning engagement	evening engagement
inanity	inactivity	inanity
coming on depressed	coming upon depressed	coming **upon** depressed
spirits, and delicate health.	spirits and delicate health.	spirits **and** delicate health.
[The other passage immediately follows; and its variants are listed below.]	[The other passage immediately precedes; but its variants are listed below.]	[The other passage follows, after two intervening paragraphs; and its variants are listed below.]
H.W., X, 549	1st Edn, II, 262-263	1st Edn, II, 312-313
Margaret did not feel as if the dinner-parties would be a panacea. [This sentence opens an earlier paragraph —*H.W.,* X, 548.] Edith piqued herself	Margaret did not feel as if the dinner-parties would be a panacea. But Edith piqued herself	Edith piqued herself
dinner parties	dinner-parties	dinner-**parties**
" So different	" so different	" so different
old heavy dowager	old dowager	old heavy **dowager**
régime;	régime;	regime,
Shaw seemed	Shaw herself seemed	Shaw seemed

deration, now that she was afresh taught by death/
what life should be. If all the world spoke, acted,/
or kept silence with intent to deceive,—if dearest/
interests were at stake, and dearest lives in peril,—/
if no one should ever know of her truth or her/
falsehood to measure out their honour or contempt/
for her by, straight alone where she stood, in the/
presence of God, she prayed that she might have/
strength to speak and act the truth for evermore.//[28]

of torpid pleasure	of pleasure	of torpid pleasure
acquaintance	acquaintances	acquaintance
herself used to give.	herself used to give.	herself had formerly given.
brotherly to Margaret	brotherly to Margaret	brotherly towards Margaret
him; excepting	him, excepting	him, excepting
impression in the	impression on the	impression in the
expressing her feelings.	expressing her feelings.	expressing her feelings.

[28] *North and South*, 2nd edn, II, 321-322: the transcript of this
paragraph corresponds linearly with the original; the separating gap indicates the beginning of the second page (p. 322) of the quotation. Whether the author, like her heroine, ever lied for a good cause is uncertain;
but she may have done so at least once, in a trivial matter, as Charles
Eliot Norton learned from A. H. Clough's letter of 23 November 1857
(*The Correspondence of Arthur Hugh Clough*, ed. Mulhauser, II, 536).
The relevant paragraph appeared in the copyright edition—[Elizabeth
Cleghorn Gaskell] *North and South*, Leipzig: Bernhard Tauchnitz, 1855,
pp. 404-405—as is noted in John Alfred Victor Chapple, '*North and
South*: A Reassessment', *Essays in Criticism*, XVII (October 1967), 472,
n. 2.

APPENDIX III

THE IRONICAL ORIGIN OF
THE LIFE OF CHARLOTTE BRONTE

In June 1855 *Sharpe's London Magazine*[1] contained ' A Few Words about " Jane Eyre " ', a piece of literary gossip on the novel and its author. A painful perusal of this by Ellen Nussey resulted in her suggestion to the Rev. A. B. Nicholls that Mrs. Gaskell should undertake a memoir of his late wife, thereby replying to, and castigating the writer of, such ' a tissue of ∧malign∧ falsehoods/'[2]. In his answer[3] Mr. Nicholls expressed the more favourable reactions of Mr. Brontë and himself to the account, and stated their view that nothing ought to be done. Despite the subsequent publication of ' other/ erroneous notices'[4], he continued in this belief, though without opposing Mr. Brontë when the latter changed his mind and asked Mrs. Gaskell[5] to embark on a biography.

The first, albeit mild, irony occurs because, as Miss Hopkins

[1] *Sharpe's London Magazine of Entertainment and Instruction, for General Reading*, N.S. VI, 339-342.

[2] Quoted in Wise and Symington, *The Brontës: Their Lives, Friendships and Correspondence*, IV, 189; but their inaccurate transcript has here been corrected from the original letter to the Rev. A. B. Nicholls of 6 June 1855 (once owned by Mr. J. T. Lancaster and now belonging to the present writer): an (unprinted) annotation to this letter states that Mr. Brontë acted on its suggestions, albeit extending them. We may note that Miss Nussey, in a 29 June 1883 letter to Mrs. Flower (a typed copy being in the Brontë Section, Brotherton Collection, Leeds University Library), affirmed that Mr. Brontë's insistence on a memoir led her to suggest Mrs. Gaskell; she quotes the future biographer as saying Charlotte's father had told her: "Madam, if you have not materials you must invent them."—cf. and cont. Hutton, 'Items from the Museum Cuttings Book', *Brontë Society Transactions*, XIV (1963), 30.

[3] Quoted in Wise and Symington, *The Brontës: Their Lives, Friendships and Correspondence*, IV, 189-190: letter of 11 June 1855.

[4] Quoted in Wise and Symington, *The Brontës: Their Lives, Friendships and Correspondence*, IV, 191; and checked against the original letter from the Rev. A. B. Nicholls to Ellen Nussey of 24 July 1855 (now bound in a volume—spine-titled 'Letters from A. B. Nicholls to Ellen Nussey'— in the Brontë Section, Brotherton Collection, Leeds University Library).

[5] In a letter of 16 June 1855 (now in the Manchester University Library), first quoted in Clement King Shorter, ed. *The Life of Charlotte Brontë*, by Mrs. Gaskell—Vol. VII of *The Life and Works of*

has shown[6], Mrs. Gaskell had, about a fortnight before receiving Mr. Brontë's request, already expressed her intention of setting down what she remembered about his distinguished daughter.

A second (and richer) irony arises from the strong probability that the future official biographer had herself had a hand in that very *Sharpe's* article which Ellen Nussey had considered highly offensive. If so, then ' A Few Words about " Jane Eyre " ' has a double claim to be the origin of *The Life of Charlotte Brontë*.

The identification of the *Sharpe's* contributor comes from Mr. Richard Gilbertson. In his judgement, the entire article ' must, surely, be by Mrs. Gaskell '[7]; yet this is probably an overstatement. The studied journalistic prose of the first and final paragraphs seems unGaskellian; the middle section, on the other hand, may well be from her pen. The second paragraph, with its opening description of the wild, bleak, moorland setting of the parsonage (aptly [mis]quoted by Gilbertson), readily connects with the graphic first chapter of Mrs. Gaskell's *Life*; it links too with a statement, in her letter to George Smith of 4 June [1855][8], that her personal record of Charlotte Brontë would depict the wildness and bleakness of the Haworth scene. If, as looks likely, Mrs. Gaskell was also responsible for writing the third paragraph, then one discovers a further irony in her there quoting her own words; for certainly she must have been the lady ' who afterwards became intimate with Miss Brontë,' since unmistakable verbal parallels exist between that lady's initial impressions of the novelist and those found in one of Mrs. Gaskell's letters to Catherine Winkworth. Both passages are reproduced below, the similarity of their phraseology being indubitable; reproduced as well, for comparison's sake, is part of the

---

Charlotte Brontë and Her Sisters (Vols. I-VI, ed. Mrs. Humphrey Ward; Vol. VII, ed. Clement King Shorter), 7 vols., 1899-1900 (The Haworth Edition)—London: Smith, Elder, & Co., 1900, pp. xxiii-xxiv.

[6] Hopkins, *Elizabeth Gaskell*, pp. 159-161. She discusses and quite accurately quotes from the relevant letters by Mrs. Gaskell to George Smith of 31 May and 4 June [1855], now in the archives of Sir John Murray; they appear as *G.L.*, Nos. 241, 242. See too *G.L.*, Nos. 244, 245.

[7] Richard Gilbertson, ' Haworth Parsonage ', *The Times Literary Supplement*, 28 June 1963, p. 477.

[8] Now in the archives of Sir John Murray, and relevantly and quite accurately quoted by Miss Hopkins (*Elizabeth Gaskell*, p. 161); it occurs as *G.L.*, No. 242.

modified extract from this letter to Catherine Winkworth which Mrs. Gaskell incorporated in her *Life of Charlotte Brontë*.

A lady, who afterwards became intimate with Miss Brontë, thus describes her first introduction to her. " I arrived late at the house of a mutual friend, tea was on the table, and be-hind it sat a little wee dark person, dressed in black, who scarcely spoke, so that I had time for a good look at her. She had soft lightish brown hair, eyes of the same tint, looking straight at you, and very good and expressive; a reddish com-plexion, a wide mouth—altogether plain; the forehead square, broad, and rather overhanging. Her hands are like birds' claws, and she is so short-sighted that she cannot see your face unless you are close to her. She is said to be frightfully shy, and almost cries at the thought of going amongst strangers."[9]

Dark when I got to Winder=/mere station; a drive along the level road/ to Low-wood, then a regular clamber up/ a steep lane; then a stoppage at a pretty/ house, and then a pretty drawing room/ much like the South End one, in which were/ Sir James & Lady K S, and a little lady/ in black silk gown, whom I could not/ see at first for the dazzle in the room—; she/ came up & shook hands with me at/ once—I went up to unbonnet &c, came/ down to tea—the little lady worked away// and hardly spoke; but I had time for a/ good look at her. She is, (as she calls herself)/ *undeveloped*; thin and more than ½ a head/ shorter than I, soft brown hair not so dark/ as mine; eyes (very good and expressive/ looking straight & open at you) of the same/ colour, a reddish face; large mouth & many/ teeth gone; altogether *plain*; the forehead/ square, broad, and *rather* overhanging./ She has a very sweet voice, rather hesitates/ in choosing her expressions, but when chosen/ they seem without an effort, *admirable,*/ and *just* befitting the occasion. There is/ nothing overstrained but perfectly simple./[10]

"Dark when I got to Windermere station; a drive along the level road to Low-wood; then a stoppage at a pretty house, and then a pretty drawing-room, in which were Sir James and Lady Kay Shuttleworth, and a little lady in a black-silk gown, whom I could not see at first for the dazzle in the room;

---

[9] 'A Few Words about " Jane Eyre " ', *Sharpe's London Magazine*, N.S. VI, 342 : cf. *G.L.*, No. 77.

[10] The extract comes from Mrs. Gaskell's letter to Catherine Wink-worth of Sunday evening [25 August 1850], now in the Gaskell Section, Brotherton Collection, Leeds University Library. Together with facsimiles of its first and last pages, the entire letter is printed, fairly exactly, in Wise and Symington, *The Brontës: Their Lives, Friendships and Corres-pondence*, III, 140-146; it is also quoted, quite accurately but slightly less fully, in Haldane, *Mrs. Gaskell and Her Friends*, pp. 123-128. This letter occurs as *G.L.*, No. 75, where our extract is slightly differently punctuated.

she came up and shook hands with me at once. I went up
to unbonnet, &c.; came down to tea; the little lady worked
away and hardly spoke, but I had time for a good look at her.
She is (as she calls herself) *undeveloped*, thin, and more than
half a head shorter than I am; soft brown hair, not very dark;
eyes (very good and expressive, looking straight and open at
you) of the same colour as her hair; a large mouth; the forehead square, broad, and rather overhanging. She has a very
sweet voice; rather hesitates in choosing her expressions, but
when chosen they seem without an effort admirable, and just
befitting the occasion; there is nothing overstrained, but perfectly simple."[11]

[11] Quoted, as part of a letter to a friend of hers, by Mrs. Gaskell
(*The Life of Charlotte Brontë,* 1st edn, 1857, II, 171). After quoting
further from this letter, Mrs. Gaskell (*op. cit.,* II, 172) concludes with
two paragraphs from a different source; but her manner of quoting
misleadingly implies that all three paragraphs come from the same
letter to her (unnamed) friend: see too, on this matter, Chapple and
Pollard, ed. *The Letters of Mrs Gaskell,* p. xxvii, and their footnotes
to *G.L.,* No. 76.

APPENDIX IV

THE COMPOSITION AND PUBLICATION OF
A DARK NIGHT'S WORK

In a letter of 27 January [1859][1] Meta, on Mrs. Gaskell's behalf, asked Charles Eliot Norton to enquire whether Messrs. Ticknor & Fields would buy the (American) rights of a story her mother was engaged on for *Household Words,* its expected length being about that of *My Lady Ludlow.* Her own letter to Norton of 9 March [1859][2] indicates that the author had initially intended merely to fill some forty pages of manuscript in order to settle a debt of £18 or so; but, the narrative running on, she realized not less than 200 pages would be needed, of which more than 100 were finished : feeling this story would not bear splitting into weekly numbers, Mrs. Gaskell expressed her preference for publication in America, either as a whole or in *The Atlantic Monthly,* she being specially reluctant for it to go to Dickens' proposed new periodical—*All the Year Round*—yet she feared W. H. Wills would try to get it. The bid by Messrs. Ticknor & Fields proved, nevertheless, too small to be accept-

---

[1] Deposited in the Harvard University Library : bMS Am 1088 (2644).
[2] Deposited in the Harvard University Library. Most of the relevant passage is not printed, but briefly summarized, by Mrs. Whitehill (ed. *Gaskell-Norton Letters,* pp. 30-31). Although no title is mentioned, the story seems almost certain to be the future *A Dark Night's Work.* Mrs. Whitehill (ed. *Gaskell-Norton Letters,* p. 31, fn. 1) suggests *Lois the Witch* as a possible candidate : however, as the author had already written upwards of 100 pages (of the intended 200), such a conjecture cannot be accepted; for *Lois* occupies only 117 pages (on 118 folios, including the ornamental water-colour title-page, in the Harvard University Library—fMS Eng 1010). Chapple and Pollard, in a footnote to Mrs. Gaskell's letter (*G.L.,* No. 418), follow Mrs. Whitehill's *Lois the Witch* suggestion. Mrs. Gaskell, incidentally, perhaps overestimated her debt : £13-15-0 (not £18) would have been the balance between the £40 she named as sent on the receipt of her two stories and the prices entered for 'The Sin of a Father' (£8-8-0) and 'The Manchester Marriage' (£17-17-0) in the *Household Words* Day (or Office) Book (in the Princeton University Library); her apparent miscalculation, Professor Anne Lohrli has indicated to me, possibly arose because the latter contribution drew a higher—Extra Christmas Number—rate. (The 'Sin of a Father' entry records also, rather puzzlingly, £25 as advanced.)

579

able, as Norton learned from Marianne's 9 May 1859 letter[3]:
Marianne wrote that Sampson Low[4] had offered £1,000 for a
work only a little longer; and added that, privately speaking,
she was glad her mother had abandoned her resolve, formed
during *The Life of Charlotte Brontë* troubles, 'of publishing
for the/ future in America.' The following month Mrs. Gaskell,
after informing George Smith[5] that Sampson Low, Son & Co.
were prepared to pay £1,000 for her next three-volume novel[6],

[3] Deposited in the Harvard University Library: bMS Am 1088 (2600).

[4] Like her mother, Marianne was wont to add 'e' to the publisher's
name.

[5] In a letter of 2 June [1859], now in the archives of Sir John
Murray, fairly accurately quoted by Miss Hopkins (*Elizabeth Gaskell,*
pp. 216-217). Perhaps this letter elicited Smith's own £1,000 offer for a
three-volume novel, of which, by late October, Mrs. Gaskell had not
written a line (*Gaskell-Norton Letters,* ed. Whitehill, p. 39); however,
on 30 October, she told Norton she was leaving for Whitby (*Gaskell-
Norton Letters,* ed. Whitehill, p. 40)—a significant remark in view of
Sylvia's Lovers. Mrs. Gaskell's letters respectively occur as *G.L.,* Nos.
430 (its year given as [?1859] by Chapple and Pollard), 444 (dated
October 25 [and 30 1859]).

[6] As is shown by her letter to Smith of Tuesday [21 June 1859]—
now in the archives of Sir John Murray—, Mrs. Gaskell had Smith
rather than Low in mind when she informed James T. Fields on Tuesday 14 June [1859] of 'an offer from// an English publisher of/
1,000£ for a three vol novel,/' the purchase price to include the American rights; she also said that, were she ever again to publish, her preference would be for a sum down rather than a percentage on copies
sold, adding that she supposed her writings more popular at home than
across the Atlantic since the rate of payment was certainly very different
—the relevant fragment being in the Harvard University Library: bMS
Am 2001 (45). In this connexion it is interesting that, by 25 October
[1859], the U.S. rights of the future *Sylvia's Lovers* had, Mrs. Gaskell
believed, been by Smith & Elder 'disposed of to Mr. Field' (*Gaskell-
Norton Letters,* ed. Whitehill, p. 39); that, according to the author's
official statement of 10 May 1862 (in the Parrish Collection at the
Princeton University Library), Ticknor & Fields had authority to bring
out an American edition of the book; that, on 4 September [1862], Mrs.
Gaskell wrote telling her English publishers that, should her delay in
finishing the novel cause Ticknor & Fields to recede, the money thus
lost could be deducted from what Smith had agreed to pay her (this
letter being in the possession of Mrs. E. M. Gordon); and that there
appeared Elizabeth Cleghorn Gaskell, *Sylvia's Lovers. A Novel,* New
York: Harper & Brothers, 1863. The foregoing letters by Mrs. Gaskell
respectively appear as *G.L.,* Nos. 433 (dated [?21 June 1859] by Chapple
and Pollard), 432, 444 (dated October 25 [and 30 1859]), 508, 512;
Chapple and Pollard, in their Appendix F, record a 31 December 1862
receipt for £1,000 (owned by Mrs. Gordon) for the entire *Sylvia's Lovers*
copyright.

spoke of having a story partly-written, which, however, seemed unlikely to reach three volumes.

On 20 December 1859[7] Dickens promised £210 (with republication rights) if, by the end of June, Mrs. Gaskell would supply a serial, around 400 of her usual pages, to run for twenty-two weeks in *All the Year Round*. In a letter to Smith of 23 December [1859][8], having referred to Dickens' offer, Mrs. Gaskell mentioned a one-volume story, 120 pages of which had been written for a year and a half : this work, which, though in her opinion below *Cornhill* standards, ' might be good enough/ for *H.W.* [*sic*][9], was, she affirmed, the one she had once thought of completing for Mr. Dickens. Four days later she wrote again[10], saying she had let Dickens know she could not comply with his request; she would, she told Smith, have greatly disliked cutting up her one-volume story, the only temptation being the quarter lying ready by her—though she had resolved never again to write for *All the Year Round*. Dickens, on the other hand, was equally determined that she should, and persisted in seeking a long serial[11].

Albeit not obtaining the long serial he had wanted, Dickens, for £150, did secure the present tale, the manuscript reaching

[7] *The Letters of Charles Dickens,* ed. Dexter, III, 139.

[8] Now in the archives of Sir John Murray, it appears as *G.L.*, No. 451a.

[9] Clearly, if our dating is correct, Mrs. Gaskell must have meant *All the Year Round,* the first number of which came out on 30 April 1859. The letter also speaks of a story she had begun, perhaps to be forty of her pages long, which, intended for *The Cornhill Magazine,* was reserved for her ' best moments '; this tale appears to have been ' Curious, if True ', her contribution to the first (January 1860) number of *The Cornhill Magazine* (I, 208-219).

[10] This letter to Smith of Tuesday 27 December [1859] is in the archives of Sir John Murray. In it (*G.L.*, No. 452) Mrs. Gaskell promised to send her *Cornhill* tale in a fortnight—see our previous footnote.

[11] His subsequent offer—£400 (with the right to republish) for an eight-month serial—was made through Wills, a copy of whose 7 August 1860 letter appears in the Office (or, rather, Letter) Book of *All the Year Round* (now in the Huntington Library: HM 17507). The details are reproduced with comment in Hopkins, ' Dickens and Mrs. Gaskell ', *The Huntington Library Quarterly,* IX (1946), 378-379; *Elizabeth Gaskell,* pp. 154-155.

London on Monday [28 April 1862][12]. The complete work was not, however, then despatched[13]. Though paid in full, the author was informed that her ending would most probably not be needed till after the publication of a tale then being negotiated for, intended to succeed 'No Name' in *All the Year Round* : having mentioned this in an [October 1862] letter to Smith[14], Mrs. Gaskell went on to say she had recently received word that the conclusion was desired by the end of the month—the conclusion, as she herself remarked, to that (probably) one-volume story which had, half-finished, been for four years lying by her.

Rather ironically, in view of Dickens' eagerness for another serial after his 'North and South' experiences, the division of the narrative presented problems[15]. Writing on 30 September [1862][16], the author asked a member of an American firm—possibly Harper & Brothers, who brought out a New York edition in 1863[17]—whether he wished to make an offer for republishing in the United States her one-volume novel, 'A Night's

[12] According to what Mrs. Gaskell wrote to Marianne on Thursday [1 May 1862] in a letter, begun on (apparently) Wednesday [30 April 1862] and post-marked 4 and 5 May 1862, in the Gaskell Section, Brotherton Collection, Leeds University Library; this letter occurs as *G.L.*, No. 505 (dated [1 and 2 May 1862] by Chapple and Pollard).

[13] Miss Hopkins—erroneously—inferred from Wills' letter of 30 April 1862 (copied in the *A.Y.R.* Office Book) that Dickens then had 'the entire manuscript under his eye'—Hopkins, 'Dickens and Mrs. Gaskell', *The Huntington Library Quarterly*, IX, 381; *Elizabeth Gaskell*, p. 153. This letter to Mrs. Gaskell mentions some sixty *A.Y.R.* pages as an estimate for her tale: when printed, it filled about sixty-six.

[14] The relevant fragment of this letter is in the archives of Sir John Murray. Its dating is made possible by the fact that the ending of the fragment overlaps with the beginning of an extract from the rest of the letter given by Ward (ed. *Works*, I, pp. xxxvii-xxxviii), who supplies both place and date—Eastbourne and October 1862—; however [?Late September 1862] is the date (*G.L.*, No. 517) suggested by Chapple and Pollard. Subsequently, from Wills' 6 December 1862 letter (copied in the *A.Y.R.* Office Book), Mrs. Gaskell learned publication would commence on 10 January 1863 (Hopkins, 'Dickens and Mrs. Gaskell', *The Huntington Library Quarterly*, IX, 380); but, 'No Name' continuing till 17 January, her first instalment only appeared with the following (24 January) number.

[15] Interesting accounts of these difficulties appear in Hopkins, 'Dickens and Mrs. Gaskell', *The Huntington Library Quarterly*, IX, 379-381; *Elizabeth Gaskell*, pp. 152-153.

[16] The letter is in the Parrish Collection at the Princeton University Library; it appears as *G.L.*, No. 518.

[17] Elizabeth Cleghorn Gaskell, *A Dark Night's Work. A Novel*, New York: Harper & Brothers, 1863.

Work'[18], which, she supposed, would occupy from ten to twelve numbers in *All the Year Round*. This estimate, made before the conclusion was penned, far exceeded what Dickens subsequently had in mind. His letter to Wills, written from Paris on 18 January 1863[19], stated that altogether the story must appear in six parts, and gave instructions concerning the contents of three of these : the following day Dickens sent Wills further details—not apparently preserved—about dividing the last two parts[20]. On 29 January 1863 he once more wrote from Paris to Wills[21], telling him to do the best he could, always trying to begin a chapter where he, Dickens, had begun one, and subdividing afterwards, if this were possible. Three days later Dickens returned all the slips of 'A Dark Night's Work' which he had marked, saying he would destroy the rest[22].

Dickens' Proposed Portions *All the Year Round* Instalments[23]

No. 1 Chapters I-III.
(*A.Y.R.*, VIII, 457-465 : 16¾ cols.[24])

No. 2 Chapter IV.
(*A.Y.R.*, VIII, 481-485 : 8⅔ cols.)

No. 3 Chapter V.
(*A.Y.R.*, VIII, 505-510 : 10½ cols.)

[18] Dickens added 'Dark' to the title (*The Letters of Charles Dickens*, ed. Dexter, III, 320). Smith's retention of the adjective when his firm published the story in book-form greatly displeased the author—as is shown by Mrs. Gaskell's letter (*G.L.*, No. 524) to Marianne of Monday [1 June 1863], now in the possession of Mrs. Margaret Trevor Jones. The relevant letter by Dickens is that to Wills of 21 November 1862.

[19] *The Letters of Charles Dickens*, ed. Dexter, III, 335.

[20] *The Letters of Charles Dickens*, ed. Dexter, III, 335: letters to Wills of 18 January 1863, 19 January 1863.

[21] *The Letters of Charles Dickens*, ed. Dexter, III, 337.

[22] In his letter from Paris to Wills (*The Letters of Charles Dickens*, ed. Dexter, III, 339).

[23] In all there were nine of these (24 January - 21 March 1863): *All the Year Round*, VIII, 457-465, 481-485, 505-510, 529-533, 553-562; IX, 1-7, 25-32, 49-57, 73-84.

[24] These are only approximate estimates. Since this story opens the numbers in which it appears, the columns of text occupying the title-page are slightly less high than those on the succeeding pages—to arrive at the amount of text reckoned in terms of the usual (tall) column, it is necessary to deduct just over a third of a column from the estimate given.

No. 4   Chapter VI.
(*A.Y.R.*, VIII, 529-533 : 9½ cols.)

3rd
Portion
Chapters VII-VIII.   No. 5   Chapters VII-VIII.
(*A.Y.R.*, VIII, 553-562 : 18⅗ cols.)

4th
Portion
Chapters IX-X   No. 6   Chapter IX (ends 'if she
(chapter IX to end   could find those priceless
' happened at a   **blessings.').**
sadder time ';   (*A.Y.R.*, IX, 1-7 : 13⅓ cols.)
chapter X to begin
' Before the June
roses were in full
bloom ', and to end
'except Dixon, could
have gone straight
to her grave.').

5th
Portion
Chapter XI onwards   No. 7   Chapters X-XI (chapter X
(to begin ' In a   begins ' Mr. Corbet was so
few days Miss   well known '; after a few
Munroe [*sic*]   paragraphs comes one ending
obtained').   'happened at a sadder time.';
                             the next begins ' Before the
                             June roses were in full bloom'
                             —*A.Y.R.*, IX, 26. This
                             chapter ends 'except Dixon,
                             could have gone straight to
                             her grave.' Chapter XI
                             begins 'In a few days Miss
                             Munro obtained').
(*A.Y.R.*, IX, 25-32 : 15 + cols.)

On 24 April 1863[25] *A Dark Night's Work* appeared in book-form (London : Smith, Elder and Co.). A superficial collation indicates that for this edition Mrs. Gaskell very slightly revized her *All the Year Round* text, having stylistic considerations in mind. Thus variants like the following occur.

All the Year Round		*A Dark Night's Work*	
VIII, 461	The eldest Mr. Corbet	p. 22	Old Mr. Corbet
VIII, 484	whose company he never refused, be it said, by the way.	p. 52	whose company, however, be it said by the way, he never refused.
VIII, 484	it was arrived at.	p. 53	it was reached.
IX, 4	Mrs. Day's	p. 157	Mrs. Kay's [26]
IX, 30	By-and-by, she, herself, won	pp. 195-196	By-and-by, Ellinor/ herself won

[25] Publication was advertized for the 24th on 18 April 1863, a week later the book being announced as ready, in *The Athenaeum Journal of Literature, Science, and the Fine Arts,* No. 1851, p. 533, No. 1852, p. 564. Apparently Mrs. Gaskell refused to name a price for the right to publish in book-form, according to what her daughter wrote—quoted in [Huxley] *The House of Smith Elder,* p. 80 (where, however, her words are differently interpreted).

[26] Perhaps 'Day' in the *All the Year Round* version resulted from a compositorial misreading of the author's manuscript.

APPENDIX V

THE FIRST TWO EDITIONS OF *SYLVIA'S LOVERS*

A cursory collation revealed numerous alterations to the second edition. The majority seem minor, largely concerned with rendering the dialogue even more dialectal, often by means of abbreviation and syncopation. Nevertheless one also came upon the odd slip rectified, as in the correction of an erroneous Biblical reference[1].

Since the comparison was far from thorough, some interesting revisions of detail (though, one trusts, none of substance) may have been overlooked. Merely to indicate the general nature of these changes the variant readings for the first four chapters appear below.

	First Edition	Second Edition
I, 3	melting sheds	melting-sheds
	half-schoolmaster	half schoolmaster
	half-sailor	half sailor
	superiority, it	superiority it
	voyages, the	voyages the
I, 7	broth :	broth;
I, 8	well furnished	well-furnished
	melting houses	melting-houses
I, 9	homeward bound	homeward-bound
I, 11	ship with	ship, with
	cargo became	cargo, became
I, 13	1777	1777[2]
I, 14	over-haste	overhaste
I, 16	yet perhaps	yet, perhaps
	them;	them :
I, 21	Sylvia.	Sylvia?

[1] In the first edition a (slightly shortened) quotation is assigned to Gehazi instead of to Hazael (II Kings 8[13])—*Sylvia's Lovers*, 1st edn, II, 53-54: cont. *Sylvia's Lovers*, 2nd edn, II, 53-54; *Works*, VI, 217.

[2] This date appears unchanged from that in the first edition, nor is it altered in the 1863 Illustrated Edition (p. 8); but possibly the year should be 1797 (as amended by Ward in *Works*, VI, 8).

I, 22 Cousin   cousin
I, 23 way-side   wayside
I, 25 the/ Greenland   t'/ Greenland
       The first   T' first
       high-water   high water
I, 26 god   God
       everyday   every-day
       action to   action, to
       shop./   shop/[³]
I, 27 Aye   Ay
       throwin'   throwing
       wi' t' best   wit' t' best
       the quay   t' quay
I, 29 Christison), ' Tell   Christison)—' tell
       that   as
       shipowners   ship-owners
I, 30 the/ Crooked   t'/ Crooked
I, 31 to cover   t' cover
       We had   We'd
I, 34 Market is   Market's
       must   mun
       th' huxters   t' huxters
I, 35 a coming   a-coming
I, 36 ever   iver
       said in   said, in
I, 37 you   yo'
       you   yo'
       ever   iver
       Father   Feyther
       must   mun
       market-place   market place
I, 41 blood-relation   blood relation
       that, if   that if
I, 42 fashion under   fashion, under
I, 43 nothing, but   nothing but
       Sylvia   Sylvie
I, 44 father's   feyther's
       and seating   and, seating

³ The stop here absent, clearly a printing error, reappears in the third
edition (I, 26)—virtually a second impression of the second edition.

I, 45 never	niver
I, 47 Molly/ had left	Molly/ left
the/ quay-side	t'/ quay-side
cry, at	cry at
I, 48 you'd	yo'd
the folk	t' folk
you'd	yo'd
never	niver
I, 49 Randyvow'se	Randyvowse
Sylvia	Sylvie
I, 50 for pressing	for, pressing
wrong were	wrong, were
I, 51 others, now	others—now
Will	will
no	not
I, 52 Jeremiah	John[4]
John	Jere-/miah
I, 53 you	yo'
goin'	going
ne'er	niver
I, 54 murmured—	murmured,
Jeremiah	John
Randyvow'se	Randyvowse
Jeremiah	John
into	in
I, 55 John's	Jeremiah's
up-stairs	upstairs
it is	it's
I, 56 Jeremiah	John
is not	isn't
Jeremiah	John
I, 58 Jeremiah's/ hospitality;	John's/ hospitality,

---

4 Apparently Mrs. Gaskell had confused the brothers, forgetting that Jeremiah, as the widower (*Sylvia's Lovers,* 1st and 2nd edns, I, 41), resided over the bridge, whereas John lived at the shop. She made other such corrections (*Sylvia's Lovers,* 1st edn, II, 115-117; III, 237: cont. *Sylvia's Lovers,* 2nd edn, II, 115-117; III, 237), though at least one inconsistency concerning the Fosters went unrectified through three editions (*Sylvia's Lovers,* 1st, 2nd, 3rd edns, III, 121: cont. Illus. edn, 1863, p. 407; *Works,* VI, 433—'said John' being corrected to 'said Jeremiah').

I, 60	bridle-path	bridal-path[5]
	sea-board	seaboard
	sea-wreck	sea-wrack
I, 63	ha	ha'
	morning	morn
	afeared	afeard
I, 64	right	reet
	Ne'er	Niver
	theesel	theesel'
	getting	gettin'
	even-/ings; and there	even-/ings; there
	that	but it
I, 65	had	received
	water	watter
	daylight	dayleet
	brow/ head	brow-/head
	other person	one else
	I/ had	I'd/
	press-/gang	press-/gang's
I, 66	no/ one	no-/body
	ever	iver
	sperits as	sperits, as
	'potticary's just	'potticary's, just
	on board	a-board
	Watson,/ 'Now	Watson,/ says I, 'Now
	you't	thee
	never	niver
	and it	and, it
I, 67	wilfull	wilfu'

5 The correct—'bridle-path' (*Works*, VI, 36)—reading was restored in the 1863 Illustrated Edition (p. 34), though not in the third edition (I, 60) which, as previously noted, is virtually a second impression of the second edition. The illustrated text seems to have been carefully revized: thus, besides modifications in spelling (usually dialect) and punctuation, Mrs. Gaskell, perhaps in response to Dr. Dixon's remarks (*G.L.*, No. 537), made Monkshaven topography accord more with that of Whitby by altering 'north side' ('north-side', 2nd and 3rd edns) to 'west side' and 'northern side' to 'western side' (1st, 2nd, 3rd edns, III, 33, 35: Illus. edn, 1863, pp. 357, 359; *Works*, VI, 379, 381), albeit leaving unchanged 'North Cliff' (1st, 2nd, 3rd edns, III, 251; Illus. edn, 1863, p. 480; *Works*, VI, 510).

I, 68	on shore	a-shore
	be— !	be d—d!
	catch	cotch
	fighting	fightin'
	bidding	biddin'
I, 69	noan	naught
	never	niver
	you	yo'
	hand down on	hand on
	every	ivery
I, 70	had not	hadn't
	I am	I'm
	you	yo'
	there	theer
	Robson/	Robson,/
I, 71	blew	puffed
	slowly,	slowly.
	there	theere
	you're	yo're
	nowhere	nowheere
	you	yo'
I, 72	house place	house-place
	flax,—	flax—
I, 73	correct/	correct,/
	hand, drew	hand drew
	would, she	would she
I, 74	Aye, aye	Ay, ay
	Mother will	Mother'll
	it, if	it if
	spot,/	spot/
	Bell/	Bell,/
	red,	red;
	off; feyther	off. Feyther
	yo,'	yo',
	ne'er	niver
	ne'er	niver
	o' coaxing	for coaxing
I, 75	did, as	did as
	ne'er	niver
	dost na'	dostn't

husband perhaps;   husband, perhaps,
he has   he's
I, 76 and   an'
Daniel. But   Daniel; but
Hollands and water   Hollands-and-water
sen-/tence.   sentence :
Therefore what   Theerefore, what
there   theere
reason, I   reason I
you   yo'
conversation, Bell   conversation Bell
I, 77 not in the least   in no way
said in   said, in
she used   she had used
ones,   ones—
Philip: Philip—
man! Ne'er   man. Niver
Philip;   Philip,

APPENDIX VI

' NIGHT FANCIES '

Among her collection of Gaskelliana Mrs. Margaret Trevor Jones has a poem which, with her kind permission, is reproduced below. The handwriting—of all that appears above, as well as below, the double line (including the initials)—looks unlike Mrs. Gaskell's.

Two original poems were considered early in our study. The first, ' On Visiting the Grave of My Stillborn Little Girl ', seemingly composed on 4 July 1836, was not printed till it appeared in the first volume of Ward's Knutsford Edition (1906)—*Works*, I, pp. xxvi-xxvii. The other, a joint production by husband and wife, came out in the January 1837 number of *Blackwood's Edinburgh Magazine* (XLI, 48-50): entitled ' Sketches among the Poor. No. 1 ', it was also the last of that projected series. ' Night Fancies ' has only recently, almost incidentally, been published—by Chapple and Pollard (whose version differs very slightly from ours) in Appendix F of *The Letters of Mrs Gaskell*, 1966, pp. 967-968. Albeit in content somewhat obscure, with the absence of a date not helping matters, one might take it, *prima facie*, to be a rather elaborate piece of invention that, among other things, seeks to refer frequently but obliquely to the childhood name by which the writer was known to parents and spouse.

[page 1]

Night Fancies

The ever rushing winds
Chasing each other o'er the trembling earth
(Like children at their games
Wild hurrying in their mirth)

———

The winds come hastening by
   Shaking my desolate room
And bring with them strange sounds
   Dead voices from the tomb.

———

593

They call me by a name,
In the deep and still midnight,
The name I heard in childhood
When heart and hope were bright.

Those voices often shouted
In the fields behind our home,—
And to our Mother murmured low,
When the hour of prayer [had *deleted*] was come.

And the name they utter now
With a clear, unearthly tone
Hath passed away,—' tis [*sic*] heard no more
From me, with the dead ' ' tis [*sic*] gone.—

[page 2]
My Mother spoke it fondly
To the child upon her knee,
My Father in a solemn tone
Named it, when blessing me.

And in my dreams I hear it
In a gentle loving voice
That like a gleam of sunshine
Once made my heart rejoice.

The voice of her I loved
When first I loved the flowers
Whom I loved through the shine & shade
Of many anxious hours—

With whom the blessed words
In the old old Church were spoken
And we were bound by a tie more strong
Than the awful grave has broken

[page 3]
She comes with her look of gentleness
In the quiet hours of sleep
And I know, I know she loves me still
Yet I cannot choose but weep

When I hear my childhood's name again
  ' Twill [*sic*] be the greeting of the Blest
Welcoming the lonely one
  To their Eternal Rest

E G.

———————
———

[I   think   deleted]   this   is   by   Elzth   Cleghorn
Stevenson
Mrs Wm Gaskell

[page 4]   [blank]

APPENDIX VII

NAMES OF CHARACTERS IN MRS. GASKELL'S FICTION

More than once we have noticed our author's repetition of personal names. Perhaps it was, as Miss Rubenius remarks, 'one of Mrs. Gaskell's difficulties to invent names for her characters'[1]. On the other hand these repetitions may have arisen from a want of care or a faulty memory; for, one recalls, besides giving several characters a similar name, she sometimes bestowed various names on the same character. Since final published editions exhibit such inconsistencies, one would expect both manuscripts and subsequently-revized printed versions to reveal corrections and afterthoughts. Thus the celebrated widow of *Wives and Daughters* made MS appearances as Mrs. Brown, Mrs. Kirkpatrick, and Mrs. Fitzpatrick, before the second designation became habitual[2]; and one Cranford gentlewoman was for *Household Words* readers Miss Matey[3], whereas for readers of the book she was Miss Matty[4].

Several scholars have commented on this aspect of Mrs. Gaskell's nomenclature, yet without attempting detailed analyses; so further investigation seemed worth while. To have listed only names that occur again and again in Gaskellian fiction might

[1] Rubenius, *The Woman Question in Mrs. Gaskell's Life and Works*, p. 73, fn. 2.
[2] This is evidenced by the manuscript of 'Wives and Daughters' (now in The John Rylands Library, Manchester—English MS. 877), which has, incidentally, many authorial corrections. Below, the relevant MS readings are set against those of the first instalment, printed in *The Cornhill Magazine*, X (1864), 129-153.

	MS		*Cornhill* Instalment
f. 13	Brown	X, 135	Kirkpatrick
f. 23	Kirkpatrick's	X, 140	Kirkpatrick's
f. 23	Kirkpatrick	X, 140	Kirkpatrick
f. 24	Kirkpatrick's	X, 141	Kirk-/patrick's
f. 24	Fitzpatrick	X, 141	Kirkpatrick
f. 25	Kirkpatrick's	X, 141	Kirkpatrick's
f. 25	Kirkpatrick	X, 141	Kirkpatrick

[3] 'Our Society at Cranford', *Household Words*, IV (1851), 270.
[4] *Cranford*, 1st edn, 1853, p. 23; *Works*, II, 14.

have been open to objection : the procedure would have ignored those which, appearing but once or twice, could well be far more numerous. The following method was accordingly adopted.

An index was compiled of every name belonging to a fictional personage or to a historical personage not easily recognized as such (often, without considerable research, it is difficult to determine whether or not a character—perhaps mentioned merely in passing—is invented or historical; hence all except the most famous historical figures were covered[5]). Surnames formed the basis of the index : however, when none could be found or deduced, and in cases of doubt, the entry went under the appropriate Christian name. The primary reference for each entry applied to the name in its fullest form, not to the first mention of the character bearing it; if a surname was inferred, if a Christian name appeared elsewhere, or if a change of name took place (whether intentionally—for instance, owing to the character's marriage—or not), then such elements were enclosed by brackets, a secondary reference sometimes being given.

It would be impractical to reproduce our findings *in toto,* since over seven hundred separate headings were indexed[6]. Nevertheless a fairly representative sample may be obtained by taking the entries under every twenty-fifth heading (personal name). These are listed below. If several characters in the same work have an identical surname, then they are related—unless there is a note to the contrary.

The impression conveyed by this (one trusts) unbiassed sample is that some of Mrs. Gaskell's characters are indeed noteworthy for having ' pseudo-relatives '. Whether or not the author's repetition of personal names sprang from a fondness for certain sounds, from poverty of invention, from obscure (possibly subconscious) sources, or simply from carelessness or forgetfulness[7] remains a matter for speculation.

[5] This explains why Sir Horace Mann, for instance, appears in our sample.

[6] A precise figure could be misleading; for the indexing was certainly not undertaken with the scrupulousness such numerical exactness would imply.

[7] It is interesting that, in the midst of writing *Wives and Daughters,* Mrs. Gaskell confessed to George Smith that she ' had forgotten/ all the names ', her letter of 6 December [1864] being in the archives of Sir John Murray: *G.L.,* No. 557.

Entries under Every Twenty-Fifth Name

25. APPLETHWAITE.
    i.   Thomas Applethwaite—'Half a Lifetime Ago'
         (*Works*, V, 307).

50. BERESFORD.
    i.   Miss Beresford (Mrs. Shaw)—*North and South*
         (*Works*, IV, 13).
    ii. Lady Beresford—*North and South* (*Works*, IV, 20).
    iii. Sir John (Beresford)—*North and South* (*Works*, IV,
         20).
    iv. The Miss Beresfords (Mrs. Shaw and Mrs. Hale)—
         North and South (*Works*, IV, 20).

75. BOUPRÉ.
    i.   Boupré—*My Lady Ludlow* (*Works*, V, 93).

100. BUCKLEY.
    i.   Anne Buckley—*North and South* (*Works*, IV, 106).

125. DE CHALABRE.
    i.   Monsieur de Chalabre—'My French Master' (*Works*,
         II, 507).
    ii. Madame Chalabre (Susan Dobson)—'My French
         Master' (*Works*, II, 524).
    iii. Aimée (Chalabre)—'My French Master' (*Works*,
         II, 525).
    iv. Anne-Marguérite de Chalabre—'My French Master'
         (*Works*, II, 527).
    v.   Suzette (Susan) Chalabre—'My French Master'
         (*Works*, II, 528, 529).

150. COURTENAY.
    i.   Mr. Courtenay—*Wives and Daughters* (*Works*, VIII,
         24).

175. DARLEY.
    i.   Darley—*Sylvia's Lovers* (*Works*, VI, 59).
    ii. Darley (senior)—*Sylvia's Lovers* (*Works*, VI, 71).
    iii. Betsy Darley—*Sylvia's Lovers* (*Works*, VI, 78).
    iv. William Darley—*Sylvia's Lovers* (*Works*, VI, 512).

200. DONALD.
    i.   Donald—*A Dark Night's Work* (*Works*, VII, 559).

225. FANNY.
   i.   Fanny—*Christmas Storms and Sunshine* (*Works*, II, 198).
   ii. Fanny—*Cranford* (*Works*, II, 29).
   iii. Miss Fanny—' My French Master ' (*Works*, II, 517).
   iv. Aunt Fanny—' The Half-Brothers ' (*Works*, V, 391).
   v.   Fanny—' The Cage at Cranford ' (*Novels and Tales*, III, 202).

250. FFOULKES.
   i.   Mr. ffoulkes—*Cranford* (*Works*, II, 77).

275. GRAHAM.
   i.   Messrs. Graham—*My Lady Ludlow* (*Works*, V, 186).

300. HAMLEY.
   i.   (Squire) Roger Hamley—*Wives and Daughters* (*Works*, VIII, 44).
   ii.   Squire Stephen (Hamley)—*Wives and Daughters* (*Works*, VIII, 44).
   iii. Mrs. Hamley (*née* Osborne)—*Wives and Daughters* (*Works*, VIII, 45, 46).
   iv.   Osborne Hamley—*Wives and Daughters* (*Works*, VIII, 48).
   v.   Roger Hamley—*Wives and Daughters* (*Works*, VIII, 48).
   vi.   Fanny (Hamley)—*Wives and Daughters* (*Works*, VIII, 232).
   vii. Mrs. Osborne Hamley = (Marie-)Aimée Hamley— *Wives and Daughters* (*Works*, VIII, 351, 660, 574).
   viii. The Irish Hamleys—*Wives and Daughters* (*Works*, VIII, 409).
   ix.   Roger Stephen Osborne Hamley—*Wives and Daughters* (*Works*, VIII, 660).

325. HAYLEY.
   i.   Hayley—*Sylvia's Lovers* (*Works*, VI, 131).

350. HILTON.
    i.   Ruth Hilton (Mrs. Denbigh)—*Ruth* (*Works*, III, 3, 129).
    ii.   Mrs. Hilton—*Ruth* (*Works*, III, 35).
    iii. Mr. Hilton—*Ruth* (*Works*, III, 35).
    iv. Master Hilton—' Morton Hall ' (*Works*, II, 455).

375. HOUBIGANT.
    i.   Houbigant—*Wives and Daughters* (*Works*, VIII, 571).

400. JENKIN.
    i.   Mr. Justice Jenkin—*A Dark Night's Work* (*Works*, VII, 553).

425. KESTER.
    i.   Kester (Christopher)—*Sylvia's Lovers* (*Works*, VI, 38, 505).

450. LILY.
    i.   Lily—*Wives and Daughters* (*Works*, VIII, 104).

475. MANN.
    i.   Sir Horace Mann—*My Lady Ludlow* (*Works*, V, 44).

500. MIDDLETON.
    i.   John Middleton—' The Heart of John Middleton ' (*Works*, II, 386).
    ii.   John Middleton (senior)—' The Heart of John Middleton ' (*Works*, II, 389).
    iii. (Mrs.) Nelly (Middleton)—' The Heart of John Middleton ' (*Works*, II, 395).
    iv. Grace (Middleton)—'The Heart of John Middleton' (*Works*, II, 402).
    v.   Middleton—*The Moorland Cottage* (*Works*, II, 379).

525. MURRAY.
    i.   Mrs. Murray—*North and South* (*Works*, IV, 173).
    ii.   Mr. Murray—*Wives and Daughters* (*Works*, VIII, 520).

550. OWEN.
 i. Miss Owen (Mrs. Owen Griffiths)—'The Doom of the Griffiths' (*Works,* V, 239).
 ii. Mrs. Owen (Mrs. Griffiths [second wife to the husband of the above])—'The Doom of the Griffiths' (*Works,* V, 245, 265).
 iii. Robert (Owen)—'The Doom of the Griffiths' (*Works,* V, 264).

575. PRATT.
 i. Miss (Jessy) Pratt—'The Squire's Story' (*Works,* II, 539, 548).
 ii. Nancy Pratt—*Sylvia's Lovers* (*Works,* VI, 148).
 iii. Josiah Pratt—*Sylvia's Lovers* (*Works,* VI, 158).

600. ROSE.
 i. Mrs. Rose—'Mr. Harrison's Confessions' (*Works,* V, 420).
 ii. Hester Rose (Hester Huntroyd)—'The Crooked Branch' (*Works,* VII, 209, 256).
 iii. Jack Rose—'The Crooked Branch' (*Works,* VII, 211).
 iv. Bessy (Elizabeth) Rose—'The Crooked Branch' (*Works,* VII, 211, 232).
 v. Hester Rose—*Sylvia's Lovers* (*Works,* VI, 25).
 vi. Alice Rose—*Sylvia's Lovers* (*Works,* VI, 79).
 vii. Jack Rose—*Sylvia's Lovers* (*Works,* VI, 254).
 viii. Miss Rose—*Wives and Daughters* (*Works,* VIII, 65).

625. SHEEPSHANKS.
 i. Sheepshanks—*Wives and Daughters* (*Works,* VIII, 6).

650. STARKEY.
 i. The Starkeys—'The Poor Clare' (*Works,* V, 329).
 ii. Mr. Patrick Byrne Starkey—'The Poor Clare' (*Works,* V, 331).
 iii. Mrs. (Madame) Starkey (Miss Byrne)—'The Poor Clare' (*Works,* V, 331, 332).
 iv. Squire Starkey—'The Poor Clare' (*Works,* V, 333).

675. TREVOR.
 i. Dr. Trevor—*My Lady Ludlow* (*Works,* V, 151).

700. **WILSON.**

    i.   Alice Wilson—*Mary Barton* (*Works*, I, 14).

    ii.   George Wilson—*Mary Barton* (*Works*, I, 16).

   iii.   Jane Wilson—*Mary Barton* (*Works*, I, 16).

   iv.   Jem (James) Wilson—*Mary Barton* (*Works*, I, 29, 265).

    v.   Tom (Wilson)—*Mary Barton* (*Works*, I, 32).

   vi.   Sally (Wilson)—*Mary Barton* (*Works*, I, 35).

  vii.   Joe (Wilson)—*Mary Barton* (*Works*, I, 87).

 viii.   Will (Wilson)—*Mary Barton* (*Works*, I, 87).

   ix.   Will (William) Wilson—*Mary Barton* (*Works*, I, 166, 343).

    x.   Edwin Wilson—*Cranford* (*Works*, II, 144).

   xi.   Frank Wilson—' The Manchester Marriage ' (*Works*, V, 493).

  xii.   Captain Wilson—' The Manchester Marriage ' (*Works*, V, 494).

 xiii.   Ailsie (Wilson)—' The Manchester Marriage ' (*Works*, V, 502).

 xiv.   Alice Wilson—' The Manchester Marriage ' (*Works*, V, 502).

  xv.   Canon Wilson—*A Dark Night's Work* (*Works*, VII, 524).

 xvi.   Dr. Wilson—*Sylvia's Lovers* (*Works*, VI, 70).

APPENDIX VIII

UNTRACED OR DUBIOUS GASKELL PUBLICATIONS

Not all Mrs. Gaskell's published writings may yet have come
to light; nor, on the other hand, did she compose everything
that has been ascribed to her. The purpose of the ensuing notes
is to raise rather than settle a few such problems.

1. In Spring 1836 Mrs. Gaskell[1] was working at compositions
on poets like Dryden, Pope, Crabbe, Wordsworth, Coleridge,
and Byron. It is conceivable, although scarcely likely, that
these found their way into print. Alternatively they may
have resulted in certain articles which, submitted to *Blackwood's* following the publication of ' Sketches among the
Poor. No. 1 ', were never inserted and which their author
later considered ' both/ poor & exaggerated in tone '[2].

2. Jean-Paul Hulin[3] has claimed that Mrs. Gaskell was the
Lancashire lady who, signing herself Lizzie, contributed
' Rich and Poor '—a philanthropic poem in octosyllabic
couplets—to the fourth (May 1842) number of *The
North of England Magazine*[4]. Nevertheless the arguments he
adduces will not bear scrutiny. Indeed one of his major
reasons for making the identification—the use of Lizzie as
a signature—tells strongly against Gaskellian authorship :
Elizabeth Cleghorn Gaskell never employed (nor ever would
have employed) such a contraction of her Christian name
for literary purposes. At best what Hulin does is to provide

---

[1] According to her letter to Eliza Gaskell, post-marked 13 May 1836
and written on the morning of Thursday [12 May 1836], now in the
possession of Mrs. Margaret Trevor Jones: *G.L.*, No. 4.

[2] As she informed John Blackwood in a letter of 9 March [1859]—
National Library of Scotland: MS. 4319, ff. 9-12 (the words quoted
being on f. 11r)—: *G.L.*, No. 417.

[3] ' Les Débuts Littéraires de Mrs. Gaskell: Réflexions sur un Poème
Oublié ', *Etudes Anglaises: Grande-Bretagne—Etats-Unis*, XVII (April-
June 1964), 128-139.

[4] I, 201-203. Signed ' Lizzie ', the verses are headed ' Rich and Poor./
By A Lancashire Lady.' The periodical (latterly absorbing *Bradshaw's
Manchester Journal*) ran from February 1842 to December 1843.

some slight evidence that the author of *Mary Barton* may have been stimulated by a reading of 'Rich and Poor'.

3. Apparently in a letter to Eliza Fox begun one Monday [17 November 1851 (?)][5], Mrs. Gaskell wrote as follows.

I have offered myself to the "Critic" as a writer. I did it in a state of rage at that Marples man[6] at Liverpool, and Chapman and I swore I would penny-a-line and have nothing to do with publishers never no more; so my critics generously offered me 7s. a column. (I never saw the paper but I heard it was a respectable dullard) and I counted up and I think its about 3*d* a line, so I think I shall do well,—Wm. is very mad about it, and calls me names which are not pretty for a husband to call a wife "great goose" etc.

[5] Although her dating is erroneous, the version printed by Miss Haldane (*Mrs. Gaskell and Her Friends,* pp. 252-254) agrees quite well with the copy of part of this letter in the Gaskell Section, Brotherton Collection, Leeds University Library: *G.L.,* No. 108a (to ?Eliza Fox and dated [?17 November 1851], according to Chapple and Pollard, whose punctuation-emendation—'Chapman[;] and I'—suggests a somewhat different interpretation of the quoted passage). There seems no evidence that Mrs. Gaskell did write for *The Critic* (which, under more than one name, flourished from November 1843 to December 1863). As early as a 19 October [1848] letter (*G.L.,* No. 28) to Edward Chapman (in the Pierpont Morgan Library: Autographs-Miscellaneous-English), Mrs. Gaskell had enquired whether she could be put 'in the way// of getting articles inserted/ in any magazine'. Perhaps as a consequence, she received requests from Charlotte Cushman and Eliza Cook for articles for the latter's proposed weekly (respectively dated 21 January 1849 and 22 January 1849, their letters—cited and relevantly quoted in Waller, ed. *Letters Addressed to Mrs Gaskell by Celebrated Contemporaries,* pp. 47-49—are in The John Rylands Library, Manchester: English MS. 730/28, 26); but, as Waller (ed. *op. cit.,* p. 48) notes, she appears not to have written for *Eliza Cook's Journal* (1849-1854). Moreover, writing to her on 20 October 1849 (the first part of the letter being in The John Rylands Library, Manchester: English MS. 731/112), Mrs. Jane Loudon regretted she could not contribute to her new paper; Mrs. Gaskell did, nevertheless, subsequently submit at least one (anonymous) item, 'Mr. Harrison's Confessions', to *The Ladies' Companion* (1850-1870)—III (February-April 1851), 1-11, 49-56, 97-106. That at the time she had many manuscripts lying to hand is suggested by a communication from Mrs. Mary Howitt (whose words may imply that the author's previous *Sartain's Union Magazine* contribution—'The Last Generation in England' (July 1849)—was not her first; post-marked 20 and 21 October 1849, this (mutilated) 20 October [1849] letter to Mrs. Gaskell (in The John Rylands Library, Manchester: English MS. 730/43) is cited but not fully summarized by Waller (ed. *op. cit.,* p. 7), who does not enclose with square brackets the year in his dating.

[6] David Marples, to whose repeated republications of *Libbie Marsh's Three Eras* Mrs. Gaskell had objected (according to her earlier remarks in the same passage). See too *G.L.,* No. 74.

4. In a letter to Marianne Gaskell of Thursday [26 February 1852][7] her mother stated she had 'had a good piece of writing to do for the Athenaeum'. Since the same letter refers to her efforts on behalf of a subscription-fund for Thomas Wright, Mrs. Gaskell may merely have supplied the journal with information about the fund, a brief account of which appeared in its number for 21 February 1852[8].

5. A letter from Charles Dickens of 21 April 1854 informed Mrs. Gaskell that he had 'safely received the paper/ from M[r] Shaen—welcomed it with/ three cheers—and instantly dispatched/ it to the printer, who'[9] then had it in hand. This paper, conjectured William Edward Armytage Axon[10], was by Mrs. Gaskell, perhaps being 'One of Our Legal Fictions'—a plea for the rights of married women, published in *Household Words*[11] on 29 April 1854. However the *Household Words* Day Book[12] lists Miss Lynn, not Mrs. Gaskell, as the author of 'One of Our Legal Fictions'; it records, moreover, no Gaskell contribution between 'Modern Greek Songs'[13] and 'Company Manners'[14], pay-

[7] Copies of which (*G.L.*, No. 116a), once owned by Mr. J. T. Lancaster, belong to the present writer.

[8] 'Our Weekly Gossip', *The Athenaeum Journal of Literature, Science, and the Fine Arts*, No. 1269, p. 226. However, according to Leslie Alexis Marchand ('*The Athenaeum*': *A Mirror of Victorian Culture,* Chapel Hill: The University of North Carolina Press, 1941, p. 225), who had access to an *Athenaeum* marked file (*op. cit.,* p. ix), Mrs. Gaskell was one of those reviewing general literature for the journal.

[9] This passage (from the letter in The John Rylands Library, Manchester: English MS. 729/20) is rather inaccurately reproduced by Dexter (ed. *The Letters of Charles Dickens,* II, 554), who encloses 1854 with square brackets, although the year appears in the original dating.

[10] William E. A. Axon and Ernest Axon, 'Bibliography of the Writings of Mrs. Elizabeth Cleghorn Gaskell, Author of "Mary Barton," and of Her Husband, the Rev. William Gaskell, M.A.', *Papers of the Manchester Literary Club,* XXI (1894-5), 467. (This bibliography was reprinted with the cover-title *Gaskell Bibliography: A List of the Writings of Mrs. E. C. Gaskell, Author of "Mary Barton," and of Her Husband, the Rev. William Gaskell, M.A.,* Manchester, London, Liverpool, Bristol, and Leeds: John Heywood, 1895—see p. 3.)

[11] IX, 257-260.

[12] Now in the Princeton University Library. Professor Anne Lohrli generously supplied information about these Office Book entries; and identified the contributor, Thomas, as William Moy Thomas.

[13] *Household Words,* IX (25 February 1854), 25-32.

[14] *Household Words,* IX (20 May 1854), 323-331.

ment for both these going to (hence presumably through)
Mrs. Shaen. (Incidentally, Axon might have suggested that
the piece Dickens had in mind was ' Missing, A Married
Gentleman ', to be found in the previous—22 April
1854—number of *Household Words*[15]. Albeit not by Mrs.
Gaskell—the Day Book attributes it to Thomas—, this
article contains a long extract from Dr. William King's
Political and Literary Anecdotes of His Own Times[16], intended as ' an interesting addition to the stories of " Disappearances " in earlier numbers of *Household Words* '[17]).

6. Mrs. Gaskell concluded a letter to Frederick James Furnivall
of 17 June [1858][18] by remarking that she would 'like
to write,/ *along with those others,*/ for that Quarterly '—which one, she did not specify; but it was that about
which Thomas Hughes wrote to her on 3 July 1858[19], whose
first number was to appear in January 1859. The project did
not reach fruition, though instead a monthly—*Macmillan's
Magazine,* ed. David Masson—began publication on 1 November 1859[20]. Solicited for contributions[21], Mrs. Gaskell, as
far as is known, submitted only her ' Robert Gould Shaw '
notice—*Macmillan's Magazine,* IX (December 1863), 113-
117.

7. According to Payne, who was a friend of the Miss Gaskells,
their mother had been ' a contributor to the columns of
the *Daily News.*'[22]

[15] IX, 227-228.
[16] London: John Murray, 1818, pp. 237-245.
[17] ' Missing, A Married Gentleman ', *Household Words,* IX, 227.
[18] In the Henry E. Huntington Library and Art Gallery—MSS Catalogue: FU 318—: *G.L.,* No. 399.
[19] His letter (in The John Rylands Library, Manchester: English MS.
730/45) is relevantly and quite accurately quoted by Waller (ed. *Letters
Addressed to Mrs Gaskell by Celebrated Contemporaries,* p. 49), who,
however, fails to include his words about it being ' from Furnivall/' that
he had learned of her willingness to contribute.
[20] Edward Clarence Mack and Walter Harry Green Armytage, *Thomas
Hughes: The Life of the Author of ' Tom Brown's Schooldays ',* London:
Ernest Benn Limited, 1952 [1953], pp. 107-109.
[21] *G.L.,* Nos. 440, 442; see too No. 237 (to ?F. J. Furnivall and dated,
doubtfully and probably incorrectly, [?May ?1855], according to Chapple
and Pollard).
[22] Payne, *Mrs. Gaskell and Knutsford,* 1905, p. 97; see too Payne,
Mrs. Gaskell: A Brief Biography, p. 45. His source may have been an
obituary—such as ' Mrs. Gaskell ', *The Inquirer,* Vol. XXIV, No. 1220

8. Acknowledging a request for her to contribute to a projected periodical, conceived along the lines of *Fraser's* but Unitarian in persuasion, Mrs. Gaskell[23] warned of the financial and other difficulties ahead, especially with John Chapman as the proposed publisher; yet she wished the venture well, and, despite an unwillingness to commit herself, held out hopes that possibly she might write something.

9. In a 10 May letter[24] Mrs. Gaskell, having expressed her obligations to the unnamed recipient and his son for trouble taken to bring about a literary engagement between herself and Dr. Noyes, regretfully declined for the moment any such engagement, her time being fully occupied.

10. Writing on 19 November 1903, W. E. A. Axon confessed to Clement Shorter that among the papers of Mrs. Gaskell's he had not traced was ' one that should/ be of interest written on the/ side of the North in the/ American Civil War.'[25] One wonders whether he had searched *The Atlantic Monthly*: for in 1857 (probably early June) Charles Eliot Norton had passed on to Mrs. Gaskell a request from its

---

(18 November 1865), p. 742. Mentioning that on good authority Mrs. Gaskell had ' contributed to the *Daily News* in the 'fifties,' Mrs. Chadwick remarked that a diligent search had nevertheless proved unsuccessful, there being ' no record in the book of payments to contributors.'—E. A. Chadwick, ' The Gaskell Collection at Manchester ', *The Bookman*, XLI (1911), 45. Mrs. Gaskell's 7 February 1862 letter, declining because of literary commitments an offer to write for *The Daily News* about a topic (probably the Lancashire Cotton Famine) on which in any case she felt far from competent, might indicate a previous connexion between writer and paper: this letter (*G.L.*, No. 500), whose unnamed recipient could have been the *Daily News* editor, Thomas Walker, is owned by Mr. John H. Samuels (784 Park Avenue, New York, U.S.A.). As early as Saturday [15 September 1849] Mrs. Gaskell had sought advice, from Susanna Winkworth, about newspaper-writing, according to the latter's Thursday 20 September [1849] letter to her sisters—Her Sister [Susanna Winkworth], ed. *Letters and Memorials of Catherine Winkworth*, I (1883), 203. *The Daily News* began in January 1846, with Dickens (albeit briefly) as its first editor; and continued throughout the century.

[23] In a letter, written one Saturday, whose first part is in the Parrish Collection at the Princeton University Library and whose second part is in the Yale University Library (MS Vault File): *G.L.*, No. 638—the correspondent is unnamed.

[24] Owned by The Historical Society of Pennsylvania, this letter (*G.L.*, No. 429) is given [?1859] for its year by Chapple and Pollard.

[25] Axon's letter resides among correspondence in the Shorter Section, Brotherton Collection, Leeds University Library.

editor, James Russell Lowell, for contributions[26]; and on
at least two occasions she considered—albeit later decided
against—submitting something[27]. However the object of
Axon's search could have been her ' Robert Gould Shaw '
memoir—*Macmillan's Magazine,* IX (1863), 113-117—,
later unearthed by John Albert Green[28].

11. According to Henry Richard Fox Bourne[29], himself a contributor, Mrs. Gaskell was among those writers gathered
together by John Malcolm Ludlow, first editor of *The
Reader* (which ran from 3 January 1863 to 12 January
1867). Although her name appears on several lists of contributors[30], the *Reader* indexes record only reviews of her
stories[31]. Nevertheless she may have sent unsigned pieces—
a possibility supported by the following [1863] letter[32].

[page 1]

46 Plymouth Grove
February 9th

My dear Mr Ludlow,/
    I am very glad/ you liked my paper;/ and
please do what/ you think best with/ the rest of the
MSS./ If you think it's being/ published will do any//

[26] The relevant part of Norton's 20 June 1857 letter to Lowell is quoted
in *Letters of Charles Eliot Norton, with Biographical Comment,* ed.
Norton and DeWolfe Howe, I, 170-171.

[27] *Gaskell-Norton Letters,* ed. Whitehill, pp. 31, 39: *G.L.,* Nos. 418,
444—see too Nos. 394, 396. *The Atlantic Monthly. A Magazine of
Literature, Art, and Politics* commenced in November 1857.

[28] Chadwick, ' The Gaskell Collection at Manchester ', *The Bookman,*
XLI (1911), 45. The memoir is listed in Green, *A Bibliographical Guide
to the Gaskell Collection in the Moss Side Library,* 1911, p. 58.

[29] *English Newspapers: Chapters in the History of Journalism,* 2 vols.,
London: Chatto & Windus, 1887, II, 314—a reference I owe to John
McVeagh, Ph.D. (Birmingham University).

[30] Such as that (for the first two volumes) in *The Reader: A Review
of Literature, Science, and Art,* Vol. III, No. 62 (5 March 1864), p. 285;
and that in *The Athenaeum Journal of Literature, Science, and the Fine
Arts,* No. 1849 (4 April 1863), p. 468.

[31] Both *Sylvia's Lovers* and *A Dark Night's Work* were reviewed in
The Reader, Vol. I—No. 9 (28 February 1863), pp. 207-208; No. 19 (9
May 1863), pp. 450-451.

[32] Watermarked 1862, this letter is in the Cambridge University
Library: MS. Add. 7348/10/128.

[page 2]

good, please let it be/ published where you/ think best,
—but/ if it is superfluous/ and unneeded, e=/=qually
please, burn/ it. Only don't let/ *me* see it's face again//

[page 3]

I am very glad a=/=bout the Reader's/ steady
progress. I/ know I like it!/
Yours very truly/
E. C. Gaskell//

[page 4]   [blank]

12. On 7 January Mrs. Gaskell acknowledged, without refusing
or promising to fulfil, a request for a contribution to a
'volume of stories published for the Lancashire Relief
Fund.'[33]

13. John Ruskin's 6 July 1865 letter[34] testifies that he had often
read in manuscript 'a little pretty book of' Mrs. Gaskell's.
This could have been a work (such as 'The Half-Brothers')
that was eventually published under her name or even one
(like, perhaps, a second 'Camorra' sketch[35]) that may never
have appeared in print.

14. In his *Dictionary of National Biography* article on Mrs.
Gaskell, Dr. Adolphus William Ward records a family tradition that she composed a poem 'on a wounded stag, as well
as the opening of a short story, probably begun even before
her marriage': apparently he had no evidence that either
was printed, though it seems just possible that the latter was
the first of the 'Two Fragments of Ghost Stories' which
in 1906 Ward himself incorporated in the penultimate

[33] A copy of this letter to an unnamed correspondent (*G.L.*, No. 519a,
its year being [?1863] according to Chapple and Pollard)—the original
apparently once having been in the Knutsford Public Library—was
generously loaned to the present writer by Mrs. Jane Whitehill.

[34] A copy of part of his letter to Mrs. Gaskell is in Shorter and
Symington, 'Correspondence, Articles & Notes Relating to Mrs. E. C.
Gaskell. Transcripts', Vol. II, Section of Extracts Relating to Mrs.
Gaskell and Her Work—a typescript in the Gaskell Section, Brotherton
Collection, Leeds University Library.

[35] *G.L.*, Nos. 523a, 524, 532.

volume of his Knutsford Edition. Other literary projects Mrs. Gaskell commenced without completing include the eighteenth-century tale, set on the Yorkshire borders, mentioned in her *Mary Barton* Preface[36]; her Mme de Sévigné study[37]; and the 'Two Mothers' (abandoned for *Wives and Daughters*)[38] : moreover she may—conceivably—have embarked, albeit with reluctance, upon a philanthropically-orientated Christmas-story[39]—this not fulfilling her publisher's expectations[40], *The Moorland Cottage* appeared instead.

The foregoing notes certainly do not exhaust the possibilities. Even when initially Mrs. Gaskell declined[41], or virtually declined[42], requests for material, she may have changed her mind. Moreover future discoveries—marked files of Victorian periodicals (identifying unsigned items), for instance, as well as letters by or about Mrs. Gaskell—may result in confident additions to the canon. Indeed information has just come : from Mrs. Walter E. Houghton (Wellesley College Library, Wellesley, Massachusetts 02181) about E[lizabeth (?)] C[leghorn (?)] G[askell (?)], 'Shams', *Fraser's Magazine for Town and Country*, LXVII (February 1863), 265-272; and from John F. Byrne (St. Procopius College, Lisle, Illinois 60532) about [Elizabeth Cleghorn Gaskell (?)], Review of *Lancashire's Lesson* by W. T. M. Torrens, in *The Reader: A Review of Literature, Science, and Art*, V (25 March 1865), 333-335.

---

36 *Works*, I, p. lxxiii.
37 *G.L.*, Nos. 499, 501, 502, 509b, 532.
38 *G.L.*, Nos. 532, 550.
39 *G.L.*, No. 81.
40 *G.L.*, No. 66. Were such a Christmas book started, it may—despite the publisher's unencouraging verdict—have been continued (even alongside what became *The Moorland Cottage*), and perhaps been variously styled 'December Days' (*aliter* 'The Fagot') and/or 'Rosemary' (*G.L.*, Nos. 87, 81): however these are mere speculations; for quite likely Mrs. Gaskell wrote only one story, that whose final title was *The Moorland Cottage*. See too *G.L.*, Nos. 79, 382.
41 As in her 11 December 1852 letter to an unnamed correspondent (in the Parrish Collection at the Princeton University Library): *G.L.*, No. 519 (the year being mistakenly transcribed as 1862 by Chapple and Pollard).
42 As in her 27 April letter to an unknown lady. Owned by the present writer, this letter (*G.L.*, No. 568) has [?1865] conjectured for its year by Chapple and Pollard.

BIBLIOGRAPHY

FOREWORD TO BIBLIOGRAPHY

The first of the ensuing sections comprises books, articles, and typescripts cited in our study. Professor James Barry has provided a useful survey of Gaskelliana up to 1962[1]. The fullest bibliographies are by Professor Whitfield[2], Dr. Northup[3], and Miss Halls[4]: of these the last is the most recent, extending the earlier two; but one must treat with circumspection Miss Halls' corrections to Northup's compilation, corrections based on a list of *errata* composed by Miss Hopkins[5]. Besides the great copyright repositories, the Manchester Central Reference Library contains the widest range of printed Gaskell material[6]. Professor Whitfield's valuable collection is lodged at Brook Street Unitarian Chapel, Knutsford; and the Knutsford Public Library houses several inscribed copies, with other items having family associations[7]. Most standard (and some rarer) editions belong to the present writer, who also owns Mr. J. T. Lancaster's Gaskell acquisitions.

[1] James Donald Barry, 'Elizabeth Cleghorn Gaskell: Charles Kingsley', in *Victorian Fiction: A Guide to Research,* ed. Lionel Stevenson, Cambridge, Massachusetts: Harvard University Press, 1964, pp. 245-263.

[2] *Mrs Gaskell,* pp. 221-253.

[3] The Bibliography by Clark Sutherland Northup in Sanders, *Elizabeth Gaskell,* pp. 163-267.

[4] Catharine Margaret Ellen Halls, 'Bibliography of Elizabeth C. Gaskell', Diploma in Librarianship dissertation, University of London, 1957. There are copies at the London University Library and the Manchester Central Reference Library.

[5] Halls, 'Bibliography of Elizabeth C. Gaskell', pp. 1-2.

[6] See Malcolm-Hayes, 'Notes on the Gaskell Collection in the Central Library', *Memoirs and Proceedings of the Manchester Literary & Philosophical Society (Manchester Memoirs),* LXXXVII (1945-1946), 149-174.

[7] Once in the Special Collection (*Knutsford Public Library. Catalogue Complete to Date, October 25th,* 1921, Knutsford: F. Alcock, Printer, 1921, pp. 182-186), not all these are now at Knutsford, perhaps having belonged to G. A. Payne, then Hon. Secretary to the Library Committee: the current holdings are noted in the comprehensive Bibliography by Graham Owens (to his Bangor M.A. thesis, 'Town and Country in the Life and Work of Mrs. Gaskell and Mary Russell Mitford', 1953)—a useful guide, incidentally, to various Gaskell miscellanea.

The second section records, very provisionally, the locations of Mrs. Gaskell's letters; it also indicates, again very provisionally, both the extent of these holdings and the nature of the recipients[8]. Our researches unearthed much of the novelist's correspondence. A far more detailed account would, therefore, have been required, if Mr. J. A. V. Chapple and Mr. Arthur Polland had not fittingly resolved that the centenary of Mrs. Gaskell's death should be followed by an edition of her letters[9]. No comprehensive list of unprinted material exists[10]; so the opportunity was taken to note the whereabouts of certain ' Gaskelliana '—pertinent primary sources other than the author's letters.

[8] Often the names of recipients need to be conjectured; but in this respect square brackets have not been used.

[9] Besides dealing exhaustively with all Mrs. Gaskell's letters known to them in 1966, Chapple and Pollard (ed. *The Letters of Mrs Gaskell*, pp. 967-971), in their ' Miscellaneous ' Appendix F, summarize or quote receipts and other Gaskelliana.

[10] Printed guides include Barry, ' Elizabeth Gaskell: Charles Kingsley ', in *Victorian Fiction: A Guide to Research*, ed. Stevenson, pp. 247-249; Hopkins, *Elizabeth Gaskell*, p. 341; Rubenius, *The Woman Question in Mrs. Gaskell's Life and Works*, p. 373; Leslie A. Marchand, ' The Symington Collection ', *Journal of Rutgers University Library*, XII (1948), 11-12; the Appendix—' Gaskell Manuscript Material in Manchester '—in Pollard, ' The Novels of Mrs. Gaskell ', *Bulletin of the John Rylands Library, Manchester*, XLIII (1961), 424-425; and Alexander D. Wainwright, ' The Morris L. Parrish Collection of Victorian Novelists: A Summary Report and an Introduction ', *The Princeton University Library Chronicle*, XVII (1956), 60, 65. Many letters are quoted in Erskine, ed *Anna Jameson: Letters and Friendships* (1812-1860); Haldane, *Mrs. Gaskell and Her Friends*; Hopkins, *Elizabeth Gaskell*; Pollard, *Mrs Gaskell: Novelist and Biographer*; Albert H. Preston, Appendix on Some Gaskell Letters, in Arthur Pollard, ' Mrs. Gaskell's *Life of Charlotte Brontë* ', *Bulletin of the John Rylands Library, Manchester*, XLVII (March 1965), 477-488; Rubenius, *The Woman Question in Mrs. Gaskell's Life and Works*; Whitehill, ed. *Gaskell-Norton Letters*; Whitfield, *Mrs Gaskell*; Wise and Symington, *The Brontës: Their Lives, Friendships and Correspondence*; and Wright, *Mrs. Gaskell*. Also noteworthy is a special selection, *Letters on Charlotte Brontë by Mrs. Gaskell* [London, c. 1916], privately printed by Clement Shorter, whose texts sometimes have greater authority than those of Chapple and Pollard (cf. and cont. *G.L.*, Nos. 48, 55, 79, 146, 274; and No. 316 [where the Shorter text, though followed, is not quite accurately reproduced]): for a background to several of these (included among letters Meta Gaskell sent Shorter, he giving her some of her mother's more private ones), see Clement King Shorter, ' Mrs. Gaskell and Charlotte Brontë ', *Brontë Society Transactions*, Vol. V, No. 4 (Part 26 of the Society's Publications), 1916, pp. 144-149 (a reprint of C.K.S., ' A Literary Letter: Mrs. Gaskell and Charlotte Brontë ', *The Sphere*, 2 October 1915).

(a) LIST OF PRINTED WORKS AND TYPESCRIPTS CITED

ADSHEAD, Joseph. *Distress in Manchester. Evidence (Tabular and Otherwise) of the State of the Labouring Classes in 1840-42*. London : Henry Hooper, 1842.

AINGER, Alfred. Article on George Louis Palmella Busson Du Maurier (1834-1896). In *The Dictionary of National Biography*.

ALLEN, Walter Ernest. ' Mrs. Gaskell in Town and Country ', *The Daily Telegraph and Morning Post*, 28 October 1965, p. 20.

ALLOTT, Miriam. *Elizabeth Gaskell*. Writers and Their Work (ed. Bonamy Dobrée), No. 124. London, Cape Town, Melbourne, New York, and Toronto : Longmans, Green & Co. for The British Council and the National Book League, 1960.

ANNUAL BIOGRAPHY AND OBITUARY. Obituary Notice of William Stevenson. In *The Annual Biography and Obituary: 1830*, XIV (London : Longman, Rees, Orme, Brown, and Green, 1830), 208-214.

ANNUAL REGISTER. The Annual Register; or, A View of the History, Politics, and Literature, [Vols.] *for the Year*[s] 1795, 1796, 1799. London : F. C. & J. Rivington.

ASHTON, Thomas Southcliffe. *Economic and Social Investigations in Manchester, 1833-1933: A Centenary History of the Manchester Statistical Society*. Intro. The Earl of Crawford and Balcarres. London : P. S. King & Son, Ltd., 1934.

ASTON, Joseph. *The Lancashire Gazetteer: an Alphabetically Arranged Account of the Hundreds, Market Towns, Boroughs, Parishes, Townships, Hamlets, Gentlemens' Seats, Rivers, Lakes, Mountains, Moors, Commons, Mosses, Antiquities, &c. in the County Palatine of Lancaster; Together with Historical Descriptions of the Chief Places, with their Fairs, Markets, Local and Metropolitan Distances, Charters, Church Livings, Patrons, &c*. London : Longman, Hurst, Rees, and Orme; County of Lancaster : All booksellers, 1808.

ATHENAEUM. Account of the Subscription-Fund for Thomas Wright. In ' Our Weekly Gossip ', *The Athenaeum Journal of Literature, Science, and the Fine Arts*, No. 1269 (21 February 1852), p. 226.

ATHENAEUM. The Athenaeum Journal of Literature, Science, and the Fine Arts.
Advertisements and Reviews.

Advertisements for Mrs. Gaskell's *A Dark Night's Work* (1st edn) —No. 1851 (18 April 1863), p. 533; No. 1852 (25 April 1863), p. 564.

Advertisements for *Garibaldi at Caprera,* pref. Mrs. Gaskell (1st edn)—No. 1790 (15 February 1862), p. 235; No. 1792 (1 March 1862), pp. 295, 306.

Advertisement for Mrs. Gaskell's *Mary Barton* (1st edn)—No. 1094 (14 October 1848), p. 1019.

Review of Mrs. Gaskell's *Mary Barton* (1st edn)—No. 1095 (21 October 1848), pp. 1050-1051.

Advertisement for Mrs. Gaskell's *North and South* (1st edn)— No. 1430 (24 March 1855), p. 356.

Advertisement for Mrs. Gaskell's *North and South* (2nd edn)— No. 1441 (9 June 1855), p. 682.

Advertisements for *The Reader: A Review of Current Literature* —No. 1836 (3 January 1863), p. 26; No. 1849 (4 April 1863), p. 468.

Advertisements for Mrs. Gaskell's *Sylvia's Lovers* (1st edn)—No. 1842 (14 February 1863), p. 212; No. 1843 (21 February 1863), p. 273.

Review of Mrs. Gaskell's *Sylvia's Lovers* (1st edn)—No. 1844 (28 February 1863), p. 291.

Advertisements for Mrs. Gaskell's *Sylvia's Lovers* (2nd edn)—No. 1848 (28 March 1863), p. 413; No. 1849 (4 April 1863), p. 469.

Advertisements for Mrs. Gaskell's *Sylvia's Lovers* (3rd edn)—No. 1851 (18 April 1863), p. 533; No. 1852 (25 April 1863), p. 564.

Advertisements for Mrs. Gaskell's *Sylvia's Lovers* (Illus. edn)— No. 1883 (28 November 1863), p. 729; No. 1884 (5 December 1863), p. 742; No. 1885 (12 December 1863), p. 788.

ATLANTIC MONTHLY. The Atlantic Monthly. A Magazine of Literature, Art, and Politics, November 1857 (inception).

[AUDIN, Jean-Marie-Vincent.] Richard. *Guide du Voyageur en France.* In the ' Guides-Joanne ' Series. 25th edn. Paris: L. Hachette, 1861. (Based on an entry in the *Catalogue Général des Livres Imprimés de la Bibliothèque Nationale.*)

AXON, William Edward Armytage and Ernest Axon. ' Bibliography of the Writings of Mrs. Elizabeth Cleghorn Gaskell, Author of " Mary Barton," and of Her Husband, the Rev. William Gaskell, 'M.A.', *Papers of the Manchester Literary Club*, XXI (1894-5), 465-486. (This was reprinted, see next item.)

AXON, William Edward Armytage and Ernest Axon. *Gaskell Bibliography: A List of the Writings of Mrs. E. C. Gaskell, Author of " Mary Barton," and of Her Husband, the Rev. William Gaskell, M.A.* Manchester, London, Liverpool, Bristol, and Leeds: John Heywood, 1895. (Cover-title of a reprint of the last item.)

BALD, Marjory Amelia. *Women-Writers of the Nineteenth Century*. Cambridge: The University Press, 1923.

BAMFORD, Samuel. *Bamford's ' Passages in the Life of a Radical' and ' Early Days'*. Ed. Henry Dunckley. 2 vols. London: T. Fisher Unwin, 1893.

BARROW, John. *The Life and Correspondence of Admiral Sir William Sidney Smith, G.C.B.* 2 vols. London: Richard Bentley, 1848.

BARRY, James Donald. ' Elizabeth Cleghorn Gaskell: Charles Kingsley '. In *Victorian Fiction: A Guide to Research*, ed. Lionel Stevenson, Cambridge, Massachusetts: Harvard University Press, 1964, pp. 245-276.

BATESON, Frederick Noel Wilse. Ed. *The Cambridge Bibliography of English Literature*. 4 vols. Cambridge: The University Press, 1940.

BAYLEY, John. ' Why Read Mrs. Gaskell?', *Sunday Telegraph*, 14 November 1965, p. 18.

[BAYLY, Ada Ellen.] Edna Lyall. ' Mrs. Gaskell '. In *Women Novelists of Queen Victoria's Reign: A Book of Appreciations*, London: Hurst & Blackett, Limited, 1897, pp. 117-145.

BEARD, Paul. Ed. *The Cage at Cranford and Other Stories*. By Mrs. Gaskell. London, Edinburgh, Paris, Melbourne, Toronto, and New York: Thomas Nelson & Sons Ltd [1937].

[BENJAMIN, Lewis Saul.] Lewis Melville. ' The Centenary of Mrs. Gaskell ', *The Nineteenth Century and After: A Monthly Review Founded by James Knowles*, LXVIII (September 1910), 467-482.

BESWICK, Thomas. Reported in " ' Old Knutsford ' recalled on author's birthdate ", *Knutsford Guardian,* 28 September 1956, p. 9.

BIBBY, R. E. ' " Mary Barton " and Greenheys Fields ', *Manchester City News,* 22 June 1878.

BLACK, Adam and Charles. *Black's Picturesque Guide to Yorkshire with Map of the County, and several Illustrations.* Edinburgh : Adam and Charles Black, 1858.

BLAND, D. S. ' *Mary Barton* and Historical Accuracy ', *The Review of English Studies,* N.S. I (January 1950), 58-60.

BLOMFIELD, Alfred. Ed. *A Memoir of Charles James Blomfield, D.D., Bishop of London, with Selections from His Correspondence.* 2 vols. London : John Murray, 1863.

BOASE, George Clement. Article on Samuel Greg (1804-1876). In *The Dictionary of National Biography.*

BOSWELL, James. *Boswell's ' Life of Johnson ', Together with Boswell's ' Journal of a Tour to the Hebrides ' and Johnson's ' Diary of a Journey into North Wales '.* Ed. George Birkbeck Hill. Rev. and enlarged by Lawrence Fitzroy Powell. 6 vols. Oxford : The Clarendon Press, 1934-1950.

BOURNE, Henry Richard Fox. *English Newspapers: Chapters in the History of Journalism.* 2 vols. London : Chatto & Windus, 1887.

BOWEN, Elizabeth Dorothea Cole. Intro. *North and South.* By Mrs. Gaskell. London : John Lehmann, 1951.

BRIDELL-FOX, Mrs. Eliza F. ' Memories ', *The Girl's Own Paper,* Vol. XI, No. 551 (19 July 1890), pp. 657-661.

BRIDGEMAN, William Clive. Intro. *Country Conversations: The Humour of Old Village Life in the Midlands.* [By Georgine Tollet.] London : John Murray, 1923. (The first, privately printed, edition—London : T. Richards—came out in 1881.)

BRITISH QUARTERLY REVIEW. Review of *Mary Barton.* In *The British Quarterly Review,* IX (February 1849), 117-136.

BROWN, William Henry. 'Mrs. Gaskell : A Manchester Influence', *Papers of the Manchester Literary Club,* LVIII (1932), 13-26.

BROWNING, Elizabeth Barrett. *The Letters of Elizabeth Barrett Browning, with Biographical Additions.* Ed. Frederic George Kenyon. 2 vols. London : Smith, Elder, & Co., 1897.

BUTLER, Samuel. *The Life and Letters of Dr. Samuel Butler, Head-Master of Shrewsbury School 1798-1836, and Afterwards Bishop of Lichfield, in So Far as They Illustrate the Scholastic, Religious, and Social Life of England,* 1790-1840. 2 vols. London: John Murray, 1896.

CALEF, Robert. *More Wonders of the Invisible World: or, The Wonders of the Invisible World, Display'd in Five Parts.* London: Nath. Hillar; and Joseph Collyer, 1700.

CARLYLE, Alexander. Ed. *New Letters and Memorials of Jane Welsh Carlyle, Annotated by Thomas Carlyle.* Intro. James Crichton-Browne. 2 vols. London and New York: John Lane, The Bodley Head, 1903.

CARLYLE, Jane Welsh. *New Letters and Memorials of Jane Welsh Carlyle, Annotated by Thomas Carlyle.* Ed. Alexander Carlyle. Intro. James Crichton-Browne. 2 vols. London and New York: John Lane, The Bodley Head, 1903.

CARLYLE, Thomas. *Chartism.* London: James Fraser, 1840.

CAZAMIAN, Louis François. *Le Roman Social en Angleterre (1830-1850): Dickens—Disraeli—Mrs. Gaskell—Kingsley.* New edn. 2 vols. Paris: H. Didier [1935]. [The one-volume first edition—Paris: Société Nouvelle de Librairie et d'Edition (Librairie Georges Bellais), 1903—appeared in 1904.]

CECIL, Edward Christian David Gascoyne. *Early Victorian Novelists: Essays in Revaluation.* Harmondsworth, Middlesex: Penguin Books, 1948. (This is a slightly revised edition of *Early Victorian Novelists: Essays in Revaluation.* London: Constable & Co. Ltd, 1934.)

CHADWICK, Esther Alice (Mrs. Ellis H.). ' The Gaskell Collection at Manchester ', *The Bookman* (London), XLI (October 1911), 45-46.

CHADWICK, Esther Alice (Mrs. Ellis H.). *In the Footsteps of the Brontës.* London: Sir Isaac Pitman & Sons, Ltd., 1914.

CHADWICK, Esther Alice (Mrs. Ellis H.). *Mrs. Gaskell: Haunts, Homes, and Stories.* London: Sir Isaac Pitman and Sons, Ltd., 1910.

CHADWICK, Esther Alice (Mrs. Ellis H.). *Mrs. Gaskell: Haunts, Homes, and Stories.* New and rev. edn. London: Sir Isaac Pitman & Sons, Ltd., 1913.

CHADWICK, Esther Alice (Mrs. Ellis H.). Review of Mrs. Chadwick's *Mrs. Gaskell: Haunts, Homes, and Stories.* 'Biographical Guesswork', 'New Books' Section, *The Manchester Guardian,* 26 September 1910, p. 5.

CHADWICK, Esther Alice (Mrs. Ellis H.). Intro. *Sylvia's Lovers.* By Mrs. Gaskell. London: J. M. Dent & Sons, Ltd.; New York: E. P. Dutton & Co. [1911.]

CHAPPLE, John Alfred Victor and Arthur Pollard. Ed. *The Letters of Mrs Gaskell.* Manchester: Manchester University Press, 1966.

[CHORLEY, Henry Fothergill.] Review of *Wives and Daughters.* In *The Athenaeum Journal of Literature, Science, and the Fine Arts,* No. 2001 (3 March 1866), pp. 295-296.

[CHRISTYN, Jean-Baptiste.] *Histoire Générale des Païs-Bas, Contenant la Description des XVII Provinces. Edition Nouvelle, Divisée en IV volumes, augmentée de plusieurs remarques curieuses, de nouvelles figures, & des evenemens les plus remarquables jusqu'à l'an MDCCXX.* 4 vols. Brussels: François Foppens, 1720.

CLAPHAM, John Harold. *An Economic History of Modern Britain.* 3 vols. Cambridge: The University Press, 1926-1938.

CLARK, Arthur Melville. *Studies in Literary Modes.* Edinburgh and London: Oliver and Boyd, 1946.

CLOUGH, Arthur Hugh. *The Correspondence of Arthur Hugh Clough.* Ed. Frederick Ludwig Mulhauser. 2 vols. Oxford: The Clarendon Press, 1957.

COLERIDGE, Christabel Rose. 'Molly Gibson'. In *Great Characters of Fiction,* ed. Mary Elizabeth Townsend, London: Wells Gardner, Darton, & Co., 1893, pp. 209-218.

COLLEY, T. 'Gleanings and Jottings in Knutsford', *Cheshire Notes and Queries,* N.S. V (1900), 159-164.

COOLIDGE, Jane Revere (Mrs. Walter Muir Whitehill). 'Life and letters of Mrs. E. C. Gaskell.' (An incomplete typescript is in the Gaskell Section, Brotherton Collection, Leeds University Library—the finished version being in the hands of Mrs. Whitehill, 44 Andover Street, North Andover, Massachusetts, U.S.A.)

C[OOLIDGE], T[heresa]. 'Mrs. Gaskell to Ruskin', 'Library Notes' Section, *More Books,* XXIII (June 1948), 229-230.

COOPER, Thompson. Article on Joseph Stevenson (1806-1895). In *The Dictionary of National Biography.*

CORNHILL MAGAZINE EDITOR. [Frederick Greenwood.] Concluding Remarks by Ed. C. M. to [Elizabeth Cleghorn Gaskell] 'Wives and Daughters. An Every-Day Story', *The Cornhill Magazine,* XIII (January 1866), 11-15.

COUSIN, Claude Henri Victor. 'La Marquise de Sablé et les Salons Littéraires au XVIIᵉ Siècle'; 'Histoire Littéraire.—La Marquise de Sablé et La Rochefoucauld'; 'La Marquise de Sablé.—III.—Mme de Sablé et Mme de Longueville'; 'La Marquise de Sablé.—IV.—Port-Royal et Mme de Longueville, dernière partie', *Revue des Deux Mondes,* 2nd Series, V (1854), 5-36, 433-472, 865-896; VI (1854), 5-36.

COUSIN, Claude Henri Victor. *Madame de Sablé: Etudes sur les Femmes Illustres de la Société du XVIIᵉ Siècle.* Paris: Didier, 1854.

CRIMES CELEBRES. Crimes Célèbres. Vols. I-VI by Alexandre Dumas (the elder); Vols. VII-VIII by Alexandre Dumas (the elder), Auguste Arnould, Narcisse Fournier, Pier-Angelo Fiorentino, and Pierre-Jean-Félicien Mallefille. 8 vols. Paris: Administration de Librairie, 1839-1840. (Based on entries in the General Catalogues of Printed Books of the British Museum and the *Bibliothèque Nationale.*)

[CUMMINS, Maria Susanna.] The Author of The "Lamplighter". *Mabel Vaughan.* Ed. Mrs. Gaskell. London: Sampson Low, Son, and Co., 1857.

[DAVIES, William Llewelyn. Ed.] *The Memoirs of Samuel Holland, One of the Pioneers of the North Wales Slate Industry.* The Merioneth Historical and Record Society (Cymdeithas Hanes a Chofnodion Sir Feirionnydd), Extra Publications (Cyhoeddiadau Ychwanegol), Series (Cyfres) I, Number (Rhif) 1. [Dolgelley (Dolgellau), 1952.] (Samuel Holland's manuscript is in the National Library of Wales—MS. 4983C.)

DAVIS, Nuel Pharr. *The Life of Wilkie Collins.* Urbana: University of Illinois Press, 1956.

DEXTER, Walter. Ed. *The Letters of Charles Dickens.* 3 vols. Bloomsbury: The Nonesuch Press, 1938.

DICKENS, Charles John Huffam. *Letters from Charles Dickens to Angela Burdett-Coutts, 1841-1865, Selected and edited from the collection in the Pierpont-Morgan Library, with a critical and biographical introduction.* Ed. Edgar Johnson. London: Jonathan Cape, 1953.

DICKENS, Charles John Huffam. *The Letters of Charles Dickens.* Ed. Walter Dexter. 3 vols. Bloomsbury: The Nonesuch Press, 1938.

DICKENS, Charles John Huffam. ' To Be Read at Dusk ', *The Keepsake,* 1852, ed. Margaret A. Power, pp. 117-131.

DICTIONARY OF NATIONAL BIOGRAPHY. The Dictionary of National Biography. Articles on :
Samuel Bamford (1788-1872) by Edward Smith;
George Louis Palmella Busson Du Maurier (1834-1896) by Alfred Ainger;
James Anthony Froude (1818-1894) by Albert Frederick Pollard;
Samuel Greg (1804-1876) by George Clement Boase;
Julius Charles Hare (1795-1855) by Augustus John Cuthbert Hare;
Sir Henry Manisty (1808-1890) by John Andrew Hamilton;
Joseph Stevenson (1806-1895) by Thompson Cooper;
Tom Taylor (1817-1880) by Charles Kent.

DICTIONARY OF WELSH BIOGRAPHY. The Dictionary of Welsh Biography, Down to 1940. 1959. Article on :
Dafydd Gam (d. 1415) by John Edward Lloyd.

DISAPPEARANCES. A Communication from a Correspondent Whose Sister Was the Daughter-in-Law of Dr. G. In ' A Disappearance ', ' Chips ' Section, *Household Words. A Weekly Journal. Conducted by Charles Dickens,* III (June 1851), 305-306.

DISAPPEARANCES. Communications from John and William Gaunt. In ' A Disappearance Cleared Up ', ' Chips ' Section, *Household Words,* IV (February 1852), 513-514.

DOBSON, Henry Austin. *Collected Poems.* London : Kegan Paul, Trench, Trübner & Co. Ltd, 1897.

DULLEMEN, Johanna Jacoba van. *Mrs. Gaskell: Novelist and Biographer.* Amsterdam : H. J. Paris, 1924.

DUMAS, Alexander (the elder). *Celebrated Crimes.* London : Chapman and Hall, 1843.

DUMAS, Alexandre (the elder). *Crimes Célèbres.* Vols. I-VI by Alexandre Dumas (the elder); Vols. VII-VIII by Alexandre Dumas (the elder), Auguste Arnould, Narcisse Fournier, Pier-Angelo Fiorentino, and Pierre-Jean-Félicien Mallefille. 8 vols.

Paris: Administration de Librairie, 1839-1840. (Based on entries in the General Catalogues of Printed Books of the British Museum and the *Bibliothèque Nationale*.)

DUNCKLEY, Henry. Ed. *Bamford's ' Passages in the Life of a Radical ' and ' Early Days '*. 2 vols. London: T. Fisher Unwin, 1893.

DUNN, Waldo Hilary. *James Anthony Froude: A Biography*. 2 vols. Oxford: The Clarendon Press, 1961-1963.

DURFEE, Charles Augustus. Compiled. *Index to ' Harper's New Monthly Magazine ', Alphabetical, Analytical, and Classified, Volumes I. to LXX. Inclusive from June, 1850, to June, 1885*. New York: Harper & Brothers, 1886.

EASTBOURNE. *The Guide to East Bourne and Its Environs. A Descriptive Account of That Beautiful Watering-Place, and the Objects of Interest in its Vicinity*. New edn. East Bourne: E. M. & E. Hopkins [1856].

ED[ITOR OF 'THE] C[ORNHILL] M[AGAZINE']. [Frederick Greenwood.] Concluding Remarks to [Elizabeth Cleghorn Gaskell] ' Wives and Daughters. An Every-Day Story ', *The Cornhill Magazine*, XIII (January 1866), 11-15.

ELIOT, Thomas Stearns. Review of *Letters of Mrs. Gaskell and Charles Eliot Norton, 1855-1865*, ed. Whitehill. In *The New England Quarterly*, VI (September 1933), 627-628.

ELIZA COOK'S JOURNAL. Eliza Cook's Journal, 1849-1854.

[ELLIS, L. and M.] Trans. *Garibaldi at Caprera*. By Colonel C. Augusto Vecchj. Pref. Mrs. Gaskell. Cambridge and London: Macmillan and Co., 1862.

ENGELS, Friedrich. *The Condition of the Working Class in England*. Trans. and ed. William Otto Henderson and William Henry Chaloner. Oxford: Basil Blackwell, 1958.

ERSKINE, Beatrice Caroline (Mrs. Steuart). Ed. *Anna Jameson: Letters and Friendships* (1812-1860). London: T. Fisher Unwin, Ltd., 1915.

ESSAYS AND REVIEWS. Essays and Reviews. [Ed. J. Parker.] London: John W. Parker and Son, 1860.

FAIRBAIRN, William. *The Life of Sir William Fairbairn, Bart., F.R.S., LL.D., D.C.L., . . . Partly Written by Himself*. Ed. and completed by William Pole. London: Longmans, Green, and Co., 1877 [1876].

FARRER, William and John Brownbill. Ed. *The Victoria History of the County of Lancaster*. 8 vols. London: (Archibald) Constable and Company Limited (and James Street), 1906-1914. Vols. IV and VI, London: Constable and Company Limited, 1911.

FAURIEL, Claude-Charles. *Chants Populaires de la Grèce Moderne, Recueillis et Publiés, avec une Traduction Française, des Eclaircissements et des Notes*. 2 vols. Paris: Firmin Didot, Père et Fils (and Dondey-Dupré, Père et Fils), 1824-1825.

FFRENCH, Yvonne. *Mrs. Gaskell*. London: Home & Van Thal Ltd., 1949.

FLETCHER, Eliza. *Autobiography of Mrs. Fletcher with Letters and Other Family Memorials*. Ed. The Survivor of Her Family [Mary Richardson]. Edinburgh: Edmonston and Douglas, 1875.

FORD, Boris. Ed. *A (The Pelican) Guide to English Literature*. 7 vols. Melbourne, London, and Baltimore: Penguin Books, 1954-1961.

FORSTER, Edward Morgan. 'The Charm and Strength of Mrs. Gaskell', *The Sunday Times*, 7 April 1957, pp. 10-11.

[GASKELL, Eliza(beth). (Mrs. Charles Holland.)] 'The Growth of Good', *Household Words. A Weekly Journal. Conducted by Charles Dickens*, V (April 1852), 54-55.

[GASKELL, Elizabeth Cleghorn.] 'An Accursed Race', *Household Words. A Weekly Journal. Conducted by Charles Dickens*, XII (August 1855), 73-80.

GASKELL, Elizabeth Cleghorn. 'Bessy's Troubles at Home', *The Sunday School Penny Magazine*, N.S. II (January-April 1852), 7-12, 21-24, 41-45, 61-64.

[GASKELL, Elizabeth Cleghorn and/or William.] 'Bran', *Household Words*, VIII (October 1853), 179-181.

[GASKELL, Elizabeth Cleghorn.] 'The Cage at Cranford', *All the Year Round. A Weekly Journal. Conducted by Charles Dickens. With Which Is Incorporated 'Household Words'*, X (November 1863), 332-336.

GASKELL, Elizabeth Cleghorn. *The Cage at Cranford and Other Stories*. Ed. Paul Beard. London, Edinburgh, Paris, Melbourne, Toronto, and New York: Thomas Nelson & Sons Ltd [1937].

[GASKELL, Elizabeth Cleghorn (?).] 'A Christmas Carol', *Household Words*, XIV (December 1856), 565.

[GASKELL, Elizabeth Cleghorn.] Cotton Mather Mills. 'Christmas Storms and Sunshine', *Howitt's Journal of Literature and Popular Progress*, III (January 1848), 4-7.

[GASKELL, Elizabeth Cleghorn.] ' Christmas Storms and Sunshine', *The Christian Socialist*, I (March-April 1851), 175-176, 183-184, 191-192, 199-200.

[GASKELL, Elizabeth Cleghorn.] ' Clopton Hall' Contribution. In William Howitt, *Visits to Remarkable Places: Old Halls, Battle Fields, and Scenes Illustrative of Striking Passages in English History and Poetry*, London : Longman, Orme, Brown, Green, & Longmans, 1840, pp. 135-139.

[GASKELL, Elizabeth Cleghorn (?).] 'A Column of Gossip from Paris', *The Pall Mall Gazette: An Evening Newspaper and Review*, Saturday 25 March 1865, p. 4 (Vol. I, No. 41, p. 388 of the bound edn).

[GASKELL, Elizabeth Cleghorn (?).] 'A Column of Gossip from Paris', *The Pall Mall Gazette*, Tuesday 28 March 1865, p. 9 (Vol. I, No. 43, p. 417 of the bound edn).

[GASKELL, Elizabeth Cleghorn.] ' Company Manners', *Household Words*, IX (May 1854), 323-331.

[GASKELL, Elizabeth Cleghorn.] ' Cousin Phillis', *The Cornhill Magazine*, VIII (November-December 1863), 619-635, 688-706; IX (January-February 1864), 51-65, 187-209.

[GASKELL, Elizabeth Cleghorn.] *Cousin Phillis. A Tale*. New York : Harper & Brothers, 1864.

GASKELL, Elizabeth Cleghorn. *Cousin Phillis. And Other Tales*. Illus. edn. London : Smith, Elder and Co., 1865. [December—Sadleir, p. 210; *Athenaeum*, No. 1985, p. 639, No. 1988, p. 751.]

GASKELL, Elizabeth Cleghorn. *Cousin Phillis*. Pref. Thomas Seccombe. London : George Bell & Sons, 1908.

[GASKELL, Elizabeth Cleghorn.] ' Cranford', *Household Words*, IV (December 1851-January 1852, March 1852), 265-274, 349-357, 588-597; V (April 1852), 55-64; VI (January 1853), 390-396, 413-420; VII (April-May 1853), 108-115, 220-227, 277-285.

[GASKELL, Elizabeth Cleghorn.] *Cranford*. London: Chapman & Hall, 1853.

GASKELL, Elizabeth Cleghorn. *Cranford*. Pref. Anne Isabella Thackeray Ritchie. London and New York: Macmillan and Co., 1891.

GASKELL, Elizabeth Cleghorn. *Cranford* [and] *Cousin Phillis*. Intro. Elizabeth Jenkins. London: John Lehmann, 1947.

[GASKELL, Elizabeth Cleghorn.] 'The Crooked Branch'. In [Elizabeth Cleghorn Gaskell] *Right at Last, and Other Tales*, London: Sampson Low, Son & Co., 1860, pp. 241-318. (This tale first appeared as 'The Ghost in the Garden Room' in *The Haunted House, All the Year Round*, Extra Christmas Number, 1859, pp. 31-48.)

GASKELL, Elizabeth Cleghorn. 'Crowley Castle'. In *The Works of Mrs. Gaskell*, ed. Adolphus William Ward, 8 vols., London: Smith, Elder & Co., 1906, VII, 681-720. [This tale is a composite of 'How the First Floor Went to Crowley Castle' (in *Mrs. Lirriper's Lodgings, All the Year Round*, Extra Christmas Number, 1863, pp. 12-25) and an incomplete manuscript, now deposited in the Manchester Central Reference Library—MS. F. 823·894 Z1.]

[GASKELL, Elizabeth Cleghorn.] 'Cumberland Sheep-Shearers', *Household Words*, VI (January 1853), 445-451.

[GASKELL, Elizabeth Cleghorn.] 'Curious, if True. (Extract from a Letter from Richard Whittingham, Esq.)', *The Cornhill Magazine*, I (February 1860), 208-219.

[GASKELL, Elizabeth Cleghorn.] 'A Dark Night's Work ', *All the Year Round*, VIII (January-February 1863), 457-465, 481-485, 505-510, 529-533, 553-562; IX (February-March 1863), 1-7, 25-32, 49-57, 73-84.

GASKELL, Elizabeth Cleghorn. *A Dark Night's Work*. London: Smith, Elder and Co., 1863. [24 April—Advertisement in a *Sylvia's Lovers* third edition; see too *Athenaeum*, No. 1851, p. 533, No. 1852, p. 564.]

GASKELL, Elizabeth Cleghorn. *A Dark Night's Work. A Novel*. New York: Harper & Brothers, 1863.

[GASKELL, Elizabeth Cleghorn.] 'Disappearances', *Household Words*, III (June 1851), 246-250.

GASKELL, Elizabeth Cleghorn. 'The Doom of the Griffiths', *Harper's New Monthly Magazine,* XVI (January 1858), 220-234.

[GASKELL, Elizabeth Cleghorn (?).] Our Manchester Correspondent. 'Emerson's Lectures', *Howitt's Journal,* II (December 1847), 370-371.

[GASKELL, Elizabeth Cleghorn (?).] Contribution to 'A Few Words about "Jane Eyre"', *Sharpe's London Magazine of Entertainment and Instruction, for General Reading,* N.S. VI (June 1855), 339-342.

[GASKELL, Elizabeth Cleghorn.] 'French Life', *Fraser's Magazine for Town and Country,* LXIX (April-June 1864), 435-449, 575-585, 739-752.

GASKELL, Elizabeth Cleghorn. Pref. *Garibaldi at Caprera.* By Colonel C. Augusto Vecchj. Trans. [L. and M. Ellis.] Cambridge and London: Macmillan and Co., 1862. [1 March— *Athenaeum,* No. 1792, pp. 295, 306; see too *Athenaeum,* No. 1790, p. 235; and Sadleir, p. 213.]

[GASKELL, Elizabeth Cleghorn.] 'The Ghost in the Garden Room'. In *The Haunted House, All the Year Round,* Extra Christmas Number, 1859, pp. 31-48. (This tale was reprinted as 'The Crooked Branch' in [Elizabeth Cleghorn Gaskell] *Right at Last, and Other Tales,* London: Sampson Low, Son & Co., 1860, pp. 241-318.)

[GASKELL, Elizabeth Cleghorn.] 'The Grey Woman', *All the Year Round,* IV (January 1861), 300-306, 321-328, 347-355.

GASKELL, Elizabeth Cleghorn. *The Grey Woman. And Other Tales.* Illus. edn. London: Smith, Elder and Co., 1865. [October —Sadleir, p. 210; *Athenaeum,* No. 1981, p. 520, No. 1982, p. 551.]

[GASKELL, Elizabeth Cleghorn.] 'Half a Life-Time Ago', *Household Words,* XII (October 1855), 229-237, 253-257, 276-282.

[GASKELL, Elizabeth Cleghorn.] 'The Half-Brothers'. In [Elizabeth Cleghorn Gaskell] *Round the Sofa,* 2 vols., London: Sampson Low, Son & Co., 1859, II, 277-297.

GASKELL, Elizabeth Cleghorn. 'Hand and Heart', *The Sunday School Penny Magazine,* II (July-August, October-December, 1849), 121-123, 141-144, 181-184, 201-205, 221-226.

[GASKELL, Elizabeth Cleghorn.] *Hand and Heart; and Bessy's Troubles at Home.* London: Chapman and Hall, 1855.

[GASKELL, Elizabeth Cleghorn.] 'The Heart of John Middleton', *Household Words,* II (December 1850), 325-334.

[GASKELL, Elizabeth Cleghorn.] 'How the First Floor Went to Crowley Castle'. In *Mrs. Lirriper's Lodgings, All the Year Round,* Extra Christmas Number, 1863, pp. 12-25. [This tale, modified from a manuscript source (now deposited in the Manchester Central Reference Library—MS. F. 823.894 Z1), was published as 'Crowley Castle' in *The Works of Mrs. Gaskell,* ed. Adolphus William Ward, 8 vols., London: Smith, Elder & Co., 1906, VII, 681-720.]

GASKELL, Elizabeth Cleghorn (?). 'An Incident at Niagara Falls', *Harper's New Monthly Magazine,* XVII (June 1858), 80-82.

[GASKELL, Elizabeth Cleghorn.] 'An Italian Institution', *All the Year Round,* IX (March 1863), 93-96.

[GASKELL, Elizabeth Cleghorn (?).] 'The Last Generation in England', *Sartain's Union Magazine,* V (July 1849), 45-48.

[GASKELL, Elizabeth Cleghorn (?).] C[otton (?)] M[ather (?)] M[ills (?)]. Letter of Enquiry of 6 December 1847. In *Howitt's Journal,* II (December 1847), 399.

[GASKELL, Elizabeth Cleghorn (?).] 'A Letter of Gossip from Paris', *The Pall Mall Gazette,* Tuesday 25 April 1865, p. 11 (Vol. I, No. 66, p. 695 of the bound edn).

GASKELL, Elizabeth Cleghorn. *The Letters of Mrs. Gaskell.* Ed. John Alfred Victor Chapple and Arthur Pollard. Manchester: Manchester University Press, 1966.

GASKELL, Elizabeth Cleghorn. *Letters of Mrs. Gaskell and Charles Eliot Norton,* 1855-1865. Ed. Jane Revere Whitehill. London: Humphrey Milford, Oxford University Press, 1932.

GASKELL, Elizabeth Cleghorn. *Letters on Charlotte Brontë by Mrs. Gaskell.* [London:] Privately printed by Clement Shorter [c. 1916].

[GASKELL, Elizabeth Cleghorn.] *Libbie Marsh's Three Eras. A Lancashire Tale.* London: Hamilton, Adams, and Co.; Liverpool: David Marples [1850].

[GASKELL, Elizabeth Cleghorn.] Cotton Mather Mills, Esq. 'Life in Manchester. Libbie Marsh's Three Eras', *Howitt's Journal,* I (June 1847), 310-313, 334-336, 345-347.

GASKELL, Elizabeth Cleghorn. *The Life of Charlotte Brontë*. 2 vols. London: Smith, Elder & Co., 1857. [27 March—*Athenaeum*, No. 1534, p. 384, No. 1535, p. 392.]

GASKELL, Elizabeth Cleghorn. *The Life of Charlotte Brontë*. London: Smith, Elder and Co., 1860. (Richard Waugh Wright's copy, bearing a MS note by Mrs. Gaskell, is in the Manchester Central Reference Library—Book No. B.R. 823· 81 B160/1.)

GASKELL, Elizabeth Cleghorn. *The Life of Charlotte Brontë*. Ed. Clement King Shorter. Vol. VII of *The Life and Works of Charlotte Brontë and Her Sisters* (Vols. I-VI, ed. Mrs. Humphrey Ward; Vol. VII, ed. Clement King Shorter), 7 vols., 1899-1900 (The Haworth Edition). London: Smith, Elder, & Co., 1900.

[GASKELL, Elizabeth Cleghorn.] ' Lizzie Leigh ', *Household Words*, I (March-April 1850), 2-6, 32-35, 60-65.

[GASKELL, Elizabeth Cleghorn.] '[From Household Words.]/ Lizzie Leigh ', *Harper's New Monthly Magazine*, I (June 1850), 38-50.

[GASKELL, Elizabeth Cleghorn.] *Lizzie Leigh and Other Tales*. London: Chapman & Hall [1854]. (An entry based on the Bibliography by Northup in Sanders, *Elizabeth Gaskell*, p. 174.)

[GASKELL, Elizabeth Cleghorn.] ' Lois the Witch ', *All the Year Round*, I (October 1859), 564-571, 587-597, 609-624.

GASKELL, Elizabeth Cleghorn. *Lois the Witch and Other Tales*. Copyright edn. Leipzig: Bernhard Tauchnitz, 1861.

[GASKELL, Elizabeth Cleghorn.] ' A Love Affair at Cranford ', *Harper's New Monthly Magazine*, IV (March 1852), 457-464.

GASKELL, Elizabeth Cleghorn. Ed. *Mabel Vaughan*. By The Author of The " Lamplighter " [Maria Susanna Cummins]. London: Sampson Low, Son, and Co., 1857. [September—Sadleir, p. 213.]

[GASKELL, Elizabeth Cleghorn.] 'The Manchester Marriage '. In *A House to Let*, *Household Words*, Extra Christmas Number, 1858, pp. 6-17.

[GASKELL, Elizabeth Cleghorn (?).] ' Martha Preston ', *Sartain's Union Magazine*, VI (February 1850), 133-138.

[GASKELL, Elizabeth Cleghorn.] *Mary Barton: A Tale of Manchester Life*. 2 vols. London: Chapman and Hall, 1848. [18 October—*Athenaeum*, No. 1094, p. 1019.]

[GASKELL, Elizabeth Cleghorn.] *Mary Barton: A Tale of Manchester Life*. 2nd edn. 2 vols. London: Chapman and Hall, 1849.

[GASKELL, Elizabeth Cleghorn.] *Mary Barton: A Tale of Manchester Life*. 3rd edn. 2 vols. London: Chapman and Hall, 1849. [(Probably) May—Box 3 of the Gaskell Boxes in the Manchester Central Reference Library contains a bookseller's advertisement for an uncut *Mary Barton* third edition, by the author presented to Eliza Fox and inscribed 15 May 1849.]

[GASKELL, Elizabeth Cleghorn.] *Mary Barton: A Tale of Manchester Life*. Copyright edn. Leipzig: Bernhard Tauchnitz, 1849.

[GASKELL, Elizabeth Cleghorn.] *Mary Barton; A Tale of Manchester Life*. 5th edn. With Appendix by William Gaskell: 'Two Lectures on the Lancashire Dialect'. London: Chapman and Hall, 1854.

[GASKELL Elizabeth Cleghorn.] *Mary Barton; A Tale of Manchester Life*. Cheap edn. London: Chapman and Hall, 1856. (Richard Waugh Wright's copy, bearing a MS note by Mrs. Gaskell and having inserted in it an interesting clipping about Signor Brunoni, is in the Manchester Central Reference Library—Book No. B.R. 823·894 P2.156.)

GASKELL, Elizabeth Cleghorn. *Mary Barton*. Intro. Thomas Seccombe. London: J. M. Dent & Sons, Ltd.; New York: E.P. Dutton & Co. [1911.] (Dated [1912] in the B.M. Catalogue.)

[GASKELL, Elizabeth Cleghorn.] 'Modern Greek Songs', *Household Words*, IX (February 1854), 25-32.

[GASKELL, Elizabeth Cleghorn.] *The Moorland Cottage*. London: Chapman & Hall, 1850. [December—Sadleir, p. 205; Northup in Sanders, p. 171.]

[GASKELL, Elizabeth Cleghorn.] 'Morton Hall', *Household Words*, VIII (November 1853), 265-272, 293-302.

[GASKELL, Elizabeth Cleghorn.] 'Mr. Harrison's Confessions', *The Ladies' Companion and Monthly Magazine*, III (February-April 1851), 1-11, 49-56, 97-106.

GASKELL, Elizabeth Cleghorn. *"My Diary": The early years of my daughter Marianne*. Intro. Clement King Shorter. London: Privately printed by Clement Shorter, 1923.

[GASKELL, Elizabeth Cleghorn.] 'My French Master', *Household Words*, VIII (December 1853), 361-365, 388-393.

[GASKELL, Elizabeth Cleghorn.] 'My Lady Ludlow', *Household Words*, XVIII (June-September 1858), 1-7, 29-34, 51-56, 85-89, 99-104, 123-128, 148-153, 175-181, 205-211, 247-252, 277-282, 299-305, 327-332, 341-346.

GASKELL, Elizabeth Cleghorn. *My Lady Ludlow. A Novel.* New York: Harper & Brothers, 1858.

GASKELL, Elizabeth Cleghorn. *My Lady Ludlow and Other Tales.* 2 vols. London: Smith, Elder & Co. [1859.] (An entry based upon the Bibliography by Northup in Sanders, *Elizabeth Gaskell*, p. 180.)

GASKELL, Elizabeth Cleghorn. *My Lady Ludlow, and Other Tales; Included in "Round the Sofa."* New edn. London: Sampson Low, Son & Co., 1861. (Northup in Sanders, p. 182.)

[GASKELL, Elizabeth Cleghorn.] 'North and South', *Household Words*, X (September 1854-January 1855), 61-68, 85-92, 109-113, 133-138, 157-162, 181-187, 205-209, 229-237, 253-259, 277-284, 301-307, 325-333, 349-357, 373-382, 397-404, 421-429, 445-453, 469-477, 493-501, 517-527, 540-551, 561-570.

[GASKELL, Elizabeth Cleghorn.] *North and South.* 2 vols. London: Chapman and Hall, 1855. [March—Sadleir, p. 207; Northup in Sanders, p. 176; *Athenaeum*, No. 1430, p. 356.]

[GASKELL, Elizabeth Cleghorn.] *North and South.* 2nd edn. 2 vols. London: Chapman and Hall, 1855. [June—*G.L.*, No. 382; *Athenaeum*, No. 1441, p. 682.]

[GASKELL, Elizabeth Cleghorn.] *North and South.* Copyright edn. Leipzig: Bernhard Tauchnitz, 1855.

GASKELL, Elizabeth Cleghorn. *North and South.* Intro. Elizabeth Dorothea Cole Bowen. London: John Lehmann, 1951.

GASKELL, Elizabeth Cleghorn. *The Novels and Tales of Mrs Gaskell.* Ed. Clement King Shorter. 11 vols. London (Edinburgh, Glasgow), New York, Toronto (Melbourne, and Bombay): Henry Frowde (Humphrey Milford for Vols. IX-XI), Oxford University Press, 1906-1919. (This is 'The World's Classics' Edition.)

[GASKELL, Elizabeth Cleghorn.] 'The Old Nurse's Story'. In *A Round of Stories by the Christmas Fire, Household Words*, Extra Christmas Number, 1852, pp. 11-20.

GASKELL, Elizabeth Cleghorn. 'On Visiting the Grave of My Stillborn Little Girl'. In *The Works of Mrs. Gaskell,* ed. Adolphus William Ward, 8 vols., London : Smith, Elder & Co., 1906, I, pp. xxvi-xxvii.

[GASKELL, Elizabeth Cleghorn (?).] M[ark] N. 'A Parson's Holiday', *The Pall Mall Gazette,* Friday 11 August 1865, p. 3 (Vol. II, No. 159, p. 51 of the bound edn); Tuesday 15 August 1865, pp. 3-4 (Vol. II, No. 162, pp. 87-88 of the bound edn); Thursday 17 August 1865, pp. 3-4 (Vol. II, No. 164, pp. 111-112 of the bound edn); Monday 21 August 1865, pp. 3-4 (Vol. II, No. 167, pp. 147-148 of the bound edn); Tuesday 5 September 1865, pp. 3-4 (Vol. II, No. 180, pp. 303-304 of the bound edn). (The fourth contribution—that of Monday 21 August 1865—bears no initials.)

[GASKELL, Elizabeth Cleghorn.] 'The Poor Clare', *Household Words,* XIV (December 1856), 510-515, 532-544, 559-565.

[GASKELL, Elizabeth Cleghorn.] *Right at Last, and Other Tales.* London : Sampson Low, Son & Co., 1860. [*Right at Last* first appeared as 'The Sin of a Father' in *Household Words,* XVIII (November 1858), 553-561.] [10 May—Sadleir, p. 208.]

GASKELL, Elizabeth Cleghorn. 'Robert Gould Shaw', *Macmillan's Magazine,* IX (December 1863), 113-117.

[GASKELL, Elizabeth Cleghorn.] *Round the Sofa.* 2 vols. London : Sampson Low, Son & Co., 1859. [19 March—*Athenaeum,* No. 1638, p. 398.]

[GASKELL, Elizabeth Cleghorn.] *Ruth. A Novel.* 3 vols. London : Chapman & Hall, 1853. [January—Sadleir, p. 206; Northup in Sanders, p. 174.]

[GASKELL, Elizabeth Cleghorn.] 'The Schah's English Gardener', *Household Words,* V (June 1852), 317-321.

[GASKELL, Elizabeth Cleghorn and/or William.] 'The Scholar's Story'. In *Another Round of Stories by the Christmas Fire, Household Words,* Extra Christmas Number, 1853, pp. 32-34.

[GASKELL, Elizabeth Cleghorn.] Cotton Mather Mills, Esq. 'The Sexton's Hero', *Howitt's Journal,* II (September 1847), 149-152.

[GASKELL, Elizabeth Cleghorn.] 'The Sexton's Hero', *The Christian Socialist*, I (March 1851), 159-160, 167-168.

[GASKELL, Elizabeth Cleghorn.] *The Sexton's Hero, and Christmas Storms and Sunshine*. Manchester: Johnson, Rawson, and Co., 1850.

GASKELL, Elizabeth Cleghorn. *The Sexton's Hero and Other Tales*. Ed. Archie Stanton Whitfield. 3rd edn. [Tokyo:] The Hokuseido Press [1932].

[GASKELL, Elizabeth Cleghorn (?).] 'The Siege of the Black Cottage', *Harper's New Monthly Magazine*, XIV (February 1857), 334-341.

[GASKELL, Elizabeth Cleghorn.] 'The Sin of a Father', *Household Words*, XVIII (November 1858), 553-561. (This tale was reprinted as *Right at Last* in [Elizabeth Cleghorn Gaskell] *Right at Last, and Other Tales*, London: Sampson Low, Son & Co., 1860, pp. 1-34.)

[GASKELL, Elizabeth Cleghorn.] 'Six Weeks at Heppenheim', *The Cornhill Magazine*, V (May 1862), 560-587.

[GASKELL, Elizabeth Cleghorn and William.] 'Sketches among the Poor. No. 1', *Blackwood's Edinburgh Magazine*, XLI (January 1837), 48-50.

[GASKELL, Elizabeth Cleghorn.] 'The Squire's Story'. In *Another Round of Stories by the Christmas Fire, Household Words*, Extra Christmas Number, 1853, pp. 19-25.

GASKELL, Elizabeth Cleghorn. *Sylvia's Lovers*. 3 vols. London: Smith, Elder and Co., 1863. [February—*Athenaeum*, No. 1842, p. 212, No. 1843, p. 273.]

GASKELL, Elizabeth Cleghorn. *Sylvia's Lovers*. 2nd edn. 3 vols. London: Smith, Elder and Co., 1863. [March or (more probably) April—*Athenaeum*, No. 1848, p. 413, No. 1849, p. 469.]

GASKELL, Elizabeth Cleghorn. *Sylvia's Lovers*. 3rd edn. 3 vols. London: Smith, Elder and Co., 1863. [April—*Athenaeum*, No. 1851, p. 533, No. 1852, p. 564.]

GASKELL, Elizabeth Cleghorn. *Sylvia's Lovers*. Illus. edn. London: Smith, Elder and Co., 1863. [November or (probably) December—*Athenaeum*, No. 1883, p. 729, No. 1884, p. 742, No. 1885, p. 788.]

GASKELL, Elizabeth Cleghorn. *Sylvia's Lovers. A Novel*. New York: Harper & Brothers, 1863.

GASKELL, Elizabeth Cleghorn. *Sylvia's Lovers.* Intro. Esther Alice (Mrs. Ellis H.) Chadwick. London : J. M. Dent & Sons, Ltd.; New York : E. P. Dutton & Co. [1911.]

GASKELL, Elizabeth Cleghorn. *Sylvia's Lovers.* Pref. Thomas Seccombe. London : G. Bell & Sons, Ltd., 1910.

[GASKELL, Elizabeth Cleghorn.] ' Traits and Stories of the Huguenots ', *Household Words,* VIII (December 1853), 348-354.

GASKELL, Elizabeth Cleghorn. ' Two Fragments of Ghost Stories '. In *The Works of Mrs. Gaskell,* ed. Adolphus William Ward, 8 vols., London : Smith, Elder & Co., 1906, VII, 721-727.

[GASKELL, Elizabeth Cleghorn.] ' The Well of Pen-Morfa ', *Household Words,* II (November 1850), 182-186, 205-210.

[GASKELL, Elizabeth Cleghorn.] ' Wives and Daughters. An Every-Day Story ', *The Cornhill Magazine,* X (August-December 1864), 129-153, 355-384, 385-408, 583-608, 695-721; XI (January-June 1865), 65-87, 197-222, 320-345, 434-460, 564-590, 682-705; XII (July-December 1865), 1-29, 129-164, 257-295, 385-425, 513-546, 641-678; XIII (January 1866), 1-15— 1-11 [by Mrs. Gaskell], 11-15 (Concluding Remarks) by Ed. C. M. [Frederick Greenwood].

GASKELL, Elizabeth Cleghorn. *Wives and Daughters. An Every-Day Story.* 2 vols. London : Smith, Elder and Co., 1866. [February—Sadleir, p. 211; Northup in Sanders, p. 187.]

GASKELL, Elizabeth Cleghorn. *Wives and Daughters.* Intro. Rosamond Nina Lehmann. London : John Lehmann, 1948.

GASKELL, Elizabeth Cleghorn. *Wives and Daughters. An Every-Day Story.* Pref. Thomas Seccombe. London : Herbert & Daniel, 1912.

GASKELL, Elizabeth Cleghorn. *The Works of Mrs. Gaskell.* Ed. Adolphus William Ward. 8 vols. London : Smith, Elder & Co., 1906. (This is the Knutsford Edition.)

GASKELL CENTENARY. ' The Gaskell Centenary ', *Manchester City News,* 3 September 1910.

GASKELL OBITUARY. ' Death of Mrs. Gaskell ', *The Manchester Guardian,* 14 November 1865, p. 5.

GASKELL OBITUARY. M[ary Jane Robberds (Mrs. Charles James Herford)]. ' The late Mrs. Gaskell ', *The Unitarian Herald,* Vol. V, No. 238 (17 November 1865), pp. 366-367.

GASKELL OBITUARY. 'Mrs. Gaskell', *The Inquirer*, Vol. XXIV, No. 1220 (18 November 1865), pp. 742-743.

GASKELL OBITUARY. 'Sudden Death of Mrs. Gaskell', *The Manchester Courier and Lancashire General Advertiser*, 14 November 1865, p. 3.

GASKELL SALE. 'The Gaskell Sale', *The Manchester Guardian*, 18 February 1913.

GASKELL SALE CATALOGUE. *Re the late Miss M. E. Gaskell, 84, Plymouth Grove, Manchester. Catalogue of the Valuable Contents of the Above House, Consisting of Furniture, Linen, Glass, China, Brass, Cutlery, Silver and Jewellery, Prints, Etchings, Engravings, Water Colours, Drawings, &c.; and about* 4000 *Vols. of Books, including many rare and valuable First Editions of the Works of Mrs. Gaskell, Charlotte Brontë, George Eliot, &c., &c. To be Sold by Auction, by Messrs. George H. Larmuth & Sons on the Premises as Above, Commencing on Monday, February 9th, 1914, and Tuesday, Wednesday, Thursday, Friday, and following Monday, 16th February.* The address of the aforenamed Auctioneers is given as 10 St. Ann's Square, Manchester; that of the Solicitors (Tatham, Worthington & Co.), as 1 St. James's Square, Manchester. (A copy of this catalogue is deposited in Box 4 of the Gaskell Boxes in the Manchester Central Reference Library.)

[GASKELL, Margaret Emily (?).] 'Helena Mathewson', *Household Words*, XVI (July 1857), 13-22.

GASKELL, Margaret Emily. Letter to the Editor. 'Mrs. Gaskell's Life', *The Guardian*, 30 September 1910, p. 1337. (The relevant cutting from this church weekly is deposited in Box 2 of the Gaskell Boxes in the Manchester Central Reference Library.)

GASKELL, Peter. *The Manufacturing Population of England, Its Moral, Social, and Physical Conditions, and the Changes Which Have Arisen from the Use of Steam Machinery; with an Examination of Infant Labour.* London: Baldwin and Cradock, 1833.

[GASKELL, William and/or Elizabeth Cleghorn.] 'Bran', *Household Words*, VIII (October 1853), 179-181.

GASKELL, William. *The Lancashire Dialect, Illustrated in Two Lectures*. London : Chapman and Hall; Manchester : Abel Heywood, 1854. (This is a cover-style for the threepenny pamphlet whose title-page announces *Two Lectures on the Lancashire Dialect*.)

[GASKELL, William and/or Elizabeth Cleghorn.] ' The Scholar's Story '. In *Another Round of Stories by the Christmas Fire, Household Words*, Extra Christmas Number, 1853, pp. 32-34.

[GASKELL, William and Elizabeth Cleghorn.] ' Sketches among the Poor. No. 1 ', *Blackwood's Edinburgh Magazine*, XLI (January 1837), 48-50.

[GASKELL, William.] *Temperance Rhymes*. London : Simpkin, Marshall and Co., 1839.

GASKELL, William. *Two Lectures on the Lancashire Dialect*. London : Chapman and Hall, 1854.

GASKELL, William. 'Two Lectures on the Lancashire Dialect'. Appendix in [Elizabeth Cleghorn Gaskell] *Mary Barton; A Tale of Manchester Life*, 5th edn, London : Chapman and Hall, 1854, pp. 1-27.

GAUNT, John and William. Communications. In ' A Disappearance Cleared Up ', ' Chips ' Section, *Household Words*, IV (February 1852), 513-514.

[GAYOT DE PITAVAL, François.] *Causes Célèbres et Intéressantes, avec les Jugements qui les ont decidées. Recueillies par M*^{XXX}. 20 vols. Paris : G. Cavelier (Le Gras, Vve Delaulne, C.-N. Poirion, and J. de Nully), 1734-1743. (An inferential expansion of an entry in the *Catalogue Général des Livres Imprimés de la Bibliothèque Nationale*.)

[GAYOT DE PITAVAL, François.] *Causes Célèbres et Intéressantes, avec les Jugemens qui les ont decidées*. 20 vols. Paris (Vols. I-XII, XV-XX: Théodore Legras, 1738-1743; Vols. XIII-XIV : Guillaume Desprez and Pierre-Guillaume Cavelier fils, 1747). (This composite edition is in the Bodleian Library, Oxford.)

GERNSHEIMER, Josephine. ' Mrs. Gaskell's Novels, Their Reception in Various Periodicals, 1848-1910 '. M.A. Essay. Columbia University, New York, 1934.

GILBERTSON, Richard. ' Haworth Parsonage ', *The Times Literary Supplement*, 28 June 1963, p. 477.

GOWLAND, T. S. *The Guide to Eastbourne and its Environs, with a Map, and Illustrations, and a Descriptive Account of the Objects of Interest in Its Vicinity.* 6th edn. Eastbourne: T. S. Gowland, 1863.

GREEN, Henry. *Knutsford, Its Traditions and History: with Reminiscences, Anecdotes, and Notices of the Neighbourhood.* London: Smith, Elder, & Co.; Macclesfield: Swinnerton & Brown; Knutsford: John Siddeley, 1859.

GREEN, John Albert. *A Bibliographical Guide to the Gaskell Collection in the Moss Side Library.* Manchester: Reference Library, King St.; Moss Side Library, Bradshaw Street, 1911.

[GREENWOOD, Frederick.] Concluding Remarks by Ed. C. M. to [Elizabeth Cleghorn Gaskell] ' Wives and Daughters. An Every-Day Story ', *The Cornhill Magazine*, XIII (January 1866), 11-15.

[GREG, William Rathbone.] Review of *Mary Barton.* In *The Edinburgh Review or Critical Journal*, LXXXIX (April 1849), 402-435. (This essay was reprinted, with several new footnotes, in William Rathbone Greg, *Mistaken Aims and Attainable Ideals of the Artizan Class*, London: Trübner & Co., 1876, pp. 111-173.)

GREY, Herbert. *The Three Paths.* 2 vols. London: Hurst & Blackett, 1859. [(Probably) January—*Athenaeum*, No. 1631, p. 142, No. 1632, p. 178.]

GRIMAREST, Jean-Léonor Le Gallois, sieur de. *Traité sur la Manière d'Ecrire des Lettres et sur le Cérémonial, avec un Discours sur Ce Qu' On Appelle Usage dans la Langue Françoise, par M. de Grimarest.* Paris: J. Estienne, 1709. (Based on an entry in the *Catalogue Général des Livres Imprimés de la Bibliothèque Nationale*.)

GUIDE DU VOYAGEUR. Guide du Voyageur en France. By Richard [Jean-Marie-Vincent Audin]. 25th edn. In the ' Guides-Joanne' Series. Paris: L. Hachette, 1861. (Based on an entry in the *Catalogue Général des Livres Imprimés de la Bibliothèque Nationale*.)

HALDANE, Elizabeth Sanderson. *Mrs. Gaskell and Her Friends.* London: Hodder and Stoughton Limited, 1930.

HALL, Edward. Ed. " ' Cranford ' again : The Knutsford Letters, 1809-1824 ". (This typescript edition of letters in the Edward Hall Collection at the Wigan Central Library is in the Manchester Central Reference Library—MS. F. 823·89 G69.)

HALLS, Catharine Margaret Ellen. ' Bibliography of Elizabeth C. Gaskell '. Diploma in Librarianship Dissertation. University of London, 1957. (There are copies at the London University Library and the Manchester Central Reference Library.)

HAMILTON, John Andrew (Lord Sumner of Ibstone). Article on Sir Henry Manisty (1808-1890). In *The Dictionary of National Biography.*

HANDLEY, Graham Roderick. ' The Chronology of " Sylvia's Lovers " ', *Notes and Queries*, CCX (N.S. XII—August 1965), 302-303.

HANDLEY, Graham Roderick. *Sylvia's Lovers (Mrs. Gaskell).* Notes on English Literature (ed. W. H. Mason). Oxford : Basil Blackwell, 1968.

HANSON, Lawrence and Elisabeth Mary. *Necessary Evil: The Life of Jane Welsh Carlyle.* London : Constable, 1952.

HARE, Augustus John Cuthbert. Article on Julius Charles Hare (1795-1855). In *The Dictionary of National Biography.*

HARE, Augustus John Cuthbert. *The Story of My Life.* 6 vols. London : George Allen, 1896-1900.

HARLAND, John and Thomas Turner Wilkinson. Compiled and ed. *Lancashire Folk-Lore: Illustrative of the Superstitious Beliefs and Practices, Local Customs and Usages of the People of the County Palatine.* London : Frederick Warne and Co.; New York : Scribner and Co., 1867.

HARPER'S NEW MONTHLY MAGAZINE. Index to ' Harper's New Monthly Magazine ', Alphabetical, Analytical, and Classified, Volumes I. to LXX. Inclusive from June, 1850, to June, 1885. Compiled by Charles Augustus Durfee. New York : Harper & Brothers, 1886.

HARTWELL, Ronald Max. ' Interpretations of the Industrial Revolution in England : A Methodological Inquiry ', *The Journal of Economic History*, XIX (June 1959), 229-249.

HARTWELL, Ronald Max. ' The Rising Standard of Living in England, 1800-1850 ', *The Economic History Review*, 2nd Series, XIII (April 1961), 397-416.

HATFIELD, Charles William and Mrs. Catherine Mabel Edgerley. ' The Reverend Patrick Brontë and Mrs. E. C. Gaskell. Sources of Biographer's Information ', *Brontë Society Transactions*, VIII (Parts 43-44 of the Society's Publications, 1933-1934), 83-100, 125-138.

HAYEK, Friedrich August von. Ed. *Capitalism and the Historians*. London : Routledge & Kegan Paul Limited, 1954.

HENDERSON, William Otto and William Henry Chaloner. Trans. and ed. *The Condition of the Working Class in England*. By Friedrich Engels. Oxford : Basil Blackwell, 1958.

HERFORD, Brooke. *Travers Madge: A Memoir*. London : Hamilton, Adams and Compy; Manchester : Johnson & Rawson; Norwich : Fletcher & Son, 1867.

HICKS, Phyllis D. *A Quest of Ladies: The Story of a Warwickshire School*. [Birmingham : Frank Juckes, 1949.]

HILL, George Birkbeck. Ed. *Boswell's ' Life of Johnson ', Together with Boswell's ' Journal of a Tour to the Hebrides ' and Johnson's ' Diary of a Journey into North Wales '*. Rev. and enlarged by Lawrence Fitzroy Powell. 6 vols. Oxford : The Clarendon Press, 1934-1950.

HOBSBAWM, Eric John Ernest and Ronald Max Hartwell. ' The Standard of Living during the Industrial Revolution : A Discussion ', *The Economic History Review*, 2nd Series, XVI (August 1963), 119-146.

HOLLAND, Bernard Henry. *The Lancashire Hollands*. London : John Murray, 1917.

HOLLAND, Bernard Henry. Selected and ed. *Letters of Mary Sibylla Holland*. London : Edward Arnold, 1898.

HOLLAND, Edgar Swinton. *A History of the Family of Holland of Mobberley and Knutsford in the County of Chester with Some Account of the Family of Holland of Upholland & Denton in the County of Lancaster, from Materials Collected by the Late Edgar Swinton Holland*. Ed. William Fergusson Irvine. Edinburgh : Privately printed at the Ballantyne Press, 1902.

HOLLAND, Henry. *Recollections of Past Life*. London : Longmans, Green, and Co., 1872.

HOLLAND, Mary Sibylla. *Letters of Mary Sibylla Holland*. Selected and ed. Bernard Henry Holland. London : Edward Arnold, 1898.

HOLLAND, Samuel. *The Memoirs of Samuel Holland, One of the Pioneers of the North Wales Slate Industry*. [Ed. William Llewelyn Davies.] The Merioneth Historical and Record Society (Cymdeithas Hanes a Chofnodion Sir Feirionnydd), Extra Publications (Cyhoeddiadau Ychwanegol), Series (Cyfres) I, Number (Rhif), 1. [Dolgelley (Dolgellau), 1952.] (Samuel Holland's manuscript is in the National Library of Wales—MS. 4983C.)

HOMPES, Mat. ' Mrs. Gaskell ', *The Gentleman's Magazine*, CCLXXIX (August 1895), 124-138.

[HOMPES, Mat.] A Manchester Correspondent. ' Mrs. Gaskell and Her Social Work among the Poor ', *The Inquirer*, Vol. LXIX, No. 3563 (N.S. No. 667—8 October 1910), p. 656.

[HOPE, Charlotte.] His Daughter. Compiled. *George Hope of Fenton Barns: A Sketch of his Life*. Edinburgh : David Douglas, 1881. (This is a slightly altered version of the privately circulated [Edinburgh] edition of 1879—His Daughter [Charlotte Hope], compiled *A Sketch of the Life of George Hope*.)

HOPE, George. *George Hope of Fenton Barns: A Sketch of his Life*. Compiled by His Daughter [Charlotte Hope]. Edinburgh : David Douglas, 1881. (This is a slightly altered version of the privately circulated [Edinburgh] edition of 1879—*A Sketch of the Life of George Hope*, compiled by His Daughter [Charlotte Hope].)

HOPKINS, Annette Brown. ' Dickens and Mrs. Gaskell ', *The Huntington Library Quarterly*, IX (August 1946), 357-385.

HOPKINS, Annette Brown. *Elizabeth Gaskell: Her Life and Work*. London : John Lehmann, 1952.

HOPKINS, Annette Brown. ' A Letter of Advice from the Author of *Cranford* to an Aspiring Novelist', *The Princeton University Library Chronicle*, XV (Spring 1954), 142-150.

HOPKINS, Annette Brown. 'Liberalism in the Social Teachings of Mrs. Gaskell ', *The Social Service Review*, V (March 1931), 57-73.

HOPKINS, Annette Brown. ' " Mary Barton " : A Victorian Best Seller ', *The Trollopian*, III (June 1948), 1-18.

[HOWARD, Edward.] *Memoirs of Admiral Sir Sidney Smith, K.C.B., &c.* 2 vols. London : Richard Bentley, 1839.

HOWITT, Margaret. Ed. *Mary Howitt: An Autobiography*. 2 vols. London : Wm. Isbister Limited, 1889.

HOWITT, Margaret. 'Stray Notes from Mrs. Gaskell', *Good Words*, XXXVI (September 1895), 604-612.

HOWITT, Mary. *Mary Howitt: An Autobiography*. Ed. Margaret Howitt. 2 vols. London: Wm. Ibister Limited, 1889.

HOWITT, William. *Visits to Remarkable Places: Old Halls, Battle Fields, and Scenes Illustrative of Striking Passages in English History and Poetry*. London: Longman, Orme, Brown, Green, & Longmans, 1840.

HULIN, Jean-Paul. 'Les Débuts Littéraires de Mrs. Gaskell: Réflexions sur un Poème Oublié', *Etudes Anglaises: Grande-Bretagne—Etats-Unis*, XVII (April-June 1964), 128-139.

HUTCHINSON, J. R. *The Press-Gang Afloat and Ashore*. London: Eveleigh Nash, 1913.

HUTT, William Harold. 'The Factory System of the Early Nineteenth Century'. In *Capitalism and the Historians*, ed. Friedrich August von Hayek, London: Routledge & Kegan Paul Limited, 1954, pp. 160-188.

HUTTON, Joanna Mary Brough. 'Items from the Museum Cuttings Book', *Brontë Society Transactions*, Vol. XIV, No. 3 (Part 73 of the Society's Publications), 1963, pp. 26-30.

[HUXLEY, Leonard.] *The House of Smith Elder*. Pref. I[sabel] M[arion] S[mith]. London: Privately printed, 1923.

INGLIS, Kenneth Stanley. *Churches and the Working Classes in Victorian England*. Studies in Social History (ed. Harold Perkin), No. 9. London: Routledge and Kegan Paul; Toronto: University of Toronto Press, 1963.

INGLIS, Kenneth Stanley. 'English Churches and the Working Classes, 1880-1900, with an Introductory Survey of Tendencies Earlier in the Century'. D. Phil. Thesis. Oxford University, 1956. (Bodley MS. D.Phil. d. 1667.)

INQUIRER. 'Mrs. Gaskell', 'Obituary' Section, *The Inquirer*, Vol. XXIV, No. 1220 (18 November 1865), pp. 742-743.

IRVINE, Hugh Colley. *The Old D.P.S. A Short History of Charitable Work in Manchester and Salford, 1833-1933*. Manchester: The Committee of the District Provident and Charity Organisation Society of Manchester and Salford [1933].

IRVINE, William Fergusson. Ed. *A History of the Family of Holland of Mobberley and Knutsford in the County of Chester with Some Account of the Family of Holland of Upholland & Denton in the County of Lancaster, from Materials Collected by the Late Edgar Swinton Holland.* Edinburgh: Privately printed at the Ballantyne Press, 1902.

[JAMES, Henry.] Review of *Wives and Daughters.* In *The Nation,* II (22 February 1866), 246-247.

JAMES, Henry. *William Wetmore Story and His Friends, from Letters, Diaries, and Recollections.* 2 vols. Edinburgh and London: William Blackwood and Sons, 1903.

JAMES, William Milburne. *The Order of Release: The Story of John Ruskin, Effie Gray and John Everett Millais, Told for the First Time in Their Unpublished Letters.* London: John Murray, 1947 [1948].

JAMESON, Anna Brownell. *Anna Jameson: Letters and Friendships* (1812-1860). Ed. Beatrice Caroline (Mrs. Steuart) Erskine. London: T. Fisher Unwin, Ltd., 1915.

JANE EYRE. [Elizabeth Cleghorn Gaskell (?).] Contribution to 'A Few Words about " Jane Eyre " ', *Sharpe's London Magazine of Entertainment and Instruction, for General Reading,* N.S. VI (June 1855), 339-342.

JEFFREY, Percy Shaw. Collected and ed. *Whitby Lore and Legend.* 3rd and rev. edn. Whitby: Horne & Son, Ltd., 1952.

JENKINS, Elizabeth. Intro. *Cranford* [and] *Cousin Phillis.* By Mrs. Gaskell. London: John Lehmann, 1947.

JOHNSON, Colin Arthur. ' Russian Gaskelliana ', *A Review of English Literature,* Vol. VII, No. 3 (July 1966), pp. 39-51.

JOHNSON, Edgar. Ed. *Letters from Charles Dickens to Angela Burdett-Coutts, 1841-1865, Selected and edited from the collection in the Pierpont-Morgan Library, with a critical and biographical introduction.* London: Jonathan Cape, 1953.

JOHNSTON, Josephine. 'The Social Significance of the Novels of Mrs. Gaskell ', *The Journal of Social Forces,* VII (December 1928), 224-227.

KAY-SHUTTLEWORTH, James Phillips. *Four Periods of Public Education as Reviewed in* 1832-1839-1846-1862. London: Longman, Green, Longman, and Roberts, 1862.

KELLY. *Post Office Directory of Westmoreland, Cumberland, Northumberland, and Durham: with Maps Engraved Expressly for the Work, and Corrected to the Time of Publication.* London : Kelly and Co., 1858.

KENT, Charles. Article on Tom Taylor (1817-1880). In *The Dictionary of National Biography.*

KENYON, Frederic George. Ed. *The Letters of Elizabeth Barrett Browning, with Biographical Additions.* 2 vols. London : Smith, Elder, & Co., 1897.

KETTLE, Arnold Charles. 'The Early Victorian Social-Problem Novel'. In *From Dickens to Hardy*—Vol. VI of *A (The Pelican) Guide to English Literature,* ed. Boris Ford, 7 vols., 1954-1961—[Melbourne, London, and Baltimore:] Penguin Books, 1958, pp. 169-187.

KING, William. *Political and Literary Anecdotes of His Own Times.* London : John Murray, 1818.

KNIPE, William. *Criminal Chronology of York Castle; with a Register of the Criminals Capitally Convicted and Executed at the County Assizes, Commencing March 1st, 1379, to the Present Time: An interesting Record to those who trace the Progress of Crime through the Change of Manners, the Increase of Population, and the Raised Complexion of the Penal Code. Carefully Compiled from Prison Documents, Ancient Papers, and Other Authentic Sources, Materially Assisted by William Knipe, Antiquarian, of Clementhorpe, York.* York : C.L. Burdekin; London : Simpkin, Marshall, & Co., 1867.

KNUTSFORD PUBLIC LIBRARY CATALOGUE. *Knutsford Public Library. Catalogue Complete to Date, October 25th,* 1921. Knutsford : F. Alcock, Printer, 1921.

LASKI, Marghanita. 'Words from Mrs. Gaskell—I', *Notes and Queries,* CCVI (N.S. VIII—September 1961), 339-341.

LEHMANN, Rosamond Nina. Intro. *Wives and Daughters.* By Mrs. Gaskell. London : John Lehmann, 1948.

LESLIE, Marion. 'Mrs. Gaskell's House and Its Memories', *The Woman at Home: Annie S. Swan's Magazine,* Vol. V, No. 45 (June 1897), pp. 761-770.

LIZZIE. A Lancashire Lady. 'Rich and Poor', *The North of England Magazine, A Monthly Journal of Politics, Literature, Science, and Art,* Vol. I, No. 4 (May 1842), pp. 201-203.

LLOYD, John Edward. Article on Dafydd Gam (d. 1415). In *The Dictionary of Welsh Biography, Down to* 1940, 1959.

LOHRLI, Anne. '*Household Words* and Its "Office Book"', *The Princeton University Library Chronicle*, XXVI (Autumn 1964), 27-47.

LOWER, Mark Antony. *Chronicles of Pevensey, with Notices Biographical, Topographical, and Antiquarian; for Visitors.* Lewes: R. W. Lower; London: J. R. Smith, 1846.

LUCAS, Frank Laurence. *Literature and Psychology.* London, Toronto, Melbourne, Sydney, and Wellington: Cassell & Company Ltd, 1951.

LYALL, Edna. [Ada Ellen Bayly.] 'Mrs. Gaskell'. In *Women Novelists of Queen Victoria's Reign: A Book of Appreciations*, London: Hurst & Blackett, Limited, 1897, pp. 117-145.

[LYNN, Eliza (Mrs. Eliza Lynn Linton).] 'One of Our Legal Fictions', *Household Words*, IX (April 1854), 257-260.

M. [Mary Jane Robberds (Mrs. Charles James Herford).] 'The late Mrs. Gaskell', *The Unitarian Herald*, Vol. V, No. 238 (17 November 1865), pp. 366-367.

M., C.M. [Elizabeth Cleghorn Gaskell (?).] Letter of Enquiry of 6 December 1847. In *Howitt's Journal*, II (December 1847), 399.

[McDERMID, Thomas Wright.] *The Life of Thomas Wright, of Manchester, the Prison Philanthropist.* Pref. The Earl of Shaftesbury. Manchester: John Heywood; London: Simpkin, Marshall, and Co., 1876.

MACK, Edward Clarence and Walter Harry Green Armytage. *Thomas Hughes: The Life of the Author of 'Tom Brown's Schooldays'.* London: Ernest Benn Limited, 1952 [1953].

MALCOLM-HAYES, Marian V. 'Notes on the Gaskell Collection in the Central Library', *Memoirs and Proceedings of the Manchester Literary & Philosophical Society (Manchester Memoirs)*, LXXXVII (1945-1946), 149-174.

MANCHESTER CITY NEWS. 'The Gaskell Centenary', *Manchester City News*, 3 September 1910.

MANCHESTER CORRESPONDENT. A Manchester Correspondent [Mat Hompes]. 'Mrs. Gaskell and Her Social Work among the Poor', *The Inquirer*, Vol. LXIX, No. 3563 (N.S. No. 667—8 October 1910), p. 656.

MANCHESTER CORRESPONDENT. Our Manchester Correspondent [Elizabeth Cleghorn Gaskell (?)]. ' Emerson's Lectures ', *Howitt's Journal*, II (December 1847), 370-371.

MANCHESTER COURIER. ' Sudden Death of Mrs. Gaskell ', *The Manchester Courier and Lancashire General Advertiser*, 14 November 1865, p. 3.

MANCHESTER GUARDIAN. ' Death of Mrs. Gaskell ', *The Manchester Guardian*, 14 November 1865, p. 5.

MANCHESTER GUARDIAN. Editorial Comment on a Letter by D. Winstanley. In *The Manchester Guardian,* 7 March 1849, p. 8.

MANCHESTER GUARDIAN. Review of *Mary Barton.* In *The Manchester Guardian,* 28 February 1849, p. 7.

MANCHESTER GUARDIAN. Review of Mrs. Chadwick's *Mrs. Gaskell: Haunts, Homes, and Stories.* ' Biographical Guesswork ', ' New Books ' Section, *The Manchester Guardian,* 26 September 1910, p. 5.

MARCHAND, Leslie Alexis. *' The Athenaeum ': A Mirror of Victorian Culture.* Chapel Hill: The University of North Carolina Press, 1941.

MARCHAND, Leslie Alexis. ' The Symington Collection ', *Journal of Rutgers University Library,* XII (1948), 1-15.

MARY BARTON. Review of *Mary Barton.* In *The British Quarterly Review,* IX (February 1849), 117-136.

MARY BARTON. Review of *Mary Barton.* In *The Manchester Guardian,* 28 February 1849, p. 7.

MASKELL, William. *Odds and Ends.* London : James Toovey, 1872.

MASSON, Flora. ' The Gaskell Centenary. The Novelist's Career ', *The Manchester Guardian,* 29 September 1910, pp. 4-5.

MELVILLE, Lewis. [Lewis Saul Benjamin.] ' The Centenary of Mrs. Gaskell ', *The Nineteenth Century and After: A Monthly Review Founded by James Knowles,* LXVIII (September 1910), 467-482.

MERIMEE, Prosper. ' The Letters of Prosper Mérimée ', " French Writing To-Day " Special Section, *The Times Literary Supplement,* 26 March 1954, p. xiii.

MILLS, Cotton Mather. [Elizabeth Cleghorn Gaskell.] ' Christmas Storms and Sunshine ', *Howitt's Journal,* III (January 1848), 4-7.

M[ILLS (?)], C[otton (?)] M[ather (?)]. [Elizabeth Cleghorn Gaskell (?).] Letter of Enquiry of 6 December 1847. In *Howitt's Journal*, II (December 1847), 399.

MILLS, ESQ., Cotton Mather. [Elizabeth Cleghorn Gaskell.] 'Life in Manchester. Libbie Marsh's Three Eras', *Howitt's Journal*, I (June 1847), 310-313, 334-336, 345-347.

MILLS, ESQ., Cotton Mather. [Elizabeth Cleghorn Gaskell.] 'The Sexton's Hero', *Howitt's Journal*, II (September 1847), 149-152.

MINTO, William. 'Mrs. Gaskell's Novels', *The Fortnightly Review*, XXX (N.S. XXIV—September 1878), 353-369.

MONNIER, Marc. *La Camorra, Mystères de Naples*. Paris: Michel-Lévy Frères, 1863. (Based on an entry in the *Catalogue Général des Livres Imprimés de la Bibliothèque Nationale*.)

M[ONNIER], M[arc]. *La Camorra, Notizie Storiche Raccolte e Documentate per Cura M.M.* Florence, 1862. (Based on an entry in the General Catalogue of Printed Books of the British Museum.)

MONTGOMERY, K. L. [Kathleen and Letitia.] 'Elizabeth Cleghorn Gaskell', *The Fortnightly Review*, XCIV (N.S. LXXXVIII—September 1910), 450-463.

MORLEY, Edith Julia. Ed. *The Correspondence of Henry Crabb Robinson with the Wordsworth Circle (1808-1866), the Greater Part Now for the First Time Printed from the Originals in Dr. Williams's Library, London, Chronologically arranged and edited with Introduction, Notes and Index.* 2 vols. Oxford: The Clarendon Press, 1927.

[MORLEY, Henry.] 'Character Murder', 'Chips' Section, *Household Words*, XIX (January 1859), 139-140.

[MORLEY, Henry.] 'An Unpaid Servant of the State', *Household Words*, IV (March 1852), 553-555.

MORTIMER, John. 'Concerning the "Mary Barton" Fields', *The Manchester Quarterly*, XXXVII (January 1911), 1-8.

MULHAUSER, Frederick Ludwig. Ed. *The Correspondence of Arthur Hugh Clough.* 2 vols. Oxford: The Clarendon Press, 1957.

N., M[ark]. [Elizabeth Cleghorn Gaskell (?).] 'A Parson's Holiday', *The Pall Mall Gazette*, Friday 11 August 1865, p. 3 (Vol. II, No. 159, p. 51 of the bound edn); Tuesday 15 August 1865, pp. 3-4 (Vol. II, No. 162, pp. 87-88 of the bound edn); Thursday 17 August 1865, pp. 3-4 (Vol. II, No. 164, pp. 111-112 of the bound edn); Tuesday 5 September 1865, pp. 3-4 (Vol. II, No. 180, pp. 303-304 of the bound edn). [N., M(ark).] [Elizabeth Cleghorn Gaskell (?).] 'A Parson's Holiday', *The Pall Mall Gazette*, Monday 21 August 1865, pp. 3-4 (Vol. II, No. 167, pp. 147-148 of the bound edn).

NASMYTH, James. *James Nasmyth, Engineer: An Autobiography*. Ed. Samuel Smiles. London: John Murray, 1883.

NORTH, Marianne. *Recollections of a Happy Life, Being the Autobiography of Marianne North*. Ed. Her Sister (Janet Catherine), Mrs. John Addington Symonds. 2 vols. London and New York: Macmillan and Co., 1892.

NORTHUP, Clark Sutherland. Bibliography. In Gerald DeWitt Sanders, *Elizabeth Gaskell*, Cornell Studies in English (ed. Joseph Quincy Adams, Clark Sutherland Northup, and Martin Wright Sampson), Vol. XIV, New Haven: Yale University Press for Cornell University; London: Humphrey Milford, Oxford University Press, for Cornell University, 1929, pp. 163-267.

NORTON, Charles Eliot. *Letters of Charles Eliot Norton, with Biographical Comment*. Ed. Sara Norton and Mark Antony DeWolfe Howe. 2 vols. London: Constable & Co. Limited; Boston and New York: Houghton Mifflin Company, 1913.

NORTON, Charles Eliot. *Letters of Mrs. Gaskell and Charles Eliot Norton, 1855-1865*. Ed. Jane Revere Whitehill. London: Humphrey Milford, Oxford University Press, 1932.

NORTON, Sara and Mark Antony DeWolfe Howe. Ed. *Letters of Charles Eliot Norton, with Biographical Comment*. 2 vols. London: Constable & Co. Limited; Boston and New York: Houghton Mifflin Company, 1913.

O'MEARA, Kathleen. *Madame Mohl, Her Salon and Her Friends: A Study of Social Life in Paris*. London: Richard Bentley & Son, 1885.

OWENS, Graham. 'Town and Country in the Life and Work of Mrs. Gaskell and Mary Russell Mitford'. M.A. Thesis. University College of North Wales, Bangor, 1953.

PAGE, William. Ed. *The Victoria History of the County of York*. 3 vols. London: (Archibald) Constable and Company Limited, 1907-1913. Index. London: The St. Catherine's Press, 1925. Vol. III, London: Constable and Company Limited, 1913.

PARKES, Mrs. William. *Domestic Duties; or, Instructions to Young Married Ladies, on the Management of Their Households, and the Regulation of Their Conduct in the Various Relations and Duties of Married Life*. London: Longman, Hurst, Rees, Orme, Brown, and Green, 1825.

PARRISH, Morris Longstreth. *Victorian Lady Novelists: George Eliot, Mrs. Gaskell, the Brontë Sisters. First Editions in the Library at Dormy House, Pine Valley, New Jersey, described with Notes*. London: Constable and Company Limited, 1933.

PAYNE, George Andrew. *An Ancient Chapel: Brook Street Chapel, Knutsford, with Allostock Chapel, Nr. Knutsford*. Banbury: "The Banbury Guardian" Office, 1934.

PAYNE, George Andrew. *Mrs. Gaskell: A Brief Biography*. Manchester: Sherratt & Hughes, 1929.

PAYNE, George Andrew. *Mrs. Gaskell and Knutsford*. 2nd edn. Manchester: Clarkson & Griffiths, Ltd.; London: Mackie & Co. Ld. [1905.] (The first edition—Manchester: Clarkson & Griffiths, Ltd.; London: Gay & Bird—appeared in 1900; but, like the second, it bore no publication-date. Northup's Bibliography—in Sanders, *Elizabeth Gaskell*, p. 247—enters the second edition under 1905, though the British Museum Catalogue attributes it to 1906.)

PIRENNE, Jean Henri O.L.M. *Histoire de Belgique*. 7 vols. Brussels: (Henri or Maurice) Lamertin, 1900-1932. Vol. V, 2nd and rev. edn, Brussels: Maurice Lamertin, 1926.

POLE, William. Ed. and completed. *The Life of Sir William Fairbairn, Bart., F.R.S., LL.D., D.C.L., . . . Partly Written by Himself*. London: Longmans, Green, and Co., 1877 [1876].

POLLARD, Albert Frederick. Article on James Anthony Froude (1818-1894). In *The Dictionary of National Biography*.

POLLARD, Arthur. ' Mrs. Gaskell's *Life of Charlotte Brontë* ', with an Appendix by Albert H. Preston on Some New Gaskell Letters, *Bulletin of the John Rylands Library, Manchester,* XLVII (March 1965), 453-488. (This article was printed separately, see next item.)

POLLARD, Arthur. *Mrs. Gaskell's ' Life of Charlotte Brontë'.* With an Appendix by Albert H. Preston on Some New Gaskell Letters. Manchester: The John Rylands Library, 1965. (This is an off-print of the last item.)

POLLARD, Arthur. ' The Novels of Mrs. Gaskell ', *Bulletin of the John Rylands Library, Manchester,* XLIII (March 1961), 403-425. (This article was printed separately, see next item.)

POLLARD, Arthur. *The Novels of Mrs. Gaskell.* Manchester: The Librarian, The John Rylands Library; and The Manchester University Press, 1961. (This is an off-print of the last item.)

POLLARD, Arthur. *Mrs Gaskell: Novelist and Biographer.* Manchester: Manchester University Press, 1965.

POPE-HENNESSY, James. *Monckton Milnes.* Vol. I, *The Years of Promise:* 1809-1851; Vol. II, *The Flight of Youth:* 1851-1885. 2 vols. London: Constable, 1949-1951.

POWELL, Lawrence Fitzroy. Rev. and enlarged. *Boswell's ' Life of Johnson ', Together with Boswell's ' Journal of a Tour to the Hebrides' and Johnson's ' Diary of a Journey into North Wales'.* Ed. George Birkbeck Hill. 6 vols. Oxford: The Clarendon Press, 1934-1950.

PRESTON, Albert H. Appendix on Some New Gaskell Letters. In Arthur Pollard, ' Mrs. Gaskell's *Life of Charlotte Brontë* ', *Bulletin of the John Rylands Library, Manchester,* XLVII (March 1965), 477-488. (This article was printed separately, see next item.)

PRESTON, Albert H. Appendix on Some New Gaskell Letters. In Arthur Pollard, *Mrs. Gaskell's ' Life of Charlotte Brontë'*, Manchester: The John Rylands Library, 1965, pp. 477-488. (This is an off-print of the last item.)

QUILLER-COUCH, Arthur Thomas. *Charles Dickens and Other Victorians.* Cambridge: The University Press, 1925.

READER CONTRIBUTORS. List of Contributors to *The Reader,* Vols. I-II. In *The Reader: A Review of Literature, Science, and Art,* Vol. III, No. 62 (5 March 1864), p. 285.

REDFORD, Arthur assisted by Ina Stafford Russell. *The History of Local Government in Manchester.* 3 vols. London, New York, and Toronto: Longmans, Green and Company, 1939-1940.

REID, Thomas Wemyss. *The Life, Letters, and Friendships of Richard Monckton Milnes, First Lord Houghton.* 2nd edn. 2 vols. London, Paris & Melbourne: Cassell & Company, Limited, 1890. (The first edition appeared in 1890.)

RICHARD. [Jean-Marie-Vincent Audin.] *Guide du Voyageur en France.* 25th edn. In the 'Guides-Joanne' Series. Paris: L. Hachette, 1861. (Based on an entry in the *Catalogue Général des Livres Imprimés de la Bibliothèque Nationale.*)

[RICHARDSON, Mary.] The Survivor of Her Family. Ed. *Autobiography of Mrs. Fletcher with Letters and Other Family Memorials.* Edinburgh: Edmonston and Douglas, 1875.

RITCHIE, Anne Isabella Thackeray. *Blackstick Papers.* London: Smith, Elder, & Co., 1908.

RITCHIE, Anne Isabella Thackeray. Pref. *Cranford.* By Mrs. Gaskell. London and New York: Macmillan and Co., 1891.

ROBINSON, Francis Kildill. *A Glossary of Words Used in the Neighbourhood of Whitby.* Publications of The English Dialect Society, Nos. 9 and 13—Part of Series C (Original Glossaries, and Glossaries with Fresh Additions). London: Trübner & Co. for The English Dialect Society, 1875-1876.

[ROBINSON, Francis Kildill.] An Inhabitant. *A Glossary of Yorkshire Words and Phrases, Collected in Whitby and the Neighbourhood. With Examples of Their Colloquial Use, and Allusions to Local Customs and Traditions.* London: John Russell Smith, 1855.

ROBINSON, Francis Kildill. *Whitby: Its Abbey, and the Principal Parts of the Neighbourhood; Or A Sketch of the Place in Its Former History and Present State, with the Topography and Antiquities of the Surrounding Country.* Whitby: S. Reed, 1860.

ROBINSON, Henry Crabb. *The Correspondence of Henry Crabb Robinson with the Wordsworth Circle* (1808-1866), *the Greater Part Now for the First Time Printed from the Originals in Dr. Williams's Library, London, Chronologically arranged and edited with Introduction, Notes and Index.* Ed. Edith Julia Morley. 2 vols. Oxford: The Clarendon Press, 1927.

RODGERS, Joseph. " Mrs. Gaskell's ' Sylvia's Lovers ' ", *Notes and Queries*, CIX (10th Series, I—March 1904), 187-188.

RUBENIUS, Aina. *The Woman Question in Mrs. Gaskell's Life and Works*. The English Institute in the University of Upsala : Essays and Studies on English Language and Literature (ed. S. B. Liljegren), No. V. Upsala : A.-B. Lundequistska Bokhandeln; Copenhagan : Ejnar Munksgaard; Cambridge, Mass. : Harvard University Press, 1950.

SADLEIR, Michael Thomas Harvey. *Excursions in Victorian Bibliography*. London : Chaundy & Cox, 1922.

SANDERS, Gerald DeWitt. *Elizabeth Gaskell*. With a Bibliography by Clark Sutherland Northup. Cornell Studies in English (ed. Joseph Quincy Adams, Clark Sutherland Northup, and Martin Wright Sampson), Vol. XIV. New Haven : Yale University Press for Cornell University; London : Humphrey Milford, Oxford University Press, for Cornell University, 1929.

SARGISSON, Conrad S. ' Mrs. Gaskell's Early Surroundings, and Their Influence on Her Writings ', *The Bookman* (London), XXXVIII (September 1910), 245-250.

SCHNURER, Clara. ' Mrs. Gaskell's Fiction '. Ph.D. Dissertation. University of Pittsburgh, Pennsylvania, 1932.

SCORESBY, William (junior). *An Account of the Arctic Regions, with a History and Description of the Northern Whale-Fishery*. 2 vols. Edinburgh : Archibald Constable and Co.; London : Hurst, Robinson and Co., 1820.

SCORESBY, William (junior). *The Northern Whale-Fishery*. London : The Religious Tract Society [1849].

SECCOMBE, Thomas. Pref. *Cousin Phillis*. By Mrs. Gaskell. London : George Bell & Sons, 1908.

SECCOMBE, Thomas. Intro. *Mary Barton*. By Mrs. Gaskell. London : J. M. Dent & Sons, Ltd.; New York : E. P. Dutton & Co. [1911.] (Dated [1912] in the B.M. Catalogue.)

SECCOMBE, Thomas. Pref. *Sylvia's Lovers*. By Mrs. Gaskell. London : G. Bell & Sons, Ltd., 1910.

SECCOMBE, Thomas. Pref. *Wives and Daughters. An Every-Day Story*. By Mrs. Gaskell. London : Herbert & Daniel, 1912.

SHAEN, Margaret Josephine. Ed. *Memorials of Two Sisters: Susanna and Catherine Winkworth*. London, New York, Bombay, and Calcutta : Longmans, Green, and Co., 1908.

SHARPE'S LONDON MAGAZINE. [Elizabeth Cleghorn Gaskell (?).] Contribution to 'A Few Words about "Jane Eyre"', *Sharpe's London Magazine of Entertainment and Instruction, for General Reading,* N.S. VI (June 1855), 339-342.

SHARPS, John Geoffrey. 'Articles by Mrs. Gaskell in "The Pall Mall Gazette" (1865)', *Notes and Queries,* CCX (N.S. XII—August 1965), 301-302.

SHARPS, John Geoffrey. "Charlotte Brontë and the Mysterious 'Miss H.' A Detail in Mrs. Gaskell's *Life* ", *English,* XIV (Autumn 1963), 236.

[SHAW, Sarah Blake.] *Memorial: RGS.* Cambridge [Mass.] : University Press, 1864.

SHERIDAN, Charles Brinsley. '*The Songs of Greece*', *from the Romaic Text, Edited by M. C. Fauriel, with Additions. Translated into English Verse.* London : Longman, Hurst, Rees, Orme, Brown, and Green, 1825.

SHORTER, Clement King. Ed. *The Life of Charlotte Brontë.* By Mrs. Gaskell. Vol. VII of *The Life and Works of Charlotte Brontë and Her Sisters* (Vols. I-VI, ed. Mrs. Humphrey Ward; Vol. VII, ed. Clement King Shorter), 7 vols., 1899-1900 (The Haworth Edition). London : Smith, Elder, & Co., 1900.

S[HORTER], C[lement] K[ing]. 'A Literary Letter : The late Miss "Meta" Gaskell', *The Sphere,* Vol. LV, No. 720 (8 November 1913), p. 154.

SHORTER, Clement King. 'Mrs. Gaskell and Charlotte Brontë', *Brontë Society Transactions,* Vol. V, No. 4 (Part 26 of the Society's Publications), 1916, pp. 144-149. (This is a reprint of C.K.S., 'A Literary Letter : Mrs. Gaskell and Charlotte Brontë', *The Sphere,* 2 October 1915.)

SHORTER, Clement King. Intro. "*My Diary*": *The early years of my daughter Marianne.* By Elizabeth Cleghorn Gaskell. London : Privately printed by Clement Shorter, 1923.

SHORTER, Clement King. Ed. *The Novels and Tales of Mrs Gaskell.* 11 vols. London (Edinburgh, Glasgow), New York, Toronto (Melbourne, and Bombay) : Henry Frowde (Humphrey Milford for Vols. IX-XI), Oxford University Press, 1906-1919. (This is 'The World's Classics' Edition.)

SHORTER, Clement King and John Alexander Symington. ' Transcripts of Letters written by, to or about Mrs. E. C. Gaskell, Together with Particulars of Her Books and Other Literary Works. Magazine Articles, Press Notices, Bibliographical Records and other Miscellaneous Biographical Notes. First Collected by Clement K. Shorter to 1914, and Now Continued, Arranged and Transcribed by J. Alex. Symington, Brotherton Librarian, 1927 '. 2 vols. (This typescript—in the Gaskell Section, Brotherton Collection, Leeds University Library— bears the spine-title, ' Correspondence, Articles & Notes Relating to Mrs. E. C. Gaskell. Transcripts.')

SHUSTERMAN, David. ' William Rathbone Greg and Mrs. Gaskell ', *Philological Quarterly*, XXXVI (April 1957), 268-272.

SICHEL, Edith Helen. *The Life and Letters of Alfred Ainger*. London : Archibald Constable and Company Limited, 1906.

SIMPSON, Mary Charlotte Mair. *Letters and Recollections of Julius and Mary Mohl*. London : Kegan Paul, Trench & Co., 1887.

SMILES, Samuel. Ed. *James Nasmyth, Engineer: An Autobiography*. London : John Murray, 1883.

SMITH, A. Cobden. ' Mrs. Gaskell and Lower Mosley Street ', *The Sunday School Quarterly*, II (January 1911), 156-161.

SMITH, Mrs. Charlotte. *The Romance of Real Life*. 3 vols. London : T. Cadell, 1787.

SMITH, Edward. Article on Samuel Bamford (1788-1872). In *The Dictionary of National Biography*.

STANLEY, Arthur Penrhyn. *The Bible in the Holy Land. Being Extracts from Canon Stanley's " Sinai and Palestine." For the Use of Schools, Village Clubs, Etc.* London : John Murray, 1862.

STANLEY, Arthur Penrhyn. *Sinai and Palestine in Connection with Their History*. London : John Murray, 1856.

STARKEY, Marion Lena. *The Devil in Massachusetts: A Modern Enquiry into the Salem Witch Trials*. London : Robert Hale Limited [1952].

STEBBINS, Lucy Poate. *A Victorian Album: Some Lady Novelists of the Period*. London : Secker & Warburg, 1946.

STEUART, Maria I. 'A Lengthening Chain'. 1942. [Written by Miss Steuart for Florence Peck (*née* Campbell) and her son (the author's godson), Dennis, this typescript is now in the National Library of Scotland—MS. 3109, ff. 233-243.]

STEVENSON, Lionel. Ed. *Victorian Fiction: A Guide to Research.* Cambridge, Massachusetts : Harvard University Press, 1964.

STEVENSON, William. Obituary Notice. Memoirs of Celebrated Persons Who Have Died within the Years 1828-1829 : ' No XIV. William Stevenson, Esq., of the Records Office, in the Treasury ', *The Annual Biography and Obituary:* 1830, XIV (London : Longman, Rees, Orme, Brown, and Green, 1830), 208-214.

SWINBURNE, Algernon Charles. *A Note on Charlotte Brontë.* London : Chatto & Windus, 1877.

SYMONDS, (Janet Catherine) Mrs. John Addington. Ed. *Recollections of a Happy Life, Being the Autobiography of Marianne North.* 2 vols. London and New York : Macmillan and Co., 1892.

TAYLOR, A. J. ' Progress and Poverty in Britain, 1780-1850 : A Reappraisal ', *History,* XLV (February 1960), 16-31.

TAYLOR, Frank. *Supplementary Hand-List of Western Manuscripts in the John Rylands Library,* 1937. Manchester : The Manchester University Press; and The Librarian, The John Rylands Library, 1937.

[THOMAS, William Moy.] ' Missing, A Married Gentleman ', *Household Words,* IX (April 1854), 227-228.

TILLOTSON, Kathleen Mary. *Novels of the Eighteen-Forties.* Corrected 2nd impression. Oxford : The Clarendon Press, 1956. (The first impression appeared in 1954.)

TIMES LITERARY SUPPLEMENT. ' The Letters of Prosper Mérimée ', " French Writing To-day " Special Section, *The Times Literary Supplement,* 26 March 1954, p. xiii.

TOLLEMACHE, Beatrix Lucia Catherine. *Cranford Souvenirs and Other Sketches.* London : Rivingtons, 1900.

TOLLEMACHE, Lionel Arthur. Letter to the Editor of *The Spectator.* ' Lady Cumnor in " Wives and Daughters " ', *The Spectator. A Weekly Review of Politics, Literature, Theology, and Art,* XCVII (6 October 1906), 490.

[TOLLET, Georgine.] *Country Conversations: The Humour of Old Village Life in the Midlands.* Intro. William Clive Bridgeman. London: John Murray, 1923. (The first, privately printed, edition—London: T. Richards—came out in 1881.)

TOOKE, Thomas and (for Vols. V-VI) William Newmarch. *A History of Prices, and of the State of the Circulation, from 1792 to 1856.* 6 vols. London: Longman (Orme), Brown, Green, Longmans (& Roberts), 1838-1857. Vols. V-VI, Tooke and Newmarch, *A History of Prices, and of the State of the Circulation, during the Nine Years* 1848-1856, 2 vols., London: Longman, Brown, Green, Longmans, & Roberts, 1857.

TOOLEY, Sarah A. 'The Centenary of Mrs. Gaskell', *The Cornhill Magazine,* N.S. XXIX (September 1910), 315-325.

TOWNSEND, Mary Elizabeth. Ed. *Great Characters of Fiction.* London: Wells Gardner, Darton, & Co., 1893.

TYSON, Moses. *Hand-List of Additions to the Collection of English Manuscripts in the John Rylands Library,* 1928-35. Manchester: The Manchester University Press; and The Librarian, The John Rylands Library, 1935.

TYSON, Moses. *Hand-List of the Collection of English Manuscripts in the John Rylands Library,* 1928. Manchester: The Manchester University Press; and The Librarian, The John Rylands Library, 1929.

UPHAM, Charles Wentworth. *Lectures on Witchcraft, Comprising a History of the Delusion in Salem, in* 1692. Boston: Carter, Hendee and Babcock, 1831.

VECCHJ, Colonel C. Augusto. *Garibaldi at Caprera.* Trans. [L. and M. Ellis.] Pref. Mrs. Gaskell. Cambridge and London: Macmillan and Co., 1862. [1 March—*Athenaeum*, No. 1792, pp. 295, 306; see too *Athenaeum*, No. 1790, p. 235; and Sadleir, p. 213.]

WAINWRIGHT, Alexander D. 'The Morris L. Parrish Collection of Victorian Novelists: A Summary Report and an Introduction', *The Princeton University Library Chronicle,* XVII (Winter 1956), 59-67.

WALLER, Ross Douglas. 'Articles by Mrs. Gaskell', *The Times Literary Supplement,* 25 July 1935, p. 477.

WALLER, Ross Douglas. 'Letters Addressed to Mrs. Gaskell by Celebrated Contemporaries. Now in the Possession of the

John Rylands Library', *Bulletin of the John Rylands Library, Manchester*, XIX (January 1935), 102-169. (This article was reprinted separately, see next item.)

WALLER, Ross Douglas. Ed. *Letters Addressed to Mrs Gaskell by Celebrated Contemporaries Now in the Possession of the John Rylands Library.* Manchester: The Manchester University Press; and The Librarian, The John Rylands Library, 1935. (This is a reprint of the last item.)

WALLER Ross Douglas. 'Mrs. Gaskell', 'Notes and News' Section, *Bulletin of the John Rylands Library, Manchester*, XX (January 1936), 25-27.

WARD, Adolphus William. 'In Memoriam Elizabeth Cleghorn Gaskell', *The Cornhill Magazine*, N.S. XXIX (October 1910), 457-466.

WARD, Adolphus William. Ed. *The Works of Mrs. Gaskell.* 8 vols. London: Smith, Elder & Co., 1906. (This is the Knutsford Edition.)

WHEELER, Mrs. Ann. *The Westmoreland Dialect in Four Familiar Dialogues, in Which an Attempt Is Made to Illustrate the Provincial Idiom.* New edn. London: John Russell Smith, 1840.

WHITAKER, Thomas Dunham. *An History of the Original Parish of Whalley, and Honor of Clitheroe. To Which Is Subjoined an Account of the Parish of Cartmell.* Ed. John Gough Nichols and Ponsonby A. Lyons. 4th edn, rev. and enlarged. 2 vols. London: George Routledge and Sons (Manchester: L. C. Gent, 1872) (and Lynch Conway Gent, 1876), 1872-1876.

WHITBY GLOSSARY. An Inhabitant [Francis Kildill Robinson]. *A Glossary of Yorkshire Words and Phrases, Collected in Whitby and the Neighbourhood. With Examples of Their Colloquial Use, and Allusions to Local Customs and Traditions.* London: John Russell Smith, 1855.

WHITBY GUIDE. *The Stranger's Guide through Whitby and the Vicinity: Comprising All That Is Requisite to Be Known by the Resident Inhabitant, or Occasional Visitor.* Whitby: R. Kirby, 1828.

WHITBY REPOSITORY. 'The "Criminal Chronology of York Castle"', *The Whitby Repository, or Album of Local Literature*, N.S. II (February 1868), 287-288.

WHITEHILL, Jane Revere (*née* Coolidge). Ed. *Letters of Mrs. Gaskell and Charles Eliot Norton,* 1855-1865. London: Humphrey Milford, Oxford University Press, 1932.

WHITFIELD, Archie Stanton. Major Entry for Elizabeth Cleghorn Gaskell, *née* Stevenson (1810-1865). In *The Cambridge Bibliography of English Literature,* ed Frederick Noel Wilse Bateson, 4 vols., Cambridge: The University Press, 1940, III, 427-429.

WHITFIELD, Archie Stanton. *Mrs Gaskell: Her Life and Work.* London: George Routledge & Sons Ltd., 1929.

WHITFIELD, Archie Stanton. Ed. *The Sexton's Hero and Other Tales.* By Elizabeth Cleghorn Gaskell. 3rd edn. [Tokyo:] The Hokuseido Press [1932].

WILLIAMS, Raymond Henry. *Culture and Society,* 1780-1950. London: Chatto & Windus, 1958.

[WILLS, William Henry.] ' A Disappearance ', 'Chips ' Section, *Household Words,* III (June 1851), 305-306.

WILSON, David Alec. *Life of Carlyle.* Vol. VI with David Wilson MacArthur. 6 vols. London: Kegan Paul, Trench, Trubner & Co., Ltd. (New York: E. P. Dutton & Co. [Inc.]), 1923-1934. Vol. IV, *Carlyle at His Zenith* (1848-53), London: Kegan Paul, Trench, Trubner & Co., Ltd.; New York: E. P. Dutton & Co., 1927.

WINKWORTH, Catherine. *Letters and Memorials of Catherine Winkworth.* Vol. I, ed. Her Sister [Susanna Winkworth]; Vol. II [ed. Susanna Winkworth and Margaret Josephine Shaen]. 2 vols. Clifton: E. Austin and Son (privately circulated), 1883-1886.

[WINKWORTH, Susanna and (for Vol. II) Margaret Josephine Shaen.] Ed. *Letters and Memorials of Catherine Winkworth.* 2 vols. Clifton: E. Austin and Son (privately circulated), 1883-1886.

WINKWORTH, Susanna and Catherine. *Memorials of Two Sisters: Susanna and Catherine Winkworth.* Ed. Margaret Josephine Shaen. London, New York, Bombay, and Calcutta: Longmans, Green, and Co., 1908.

WINSTANLEY, D. Editorial Comment on a Letter by D. Winstanley. In *The Manchester Guardian,* 7 March 1849, p. 8.

WISE, Thomas James and John Alexander Symington. *The Brontës: Their Lives, Friendships and Correspondence.* 4 vols. Oxford: Basil Blackwell for The Shakespeare Head Press, 1932.

WOODRING, Carl Ray. *Victorian Samplers: William and Mary Howitt.* Lawrence, Kansas: University of Kansas Press, 1952.

WORRALL, John. *Worrall's Directory of North Wales, Comprising the Counties of Anglesey, Carnarvon, Denbigh, Flint, Merioneth, and Montgomery, with Chester, Shrewsbury, Oswestry, and Aberystwith.* Oldham: John Worrall, 1874.

WRIGHT, Edgar. *Mrs. Gaskell: The Basis for Reassessment.* London, New York, and Toronto: Oxford University Press, 1965.

WRIGHT, Joseph. Ed. *The English Dialect Dictionary, Being the Complete Vocabulary of All Dialect Words Still in Use, or Known to Have Been in Use during the Last Two Hundred Years, Founded on the Publications of the English Dialect Society and on a Large Amount of Material Never Before Printed.* 6 vols. London: Henry Frowde; Oxford: 116 High Street; New York: G. P. Putnam's Sons, 1898-1905.

WRIGHT, Thomas. Account of the Subscription-Fund for Wright. In 'Our Weekly Gossip', *The Athenaeum Journal of Literature, Science, and the Fine Arts,* No. 1269 (21 February 1852), p. 226.

YORK CASTLE. *Criminal Chronology of York Castle; with a Register of the Criminals Capitally Convicted and Executed at the County Assizes, Commencing March 1st, 1379, to the Present Time: An interesting Record to those who trace the Progress of Crime through the Change of Manners, the Increase of Population, and the Raised Complexion of the Penal Code. Carefully Compiled from Prison Documents, Ancient Papers, and Other Authentic Sources, Materially Assisted by William Knipe, Antiquarian, of Clementhorpe, York.* York: C. L. Burdekin; London: Simpkin, Marshall, & Co., 1867.

YORK CASTLE. 'The "Criminal Chronology of York Castle" ', *The Whitby Repository, or Album of Local Literature,* N.S. II (February 1868), 287-288.

YOUNG, George. *A History of Whitby, and Streoneshalh Abbey; with a Statistical Survey of the Vicinity to the Distance of Twenty-five Miles.* 2 vols. Whitby: Clark and Medd; London: Longman and Co., and R. Fenner; Edinburgh: Oliphant, Waugh and Co., 1817.

YOUNG, George. *A Picture of Whitby and Its Environs.* 2nd edn. Whitby: Horne and Richardson, 1840. (The first edition appeared in 1824.)

Addenda

BELLOC, Mme Louise Swanton. Prefatory Notice. To *Cousine Phillis, L'Oeuvre d'une Nuit de Mai, Le Héros du Fossoyeur.* By Mrs. Gaskell. Trans. Emile-D. Forgues. Paris: Librairie de L. Hachette et Cie, 1867.

COOK, Edward Tyas. *The Life of Florence Nightingale.* 2 vols. London: Macmillan and Co., Limited, 1913.

CHAPPLE, John Alfred Victor. Ed. *North and South.* By Mrs. Gaskell. New English Library (forthcoming publication).

CRITIC. *The Critic* . . . , November 1843-December 1863.

GANZ, Margaret. *Elizabeth Gaskell: The Artist in Conflict.* New York: Twayne Publishers, Inc., 1969.

[GASKELL, Elizabeth Cleghorn.] *Lizzie Leigh; and Other Tales.* Cheap edn. London: Chapman and Hall [1855]. (See M[ichael] J[oseph] H[arkin], ' "Lizzie Leigh": A Bibliographical Inquiry ', *The Manchester Review*, XI [1967], 132-133.)

[GASKELL, Elizabeth Cleghorn.] *Lizzie Leigh; and Other Tales.* Cheap edn. London: Chapman and Hall, 1855. [September— Sadleir, p. 206.]

GASKELL, Elizabeth Cleghorn. *My Lady Ludlow, and Other Tales; Included in " Round the Sofa."* London: Sampson Low, Son and Co., 1861.

[GASKELL, Elizabeth Cleghorn (?).] Review of *Lancashire's Lesson* by W. T. M. Torrens. In *The Reader: A Review of Literature, Science, and Art*, V (25 March 1865), 333-335.

G[ASKELL (?)], E[lizabeth (?)] C[leghorn (?)]. 'Shams', *Fraser's Magazine for Town and Country*, LXVII (February 1863), 265-272.

GERIN, Winifred (Mrs. John Lock). *Charlotte Brontë: The Evolution of Genius.* Oxford : The Clarendon Press, 1967.

HOWITT, William. Extract from a Letter by Howitt of 1849, Quoted by a Correspondent to *The Manchester Guardian.* (The relevant cutting—sent by Clement Shorter to Dr. W. E. A. Axon —is in Box 1 of the Gaskell Boxes in the Manchester Central Reference Library.)

KNIGHT, William Angus. *Retrospects.* 1st Series. London : Smith, Elder, & Co., 1904.

LUTYENS, Mary (Mrs. J. G. Links). Ed. *Effie in Venice: Unpublished Letters from Mrs John Ruskin written from 1849-1852.* London : John Murray, 1965.

LUTYENS, Mary (Mrs. J. G. Links). Letters to the Editor about Effie Gray from Mary Lutyens and Other Correspondents. In *The Times Literary Supplement,* Nos. 3395-3401 (23 March-4 May 1967). See too No. 3394 (16 March 1967).

LUTYENS, Mary (Mrs. J. G. Links). *Millais and the Ruskins.* London : John Murray, 1967.

SHORTER, Clement King. *The Brontës: Life and Letters. Being an Attempt to Present a Full and Final Record of the Lives of the Three Sisters, Charlotte, Emily and Anne Brontë from the Biographies of Mrs. Gaskell and Others, and from Numerous Hitherto Unpublished Manuscripts and Letters.* 2 vols. London : Hodder and Stoughton, 1908.

WALFORD, Mrs. Lucy Bethia (Colquhoun). *Twelve English Authoresses.* London and New York : Longmans, Green, and Co., 1892.

(b) HOLDERS OF GASKELL MANUSCRIPTS

(i) Holdings by Institutions

The Birmingham University Library (Martineau Papers), Edgbaston, Birmingham 15.

8 Letters[1].	To Harriet Martineau and Maria Martineau.
Gaskelliana.	Letter by[2] the Rev. Arthur Bell Nicholls to Harriet Martineau.

The Boston Public Library, Boston 17, Massachusetts, U.S.A. (Acknowledgement to the Trustees of the Boston Public Library.)

2 Letters.	To Geraldine Endsor Jewsbury and John Ruskin—see T[heresa] C[oolidge], 'Mrs. Gaskell to Ruskin', 'Library Notes' Section, *More Books*, XXIII (1948), 229-230.

The British Museum (Department of Manuscripts), London W.C.1. (Acknowledgement to the Trustees of the British Museum.)

13 Letters.	To John Forster, Frederick James Furnivall, and Marianne Gaskell[3].
Gaskelliana.	Copied letters (among Florence Nightingale papers) from J. Hilary Bonham Carter, Florence Nightingale, and Frances Parthenope Nightingale.

The Brontë Parsonage Museum, Haworth, Keighley, Yorkshire.

4 Letters (3 *G.L.*[4]).	To Martha Brown, *Anne (Burnett*[5]?[6]), and the Rev. R. S. Oldham.

---

[1] 'Letter', for this survey, signifies a part of a letter as well as a whole one.

[2] 'Letters by' are addressed to recipients other than Mrs. Gaskell, whose names have sometimes been given; 'letters from' were received by Mrs. Gaskell.

[3] Marianne Gaskell later became Mrs. Edward Thurstan Holland; but women (whether married or unmarried) are usually designated by their Christian names and their surnames at the period of the correspondence, though nicknames and maiden names have occasionally been included.

[4] Thus one of the four letters was unavailable to Chapple and Pollard (ed. *The Letters of Mrs Gaskell*).

[5] Such italics indicate that not every letter to the recipient appears in *The Letters of Mrs Gaskell*, ed. Chapple and Pollard.

[6] Queries mark uncertain attributions, sometimes (as here) owing to difficulties in deciphering the correspondent's script: *Bennett* is possible.

Gaskelliana.   Letter by Margaret Emily (Meta) Gaskell
                          to Ellen Nussey; various material, largely
                          relating to *The Life of Charlotte Brontë*
                          (including correspondence between Ellen
                          Nussey and George Smith or his firm).

The Brown University Library (Special Collections), Providence,
Rhode Island 02912, U.S.A.
1 Letter.   To Anna Brownell Jameson.
Gaskelliana.   Letters from Julia U. (?) Hallam.

The University of California Library (Department of Special
Collections), 405 Hilgard Avenue, Los Angeles 24, California,
U.S.A.
11 Letters.   The recipients include Georgina (Behrens?),
                          Edward Chapman, Charles Dickens, Ed-
                          mund Evans, Samuel Lawrence, Mrs.
                          Montagu, Anne (Nancy) Robson (Gaskell),
                          Mme Weigermann, Laetitia Wheelwright,
                          and Mr. Wilbraham.

The Cambridge University Library, Cambridge.
15[7] Letters   To Dr. James Dixon and *John Malcolm*
(1 *G.L.*).   *Forbes Ludlow.*
Gaskelliana.   Letters to John Malcolm Forbes Ludlow
                          by Margaret Emily (Meta) Gaskell and
                          William Gaskell.

The Library of Congress (Manuscript Division), Washington,
D.C. 20540, U.S.A.
1 Letter.   To Elizabeth Barrett Browning.

The Cornell University Library (Department of Rare Books),
Ithaca, N.Y. 14850, U.S.A.
2 Letters.   The recipients include John Seely Hart.

The Curtis Museum, Alton, Hampshire.
3 Letters.   The recipients include Mr. (David?) Grundy
                          and Miss Leo.

The Dickens House, 48 Doughty Street, London W.C.1.
3 Letters.   The recipients include Anne Green.

---

[7] Or 14—for one may well be a postscript to that which precedes it in
the group of letters addressed to Ludlow.

The Fitzwilliam Museum, Cambridge. (Acknowledgement to the Syndics of the Fitzwilliam Museum.)

2 Letters.	The recipients include Margaret Wooler— see Wise & Symington, *Brontës*, IV, 195.

La Bibliothèque de l'Institut de France, 23 Quai de Conti, Paris IVe.

Gaskelliana.	Letter by Margaret Emily (Meta) Gaskell to Julius Mohl.

The Harvard University Library (Houghton Library and Widener Collection), Cambridge, Massachusetts 02138, U.S.A.

39 Letters (36 *G.L.*).	The recipients include Abigail B. Adams, Mr. Anderson, James T. Fields, *Mrs. Horner*, James Russell Lowell, Charles Eliot Norton, *John Ruskin*[8], *William Wetmore Story*, and Messrs. Ticknor & Fields.
Gaskelliana.	(Corrected) MS (118 folios) of *Lois the Witch*; letters from Charles B. P. Bosanquet, Charlotte Brontë, Annie and H. C. Fleeming Jenkin, Charles Eliot Norton, Grace Norton, and Sampson Low (Son & Co.); letters to Margaret Emily (Meta) Gaskell by Charles Eliot Norton and Susan Norton; letters to Charles Eliot Norton by Charles Crompton, Florence Elizabeth Crompton (Gaskell), Marianne Gaskell, Meta Gaskell, William Gaskell, and Edward Thurstan Holland; letter to Sara Norton by Meta Gaskell; letters to Susan Norton by Meta Gaskell and Marianne Holland (Gaskell); copy in Meta Gaskell's hand of a letter by Marianne Lumb to Hannah Lumb (her mother)[9]; notes by Elizabeth Gaskell Norton; editions of *The Life of Charlotte Brontë* annotated by Charles Eliot Norton, Harriet Martineau, and others.

---

[8] The original letter to Ruskin was unknown to Chapple and Pollard whose text (*G.L.*, No. 562) is copy-based.

[9] Two other copies are in the Gaskell Section, Brotherton Collection, Leeds University Library; all differ slightly from one another.

The Henry E. Huntington Library and Art Gallery (Department of Manuscripts), San Marino, California 91108, U.S.A.

11 Letters (10 *G.L.*).	To Mrs. Booth, *John Forster*[10], Frederick James Furnivall, and a publisher—probably Sampson Low.
Gaskelliana.	*All the Year Round* Letterbook (containing copies of letters from William Henry Wills); letters by Charles Dickens to William Henry Wills.

The Illinois University Library (Rare Book Room), Urbana, Illinois 61803, U.S.A.

3 Letters.	To Richard Bentley and William Shaen.
Gaskelliana.	Letter by Margaret Emily (Meta) Gaskell to Mrs. Pawling.

The State University of Iowa Library (Special Collections), Iowa City, Iowa 52240, U.S.A.

1 Letter.	To Eliza Fox.

The Knutsford Public Library, Knutsford, Cheshire.

Gaskelliana.	Several books inscribed by Mrs. Gaskell and members of her family; various mementos; water-colour by Margaret Emily (Meta) Gaskell of her mother (c. 1865)— see Hopkins, *Elizabeth Gaskell*, reproduction as frontispiece.

The (Knutsford) Unitarian Chapel (A. Stanton Whitfield Collection on deposit), Brook Street, Knutsford, Cheshire.

6 Letters.	To Leigh Hunt, Mary Ann Milman, Anne Nasmyth, George Richmond (?), Messrs. Williams & Norgate, and a nephew of Mme Mohl.
1 Copied (?) Letter.	To Mrs. Heywood (perhaps dictated).

Leeds City Archives Department, Sheepscar Library, Leeds 7.

Gaskelliana.	Miscellanea collected by John Alexander Symington. (See Late Information.)

---

[10] This unprinted fragment of a 3 May [1853] letter to Forster concerns the possible (book-form) publication by Chapman of Mrs. Gaskell's *Household Words* 'Cranford' series—whose instalment-titles, we learn, were supplied for the author (doubtless by Charles Dickens).

The Leeds University Library (Brontë, Egerton Leigh, Gaskell, Novello & Cowden Clarke, Shorter, and Rossetti Sections of the Brotherton Collection), Leeds 2.

86 Letters (85 *G.L.*).	To Mary Victoria Cowden Clarke, *John Forster*[11], Florence Elizabeth Gaskell, Julia Bradford Gaskell, Marianne Gaskell, Margaret Emily (Meta) Gaskell, Elizabeth (Eliza) Holland (Gaskell), Anne (Nancy) Robson (Gaskell), Ann Scott, Ann A. Shaen, Emily Shaen (Winkworth), Laetitia Wheelwright, and Catherine Winkworth.
57 Copied Letters[12].	The recipients include Mary Beaver, Robert Chambers, William Chambers, Mary Ewart, Eliza (Bridell-)Fox, William Johnson Fox, Eliza Gaskell, Marianne Gaskell, Meta Gaskell, Anna Brownell Jameson, Mary, Mr. C. C. Perkins, Mr. Richies (Leitch Ritchie?), Nancy Robson, William Smith Williams, and (Mr. or Mrs.) Wilmot (?).
Gaskelliana.	Letters from Frederika Bremer, Samuel Dukinfield Darbishire, William Gaskell, Frances Parthenope Nightingale, Ellen Nussey, and Eliza Thornborrow; copied letters from Mrs. Thomas Arnold, Hilary Bonham Carter, Edward Chapman, Samuel Dukinfield Darbishire, William Fairbairn, John Forster, Mrs. (Henry?) Green, Esther Hare, Mary Howitt, William Howitt, Anna Brownell Jameson, Mary Mohl, Charles Eliot Norton, and John Ruskin; letters by Charlotte Brontë to Emily Shaen and William Smith Williams; letters by Meta Gaskell to Marianne Gaskell and Clement King

[11] One of the letters to Forster was unknown to Chapple and Pollard, whose text (*G.L.*, No. 166) is copy-based.

[12] Transcripts formerly belonging to Mr. J. T. Lancaster and now owned by the present writer sometimes provide better versions than the Brotherton copies available to Chapple and Pollard, who, moreover, occasionally took their texts from Coolidge's 'Life and letters of Mrs. E. C. Gaskell' although the Shorter-Symington typescripts would probably have been preferable—as, for instance, with *G.L.*, Nos. 1, 19, 36, 100, 148.

Shorter[13]; letter by William Gaskell to Eliza Gaskell; letter by A. J. Hiscock to Mr. Higgs; letters by Bryan Thurstan Holland to Sir Edward Allen Brotherton and Clement King Shorter; letters by the Rev. Arthur Bell Nicholls to Ellen Nussey and Clement King Shorter; letter by Dante Gabriel Rossetti to William Michael Rossetti; letters to Clement King Shorter by William Edward Armytage Axon, William Copeland Bowie, Arthur Henry Bullen, M.T.C. (of Messrs. Longmans, Green & Co.), the Rev. R. H. Faires, Frederick Greenwood, Marianne Holland (Gaskell), George Smith, Reginald John Smith, Messrs. Smith, Elder & Co., and Messrs. Tatham, Worthington & Co.; copied letter by William Fairbairn; copied letter by Jane Martha Forster to Thomas Arnold; copied letter by William Gaskell to Eliza Gaskell; copied letter by Lady Caroline Anne Hatherton to one of Mrs. Gaskell's daughters; copied letter by Marianne Lumb to Hannah Lumb (her mother)[14]; copied letter by Ellen Nussey to Mrs. Flower; copied letter by Mrs. Stanley; copied letter by Catherine Stevenson (William Stevenson's second wife) to Hannah Lumb; MS review by Emily Winkworth of *Mary Barton*; copied extract from notes by Susanna Winkworth relating

---

[13] A fuller (and fairly accurate, though still incomplete) version of one of Meta's letters to him than the extant fragment in the Brotherton Collection was published by Shorter (ed. *Novels and Tales*, VIII, pp. x-xi); this printed text includes Meta's statements that part of 'French Life' was written at Avignon where she, her mother, Florence, and Julia passed a few nights in 1863 on their way from Paris to Rome, and that part of *Wives and Daughters* was composed during Mrs. Gaskell's Paris stay with Mme Mohl in Spring 1865.

[14] The Brotherton Collection contains both a typescript copy and part of a handwritten copy of this letter; they differ slightly from each other, and from the copy in Meta Gaskell's hand in the Harvard University Library.

to *Mary Barton*; biographical and bibliographical notes on Mrs. Gaskell, largely
compiled and collected by Clement King
Shorter and John Alexander Symington.

The Leicester University Library, Leicester.

1 Letter	To (*Sir*) *Benjamin Collins Brodie*.

(0 *G.L.*).

The Liverpool University Library (Special Collections), Liverpool 3.

1 Letter.	To Alice.
Gaskelliana.	MS fragment of *Sylvia's Lovers* (cf. and cont. 1st edn, 1863, III, 193-194; *Works*, VI, 476).

The McGill University Library (Redpath Library), Montreal 2,
P.Q., Canada.

1 Letter.	To a cousin—perhaps Samuel Holland.

The Manchester Central Reference Library, St. Peter's Square,
Manchester 2. (Acknowledgement to the Manchester Libraries

Committee.)	To James Crossley, Mrs. Henry A. Fielden,
13 Letters.	Dr. James Bower Harrison, Ellen Nussey, Sir John Potter, Grace Schwabe, Julius Salis Schwabe, Messrs. Williams & Norgate, and a publisher—perhaps Sampson Low.
Gaskelliana.	Incomplete (corrected) MS (45 folios) of 'Crowley Castle'; MS fragment of *The Life of Charlotte Brontë*, 3rd edn, rev. and corrected (cf. and cont. 3rd edn, 2 vols, London: Smith, Elder, and Co., 1857, I, 30; *Novels and Tales*, XI, 22-23); MS fragment about a French girl (Mlle Berthe); stanzas from Tennyson's *In Memoriam* copied by Mrs. Gaskell as an autograph for Isabella Banks; letter from Charles Dickens; letter by the Rev. Patrick Brontë to William Gaskell; letters by Julia Brad-ford Gaskell and Margaret Emily (Meta) Gaskell; correspondence by and/or to H. Allen-Maltby, William Edward Armytage Axon, the Hon. George Rothe Bellew, O. S. Blomberg, W. R. Credland, Alfred E.

Dillon, Johanna Jacoba van Dullemen, John Albert Green, Annette Brown Hopkins, C. E. Larter, Marian V. Malcolm-Hayes, Charles Nowell, John J. Potts, Clement King Shorter, Lord Shuttleworth, W. Smith, Charles Sutton, and A. P. Wadsworth; Elizabeth Cleghorn Stevenson's autographed manuscript music books; printed books inscribed by Mrs. Gaskell and members of her family; numerous miscellanea, including newspaper-cuttings, catalogues, typescripts, and illustrative material of various kinds.

The Manchester Literary Club (per Mr. Arthur Hyde, 27 Viceroy Court, Didsbury, Manchester 20).

1 Letter.	To Henry Somerset.

The (Manchester) Unitarian College Library, Victoria Park, Manchester 14.

9 Letters.	The recipients include the Rev. John Relly Beard and the Rev. Samuel Alfred Steinthal.

The Manchester University Library (Special Collections), Manchester 13.

13 Letters.	To Charles B. P. Bosanquet, Mrs. Heald, Charles Kingsley, and Henry Morley.
2 Copied Letters[15].	To unknown recipients.
Gaskelliana.	(Corrected) MS (665 folios + 24 folios of corrections) of *The Life of Charlotte Brontë*; (corrected) MS (65 folios) of 'The Crooked Branch'; letters from Charlotte Brontë, the Rev. Patrick Brontë (including a copy by Mrs. Gaskell and her daughter, Marianne, of one to her) [see Charles William Hatfield and Catherine Mabel Edgerley, 'The Reverend Patrick Brontë and Mrs. E. C. Gaskell. Sources of Biographer's Information', *Brontë Society Transactions*, VIII

---

[15] These copies occur in the *Life of Charlotte Brontë* MS.

(1933-1934), 83-100, 125-138], and Constantin Heger; letter by the Rev. Patrick Brontë to William Gaskell; letter by Mary (Polly) Taylor to Charlotte Brontë; Brontë-ana, including a memorandum of facts for the *Life*; first edition of *A Dark Night's Work* inscribed for Harriette Bright on 28 July 1863 by the author; various mementos; miniature by William John Thomson of Elizabeth Cleghorn Stevenson (June 1832, Edinburgh)[16] and marble replica (1895) by William Hamo Thornycroft of David Dunbar's bust of her (1829)[17]— see Hopkins, *Elizabeth Gaskell*, reproductions facing pp. 48, 49.

The Pierpont Morgan Library (Autograph Manuscripts, including the deposited Bonnell Collection), 33 East 36th Street, New York, N.Y. 10016, U.S.A. (Acknowledgement to the Pierpont Morgan Library and to Mrs. Henry H. Bonnell.)

20 Letters (18 *G.L.*).	To Edward Chapman, Charles Dickens (see Edgar Johnson, ed. *Letters from Charles Dickens to Angela Burdett-Coutts, 1841-1865*, 1953, pp. 159-163), *Maria James*, and *the Rev. John Pierpont*.
Gaskelliana.	Letter from Charlotte Brontë; letter by William Gaskell to Edward Chapman; memoranda of agreements by Edward Chapman (& Hall), Mrs. Gaskell, and William Gaskell; receipts signed by William Gaskell; edition of *New Friends* inscribed for Julia Bradford Gaskell in September 1853 by Charlotte Brontë.

[16] Thus dated and located on the back of the picture, where the painter's name appears as W. J. Thomson—an alternative spelling being Thompson.

[17] On the back of the replica is 'D. Dunbar. 1831'; but authorities differ about both the date of the original and the form of the copyist's name—Ward, ed. *Works*, VI, frontispiece, p. ix; Whitfield, *Mrs Gaskell*, pp. 11, 253: cont. Chadwick, *Mrs. Gaskell*, pp. 120-121, 312: cont. Hopkins, *Elizabeth Gaskell*, pp. vii, 42, 344.

The New York Public Library (Berg Collection), Fifth Avenue
and 42nd Street, New York, N.Y. 10018, U.S.A. (Acknowledgement to the Henry W. and Albert A. Berg Collection of the New
York Public Library, Astor, Lennox and Tilden Foundations.)

15 Letters.	The recipients include Mary Carpenter, John Forster, Charlotte Froude, Marianne Gaskell, Maria James, Anna Brownell Jameson, Sampson Low, Ellen Nussey, Emelyn Story, William Wetmore Story, and the Miss Wheelwrights.
Gaskelliana.	MS of ghost story (the basis for that in *Sylvia's Lovers*: *Works*, VI, 457-458); letters from Charles Dickens.

The New York University Libraries (Fales Collection, Division of
Special Collections), 13-19 University Place, New York 3, N.Y.,
U.S.A.

12 Letters.	The recipients include Henry Arthur Bright, Henry Fothergill Chorley, Mrs. (Caroline?) Clive, Marianne Gaskell, Mrs. Granville, Charles Hallé, Miss James, F. P. B. Martin (?), and Mr. Ollivant.
Gaskelliana.	Letterless envelope to Mrs. Ames; letter by Margaret Emily (Meta) Gaskell.

The Oxford University (Bodleian) Library (Department of Western Manuscripts), Oxford.

3 Letters.	To James Bryce, the Rev. Greville J. Chester, and Mark Pattison.
Gaskelliana.	Letter by Margaret Emily (Meta) Gaskell to Blanche M. Clough.

The Historical Society of Pennsylvania, 1300 Locust Street,
Philadelphia 7, Pa., U.S.A.

4 Letters.	The recipients include Robert Chambers and Annabel Milnes, Lady Houghton.

The Carl H. Pforzheimer Library, Room 815, 41 East 42nd
Street, New York, N.Y. 10017, U.S.A. (Acknowledgement for
permission from the Carl and Lily Pforzheimer Foundation,
Incorporated, on behalf of the Carl H. Pforzheimer Library.)

2 Letters (0 *G.L.*).	To *Edward* (*or Frederic*) *Chapman* (?) and *Mrs. Ogden*.

The Princeton University Library (Morris L. Parrish Collection), Princeton, New Jersey 08540, U.S.A.

45 Letters (38 *G.L.*).	The recipients include Mrs. Alcock, Georgina (Behrens?), Miss (Louisa?) Bell, Isa Blagden, Mrs. Booth, Edward Chapman, Mr. Deane, 'George Eliot', Mrs. Henry A. Fielden, John Forster, Charlotte Froude, Harriette, Anna Brownell Jameson, Miss Lamont, Sampson Low[18], Mr. (Godfrey?) Lushington, *Vernon Lushington*, Rosa (Mitchell?), Miss (Catherine?) North, William Robson, *Messrs. Routledge & Warne*, the Rev. Howard Ryland, *Mme Schérer*[19], William Shaen (?), Emile[20] Souvestre (see M. L. Parrish, *Victorian Lady Novelists*, 1933, pp. 57-58), Emily (Tagart?), Thomas A. Trollope, *Thomas Wright*, and a would-be writer—see A. B. Hopkins, 'A Letter of Advice from the Author of *Cranford* to an Aspiring Novelist', *The Princeton University Library Chronicle*, XV (1954), 142-150.
1 Copied Letter.	To Harriet Martineau[21].
Gaskelliana.	Memorandum of agreement for *Ruth* signed by Edward Chapman and Mrs. Gaskell; letters from Robert Dawson and E. A. Ship (?); letter by Margaret Emily (Meta) Gaskell to Charlotte Kingsley; letter by William Gaskell; letter by Harriet Martineau to Charles H. Bracebridge; copied letter by Edward Thurstan Holland to Charles Eliot Norton[22]; *Household Words* Office (or Day) Book.

[18] As here, Mrs. Gaskell often used the form 'Lowe'.
[19] 'Schérer' appears on the envelope, 'Scherer' in the letter.
[20] The envelope is addressed to 'M. Emil Souvestre'.
[21] The original of this handwritten copy is in the Birmingham University Library.
[22] The original of this handwritten copy is in the Harvard University Library.

The Rutgers University Library (Special Collections Department), New Brunswick, New Jersey 08901, U.S.A.

5 Letters.	To Edward Thurstan Holland, John Stuart Mill (see Haldane, *Mrs. Gaskell and Her Friends*, pp. 265-271), and Mr. Proby.
Copied Letters.	The greatest number are to Mrs. Gaskell's relatives[23].
Gaskelliana.	Letter from William Gaskell; letter by Margaret Emily (Meta) Gaskell to Ellen Nussey; letters by William Gaskell to Marianne Gaskell and Ellen Nussey; miscellanea collected by John Alexander Symington.

The John Rylands Library, Deansgate, Manchester 3.

2 Letters.	The recipients include Ann Scott.
Gaskelliana.	(Corrected) MS (72 folios) of *The Grey Woman*; (corrected) MS (920 folios) of *Wives and Daughters*; numerous letters from celebrities (see R. D. Waller, ed. *Letters Addressed to Mrs Gaskell by Celebrated Contemporaries*, 1935; Moses Tyson, *Hand-List of the Collection of English Manuscripts in the John Rylands Library*, 1928, 1929; Tyson, *Hand-List of Additions to the Collection of English Manuscripts in the John Rylands Library*, 1928-1935, 1935; Frank Taylor, *Supplementary Hand-List of Western Manuscripts in the John Rylands Library*, 1937, 1937; Dickensiana; Landoriana; Gaskell collection of autographs; photograph (perhaps last one taken) of Mrs. Gaskell (c. 1864)[24]—cf. and cont. Chadwick, *Mrs. Gaskell*, reproduced photograph facing p. 299, see too p. xv.

---

[23] These are mostly copies of originals in the Brotherton Collection at the Leeds University Library.

[24] Presented to the Library on 30 May 1933 by John Alexander Symington, to whom it had been given by Margaret Josephine Shaen.

The National Library of Scotland (Department of Manuscripts), Edinburgh 1. (Acknowledgement to the Trustees of the National Library of Scotland.)

10 Letters.	The recipients include Miss (Louisa?) Bell, John Blackwood, John Forster, Mrs. (Jane?) Loudon, and Catherine Winkworth.
Gaskelliana.	Letterless envelope to Catherine Winkworth; Elizabeth Sanderson Haldane papers (including letters to her by James Caithness, Bryan Thurstan Holland, Flora Masson, the Rev. George Andrew Payne, Margaret Josephine Shaen, Annie Doris Shorter, Clement King Shorter, Georgina E. Sington, John Alexander Symington, and Sarah A. Tooley; and typed remarks by Charles William Hatfield on her *Mrs. Gaskell and Her Friends*); letters by William Stevenson and William Stevenson junior (his son) to William Blackwood; 'A Lengthening Chain' by Maria I. Steuart.

The Smith College Library (Hale Papers in the Sophia Smith Collection), Northampton, Massachusetts 01060, U.S.A.

3 Letters (0 *G.L.*).	To *the Rev. Dr. Edward Everett Hale*.
Gaskelliana.	Letters to the Rev. Dr. Edward Everett Hale by Florence Elizabeth Gaskell, Julia Bradford Gaskell, Marianne Gaskell, Margaret Emily (Meta) Gaskell, and William Gaskell; letter to Mr. Stewart (?) by William Gaskell (apparently in Marianne's hand).

The Staffordshire County Record Office (Hatherton Papers), County Buildings, Eastgate Street, Stafford.

3 Letters.	To the First Baron Hatherton.
Gaskelliana.	Lord Hatherton's estate books.

The University of Texas Library (Miriam Lutcher Stark Library), Austin, Texas 78712, U.S.A.

6 Letters.	To Grace Schwabe, Emelyn Story, and William Wetmore Story.

Gaskelliana.   Letters from Elizabeth Gurney Fry, William
                      Smyth, and William Wetmore Story; mis-
                      cellanea collected by John Alexander Sym-
                      ington.

The Trinity College Library, Cambridge. (Acknowledgement to
the Master and Fellows.)
11 Letters   To Lady Houghton, Richard Monckton
(10 *G.L.*).   Milnes, and *the English publisher—Samp-
                      son Low—of 'Right at Last'.*

Universitätsbibliothek Tübingen, 74 Tübingen, Wilhelmstrasse
32, Postfach 149.
1 Letter   To *Robert (von) Mohl.*
(0 *G.L.*).

The Victoria & Albert Museum Library (Forster Collection),
South Kensington, London S.W.7.
2 Letters.   To Walter Savage Landor.
Gaskelliana   MS of proposed conclusion to *Mary Barton.*

The Wigan Central Library (Edward Hall Collection), Rodney
Street, Wigan, Lancashire.
Gaskelliana.   Letters to John William Whittaker by
                      Knutsford correspondents.

The National Library of Wales, Aberystwyth, Cardiganshire.
Gaskelliana.   MS of Samuel Holland's *Memoirs.*

The Yale University Library, New Haven, Connecticut, U.S.A.
22 Letters.   The recipients include Mr. (Henry Arthur
                      or John) Bright, 'George Eliot', Marianne
                      Gaskell, Margaret Emily (Meta) Gaskell (?),
                      Edward Thurstan Holland, Anna Brownell
                      Jameson, Mrs. Ouvry, Anne (Nancy)
                      Robson (Gaskell).
Gaskelliana.   Letters from Marianne Leisler, Ellen
                      Nussey, and John Ruskin; letter by Julia
                      Bradford Gaskell to Nancy Robson; letters
                      by Meta Gaskell to Marianne Gaskell;
                      letter by Meta Gaskell[25].

---

[25] This fragment (*G.L.*, Appendix F) appears to be in Meta's hand,
and may be of her composition; possibly, however, it was written at her
mother's dictation.

(ii) Holdings by Individuals

Mrs. Helen Hunt Arnold, 55 Emmonsdale Road, West Roxbury
32, Massachusetts, U.S.A.

1 Letter.	To Mr. Parker—see *Brontë Society Transactions*, XIII (1957), 166.

Mr. P. Bayliss, 26 Westland Road, Wolverhampton.

1 Letter.	To John Duke Coleridge.

Mrs. Joyce Buckley, A4 Albany, Piccadilly, London W.1.

1 Letter.	To Edward Coward (?).

Mr. Alan Gill, 19 Audley Street, Blackburn, Lancashire.

1 Letter.	To the Duchess of Sutherland.

Mrs. Elizabeth M. Gordon, Biddlesden Park, Brackley, Northants.

7 Letters.	To Elizabeth Smith, George Smith, Messrs. Smith, Elder & Co., and William Smith Williams.
Gaskelliana.	Receipts for various copyrights; portrait by Samuel Lawrence of Mrs. Gaskell (c. 1864) —see Hopkins, *Elizabeth Gaskell*, reproduction facing p. 320.

Miss Elspeth Holland, St. John's House, St. Mary's Road, Oxford.

4 Letters.	To Anne Holland.

The Hon. Mrs. Bernard Ramsden James, Cutlers, Lane End, High Wycombe, Bucks.

7 Copied Letters[1].	To Lady (Janet, wife of Sir James Phillips) Kay-Shuttleworth.

Mrs. Margaret Evelyn Averia Trevor Jones, 56 Heol Isaf (formerly of Monkstone), Radyr, Cardiff.

51 Letters.	To Julia Bradford Gaskell, Marianne Gaskell, Margaret Emily (Meta) Gaskell, Edward Holland, Edward Thurstan Holland, Elizabeth (Eliza) Holland (Gaskell), and Anne (Nancy) Robson (Gaskell).
Gaskelliana.	MS of *"My Diary"*; MS (apparently not in Mrs. Gaskell's hand) of 'Night Fancies'; MS (with tail-piece in Meta Gaskell's hand) of 'Precepts for the guidance of a

---

[1] The originals are in the hands of Lord Shuttleworth.

Daughter'; MS (not apparently in Mrs.
Gaskell's hand) of 'Extract from a letter
relating to the Coppock family at Stock-
port. February—1838'; letters from Mary
Mackintosh and G. H. Tollet; letters by
Meta Gaskell to Marianne Gaskell; Mrs.
Gaskell's passport; Holland-Gaskell family
Bible; editions of her books presented and
inscribed to Mr. Gaskell by his wife; various
mementos; portrait of Marianne Holland in
middle age (see Hopkins, *Elizabeth Gaskell*,
p. 116); group-picture by A. C. Duval of
Meta, Florence Elizabeth (Flossy), and
Marianne Gaskell (1845) and drawing by
Samuel Lawrence of their mother (Dec.
1854-5)[2]—see Winifred Gérin, *Charlotte
Brontë: The Evolution of Genius*, Oxford :
The Clarendon Press, 1967, reproductions
facing p. 360.

John Murray (Publishers) Ltd., 50 Albemarle Street, London
W.1. (Acknowledgement to the late Sir John Murray for access
to these archives.)

93 Letters.	To George Smith.
Gaskelliana.	Letterless envelope to George Smith; letters from the Rev. Patrick Brontë, James T. Fields, John Greenwood, and George Smith.

Mrs. Mary Preston, 4 Mytholmes Lane, Haworth, Keighley,
Yorkshire.

9 Letters.	To John Greenwood.

Mr. Peter P. Rhodes, Church Cottage, Iffley, Oxford.

1 Letter.	To a member of Messrs. Chapman & Hall —perhaps Frederic Chapman.

Mr. S. Roscoe, Dunsmore, South Hill Avenue, Harrow.

1 Letter.	To Jane (a cousin).

Miss P. L. Ruddock, Wyche Keep, 22 Wyche Road, Malvern,
Worcestershire.

1 Letter.	To Holbrook Gaskell.

---

[2] Mrs. Trevor Jones most helpfully informed me that the Duval date
is distinct, whereas that of the Lawrence is not; nor do her years for the
latter tally with 1864-5 given in Ward, ed. *Works*, VII, frontispiece, p. ix.

Mr. John H. Samuels, 785 Park Avenue, New York, N.Y., U.S.A.

1 Letter.   To Thomas Walker (?)—a *Daily News* editor.

Mr. John Geoffrey Sharps, Sarda Lapis, 25 Cornelian Drive, Scarborough, Yorkshire (and also of High Bank, 12 Forest Street, Weaverham, Northwich, Cheshire). (His collection includes Gaskell material once belonging to Mr. Walter Carter, Mr. Joseph Torry Lancaster[3], Mrs. M. E. Miller, and Mrs. Ethel Smith.)

6 Letters.   The recipients include William Cox Bennett, Edward Chapman, Eliza Fox, the Rev. R. S. Oldham, and Mr. N. Sherman.

87 Copied Letters   The recipients include William Chambers,
(86 *G.L.*[4]).   Marianne Gaskell, Margaret Emily (Meta) Gaskell, Edward Holland, Elizabeth (Eliza) Holland (Gaskell), Lady (Janet, wife of Sir James Phillips) Kay-Shuttleworth, *Ellen Nussey*, and William Smith Williams.

Gaskelliana.   Letters from Ellen Nussey and John Stevenson; letter by Marianne Gaskell to the Rev. R. S. Oldham; letter by M(eta?) Gaskell to the Hon. Mrs. Llewellyn Charles Robert Irby (Margaret Emily Bullock); letters by Meta Gaskell to Thomas Seccombe[5]; letters

---

[3] Chapple and Pollard had not access to all the late Mr. Lancaster's numerous transcripts of letters by Mrs. Gaskell, her two eldest daughters, and others. These consist of typed and of handwritten copies: the former almost certainly possess the greater authority; and some copies occur only in typescript. However two or more typed versions usually exist for the same letter, and distinguishing priorities poses problems; although the differences are often slight, occasionally they have importance (thus one version supplies a date—9 August—for *G.L.*, No. 264a). Moreover certain Lancaster typescripts offer better texts than the corresponding Brotherton copies—for example, in the cases of *G.L.*, Nos. 277, 310, 636, 637.

[4] Included here are those written on their mother's behalf by Marianne Gaskell and Meta Gaskell.

[5] Most concern his *Sylvia's Lovers* edition. However in one (dated 24 January 1911) Meta affirmed that, beyond implying a happy outcome, her mother had never discussed the end of *Wives and Daughters*; nor, according to her, did she know anything of Mrs. Gaskell's intentions about the happy meeting of Molly and Roger as the close of the story—cf. and cont. Shorter, ed. *Novels and Tales*, VI, pp. vii-ix; [Susanna Winkworth and Margaret Josephine Shaen, ed.] *Letters and Memorials of Catherine Winkworth*, II (1886), 429.

by Elizabeth Sanderson Haldane to the
Rev. George Andrew Payne; letter to
Henry Thurstan Holland (First Viscount
Knutsford) by Julia Bradford Gaskell and
Meta Gaskell; letters to Joseph Torry
Lancaster by Esther Alice (Mrs. Ellis H.)
Chadwick, Jane Revere Coolidge, the Rev.
George Andrew Payne, Clement King
Shorter, and others; letter by Marianne
Lumb to Hannah Lumb (her mother)[6];
letters by Ellen Nussey to the Rev. Arthur
Bell Nicholls; letters to Thomas Seccombe
by Edward Bell, the Rev. George Andrew
Payne, and others; letter by Clement King
Shorter to Marjory Amelia Bald; letter by
John Stevenson to Hannah Lumb (his
aunt); letters to a Mr. Stevenson (her
brother) by Dorothy Landles (Stevenson)
and James Smith; copied letters from the
Duke of Argyll, Jane Margaret Byerley[7],
Constantin Heger, John Whitmore Isaac,
Louy V. Jackson, Harriet Martineau, Mary
Mohl, Ellen Nussey, John Stevenson, and
William Stevenson (father to John and
Elizabeth Cleghorn); copied letter by
Marianne Gaskell to Ellen Nussey; copied
letters by Meta Gaskell to Marianne Gas-
kell, Ellen Nussey, and Thomas Seccombe;
copied letter by Sir James Phillips Kay-
Shuttleworth to William Gaskell; copied
letter by Marianne Lumb to Hannah
Lumb; copied letters by Harriet Martineau
(including one to George Smith); copied
letters by Ellen Nussey to the Rev. Arthur
Bell Nicholls, Mr. Nussey (her brother),
Clement King Shorter, George Smith, and

---

[6] This is a fragment: the typescript copies are fuller (though not
complete).

[7] According to the typed transcripts, the correspondent was Jane C.
Byerly—almost surely Jane Margaret Byerley.

Thomas James Wise; Book of Common Prayer with Mrs. Gaskell's autograph and by her dated 28 June 1855; first edition of Henry Green's *Knutsford* inscribed to M. Radcliffe in May 1859 by Mrs. Gaskell; Meta Gaskell's handwritten corrections for Seccombe's Preface to his *Sylvia's Lovers* edition (1910); Seccombe's edition of *Sylvia's Lovers* with the Preface annotated and corrected by him; first edition of Chadwick's *Mrs. Gaskell: Haunts, Homes, and Stories* annotated by Lancaster (incorporating notes by Seccombe, perhaps originating from Meta Gaskell); first edition of Payne's *Mrs. Gaskell: A Brief Biography* inscribed by him to Lancaster and textually corrected by the author; second edition of Payne's *Mrs. Gaskell and Knutsford* annotated by Lancaster; first edition of Haldane's *Mrs. Gaskell and Her Friends* annotated by Payne; privately circulated edition of *Letters and Memorials of Catherine Winkworth* with Margaret Josephine Shaen's autograph; first edition of Anne Ritchie's *Blackstick Papers* inscribed by the author; privately printed editions of Mrs. Gaskell's *"My Diary"* inscribed by Shorter; set of Ward's Knutsford Edition— *The Works of Mrs. Gaskell*—once owned by Henry Thurstan Holland (First Viscount Knutsford); odd volumes of the Knutsford Edition formerly belonging to Shorter; various books by Gaskell scholars inscribed by their authors; photograph of Meta Gaskell; memorial picture to Julia Gaskell; photograph of Charles Darwin received by Meta Gaskell on 4 July 1892 from William Erasmus Darwin; Wedgwood tea-pot (reputably) used by Mrs. Gaskell.

Charles Ughtred John Kay-Shuttleworth, Fourth Baron Shuttleworth, Leck Hall, Carnforth, Lancashire.
   9 Letters.   To Lady (Janet, wife of Sir James Phillips)
                           Kay-Shuttleworth.

Frau Ellen von Siemens (Helmholtz), a grand-niece of Mme
Mary Mohl. Her collection perished during World War II,
according to Herr Hans von Mohl (Berlin-Dahlem, Reichshofer
Strasse 74B). Some extracts from correspondence about Mrs.
Gaskell by members of the Mohl family were copied by Miss
Jane Revere Coolidge (now Mrs. Walter Muir Whitehill, 44
Andover Street, North Andover, Massachusetts, U.S.A.).

Miss Edith S. Spence, 27 Fern Avenue, Newcastle upon Tyne 2.
   1 Letter.   To Lawrence Shadwell.

Mr. William P. Telfer, 9 Gaskell Avenue, Knutsford, Cheshire.
   1 Copied Letter.   To Miss Watkins.
   Gaskelliana.   Quotation, with autograph and remarks on
                           Fryston Hall.

Sir Harry Calvert Williams Verney, Bart., Ballams, Middle
Claydon, Bletchley, Bucks.
   12 Letters.   To Frances Nightingale and Frances Par-
                           thenope Nightingale.

Dr. Helen Gill Viljoen, 167-10 Crocheron Avenue, Flushing,
N.Y. 11358, U.S.A. She has the F. J. Sharp Collection of
Ruskiniana, deposited at Queens College, The City University of
New York, Flushing, N.Y. 11367, U.S.A.
   1 Letter   To *John Ruskin.*
   (0 *G.L.*).
   Gaskelliana.   Letter by Margaret Emily (Meta) Gaskell
                           to Joan Severn.

Mrs. Douglas Walker, 60 Avenue de New York, Paris XVIᵉ.
(This collection was formerly in the possession of the Hon. Mrs.
Charles Symonds Leaf, 2 Fingest Cottage, Lane End, High
Wycombe, Bucks.)
   3 Letters.   To Hannah Kay and Lady (Janet, wife of
                           Sir James Phillips) Kay-Shuttleworth.

Mrs. Walter Muir Whitehill (Jane Revere Coolidge), 44 Andover Street, North Andover, Massachusetts, U.S.A.

3 Copied Letters (2 *G.L.*).[8]	The recipients include Emelyn Story.
Gaskelliana.	Photostat of letter from Sarah Blake Shaw[9]; extracts from Mohl family correspondence about the Gaskells; extracts from Clement King Shorter's Gaskell miscellany (when held by Lord Brotherton's librarian, John Alexander Symington); letters addressed to Jane Revere Coolidge by (among others) Messrs. Chapman & Hall, Ltd., W. H. Lee Ewart, Edward Garnett (W. J. Fox's biographer), Bryan Thurstan Holland, Henry James (nephew of W. W. Story's biographer), Messrs. Sampson Low, Marston & Co., Ltd., Sophy Martin, one of the von Mohls, John Murray, Margaret Josephine Shaen, Frank Smith (Sir James Kay-Shuttleworth's biographer), Marion Elmina Smith, Maud Waldo Story, and Messrs. Tatham, Worthington & Co.; various notes and other material assembled by Miss Coolidge in the preparation of her elegant 'Life and letters of Mrs. E. C. Gaskell' (an incomplete typescript of which is in the Gaskell Section, Brotherton Collection, Leeds University Library—the more finished version being in its author's hands).

[8] Not enumerated are the copies of seven letters once owned by (as she then was) Miss Coolidge, whose recipients include Mary Beaver, Anna Brownell Jameson, Mary, Mr. C. C. Perkins, and Wilmot (?): there are copies of these in Shorter and Symington, 'Correspondence, Articles & Notes Relating to Mrs. E. C. Gaskell. Transcripts', Vol. II (a typescript in the Gaskell Section, Brotherton Collection, Leeds University Library) as well as those held by Mrs. Whitehill. The original letter to Mary Beaver was presented to the Rev. George Andrew Payne; and one to an unnamed lady was given to Mrs. Catherine Mabel Edgerley.

[9] Taken from the letter to Mrs. Gaskell deposited at Harvard (though this original cannot at present be traced by the Houghton Library staff).

(iii) Auctioneers and Booksellers

B. H. Blackwell Ltd., Broad Street, Oxford.
1 Letter   To *Mrs. C. M. Hozier* (for sale in 1959).
(0 *G.L.*).

Christie, Manson & Woods, Ltd., 8 King Street, St. James's, London S.W.1.
Gaskelliana.   Letter from Charlotte Brontë (sold on 18 December 1964).

The House of El. Dieff Inc., 30 East 62nd Street, New York 21, N.Y., U.S.A.
1 Letter   To Frederic Chapman (?)—once for sale.
(0? *G.L.*).

Francis Edwards Ltd., 83 Marylebone High Street, London W.1.
1 Letter   To *Frances Holland* (bought at Sotheby's
(0 *G.L.*).   29 October 1968 sale).

H. M. Fletcher, Enfield, Middlesex.
1 Letter   To *an artist* (for sale in 1939).
(0? *G.L.*).

Messrs. Hofmann & Freeman, Holly Place Cottage, High Street, Shoreham, Sevenoaks, Kent.
Gaskelliana.   Letters from Mary Victoria Cowden Clarke, Charles Dickens, and Adelaide Ann Procter; letter by Catherine Dickens to Miss Holland —all bought at Sotheby's 29 October 1968 sale.

Pickering & Chatto Ltd., 95 Wimpole Street, London W.1.
1 Copied Letter.   To John Ruskin (bought at Christie's 18 December 1964 sale)[1].
Gaskelliana.   Papers of John Alexander Symington, including letters by Margaret Emily (Meta) Gaskell (bought at Christie's 18 December 1964 sale; subsequently sold).

---

[1] This hand-copied part of a letter was probably prepared for Dr. Ward, who (ed. *Works*, II, pp. xi-xii) quotes extensively therefrom: it (*G.L.*, No. 562) was also used by Chapple and Pollard. The complete original is in the Harvard University Library.

Sotheby & Co., 34-35 New Bond Street, London W.1.

2 Letters (0 *G.L.*).	To *unknown recipients* (sold : on 29 April 1969 to F. Edwards Ltd.; on 4 November 1969 to Goodspeed's Bookshop, Boston 8, U.S.A.).
Gaskelliana.	Note from Charlotte Brontë, written on the verso of the half-title of a copy (purportedly Jane Austen's) of L. C. Morlet, *Les Beautés de l'Histoire* (sold on 8 May 1961).

B. F. Stevens & Brown Ltd., Ardon House, Mill Lane, Goldalming, Surrey.

2 Letters (0 *G.L.*).	To *unknown recipients*—in an album of autographs (bought at Christie's 28 April 1966 sale; subsequently sold).

(iv) Manuscripts Quoted or Cited in Printed Works

Esther Alice (Mrs. Ellis H.) Chadwick, *In the Footsteps of the Brontës*, London : Sir Isaac Pitman & Sons, Ltd., 1914, p. 418.

Cited Letters   To *members of the Arnold family* (?)—c.
(0 *G.L.*).   1910 in the hands of Miss Frances Arnold,
                    Fox How, Ambleside, Westmoreland.

Edward Tyas Cook, *The Life of Florence Nightingale*, 2 vols., London : Macmillan and Co., Limited, 1913, I, 347.

1 Quoted Letter.   To Florence Nightingale.

Beatrice Caroline (Mrs. Steuart) Erskine, ed. *Anna Jameson: Letters and Friendships* (1812-1860), London : T. Fisher Unwin, Ltd., 1915, pp. 293-294.

2 Quoted Letters.   To Anna Brownell Jameson.

'A Few Words about "Jane Eyre" ', *Sharpe's London Magazine of Entertainment and Instruction, for General Reading*, N.S. VI (1855), 342.

1 Quoted Letter.   To an unknown recipient.

Elizabeth Sanderson Haldane, *Mrs. Gaskell and Her Friends*, London : Hodder and Stoughton Limited, 1930, pp. 68, 90-97, 118-120, 184-189, 239-240, 242-243, 251-252, 284-285, 287-288, 296-300.

13 Quoted   The recipients include Ann A. Shaen,
Letters[1].   Emily Shaen (Winkworth), and Catherine
                  Winkworth.

Gaskelliana.   Quoted letter by Margaret Emily (Meta)
                  Gaskell to Emily Shaen.

[Charlotte Hope] His Daughter, compiled *George Hope of Fenton Barns: A Sketch of his Life*, Edinburgh : David Douglas, 1881, pp. 177-178.

1 Quoted Letter.   To George Hope.

---

[1] The Brontë Section of the Brotherton Collection at the Leeds University Library contains the original manuscript for one Haldane quotation (*op. cit.*, pp. 141-148), Chapple and Pollard basing their text (*G.L.*, No. 166) on this printed version; another quotation (*G.L.*, No. 624) they take from Haldane (*op. cit.*, p. 25) is not—as she states—by Mrs. Gaskell, but by Charlotte Brontë.

Margaret Howitt, 'Stray Notes from Mrs. Gaskell', *Good Words*, XXXVI (1895), 604-612.

    4 Quoted Letters To *Mary Howitt* and William Howitt. (4 *G.L.*[2]).

[Leonard Huxley] *The House of Smith Elder*, Pref. I[sabel] M[arion] S[mith], London : Privately printed, 1923, pp. 73-81, 205-208.

c. 12 Quoted Letters (0 *G.L.*)[3].	To *George Smith*.
Gaskelliana.	Quoted letter to George Smith by one of Mrs. Gaskell's daughters; quoted letters to Reginald John Smith by Julia Bradford Gaskell and Margaret Emily (Meta) Gaskell.

Henry James, *William Wetmore Story and His Friends, from Letters, Diaries, and Recollections*, 2 vols., Edinburgh and London : William Blackwood and Sons, 1903, I, 353-359.

    8 Quoted Letters. To Emelyn Story and William Wetmore Story.

William Angus Knight, 'Whitwell Elwin', *Retrospects*, 1st Series, London : Smith, Elder, & Co., 1904, pp. 271-272.

    1 Quoted Letter. To John Forster.

Letters on Charlotte Brontë by Mrs. Gaskell, [London :] Privately printed by Clement Shorter [c. 1916], p. [12].

    1 Quoted Letter[4]. To an unknown recipient.

William Pole, ed. and completed *The Life of Sir William Fairbairn, Bart., F.R.S., LL.D., D.C.L., . . . Partly Written by Himself*, London : Longmans, Green, and Co., 1877 [1876], pp. 460-462.

    2 Quoted Letters. To William Fairbairn.

---

[2] Part of the last (fourth) quoted letter appears as *G.L.*, No. 617, based on a Shorter-Symington typescript copy (in the Gaskell Section, Brotherton Collection, Leeds University Library) rather than on the more authoritative *Good Words* source—where is quoted from (possibly) the same letter to Mary Howitt a further passage, not reproduced by Chapple and Pollard.

[3] Clearly not all Mrs. Gaskell's letters to George Smith were available to Chapple and Pollard; for instance, they print a letter (*G.L.*, No. 363) that refers back to one not included in their edition.

[4] *G.L.*, No. 316 follows (not quite accurately) this Shorter text; moreover, where applicable, Shorter's printed versions may provide better readings than the copy-texts used for *G.L.*, Nos. 48, 55, 79, 146, 274.

Thomas Wemyss Reid, *The Life, Letters, and Friendships of Richard Monckton Milnes, First Lord Houghton*, 2nd edn, 2 vols., London, Paris & Melbourne : Cassell & Company, Limited, 1890, I, 481.

    1 Quoted Letter.   To Richard Monckton Milnes.

[Sarah Blake Shaw] *Memorial: RGS*, Cambridge [Mass.] : University Press, 1864, pp. 149-150.

    1 Quoted Letter[5]. To Sarah Blake Shaw.

Clement King Shorter, *The Brontës: Life and Letters. Being an Attempt to Present a Full and Final Record of the Lives of the Three Sisters, Charlotte, Emily and Anne Brontë from the Biographies of Mrs. Gaskell and Others, and from Numerous Hitherto Unpublished Manuscripts and Letters*, 2 vols., London : Hodder and Stoughton, 1908, II, 292 fn., 396-399.

    2 Quoted Letters. To Ellen Nussey and William Smith Williams.

Lucy Bethia Walford (Colquhoun), ' Elizabeth Gaskell ', *Twelve English Authoresses*, London and New York : Longmans, Green, and Co., 1892, p. 155.

    1 Cited Letter   Written (c. 1826) *to an unknown correspondent*.
    (0 *G.L.*).   *pondent.*

Adolphus William Ward, ed. *The Works of Mrs. Gaskell*, 8 vols., London : Smith, Elder & Co., 1906, I, pp. xxxviii, lxii-lxiv; II, p. xvii; VI, pp. xii, xiv, xxvi-xxvii; VII, p. xxv; VIII, p. xvi.

    8 (?) Quoted   The recipients include Mary Greg and
    Letters (3 *G.L.*)[6]. *George Smith.*

---

    [5] *G.L.*, No. 530 is based on an accurate typed-copy (in the Gaskell Section, Brotherton Collection, Leeds University Library) of this printed text.

    [6] Whether or not Ward is using what Mrs. Gaskell said or what she wrote is sometimes difficult to determine. Thus, in one place it may be hearsay not written testimony which he (ed. *Works*, II, p. xvii) quotes, to the effect that the novelist often contemplated an epistolary 'Cranford Abroad' (foreign letters from Miss Pole to Miss Matty); whereas elsewhere he (ed. *Works*, VIII, p. xvi) may well be quoting from her correspondence, in his comments that the author of *Wives and Daughters* half-considered deferring the Molly-Roger love-story to a subsequent, one-volume, work.

Jane Revere Whitehill, ed. *Letters of Mrs. Gaskell and Charles Eliot Norton*, 1855-1865, London : Humphrey Milford, Oxford University Press, 1932, pp. xviii-xix.

   1 Quoted Letter[7]. To Emelyn Story.

[Susanna Winkworth and (for Vol. II) Margaret Josephine Shaen] ed. *Letters and Memorials of Catherine Winkworth*, 2 vols., Clifton : E. Austin and Son (privately circulated), 1883-1886, I, 160-162, 165-167, 197-200, 480-481; II, 428.

   7 Quoted Letters[8]. To Catherine Winkworth.

   Gaskelliana.   Quoted letter from Catherine Winkworth.

Thomas James Wise and John Alexander Symington, *The Brontës: Their Lives, Friendships and Correspondence*, 4 vols., Oxford : Basil Blackwell for The Shakespeare Head Press, 1932, IV, 136.

   1 Quoted Letter.   To Geraldine Endsor Jewsbury.

---

   [7] This printed version (*G.L.*, No. 342) quite accurately follows the copy which Mrs. Maud Waldo Story made for—as she then was—Jane Revere Coolidge (now Mrs. Whitehill), and sent together with a letter written when Emelyn Story died by one of Mrs. Gaskell's daughters.

   [8] The seventh letter-quotation consists merely of a few words (*G.L.*, No. 590, fn.).

Late Information

Leeds City Archives Department (Symington Collection: Box 7 and Box of Shaen Papers), Sheepscar Library, Leeds 7.

5 Letters (0 *G.L.*).	The recipients[1] include *Emily Shaen (Winkworth)*[2], *William Shaen, and Susan (Holland?).*
4 Copied Letters (4 *G.L.*)[3].	To *Emily Shaen (Winkworth), William Smith Williams, and Catherine Winkworth.*
Gaskelliana.	Letter from Sydney Williams; letters to John Alexander Symington by various correspondents (including Mme G. H. Imbert and Margaret Josephine Shaen); various correspondence and photographs relating to the Shaens; numerous other miscellanea collected by Symington.

---

[1] A letter of 30 December [1851] to an unnamed recipient concerns the Rev. Newenham Travers: like Mr. Hale (in *North and South*), he had left the Church for reasons of conscience, and was seeking employment as a tutor—he reminds one of J. A. Froude. Cf. *G.L.*, No. 249.

[2] The original Sunday [26 March 1865] letter to Emily Shaen indicates that the copy-based text (*G.L.*, No. 564) of Chapple and Pollard is incomplete and somewhat inaccurate.

[3] Two of these typed copies supply better versions than those available to Chapple and Pollard: that corresponding to *G.L.*, No. 335 is more fully dated (Monday. October, 1856); that corresponding to *G.L.*, No. 217 has a week-day heading (Thursday), and provides a completer and doubtless more accurate text.

INDEX FOR MRS. GASKELL'S WRITINGS

(Including Projected Works and Attributions, Excluding
Collective Editions and Editions of Her Letters)